Philosophic Classics, Second Edition
Volume IV

NINETEENTH-CENTURY PHILOSOPHY

FORREST E. BAIRD, EDITOR
Whitworth College

WALTER KAUFMANN
Late, of Princeton University

Prentice Hall, Upper Saddle River, New Jersey 07458

Library of Congress Cataloging-in-Publication Data

Philosophic classics / Forrest E. Baird, editor.—3rd ed.
   p.   cm.
   "Walter Kaufmann, late, of Princeton University."
   Includes bibliographical references.
   Contents: v. 1. Ancient philosophy—v. 2. Medieval philosophy—
v. 3. Modern philosophy—v. 4. Nineteenth-century philosophy. 2nd
ed.—v. 5. Twentiety-century philosophy. 2nd ed.
   ISBN 0–13–021314–4 (v. 1).—ISBN 0–13–021315–2 (v. 2).—ISBN
0–13–021316–0 (v. 3).—ISBN 0–13–021533–3 (v. 4).—ISBN
0–13–021534–1 (v. 5)
   1. Philosophy.   I. Baird, Forrest E.   II. Kaufmann, Walter
Arnold.
   B21.P39 2000
   100—dc21   98–32332
                                                        CIP

Editor-in-chief: Charlyce Jones-Owen
Acquisitions editor: Karita France
Editorial assistant: Jennifer Ackerman
Production liaison: Fran Russello
Editorial/production supervision:
   Bruce Hobart (Pine Tree Composition)
Prepress and manufacturing buyer:
   Tricia Kenny
Cover director: Jayne Conte
Cover photo: Vincent Van Gogh *"Wheatfield with Cypresses,"* 1853–1890, Dutch. Private
   Collection/A. K. G., Berlin/Superstock.
Marketing manager: Ilse Wolfe

This book was set in 10/12 Times Roman by Pine Tree Composition, Inc.,
and was printed and bound by R.R. Donnelley & Sons Company.
The cover was printed by Phoenix Color Corp.

©2000, 1997 by Prentice-Hall, Inc.
Upper Saddle River, New Jersey 07458

ISBN 0-13-021533-3

Prentice-Hall International (UK) Limited, *London*
Prentice-Hall of Australia Pty. Limited, *Sydney*
Prentice-Hall Canada, Inc., *Toronto*
Prentice-Hall Hispanoamericana, S.A., *Mexico*
Prentice-Hall of India Private Limited, *New Dehli*
Prentice-Hall of Japan, Ltd., *Tokyo*
Pearson Education Asia Pte. Ltd., *Singapore*
Editora Prentice-Hall do Brasil, Ltda., *Rio de Janeiro*

This volume is dedicated to:
  TAMMY R. REID, Academic Vice-President
  and
  WILLIAM P. ROBINSON, President
  Whitworth College

Contents

Preface

Nineteenth-century European philosophy is characterized by a growing skepticism of the assumptions of earlier "modern philosophy." The pre-Kantian thinkers of the seventeenth and eighteenth century had believed there was a knowable, nonhuman rational order upon which thinking persons could willfully choose to act. The debates of these "modern philosophers" centered on where that order was to be found, how one was to know it, and what actions should follow. But following the monumental work of Immanuel Kant, a shift took place. Kant had concluded that while there *is* a rational nonhuman order (the "things-in-themselves" or "noumenal world"), it cannot be known or used as a basis for morality. The nineteenth-century thinkers which followed were dissatisfied with this conclusion. Some maintained that there was a knowable, rational order, but claimed that it constituted reality and hence one could not really *choose* to act upon it. Others concluded that there was a nonhuman order, but it was anything but rational. Still others denied that there is anything beyond the "space-time manifold" of phenomenal experience to direct human affairs.

The nineteenth-century philosophers included in this volume represent a variety of different responses to these issues. It is often commonplace to group nineteenth- (and twentieth-) century philosophers into two groups: Continental thinkers and Anglo-American thinkers. In choosing readings for this volume, I have tried to provide a balance between these two approaches to philosophy. Accordingly, it is possible to trace the development of Continental thought beginning with Fichte and moving through Hegel, Schopenhauer, Comte, Feuerbach, Kierkegaard, Marx, and Nietzsche. Likewise, one can follow the Anglo-American concerns beginning with Bentham and continuing on through Mill, Peirce, and James. (Of course the development of nineteenth-century is hardly that neat and tidy. Comte's writing, for instance, had a major influence on several British and American thinkers and the later "Anglo-American" philosophy of Logical Positivism—a philosophy which began on the Continent of Europe in Vienna.)

For this third edition I have added a selection from Ludwig Feuerbach as well as new selections from Kierkegaard and Nietzsche and considerably more material from Nietzsche's *Twilight of the Idols.* To make room for these additional texts, I have cut portions of Hegel's *Encyclopaedia* and Comte's *Course in Positive Philosophy.* There are dozens of other minor changes throughout the volume. In choosing texts for this volume, I have tried wherever possible to follow three principles: (1) to use complete works or, where more appropriate, complete sections of works (2) in clear translations (3) of texts central to the thinker's philosophy or widely accepted as part of the "canon." To make the works more accessible to students, most footnotes treating textual matters (variant readings, etc.) have been omitted and all Greek words have been transliterated and put within angle brackets. In addition, each thinker is introduced by a brief essay composed of three sections: (1) biographical (a glimpse of the life), (2) philosophical (a résumé of the philosopher's thought), and (3) bibliographical (suggestions for further reading).

* * *

I would like to thank the many people who assisted me in this volume, including the library staff of Whitworth College, especially Hans Bynagle, Gail Fielding, and Jeanette Langston; my colleagues F. Dale Bruner, who made helpful suggestions on all the introductions, and Barbara Filo, who helped make selections for artwork; Stephen Davis, Claremont McKenna College; Jerry H. Gill, The College of St. Rose; Rex Hollowell, Spokane Falls Community College; Stanley Obitts, Westmont College; and Charles Young, The Claremont Graduate School, who each read some of the introductions and gave helpful advice; my secretary, Michelle Seefried; and my production editor, Bruce Hobart, my acquisitions editor, Karita France of Prentice Hall; and my former acquisitions editors, Angela Stone and Ted Bolen. I would also like to acknowledge the following reviewers: James W. Allard, Montana State University; Robert C. Bennett, El Centro College; Herbert L. Carson, Ferris State University; Steven M. Emmanuel, Virginia Wesleyan College; Daniel Graham, Brigham Young University; John Lachs, Vanderbilt University; Helen S. Lang, Trinity College; Michael Losonsky, Colorado State University; Scott MacDonald, University of Iowa; Terry Pinkard, Georgetown University; Robert Redmond, Virginia Commonwealth University; Reginald Savage, North Carolina State University; Gregory Schultz, Wisconsin Lutheran College; Stephen Scott, Eastern Washington University; Howard N. Tuttle, University of New Mexico; Richard J. Van Iten, Iowa State University; Donald Phillip Verene, Emory University; and Wilhelm S. Wurzer, Duquesne University.

I am especially thankful to my wife, Joy Lynn Fulton Baird, and to our children, Whitney Jaye, Sydney Tev, and Soren David, who have supported me in this enterprise.

Finally I would like to thank my dean, Tammy Reid, and my president, Bill Robinson, who have both been supportive friends as well as respected leaders.

Forrest E. Baird
Professor of Philosophy
Whitworth College
Spokane, WA 99251
email: fbaird@whitworth.edu

Philosophers In This Volume

Jeremy Bentham
　　Johann Gottlieb Fichte
　　　　G.W.F. Hegel

　　　　　　Arthur Schopenhauer
　　　　　　　Auguste Comte
　　　　　　　　John Stuart Mill
　　　　　　　　　Søren Kierkegaard

Other Important Figures

　　Johan Wolfgang von Goethe
　　　　Napoleon Bonaparte
　　　　Ludwig van Beethoven
　　　　　Friedrich von Schelling

　　　　　　　Ralph Waldo Emerson
　　　　　　　Ludwig Feuerbach
　　　　　　　Charles Darwin
　　　　　　　Charles Dickens

A Sampling of Major Events

　　　　　American revolution
　　　　British gain control of India
　　　　　　French Revolution
　　　　　　Napoleon crowns
　　　　　　himself emperor
　　　　　　　Slave trade abolished in
　　　　　　British Empire
　　　　　　　Several latin American
　　　　　　countries achieve
　　　　　　Independence
　　　　　　　Britain and U.S. fight
　　　　　　War of 1812

1740　　　　　1760　　　　　1780　　　　　1800

Karl Marx

Charles Sanders Peirce
William James
Friedrich Nietzsche

Henry David Thoreau
Queen Victoria
Susan B. Anthony
Herbert Spencer
Fyodor Dostoevsky

F. H. Bradley
Josiah royce

Napoleon defeated at Waterloo
Chaka founds Zulu empire
Opium War between Britain and China
Revolutions sweep Europe
David Livingstone crosses Africa
American Civil War
Suez Canal opened
1st Boer War in South Africa
Spanish
American War

1820   1840   1860   1880

JEREMY BENTHAM
1748–1832

The elder of two sons born to a successful London attorney and his wife, Jeremy Bentham never really had a childhood. Young Jeremy started reading Latin when he was three years old, began the violin at five, and was sent away to Westminster School at seven. His mother died when he was ten. During this time, his father ensured that Jeremy would learn the social graces that come from studying dancing, drawing, and French. Jeremy rarely had social contact with children his own age and frivolous play was discouraged.

Bentham entered Queen's College, Oxford, when he was only twelve years old. He was not socially active, being far younger than most of his classmates and lacking funds, because of the meager allowance provided by his father. Bentham studied law, and, following graduation at age sixteen, he was admitted to the bar. Although briefly employed to give some legal opinions, Bentham never pled a case in court. Instead, he turned his attention to legal reform and moral theory.

In the 1770s and 1780s, Bentham wrote extensively on the nature of law. He began by completing a major review of the standard current theory of law, Sir William Blackstone's *Commentaries on the Laws of England*. Bentham's first published book, *A Fragment on Government* (1776), was taken from this review of Blackstone. In 1789, Bentham published his most famous and influential work, *An Introduction to the Principles of Morals and Legislation*. During this period, Bentham also worked on the practical application of his legal theories. In the late-1780s, he wrote *Panopticon; or, The Inspection House,* which described a plan for a circular prison. Not merely content to theorize about penal reform, Bentham spent the next decade attempting to get such facilities built. His proposal was favorably received by Parliament, and land was designated to build a model prison. Bentham's endeavor ultimately proved futile, however, as the intransigence of the powerful and the apathy of the masses doomed his project to failure.

In his later years, Bentham became the leader of a group of disciples, including James Mill and his son, John Stuart Mill, who shared Bentham's concern for political change. In 1813, Parliament reimbursed Bentham £23,000 for the time and money he had spent on the Panopticon. Bentham used some of the money to establish a radical journal for his movement, the *Westminster Review*. Bentham also helped found University College, London, to carry on his ideas.

Bentham died in 1832. After his death, as Bentham directed, his body was dissected in the presence of his friends, embalmed, and placed in a glass case at University College.

* * *

According to Bentham, ethics should be empirical and scientific. Whereas thinkers prior to Bentham had grounded ethics on divine command (e.g., Thomas Aquinas), moral intuition (e.g., David Hume), or duty (e.g., Immanuel Kant), Bentham thought all of these inadequate. Instead, he asserted a frank, psychological hedonism, claiming that, in fact, all people act to avoid pain and gain pleasure. As he says in our selection from *An Introduction to the Principles of Morals and Legislation,*

> Nature has placed mankind under the governance of two sovereign masters, *pain* and *pleasure.* . . . They govern us in all we do, in all we say, in all we think: every effort we can make to throw off our subjection, will serve but to demonstrate and confirm it. In words a man may pretend to abjure their empire: but in reality he will remain subject to it all the while.

It is not even necessary to develop a complex philosophical definition of "pain" and "pleasure." These words refer to the simple sensations of displeasure and enjoyment that govern everyone's lives. Bentham's definition of pleasures includes eating and drinking, having wealth, and listening to good music.

Given the undeniable existence of *psychological* hedonism (i.e., that people *do* avoid pain and seek pleasure), Bentham argues for *ethical* hedonism (i.e., that people *should* avoid pain and seek pleasure). As Bentham says, "It is for them [pain and pleasure] alone to point out what we ought to do, as well as to determine what we shall do." The "good," then, is simply that which promotes pleasure and happiness, whereas the "bad" or "evil" do the opposite.

It might seem odd to tell people that they should do what they in fact already do. But people are often mistaken about what gives pleasure, or they may act in ways that will increase immediate pleasure but diminish their sum total of pleasure. Accordingly, Bentham developed what he called the "Principle of Utility." Borrowing a phrase from the French thinker Cesare Beccaria, Bentham argued that we should always act to promote "the greatest good for the greatest number." Any action, any rule, any legislation, is good if

> it tends to produce benefit, advantage, pleasure, good, or happiness (all this in the present case comes to the same thing), or (what comes again to the same thing) to prevent the happening of mischief, pain, evil, or unhappiness to the party whose in-

terest is considered: if that party be the community in general, then the happiness of the community: if a particular individual, then the happiness of that individual.

The job of the ethicist, then, is not to find eternal verities on which to base the "Good," it is to articulate those scientific principles that will yield the legislation that, in turn, will increase the total amount of happiness for the greatest number. In Chapter 4 of our reading, Bentham elaborates a "hedonic calculus" for measuring pleasures and pains. Pleasures and pains differ in intensity, duration, certainty or uncertainty, propinquity (nearness) or remoteness, fecundity (future-

Jeremy Bentham, University College, London. According to the terms of his will, Bentham's body was dissected in the presence of his friends and his embalmed body placed in a glass case at University College. The mummified head was long ago replaced with a wax copy, but his skeleton, fully clothed, remains on display to this day. *(The Bettmann Archive)*

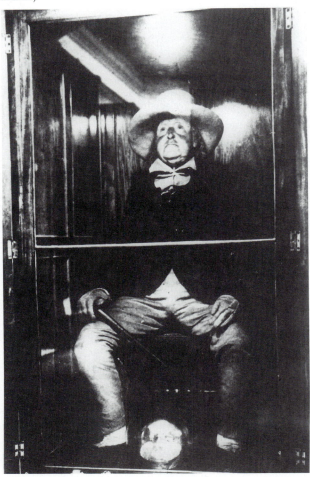

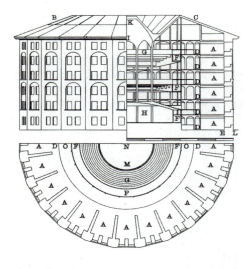

EXPLANATION

A	Cells
B to C	Great Annular Sky Light
D	Cell Galleries
E	Entrance
F	Inspection Galleries
G	Chapel Galleries
H	Inspectors Lodge
I	Dome of the Chapel
K	Sky Light to D°
L	Store Rooms &c with their Galleries immediately within the outer wall all round place for an annular Cistern Q
M	Floor of the Chapel
N	Circular Opening in d°/open except at Church times to light the Inspectors Lodge
O	Annular Wall from top to bottom, for light air and seperation

In the late-1780s, Bentham wrote *Panopticon; or, The Inspection House,* which described his plan for a circular prison. Not merely content to theorize about penal reform, Bentham spent the next decade attempting to get such a facility built. His proposal was favorably received by Parliament, and land was designated to build a model prison. Bentham's endeavor ultimately proved futile, however, as the intransigence of the powerful and the apathy of the masses doomed his project to failure. *(Bodleian Library)*

pleasure quotient), purity, and extent. Accordingly, we must consider the whole calculus when making legislation. For example, if determining whether to legalize marijuana, we must consider the intensity of the pleasure marijuana gives, for how long, how certain it is to give such pleasure, how close the pleasure is, whether it is likely to lead to later pain, how pure the pleasure is, and how many people will be affected. According to Bentham, there are *no other* relevant considerations.

Bentham's focus on the pleasurable *consequences* of an action or rule (in opposition to Kant's emphasis on the *intention* to do one's duty) has been enormously influential. But Bentham's followers have softened his claim that only the quantity of pleasurable consequences are ethically relevant. John Stuart Mill, for example, argues that there is a distinction between the *quality* of pleasures. A pig might gain a great *quantity* of pleasure from wallowing in the mud, but that would be a low-*quality* pleasure; and "It is better to be a human being dissatisfied than a pig satisfied." Still, modified versions of Utilitarianism (as Bentham's ethics came to be called) are alive in the beliefs of many people today.

* * *

A good place to begin further study of Bentham is John Dinwiddy, *Bentham* (Oxford: Oxford University Press, 1989), part of the acclaimed Past Masters series. Charles Milner Atkinson, *Jeremy Bentham: His Life and Works* (London: Methuen, 1905) is the classic study of Bentham, whereas Elie Halevy, *The Growth of Philosophic Radicalism,* translated by Mary Morris (Boston: Beacon Press, 1955); D.J. Manning, *The Mind of Jeremy Bentham* (New York: Barnes & Noble, 1968); James Steintrager, *Bentham* (Ithaca, NY: Cornell University Press, 1977); and Ross Harrison, *Bentham* (London: Routledge, 1983) provide general overviews. Charles W. Everett, *Jeremy Bentham* (New York: Dell, 1966) combines biography with extensive selections from Bentham's works, while Janet Semple, *Bentham's Prison: A Study of the Panopticon Peniteniary* (Oxford: Oxford University Press, 1993), chronicles the history of Bentham's proposed prison. There are a number of books on Bentham as a political theorist, including William Leslie Davidson, *Political Thought in England: The Utilitarians from Bentham to Mill* (Oxford: Oxford University Press, 1947); David Lyons, *In the Interest of the Governed: A Study in Bentham's Philosophy of Utility and Law* (Oxford: Clarendon Press, 1973); Douglas G. Long, *Bentham on Liberty: Jeremy Bentham's Idea of Liberty in Relation to His Utilitarianism* (Toronto: University of Toronto Press, 1977); Nancy L. Rosenblum, *Bentham's Theory of the Modern State* (Cambridge, MA: Harvard University Press, 1978); H.L.A. Hart, *Essays on Bentham: Studies in Jurisprudence and Political Theory* (Oxford: Clarendon Press, 1982); and Gerald J. Postema, *Bentham and the Common Law Tradition* (Oxford: Clarendon Press, 1986). The collection of essays, Bhikhu Parekh, ed., *Jeremy Bentham: Ten Critical Essays* (London: Frank Cass, 1974), includes an essay by John Stuart Mill.

INTRODUCTION TO THE PRINCIPLES OF MORALS AND LEGISLATION (in part)

CHAPTER 1: OF THE PRINCIPLE OF UTILITY.

I. Nature has placed mankind under the governance of two sovereign masters, *pain* and *pleasure*. It is for them alone to point out what we ought to do, as well as to determine what we shall do. On the one hand the standard of right and wrong, on the other the chain of causes and effects, are fastened to their throne. They govern us in all we do, in all we say, in all we think: every effort we can make to throw off our subjection, will serve but to demonstrate and confirm it. In words a man may pretend to abjure their empire: but in reality he will remain subject to it all the while. The *principle of utility* recognises this subjection, and assumes it for the foundation of that system, the object of which is to rear the fabric of felicity by the hands of reason and of law. Systems which attempt to question it, deal in sounds instead of sense, in caprice instead of reason, in darkness instead of light.

But enough of metaphor and declamation: it is not by such means that moral science is to be improved.

II. The principle of utility is the foundation of the present work: it will be proper therefore at the outset to give an explicit and determinate account of what is meant by it. By the principle of utility is meant that principle which approves or disapproves of every action whatsoever, according to the tendency which it appears to have to augment or diminish the happiness of the party whose interest is in question: or, what is the same thing in other words, to promote or to oppose that happiness. I say of every action whatsoever; and therefore not only of every action of a private individual, but of every measure of government.

III. By utility is meant that property in any object, whereby it tends to produce benefit, advantage, pleasure, good, or happiness (all this in the present case comes to the same thing), or (what comes again to the same thing) to prevent the happening of mischief, pain, evil, or unhappiness to the party whose interest is considered: if that party be the community in general, then the happiness of the community: if a particular individual, then the happiness of that individual.

IV. The interest of the community is one of the most general expressions that can occur in the phraseology of morals: no wonder that the meaning of it is often lost. When it has a meaning, it is this. The community is a fictitious *body,* composed of the individual persons who are considered as constituting as it were its *members.* The interest of the community then is, what?—the sum of the interests of the several members who compose it.

V. It is in vain to talk of the interest of the community without understanding what is the interest of the individual. A thing is said to promote the interest, or to be *for* the interest, of an individual, when it tends to add to the sum total of his pleasures: or, what comes to the same thing, to diminish the sum total of his pains.

VI. An action then may be said to be conformable to the principle of utility, or, for shortness sake, to utility (meaning with respect to the community at large), when the tendency it has to augment the happiness of the community is greater than any it has to diminish it.

VII. A measure of government (which is but a particular kind of action, performed by a particular person or persons) may be said to be conformable to or dictated by the principle of utility, when in like manner the tendency which it has to augment the happiness of the community is greater than any which it has to diminish it.

VIII. When an action, or in particular a measure of government, is supposed by a man to be conformable to the principle of utility, it may be convenient, for the purposes of discourse, to imagine a kind of law or dictate, called a law or dictate of utility: and to speak of the action in question, as being conformable to such law or dictate.

IX. A man may be said to be a partizan of the principle of utility, when the approbation or disapprobation he annexes to any action, or to any measure, is determined, by and proportioned to the tendency which he conceives it to have to augment or to diminish the happiness of the community: or in other words, to its conformity or unconformity to the laws or dictates of utility.

X. Of an action that is conformable to the principle of utility, one may always say either that it is one that ought to be done, or at least that it is not one that ought not to be done. One may say also, that it is right it should be done: that it is a right action: at least that it is not a wrong action. When thus interpreted, the words *ought,* and *right* and *wrong,* and others of that stamp, have a meaning: when otherwise, they have none.

XI. Has the rectitude of this principle been ever formally contested? It should seem that it had, by those who have not known what they have been meaning. Is it susceptible of any direct proof? It should seem not: for that which is used to prove every thing else, cannot itself be proved: a chain of proofs must have their commencement somewhere. To give such proof is as impossible as it is needless.

XII. Not that there is or ever has been that human creature breathing, however stupid or perverse, who has not on many, perhaps on most occasions of his life, deferred to it. By the natural constitution of the human frame, on most occasions of their lives men in general embrace this principle, without thinking of it: if not for the ordering of their own actions, yet for the trying of their own actions, as well as of those of other men. There have been, at the same time, not many, perhaps, even of the most intelligent, who have been disposed to embrace it purely and without reserve. There are even few who have not taken some occasion or other to quarrel with it, either on account of their not understanding always how to apply it, or on account of some prejudice or other which they were afraid to examine into, or could not bear to part with. For such is the stuff that man is made of: in principle and in practice, in a right track and in a wrong one, the rarest of all human qualities is consistency.

XIII. When a man attempts to combat the principle of utility, it is with reasons drawn, without his being aware of it, from that very principle itself. His arguments, if they prove any thing, prove not that the principle is *wrong,* but that, according to the applications he supposed to be made of it, it is *misapplied.* Is it possible for a man to move the earth? Yes; but he must first find out another earth to stand upon.

XIV. To disprove the propriety of it by arguments is impossible; but, from the causes that have been mentioned, or from some confused or partial view of it, a man may happen to be disposed not to relish it. Where this is the case, if he thinks the settling of his opinions on such a subject worth the trouble, let him take the following steps, and at length, perhaps, he may come to reconcile himself to it.

1. Let him settle with himself, whether he would wish to discard this principle altogether; if so, let him consider what it is that all his reasonings (in matters of politics especially) can amount to?

2. If he would, let him settle with himself, whether he would judge and act without any principle, or whether there is any other he would judge and act by?

3. If there be, let him examine and satisfy himself whether the principle he thinks he has found is really any separate intelligible principle: or whether it be not a mere principle in words, a kind of phrase, which at bottom expresses neither more nor less than the mere averment of his own unfounded sentiments: that is, what in another person he might be apt to call caprice?

4. If he is inclined to think that his own approbation or disapprobation, annexed to the idea of an act, without any regard to its consequences, is a sufficient foundation for him to judge and act upon, let him ask himself whether his sentiment is to be a standard of right and wrong, with respect to every other man, or whether every man's sentiment has the same privilege of being a standard in itself?

5. In the first case, let him ask himself whether his principle is not despotical, and hostile to all the rest of [the] human race?

6. In the second case, whether it is not anarchical, and whether at this rate there are not as many different standards of right and wrong as there are men? and whether even in the same man, the same thing, which is right to-day, may not (without the least change in its nature) be wrong to-morrow? and whether the same thing is not right and wrong in the same place at the same time? and in either case, whether all argument is not at an end? and whether, when two men have said, "I like this," and "I don't like it," they can (upon such a principle) have any thing more to say?

7. If he should have said to himself, No: for that the sentiment which he proposes as a standard must be grounded on reflection, let him say on what particulars the reflection is to turn? If on particulars having relation to the utility of the act, then let him say whether this is not deserting his own principle, and borrowing assistance from that very one in opposition to which he sets it up: or if not on those particulars, on what other particulars?

8. If he should be for compounding the matter, and adopting his own principle in part, and the principle of utility in part, let him say how far he will adopt it?

9. When he has settled with himself where he will stop, then let him ask himself how he justifies to himself the adopting it so far? and why he will not adopt it any farther?

10. Admitting any other principle than the principle of utility to be a right principle, a principle that it is right for a man to pursue: admitting (what is not true) that the word *right* can have a meaning without reference to utility, let him say whether there is any such thing as a *motive* that a man can have to pursue the dictates of it: if there is, let him say what that motive is, and how it is to be distinguished from those which enforce the dictates of utility: if not, then lastly let him say what it is this other principle can be good for?

CHAPTER 2: OF PRINCIPLES ADVERSE TO THAT OF UTILITY.

I. If the principle of utility be a right principle to be governed by, and that in all cases, it follows from what has been just observed, that whatever principle differs from it in any case must necessarily be a wrong one. To prove any other principle, therefore, to be a wrong one, there needs no more than just to show it to be what it is, a principle of which the dictates are in some point or other different from those of the principle of utility: to state it is to confute it.

II. A principle may be different from that of utility in two ways: 1. By being constantly opposed to it: this is the case with a principle which may be termed the principle of asceticism. 2. By being sometimes opposed to it, and sometimes not, as it may happen: this is the case with another, which may be termed the principle of *sympathy* and *antipathy*.

III. By the principle of asceticism I mean that principle, which, like the principle of utility, approves or disapproves of any action, according to the tendency which it appears to have to augment or diminish the happiness of the party whose interest is in question; but in an inversive manner: approving of actions in as far as they tend to diminish his happiness: disapproving of them in as far as they tend to augment it.

*   *   *

IX. The principle of asceticism seems originally to have been the reverie of certain hasty speculators, who having perceived, or fancied, that certain pleasures, when reaped in certain circumstances, have, at the long run, been attended with pains more than equivalent to them, took occasion to quarrel with every thing that offered itself under the name of pleasure. Having then got thus far, and having forgot the point which they set out from, they pushed on, and went so much further as to think it meritorious to fall in love with pain. Even this, we see, is at bottom but the principle of utility misapplied.

X. The principle of utility is capable of being consistently pursued; and it is but tautology to say, that the more consistently it is pursued, the better it must ever be for humankind. The principle of asceticism never was, nor ever can be, consistently pursued by any living creature. Let but one tenth part of the inhabitants of this earth pursue it consistently, and in a day's time they will have turned it into a hell.

XI. Among principles adverse to that of utility, that which at this day seems to have most influence in matters of government, is what may be called the principle of sympathy and antipathy. By the principle of sympathy and antipathy, I mean that principle which approves or disapproves of certain actions, not on account of their tending to augment the happiness, nor yet on account of their tending to diminish the happiness of the party whose interest is in question, but merely because a man finds himself disposed to approve or disapprove of them: holding up that approbation or disapprobation as a sufficient reason for itself, and disclaiming the necessity of looking out for any extrinsic ground. Thus far in the general department of morals: and in the particular department of politics, measuring out the quantum (as well as determining the ground) of punishment, by the degree of the disapprobation.

*   *   *

XIV. The various systems that have been formed concerning the standard of right and wrong, may all be reduced to the principle of sympathy and antipathy. One account may serve for all of them. They consist all of them in so many contrivances for avoiding the obligation of appealing to any external standard, and for prevailing upon the reader to accept of the author's sentiment or opinion as a reason, and that a sufficient one, for itself. The phrases are different, but the principle the same.

*   *   *

CHAPTER 3: OF THE FOUR SANCTIONS OF SOURCES OF PAIN AND PLEASURE.

I. It has been shown that the happiness of the individuals, of whom a community is composed, that is, their pleasures and their security, is the end and the sole end which the legislator ought to have in view: the sole standard, in conformity to which each individual ought, as far as depends upon the legislator, to be *made* to fashion his behaviour. But whether it be this or any thing else that is to be *done,* there is nothing by which a man can ultimately be *made* to do it, but either pain or pleasure. Having taken a general view of these two grand objects (*viz.* pleasure, and what comes to the same thing, immunity from pain) in the character of *final* causes; it will be necessary to take a view of pleasure and pain itself, in the character of *efficient* causes or means.

II. There are four distinguishable sources from which pleasure and pain are in use to flow: considered separately, they may be termed the *physical,* the *political,* the *moral,* and the *religious:* and inasmuch as the pleasures and pains belonging to each of them are capable of giving a binding force to any law or rule of conduct, they may all of them be termed sanctions.

III. If it be in the present life, and from the ordinary course of nature, not purposely modified by the interposition of the will of any human being, nor by any extraordinary interposition of any superior invisible being, that the pleasure or pain takes place or is expected, it may be said to issue from, or to belong to, the *physical sanction.*

IV. If at the hands of a *particular* person or set of persons in the community, who under names correspondent to that of *judge,* are chosen for the particular purpose of dispensing it, according to the will of the sovereign or supreme ruling power in the state, it may be said to issue from the *political sanction.*

V. If at the hands of such chance persons in the community, as the party in question may happen in the course of his life to have concerns with, according to each man's spontaneous disposition, and not according to any settled or concerted rule, it may be said to issue from the *moral* or *popular sanction.*

VI. If from the immediate hand of a superior invisible being, either in the present life, or in a future, it may be said to issue from the *religious sanction.*

VII. Pleasures or pains which may be expected to issue from the *physical, political,* or *moral* sanctions, must all of them be expected to be experienced, if ever, in the present life: those which may be expected to issue from the *religious* sanction, may be expected to be experienced either in the *present* life or in a *future.*

VIII. Those which can be experienced in the present life, can of course be no others than such as human nature in the course of the present life is susceptible of: and from each of these sources may flow all the pleasures or pains of which, in the course of the present life, human nature is susceptible. With regard to these, then (with which alone we have in this place any concern), those of them which belong to any one of those sanctions differ not ultimately in mind from those which belong to any one of the other three: the only difference there is among them lies in the circumstances that accompany their production. A suffering which befals a man in the natural and spontaneous course of things, shall be styled, for instance, a *calamity;* in which case, if it be supposed to befal him through any imprudence of his, it may be styled a punishment issuing from the physical sanction. Now this same suffering, if inflicted by the law, will be what is commonly called a *punishment;* if incurred for want of any friendly assistance, which the misconduct, or supposed misconduct, of the sufferer has occasioned to be withholden, a punishment issuing from the *moral* sanction; if through the immediate interposition of a particular providence, a punishment issuing from the religious sanction.

IX. A man's goods, or his person, are consumed by fire. If this happened to him by what is called an accident, it was a calamity: if by reason of his own imprudence (for instance, from his neglecting to put his candle out), it may be styled a punishment of the physical sanction: if it happened to him by the sentence of the political magistrate, a punishment belonging to the political sanction—that is, what is commonly called a punishment: if for want of any assistance which his *neighbour* withheld from him out of some dislike to his *moral* character, a punishment of the *moral* sanction: if by an immediate act of *God's* displeasure, manifested on account of some sin committed by him, or through any distraction of mind, occasioned by the dread of such displeasure, a punishment of the *religious* sanction.

X. As to such of the pleasures and pains belonging to the religious sanction, as regard a future life, of what kind these may be, we cannot know. These lie not open to our observation. During the present life they are matter only of expectation: and, whether that expectation be derived from natural or revealed religion, the particular kind of pleasure or pain, if it be different from all those which lie open to our observation, is what we can have no idea of. The best ideas we can obtain of such pains and pleasures are altogether unliquidated in point of reality. In what other respects our ideas of them may be liquidated, will be considered in another place.

XI. Of these four sanctions, the physical is altogether, we may observe, the ground-work of the political and the moral: so is it also of the religious, in as far as the latter bears relation to the present life. It is included in each of these other three. This may operate in any case (that is, any of the pains or pleasures belonging to it may operate) independently of *them:* none of *them* can operate but by means of this. In a word, the powers of nature may operate of themselves; but neither the magistrate, nor men at large, *can* operate, nor is God in the case in question *supposed* to operate, but through the powers of nature.

XII. For these four objects, which in their nature have so much in common, it seemed of use to find a common name. It seemed of use, in the first place, for the convenience of giving a name to certain pleasures and pains, for which a name equally characteristic could hardly otherwise have been found: in the second place, for the sake of holding up the efficacy of certain moral forces, the influence of which is apt not to be sufficiently attended to. Does the political sanction exert an influence over the conduct of mankind? The moral, the religious sanctions, do so too. In every inch of his career are the operations of the political magistrate liable to be aided or impeded by these two foreign powers: who, one or other of them, or both, are sure to be either his rivals or his allies. Does it happen to him to leave them out in his calculations? He will be sure almost to find himself mistaken in the result. Of all this we shall find abundant proofs in the sequel of this work. It behooves him, therefore, to have them continually before his eyes; and that under such a name as exhibits the relation they bear to his own purposes and designs.

Chapter 4: Value of a Lot of Pleasure or Pain, How to be Measured.

I. Pleasures then, and the avoidance of pains are the *ends* which the legislator has in view: it behooves him therefore to understand their *value*. Pleasures and pains are the *instruments* he has to work with: it behooves him therefore to understand their force, which is again, in another point of view, their value.

II. To a person considered *by himself* the value of a pleasure or pain considered *by itself* will be greater or less, according to the four following circumstances:

1. Its *intensity.*

2. Its *duration.*

3. Its *certainty* or *uncertainty.*

4. Its *propinquity* or *remoteness.*

III. These are the circumstances which are to be considered in estimating a pleasure or a pain considered each of them by itself. But when the value of any pleasure or pain is considered for the purpose of estimating the tendency of any act by which it is produced, there are two other circumstances to be taken into the account; these are,

> 5. Its *fecundity,* or the chance it has of being followed by sensations of the *same* kind: that is, pleasures, if it be a pleasure: pains, if it be a pain.

> 6. Its *purity,* or the chance it has of *not* being followed by sensations of the *opposite* kind: that is, pains, if it be a pleasure: pleasures, if it be a pain.

These two last, however, are in strictness scarcely to be deemed properties of the pleasure or the pain itself; they are not, therefore, in strictness to be taken into the account of the value of that pleasure or that pain. They are in strictness to be deemed properties only of the act, or other event, by which such pleasure or pain has been produced; and accordingly are only to be taken into the account of the tendency of such act or such event.

IV. To a *number* of persons, with reference to each of whom the value of a pleasure or a pain is considered, it will be greater or less, according to seven circumstances: to wit, the six preceding ones; viz.

1. Its *intensity.*

2. Its *duration.*

3. Its *certainty* or *uncertainty.*

4. Its *propinquity* or *remoteness.*

5. Its *fecundity.*

6. Its *purity.*

And one other, to wit:

> 7. Its *extent*; that is, the number of persons to whom it *extends;* or (in other words) who are affected by it.

V. To take an exact account, then, of the general tendency of any act, by which the interests of a community are affected, proceed as follows. Begin with any one person of those whose interests seem most immediately to be affected by it: and take an account,

1. Of the value of each distinguishable *pleasure* which appears to be produced by it in the *first* instance.

2. Of the value of each *pain* which appears to be produced by it in the *first* instance.

3. Of the value of each pleasure which appears to be produced by it *after* the first. This constitutes the *fecundity* of the first *pleasure* and the *impurity* of the first *pain*.

4. Of the value of each *pain* which appears to be produced by it after the first. This constitutes the *fecundity* of the first *pain,* and *impurity* of the first pleasure.

5. Sum up all the values of all the *pleasures* on the one side, and those of all the pains on the other. The balance, if it be on the side of pleasure, will give the *good* tendency of the act upon the whole, with respect to the interests of that *individual* person; if on the side of pain, the *bad* tendency of it upon the whole.

6. Take an account of the *number* of persons whose interests appear to be concerned; and repeat the above process with respect to each. *Sum up* the numbers expressive of the degrees of *good* tendency, which the act has, with respect to each individual, in regard to whom the tendency of it is *good* upon the whole: do this again with respect to each individual, in regard to whom the tendency of it is *bad* upon the whole. Take the *balance;* which, if on the side of *pleasure,* will give the general *good tendency* of the act, with respect to the total number or community of individuals concerned; if on the side of pain, the general *evil tendency,* with respect to the same community.

VI. It is not to be expected that this process should be strictly pursued previously to every moral judgment, or to every legislative or judicial operation. It may, however, be always kept in view: and as near as the process actually pursued on these occasions approaches to it, so near will such process approach to the character of an exact one.

VII. The same process is alike applicable to pleasure and pain, in whatever shape they appear; and by whatever denomination they are distinguished: to pleasure, whether it be called *good* (which is properly the cause or instrument of pleasure), or *profit* (which is distant pleasure, or the cause or instrument of distant pleasure), or *convenience,* or *advantage, benefit, emolument, happiness,* and so forth: to pain, whether it be called *evil* (which corresponds to good), or *mischief* or *inconvenience,* or *disadvantage,* or *loss,* or *unhappiness,* and so forth.

VIII. Nor is this a novel and unwarranted, any more than it is a useless theory. In all this there is nothing but what the practice of mankind, wheresoever they have a clear view of their own interest, is perfectly conformable to. An article of property, an estate in land, for instance, is valuable: on what account? On account of the pleasures of all kinds which it enables a man to produce, and, what comes to the same thing, the pains of all kinds which it enables him to avert. But the value of such an article of property is universally understood to rise or fall according to the length or shortness of the time which a man has in it: the certainty or uncertainty of its coming into possession: and the nearness or remoteness of the time at which, if at all, it is to come into possession. As to the *intensity* of the pleasures which a man may derive from it, this is never thought of, because it depends upon the use which each particular person may come to make of it; which cannot be estimated till the particular pleasures he may come to derive from it, or the particular pains he may come to exclude by means of it, are brought to view. For the same reason, neither does he think of the *fecundity* or *purity* of those pleasures.

Thus much for pleasure and pain, happiness and unhappiness, in *general.* . . .

JOHANN GOTTLIEB FICHTE
1762–1814

Johann Gottlieb Fichte's life covered an important period in history. During his brief life span, Fichte observed both the American and French Revolutions, the rise and fall of Napoleon, and the first steps toward the unification of Germany. Fichte was a zealous advocate of German nationalism.

Fichte was born in Rammenau, Saxony, the eldest of eight children. His parents belonged to the emerging bourgeoisie; his mother was the daughter of a wealthy linen-factory owner and Fichte's father was a ribbon maker. Fichte's childhood was not particularly happy: His parents had financial problems and quarreled often with each other and with him. But in 1771, a minor incident allowed Fichte to escape his difficult family. A local nobleman, Baron von Militz, late in arriving at the village church, missed the sermon of his esteemed pastor. The villagers told the baron not to worry, for there was a local boy who could repeat any sermon verbatim. They fetched the nine-year-old Fichte, who then gave a flawless repetition of the sermon he had just heard. Von Militz was so impressed, he arranged for Fichte's education, sending him to the famous boarding school at Pforta (which Nietzsche later attended).

With the death of his benefactor in 1774, Fichte entered a long period of financial duress. But he somehow managed to finish at Pforta, graduating with honors in 1780. Over the next four years, Fichte studied theology at the universities of Jena, Wittenberg, and Leipzig, but by the time of his graduation, Fichte no longer desired a pastorate. Without a vocation and cut off from his family, Fichte found temporary employment as a tutor in Zürich. Here he met and became engaged to Johanna Rahn, but his financial situation delayed their marriage for five years.

Returning to Leipzig in 1790, Fichte's whole life changed when he read Kant's *Critique of Pure Reason*. Gathering his meager resources, Fichte immediately set out for Königsberg to meet the great man himself. Fichte did manage an audience with the elderly Kant, but he was received coolly. Undaunted, Fichte resolved to make an impression. Working feverishly, in four weeks he wrote and forwarded to Kant his *Essay Toward a Critique of All Revelations*. The *Essay* applied Kant's ethics of duty to the study of religion. Kant was delighted with the work, warmly accepted Fichte into his circle of friends, arranged for a tutoring position for Fichte, and even assisted Fichte in the publication of his manuscript. By accident, the *Essay* was published in 1792 without Fichte's name. This seeming disaster was the turning point of his professional life. Everyone assumed that the *Essay* had been written by Kant, and it received great critical acclaim. Kant quickly corrected the misconception and lauded Fichte's work. Overnight, Fichte was transformed from a struggling private tutor into Kant's philosophical successor. The University of Jena offered Fichte a chair of philosophy, and he was finally able to marry Johanna Rahn.

Fichte was an immediate success in Jena. His lectures drew standing-room-only crowds as he expounded his unique adaptations of Kant's work. In this period, Fichte wrote a number of technical works continuing the Kantian tradition, including *Basis of the Entire Theory of Science* (1794), *Basis of Natural Right* (1796), *The System of Ethics* (1798), and *The Closed Commercial State* (1800). But a few years later, his situation at Jena changed. Fichte was accused of being too harsh with students (for example, he opposed student societies, which were the fraternities of his day). He was critical of fellow professors and impolitic in his expression of criticism. Moreover, his favoring of French Revolutionary individualism alarmed conservative university officials. Finally, his religious views in the *Essay Toward a Critique of All Revelations* struck many as tending toward atheism. Even Kant, concerned with Fichte's interpretation of his philosophy, distanced himself from his protégé.

By 1799, the situation at Jena had become so intolerable that Fichte was forced to leave. Encouraged by his friends, Friedrich Schlegel and Friedrich Schleiermacher, Fichte came to Berlin where he published his most important philosophical work, *The Vocation of Man* (1800). Though he did not have a regular academic position, Fichte once again lectured to packed houses. And once again Fichte's stern moral commitment and argumentative nature eventually alienated most friends.

In 1806, Napoleon defeated the Prussians at Jena and occupied Berlin. This defeat led Fichte to write his famous *Addresses to the German Nation*. The French apparently considered Fichte too abstract and idealistic to censor and so allowed him to deliver the *Addresses* in public lectures in 1807 to 1808. These *Addresses* argued the superiority of all things German—the German nation, the German language, the German reformation, and German philosophy. Fichte called on all German states to unite around Prussia and to teutonize the world. To accomplish this, Fichte proposed a complete overhaul of the educational system in the German states.

Fichte got the chance to implement his educational reforms when he was appointed dean of the philosophical faculty at the new University of Berlin in 1810. Once again, Fichte's inability to compromise and his harsh manner made it impossible for him to carry out this task. As one of his students later wrote, "For the smallest fault he treats students as if they were imps of hell."* He resigned within months of his appointment.

In 1813, Prussia joined Russia to fight Napoleon. Johanna Fichte volunteered to nurse wounded soldiers returning to Berlin. She contracted typhus, from which she recovered, but Fichte died of the disease while caring for his convalescing wife.

*   *   *

Although Fichte appreciated Kant's works, he could not accept the Kantian notion of a thing-in-itself apart from the world of experience. Kant had argued that the world of experience, or the phenomenal world, is constructed out of sensory data ordered by the categories of the mind. But Kant had also stated that there must be a reality beyond the phenomenal world responsible for sensory data: the *Ding an sich* ("thing-in-itself"). But a thing-in-itself cannot *cause* sensations because causality is itself one of the categories of the mind. Further, since our experience and knowledge are limited to the phenomenal world, the *Ding an sich* cannot be experienced or known.

Fichte believed the only acceptable alternative was to discard the notion of a thing-in-itself entirely. According to Fichte, the entire phenomenal world of experience is a construction of the self. All experience is grounded in the spontaneous activity of the ego. As Fichte explains in the article *On the Foundation of Our Belief in a Divine Government of the Universe* (1798), given here in the Paul Edwards translation, "There is then no longer an independent world: everything is now simply a reflection of our inner activity."

The ego, or "I," as it becomes self-conscious, understands itself to be an ethical agent. But in order to be ethical, there must be others to whom the self is obligated and in relation to whom the self must act. Accordingly, the ego posits a non-ego as something outside of itself so that it can distinguish itself from that which it is not. Such a non-ego provides the "sensualized material" with a world of experience in which the ego can perform its duties. As Fichte explains in our reading from Book III of *The Vocation of Man,* given here (in part) in the William Smith translation:

> I have, most certainly and truly, these determinate duties, which announce themselves to me as duties towards certain objects, to be fulfilled by means of certain materials;—duties which I cannot otherwise conceive of, and cannot otherwise fulfil, than within such a world as I represent to myself.

The ego, then, is the acting subject and the non-ego the necessary object upon which it acts. In other words, what I experience as being me and what I experience as being not-me are both essential for the existence of an "I" and for moral action.

But this implies that there is a transcendent thinker or "I" beyond my experiences of "me" and "not-me." Such a transcendent thinker Fichte calls the Ab-

---

*Quoted in Patrick Gardiner, ed., *Nineteenth-Century Philosophy* (New York: Macmillan/The Free Press, 1969), p. 18.

solute Ego. It is the Absolute Ego that creates the experiences in which individual selves distinguish themselves from that which they consider to be external to them. This Absolute Ego is a part of the moral world order that is, in turn, "identical with God."

Although many applauded Fichte's ethical idealism, his work was immediately criticized by his peers. Besides the accusation of atheism, critics claimed that Fichte reduced nature, or the non-ego, to a passive creation of the ego. One colleague at Jena, Friedrich Schelling (1755–1854), argued that nature is not a mere passive limit to the activities of the ego, but an active force with internal laws. G.W.F. Hegel (1770–1831) pointed out that although he had rejected the Kantian thing-in-itself, Fichte's Absolute Ego was still a kind of substance underlying the finite ego and non-ego. Despite these criticisms, Fichte's thought had a lasting impact. His moral rigor inspired many, including Thomas Carlyle; his claim that the self declares its own existence anticipates some existentialist themes; and more unhappily than happily, Fichte's call for German nationalism was heard all too adamantly in the twentieth century.

*   *   *

Good places to begin a study of Fichte include the article on Fichte in Josiah Royce, *The Spirit of Modern Philosophy* (Boston, MA: Houghton Mifflin, 1931); Frederick Copleston, *A History of Philosophy: Volume VII, Fichte to Nietzsche* (Garden City, NY: Image Books, 1965); and the introduction to Johann Gottlieb Fichte, *Fichte: Early Philosophical Writings,* edited and translated by Daniel Breazeale (Ithaca, NY: Cornell University Press, 1988). The classic studies of Fichte's thought are the early nineteenth-century work, G.W.F. Hegel, *The Difference between Fichte's and Schelling's System of Philosophy,* translated by H.S. Harris and Walter Cerf (Albany, NY: SUNY Press, 1977) and Robert Adamson, *Fichte* (1903; reprinted Freeport, NY: Books for Libraries Press, 1969). More recent publications include Tom Rockmore, *Fichte, Marx, and the German Philosophical Tradition* (Carbondale: Southern Illinois University Press, 1980); Frederick Neuhouser, *Fichte's Theory of Subjectivity* (Cambridge: Cambridge University Press, 1990); and Robert R. Williams, *Recognition: Fichte and Hegel on the Other* (Albany, NY: SUNY Press, 1992). For a collection of critical essays, see Daniel Breazeale and Tom Rockmore, eds., *Fichte: Historical Contexts/Contemporary Controversies* (Atlantic Highlands, NJ: Humanities Press, 1994).

ON THE FOUNDATION OF OUR BELIEF
IN A DIVINE GOVERNMENT
OF THE UNIVERSE

The author of the present essay has for some time recognized it as his duty to set before a larger public the results of his philosophical work on the above subject. Hitherto this has been made available only to the auditors of his academic lectures. He had intended to present his ideas on this subject with the definiteness and precision that is appropriate to the sanctity which it possesses for so many honorable persons. Unfortunately the author's time was occupied with other tasks and the execution of his plan had to be repeatedly postponed.

As coeditor of the present journal, the author is obliged to put before the public the following essay of an excellent philosopher and this has facilitated the execution of the plan just mentioned. The [Forberg's] essay* coincides on many points with the present author's own convictions and hence he can on several matters simply refer the reader to it as an exposition of his own position as well. In other respects, however, the [Forberg's] essay, although not exactly opposed to the present author's views, has not quite reached the latter's position; and this makes it imperative to make the present writer's position publicly known, especially since he believes that his special intellectual approach involves more basic issues than those usually raised by philosophers. However, for the time being nothing more is attempted than a sketch of this approach. A more elaborate treatment will have to wait for another occasion.

The tendency to treat the so-called moral proof or any of the other arguments for the existence of God as genuine proofs has been a source of almost universal confusion and is likely to remain so for a long time. The assumption is apparently made that belief in God was for the first time given to the human race by means of such argumentation. Poor philosophy! I should like to know how your representatives who, after all, are also only human beings obtain what they wish to give us by means of their proofs; or if these representatives are in fact beings of a higher nature, one wonders how they can count on obtaining acceptance and understanding in us others without presupposing something analogous to their belief. No, this is not how things stand. Philosophy can explain facts—it cannot bring them into existence except for the one fact of philosophy itself. As little as it will occur to the philosopher to persuade mankind to believe from now on in the existence of material objects in space or to treat the changes of these objects as successive events in time, so little should he be inclined to persuade mankind to believe in a divine government of the world. All of this happens without any persuasion on the philosopher's part and he accepts these facts without question. It is the business of the philosopher to deduce these facts as necessarily implied in the essence of rational beings as such. Hence our procedure must not be regarded as a con-

*[Fichte here refers to Forberg's *"Entwickelung des Begriffs der Religion"* ("The Development of the Concept of Religion"), which was published in the same issue of the *Philosophisches Journal*.]

Fichte, "On the Foundation of Our Belief in a Divine Government of the Universe," translated by Paul Edwards, from Patrick L. Gardiner, ed., *Nineteenth-Century Philosophy* (New York: The Free Press, 1969), from "Readings in the History of Philosophy," Paul Edwards and Richard H. Popkin, series eds. (Originally published as *"Über der Grund unsers Glaubens an eine Göttliche Weltregierung"* in the *Philosophisches Journal*, Vol. VIII, 1798.)

version of the unbeliever but as a deduction of the believer's conviction. Our only task is to deal with the causal question, "How does man arrive at his belief?"

In dealing with this question it is essential to realize that this belief must not be represented as an arbitrary assumption which a human being may make or not make as he sees fit—as a freely chosen decision to take as true what the heart desires and because the heart desires it and as a supplement or substitute for the insufficiency of the available logical arguments. What is founded in reason is absolutely necessary; and what is not necessary is therefore a violation of reason. A person who regards the latter as fact is a deluded dreamer, however pious his attitude may be.

Where now will the philosopher, who presupposes belief in God, search for the necessary ground which he is supposed to furnish? Should he base himself on the alleged necessity with which the existence or the nature of the world of the senses implies a rational author? The answer must be an emphatic "no." For he knows only too well that such an inference is totally unwarranted, although misguided thinkers have made such a claim in their embarrassment to explain something whose existence they cannot deny but whose true ground is hidden from them. The original understanding, which is placed under the guardianship of reason and the direction of its mechanism, is incapable of such a step. One may regard the world of the senses either from the point of view of common sense which is also that of the natural sciences or else from the transcendental standpoint. In the former case reason is required to stop at the existence of the world as something absolute: the world exists simply because it does and it is the way it is simply because it is that way. From this point of view something absolute is accepted and this absolute being simply is the universe: the two are identical. The universe is regarded as a whole which is grounded in itself and complete by itself. From this point of view, the world is an organized and organizing whole containing the ground of all phenomena within itself and its immanent laws. If, while occupying the standpoint of the pure natural sciences, we demand an explanation of the existence and nature of the universe in terms of an intelligent cause, our demand is total nonsense.

Moreover, the assertion that an intelligent being is the author of the world of the senses does not help us in the least—it is not really an intelligible pronouncement and what we get are a few empty words instead of a genuine answer to a question that should not have been raised in the first place. An intelligent being is unquestionably constituted by thoughts; and the first intelligible word has yet to be spoken on the subject of how, in the monstrous system of a creation out of nothing, thoughts can be transmuted into matter, or how, in a system that is hardly more rational, the world can become what it is as the result of the action of thoughts upon self-sufficient eternal matter.

It may be admitted that these difficulties vanish if we adopt the transcendental standpoint. There is then no longer an independent world: everything is now simply a reflection of our inner activity. However, one cannot inquire into the ground of something that does not exist and we cannot thus assume something outside of it in terms of which it is to be explained.

We cannot start from the world of the senses in order to climb to the notion of a moral world order so long, that is, as we really start with the sense-world and do not surreptitiously introduce a moral order into it.

Our belief in a moral world order must be based on the concept of a supersensible world.

There is such a concept. I find myself free from any influence of the sense-world, absolutely active in and through myself, and hence I am a power transcending all that is sensuous. This freedom is not, however, indefinite: it has its purpose, and this is not a purpose received from the outside but rather one posited by the free self from its inner nature. My own self and my necessary goal are the supersensible reality.

I cannot doubt this freedom or its nature without giving up my own self.

I cannot doubt this, I say—I cannot even think of the possibility that things are not this way, that this inner voice might deceive me and that it requires to be authorized and justified by reference to something external. Concerning this insight I cannot engage in any further rationalizations, interpretations, or explanations. It is what is absolutely positive and categorical.

I cannot transcend this insight unless I decide to destroy my inner nature—I cannot question it because I cannot *will* to question it. Here is the limit to the otherwise untamed flight of reason—here we find the voice that constrains the intellect because it also constrains the heart. Here is the point where thinking and willing are united and where harmony is brought into my being. I could indeed question the insight concerning my freedom if I wanted to fall into contradiction with my own self, for there is no immanent limitation confining the reasoning faculty: it freely advances into the infinite and must be able to do this since I am free in all my utterances and only I myself can set a limit to myself through my own will. Our moral vocation is therefore itself the outcome of a moral attitude and it is identical with our faith. One is thus quite right in maintaining that faith is the basis of all certainty. This is how it must be; since morality, if it is really morality, can be constructed only out of itself and not out of any logically coercive argumentation.

I could question the insight of my moral freedom if I were ready to plunge into a bottomless abyss (if only in a theoretical fashion); if I were ready to forego absolutely any firm point of reference; if I were prepared to do without that certainty that accompanies all my thinking and without which I could not even set out on speculative inquiries. For there is no firm point of reference except the one indicated here: it is founded in the moral sentiment and not in logic; if our rational faculty does not get to it or else proceeds beyond it, the result is that we find ourselves in an unbounded ocean in which each wave is pushed along by some other wave.

By adopting the goal set before me by my own nature, and by making it the purpose of my real activity, I *ipso facto* posit the possibility of achieving this purpose through my actions. The two statements are identical—to adopt something as my purpose means that I posit it as something real at some future time; if something is posited as real, its possibility is thereby necessarily implied. I must, if I am not to deny my own nature, first set myself the execution of this goal: and I must, secondly assume that it can be realized. These are in fact absolutely identical: they are not two acts but the one indivisible act dictated by the moral sentiment.

One should note the absolute necessity of what has here been shown. (The reader is requested to grant me for the moment that the possibility of realizing the ultimate moral goal has been demonstrated.) We are not dealing with a wish, a hope, a piece of reflection and consideration, of grounds pro and con, a free decision to assume something whose opposite one also regards as possible. Given the decision to obey the laws of one's inner nature, the assumption is strictly necessary: it is immediately contained in the decision; it is in fact that decision.

One should also observe the logical sequence of the ideas here presented. The inference is not from possibility to reality, but the other way around. Our contention is not: I ought since I can; it is rather: I can since I ought. That I ought and what I ought to do comes first and is most immediately evident. It requires no further explanation, justification, or authorization. It is intrinsically true and evident. It is not based on or conditioned by any other truth, but on the contrary all other truths are conditioned by it. This logical order has frequently been overlooked. A person who maintains that I must first know whether I can do something before I can judge that I ought to do it, is thereby, if he is making a practical judgment, negating the primacy of the moral law and hence the moral law itself, while, if he is making a theoretical judgment, he thereby totally misconstrues the original sequence of our rational processes.

To say that I must simply adopt the goal of morality, that its realization is possible and possible through me, means that every action which I ought to perform and the circumstances that condition such an action are means to my adopted goal. It is in the light of this that my existence, the existence of other moral beings and of the world of the senses as our common stage receive their relation to morality. A wholly new order is thus brought into being and the sense-world with all its immanent laws is no more than the support underlying this order. The world of the senses proceeds in its course according to its eternal laws in order to provide freedom with a sphere of operation, but it does not have the slightest influence on morality or immorality, it does not in any way control a free being. The latter soars above all nature in self-sufficiency and independence. The realization of the purpose of reason can be accomplished only through the efforts of free beings, but because of a higher law this purpose will unquestionably be attained. It is possible to do what is right and every situation is geared to this through the higher law just mentioned: because of this law the moral deed succeeds infallibly and the immoral deed fails just as certainly. The entire universe now exhibits a totally different appearance to us.

This change in appearance will be further illuminated if we raise ourselves to the transcendental viewpoint. Transcendental theory teaches that the world is nothing but the sensuous appearance, given according to intelligible rational laws, of our own inner activity, our own intelligence operating within boundaries that must remain incomprehensible; and a human being cannot be blamed if he has an uncanny feeling when faced with the total disappearance of the ground underneath him. The boundaries just mentioned are admittedly beyond our understanding as far as their origin is concerned. However, practical philosophy teaches that this does not significantly affect anything of practical importance. The boundaries are the clearest and most certain of all things—they determine our fixed position in the moral arrangement of things. What you perceive as a consequence of your position in this moral order has reality and, moreover, the only reality that concerns you: it is the permanent interpretation of the injunction of your duty, the living expression of what you ought to do simply because you ought to do it. Our world is the sensualized material of our duty; the latter is the truly real in things, the genuine primal stuff of all appearances. The compulsion with which our belief in things is forced upon us is a moral compulsion—the only one that can be exerted upon a free being. Nobody can, without destruction of his nature, surrender his moral calling to such a degree that it cannot preserve him, within the limits previously mentioned, for a higher and nobler future state. Considered as the result of a moral world order, this belief in the reality of the sense-world can even be regarded as a kind of revelation. It is our duty that is revealed in the world of the senses.

This is the true faith: this moral order is the Divine which we accept. It is constituted by acting rightly. This is the only possible confession of faith: to do what duty prescribes and to do this gaily and naturally, without doubt or calculation of consequences. As a result, this Divine becomes alive and real in us; every one of our deeds is performed in the light of this presupposition and all their consequences will be preserved in the Divine.

True atheism, unbelief and godlessness in the real sense, consists in calculation of consequences, in refusing to obey the voice of one's conscience until one thinks one can foresee the success of one's actions and in thus elevating one's own judgment above that of God and in making oneself into God. He who wills to do evil in order to produce good is a godless person. Under a moral government of the world good cannot come out of evil; and as certainly as one believes in the former, so one cannot believe the latter. You must not lie even, as a result, the world were to collapse and become a heap of ruins. But this last is only a manner of speaking: if you were permitted to believe seriously that the world would collapse, then at the very least your own nature would be self-contradictory and self-destroying. In fact you do not believe this, you cannot believe it, and you are not even permitted to believe it: you know that the plan of the world's preservation does not contain a lie.

The faith just stated is the whole and complete faith. This living and effective moral order is identical with God. We do not and cannot grasp any other God. There is no rational justification for going beyond this moral world order and for inferring the existence of a separate entity as its cause. Our original reason certainly does not make any such inference and it does not know any such separate entity—only a philosophy that misunderstands its own nature draws such an inference. Is this moral world order no more than a contingent entity, something that might not be, that might be as it is or otherwise so that its existence and nature requires to be explained in terms of a cause, so that belief in it requires to be legitimized by showing its ground? If you will stop listening to the demands of a worthless system and if instead you will consult your own inner nature, then you will find that the moral world order is the absolute beginning of all objective knowledge (just as your freedom and your moral vocation are the absolute beginning of all subjective knowledge) and all other objective knowledge must be founded and conditioned by it, while the moral world order itself cannot be conditioned by anything else, since outside of it there is nothing else. You cannot even attempt the explanation [of the moral order] without falsifying and endangering the nature of the original assumption. The assumption of a moral world order is such that it is absolutely self-evident and it does not tolerate any supporting arguments. Yet you wish to make the assumption dependent on such argumentation.

And this ratiocination, how can you succeed with it? After you have undermined the immediate conviction, how do you then proceed to fortify it? Indeed, it does not stand well with your faith if you can embrace it only on condition that it has an external source and if it collapses in the absence of such a support.

Even if one were to permit you to draw this inference and, as a consequence, to conclude that an author of the moral world order exists, what would that conclusion amount to? This entity is supposed to be distinct from you and from the world, it is supposed to engage in activities in the world in accordance with its plans and must therefore be capable of having ideas, of having personality and consciousness. But what do you mean by "personality" and "consciousness"? It is plain that when you use these words, you refer to what you have found and come to know in yourself under these labels. The least attention to these notions will teach you that they can be properly employed only if what they refer to is limited and finite. You therefore make the entity to which you apply these predicates into something finite. You have not, as you intended to, succeeded in thinking about God—you have merely multiplied yourself in your thoughts. You can no more explain the moral world order by reference to this entity than by reference to yourself: the moral world order remains unexplained and absolute as before. Indeed, in talking the way you do, you have not engaged in any genuine thinking at all, but you have merely disturbed the air with empty sounds. You could have predicted this outcome without difficulty. You are a finite being and how can that which is finite grasp and understand the infinite?

If faith keeps to what is immediately given, it remains firm and unshakable; if it is made dependent on the concept [of the personal God just discussed] then it becomes shaky, for the concept is impossible and full of contradictions.

It is therefore a misunderstanding to maintain that it is doubtful whether or not there is a God. On the contrary, that there is a moral world order, that in this order a definite position has been assigned to every rational individual and that his work counts, that the destiny of every person (unless it is the consequence of his own conduct) is derived from this plan, that without this plan no hair drops from a head, nor a sparrow from a roof, that every good deed succeeds while every evil one fails and that everything must go well for those who love only the good—all this is not doubtful at all but the most certain thing in the world and the basis of all other certainty, in fact the only truth that is objectively absolutely valid. On the other side, anybody who reflects just a moment and who is candid about the outcome of this reflection cannot doubt that the concept of God as a separate substance is impossible and contradictory. It is permissible to say this openly and put down the idle chatter of the schools in order to elevate the true religion of joyful morality.

THE VOCATION OF MAN (in part)

BOOK III

I demand something beyond a mere presentation or conception; something that is, has been, and will be, even if the presentation were not; and which the presentation only records, without producing it, or in the smallest degree changing it. A mere presentation I now see to be a deceptive show; my presentations must have a meaning beneath them, and if my entire knowledge revealed to me nothing but knowledge, I would be defrauded of my whole life. That there is nothing whatever but my presentations or conceptions, is, to the natural sense of mankind, a silly and ridiculous conceit which no man can seriously entertain, and which requires no refutation. To the better informed judgment, which knows the deep, and, *by mere reasoning,* irrefragable grounds for this assertion, it is a prostrating, annihilating thought.

And what is, then, this something lying beyond all presentation, towards which I stretch forward with such ardent longing? What is the power with which it draws me towards it? What is the central point in my soul to which it is attached, and with which only it can be effaced?

"Not merely TO KNOW, but according to thy knowledge TO DO, is thy vocation":—thus is it loudly proclaimed in the innermost depths of my soul, as soon as I recollect myself for a moment, and turn my observation upon myself. "Not for idle contemplation of thyself, not for brooding over devout sensations;—no, for action art thou here; thine action, and thine action alone, determines thy worth."

Fichte, Book III of *"The Vocation of Man,"* translated by William Smith, in *The Popular Works of J.G. Fichte* (London, 1848), Vol. I, pp. 469–489.

This voice leads me from presentation, from mere cognition, to something which lies beyond it, and is entirely opposed to it; to something which is greater and higher than all knowledge, and which contains within itself the end and object of all knowledge. When I act, I doubtless know that I act, and how I act; but this knowledge is not the act itself, but only the observation of it. This voice thus announces to me precisely that which I sought; a something lying beyond mere knowledge, and, in its nature, wholly independent of it.

Thus it is, I know it immediately. But having once entered within the domain of speculation, the doubt which has been awakened within me, will secretly endure, and will continue to disturb me. Since I have placed myself in this position, I can obtain no complete satisfaction until everything which I accept is justified before the tribunal of speculation. I have thus to ask myself,—how is it thus? Whence arises that voice in my soul which directs me to something beyond mere presentation and knowledge?

There is within me an impulse to absolute, independent self-activity. Nothing is more insupportable to me, than to be merely by another, for another, and through another; I must be something for myself and by myself alone. This impulse I feel along with the perception of my own existence, it is inseparably united to my consciousness of myself.

I explain this feeling to myself, by reflection; and add to this blind impulse the power of sight, by thought. According to this impulse I must act as an absolutely independent being:—thus I understand and translate the impulse. I must be independent. Who am I? Subject and object in one,—the conscious being and that of which I am conscious, gifted with intuitive knowledge and myself revealed in that intuition, the thinking mind and myself the object of the thought—inseparable, and ever present to each other. As both, must I be what I am, absolutely by myself alone;—by myself originate conceptions,—by myself produce a condition of things lying beyond these conceptions. But how is the latter possible? To nothing I cannot unite any being whatever; from nothing there can never arise something; my objective thought is necessarily mediative only. But any being which is united to another being, does thereby, by means of this other being, become dependent;—it is no longer a primary, original, and genetic, but only a secondary and derived being. I am constrained to unite myself to something;—to another being I cannot unite myself, without losing that independence which is the condition of my own existence.

My conception and origination of a purpose, however, is, by its very nature, absolutely free,—producing something out of nothing. To such a conception I must unite my activity, in order that it may be possible to regard it as free, and as proceeding absolutely from myself alone.

In the following manner, therefore, do I conceive of my independence as *I*. I ascribe to myself the power of originating a conception simply because I originate it, of originating *this* conception simply because I originate *this* one,—by the absolute sovereignty of myself as an intelligence. I further ascribe to myself the power of manifesting this conception beyond itself by means of an action;—ascribe to myself a real, active power, capable of producing something beyond itself,—a power which is entirely different from the mere power of conception. These conceptions, which are called conceptions of design, or purposes, are not, like the conceptions of mere knowledge, copies of something already given, but rather types of something yet to be produced; the real power lies beyond them, and is *in itself* independent of them;—it only receives from them its immediate determinations, which are apprehended by knowledge. Such an independent power it is that, in consequence of this impulse, I ascribe to myself.

Here then, it appears, is the point to which the consciousness of all reality unites itself;—the real efficiency of my conception, and the real power of action which, in consequence of it, I am compelled to ascribe to myself, is this point. Let it be as it may with the reality of a sensible world beyond me; I possess reality and comprehend it,—it lies within my own being, it is native to myself.

I conceive this, my real power of action, in thought, but I do not create it by thought. The immediate feeling of my impulse to independent activity lies at the foundation of this thought; the thought does no more than portray this feeling, and accept it in its own form,—the form of thought. This procedure may, I think, be vindicated before the tribunal of speculation.

What! Shall I, once more, knowingly and intentionally deceive myself? This procedure can by no means be justified before that strict tribunal.

I feel within me an impulse and an effort towards outward activity; this appears to be true, and to be the only truth which belongs to the matter. Since it is I who feel this impulse, and since I cannot pass beyond myself, either with my whole consciousness, or in particular with my capacity of sensation,—since this *I* itself is the last point at which I feel this impulse, therefore it certainly appears to me as an impulse founded in myself, to an activity also founded in myself. Might it not be however that this impulse, although unperceived by me, is in reality the impulse of a foreign power invisible to me, and that notion of independence merely a delusion, arising from my sphere of vision being limited to myself alone? I have no reason to assume this, but just as little reason to deny it. I must confess that I absolutely know nothing, and can know nothing, about it.

Do I then indeed *feel* that real power of free action, which, strangely enough, I ascribe to myself without knowing anything of it? By no means;—it is merely the *determinable* element, which, by the well known laws of thought whereby all capacities and all powers arise, we are compelled to add in imagination to the *determinate* element—the real action, which itself is, in like manner, only an assumption.

Is that procession, from the mere conception to an imaginary realization of it, anything more than the usual and well-known procedure of all objective thought, which always strives to be, not mere thought, but something more? By what dishonesty can this procedure be made of more value here than in any other case?—can it possess any deeper significance, when to the conception of a thought it adds a realization of this thought, than when to the conception of this table it adds an actual and present table? "The conception of a purpose, a particular determination of events in me, appears in a double shape,—partly as *subjective*—a Thought; partly as *objective*—an Action." What reason, which would not unquestionably itself stand in need of a genetic deduction, could I adduce against this explanation?

I say that I feel this impulse:—it is therefore I myself who say so, and think so while I say it? Do I then really feel, or only think that I feel? Is not all which I call feeling only a presentation produced by my objective process of thought, and indeed the first transition point of all objectivity? And then again, do I really think, or do I merely think that I think? And do I think that I really think, or merely that I possess the idea of thinking? What can hinder speculation from raising such questions, and continuing to raise them without end? What can I answer, and where is there a point at which I can command such questionings to cease? I know, and must admit, that each definite act of consciousness may be made the subject of reflection, and a new consciousness of the first consciousness may thus be created; and that thereby the immediate consciousness is raised a step higher, and the first consciousness darkened and made doubtful; and that to this ladder there is no highest step. I know that all scepticism rests upon this process, and that the system which has so violently prostrated me is founded on the adoption and the clear consciousness of it.

I know that if I am not merely to play another perplexing game with this system, but intend really and practically to adopt it, I must refuse obedience to that voice within me. I cannot *will* to act, for according to that system I cannot *know* whether I can really act or not:—I can never believe that I truly act; that which seems to be my action must appear to me as entirely without meaning, as a mere delusive picture. All earnestness and all interest is withdrawn from my life; and life, as well as thought, is transformed into a mere play, which proceeds from nothing and tends to nothing.

Shall I then refuse obedience to that inward voice? I will not do so. I will freely accept the vocation which this impulse assigns to me, and in this resolution I will lay hold at once of thought, in all its reality and truthfulness, and on the reality of all things which are presupposed therein. I will restrict myself to the position of natural thought in which this impulse places me, and cast from me all those over-refined and subtle inquiries which alone could make me doubtful of its truth.

I understand thee now, sublime Spirit! I have found the organ by which to apprehend this reality, and, with this, probably all other reality. Knowledge is not this organ:—no knowledge can be its own foundation, its own proof; every knowledge presupposes another higher knowledge on which it is founded, and to this ascent there is no end. It is FAITH, that voluntary acquiescence in the view which is naturally presented to us, because only through this view we can fulfil our vocation;—this it is, which first lends a sanction to knowledge, and raises to certainty and conviction that which without it might be mere delusion. It is not knowledge, but a resolution of the will to admit the validity of knowledge.

Let me hold fast for ever by this doctrine, which is no mere verbal distinction, but a true and deep one, bearing with it the most important consequences for my whole existence and character. All my conviction is but faith; and it proceeds from the character, not from the understanding. Knowing this, I will enter upon no disputation, because I foresee that thereby nothing can be gained; I will not suffer myself to be perplexed by it, for the source of my conviction lies higher than all disputation; I will not suffer myself to entertain the desire of pressing this conviction on others by reasoning, and I will not be surprised if such an undertaking should fail. I have adopted my mode of thinking first of all for myself, not for others, and before myself only will I justify it. He who possesses the honest, upright purpose of which I am conscious, will also attain a similar conviction; but without that, this conviction can in no way be attained. Now that I know this, I also know from what point all culture of myself and others must proceed; from the will, not from the understanding. If the former be only fixedly and honestly directed towards the Good, the latter will of itself apprehend the True. Should the latter only be exercised, whilst the former remains neglected, there can arise nothing whatever but a dexterity in groping after vain and empty refinements, throughout the absolute void inane. Now that I know this, I am able to confute all false knowledge that may rise in opposition to my faith. I know that every pretended truth, produced by mere speculative thought, and not founded upon faith, is assuredly false and surreptitious; for mere knowledge, thus produced, leads only to the conviction that we can know nothing. I know that such false knowledge never can discover anything but what it has previously placed in its premises through faith, from which it probably draws conclusions which are wholly false. Now that I know this, I possess the touchstone of all truth and of all conviction. Conscience alone is the root of all truth: whatever is opposed to conscience, or stands in the way of the fulfilment of her behests, is assuredly false; and it is impossible for me to arrive at a conviction of its truth, even if I should be unable to discover the fallacies by which it is produced.

So has it been with all men who have ever seen the light of this world. Without being conscious of it, they apprehend all the reality which has an existence for them, through faith alone; and this faith forces itself on them simultaneously with their existence;—it is born with them. How could it be otherwise? If in mere knowledge, in mere perception and reflection, there is no ground for regarding our mental presentations as more than mere pictures which necessarily pass before our view, why do we yet regard all of them as more than this, and assume, as their foundation, something which exists independently of all presentation? If we all possess the capacity and the instinct to proceed beyond our first natural view of things, why do so few actually go beyond it, and why do we even defend ourselves, with a sort of bitterness, from every motive by which others try to persuade us to this course? What is it which holds us confined within this first natural belief? Not inferences of reason, for there are none such; it is the interest we have in a reality which we desire to produce;—the good, absolutely for its own sake,—the common and sensuous, for the sake of the enjoyment they afford. No one who lives can divest himself of this interest, and just as little can he cast off the faith which this interest brings with it. We are all born in faith;—he who is blind, follows blindly the secret and irresistible impulse; he who sees, follows by sight, and believes because he resolves to believe.

What unity and completeness does this view present—what dignity does it confer on human nature! Our thought is not founded on itself alone, independently of our impulses and affections;—man does not consist of two independent and separate elements; he is absolutely one. All our thought is founded on our impulses—as a man's affections are, so is his knowledge. These impulses compel us to a certain mode of thought only so long as we do not perceive the constraint; the constraint vanishes the moment it is perceived; and it is then no longer the impulse by itself, but we ourselves, according to our impulse, who form our own system of thought.

But I shall open my eyes; shall learn thoroughly to know myself; shall discover that constraint;—this is my vocation. I shall thus, and under that supposition I shall necessarily, form my own mode of thought. Then shall I stand absolutely independent, thoroughly equipt and perfected through my own act and deed. The primitive source of all my other thought and of my life itself, that from which everything proceeds which can have an existence in me, for me, or through me, the innermost spirit of my spirit,—is no longer a foreign power, but it is, in the strictest possible sense, the product of my own will. I am wholly my own creation. I might have followed blindly the leading of my spiritual nature. But I would not be a work of Nature but of myself, and I have become so even by means of this resolution. By endless subtleties I might have made the natural conviction of my own mind dark and doubtful. But I have accepted it with freedom, simply because I resolved to accept it. I have chosen the system which I have now adopted with settled purpose and deliberation from among other possible modes of thought, because I have recognized in it the only one consistent with my dignity and my vocation. With freedom and consciousness I have returned to the point at which Nature had left me. I accept that which she announces;—but I do not accept it because I must; I believe it because I will.

The exalted vocation of my understanding fills me with reverence. It is no longer the deceptive mirror which reflects a series of empty pictures, proceeding from nothing and tending to nothing; it is bestowed upon me for a great purpose. Its cultivation for this purpose is entrusted to me; it is placed in my hands, and at my hands it will be required.—It is placed in my hands. I know immediately—and here my faith accepts the testimony of my consciousness without farther criticism—I know that I am not placed under the necessity of allowing my thoughts to float about without direction or purpose, but that I can voluntarily arouse and direct my attention to one object, turn it away again towards another;—know that it is neither a blind necessity which compels me to a certain mode of thought, nor an empty chance which runs riot with my thoughts; but that it is I who think, and that I can think of that whereof I determine to think. Thus by reflection I have discovered something more; I have discovered that I myself, by my own act alone, produce my whole system of thought, and the particular view which I take of truth in general; since it remains with me either to deprive myself of all sense of truth by means of over-refinement, or to yield myself to this view with faithful obedience. My whole mode of thought, and the cultivation which my under-standing receives, as well as the objects to which I direct it, depend entirely on myself. True insight is merit;—the perversion of my capacity for knowledge, thoughtlessness, obscurity, error, and unbelief, are guilt.

There is but one point towards which I have unceasingly to direct all my atten-tion,—namely what I ought to do, and how I may most suitably fulfil the obligation which binds me to do it. All my thoughts must have a bearing on my actions, and must be capable of being considered as means, however remote, to this end; otherwise they are an idle and aimless show, a mere waste of time and strength, and the perversion of noble power, which is entrusted to me for a very different end.

I dare hope, I dare surely promise myself, to follow out this undertaking with good results. The Nature on which I have to act is not a foreign element, called into ex-istence without reference to me, into which I cannot penetrate. It is moulded by my own laws of thought, and must be in harmony with them; it must be thoroughly trans-parent, knowable and penetrable to me, even to its inmost recesses. In all its phenom-ena it expresses nothing but the connexions and relations of my own being to myself, and as surely as I may hope to know myself, so surely may I expect to comprehend it. Let me seek only that which I ought to seek, and I shall find; let me ask only that which I ought to ask, and I shall receive an answer.

That voice within my soul in which I believe, and on account of which I believe in every other thing to which I attach credence, does not merely command me to act *in general*. This is impossible; all these general principles are formed only through my own voluntary observation and reflection, applied to many individual facts; but never in themselves express any fact whatever. This voice of my conscience announces to me precisely what I ought to do, and what leave undone, in every particular situation of life; it accompanies me, if I will but listen to it with attention, through all the events of my life, and never refuses me my reward where I am called upon to act. It carries with it immediate conviction, and irresistibly compels my assent to its behests:—it is im-possible for me to contend against it.

To listen to it, to obey it honestly and unreservedly, without fear or equivoca-tion,—this is my true vocation, the whole end and purpose of my existence. My life ceases to be an empty play without truth or significance. There is something that must absolutely be done for its own sake alone;—that which conscience demands of me in this particular situation of life it is mine to do, for this only am I here;—to know it, I have understanding; to perform it, I have power. Through this edict of conscience alone, truth and reality are introduced into my conceptions. I cannot refuse them my at-tention and my obedience without thereby surrendering the very purpose of my own existence.

Hence I cannot withhold my belief from the reality which they announce, with-out at the same time renouncing my vocation. It is absolutely true, without farther proof or confirmation,—nay, it is the first truth, and the foundation of all other truth and certainty, that this voice must be obeyed; and therefore everything becomes to me true and certain, the truth and certainty of which is assumed in the possibility of such an obedience.

There appear before me in space, certain phenomena, to which I transfer the idea of myself;—I conceive of them as beings like myself. Speculation, when carried out to its last results, has indeed taught me, or would teach me, that these supposed rational beings out of myself are but the products of my own presentative power; that, according to certain laws of my thought, I am compelled to represent out of myself my conception of myself; and that, according to the same laws, I can only transfer this conception to certain definite intuitions. But the voice of my conscience thus speaks:— "Whatever these beings may be in and for themselves, thou shall act towards them as self-existent, free, substantive beings, wholly independent of thee. Assume it as already known, that they can give a purpose to their own being wholly by themselves, and quite independently of thee; never interrupt the accomplishment of this purpose, but rather further it to the utmost of thy power. Honour their freedom, lovingly take up their purposes as if they were thine own." Thus ought I to act:—by this course of action *ought* all my thought to be guided,—nay, it *shall* and *must* necessarily be so, if I have resolved to obey the voice of my conscience. I shall therefore always regard these beings as in possession of an existence for themselves wholly independent of mine, as capable of forming and carrying out their own purposes;—from this point of view, I shall never be able to regard them otherwise, and my previous speculations shall vanish from before me like an empty dream.—I *think* of them as beings like myself, I have said; but strictly speaking, it is not mere thought by which they are first presented to me as such. It is by the voice of my conscience,—the command:—"Here set a limit to thy freedom; here recognize and reverence purposes which are not thine own." This it is which is first translated into the thought, "Here, certainly and truly, are beings like myself, free and independent." To view them otherwise, I must in action renounce, and in speculation disregard, the voice of my conscience.

Other phenomena present themselves before me which I do not regard as beings like myself, but as things irrational. Speculation finds no difficulty in showing how the conception of such things is developed solely from my own presentative faculty, and its necessary modes of activity. But I apprehend these things, also, through want, desire, and enjoyment. Not by the mental conception, but by hunger, thirst, and their satisfaction, does anything become for me food and drink. I am necessitated to believe in the reality of that which threatens my sensuous existence, or in that which alone is able to maintain it. Conscience enters the field in order that it may at once sanctify and restrain this natural impulse. "Thou shalt maintain, exercise, and strengthen thyself and thy physical powers, for they have been counted upon in the plans of reason. But thou canst only maintain them by using them in a legitimate manner, conformable to the inward nature of such things. There are also, besides thee, many other beings like thyself, whose powers have been counted upon like thine own, and can only be maintained in the same way as thine own. Concede to them the same privilege that has been allowed to thee. Respect what belongs to them, as their possession;—use what belongs to thee, legitimately as thine own." Thus ought I to act,—according to this course of action must I think. I am compelled to regard these things as standing under their own natural laws, independent of, though perceivable by, me; and therefore to ascribe to them an independent existence. I am compelled to believe in such laws; the task of investigating them is set before me, and that empty speculation vanishes like a mist when the genial sun appears.

In short, there is for me absolutely no such thing as an existence which has no relation to myself, and which I contemplate merely for the sake of contemplating it;— whatever has an existence for me, has it only through its relation to myself. But there is, in the highest sense, only one relation to me possible, all others are but subordinate forms of this:—my vocation to moral activity. My world is the object and sphere of my duties, and absolutely nothing more; there is no other world for me, and no other qualities of my world than what are implied in this;—my whole united capacity, all finite capacity, is insufficient to comprehend any other. Whatever possesses an existence for me, can bring its existence and reality into contact with me only through this relation, and only through this relation do I comprehend it:—for any other existence than this I have no organ whatever.

To the question, whether, in deed and in fact, such a world exists as that which I represent to myself, I can give no answer more fundamental, more raised above all doubt, than this:—I have, most certainly and truly, these determinate duties, which announce themselves to me as duties towards certain objects, to be fulfilled by means of certain materials;—duties which I cannot otherwise conceive of, and cannot otherwise fulfil, than within such a world as I represent to myself. Even to one who had never meditated on his own moral vocation, if there could be such a one, or who, if he had given it some general consideration, had, at least, never entertained the slightest purpose of fulfilling it at any time within an indefinite futurity,—even for him, his sensuous world, and his belief in its reality, arises in other manner than from his ideas of a moral world. If he do not apprehend it by the thought of his duties, he certainly does so by the demand for his rights. What he perhaps never requires of himself, he does certainly exact from others in their conduct towards him,—that they should treat him with propriety, consideration, and respect, not as an irrational thing, but as a free and independent being;—and thus, in supposing in them an ability to comply with his own demands, he is compelled also to regard them as themselves considerate, free, and independent of the dominion of mere natural power. Should he never propose to himself any other purpose in his use and enjoyment of surrounding objects, but simply that of enjoying them, he at least demands this enjoyment as a right, in the possession of which he must be left undisturbed by others; and thus he apprehends even the irrational world of sense, by means of a moral idea. These claims of respect for his rationality, independence, and preservation, no one can resign who possesses a conscious existence; and with these claims, at least, there is united in his soul, earnestness, renunciation of doubt, and faith in a reality, even if they be not associated with the recognition of a moral law within him. Take the man who denies his own moral vocation, and thy existence, and the existence of a material world, except as a mere futile effort in which speculation tries her strength,—approach him practically, introduce his own principles into life, and act as if either he had no existence at all, or were merely a portion of rude matter,—he will soon lay aside his scornful indifference, and indignantly complain of thee; earnestly call thy attention to thy conduct towards him; maintain that thou oughtst not and darest not so to act; and thus prove to thee, by deeds, that thou art assuredly capable of acting upon him; that *he is,* and that *thou art,*—that there is a medium by which thou canst influence him, and that thou, at least, hast duties to perform towards him.

Thus, it is not the operation of supposed external objects, which indeed exist for us, and we for them, only in so far as we already know of them; and just as little an empty vision evoked by our own imagination and thought, the products of which must, like itself, be mere empty pictures;—it is not these, but the necessary faith in our own freedom and power, in our own real activity and in the definite laws of human action, which lies at the root of all our consciousness of a reality external to ourselves;—a consciousness which is itself but faith, since it is founded on another faith, of which however it is a necessary consequence. We are compelled to believe that we act, and that we ought to act in a certain manner; we are compelled to assume a certain sphere for this action; this sphere is the real, actually present world, such as we find it;—and on the other hand, the world is absolutely nothing more than this sphere, and cannot, in any other way, extend itself beyond it. From this necessity of action proceeds the consciousness of the actual world; and not the reverse way, from the consciousness of the actual world the necessity of action:—this, not that, is the first; the former is derived from the latter. We do not act because we know, but we know because we are called upon to act:—the practical reason is the root of all reason. The laws of action for rational beings are *immediately certain;* their world is only certain through that previous certainty. We cannot deny these laws without plunging the world, and ourselves with it, into absolute annihilation;—we raise ourselves from this abyss, and maintain ourselves above it, solely by our moral activity.

There is something which I am called upon to do, simply in order that it may be done; something to avoid doing, solely that it may be left undone. But can I act without having an end in view beyond the action itself, without directing my attention to something which can become possible through my action, and only through that? Can I will, without having something which I will? No:—this would entirely contradict the nature of my mind. To every action there is united in my thought, immediately and by the laws of thought itself, a condition of things placed in futurity, to which my action is related as the efficient cause to the effect produced. But this purpose or end of my action must not be given to me for its own sake,—perhaps through some necessity of Nature,—and then my course of action determined according to this end; I must not have an end assigned to me, and then inquire how I must act in order to attain this end; my action must not be dependent on the end; but I must act in a certain manner, simply because I ought so to act;—this is the first point. That a result will follow from this course of action, is proclaimed by the voice within me. This result necessarily becomes an end to me, since I am bound to perform the action which brings it, and it alone, to pass. I will that something shall come to pass, because I must act so that it may come to pass;—thus as I do not hunger because food is before me, but a thing becomes food for me because I hunger; so I do not act as I do because a certain end is to be attained, but the end becomes mine because I am bound to act in the particular manner by which it may be attained. I have not first in view the point towards which I am to draw my line, and then, by its position, determine the direction of my line, and the angle that it shall make; but I draw my line absolutely in a right angle, and thereby the points are determined through which my line must pass. The end does not determine the commandment; but, on the contrary, the primitive purport of the commandment determines the end.

I say, it is the law which commands me to act that of itself assigns an end to my action; the same inward voice that compels me to think that I ought to act thus, compels me also to believe that from my action some result will arise; it opens to my spiritual vision a prospect into another world,—which is really a world, a state, namely, and not an action,—but another and better world than that which is present to the physical eye; it makes me aspire after this better world, embrace it with every impulse, long for its realization, live only in it, and in it alone find satisfaction. The law itself is my guarantee for the certain attainment of this end. The same resolution by which I devote my whole thought and life to the fulfilment of this law, and determine to see nothing beyond it, brings with it the indestructible conviction, that the promise it implies is likewise true and certain, and renders it impossible for me to conceive the possibility of the opposite. As I live in obedience to it, I live also in the contemplation of its end; live in that better world which it promises to me. . . .

G.W.F. Hegel
1770–1831

Georg Wilhelm Friedrich Hegel was born in Stuttgart, in southern Germany. Hegel and his father, a minor government official; his mother, a loving hausfrau (housewife); and his sister and brother were all close, affectionate, and loving. It is easy to see why Hegel would later describe the family as the "immediate Ethical Substance." Following grade school in Stuttgart, at age eighteen, Hegel won a scholarship to Tübingen University, where he studied theology. While there, he met and befriended the poet Johann Christian Friedrich Hölderlin and the philosopher Friedrich Wilhelm Joseph Schelling. The work Hegel submitted to his professors at the university gave no indication of the brilliant philosophical career that was to follow. In fact, his diploma from the university recorded that his knowledge of theology was fair, but his knowledge of philosophy was inadequate. Nevertheless, Hegel was already beginning to write insightful essays, not for classroom assignments, but to clarify his own thoughts.

After graduating from the university in 1793, Hegel spent seven years as a tutor for wealthy families in Bern and Frankfurt. During this time he continued to write essays—mostly on religious topics—that indicated he had moved far away from orthodox Christianity. For example, one early essay compared Jesus and Socrates, and Socrates' ethical teaching was seen as superior.

Following his father's death in 1799, Hegel inherited a modest sum of money, quit tutoring, and joined his friend Schelling at the University of Jena. There Hegel became a *Privatdozent* (an unsalaried lecturer) and coedited a philosophic journal with Schelling. While at Jena, Hegel wrote his first great work, *The Phenomenology of Spirit* (1807), which laid out the major themes of his philosophy. This work included a critique of Schelling's ideas, which ended the friendship.

Before this important work could be published, Napoleon's war with Prussia closed the University of Jena, and so Hegel, whose inheritance had now been exhausted, was forced to find other employment.

After a stint as a newspaper editor, Hegel served eight years in Nürnberg as the rector of a *Gymnasium* (high school). There he published his second major work, *Science of Logic* (1812–1816). He also met and married a young woman from a distinguished family who was half his age, and they had two sons. In 1816, Hegel accepted a chair of philosophy at the University of Heidelberg. He continued his practice of producing a major book at each place he worked by publishing the *Encyclopedia of the Philosophical Sciences in Outline* in 1817. In 1818, Hegel moved to his final institution, the University of Berlin. There he published his *Philosophy of Right* (1821)—and became famous throughout Europe. He remained in Berlin until his death from cholera in 1831.

Following his death, a group of his friends published an eighteen-volume collection of his works, including his early essays and his lectures on aesthetics, the history of philosophy, the philosophy of history (portions of which are reprinted here), and the philosophy of religion.

*   *   *

Like all philosophers of his age, Hegel was greatly influenced by Kant. Kant had managed to synthesize two previously disparate realities—the rational world of ideas (emphasized by rationalists) with the phenomenal world of perception (emphasized by empiricists). But in so doing, Kant separated the noumenal world of "things-in-themselves" from the phenomenal world of experience and declared the noumenal world unknowable. In a sense, he had reconciled two competing epistemologies—Continental Rationalism and British Empiricism—at the expense of abandoning metaphysics. Hegel sought to go one step further than Kant and effect a complete synthesis that would not only draw together competing epistemologies but would also show the connection between epistemology and metaphysics. The key to this synthesis is the recognition that consciousness is the ultimate reality, or, to use his famous phrase, "What is real is rational—what is rational is real." That is, metaphysical reality (the real) *is* Idea or Spirit or Mind (that which knows). The resulting philosophy is called "Absolute Idealism" because all things that exist are essentially related to absolute Idea or Spirit or Mind.

According to Hegel, traditional rationalism (what he calls *raisonnement*) tends to classify all experience formally into abstract, lifeless universals. Taken to its logical extreme, rationalists end up with the abstraction "Being": "But this mere Being, as it is mere abstraction, is therefore the absolutely negative: which, in a similarly immediate aspect, is just NOTHING." By abstracting away the concreteness or particularity of actual experience, one is left with Being which is Nothing. The short article "Who Thinks Abstractly?" (1807–1808?), reprinted here in Walter Kaufmann's translation, clearly conveys Hegel's contempt for the process of abstraction.

Whereas Being and Nothing are both identical and yet contradictory, according to Hegel, "the truth of Being and Nothing is . . . the unity of the two: and this unity is BECOMING." The unity of Becoming does not obliterate Being and Nothing but holds both in tension in a higher truth. The two parts of the contradiction, together with that which unites or overcomes them, make up a triad. This method of overcoming contradictions by moving to a higher level of truth is known as the "dialectic." Hegel proposed to develop a complete dialectical system of reality based on the three foundational triads of "Being—Nothing—Becoming," "Being—Essence—Notion," and "Idea—Nature—Mind." Though he developed several proposals for this system, Hegel never completed any of them. Our selection from the *Encyclopedia of the Philosophical Sciences in Outline*, translated by William Wallace, with revisions by M.J. Inwood, presents the introduction to one such uncompleted proposal.

Although Hegel never developed a complete system, he did use the dialectical method to explain consciousness. In the section entitled "Relations of Master and Servant" from *The Phenomenology of Spirit* (1807), reprinted here in the J.L.H. Thomas translation, Hegel explains one stage in the dialectical development of consciousness. He begins by pointing out that only by acknowledging an "other" is self-consciousness possible. But if there is an other, then the original self-consciousness feels threatened and asserts its freedom by trying to dominate that other and force acknowledgment of its dominance. The ensuing struggle results in a master who dominates and a servant who is dominated. The master then forces the servant to produce material goods for the enjoyment of the master.

But at this point, the master now depends upon the servant he has dominated. In the first place, his self-consciousness as master is subject to his recognition as master by the servant. But more important, while the master has been consuming or destroying what the servant makes, the servant has been learning to create—to bend nature to his will—and so has established his own self-consciousness in relation to what he has created. Furthermore, the labor of the servant has a permanent quality whereas the master's consumption again depends on the servant's production. So by dominating the servant, the master is dominated.

The solution to this contradiction is to acknowledge that neither master nor servant is free and that freedom is not possible in relationships of domination. The next stage in the dialectic is for the mind to seek freedom within itself.

This dialectical development of the consciousness of freedom can also be understood in relation to world history. As Hegel says in his "General Introduction" to the *Philosophy of History* (1832), presented here in the Robert S. Hartman translation, "the study of world history . . . represents the rationally necessary course of the World Spirit, the Spirit whose nature is indeed always one and the same, but whose one nature unfolds in the course of the world." In other words, the Absolute Spirit as manifested in history through human consciousness is the World Spirit (*Weltgeist*), and all of human history is a process whereby this World Spirit comes to self-consciousness of itself as free. To understand this development of Spirit, Hegel examines the three elements that structure historical movement: (1) the nature of Spirit, (2) its means of actualization, and (3) the shape of its perfect embodiment. This final embodiment of Spirit as freedom is found in the State. As Hegel explains each of these three elements, he makes it clear that the individual is unimportant: "In world history the 'individuals' that we have to deal with are peoples." In fact, the individual as an individual is outside of history entirely and only finds freedom and meaning within the unified self-consciousness of a people known as the State.

In our final selection, the concluding chapter from *Lectures on the History of Philosophy,* translated by E.S. Haldane and F.H. Simson (with revisions by M.J. Inwood), Hegel explains that the entire history of philosophy is a "necessary development." The dialectical movement from one philosophy to the next is not a "blind collection of brain-waves, nor a fortuitous progression." Instead, it is the gradual unfolding of Idea or Spirit or Mind. The question left for succeeding philosophers was whether *Hegel's* philosophy was the final statement of Absolute Spirit or only another step in the dialectical movement.

Hegel's ideas have been both lauded and attacked. His insights on the master-servant relationship made a powerful impression on Marx and Nietzsche. Indeed, Hegel's understanding of dialectical development became a central feature of Marx's thought—though Marx rejected the notion of Absolute Spirit. Phenomenology developed Hegel's insights about the different types of consciousness. The sociology of knowledge developed his notions about the connection between consciousness and the culture of a particular epoch. Chief among Hegel's critics was Kierkegaard, who objected strenuously to the devaluing of the individual, questioned the implicit optimism of the dialectic, and mocked the incompleteness of Hegel's "System." Perhaps Hegel's greatest legacy was not any specific idea, but the vision of a complete historical development of thought.

*   *   *

For a selection of primary source readings for Hegel, see *Hegel, The Essential Writings,* edited by Frederick G. Weiss (New York: Harper & Row, 1974). Many secondary books about Hegel are difficult for beginning students. Two accessible classics are W.T. Stace, *The Philosophy of Hegel* (1924; reprinted New York: Dover, 1955) and G.R.G. Mure, *An Introduction to Hegel* (Oxford: Clarendon Press, 1940). Recent helpful studies include J.N. Findlay, *Hegel: A Re-examination* (New York: Macmillan, 1958); Walter Kaufmann, *Hegel: Reinterpretation, Texts and Commentary* (Garden City, NY: Doubleday, 1965); and, especially, Peter Singer, *Hegel* (Oxford: Oxford University Press, 1983). Charles Taylor's massive *Hegel* (Cambridge: Cambridge University Press, 1975) can be consulted for particular topics. For specialized topics, see H.A. Reyburn, *Ethical Theory of Hegel* (Oxford: Oxford University Press, 1965); Ivan Soll, *An Introduction to Hegel's Metaphysics* (Chicago: University of Chicago Press, 1969); Walter Kaufmann, ed., *Hegel's Political Philosophy* (New York: Atherton Press, 1970); Quentin Lauer, *Hegel's Idea of Philosophy* (New York: Fordham University Press, 1971); Quentin Lauer, *A Reading of Hegel's "Phenomenology of Spirit"* (New York: Fordham University Press, 1976); Robert C. Solomon, *From Hegel to Existentialism* (New York: Oxford University Press, 1987); Michael N. Forster, *Hegel and Skepticism* (Cambridge, MA: Harvard University Press, 1989); and Merold Westphal, *History and Truth in Hegel's "Phenomenology"* (Atlantic Highlands, NJ: Humanities Press, 1990). H. S. Harris, *Hegel: Phenomenology and System* (Cambridge, MA: Hackett, 1995); John Russon, *The Self and Its Body in Hegel's Phenomenology of Spirit* (Toronto: University of Toronto Press, 1997); and Justus Hartnack, *An Introduction to Hegel's Logic,* translated by Lars Aagaard-Mogensen (Cambridge, MA: Hackett, 1998). Karl Marx, *Critique of Hegel's "Philosophy of Right,"* edited by Joseph O'Malley (Cambridge: Cambridge University Press, 1970) is both a critical review of Hegel's work and a major work in its own right. Michael Inwood, *A Hegel Dictionary* (Oxford: Basil Blackwell, 1992) provides a useful reference work. General collections of critical essays include W.E. Steinkraus, ed., *New Studies in Hegel's Philosophy* (New York: Holt, Rinehart & Winston, 1971); Alasdair MacIntyre, ed., *Hegel: A Collection of Critical Essays* (Notre Dame, IN: University of Notre Dame Press, 1972); Michael Inwood, ed., *Hegel* (Oxford: Oxford University Press, 1985); Frederick C. Beiser, ed., *The Cambridge Companion to Hegel* (Cambridge:

Cambridge University Press, 1993); the multi-volume Robert Stern, ed., *G.W.F. Hegel: Critical Assessments* (London: Routledge, 1993); Patricia Jagentowicz Mills, ed., *Feminist Interpretations of Hegel* (College Park, PA: Pennsylvania State University Press, 1996); and Micahel Baur and John Russon, eds., *Hegel and the Tradition* (Toronto: University of Toronto Press, 1998).

PHENOMENOLOGY OF SPIRIT

INDEPENDENCE AND DEPENDENCE OF SELF-CONSCIOUSNESS: RELATIONS OF MASTER AND SERVANT

Self-consciousness is *in* and *for itself* in and through being in and for itself for another self-consciousness; that is, it is only as something acknowledged, or recognized. The concept of this unity of self-consciousness in its duplication, of the infinitude realising itself in self-consciousness, is a many-sided and many-sensed complex, so that the moments of this complex must both be held carefully apart, and at the same time taken and understood in this differentiation as not distinct, or always also in their opposed sense. The double-sensedness of what is distinguished lies in the essence of self-consciousness, of being infinite, or boundless, that is, immediately the contrary of the determination in which it is established. The laying-apart of the concept of this spiritual unity in its duplication presents to us the movement of *acknowledging*.

There is for self-consciousness another self-consciousness; it has come *outside itself*. This has a twofold significance: *first,* self-consciousness has lost itself, for it finds itself as *another* being; *second,* it has thereby done away with the other, for it does not see the other either as the essential being, but *it itself* in the *other*.

Self-consciousness must do away with this *otherness it* has; this is the doing away with of the first double-sense, and hence itself a second double-sense: *first,* it must set out to do away with *the other* independent being in order thereby to become certain of *itself* as the essential being; *second,* in so doing it sets out to do away with *itself,* for this other being is itself.

This double-sensed doing away with its double-sensed otherness is equally a double-sensed return *into itself;* for, *first,* through doing away it gets itself back, for it becomes once more equal to itself through doing away with *its* otherness; *second,* however, it no less gives back the other self-consciousness to the latter again, for it had itself in the other, it does away with this being *it* has in the other, thus letting the other go free again.

This movement of self-consciousness in its relation to another self-consciousness has been presented in this way now, as *the doing of the one;* but this doing of the one has itself the two-fold significance of being as much *its doing* as *the doing of the*

Hegel, *Phenomenology of Spirit*, (B, IV, A: "Independence and Dependence of Self-Consciousness: Relations of Master and Servant"). Translated by J.L.H. Thomas. Reprinted from *Hegel: Selections,* edited by M.J. Inwood, *The Great Philosophers* series, Paul Edwards, general editor (New York: Macmillan, 1989).

other; for the other is no less independent, shut up within itself, and there is nothing in it that is not owing to itself. The first self-consciousness does not have the object before it as the latter to begin with is merely for desire, but an independent object existing for itself, over which therefore it has of itself no power, unless the object does with itself what self-consciousness does with it. The movement is thus in all respects the double movement of both self-consciousnesses. Each sees the *other one* do the same as it does; each does itself what it demands of the other, and so does what it does only inasmuch as the other does the same; a one-sided doing would be unavailing, because what it is intended should occur can come about only through both.

The doing is therefore double-sensed not only inasmuch as it is a doing as much *to itself* as *to the other,* but also inasmuch as it is undividedly as much the *doing of the one* as *of the other.*

In this movement we see the process repeat itself which presented itself as the play of forces, but in consciousness. What in the earlier process was for us, is here for the extremes themselves. The centre is self-consciousness, which puts itself apart into the extremes; and each extreme is this exchanging of its determination and absolute going over into the opposed extreme. But though, as consciousness, it does indeed come *out of itself,* yet it is in its being-out-of-itself at the same time held back within itself, is *for itself,* and its "outside-itself" is *for it.* It is for consciousness that it immediately *is* and *is not* another consciousness; and, equally, that this other is only for itself in doing away with itself as something being for itself, and only in the being-for-itself of the other is for itself. Each is to the other the centre through which each brings into relation and connects itself with itself, and each is to itself and to the other an immediate entity existing for itself, which at the same time is thus for itself only through this relating, or mediation. They *acknowledge* one another as *mutually acknowledging one other.*

This pure concept of acknowledgement, the duplication of self-consciousness in its unity, will now be studied in the way in which its process appears for self-consciousness. This process will first present the facet of the *inequality* of the two, or the coming out of the centre into the extremes, which, being extremes, are opposed to one another, the one acknowledged only, the other acknowledging only.

Self-consciousness is to begin with simple being-for-itself, equal-with-itself through the exclusion of everything *other from itself;* its essence and absolute object is to it "*I*"; and it is in this *immediacy,* or in this *being* of its being-for-itself, an *individual.* Whatever else there is for it, is as an inessential object, one marked with the character of the negative. But the other is also a self-consciousness: an individual comes on opposite an individual. Thus *immediately* coming on, they are for each other in the way of common objects: *independent* forms, consciousnesses immersed in the *existence* of *life*—for it is as life that the existent object has here determined itself—which have not yet carried out *for each other* the movement of absolute abstraction, of expunging all immediate existence and of being merely the purely negative existence of consciousness equal-with-itself, or which have not yet presented themselves to each other as pure *being-for-self,* that is, as *self*-consciousness. Each is indeed certain of itself, but not of the other, and consequently each's own certainty of itself has as yet no truth; for its truth could only be that its own being-for-itself had presented itself to it as an independent object or, what amounts to the same thing, that the object had presented itself as this pure certainty of itself. This, however, on the concept of acknowledgement is not possible, save that as the other does for the one, so the one does for the other, each with itself through its own activity, and again through the activity of the other, carrying out this pure abstraction of being-for-itself.

The *presentation* of oneself as the pure abstraction of self-consciousness, however, consists in showing oneself to be the pure negation of one's objective way of being, that is, in showing oneself not to be attached to a particular *concrete existence,* nor to the universal individuality of concrete existence in general, nor even to life. This presentation is a *double* doing: doing of the other, and doing through oneself. Inasmuch as it is the doing *of the other,* each then is set upon the death of the other. But in this there is present also the second doing, *the doing through oneself;* for the former contains within itself the staking of one's own life. The relation of the two self-consciousnesses is hence determined in such a way that through the combat for life and death they *prove* themselves and each other.—They must enter this combat, for they must raise the certainty of themselves, *of being for themselves,* to truth in the other and in themselves. And it is solely through the staking of life that freedom arises, that it is confirmed to self-consciousness that it is not *being,* not the *immediate* way in which it comes on, not its being immersed in the expanse of life which is its essence—but that there is nothing present in it which is not for it a vanishing moment, that it is just pure *being-for-itself.* The individual that has not risked life can indeed be acknowledged as a *person;* but it has not attained the truth of this state of acknowledgement as that of an independent self-consciousness. Likewise, each must as much aim at the death of the other as it stakes its own life; for the other means no more to it than it itself does; the individual's essence presents itself to it as another, it is outside itself, it must do away with its being-outside-itself; the other is a consciousness engaged and existing in manifold ways; it must view its otherness as pure being-for-self, or as absolute negation.

This proving through death does away, however, with the truth that was to result from it, just as much as it thereby also does away with the certainty of oneself altogether; for just as life was the *natural* position of consciousness, independence without absolute negativity, so death is the *natural* negation of consciousness, negation without independence, which therefore remains without the required sense of acknowledgement. Through death the certainty has indeed arisen that both risked their life and despised it in themselves and in the other; though not for those who underwent this combat. They do away with their consciousness set in this alien essentiality that is natural concrete existence, or they do away with themselves, and are done away with as the *extremes* which would be for themselves. There thereby vanishes, however, from the play of exchange the essential moment of setting oneself apart into extremes of opposed determinations; and the centre collapses into a dead unity, which is set apart into dead, merely existent, not opposed, extremes; and the two do not mutually give back and receive back themselves from each other through consciousness, but let each other free merely indifferently, as things. Their deed is abstract negation, not the negation of consciousness, which *does away* in such a manner that it *puts by* and *preserves* what is done away, and consequently survives its being-done-away.

In this experience self-consciousness comes to realise that life is as essential to it as pure self-consciousness is. In immediate self-consciousness the simple "I" is the absolute object, which however, for us or in itself, is absolute mediation and has existent independence as an essential moment. The dissolution of that simple unity is the result of the first experience; through it there is established a pure self-consciousness, and a consciousness which is not purely for itself, but is for another consciousness, that is, is as *existent,* or is consciousness in the form of *thinghood.* Both moments are essential;—but as they are to begin with unequal and opposed, and their reflexion into unity is not yet a reality, they are as two opposed forms of consciousness: one, the independent consciousness, to which being-for-self is the essence; the other, the dependent consciousness, to which life or being for another is the essence: the former is the *master,* the latter the *servant.*

The master is the consciousness existing *for itself,* though no longer merely the concept of the latter, but a consciousness existing for itself which is in mediate relation with itself through *another* consciousness, namely through one to whose essence it pertains to be synthesised with independent *being* or thinghood in general. The master relates himself to both these moments, to a *thing* as such, the object of desire, and to the consciousness to whom thinghood is what is essential; and since he (a), *qua* concept of self-consciousness, is immediate relation of *being-for-himself,* but (b) now is also as mediation, or as a being-for-self which is for itself only through another, so he relates himself (a) immediately to both and (b) mediately to each through the other. The master relates himself *to the servant mediately through independent being;* for it is precisely to this that the servant is kept; it is his chain, from which in the combat he could not abstract, and consequently showed himself to be dependent, to have his independence in thinghood. The master, however, is the power over the being in question, for he showed in the combat that it meant merely something negative to him; since he is the power over this being, while this being is the power over the other, the master thus has in this conjunction the other under himself. Likewise the master relates himself *mediately through the servant to the thing,* the servant relates himself, *qua* self-consciousness as such, to the thing negatively also, and does away with it; but the thing is at the same time independent for him, and hence he cannot through his negating dispose of it so far as to destroy it, or he *works* it merely. The master on the other hand *gains* through this mediation the *immediate* relation as the pure negation of the thing, or the *enjoyment;* where desire did not succeed, he succeeds, namely in disposing of the thing and in satisfying himself in the enjoyment of it. Desire did not succeed in this on account of the independence of the thing; the master, however, who has interposed the servant between the thing and himself, thereby connects himself only with the non-independence of the thing, and enjoys it in its purity; the facet of independence, on the other hand, he leaves to the servant, who works it.

In these two moments the master has his acknowledgement, or recognition, by another consciousness granted him; for the other consciousness establishes itself in these moments as something inessential, first, in the working of the thing, second, in the dependence upon a particular existence; in both it cannot achieve mastery over being and attain absolute negation. There is therefore present here the following moment of recognition, that the other consciousness does away with itself as being-for-itself, and so itself does what the other does to it. Likewise the other moment is present, that this doing of the second consciousness is the first's own doing for what the servant does is really the doing of the master; to the latter, solely being-for-himself is the essence; he is the pure negative power to which the thing is nothing, and hence the pure essential doing in this situation; while the servant is not a pure doing, but an inessential one. But for true recognition there is lacking the moment that what the master does to the other he also does to himself, and what the servant does to himself he also does to the other. Thus there has arisen a one-sided and unequal recognizing.

The inessential consciousness is here for the master the object which constitutes the *truth* of the certainty of oneself. But it is evident that this object does not match its concept, and that there where the master has fulfilled himself, he has instead had something quite other than an independent consciousness come to be. It is not such a consciousness that is for him, but a dependent one rather; he is consequently not certain of *being-for-himself* as the truth, and his truth is rather the inessential consciousness, and the inessential doing of the latter.

The *truth* of independent consciousness is accordingly the servile or *subject consciousness.* The latter admittedly appears at first *outside* itself, and not as the truth of self-consciousness. But just as masterhood or dominion, showed that its essence is the converse of what it itself would be, so too, as we shall see, subjection will in its fulfillment turn rather into the contrary of what it is immediately; it will, *qua* consciousness *driven back* into itself, go into itself and turn about to true independence.

We have seen only what subjection is in the context of dominion. But the former is self-consciousness, and accordingly we shall now see what it is in and for itself. First of all, for subjection the master is the essence; hence the *independent consciousness existing for itself* is to subjection *the truth,* which however *for subjection* is not yet *in subjection.* But it has this truth of pure negativity and of *being-for-itself in the event in itself;* for subjection has *experienced* this essence within itself. This consciousness was, namely, not afraid for this or that, or for this instant or that, but for its whole being; for it has felt the fear of death, the absolute lord, or master. In this fear it has been internally broken up, it has been thoroughly shaken in itself, and everything fixed has trembled within it. This pure universal movement, the absolute becoming fluid of all that is permanent, is however the simple essence of self-consciousness, absolute negativity, *pure being-for-itself,* which is consequently *in* this consciousness. This moment of pure being-for-itself is also *for it,* for in the master it has it as its *object.* It is further not merely this universal dissolution *in general,* but in serving it *actually* brings it about; in serving it does away in all *particular* moments with its dependency on natural existence, and works that existence off.

But the feeling of absolute power, in general and in the particulars of service, is only the dissolution *in itself,* and although "the fear of the Lord is the beginning of wisdom," consciousness in this fear is *for its self,* not *being-for-itself.* Through work, however, it comes to itself. In the moment which corresponds to desire in the consciousness of the master, the facet of the inessential relation to the thing seemed to have fallen to the consciousness that serves, inasmuch as in this relation the thing retains its independence. Desire has reserved to itself the pure negating of the object and thereby the unmixed feeling-of-self. This satisfaction is on that account, however, itself just a vanishing, for it lacks the facet of the *object,* or *permanency.* Work by contrast is *contained* desire, *arrested* vanishing, or work *improves.* The negative relation to the object turns into the *form* of the object and into something *enduring,* precisely because to the worker the object has independence. This *negative* centre, or the *activity* that forms, or fashions, is at the same time *the particularity,* or the pure being-for-self of consciousness, which now in work steps out of consciousness into the element of permanency; the consciousness that works therefore attains as a consequence a view of independent being *as itself.*

The fashioning has not only this positive significance, however, that in it the consciousness that serves has itself as pure *being-for-itself* become something *existent;* but also a negative significance as against its first moment, the fear. For, in the improving of the thing, the consciousness which serves has its own negativity, its being-for-itself, become object only by doing away with the opposed existent *form.* But this objective, *negative* thing is precisely the alien being before which it trembled. Now, however, it destroys this alien negative thing, sets *itself* as something negative into the element of permanency, and thereby comes to be *for itself,* something *existing-for-itself.* In the master it has being-for-self as *an other,* or as merely *for it;* in the fear being-for-self is *in the consciousness itself that serves;* in the improving being-for-self comes to be for the consciousness that serves as *its own,* and the latter becomes conscious that it itself is in and for itself. Through being *set outside,* the form does not become to the consciousness that serves something other than the consciousness itself; for it is precisely the form that is its pure being-for-itself, which thereby to consciousness becomes the truth. Through this refinding of itself by itself, then, the consciousness that serves becomes a mind or *sense of its own,* and in the very work in which it seemed to be only *another's sense.*—For this reflexion both moments, that of fear and service in general, as well as that of improving, are necessary, and at the same time both in a general way. Without the discipline of service and obedience, fear remains at the formal stage, and does not spread itself upon the known reality of concrete existence. Without the improving, fear remains inward and silent, and consciousness does not become for itself. If consciousness fashions, or forms, without the initial absolute fear, it is merely a vain sense of self; for its form or negativity is not negativity *in itself,* and its fashioning cannot therefore give it the consciousness of itself as the essence. If it has not endured absolute fear, but only some anxiety, then it has the negative essence remain something external, its substance has not been infected through and through by the negative essence. Inasmuch as not all aspects of its natural consciousness have become insecure, it still *in itself* belongs to some particular existence; its self-sense is *self-will,* a freedom which as yet remains within subjection. No more than it can have the pure form become essence, no more is the form, regarded as something spread over individual things, a universal cultivating, an absolute concept, but is instead a dexterity which has power over merely some things, not over universal power and the whole objective realm of being.

ENCYCLOPAEDIA (in part)

INTRODUCTION

1. Philosophy lacks an advantage enjoyed by the other sciences. It cannot like them presuppose its objects on the immediate admissions of conception, nor can it assume that its method of cognition, either for beginning or continuing, is already accepted. The objects of philosophy, it is true, are to begin with the same as those of religion. In both the object is truth, in that supreme sense in which God and God alone is truth. Both then go on to consider the finite realm of nature and the human mind, with their relation to each other and to their truth in God. Thus philosophy may—indeed must— presume some acquaintance with its objects, and an interest in them besides, if only for the reason that in point of time consciousness forms *conceptions* of objects before it forms *concepts* of them, and that it is only through conception, and by recourse to it, that the thinking mind rises to know and comprehend *thinkingly.*

But in the thinking study of things, it soon becomes clear that it involves the requirement of showing the *necessity* of its content, of demonstrating the being of its objects, as well as their determinations. Our original acquaintance with them thus appears inadequate. We can assume nothing, and assert nothing dogmatically; nor can we

From the third (1830) edition of *The Encyclopedia of the Philosophical Sciences in Outline,* translated by William Wallace, with revisions by M.J. Inwood. Reprinted from *Hegel: Selections,* edited by M.J. Inwood, *The Great Philosophers* series, Paul Edwards, general ed., Macmillan, 1989.

accept the assertions and assumptions of others. Yet we must make a beginning; and a beginning, as immediate, involves, or rather is, an assumption. Thus it is difficult to *begin* at all.

2. This *thinking study of objects* may serve in general as a definition of philosophy. But the definition is too wide. If it is correct to say that thought makes the difference between man and animals, then everything human is human for the sole and simple reason that it is due to the operation of thought. Philosophy, on the other hand, is a peculiar mode of thinking, a mode in which thinking becomes knowledge, and conceptual knowledge. Thus however great the identity and essential unity of the two modes of thought, the philosophical mode will be *different* from the thinking that is active in all that is human and gives humanity its distinctive character. This difference relates to the fact that the strictly human and thought-induced contents of consciousness do not originally appear in the form of a thought, but as feeling, intuition, conception—all of which forms must be distinguished from the form of thought proper.

According to an old prejudice, which has become a commonplace, it is thought that marks man off from animals. Yet trivial as this old belief may seem, it must, strangely enough, be recalled to mind in view of a prejudice of the present day. This prejudice sets feeling and thought so far apart as to make them opposites, and supposes them to be so antagonistic that feeling, particularly religious feeling, is contaminated, perverted and even annihilated by thought, and religion and religiosity do not essentially grow out of and rest on thinking. But those who make this separation forget that only man has the capacity for religion, and animals no more have religion than law and morality.

Those who insist on this separation of religion from thinking usually have in mind the sort of thinking that may be called "meta-thinking," reflective thinking that considers thoughts as thoughts and brings them into consciousness. Failure to see and observe this definite distinction that philosophy draws in respect of thinking is the source of the crudest ideas and reproaches against philosophy. Man, just because it is his essence to think, is the only being that possesses law, religion, and ethics. In these spheres, therefore, thinking, in the guise of feeling, faith, or conception, has not been inactive; its activity and productions are present and contained in them. But it is one thing to have such feelings and conceptions determined and permeated by thought, and another to have thoughts about them. The thoughts to which meta-thinking on those modes of consciousness gives rise are what comprise reflection, argumentation, and the like, as well as philosophy itself.

Neglect of this distinction has led to another frequent misunderstanding. Such meta-thinking has often been held to be the condition, or even the only way, of attaining a conception and certainty of the eternal and true. The (now somewhat antiquated) metaphysical proofs of God's existence, for example, have been treated as if knowledge of them and a conviction of their validity were the sole and essential means of producing a belief and conviction that there is a God. This claim would find its parallel, if we said that eating was impossible before we had acquired a knowledge of the chemical, botanical, and zoological characters of our food; and that we must delay digestion until we have completed the study of anatomy and physiology. Were it so, these sciences in their field, like philosophy in its, would gain greatly in utility; in fact, their utility would rise to absolute and universal indispensableness. Or rather, instead of being indispensable, they would not exist at all.

3. The *content,* of whatever kind, that fills our consciousness, constitutes the *determinacy* of our feelings, intuitions, images, and ideas; of our aims and duties; and of our thoughts and concepts. Thus feeling, intuition, image, etc. are the *forms* assumed

by these contents. The contents remain the same whether they are felt, intuited, represented or willed, and whether they are merely felt, or felt with an admixture of thoughts, or merely and simply thought. In any one of these forms, or in the mixture of several, the content is consciousness' *object*. But when they are thus objects of consciousness, the *determinacies of these forms* ally themselves with the content, so that each form seems to give rise to a particular object. Thus, what is at bottom the same may look like a different content.

The determinacies of feeling, intuition, desire, and will, so far as we are *aware* of them, are in general called "ideas" or "conceptions"; and, roughly speaking, philosophy puts thoughts, categories, or, more precisely, concepts, in the place of ideas. Ideas in general may be regarded as metaphors of thoughts and concepts. But to have these ideas does not imply that we appreciate their meaning for thinking, i.e., their thoughts and concepts. Conversely, it is one thing to have thoughts and concepts, and another to know what ideas, intuitions, and feelings correspond to them.

This explains in part what people call the "unintelligibility" of philosophy. The difficulty lies partly in an incapacity—which in itself is just want of habit—for abstract thinking, an inability to grasp pure thoughts and move about in them. In our ordinary consciousness the thoughts are clothed in and combined with familiar sensuous and spiritual material; and in meta-thinking, reflection, and argumentation we introduce a blend of thoughts into feelings, ideas, and intuitions. (Thus in propositions where the content is wholly sensuous—e.g., "This leaf is green"—such categories as being and individuality are introduced.) But to make thoughts pure and simple our object is a different matter.

But there is also another reason for the complaint that philosophy is unintelligible: an impatience to have before one as an idea that which is in consciousness as a thought or concept. When people are asked to apprehend some concept, they often complain that they do not know what they are supposed to *think*. In a concept there is nothing more to be thought than the concept itself. What the phrase reveals is a hankering after an idea with which we are already familiar. Consciousness, denied its familiar ideas, feels the ground where it once stood firm and at home taken from it, and, when transported into the pure region of concepts, cannot tell where in the world it is. Thus authors, preachers, and orators are found most intelligible when they speak of things that their readers or hearers already know by rote, which are familiar to them and are understood as a matter of course.

4. In connection with our ordinary consciousness, philosophy will first have to prove and even to awaken the need for its peculiar mode of knowledge. But in connection with the objects of religion, with truth in general, it will have to show that it is capable of knowing them from its own resources; and if a difference from religious conceptions comes to light, it will have to *justify* the points in which it diverges.

5. To give a preliminary explanation of this distinction and of the connected insight that the real content of our consciousness is retained, and even put in its proper light for the first time, when translated into the form of the thought and the concept, it may be well to recall another old prejudice: that to learn the truth of any object or event, even of feelings, intuitions, opinions, and ideas, we must first think it over. Now in any case to think things over is at least to transform feelings, ideas, etc. into thoughts.

Nature has given everyone an ability to think. But thought is all that philosophy claims as the form proper to her business: and thus neglect of the distinction stated in §3 leads to a new delusion, the reverse of the complaint about the unintelligibility of philosophy. This science must often submit to the slight of hearing even people who have never taken any trouble with it talk as if they thoroughly understood all about it. With no preparation beyond an ordinary education they do not hesitate, especially under the influence of religious feelings, to philosophize and to criticize philosophy. Everybody allows that to know any other science you must have first studied it, and that you can express a judgement on it only in virtue of such knowledge. Everybody allows that to make a shoe you must have learned and practised the craft of the shoe-maker, though every man has a model in his own foot, and possesses in his hands the natural endowments for the operations required. For philosophy alone, it is supposed, such study, care, and application are not requisite. This comfortable view has recently received corroboration through the theory of immediate or intuitive knowledge.

6. So much for the form of philosophical knowledge. It is no less desirable, on the other hand, that philosophy should understand that its content is no other than *actuality,* that content which, originally produced and producing itself within the precincts of the living mind, has become the *world,* the inward and outward world, of consciousness. At first we become aware of these contents in what we call experience. Even a judicious consideration of the world, of the wide range of inward and outward existence, enables us to distinguish mere appearance, transient and meaningless, from what in itself really deserves the name of actuality. As it is only in form that philosophy is distinguished from other modes of attaining an awareness of this same content, it must necessarily be in harmony with actuality and experience. In fact, this harmony may be viewed as at least an extrinsic test of the truth of a philosophy. Similarly it may be held the highest and final aim of philosophic science to bring about, by knowledge of this harmony, a reconciliation of the self-conscious reason with the reason that is in the world, with actuality.

In the preface to my *Philosophy of Right,* are found the propositions:

> What is rational is actual;
>   and,
> What is actual is rational.

These simple statements have given rise to expressions of surprise and hostility, even in quarters where it would be reckoned an insult to presume absence of philosophy, and still more of religion. Religion at least need not be brought in evidence; its doctrines of the divine government of the world affirm these propositions too decidedly. For their philosophic sense, we must presuppose cultivation enough to know, not only that God is actual, that He is the supreme actuality, that He alone is truly actual; but also, as regards the formal side, that existence is in part appearance, and only in part actuality. In common life, any brain wave, error, evil, and everything of the nature of evil, as well as every degenerate and transitory existence whatever, gets indiscriminately called an actuality. But even our ordinary feelings forbid a contingent existence getting the emphatic name of an actual; for the contingent is an existence that has no greater value than that of something possible, which may as well not be as be. As for the term "actuality," these critics would have done well to consider the sense in which I employ it. In a detailed Logic I have treated among other things of actuality, and accurately distinguished it not only from the contingent, which, after all, has existence, but more precisely from determinate being, existence, and other determinations.

The actuality of the rational is opposed by the notion that Ideas and ideals are nothing but chimeras, and philosophy a mere system of such figments. It is also opposed by the contrary notion that Ideas and ideals are too excellent to have actuality, too impotent to procure it for themselves. This divorce between idea and reality is especially dear to the understanding that regards its dreamlike abstractions as something true and real, and prides itself on the "ought," which it takes especial pleasure in prescribing even in the field of politics. As if the world had waited on it to learn how it ought to be, and was not! For, if it were as it ought to be, what would come of the precocious wisdom of that "ought"? When understanding turns this "ought" against trivial external and transitory objects, against social regulations or conditions, which very likely possess a great relative importance for a certain time and special circles, it may often be right, and in such a case may find much that fails to satisfy general requirements; for who is not acute enough to see a great deal in his own surroundings which is really far from being as it ought to be? But such acuteness is mistaken to imagine that, in these objects and their "ought," it is dealing with questions of philosophical interest. The sole concern of philosophy is the Idea: and the Idea is not so impotent that it merely ought to be without actually being. The object of philosophy is an actuality of which those objects, social regulations, and conditions, are only the superficial surface.

7. Thus meta-thinking in general contains the principle (which also means the beginning) of philosophy, and when it arose again in its independence in modern times, after the epoch of the Lutheran Reformation, it did not, as in the philosophical beginnings among the Greeks, stand merely aloof and abstract, but at once turned its energies also on the apparently illimitable material of the phenomenal world. In this way the name "philosophy" came to be applied to all those branches of knowledge that are engaged in ascertaining the fixed measure and universal in the ocean of empirical individualities, as well as the necessity, the laws, in the apparent disorder of the endless masses of the contingent; and which thus derive their content from their own intuition and perception of the external and internal world, from the very presence of nature and of the mind and heart of man.

The principle of experience involves the infinitely important condition that, to accept and believe any fact the person must be present; or, more exactly, that he must find the fact unified and combined with the certainty of his own self. He must himself be present, whether only with his external senses, or else with his profounder mind, his essential self-consciousness. This principle is the same as that which has in the present day been termed faith, immediate knowledge, the revelation in the outward world, and, above all, in our own heart. Those sciences, which thus got the name of philosophy, we call *empirical* sciences, since they take their departure from experience. Still the essential results that they aim at and provide, are laws, general propositions, a theory—the thoughts of what is found existing. Thus Newtonian physics was called Natural Philosophy. Hugo Grotius, again, by putting together and comparing the behavior of nations toward each other in history, set up, with the help of the ordinary general reasoning, general principles, a theory that may be termed the Philosophy of International Law. In England this is still the usual signification of the term philosophy. Newton continues to be celebrated as the greatest of philosophers: and the name goes down as far as the price-lists of instrument makers. All instruments, such as the thermometer and barometer, that do not come under the special head of magnetic or electric apparatus are styled philosophical instruments. Surely thought, and not a mere combination of wood, iron, etc. ought to be called the instrument of philosophy! The recent science of Political Economy in particular is also called philosophy—what we are wont to call "rational" political economy, or, perhaps, the political economy of *intelligence.*

8. In its own field this knowledge may at first give satisfaction; but in two ways it falls short. In the first place there is another realm of objects that it does not embrace—freedom, spirit, and God. They are excluded, not because it can be said that they have nothing to do with experience; for though they are certainly not experiences of the

senses, it is quite a tautological proposition to say that whatever is in consciousness is experienced. The reason for their exclusion is that in their *content* these objects evidently show themselves as infinite.

There is an old dictum often wrongly attributed to Aristotle, and supposed to express the general tenor of his philosophy. "*Nihil est in intellectu quod non fuerit in sensu*": there is nothing in thought that has not been in sense, in experience. If speculative philosophy refused to admit this maxim, it can have done so only by a misunderstanding. It will, however, conversely, also assert: "*Nihil est in sensu quod non fuerit in intellectu.*" And this in two senses: in the general sense that *nous* or spirit (the more profound counterpart of *nous*) is the cause of the world; and in the specific sense (§2) that the feeling of right, ethics and religion is a feeling (and thus an experience) of such content as can only spring from and rest on thought.

9. In the second place in point of *form* the subjective reason requires further satisfaction; this form is, in general, necessity (§1). The method of empirical science exhibits two defects. The first is that the universal contained in it—the genus, etc.—is, on its own account, indeterminate, and therefore not on its own account connected with the particular. Each is external and accidental to the other; and it is the same with the particulars that are brought into union: each is external and accidental to the others. The second defect is that the beginnings are in every case data and postulates, neither accounted for nor deduced. In both these points the form of necessity fails to get its due. Hence meta-thinking, whenever it sets itself to remedy these defects, becomes speculative thinking, strictly philosophical thinking. As a species of meta-thinking, therefore, that, though it has much in common with the first variety, is nevertheless different from it, it thus possesses, in addition to the common forms, some forms of its own, of which the concept is the universal one.

The relation of speculative science to the other sciences is just this. It does not neglect the empirical content of the sciences, but recognizes and adopts it; it recognizes and applies to its own content the universal of these sciences, their laws and classifications: but besides all this, into the categories of science it introduces and applies other categories. The difference thus relates only to this change of categories. Speculative logic contains all previous logic and metaphysics: it preserves the same forms of thought, laws, and objects,—while at the same time remodeling and expanding them with further categories.

From concept in the speculative sense we should distinguish what is ordinarily called a concept. The claim that no concept can comprehend the infinite, a claim that has been repeated over and over again till it has grown axiomatic, is based on this ordinary, one-sided sense of "concept."

10. The thinking involved in philosophical knowledge itself calls for explanation. We must understand in what way it possesses necessity, and its claim to be able to apprehend absolute objects (God, spirit, freedom) must be substantiated. Such an insight, however, is itself a philosophical cognition and thus falls within philosophy itself. A preliminary attempt to make matters plain would only be unphilosophical, and consist of a tissue of assumptions, assertions, and inferential pros and cons, of dogmatism without cogency, against which there would be an equal right of counter-dogmatism.

A main line of argument in the Critical Philosophy bids us pause before proceeding to inquire into God or the essence of things, and first of all examine the faculty of cognition and see whether it is equal to the task. We ought, says Kant, to become acquainted with the instrument, before we undertake the work for which it is to be employed; for if the instrument be insufficient, all our trouble will be in vain. The plausibility of this thought has won general assent and admiration; the result of which has been to withdraw cognition from an interest in its objects and absorption in them, and to direct it back to itself, to the question of form. Unless we wish to be deceived by words, it is easy to see through this. In the case of other instruments, we can examine and assess them in other ways than by setting about the special work for which they are destined. But the examination of knowledge can only be carried out by *knowing*. To examine this so-called instrument is the same thing as to know it. But to seek to know before we know is as absurd as the wise resolution of the scholastic, not to venture into the water until he had learned to swim.

Reinhold saw the confusion in this style of beginning, and tried to get out of the difficulty by starting with a hypothetical and problematical stage of philosophizing, and by continuing in it, somehow, until we find ourselves, further on, at the primary truth. His method, when closely looked into, will be seen to amount to a common procedure. It starts from a substratum of experiential fact, or from a provisional assumption that has been brought into a definition; and then proceeds to analyze this starting point. We can detect in Reinhold's argument a perception of the truth, that the usual course that proceeds by assumptions and anticipations is a hypothetical and problematical procedure. But perceiving this does not alter the character of this method; it only makes clear its imperfections.

11. The need for philosophy may be specified thus. The mind, when it feels or intuits, finds its object in something sensuous; when it imagines, in an image; when it wills, in an aim. But in contrast to, or it may be only in distinction from, these forms of its existence and of its objects, the mind has also to gratify its highest and most inward life, *thought*. Thus the mind renders thought its object. In the deepest meaning of the phrase, it comes *to itself;* for thought is its principle, its unadulterated self. But while thus occupied, thought entangles itself in contradictions, loses itself in the hard-and-fast nonidentity of thoughts, and so, instead of reaching itself, is caught in its opposite. This result of the thinking of the mere understanding is resisted by the higher need, which is grounded in the perseverance of thought, which continues true to itself, even in this conscious loss of its consonance with itself, "that it may overcome" and work out in thinking itself the solution of its own contradictions.

To see that thought in its very nature is dialectical, and that, as understanding, it must fall into contradictions, the negative of itself, forms one of the main lessons of logic. When thought despairs of achieving, by its own means, the solution of the contradiction that it has brought upon itself, it turns back to those solutions with which the mind has learned to console itself in some of its other modes and forms. Unfortunately, however, the retreat of thought has led it, as Plato noticed even in his time, to an unnecessary "misology"; and it then takes up against itself that hostile attitude of which an example is seen in the doctrine that immediate knowledge, as it is called, is the exclusive form in which we are conscious of the truth.

12. The rise of philosophy is due to this need. Its point of departure is experience; our immediate and our inferential consciousness. Awakened by this stimulus, thought's essential procedure is to raise itself above natural consciousness, above the senses and inferences, into its own unadulterated element, and to assume, accordingly, at first a stand-aloof, negative attitude toward that beginning. Its first satisfaction it finds in itself, in the Idea of the universal essence of these phenomena: this Idea (the absolute, God) may be more or less abstract. Conversely, the experiential sciences contain a stimulus to overcome the form in which their varied contents are presented, and to elevate these contents to necessity. For these contents have the form of a vast conglomerate, one thing side by side with another, as if they were merely given and imme-

diate,—as in general contingent. This stimulus drags thought out of that universality and its merely *implicit* guarantee of satisfaction, and impels it on to a development out of itself. This development involves, on the one hand, merely receiving the content and the determinations that it presents; but, on the other, it also gives the content a new form: it lets it emerge freely, in the sense of original thinking and in accordance only with the necessity of the subject-matter itself.

On the relation between "immediacy" and "mediation" in consciousness we shall speak later, expressly and with more detail. Here it may suffice that, though the two moments present themselves as distinct, still neither of them can be absent, nor can one exist apart from the other. Thus the knowledge of God, as of every supersensible reality, is essentially an elevation above sensations or intuitions: it consequently involves a negative attitude to the initial data, and to that extent mediation. For to mediate is to begin and to go on to a second thing; so that the existence of this second thing depends on our having reached it from something other than it. In spite of this, the knowledge of God is no less independent of the empirical phase: in fact, its independence is essentially secured through this negation and elevation. If we attach an unfair prominence to mediation, and represent it as conditionedness, it may be said—not that it would amount to much—that philosophy is the child of experience, of the *a posteriori*. (In fact, thinking is the negation of what we have immediately before us.) With as much truth, however, we may be said to owe eating to the means of nourishment, for we cannot eat without them. If we take this view, eating is certainly represented as ungrateful: it devours that to which it owes itself. Thinking, in this sense, is equally ungrateful.

But there is also an *a priori* aspect of thought, where by a mediation, not made by anything external but by a reflection into self, we have that immediacy that is universality, the self-containment of thought that is so much at home with itself that it feels an innate indifference to particularization, and thus to development of itself. It is thus also with religion, which, whether it be rude or elaborate, whether it be developed to scientific consciousness or confined to the simple faith of the heart, possesses the same intensive nature of contentment and felicity. But if thought gets no further than the universality of Ideas, as was perforce the case in the first philosophies (e.g., Eleatic being, or Heraclitus' becoming), it is open to the charge of formalism. Even in a developed philosophy, we may find a mastery merely of abstract propositions or determinations such as, "In the absolute all is one," and "Subject and object are identical," which are only repeated when it comes to particulars. In respect of this first period of thought, the period of mere generality, we may safely say that experience is the real author of *growth* and *advance* in philosophy. For, first, the empirical sciences do not stop short at the mere perception of the individual features of a phenomenon. By the aid of thought, they have met philosophy with materials prepared for it, in the form of general uniformities, laws, and classifications of phenomena. Thus the content of the particular is made ready to be received into philosophy. This, second, implies a compulsion on thought itself to proceed to these concrete determinations. The reception of these contents, now that thought has removed their immediacy and made them cease to be mere data, forms at the same time a development of thought out of itself. Philosophy, then, owes its development to the empirical sciences. In return it gives their contents the most essential form: the *freedom* (the *a priori*) of thinking. The contents are now warranted necessary, and no longer depend on the evidence of facts merely, that they were so found and so experienced. The fact as experienced thus becomes an illustration and a copy of the original and completely self-supporting activity of thought.

13. In the peculiar form of external history the origin and development of philosophy is presented as the history of the science. The stages in the evolution of the Idea

there seem to follow each other by accident, and to present merely a number of different and unconnected principles, which the several philosophies develop. But for thousands of years the same architect has directed the work: the one living mind whose nature is to think, to bring to consciousness what it is, and, with this thus set as object before it, to be at the same time raised above it, and so to reach a higher stage of its own being. The different systems that the history of philosophy presents are, first, only one philosophy at different degrees of maturity; second, the particular principle, which is the groundwork of each system, is but a branch of one and the same whole. The last philosophy in time is the result of all the systems that preceded it, and must include their principles; and so, if indeed it is philosophy, will be the fullest, most comprehensive, and most adequate philosophy.

The spectacle of so many and so various philosophies suggests the necessity of defining strictly the universal and the particular. When the universal is taken formally and *coordinated* with the particular, it sinks into a particular itself. Even common sense in everyday matters is above the absurdity of setting a universal *beside* the particulars. Would anyone who wished for fruit reject cherries, pears, and grapes, on the ground that they were cherries, pears, or grapes, and not fruit? But when philosophy is in question, the excuse of many is that philosophies are so different, and none of them is *the* philosophy, each is only *a* philosophy. Such a plea is assumed to justify contempt for philosophy. And yet cherries too are fruit. Often, too, a system, of which the principle is the universal, is put on a level with another of which the principle is a particular, and with theories that deny the existence of philosophy altogether. Such systems are said to be only different views of philosophy. With equal justice, light and darkness might be styled different kinds of light.

14. The same development of thought that is exhibited in the history of philosophy is presented in philosophy itself, only *purely in the element of thinking* and freed of that historical externality. The free and genuine thought is internally concrete, and is thus an Idea; and in its whole universality, it is *the* Idea or *the absolute*. The science of it is essentially a system. For the truth is concrete; it unfolds within itself, and gathers and holds itself together in unity; that is, it is a totality; and the freedom of the whole, as well as the necessity of its distinct moments, are possible only when these are discriminated and defined.

Unless it is a system, philosophy is not in the least scientific. Unsystematic philosophising can only express personal peculiarities of mind, and is contingent in its contents. Apart from the whole of which it is a moment, a content lacks justification, and is a baseless assumption, or personal conviction. Yet many philosophical treatises confine themselves to such an exposition of opinions and sentiments.

The term "*system*" is often misunderstood. It does not denote a philosophy, the principle of which is narrow and distinguished from others. On the contrary, a genuine philosophy makes it a principle to include every particular principle.

15. Each of the parts of philosophy is a philosophical whole, a circle rounded and complete in itself. In each of these parts, however, the philosophical Idea is found in a particular specificality or medium. The individual circle, because it is internally a totality, bursts through the limits imposed by its special medium, and gives rise to a wider circle. The whole thus resembles a circle of circles. The Idea appears in each single circle, but the whole Idea is constituted by the system of these peculiar media and each is a necessary moment.

16. In the form of an encyclopaedia, science has no room for a detailed exposition of particulars, and must be limited to setting forth the beginnings of the special sciences and their basic concepts.

How much of the particular parts is requisite to constitute a particular science is indeterminate; but the part, if it is to be something true, must be not an isolated moment merely, but itself a totality. The entire field of philosophy therefore really forms a single science; but it may also be viewed as a whole composed of several particular sciences. The encyclopaedia of philosophy must not be confounded with ordinary encyclopaedias. An ordinary encyclopaedia does not pretend to be more than an aggregation of sciences, regulated by no principle, and merely as experience offers them. Sometimes it even includes what merely bear the name of sciences, but are merely collections of information. In an aggregate like this, the sciences owe their place in it to extrinsic reasons and their unity is therefore extrinsic: an *arrangement.* For the same reason, especially as the materials also depend on no principle, the arrangement is at best an experiment, and will always exhibit awkwardnesses. An encyclopaedia of philosophy excludes three kinds of partial science: (I) Mere aggregates of information. Philology *prima facie* belongs to this class. (II) The quasi sciences, founded on arbitrary will alone, such as heraldry. Sciences of this class are positive from beginning to end. (III) In other sciences, also styled positive, but which have a rational basis and beginning, philosophy claims that constituent as its own. The positive features remain the property of the sciences themselves.

The positive element in sciences is of different sorts. (I) Their beginning, though implicitly rational, yields to contingency, when they have to bring the universal into contact with empirical individuality and actuality. In this region of chance and change, the concept cannot be brought to bear, only *grounds.* Thus *e.g.* jurisprudence, or the system of direct and indirect taxation, require certain precise and definitive decisions that lie beyond the absolute determinacy of the concept. A latitude for settlement is accordingly left, which may be determined in one way on one principle, in another way on another, and admits of no definitive certainty. Similarly the Idea of nature, when individualized, is dissipated into contingencies. Natural history, geography, and medicine stumble on determinations of existence, on kinds and distinctions, which are not determined by reason, but by hazard and external chance. Even history belongs here. The Idea is its essence; but its appearance lies in contingency and in the field of self-will. (II) These sciences are positive also in failing to recognize the finite nature of their determinations and to show how they and their whole sphere pass into a higher. They assume them to possess an authority beyond appeal. Here finitude lies in the form, as in the previous instance it lay in the matter. (III) Related to this is the ground of cognition: partly inference, partly feeling, faith, and the authority of others, in general the authority of inward and outward intuition. Under this head falls also the philosophy that proposes to build on anthropology, facts of consciousness, inner or outward experience. It may happen, however, that only the form of scientific exposition is empirical; while intuitive sagacity arranges what are mere phenomena, according to the inner sequence of the concept. In such a case the contrasts between the varied phenomena brought together serve to eliminate the external, contingent circumstances of the conditions, and the universal thus comes into view. A judicious experimental physics in this way will present the rational science of nature,—as history will present the science of human affairs and actions—in an external picture, which mirrors the concept.

17. It may seem as if philosophy, in order to begin, had, like the rest of the sciences, to start with a subjective presupposition, viz to make a particular object, thinking, the object of thinking, just as space, number, etc. are objects elsewhere. However, it is by a free act of thought that it occupies the point of view in which it is for its own self, and thus gives itself an object of its own production. Moreover the point of view, which thus appears as *immediate,* must within science be converted to a result,—the

ultimate result in which philosophy returns into itself and reaches the point with which it began. In this manner philosophy exhibits the appearance of a circle which closes with itself, and has no beginning in the same way as the other sciences. It has a beginning only in relation to a person who proposes to study it, and not in relation to the science as science. In other words, the concept of science—the first concept, which, since it is the first, implies a separation between the thought that is our object, and the subject philosophizing that is, as it were, external—must be grasped by science itself. This is even the one single aim, action, and goal of philosophy—to arrive at the concept of its concept, and thus secure its return and its satisfaction.

18. As only the whole of science can exhibit the Idea, it is impossible to give a preliminary general conception of a philosophy. Nor can the division of philosophy be intelligible, except in connection with the Idea. A preliminary division, like the conception from which it comes, can only be an anticipation. But the Idea turns out to be the thinking that is completely identical with itself and this also in its activity of setting itself over against itself, so as to be for itself, and of being in full possession of itself in this other. Thus philosophy falls into three parts:

    I. Logic, the science of the Idea in and for itself.
   II. The Philosophy of Nature: the science of the Idea in its otherness.
  III. The Philosophy of Mind, of the Idea come back to itself out of that otherness.

As observed in §15, the differences between the particular philosophical sciences are only determinations of the Idea that alone is exhibited in these different media. In nature nothing else would be discerned, except the Idea: but the Idea has the form of alienation. In mind, again, the Idea is for itself, and is becoming absolute. Every such determination in which the Idea appears, is at the same time a fleeting stage; hence each subdivision has not only to know its contents as an object that has being, but also how these contents pass into their higher circle. To represent it as a division, therefore, leads to misconception; for it coordinates the several parts or sciences one beside another, as if they had no development, but were, like species, radically distinct.

WHO THINKS ABSTRACTLY?

Think? Abstractly?—*Sauve qui peut!* Let those who can save themselves! Even now I can hear a traitor, bought by the enemy, exclaim these words, denouncing this essay because it will plainly deal with metaphysics. For *metaphysics* is a word, no less than *abstract,* and almost *thinking* as well, from which everybody more or less runs away as from a man who has caught the plague.

But the intention here really is not so wicked, as if the meaning of thinking and of abstract were to be explained here. There is nothing the beautiful world finds as intolerable as explanations. I, too, find it terrible when somebody begins to explain, for when worst comes to worst I understand everything myself. Here the explanation of

Translated by Walter Kaufmann.

thinking and abstract would in any case be entirely superfluous; for it is only because the beautiful world knows what it means to be abstract that it runs away. Just as one does not desire what one does not know, one also cannot hate it. Nor is it my intent to try craftily to reconcile the beautiful world with thinking or with the abstract as if, under the semblance of small talk, thinking and the abstract were to be put over till in the end they had found their way into society incognito, without having aroused any disgust; even as if they were to be adopted imperceptibly by society, or, as the Swabians say, *hereingezäunselt,* before the author of this complication suddenly exposed this strange guest, namely the abstract, whom the whole party had long treated and recognized under a different title as if he were a good old acquaintance. Such scenes of recognition which are meant to instruct the world against its will have the inexcusable fault that they simultaneously humiliate, and the wirepuller tries with his artifice to gain a little fame; but this humiliation and this vanity destroy the effect, for they push away again an instruction gained at such a price.

In any case, such a plan would be ruined from the start, for it would require that the crucial word of the riddle is not spoken at the outset. But this has already happened in the title. If this essay toyed with such craftiness, these words should not have been allowed to enter right in the beginning; but like the cabinet member in a comedy, they should have been required to walk around during the entire play in their overcoat, unbuttoning it only in the last scene, disclosing the flashing star of wisdom. The unbuttoning of the metaphysical overcoat would be less effective, to be sure, than the unbuttoning of the minister's: it would bring to light no more than a couple of words, and the best part of the joke ought to be that it is shown that society has long been in possession of the matter itself, so what they would gain in the end would be the mere name, while the minister's star signifies something real—a bag of money.

That everybody present should know what thinking is and what is abstract is presupposed in good society, and we certainly are in good society. The question is merely *who* thinks abstractly. The intent, as already mentioned, is not to reconcile society with these things, to expect it to deal with something difficult, to appeal to its conscience not frivolously to neglect such a matter that befits the rank and status of beings gifted with reason. Rather it is my intent to reconcile the beautiful world with itself, although it does not seem to have a bad conscience about this neglect, still, at least deep down, it has a certain respect for abstract thinking as something exalted, and it looks the other way not because it seems too lowly but because it appears too exalted, not because it seems too mean but rather too noble, or conversely because it seems an *Espèce,* something special; it seems something that does not lend one distinction in general society, like new clothes, but rather something that—like wretched clothes, or rich ones if they are decorated with precious stones in ancient mounts or embroidery that, be it ever so rich, has long become quasi–Chinese—excludes one from society or makes one ridiculous in it.

Who thinks abstractly? The uneducated, not the educated. Good society does not think abstractly because it is too easy, because it is too lowly (not referring to the external status)—not from an empty affectation of nobility that would place itself above that of which it is not capable, but on account of the inward inferiority of the matter.

The prejudice and respect for abstract thinking are so great that sensitive nostrils will begin to smell some satire or irony at this point; but since they read the morning paper they know that there is a prize to be had for satires and that I should therefore sooner earn it by competing for it than give up here without further ado.

I have only to adduce examples for my proposition: everybody will grant that they confirm it. A murderer is led to the place of execution. For the common populace he is nothing but a murderer. Ladies perhaps remark that he is a strong, handsome, interesting man. The populace finds this remark terrible: What? A murderer handsome? How can one think so wickedly and call a murderer handsome; no doubt, you yourselves are something not much better! This is the corruption of morals that is prevalent in the upper classes, a priest may add, knowing the bottom of things and human hearts.

One who knows men traces the development of the criminal's mind: he finds in his history, in his education, a bad family relationship between his father and mother, some tremendous harshness after this human being had done some minor wrong, so he became embittered against the social order—a first reaction to this that in effect expelled him and henceforth did not make it possible for him to preserve himself except through crime.—There may be people who will say when they hear such things: he wants to excuse this murderer! After all I remember how in my youth I heard a mayor lament that writers of books were going too far and sought to extirpate Christianity and righteousness altogether; somebody had written a defense of suicide; terrible, really too terrible!—Further questions revealed that *The Sufferings of Werther* [by Goethe, 1774] were meant.

This is abstract thinking: to see nothing in the murderer except the abstract fact that he is a murderer, and to annul all other human essence in him with this simple quality.

It is quite different in refined, sentimental circles—in Leipzig. There they strewed and bound flowers on the wheel and on the criminal who was tied to it.—But this again is the opposite abstraction. The Christians may indeed trifle with Rosicrucianism, or rather cross-rosism, and wreathe roses around the cross. The cross is the gallows and wheel that have long been hallowed. It has lost its one-sided significance of being the instrument of dishonorable punishment and, on the contrary, suggests the notion of the highest pain and the deepest rejection together with the most joyous rapture and divine honor. The wheel in Leipzig, on the other hand, wreathed with violets and poppies, is a reconciliation à la Kotzebue, a kind of slovenly sociability between sentimentality and badness.

In quite a different manner I once heard a common old woman who worked in a hospital kill the abstraction of the murderer and bring him to life for honor. The severed head had been placed on the scaffold, and the sun was shining. How beautifully, she said, the sun of God's grace shines on Binder's head!—You are not worthy of having the sun shine on you, one says to a rascal with whom one is angry. This woman saw that the murderer's head was struck by the sunshine and thus was still worthy of it. She raised it from the punishment of the scaffold into the sunny grace of God, and instead of accomplishing the reconciliation with violets and sentimental vanity, saw him accepted in grace in the higher sun.

Old woman, your eggs are rotten! the maid says to the market woman. What? she replies, my eggs rotten? You may be rotten! You say that about my eggs? You? Did not lice eat your father on the highways? Didn't your mother run away with the French, and didn't your grandmother die in a public hospital? Let her get a whole shirt instead of that flimsy scarf; we know well where she got that scarf and her hats: if it were not for those officers, many wouldn't be decked out like that these days, and if their ladyships paid more attention to their households, many would be in jail right now. Let her mend the holes in her stockings!—In brief, she does not leave one whole thread on her. She thinks abstractly and subsumes the other woman—scarf, hat, shirt, etc., as well as her fingers and other parts of her, and her father and whole family, too—solely under the crime that she has found the eggs rotten. Everything about her is colored through and through by these rotten eggs, while those officers of which the market woman spoke—if, as one may seriously doubt, there is anything to that—may have got to see very different things.

To move from the maid to a servant, no servant is worse off than one who works for a man of low class and low income; and he is better off the nobler his master is. The common man again thinks more abstractly, he gives himself noble airs vis-à-vis the servant and relates himself to the other man merely as to a servant; he clings to this one predicate. The servant is best off among the French. The nobleman is familiar with his servant, the Frenchman is his friend. When they are alone, the servant does the talking: see Diderot's *Jacques et son maître;* the master does nothing but take snuff and see what time it is and lets the servant take care of everything else. The nobleman knows that the servant is not merely a servant, but also knows the latest city news, the girls, and harbors good suggestions; he asks him about these matters, and the servant may say what he knows about these questions. With a French master, the servant may not only do this; he may also broach a subject, have his own opinions and insist on them; and when the master wants something, it is not done with an order but he has to argue and convince the servant of his opinion and add a good word to make sure that this opinion retains the upper hand.

In the army we encounter the same difference. Among the Austrians a soldier may be beaten, he is canaille; for whatever has the passive right to be beaten is canaille. Thus the common soldier is for the officer this *abstractum* of a beatable subject with whom a gentleman who has a uniform and port *d'epée* must trouble himself—and that could drive one to make a pact with the devil.

REASON IN HISTORY (in part)

I. THE THREE METHODS OF WRITING HISTORY

*   *   *

3. The third method of history, the *philosophical.* * There was little in the two preceding methods that had to be clarified; their concept was self-explanatory. But it is different with this last one, which indeed seems to require some commentary or justification. The most universal definition would be that philosophy of history is nothing but the thoughtful contemplation of history. To think is one of those things we cannot help doing; in this we differ from the animals. In our sensation, cognition, and intellection, in our instincts and volitions, in as far as they are human, there is an element of thinking. But reference to thinking may here appear inadequate. In history, thinking is subordinate to the data of reality, which latter serve as guide and basis for historians. Phi-

---

*[The first two kinds are "Original History" (descriptions of events which the historian has witnessed) and "Reflective History" (a general history which includes events and deeds the historian has not observed).]

Hegel, *Reason in History: A General Introduction to the Philosophy of History,* (1–3), translated by Robert S. Hartman (New York: Macmillan/Library of the Liberal Arts, 1953).

losophy, on the other hand, allegedly produces its own ideas out of speculation, without regard to given data. If philosophy approached history with such ideas, it may be held, it would treat history as its raw material and not leave it as it is, but shape it in accordance with these ideas, and hence construct it, so to speak, *a priori.* But since history is supposed to understand events and actions merely for what they are and have been, and is the truer, the more factual it is, it seems that the method of philosophy would be in contradiction to the function of history. This contradiction and the charge consequently brought against philosophy shall here be explained and refuted. But we shall not, for that matter, attempt to correct the innumerable specific misrepresentations which are current and continuously recur about the aims, interests, and methods of history, and its relations to philosophy.

II. REASON AS THE BASIS OF HISTORY

The sole thought which philosophy brings to the treatment of history is the simple concept of *Reason:* that Reason is the law of the world and that, therefore, in world history, things have come about rationally. This conviction and insight is a presupposition of history as such; in philosophy itself it is not presupposed. Through its speculative reflection philosophy has demonstrated that Reason—and this term may be accepted here without closer examination of its relation to God—is both *substance and infinite power,* in itself the infinite material of all natural and spiritual life as well as the *infinite form,* the actualization of itself as content. It is *substance,* that is to say, that by which and in which all reality has its being and subsistence. It is infinite *power,* for Reason is not so impotent as to bring about only the ideal, the ought, and to remain in an existence outside of reality—who knows where—as something peculiar in the heads of a few people. It is the infinite *content* of all essence and truth, for it does not require, as does finite activity, the condition of external materials, of given data from which to draw nourishment and objects of its activity; it supplies its own nourishment and is its own reference. And it is infinite *form,* for only in its image and by its fiat do phenomena arise and begin to live. It is its own exclusive presupposition and absolutely final purpose, and itself works out this purpose from potentiality into actuality, from inward source to outward appearance, not only in the natural but also in the spiritual universe, in world history. That this *Idea* or *Reason* is the True, the Eternal, the Absolute Power and that it and nothing but it, its glory and majesty, manifests itself in the world—this, as we said before, has been proved in philosophy and is being presupposed here as proved.

     Those among you, gentlemen, who are not yet acquainted with philosophy could perhaps be asked to come to these lectures on world history with the belief in Reason, with a desire, a thirst for its insight. It is indeed this desire for rational insight, for cognition, and not merely for a collection of various facts, which ought to be presupposed as a subjective aspiration in the study of the sciences. For even though one were not approaching world history with the thought and knowledge of Reason, at least one ought to have the firm and invincible faith that there is Reason in history and to believe that the world of intelligence and of self-conscious willing is not abandoned to mere chance, but must manifest itself in the light of the rational Idea. Actually, however, I do not have to demand such belief in advance. What I have said here provisionally, and shall have to say later on, must, even in our branch of science, be taken as a summary view of the whole. It is not a presupposition of study; it is a *result* which happens to be known to myself because I already know the whole. Therefore, only the study of world history itself can show that it has proceeded rationally, that it represents the rationally necessary course of the World Spirit, the Spirit whose nature is indeed always one and the same, but whose one nature unfolds in the course of the world. This, as I said, must be the result of history. History itself must be taken as it is; we have to proceed historically, empirically. Among other things, we must not let ourselves be tempted by the professional historians, for these, particularly the Germans, who possess great authority, practice precisely what they accuse the philosophers of, namely, *a priori* historical fiction. For example, it is a widespread fabrication that there was an original, primeval people taught immediately by God, endowed with perfect insight and wisdom, possessing a thorough knowledge of all natural laws and spiritual truths; or that there were such or such sacerdotal peoples; or, to mention a more specific matter, that there was a Roman epos from which the Roman historians derived the earliest history—and so on. Apriorities of this kind we shall leave to these talented professional historians, among whom, at least in our country, their use is quite common. As our first condition we must therefore state that we apprehend the historical faithfully. In such general terms, however, as "faithfully" and "apprehend" lies an ambiguity. Even the average and mediocre historian, who perhaps believes and pretends that he is merely receptive, merely surrendering himself to the data, is not passive in his thinking. He brings his categories with him and sees the data through them. In everything that is supposed to be scientific, Reason must be awake and reflection applied. To him who looks at the world rationally the world looks rationally back. The relation is mutual. But we cannot treat here the various modes of reflection, of points of view, of judgment, not even those concerning the relative importance or unimportance of facts—the most elementary category.

Only two aspects of the general conviction that Reason has ruled in the world and in world history may be called to your attention. They will give us an immediate opportunity to examine our most difficult question and to point ahead to the main theme.

1. The first is the historical fact of the Greek, Anaxagoras, who was the first to point out that *nous,* understanding in general or Reason, rules the world—but not an intelligence in the sense of an individual consciousness, not a spirit as such. These two must be carefully distinguished. The motion of the solar system proceeds according to immutable laws; these laws are its reason. But neither the sun nor the planets, which according to these laws rotate around it, have any consciousness of it. Thus, the thought that there is Reason in nature, that nature is ruled by universal, unchangeable laws, does not surprise us; we are used to it and make very little of it. Also, this historical circumstance teaches us a lesson of history: things which may seem trivial to us have not always been in the world; a new thought like this one marks an epoch in the development of the human spirit. Aristotle says of Anaxagoras, as the originator of this thought, that he appeared like a sober man among the drunken. From Anaxagoras, Socrates adopted the doctrine, which became forthwith the ruling idea in philosophy, except in the school of Epicurus, who ascribed all events to chance. "I was delighted about this," Plato makes Socrates say, "and hoped to have found a teacher who would interpret Nature by Reason and would show me in the particular its particular purpose, and in the universal, the universal purpose. I should not have given up this hope for anything. But how greatly was I disappointed when, having zealously applied myself to the writings of Anaxagoras, I found that he mentions only external causes, such as

Air, Ether, Water, and the like, instead of Reason."* It is evident that the insufficiency which Socrates found in the principle of Anaxagoras has nothing to do with the principle itself, but with Anaxagoras' failure to apply it to concrete nature. Nature was not understood or comprehended through this principle; the principle remained abstract— nature was not understood as a development of Reason, as an organization brought forth by it. I wish at the very outset to draw your attention to this difference between a concept, a principle, a truth, as confined to the abstract and as determining concrete application and development. This difference is fundamental; among other things we shall come back to precisely this point at the end of our world history, when we deal with the most recent political events.

2. The second point is the historical connection of the thought that Reason rules the world with another form of it, well known to us—that of religious truth: that the world is not abandoned to chance and external accident but controlled by *Providence*. I said before that I do not make any demand on your belief in the principle announced; but I think I may appeal to this belief in its religious form, unless the nature of scientific philosophy precludes, as a general rule, the acceptance of any presuppositions; or, seen from another angle, unless the science itself which we want to develop should first give the proof, if not of the truth, at least of the correctness of our principle. The truth that a Providence, that is to say, a divine Providence, presides over the events of the world corresponds to our principle; for divine Providence is wisdom endowed with infinite power which realizes its own aim, that is, the absolute, rational, final purpose of the world. Reason is Thought determining itself in absolute freedom.

On the other hand, a difference, indeed an opposition, now appears between this faith and our principle, very much like that between Socrates' expectation and the principle of Anaxagoras. For this faith is also indefinite, it is what is called faith in Providence in general; it is not followed up in definite application to the whole, the comprehensive course of world history. To explain history means to reveal the passions of men, their genius, their active powers. This definiteness of Providence is usually called its *plan*. Yet this very plan is supposed to be hidden from our view; indeed, the wish to recognize it is deemed presumption. The ignorance of Anaxagoras about the manifestation of Reason in reality was naïve; the knowledge of the principle had not yet developed, either in him or in Greece in general. He was not yet able to apply his general principle to the concrete, to deduce the latter from the former. Only Socrates took the first step in comprehending the union of the concrete and the universal. Anaxagoras, then, was not opposed to such application; but the faith in Providence *is*. It is opposed at least to the application at large of our principle, to the *cognition* of the plan of Providence. In particular cases, it is true, one allows it here and there, when pious minds see in particular events not only chance but God's will—when, for example, an individual in great perplexity and need gets unexpected help. But these instances are limited to the particular purposes of this individual. In world history the "individuals" that we have to deal with are peoples; they are totalities which are states. We cannot, therefore, be satisfied with what we may call this "retail" view of faith in Providence, nor with the merely abstract, undetermined faith in the universal statement that there is a Providence, without determining its definite acts. On the contrary, we must seriously try to recognize the ways of Providence, its means and manifestations in history, and their relation to our universal principle.

---

*[*Phaedo,* 97–98. Hegel paraphrases this passage.]

But in mentioning at all the recognition of the plan of divine Providence I have touched on a prominent question of the day, the question, namely, whether it is possible to recognize God—or, since it has ceased to be a question, the doctrine, which has now become a prejudice, that it is impossible to know God. Following this doctrine we now contradict what the Holy Scripture commands as our highest duty, namely, not only to love but also to know God. We now categorically deny what is written, namely, that it is the spirit which leads to truth, knows all things, and penetrates even the depths of divinity. Thus, in placing the Divine Being beyond our cognition and the pale of all human things, we gain the convenient license of indulging in our own fancies. We are freed from the necessity of referring our knowledge to the True and Divine. On the contrary, the vanity of knowledge and the subjectivity of sentiment now have ample justification. And pious humility, in keeping true recognition of God at arm's length, knows very well what it gains for its arbitrary and vain striving.

I wanted to discuss the connection of our thesis—that Reason governs and has governed the world—with the question of the possible knowledge of God, chiefly in order to mention the accusation that philosophy avoids, or must avoid, the discussion of religious truths because it has, so to speak, a bad conscience about them. On the contrary, the fact is that in recent times philosophy has had to take over the defense of religious truths against many a theological system. In the Christian religion God has revealed Himself, which means He has given man to understand what He is, and thus is no longer concealed and secret. With this *possibility* of knowing God the *obligation* to know Him is imposed upon us. God wishes no narrow souls and empty heads for his children; He wishes our spirit, of itself indeed poor, rich in the knowledge of Him and holding this knowledge to be of supreme value. The development of the thinking spirit only *began* with this revelation of divine essence. It must now advance to the intellectual comprehension of that which originally was present only to the feeling and imagining spirit.

[*Feeling is the lowest form in which any mental content can exist. God is the Eternal Being in and for itself; and what is universal in and for itself is subject of thought, not of feeling. It is true that everything spiritual, every content of consciousness, anything that is product and subject of thought—in particular religion and morality—must also, and originally does, exist in the mode of feeling. But feeling is not the fount from which this content flows to man, but only a primal mode in which it exists in him. It is indeed the worst mode, a mode which he has in common with the animal. What is substantial must also exist in feeling, but it does mainly exist in a higher, more dignified form. If one wants to relegate the moral, the true, the most spiritual mental content necessarily to feeling and emotion and keep it there on general principle, one would ascribe to it essentially the animalic form; but this is not at all capable of containing the spirit. In feeling, the mental content is the smallest possible; it is present in its lowest possible form. As long as it is still in feeling it is veiled and entirely indefinite. It is still entirely subjective, present exclusively in the subjective form. If one says: "I feel such and such and so and so," then one has secluded himself in himself. Everybody else has the same right to say: "I don't feel it that way." And hence one has retreated from the common soil of understanding. In wholly particular affairs feeling is entirely in its right. But to maintain that all men had this or that in their feeling is a contradiction in terms; it contradicts the concept of feeling, the point of view of the individual subjectivity of each which one has taken with this statement. As soon as mental content is placed into feeling, everybody is reduced to his subjective point of view. If someone called anyone else by this or that epithet, the other would be entitled to give it back; and both, from their respective points of view, would be entitled to offend each other. If someone says he has religion in his feeling and the other that he does not find any God in his feeling, then both are right. If in this manner the divine content—the revelation of God, the relationship of man to God, the being of God for man—is reduced to pure feeling, then it is reduced to pure subjectivity, to the arbitrary, to whim. In this way one actually gets rid of truth as it is in and for itself. The true is universal in and for itself, essential, substantial; as such it can be only in and for thought.]* The time has finally come to understand also the rich product of creative Reason which is world history.

It was for a while the fashion to admire God's wisdom in animals, plants, and individual lives. If it is conceded that Providence manifests itself in such objects and materials, why not also in world history? Because its scope seems to be too large. But the divine wisdom, or Reason, is the same in the large as in the small. We must not deem God too weak to exercise his wisdom on a grand scale. Our intellectual striving aims at recognizing that what eternal wisdom *intended* it has actually *accomplished,* dynamically active in the world, both in the realm of nature and that of the spirit. In this respect our method is a theodicy, a justification of God, which Leibniz attempted metaphysically, in his way, by undetermined abstract categories. Thus the evil in the world was to be comprehended and the thinking mind reconciled with it. Nowhere, actually, exists a larger challenge to such reconciliation than in world history. This reconciliation can only be attained through the recognition of the positive elements in which that negative element disappears as something subordinate and vanquished. This is possible through the consciousness, on the one hand, of the true ultimate purpose of the world and, on the other hand, of the fact that this purpose has been actualized in the world and that the evil cannot ultimately prevail beside it. But for this end the mere belief in *nous* and providence is not sufficient. "Reason," which is said to govern the world, is as indefinite a term as "Providence."

One always speaks of Reason without being able to indicate its definition, its content, which alone would enable us to judge whether something is rational or irrational. What we need is an adequate definition of Reason. Without such definition we can get no further than mere words. With this let us proceed to the second point that we want to consider in this introduction.

III. The Idea of History and Its Realization

The question of how Reason is determined in itself and what its relation is to the world coincides with the question, *What is the ultimate purpose of the world?* This question implies that the purpose is to be actualized and realized. Two things, then, must be considered: first, the content of this ultimate purpose, the determination as such, and, secondly, its realization.

To begin with, we must note that world history goes on within the realm of Spirit. The term "world" includes both physical and psychical nature. Physical nature does play a part in world history, and from the very beginning we shall draw attention to the fundamental natural relations thus involved. But Spirit, and the course of its development, is the substance of history. We must not contemplate nature as a rational system in itself, in its own particular domain, but only in its relation to Spirit.

Coalbrookdale by Night, 1801, by Phillip James De Loutherbourg. The coal furnaces in the background light the sky and illuminate the fragments from the past in the foreground, symbolizing the onward march of history. *(Science Museum, London)*

[*After the creation of nature appears Man. He constitutes the antithesis to the natural world; he is the being that lifts itself up to the second world. We have in our universal consciousness two realms, the realm of Nature and the realm of Spirit. The realm of Spirit consists in what is produced by man. One may have all sorts of ideas about the Kingdom of God; but it is always a realm of Spirit to be realized and brought about in man.*

The realm of Spirit is all-comprehensive; it includes everything that ever has interested or ever will interest man. Man is active in it; whatever he does, he is the creature within which the Spirit works. Hence it is of interest, in the course of history, to learn to know spiritual nature in its existence, that is, the point where Spirit and Nature unite, namely, human nature. In speaking of human nature we mean something permanent. The concept of human nature must fit all men and all ages, past and present. This universal concept may suffer infinite modifications; but actually the universal is one and the same essence in its most various modifications. Thinking reflection disregards the variations and adheres to the universal, which under all circumstances is active in the same manner and shows itself in the same interest. The universal type appears even in what seems to deviate from it most strongly; in the most distorted figure we can still discern the human. . . .

This kind of reflection abstracts from the content, the purpose of human activity. . . . But the cultured human mind cannot help making distinctions between inclinations and desires as they manifest themselves in small circumstances and as they appear in the struggle of world-wide historical interests. Here appears an objective interest, which impresses us in two aspects, that of the universal aim and that of the individual who represents this aim. It is this which makes history so fascinating. These are the aims and individuals whose loss and decline we mourn. When we have before us the struggle of the Greeks against the Persians or Alexander's mighty dominion, we know very well what interests us. We want to see the Greeks saved from barbarism, we want the Athenian state preserved, and we are interested in the ruler under whose leadership the Greeks subjugated Asia. If it were only a matter of human passion, we would not feel any loss in imagining that Alexander would have failed in his enterprise. We could very well content ourselves in seeing here a mere play of passions, but we would not feel satisfied. We have here a substantial, an objective interest. . . .

In contemplating world history we must thus consider its ultimate purpose. This ultimate purpose is what is willed in the world itself. We know of God that He is the most perfect; He can will only Himself and what is like Him. God and the nature of His will are one and the same; these we call, philosophically, the Idea. *Hence, it is the Idea in general, in its manifestation as human spirit, which we have to contemplate. More precisely, it is the idea of human freedom. The purest form in which the Idea manifests itself is Thought itself. In this aspect the Idea is treated in Logic. Another form is that of physical Nature.* The third form, finally, is that of Spirit in general.*] Spirit, on the stage on which we observe it, that of world history, is in its most concrete reality. But nevertheless—or rather in order to understand also the general idea of this concrete existence of Spirit—we must set forth, first, some general definition of the *nature of Spirit*. But this can only be done here as a mere assertion; this is not the place to develop the idea of Spirit through philosophical speculation. As was mentioned above, what can be said in an introduction can be taken only historically—as an assumption to be explained and proved elsewhere or to be verified by the science of history itself.

We have therefore to indicate here:

(1) The abstract characteristics of the nature of Spirit.
(2) The means Spirit uses in order to realize its Idea.
(3) The form which the complete realization of Spirit assumes in existence—the State.

1. THE IDEA OF FREEDOM

The nature of Spirit may be understood by a glance at its direct opposite—Matter. The essence of matter is gravity, the essence of Spirit—its substance—is Freedom. It is immediately plausible to everyone that, among other properties, Spirit also possesses Freedom. But philosophy teaches us that *all* the properties of Spirit exist only through Freedom. All are but means of attaining Freedom; all seek and produce this and this alone. It is an insight of speculative philosophy that Freedom is the sole truth of Spirit. Matter possesses gravity by virtue of its tendency toward a central point; it is essentially composite, consisting of parts that exclude each other. It seeks its unity and thereby its own abolition; it seeks its opposite. If it would attain this it would be matter no longer, but would have perished. It strives toward ideality, for in unity it exists ide-

---

*[In this aspect the Idea is treated in the Philosophy of Nature.]

ally. Spirit, on the contrary, is that which has its center in itself. It does not have unity outside of itself but has found it; it is in itself and with itself. Matter has its substance outside of itself; Spirit is Being-within-itself (self-contained existence). But this, precisely, is Freedom. For when I am dependent, I refer myself to something else which I am not; I cannot exist independently of something external. I am free when I am within myself. This self-contained existence of Spirit is self-consciousness, consciousness of self.

Two things must be distinguished in consciousness, first, *that* I know and, secondly, *what* I know. In self-consciousness the two coincide, for Spirit knows itself. It is the judgment of its own nature and, at the same time, the operation of coming to itself, to produce itself, to make itself (actually) into that which it is in itself (potentially). Following this abstract definition it may be said that world history is the exhibition of spirit striving to attain knowledge of its own nature. As the germ bears in itself the whole nature of the tree, the taste and shape of its fruit, so also the first traces of Spirit virtually contain the whole of history. Orientals do not yet know that Spirit—Man as such—is free. And because they do not know it, they are not free. They only know that *one* is free; but for this very reason such freedom is mere caprice, ferocity, dullness of passion, or, perhaps, softness and tameness of desire—which again is nothing but an accident of nature and thus, again, caprice. This *one* is therefore only a despot, not a free man. The consciousness of freedom first arose among the Greeks, and therefore they were free. But they, and the Romans likewise, only knew that some are free—not man as such. This not even Plato and Aristotle knew. For this reason the Greeks not only had slavery, upon which was based their whole life and the maintenance of their splendid liberty, but their freedom itself was partly an accidental, transient, and limited flowering and partly a severe thralldom of human nature. Only the Germanic peoples came, through Christianity, to realize that man as man is free and that freedom of Spirit is the very essence of man's nature. This realization first arose in religion, in the innermost region of spirit; but to introduce it in the secular world was a further task which could only be solved and fulfilled by a long and severe effort of civilization. Thus slavery did not cease immediately with the acceptance of the Christian religion. Liberty did not suddenly predominate in states nor reason in governments and constitutions. The application of the principle to secular conditions, the thorough molding and interpenetration of the secular world by it, is precisely the long process of history. I have already drawn attention to this distinction between a principle as such and its application, its introduction and execution in the actuality of life and spirit. This is a fundamental fact in our science and must be kept constantly in mind. Just as we noted it in the Christian principle of self-consciousness and freedom, so it shows itself in the principle of freedom in general. World history is the progress of the consciousness of freedom—a progress whose necessity we have to investigate.

The preliminary statement given above of the various grades in the consciousness of freedom—that the Orientals knew only that *one* is free, the Greeks and Romans that *some* are free, while we know that *all* men absolutely, that is, as men, are free—is at the same time the natural division of world history and the manner in which we shall treat it. But this is only mentioned in passing; first, we must explain some other concepts.

We have established Spirit's consciousness of its freedom, and thereby the actualization of this Freedom as the final purpose of the world. For the spiritual world is the substance of reality, and the physical world remains subordinate to it, or, in terms of speculative philosophy, has no truth compared with the former. But the term "freedom," without further qualification, is indefinite and infinitely ambiguous. Being the highest concept, it is liable to an infinity of misunderstandings, confusions, and errors and may give rise to all possible kinds of extravagances. All this has never been more clearly known and experienced than today. Yet for the time being we must content ourselves with this general, as yet undefined term. Attention was also drawn to the importance of the infinite difference between the principle, as that which so far is only in itself, and that which is real. At the same time, it is Freedom in itself that comprises within itself the infinite necessity of bringing itself to consciousness and thereby, since knowledge about itself is its very nature, to reality. Freedom is itself its own object of attainment and the sole purpose of Spirit. It is the ultimate purpose toward which all world history has continually aimed. To this end all the sacrifices have been offered on the vast altar of the earth throughout the long lapse of ages. Freedom alone is the purpose which realizes and fulfills itself, the only enduring pole in the change of events and conditions, the only truly efficient principle that pervades the whole. This final aim is God's purpose with the world. But God is the absolutely perfect Being and can, therefore, will nothing but Himself, His own will. The nature of His own will, His own nature, is what we here call the Idea of freedom. Thus we translate the language of religion into that of philosophy. Our next question then is: what are the means the Idea uses for its realization? This is the second point that we have to consider.

2. The Means of Realization

(A) The Idea and the Individual

The question of the *means* whereby Freedom develops itself into a world leads us directly to the phenomenon of history. Although Freedom as such is primarily an internal idea, the means it uses are the external phenomena which in history present themselves directly before our eyes. The first glance at history convinces us that the actions of men spring from their needs, their passions, their interests, their characters, and their talents. Indeed, it appears as if in this drama of activities these needs, passions, and interests are the sole springs of action and the main efficient cause. It is true that this drama involves also universal purposes, benevolence, or noble patriotism But such virtues and aims are insignificant on the broad canvas of history. We may, perhaps, see the ideal of Reason actualized in those who adopt such aims and in the spheres of their influence; but their number is small in proportion to the mass of the human race and their influence accordingly limited. Passions, private aims, and the satisfaction of selfish desires are, on the contrary, tremendous springs of action. Their power lies in the fact that they respect none of the limitations which law and morality would impose on them; and that these natural impulses are closer to the core of human nature than the artificial and troublesome discipline that tends toward order, self-restraint, law, and morality.

When we contemplate this display of passions and the consequences of their violence, the unreason which is associated not only with them, but even—rather we might say *especially*—with *good* designs and righteous aims; when we see arising therefrom the evil, the vice, the ruin that has befallen the most flourishing kingdoms which the mind of man ever created, we can hardly avoid being filled with sorrow at this universal taint of corruption. And since this decay is not the work of mere nature, but of human will, our reflections may well lead us to a moral sadness, a revolt of the good will (spirit)—if indeed it has a place within us. Without rhetorical exaggeration, a simple, truthful account of the miseries that have overwhelmed the noblest of nations and politics and the finest exemplars of private virtue forms a most fearful picture and excites emotions of the profoundest and most hopeless sadness, counter-balanced by no consoling result. We can endure it and strengthen ourselves against it only by thinking that this is the way it had to be—it is fate; nothing can be done. And at last, out of the boredom with which this sorrowful reflection threatens us, we draw back into the vitality of the present, into our aims and interests of the moment; we retreat, in short, into the selfishness that stands on the quiet shore and thence enjoys in safety the distant spectacle of wreckage and confusion.

But in contemplating history as the slaughter-bench at which the happiness of peoples, the wisdom of states, and the virtue of individuals have been sacrificed, a question necessarily arises: To what principle, to what final purpose, have these monstrous sacrifices been offered?

From here one usually proceeds to the starting point of our investigation: the events which make up this picture of gloomy emotion and thoughtful reflection are only the means for realizing the essential destiny, the absolute and final purpose, or, what amounts to the same thing, the true result of world history. We have all along purposely eschewed that method of reflection which ascends from this scene of particulars to general principles. Besides, it is not in the interest of such sentimental reflections really to rise above these depressing emotions and to solve the mysteries of Providence presented in such contemplations. It is rather their nature to dwell melancholically on the empty and fruitless sublimities of their negative result. For this reason we return to our original point of view. What we shall have to say about it will also answer the questions put to us by this panorama of history.

The first thing we notice—something which has been stressed more than once before but which cannot be repeated too often, for it belongs to the central point of our inquiry—is the merely general and abstract nature of what we call principle, final purpose, destiny, or the nature and concept of Spirit. A principle, a law is something implicit, which as such, however true in itself, is not completely real (actual). Purposes, principles, and the like, are at first in our thoughts, our inner intention. They are not yet in reality. That which is in itself is a possibility, a faculty. It has not yet emerged out of its implicitness into existence. A second element must be added for it to become reality, namely, activity, actualization. The principle of this is the will, man's activity in general. It is only through this activity that the concept and its implicit ("being-in-themselves") determinations can be realized, actualized; for of themselves they have no immediate efficacy. The activity which puts them in operation and in existence is the need, the instinct, the inclination, and passion of man. When I have an idea I am greatly interested in transforming it into action, into actuality. In its realization through my participation I want to find my own satisfaction. A purpose for which I shall be active must in some way be my purpose; I must thereby satisfy my own desires, even though it may have ever so many aspects which do not concern me. This is the infinite right of the individual to find itself satisfied in its activity and labor. If men are to be interested in anything they must have "their heart" in it. Their feelings of self-importance must be satisfied. But here a misunderstanding must be avoided. To say that an individual "has an interest" in something is justly regarded as a reproach or blame; we imply that he seeks only his private advantage. Indeed, the blame implies not only his disregard of the common interest, but his taking advantage of it and even his sacrificing it to his own interest. Yet, he who is active for a cause is not simply "interested," but "interested *in it.*" Language faithfully expresses this distinction. Nothing therefore happens, nothing is accomplished, unless those concerned with an issue find their own satisfaction in it. They are particular individuals; they have their special needs, instincts, and interests. They have their own particular desires and volitions, their own insight and conviction, or at least their own attitude and opinion, once the aspirations to reflect, understand, and reason have been awakened. Therefore people demand that a cause for which they should be active accord with their ideas. And they expect their opinion—concerning its goodness, justice, advantage, profit—to be taken into account. This is of particular importance today when people are moved to support a cause not by faith in other people's authority, but rather on the basis of their own independent judgment and conviction.

We assert then that nothing has been accomplished without an interest on the part of those who brought it about. And if "interest" be called "passion"—because the whole individuality is concentrating all its desires and powers, with every fiber of volition, to the neglect of all other actual or possible interests and aims, on one object—we may then affirm without qualification that *nothing great in the world* has been accomplished without passion.

Two elements therefore enter into our investigation: first, the Idea, secondly, the complex of human passions; the one the warp, the other the woof of the vast tapestry of world history. Their contact and concrete union constitutes moral liberty in the state. We have already spoken of the Idea of freedom as the essence of Spirit and absolutely final purpose of history. Passion is regarded as something wrong, something more or less evil; man is not supposed to have passions. "Passion," it is true, is not quite the right word for what I wish to express. I mean here nothing more than human activity resulting from private interest, from special or, if you will, self-seeking designs—with this qualification: that the whole energy of will and character is devoted to the attainment of one aim and that other interests or possible aims, indeed everything else, is sacrificed to this aim. This particular objective is so bound up with the person's will that it alone and entirely determines its direction and is inseparable from it. It is that which makes the person what he is. For a person is a specific existence. He is not man in general—such a thing does not exist—but a particular human being. The term "character" also expresses this uniqueness of will and intelligence. But character comprises all individual features whatever—the way in which a person conducts himself in his private and other relations. It does not connote this individuality itself in its practical and active phase. I shall therefore use the term "passion" to mean the particularity of a character insofar as its individual volitions not only have a particular content but also supply the impelling and actuating force for deeds of universal scope. Passion is thus the subjective and therefore the formal aspect of energy, will, and activity, whose content and aim are at this point still undetermined. And a similar relation exists between individual conviction, insight, and conscience, on the one hand, and their content, on the other. If someone wants to decide whether my conviction and passion are true and substantial, he must consider the *content* of my conviction and the *aim* of my passion. Conversely, if they are true and substantial, they cannot help but attain actual existence.

From this comment on the second essential element in the historical embodiment of an aim, we infer—considering for a moment the institution of the state—that a state is then well constituted and internally vigorous when the private interest of its citizens is one with the common interest of the state, and the one finds gratification and realization in the other—a most important proposition. But in a state many institutions are necessary—inventions, appropriate arrangements, accompanied by long intellectual struggles in order to find out what is really appropriate, as well as struggles with private interests and passions, which must be harmonized in difficult and tedious discipline. When a state reaches this harmony, it has reached the period of its bloom, its excellence, its power and prosperity. But world history does not begin with any conscious aim, as do the *particular* circles of men. Already the simple instinct of living together contains the conscious purpose of securing life and property; once this primal society has been established, the purpose expands. But world history begins its *general* aim—to realize the idea of Spirit—only in an implicit form (*an sich*), namely, as Nature—as an innermost, unconscious instinct. And the whole business of history, as already observed, is to bring it into consciousness. Thus, appearing in the form of nature, of natural will, what we have called the subjective side is immediate, actual existence (*für sich*): need, instinct, passion, private interest, even opinion and subjective representation. These vast congeries of volitions, interests, and activities constitute the tools and means of the World Spirit for attaining its purpose, bringing it to consciousness, and realizing it. And this purpose is none other than finding itself—coming to itself—and contemplating itself in concrete actuality. But one may indeed question whether those manifestations of vitality on the part of individuals and peoples in which they seek and satisfy their own purposes are, at the same time, the means and tools of a higher and broader purpose of which they know nothing, which they realize unconsciously. This purpose has been questioned, and in every variety of form denied, decried, and denounced as mere dreaming and "philosophy." On this point, however, I announced my view at the very outset, and asserted our hypothesis—which eventually will appear as the result of our investigation—namely, that Reason governs the world and has consequently governed its history. In relation to this Reason, which is universal and substantial, in and for itself, all else is subordinate, subservient, and the means for its actualization. Moreover, this Reason is immanent in historical existence and reaches its own perfection in and through this existence. The union of the abstract universal, existing in and for itself, with the particular or subjective, and the fact that this union alone constitutes truth are a matter of speculative philosophy which, in this general form, is treated in logic. But in its historical development [*the subjective side, consciousness, is not yet able to know what is*] the abstract final aim of history, the idea of Spirit, for it is then itself in process and incomplete. The idea of Spirit is not yet its distinct object of desire and interest. Thus desire is still unconscious of its purpose; yet it already exists in the particular purposes and realizes itself through them. The problem concerning the union of the general and the subjective may also be raised under the form of the union of freedom and necessity. We consider the immanent development of the Spirit, existing in and for itself, as necessary, while we refer to freedom the interests contained in men's conscious volitions. Since, as was said, the speculative, that is, the conceptual aspect of this connection belongs to logic, it would be out of place to analyze it here. But the chief and cardinal points may be mentioned.

In philosophy we show that the Idea proceeds to its infinite antithesis. . . . [*The Idea has within itself the determination of its self-consciousness, of activity. Thus it is God's own eternal life, as it was, so to speak, before the creation of the world, (the) logical connection (of all things). It still lacks at this point the form of being which is actuality. It still is the universal, the immanent, the represented. The second stage begins when the Idea satisfies the contrast which originally is only ideally in it and posits the difference between itself in its free universal mode, in which it remains within itself, and itself as purely abstract reflection in itself. In thus stepping over to one side (in order to be object of reflection) the Idea sets the other side as formal actuality (Für-*

sichsein), *as formal freedom, as abstract unity of self-consciousness, as infinite reflection in itself, and as infinite negativity (antithesis). Thus it becomes Ego, which, as an atom (indivisible), opposes itself to all content and thus is the most complete antithesis—the antithesis, namely, of the whole plenitude of the Idea. The absolute Idea is thus, on the one hand, substantial fullness of content and, on the other hand, abstract free volition. God and universe have separated, and set each other as opposites. Consciousness, the Ego, has a being such that the other (everything else) is for it (its object). In developing this train of thought one arrives at the creation of free spirits, the world, and so on. The absolute antithesis, the atom (i.e., the Ego), which at the same time is a manifold (of contents of consciousness), is finiteness itself. It is for itself (in actuality) merely exclusion of its antithesis (the absolute Idea). It is its limit and barrier. Thus it is the Absolute itself become finite. Reflection in itself, individual self-consciousness, is the antithesis of the absolute Idea and hence the Idea in absolute finiteness. This finitude, the acme of freedom, this formal knowledge—when referred to the glory of God as to the absolute Idea which recognizes what ought to be—is the soil on which the spiritual element of knowledge as such is falling; thus it constitutes the absolute aspect of its actuality, though it remains merely formal.]*

To comprehend the absolute connection of this opposition is the profound task of metaphysics. *[The Divine, and hence religion, exists for the Ego, and likewise also the world in general, that is, the universal totality of finite existence, exists for the Ego. The Ego, in this relation, is itself its own finiteness and comprehends itself as finite. Thus it is the viewpoint of finite purposes, of mere appearance. (At the same time it is particularity of consciousness.) Consciousness in itself, freedom abstractly considered, is the formal aspect of the activity of the absolute Idea. This self-consciousness, first of all, wills itself in general and, secondly, wills itself in every particular. This self-knowing subjectivity projects itself into all objectivity. This constitutes the Ego's certainty of its own existence. Inasmuch as this subjectivity has no other content, it must be called the rational desire—just as piety is nothing but the desire for the subject's salvation. The Ego thus wills itself primarily not as conscious but as finite in its immediacy. This is the sphere of its phenomenality. It wills itself in its particularity. At this point we find the passions, where individuality realizes its particularity. If it succeeds in thus realizing its finiteness, it doubles itself (its potential finiteness becomes actual finiteness). Through this reconciliation of the atom and its othernesses individuals are what we call happy, for happy is he who is in harmony with himself. One may contemplate history from the point of view of happiness.]* But actually history is not the soil of happiness. The periods of happiness are blank pages in it. *[There is, it is true, satisfaction in world history. But it is not the kind that is called happiness, for it is satisfaction of purposes that are above particular interests. Purposes that are relevant for world history must be grasped in abstract volition and with energy. The world-historical individuals who have pursued such purposes have satisfied themselves, it is true, but they did not want to be happy.**

This element of abstract action] is to be regarded as the bond, the middle term, between the universal Idea, which reposes in the inner recesses of Spirit, and the external world. *[It is that which carries the Idea from its immanence into its external state. Universality, in being externalized, is at the same time made particular. The immanent by itself would be dead, abstract. Through action it becomes existent. Conversely, ac-*

---

*[They wanted to be great. Greatness is satisfaction in large situations, happiness satisfaction in small situations.]

tivity elevates (the) empty objectivity (of nature) to be the appearance of the essence which is in and for itself.]

(B) The Individual as Subject of History

[*In world history we deal with the Idea as it manifests itself in the element of human will, of human freedom. . . . Objectively seen, the Idea and the particular individual stand in the great opposition of Necessity and Freedom—the struggle of man against fate. But we take necessity not as the external necessity of fate, but as that of the divine Idea. The question then is: How is this high Idea to be united with human freedom? The will of the individual is free when it can posit abstractly, absolutely, and in and for itself that which it wills. How then can the universal, the rational in general, be determinant in history? This contradiction cannot be clarified here in complete detail. But think of the following:*

The flame consumes the air; it is nourished by wood. The air is the sole condition for the growing of trees. In the wood's endeavor to consume the air through fire, it fights against itself and against its own source. And yet oxygen continues in the air and the trees do not cease to grow green. So also when someone starts building a house, his decision to do so is freely made. But all the elements must help. And yet the house is being built to protect man against the elements. Hence the elements are here used against themselves. But the general law of nature is not disturbed thereby.] The building of a house is, in the first instance, a subjective aim and design. On the other hand we have, as means, the several substances required for the work—iron, wood, stones. The elements are used in preparing this material: fire to melt the iron, wind to blow the fire, water to set wheels in motion in order to cut the wood, etc. The result is that the wind, which has helped to build the house, is shut out by the house; so also are the violence of rains and floods and the destructive powers of fire, so far as the house is made fire-proof. The stones and beams obey the law of gravity and press downwards so that the high walls are held up. Thus the elements are made use of in accordance with their nature and cooperate for a product by which they become constrained. In a similar way the passions of men satisfy themselves; they develop themselves and their purposes in accordance with their natural destination and produce the edifice of human society. Thus they fortify a structure for law and order *against* themselves. [*Thus the passions are by no means always opposed to morality but actualize the universal. As far as their own morality is concerned, it is true, they strive to realize their own interests. Thus they* appear *bad and self-seeking. But action is always individual; it is always* I *who act. It is* my *purpose which I want to fulfill. This purpose may be a good one, a universal aim; on the other hand, the interest may be a particular, a private one. This does not mean that it is necessarily opposed to the universal good. On the contrary, the universal must be actualized through the particular.*]

This connection implies that human actions in history produce additional results, beyond their immediate purpose and attainment, beyond their immediate knowledge and desire. They gratify their own interests; but something more is thereby accomplished, which is latent in the action though not present in their consciousness and not included in their design. An analogous example is offered in the case of a man who, thirsting for revenge perhaps justly to redress an unjust injury, sets fire to another man's house. The deed immediately establishes a train of circumstances not directly connected with it, taken in itself. In itself it consists in merely presenting a small flame to a small portion of a beam. Events not involved in that simple act follow of themselves. The part of the beam which was set afire is connected with its remote portions; the beam itself is united with the woodwork of the house and this with other houses, and a wide conflagration ensues. It destroys the goods and chattels of many other persons besides those of the original victim and may even cost their lives. This lay neither in the deed itself, nor in the design of the man who committed it. But the action has a further general bearing. In the design of the doer it was only revenge executed against an individual through the destruction of his property. But it is moreover a crime, and that involves punishment. All this may not have been present to the mind of the perpetrator, still less in his intention; but his deed itself, the general principles that it calls into play, its substantial content, entail it. By this example I wish only to impress on you the consideration that in a simple act something further may be implicated than lies in the intention and consciousness of the agent. The example before us involves, however, this additional consideration, that the substance of the act—consequently we may say the act itself—recoils upon the perpetrator, reacts upon him and destroys him.

This union of the two extremes—the embodiment of a general idea in immediate actuality and the elevation of a particularity into universal truth—comes about under the condition of the diversity and mutual indifference of the two extremes. The human agents have before them limited aims, special interests. But they are also intelligent, thinking beings. Their purposes are interwoven with general and essential considerations of law, the good, duty, etc. For mere desire, volition in its raw and savage form, falls outside the scene and sphere of world history. These general considerations, which at the same time form norms for directing purposes and actions, have a definite content. For such empty abstractions as "good for its own sake" have no place in living actuality. If men are to act, they must not only intend the good but must know whether this or that particular course is good. What special course of action is good or not, right or wrong, is determined, for the ordinary circumstances of private life, by the laws and customs of a state. It is not too difficult to know them. [*It is part of the freedom in the state . . . that no apportionment in castes determines to which business an individual should dedicate himself. The* morality *of the individual, then, consists in his fulfilling the duties of his social position. And it is an easy matter to know what these duties are; they are determined by this position. The substantial content of such a relationship, its rationale, is known. It is, precisely, what is called duty. To investigate the content of duty is unnecessary speculation; in the tendency to regard the moral as a difficult problem, we rather sense the desire to get rid of one's duties.*] Each individual has his position; he knows, on the whole, what a lawful and honorable course of conduct is. To assert in ordinary private relations that it is difficult to choose the right and good, and to regard it as mark of an exalted morality to find difficulties and raise scruples on that score indicates an evil and perverse will. It indicates a will that seeks to evade obvious duties or, at least, a petty will that gives its mind too little to do. The mind, then, in idle reflection, busies itself with itself and indulges in moral smugness.

[*The essence of a moral relation lies in the substantial nature that duty indicates. Thus, the nature of the relation between children and parents simply lies in the duty to behave accordingly. Or, to mention a legal relationship, if I owe money to someone, I just have to act according to law and the nature of the relation and return the money. There is nothing problematic in all this. The basis of duty is the civil life: the individuals have their assigned business and hence their assigned duties. Their morality consists in acting accordingly. . . .*

But each individual is also the child of a people at a definite stage of its development. One cannot skip over the spirit of his people any more than one can skip over the earth. The earth is the center of gravity; a body imagined as leaving this center can] *only be imagined as exploding into the air. So it is with an individual. But only through his own effort can he be in harmony with his substance; he must bring the will demanded by his people to his own consciousness, to articulation. The individual does not invent his own content; he is what he is by acting out the universal as his own content.*

This universal content everyone must activate within himself. Through this activity he maintains the whole of ethical life. But there is another element active in history which does bring about just this difficulty of acting according to ethical norms. We saw earlier, in the discussion of the dialectic of the Idea, where this universal content originates. It cannot originate within the ethical community. There particular events may occur that violate its determinate universality, such as vice, fraud, and the like, which are suppressed. But a moral whole, as such, is limited. It must have above it a higher universality, which makes it disunited in itself. The transition from one spiritual pattern to the next is just this, that the former moral whole, in itself a universal, through being thought (in terms of the higher universal), is abolished as a particular.* The later universal, so to speak, the next higher genus of the preceding species, is potentially but not yet actually present in the preceding one. This makes all existing reality unstable and disunited.

In the course of history two factors are important. One is the preservation of a people, a state, of the well-ordered spheres of life. This is the activity of individuals participating in the common effort and helping to bring about its particular manifestations. It is the preservation of ethical life. The other important factor, however, is the decline of a state. The existence of a national spirit is broken when it has used up and exhausted itself. World history, the World Spirit, continues on its course. We cannot deal here with the position of the individuals within the moral whole and their moral conduct and duty. We are concerned with the Spirit's development, its progression and ascent to an ever higher concept of itself. But this development is connected with the degradation, destruction, annihilation of the preceding mode of actuality which the concept of the Spirit had evolved. This is the result, on the one hand, of the inner development of the Idea and, on the other, of the activity of individuals, who are its agents and bring about its actualization.] It is at this point that appear those momentous collisions between existing, acknowledged duties, laws, and rights and those possibilities which are adverse to this system, violate it, and even destroy its foundations and existence. Their tenor may nevertheless seem good, on the whole advantageous—yes, even indispensable and necessary. These possibilities now become historical fact; they involve a universal of an order different from that upon which depends the permanence of a people or a state. This universal is an essential phase in the development of the creating Idea, of truth striving and urging toward itself. The historical men, *world-historical individuals,* are those [*who grasp just such a higher universal, make it their own purpose, and realize this purpose in accordance with the higher law of the spirit*].

Caesar was such a man. Before reaching his position of superiority he was in danger of losing his place of equality with the other leaders of Rome. He was about to succumb to those who were just becoming his enemies. These enemies, who at the same time pursued their own personal interests, had on their side the formal constitution of Rome and the power of legal appearance. Caesar fought to keep his position, honor, and safety. But victory over his enemies, who held the power over all the Roman provinces, became at the same time conquest of the entire empire. Thus Cae-

---

*[For it is elevated into the universal.]

sar, without changing the form of the constitution, became the sole ruler of the state. In accomplishing his originally negative purpose—the autocracy over Rome—he at the same time fulfilled the necessary historical destiny of Rome and the world. Thus he was motivated not only by his own private interest, but acted instinctively to bring to pass that which the times required. It is the same with all great historical individuals: their own particular purposes contain the substantial will of the World Spirit. They must be called "heroes," insofar as they have derived their purpose and vocation not from the calm, regular course of things, sanctioned by the existing order, but from a secret source whose content is still hidden and has not yet broken through into existence. The source of their actions is the inner spirit, still hidden beneath the surface but already knocking against the outer world as against a shell, in order, finally, to burst forth and break it into pieces; for it is a kernel different from that which belongs to the shell. They are men, therefore, who appear to draw the impulses of their lives from themselves. Their deeds have produced a condition of things and a complex of historical relations that appear to be their own interest and their own work.

Such individuals have no consciousness of the Idea as such. They are practical and political men. But at the same time they are thinkers with insight into what is needed and timely. They see the very truth of their age and their world, the next genus, so to speak, which is already formed in the womb of time. It is theirs to know this new universal, the necessary next stage of their world, to make it their own aim and put all their energy into it. The world-historical persons, the heroes of their age, must therefore be recognized as its seers—their words and deeds are the best of the age. Great men have worked for their own satisfaction and not that of others. Whatever prudent designs and well-meant counsels they might have gotten from others would have been limited and inappropriate under the circumstances. For it is they who knew best and from whom the others eventually learned and with whom they agreed or, at least, complied. For Spirit, in taking this new historical step, is the innermost soul of all individuals—but in a state of unconsciousness, which the great men arouse to consciousness. For this reason their fellow men follow these soul-leaders, [*they stream to their banner*]. For they feel the irresistible power of their own spirit embodied in them.

Let us now cast a look at the fate of these world-historical individuals. [*They were fortunate in being the agents of a purpose which constitutes a step in the progress of the universal Spirit. But as individuals distinguished from their substantial aim, they were not what is commonly called happy, nor did they want to be. They wanted to achieve their aim, and they achieved it by their toil and labor. They succeeded in finding their satisfaction in bringing about their purpose, the universal purpose. With such a grand aim they had the boldness to challenge all the opinions of men.*] Thus they attained no calm enjoyment. Their whole life was labor and trouble, their whole being was in their passion. Once their objective is attained, they fall off like empty hulls from the kernel. They die early like Alexander, they are murdered like Caesar, transported to Saint Helena like Napoleon. This awful fact, that historical men were not what is called happy—for only private life in its manifold external circumstances can be "happy"—may serve as a consolation for those people who need it, the envious ones who cannot tolerate greatness and eminence. They strive to criticize the great and belittle greatness. Thus in modern times it has been demonstrated *ad nauseam* that princes are generally unhappy on their thrones. For this reason one does not begrudge them their position and finds it tolerable that *they* rather than oneself sit on the throne. The free man, however, is not envious, but gladly recognizes what is great and exalted and rejoices in its existence. . . . [*But to such great men attaches a whole train of envy, which tries to demonstrate that their passion is a vice. One can indeed apply the term "passion" to the phenomenon of the great men and can judge them morally by saying that passion had driven them. They were indeed men of passion: they had the passion of their conviction and put their whole character, genius, and energy into it. Here, then, what is necessary in and for itself appears in the form of passion. These great men seem only to follow their passion and their arbitrary wills. But what they pursue is the universal; that alone is their pathos. The passion precisely has been the energy of their ego; without it they would not have been able to achieve anything.*

In this way the purpose of passion and the purpose of the Idea are one and the same. Passion is the absolute unity of individual character and the universal. It is something almost animalic how the spirit in its subjective particularity here becomes identified with the Idea. . . .

By fulfilling their own great purpose in accordance with the necessity of the universal Spirit, these world-historical men also satisfy themselves. These two things belong inseparably together: the cause and its hero. They must both be satisfied. . . . It is psychological pedantry to make a separation and, by giving passion the name of addiction, to suspect the morality of these men. By saying they acted only from morbid craving, one presents the consequences of their actions as their purposes and degrades the actions themselves to means.] Alexander of Macedon partly conquered Greece and then Asia; it is said, therefore, that he craved conquest, and as proof it is offered that he did things which resulted in fame. What schoolmaster has not demonstrated that Alexander the Great and Julius Caesar were driven by such passions and were, consequently, immoral? From which it immediately follows that he, the schoolmaster, is a better man than they because he has no such passions, and proves it by the fact that he has not conquered Asia nor vanquished Darius and Porus, but enjoys life and allows others to enjoy it too. These psychologists are particularly fond of contemplating those peculiarities that belong to great historical figures as private persons. Man must eat and drink; he has relations with friends and acquaintances; he has emotions and fits of temper. "No man is a hero to his *valet de chambre*," is a well-known proverb; I have added—and Goethe repeated it two years later—"but not because the former is no hero, but because the latter is a valet." He takes off the hero's boots, helps him into bed, knows that he prefers champagne, and the like. Historical personages fare badly in historical literature when served by such psychological valets. These attendants degrade them to their own level, or rather a few degrees below the level of their own morality, these exquisite discerners of spirits. Homer's Thersites, who abuses the kings, is a standing figure for all times. Not in every age, it is true, does he get blows— that is, beating with a solid cudgel—as in the Homeric one. But his envy, his egotism, is the thorn that he has to carry in his flesh; and the undying worm that gnaws him is the tormenting thought that his excellent intentions and criticisms get absolutely no result in the world. One may be allowed a certain glee over Thersites' fate.

A world-historical individual is not so sober as to adjust his ambition to circumstances; nor is he very considerate. He is devoted, come what may, to one purpose. Therefore such men may treat other great and even sacred interests inconsiderately—a conduct which indeed subjects them to moral reprehension. But so mighty a figure must trample down many an innocent flower, crush to pieces many things in its path.

(C) THE INDIVIDUAL AS OBJECT OF HISTORY

The special interest of passion is thus inseparable from the actualization of the universal; for the universal results from the particular and definite and its negation. [*The par-*

ticular has its own role to play in world history; it is finite and must, as such, perish.] It is the particular which exhausts itself in the struggle and part of which is destroyed. [*But the universal results precisely from this struggle, from the destruction of the particular.*] It is not the general Idea that involves itself in opposition and combat and exposes itself to danger; it remains in the background, untouched and uninjured. This may be called the *cunning of Reason*—that it sets the passions to work for itself, while that through which it develops itself pays the penalty and suffers the loss. For it is the phenomenal which in part is negative, in part positive. The particular in most cases is too trifling as compared with the universal; the individuals are sacrificed and abandoned. The Idea pays the tribute of existence and transience, not out of its own funds but with the passions of the individuals.

We might find it tolerable that individuals, their purposes and gratifications, are thus sacrificed, their happiness abandoned to the realm of [*natural forces and hence of*] chance to which it belongs; and that individuals in general are regarded under the category of means. Yet there is one aspect of human individuality that we must refuse to take exclusively in this light even in relation to the highest, an element which is absolutely not subordinate but exists in individuals as essentially eternal and divine. I mean morality, ethics, religion. Already in discussing the role of individuals in the realization of the rational aim we said that the subjective element in them, their interests, cravings, and impulses, their views and judgments had an infinite right to be satisfied, although we regarded these as only the formal aspect of the process. In speaking of means we imagine, first of all, something external to the end which has no share in it. But actually even merely natural things, the most common lifeless objects used as means, must somehow be adapted to their purpose; they must have something in common with it. This bare external relation of mere means is the least relation human beings have to the rational purpose. In the very act of realizing it they make it the occasion of satisfying their personal desires, whose import is different from that purpose. Moreover, they share in the rational purpose itself and for that very reason are ends in themselves—not merely formally, as is the world of other living beings, whose individual life is essentially subordinate to that of man and is properly used up as an instrument. Men, on the contrary, are ends in themselves in regard to the content of the end. This defines those elements which we demand to be exempt from the category of means: morality, ethics, religion.

Man is an end in himself only by virtue of the divine in him—that which we designated at the outset as *Reason,* or, insofar as it has activity and power of self-determination, as *Freedom.* And we say—without entering at present into further discussion—that religiosity, morality, etc., have their foundation and source in it and are thus essentially exempt from external necessity and chance. [*But we must not forget that here we speak of morality, religiosity, etc., only insofar as they exist in individuals, hence, subject to individual freedom. In this sense, that is,*] to the extent of their freedom, individuals are responsible for the depravation and enfeeblement of morality and religion. This is the seal of the absolute and sublime destiny of man, that he knows what is good and what is evil, and that his destiny is his very ability to will either good or evil. In one word, he can be guilty—guilty not only of evil but of good, and not only concerning this or that particular matter and all that happens in and around him (*Sittlichkeit*), but also the good and evil attaching to his individual freedom (*Moralität*). The animal alone is truly innocent. It would, however, require an extensive explanation—as extensive as that of freedom itself—to avoid or refute all the misunderstandings which usually arise from the statement that the word "innocence" means ignorance of evil.

In contemplating the fate which virtue, morality, even piety have in history, we must not fall into the litany of lamentations that the good and pious often, or for the most part, fare ill in the world, while the evil and wicked prosper. By prosperity one may understand a variety of things—riches, outward honor, and the like. But in speaking of purpose in and for itself, the so-called prosperity or misfortune of this or that isolated individual cannot be regarded as an essential element in the rational order of the universe. With more reason than merely the happiness or fortunate circumstances of individuals we demand of the purpose of the world that good, moral, righteous purposes should find in and under it their satisfaction and security. What makes men morally discontented—a discontent on which they pride themselves—is that they do not find the present appropriate for the realization of aims which in their opinion are right and good—especially the ideals of political institutions of our time. They contrast things as they are with their ideal of things as they ought to be. In this case it is neither private interest nor passion that desires gratification, but reason, justice, liberty. In their name people demand their due and often are not merely discontent but rebellious against the condition of the world. To estimate such views and feelings one would have to examine the stubborn demands and dogmatic opinions in question. At no time as much as in our own have such general principles and notions been advanced with so much pretentiousness. At other times history seems to present itself as a struggle of passions. In our time, however, though passions are not wanting, history exhibits partly and predominantly a struggle of justifiable ideas and partly a struggle of passions and subjective interests under the mask of such higher pretensions. These pretensions, regarded as legitimate in the name of the supposed destiny of Reason, are thereby validated as absolute ends—in the same way as religion, morality, ethics.

As was said earlier, nothing is now more common than the complaint that the *ideals* which imagination sets up are not actualized, that these glorious dreams are destroyed by cold actuality. These ideals, which in the voyage of life founder on the rocks of hard reality, may be merely subjective to begin with and belong to the peculiarity of an individual who regards himself as supremely wise. Such ideals do not belong here. For what an individual fancies for himself in his isolation cannot be the norm for universal reality. The universal law is not designed for individuals, as such, who indeed may find themselves very much the losers. But by the term "ideal" we also understand the ideal of Reason, of the good and true. Poets, like Schiller, have painted such ideals touchingly and with strong emotion, and with the deeply melancholy conviction that they could never be actualized. In affirming, on the contrary, that the universal Reason *does* actualize itself, we have nothing to do with the empirical detail. For this can be better or worse; here chance and particularity have received authority to exercise their tremendous power. Much fault, therefore, might be found in phenomenal details. This subjective fault-finding is easy, particularly since it keeps in view only the detail and its deficiency, without understanding the universal Reason in it. In asserting good intentions for the welfare of the whole and exhibiting a semblance of good-heartedness, it can swagger about with great airs. It is easier to discover the deficiency in individuals, in states, and in Providence, than to see their real meaning. For in negative fault-finding one stands nobly and with proud mien above the matter, without penetrating into it and without comprehending its positive aspects. Age generally makes people more tolerant; youth is always discontented. For older people have a more mature judgment, which accepts even the bad, not out of mere indifference but because it has been more deeply taught by the grave experience of life. It has thus been led to the essence, the intrinsic value of the matter in question.

The insight then to which—in opposition to these ideals—philosophy should lead us is that the actual world is as it ought to be, that the truly good, the universal divine Reason is the power capable of actualizing itself. This good, this Reason, in its most concrete representation, is God. God governs the world. The actual working of His government, the carrying out of His plan is the history of the world. Philosophy strives to comprehend this plan, for only that which has been carried out according to it has reality; whatever does not accord with it is but worthless existence. Before the pure light of this divine Idea, which is no mere ideal, the illusion disappears as though the world were a crazy, inane process. Philosophy wishes to recognize the content, the reality of the divine Idea, and to justify the spurned actuality; for Reason is the comprehension of the divine work.

But then what about the atrophy, corruption, and ruin of religious, ethical, and moral purposes and social conditions in general? It must be said that essentially these purposes are infinite and eternal. But the forms that they assume may be of a limited order and consequently belong to the realm of mere nature, subject to the sway of chance. They are therefore transitory and exposed to atrophy and corruption. Religion and morality, as the universal essences in themselves, have the peculiarity of being present, conformably to their concepts and therefore truthfully, in the individual soul, although they may not be represented there fully elaborated and applied to completely developed conditions. The religiousness, the morality of a limited life—of a shepherd, a peasant—in their concentrated inward limitation to a few and quite simple circumstances of life, has infinite value. It has the same value as the religiousness and morality of a trained intellect and of an existence rich in scope of relations and activities. This inner focus, this simple region of the claims of subjective freedom—the seat of volition, resolution, and action, the abstract content of conscience, that wherein responsibility and worth of the individual are enclosed—remains untouched. It is quite shut out from the noisy din of world history, not only from its external and temporal changes but also from all alterations entailed by the absolute necessity of the concept of freedom itself. In general, however, it must be noted that for whatever in the world is acclaimed as noble and glorious there is something even higher. The claim of the World Spirit rises above all special claims.

So much concerning the means which the World Spirit uses for actualizing its concept. Simply and abstractedly, it is the activity of the subjects in whom Reason is present as their substantial essence in itself, but still obscure and concealed from them. The matter becomes more complicated and difficult when we regard the individuals not merely as active but, more concretely, consider the definite content of their religion and morality—features which have part in Reason and thereby in its absolute claims. Here the relation of mere means to an end disappears. The main points of this seeming difficulty with regard to the absolute purpose of Spirit have been briefly considered.

3. THE STATE

(A) THE STATE AS REALIZATION OF THE IDEA

The third point, then, concerns the end to be attained by these means, that is, the form it assumes in the realm of the actual. We have spoken of means; but the carrying out of a subjective, limited aim also requires a *material* element, either already present or to be procured or to serve this actualization. Thus the question would arise: What is the material in which the final end of Reason is to be realized? It is first of all the subjective agent itself, human desires, subjectivity in general. In human knowledge and volition, as its material basis, the rational attains existence. We have considered subjective volition with its purpose, namely, the truth of reality, insofar as moved by a great world-historical passion. As a subjective will in limited passions it is dependent; it can gratify its particular desires only within this dependence. But the subjective will has also a substantial life, a reality where it moves in the region of essential being and has the essential itself as the object of its existence. This essential being is the union of the subjective with the rational will; it is the moral whole, the *State*. It is that actuality in which the individual has and enjoys his freedom, but only as knowing, believing, and willing the universal. This must not be understood as if the subjective will of the individual attained its gratification and enjoyment through the common will and the latter were a means for it—as if the individual limited his freedom among the other individuals, so that this common limitation, the mutual constraint of all, might secure a small space of liberty for each. (This would only be negative freedom.) Rather, law, morality, the State, and they alone, are the positive reality and satisfaction of freedom. The caprice of the individual is not freedom. It is this caprice which is being limited, the license of particular desires.

The subjective will, passion, is the force which actualizes and realizes. The Idea is the interior; the State is the externally existing, genuinely moral life. It is the union of the universal and essential with the subjective will, and as such it is *Morality*. The individual who lives in this unity has a moral life, a value which consists in this substantiality alone.* Sophocles' Antigone says: "The divine commands are not of yesterday nor of today; no, they have an infinite existence, and no one can say whence they came." The laws of ethics are not accidental, but are rationality itself. It is the end of the State to make the substantial prevail and maintain itself in the actual doings of men and in their convictions. It is the absolute interest of Reason that this moral whole exist; and herein lies the justification and merit of heroes who have founded states, no matter how crude.

[*What counts in a state is the practice of acting according to a common will and adopting universal aims. Even in the crude state there is subjection of one will under another; but this does not mean that the individual does not have a will of his own. It means that his particular will has no validity. Whims, lusts are not valid. The particularity of the will is being renounced already in such crude political formations. What counts is the common will. In thus being suppressed the individual will retires into itself. And this is the first condition necessary for the existence of the universal, the condition, namely, of knowledge, of thought—for it is thought that man has in common with the divine. It thus makes its appearance in the state. Only on this soil, that is, in the state, can art and religion exist. The objects of our considerations are peoples that have organized themselves rationally.*] In world history only those peoples that form states can come to our notice. [*One must not imagine that such organizations could appear on a desert island or in isolation. Although it is true that all great men have*

---

*[Social institutions, originally extrinsic to the individual and his intrinsic morality, grow up to complete this morality in the course of their development. Their totality, the State, thus becomes itself intrinsic morality, both with respect to the individual, as completion of his intrinsic freedom, and to the World Spirit, as concretion of its universal Freedom.]

formed themselves in solitude, they have done so only by assimilating what the state had already created. The universal must be not only something which the individual merely intends, but which is in existence. As such it is present in the state; it is that which is valid in it. Here inwardness is at the same time actuality. It is but actuality of an external manifold, yet comprehended here in universality.

The universal Idea manifests itself in the state. The term "manifestation" has here a meaning different from the usual one. Usually we distinguish between power (potentiality) and manifestation, as if the former were the essential, the latter the unessential or external. But no concrete determination lies as yet in the category of power itself, while where Spirit is, or the concrete concept, manifestation itself is the essential. The criterion of Spirit is its action, its active essence. Man is his own action, the sequence of his actions, that into which he has been making himself. Thus Spirit is essentially Energy; and in regard to Spirit one cannot set aside its manifestation. The manifestation of Spirit is its actual self-determination, and this is the element of its concrete nature. Spirit which does not determine itself is an abstraction of the intellect. The manifestation of Spirit is its self-determination, and it is this manifestation that we have to investigate in the form of states and individuals.

The spiritual individual, the people, insofar as it is organized in itself, an organic whole, is what we call the State. This designation is ambiguous in that by "state" and "constitutional law" one usually means the simple political aspect as distinct from religion, science, and art. But when we speak of the manifestation of the spiritual we understand the term "state" in a more comprehensive sense, similar to the term Reich *(empire, realm). For us, then, a people is primarily a spiritual individual. We do not emphasize the external aspects but concentrate on what has been called the spirit of a people. We mean its consciousness of itself, of its own truth, its own essence, the spiritual powers which live and rule in it. The universal which manifests itself in the State and is known in it—the* form *under which everything that is, is subsumed—is that which constitutes the* culture *of a nation. The definite* content *which receives this universal form and is contained in the concrete actuality of the state is the* spirit of the people. *The actual state is animated by this spirit in all its particular affairs, wars, institutions, etc. This spiritual content is something definite, firm, solid, completely exempt from caprice, the particularities, the whims of individuality, of chance. That which is subject to the latter is not the nature of the people: it is like the dust playing over a city or a field, which does not essentially transform it. This spiritual content then constitutes the essence of the individual as well as that of the people. It is the holy bond that ties the men, the spirits together. It is one life in all, a grand object, a great purpose and content on which depend all individual happiness and all private decisions.*] [*The state does not exist for the citizens; on the contrary, one could say that the state is the end and they are its means. But the means-end relation is not fitting here. For the state is not the abstract confronting the citizens; they are parts of it, like members of an organic body, where no member is end and none is means.*] It is the realization of Freedom, of the absolute, final purpose, and exists for its own sake. All the value man has, all spiritual reality, he has only through the state. For his spiritual reality is the knowing presence to him of his own essence, of rationality, of its objective, immediate actuality present in and for him. Only thus is he truly a consciousness, only thus does he partake in morality, in the legal and moral life of the state. For the True is the unity of the universal and particular will. And the universal in the state is in its laws, its universal and rational provisions. The state is the divine Idea as it exists on earth.

Thus the State is the definite object of world history proper. In it freedom achieves its objectivity and lives in the enjoyment of this objectivity. For law is the objectivity of Spirit; it is will in its true form. Only the will that obeys the law is free, for it obeys itself and, being in itself, is free. In so far as the state, our country, constitutes a community of existence, and as the subjective will of man subjects itself to the laws, the antithesis of freedom and necessity disappears. The rational, like the substantial, is necessary. We are free when we recognize it as law and follow it as the substance of our own being. The objective and the subjective will are then reconciled and form one and the same harmonious whole. For the ethos of the state is not of the moral, the reflective kind in which one's own conviction rules supreme. This latter is rather the peculiarity of the modern world. The true and antique morality is rooted in the principle that everybody stands in his place of duty. An Athenian citizen did what was required of him, as it were from instinct. But if I reflect on the object of my activity, I must have the consciousness that my will counts. Morality, however, is the duty, the substantial law, the second nature, as it has been rightly called; for the first nature of man is his immediate, animalic existence.

(B) Law as Realization of Freedom

The detailed development of the state is the subject of legal philosophy. But it must be observed that in present-day theories various errors are current respecting the state, which pass for established truths and have become prejudices. We will mention only a few of them, particularly those which refer to the subject of history.

The first error that we encounter is the direct contradiction of our principle that the State is the realization of freedom: the view, namely, that man is free by nature but that in society and in the state, to which he necessarily belongs, he must limit this natural freedom. That man is free "by nature" is quite correct in the sense that he is free according to the very concept of man, that is, in his *destination* only, as he is, in himself; the "nature" of a thing is indeed tantamount to its concept. But the view in question also introduces into the concept of man his immediate and natural way of *existence*. In this sense a state of nature is assumed in which man is imagined in the possession of his natural rights and the unlimited exercise and enjoyment of his freedom. This assumption is not presented as a historical fact; it would indeed be difficult, were the attempt seriously made, to detect any such condition anywhere, either in the present or the past. Primitive conditions can indeed be found, but they are marked by brute passions and acts of violence. Crude as they are, they are at the same time connected with social institutions which, to use the common expression, restrain freedom. The assumption (of the noble savage) is one of those nebulous images which theory produces, an idea which necessarily flows from that theory and to which it ascribes real existence without sufficient historical justification.

Such a state of nature is in theory exactly as we find it in practice. Freedom as the *ideal* of the original state of nature does not *exist* as original and natural. It must first be acquired and won; and that is possible only through an infinite process of the discipline of knowledge and will power. The state of nature, therefore, is rather the state of injustice, violence, untamed natural impulses, of inhuman deeds and emotions. There is, it is true, a limitation by society and the state, but it is a limitation of the brute emotions and rude instincts, as well as (in a more advanced stage of culture) of self-reflecting caprice and passion. This constraint is part of the process through which is first produced the consciousness of and the desire for freedom in its true, that is, rational and ideal form. The idea of freedom necessarily implies law and morality. These are in and for themselves universal essences, objects, and aims, to be discovered only by the activity of thought, emancipating itself from, and developing itself in opposition to, the merely sensuous; it must be assimilated to and incorporated with the originally sensuous will against its natural inclination. The perpetual misunderstanding of freedom is this: that one knows it only in its formal subjective sense, abstracted from its essential objects and aims. Thus the limitation of impulse, desire, passion—pertaining merely to the particular individual as such—of caprice and willfulness, is taken as a limitation of freedom. On the contrary, such limitation is the very condition leading to liberation; and society and the state are the very conditions in which freedom is realized.

Secondly, there is another theory that objects to the development of morality into legal form. The *patriarchal* state is viewed, either in relation to the whole or to some branches (of the human family), as that condition in which, together with the legal element, the moral and emotional find their fulfillment. Hence justice, it is believed, can be truly carried out only through the union of its content with the moral and emotional elements. The basis of the patriarchal condition is the family relation. It develops as the first phase of conscious morality, to be followed by that of the state as its second phase. The patriarchal condition is one of transition, in which the family has already advanced to a race or people. The union, therefore, has already ceased to be simply a bond of love and confidence and has become one of service. To understand this transition we must first examine the ethical principle of the family. The family is a single person; its members have either, as parents, mutually surrendered their individuality—and consequently their legal relations to one another, as well as their particular interests and desires—or have not yet attained individuality, as children, who are at first in the merely natural condition already mentioned. They live therefore in a unity of feeling, love, confidence, and faith in each other. In love, the one individual has the consciousness of himself in the consciousness of the other; he lives selflessly. In this mutual self-renunciation each gains the life of the other, as well as his own which is one with the other. All other interests of life, its necessities and external concerns, education of the children, form a common purpose for the members of the family. The spirit of the family—the Penates—are as much one substantial being as the spirit of a people in the State. Morality in both cases consists in a feeling, a consciousness, and a will not of the individual personality and its interests but of the common personality, the interest of all members as such. But this unity is in the case of the family essentially one of feeling, remaining within the limits of the natural. The sacredness of the family relation should be respected in the highest degree by the state. Through it the state has as members individuals who are already, as such and in themselves, moral—for as mere persons they are not; and who, in uniting to form a state, bring with them the sound basis of a political edifice, the capacity of feeling one with a whole. But the expansion of the family to a patriarchal whole extends beyond the ties of blood relationship, the simple, natural basis of the state. Beyond that the individuals must acquire the status of personality. A detailed review of the patriarchal condition would lead us to the discussion of theocracy. The head of the patriarchal clan is also its priest. When the family is not yet distinct from civil society and the state, the separation of religion from it has not yet taken place either; and so much the less since its piety is itself (like religion) an inwardness of feeling.

(C) THE LEGAL FOUNDATION OF THE STATE (THE CONSTITUTION)

We have discussed two aspects of freedom, the objective and the subjective. If freedom implies the consent of each individual, then of course only the subjective aspect is meant. From this principle follows as a matter of course that no law is valid except by agreement of all. This implies that the majority decides; hence the minority must yield to the majority. But already Rousseau has remarked that this means the absence of freedom, for the will of the minority is disregarded. In the Polish diet all decisions had to be unanimous, and it was from this kind of freedom that the state perished. Moreover, it is a dangerous and false presupposition that the people *alone* has reason and insight and knows what is right; for each popular faction can set itself up as the People. What constitutes the state is a matter of trained intelligence, not a matter of "the people."

If the principle of individual will and consent of all is laid down as the only basis of constitutional freedom, then actually there is no *Constitution*. The only institution necessary would be a neutral, centrally located observer who would announce what in his opinion were the needs of the state, a mechanism of assembling the individuals, casting their vote, and the arithmetical counting and comparison of the votes on the various propositions—and this would already be the decision. The state is an abstract entity which has its—merely general—reality in the citizens. But it is real, and the merely general existence must be translated into individual will and activity. Thus arises the necessity of government and administration, the selection of individuals who have to take the helm of political administration, decide its execution, and command the citizens entrusted with it. Thus, even in a democracy the people's decision on a war requires a general as leader of the army. Only in the constitution does the abstract entity of the state assume life and reality; but this involves a distinction between those who command and those who obey. Yet, it does not seem to be in accordance with freedom to obey, and those who command seem to act in opposition to the concept of freedom, the very basis of the state.

Thus the distinction between commanding and obeying seems necessary for the very function of the state. Hence one recommends—as a matter of purely external necessity, which is in opposition to the nature of freedom in its abstract aspect—that the constitution should at least be so framed that the citizens have to obey as little as possible and the authorities are allowed to command as little as possible. The nature and degree of whatever authority is necessary should be determined and decided in large measure by the people, that is to say, by the will of the majority; yet, at the same time the state, as reality, as individual unit, should have power and strength.

The primary distinction to be made is, then, between the governing and the governed. Constitutions have rightly been classified as monarchic, aristocratic, and democratic; the monarchy proper, however, must be distinguished again from despotism. Also, it must be understood that such classifications are drawn from abstract concepts so as to emphasize the fundamental differences only. They are types or genera or species which cannot exhaustively account for the concrete realities. Particularly, they admit of a great number of special modifications, not only within the types but also among the types; even though such fusions or mixtures of type conduce to misshapen, unstable, and inconsistent forms. The problem, in such collisions, therefore, is to determine the *best constitution,* namely, that institution, organization, or mechanism of government which most securely guarantees the purpose of the state. This goal can of course be considered in various ways, for example, as the quiet enjoyment of life, as universal happiness. Such aims have brought about the so-called ideals of government and, particularly, the ideals of the education of princes, as in Fénelon,* or of the rulers

---

*[In his *Télémaque* (1699), written after Fénelon's tutorship of the Duke of Burgundy, who for a year (1711–1712) was heir-apparent to the throne of Louis XIV. Fénelon (1651–1715) also wrote a *Treatise on the Education of Girls,* which for a century became the standard handbook on the subject. In 1695 he became archbishop of Cambrai. His writings form the transition from absolutism to enlightenment.]

or the aristocracy in general, as in Plato. The emphasis is here put on the nature of the ruling individuals; the content of the organic institutions of the state is not at all considered. It is often thought that the question of the best or a better constitution is not only in theory a matter of free individual conviction, but that its actual introduction could also be only a matter of purely theoretical decisions; so that the constitution would be a matter of free choice, determined by nothing but reflection. In this quite naïve sense the Persian magnates—though not the Persian people—deliberated upon the constitution which they wanted to introduce in Persia, after their conspiracy against the pseudo-Smerdis and the Magi had succeeded and there was no royal heir. And the account that Herodotus gives of this deliberation is equally naïve.

Today the constitution of a country and people is not regarded as so entirely dependent upon free choice. The underlying, but abstractly entertained conception of freedom has resulted in the Republic's being quite universally regarded—in theory—as the only just and true constitution. Many of those who even have high official positions under monarchical constitutions do not resist but rather incline toward such views. They understand, however, that such a constitution, though ideal, cannot be realized under all circumstances. People being what they are, one has to be content with less freedom; so that the monarchical constitution, under the given circumstances and the moral condition of the people, is regarded the most useful. Even in this view the actual condition on which the constitution is thought to depend is regarded as a merely external accident. This opinion is based on the separation which reflection and understanding make between the concept and its reality. Holding to an abstract and hence untrue concept they do not grasp the idea; or—which comes to the same thing insofar as the content, though not the form, is concerned—they have no concrete view of a people and a state. We shall show later that the constitution of a people is of the same substance, the same spirit as its art and philosophy, or at least its imagination, its thoughts, and its general culture—not to mention the additional, external influences of climate, neighbors, and global position. A state is an individual totality from which no particular aspect, not even one as highly important as the constitution, can be separated and considered by itself alone. Nor can this constitution be considered, discussed, and selected in isolation. Not only is the constitution intimately connected with those other spiritual forces and dependent on them, but the determination of the whole spiritual individuality, including all its forces, is only a moment in the history of the whole and predetermined in its course. It is this that gives to the constitution its highest sanction and necessity. The origin of the state is domination on the one hand, instinctive obedience on the other. But obedience and force, fear of a ruler, is already a connection of wills. Already in primitive states we found that the will of the individual does not count, that particularity is renounced and the universal will is the essential. This unity of the universal and the particular is the Idea itself, present as the State and as such developing itself further. The abstract but necessary course of the development of truly independent states begins then with royal power, either patriarchal or military. After that, individuality and particularity must assert themselves in aristocracy and democracy. The end is the subjection of this particularity under one power which must be absolutely of such a nature that the two spheres have their independence outside of it: it must be monarchical. Thus we must distinguish a first (or original) and a second phase of royalty. This course is a necessary one; each concrete constitution must enter it. A constitution is therefore not a matter of choice but depends on the stage of the people's spiritual development.

What is important in a constitution is the internal development of the rational, that is, the political condition, the setting free of the successive moments of the concept. The particular powers must become distinct, each one completing itself, but at the same time they must freely cooperate for one purpose and be held together by it, thus forming an organic whole. Thus the State is rational and self-conscious freedom, objectively knowing itself. For its objectivity resides precisely in the fact that its moments are not merely ideally present but actualized in their particularity; that they pass over from their own self-related activity into that activity from which results the whole, the soul, the individual unity.

The State is the idea of Spirit in the externality of human will and its freedom. It therefore is essentially the medium of historical change, and the stages of the Idea represent in it various *principles.* The constitutions wherein world-historical peoples have reached their flowering are peculiar to them, hence give us no universally valid basis. Their differences consist not in the individual manners of elaboration and development, but rather in the differences of principles. Thus we can learn little for the political principle of our time, as the last constitutional principle, from a comparison with the constitutions of earlier world-historical peoples. It is different with science and art. The philosophy of the ancients, for example, is so much the basis of modern philosophy that it must be contained in the latter as its fundament. The relation is here one of uninterrupted development of an identical structure, whose foundations, walls, and roof are still the same. In art that of the Greeks is the highest model. But in respect to the constitution it is different; here the old and the new do not have the essential principle in common, although we do have in common abstract speculations and doctrines of just government, of insight and virtue of the ruler. Yet, nothing is so inappropriate as to use as models for our constitutional institutions examples from Greece, Rome, or the Orient. From the Orient we can take agreeable pictures of patriarchal conditions, fatherly government, popular devotion; from the Greeks and Romans descriptions of popular liberty. The Greeks and Romans understood the concept of a free constitution as granting all citizens a share in the council and decisions of communal affairs and laws. Also in our times this is the general opinion, but with one modification: our states are so big and their people so many, that they cannot directly, but only indirectly through representatives, contribute their will to political decisions. For purposes of legislation the people must be represented by deputies. A free constitution is for us dependent upon the idea of representative government, and this has become a firm prejudice. Thus people and government are separated. But there is something malicious in this opposition, a trick of bad will, as if the people were the whole. Also, at the bottom of this idea lies the principle of individuality, the absoluteness of the subjective will of which we spoke above. The main thing is that freedom, as it is determined by the concept, is *not* based on the subjective will and caprice but on the understanding of the general will, and that the system of freedom is the free development of its stages. The subjective will is a purely formal concept which does not say at all *what* it wills. Only the rational will is the universal which determines and develops itself in itself and unfolds its successive moments in an organic manner. Of such Gothic cathedral architecture the ancients knew nothing.

(D) The Religious Foundation of the State

We have established as the two points of our discussion, first, the idea of Freedom as absolute final aim, and, secondly, the means of its realization, the subjective side of knowledge and volition with their vitality, mobility, and activity. We then discussed the State as the moral whole and the reality of freedom, and thus as the objective unity of the two preceding factors. Although for analysis we separated the two elements, it must be well remembered that they are closely connected and that this connection is within each of them when we examine them singly. On the one hand we recognized the Idea in its determination, as self-knowing and self-willing freedom which has only itself as its aim. As such, it is at the same time the simple idea of reason and likewise that which we have called subject, the consciousness of self, the Spirit existing in the world. On the other hand, in considering this subjectivity, we find that subjective knowing and willing are Thinking. But in thoughtful knowing and willing I will the universal object, the substance of actualized rationality (of what is in and for itself rational). We thus observe a union which is in itself, between the objective element, the concept, and the subjective element. The objective existence of this unity is the State. The State, thus, is the foundation and center of the other concrete aspects of national life, of art, law, morality, religion, science. All spiritual activity, then, has the aim of becoming conscious of this union, that is, of its freedom. Among the forms of these conscious unions *religion* is the highest. In it the spirit existing in the world becomes conscious of absolute Spirit. In this consciousness of actualized ("being-in-and-for-itself") essence the will of man renounces particular interest; it puts it aside in devotion in which he is not concerned any more with particulars. Through sacrifice man expresses his renunciation of property, his will, his private feelings. The religious concentration of the mind appears as emotion, but passes also into contemplation; ritual is an expression of contemplation. The second form of the spiritual union between the objective and the subjective is *Art:* it appears more in sensible reality than does religion; in its most noble attitude it has to represent, not indeed the spirit of God but the form of the God—and then the divine, the spiritual in general. It renders the divine visible to imagination and the senses. The True, however, not only achieves representation and feeling, as in religion, and for the senses, as in art, but also for the thinking spirit; this leads to the third form of the union, *Philosophy.* It is in this respect the highest, freest, and wisest product. We cannot here discuss these three forms in any detail. They had to be mentioned only because they occupy the same ground as the object of our study, the *State.*

The universal which appears and becomes known in the state, the form into which is cast all reality, constitutes what is generally called the *culture* of a nation. The definite content, however, which receives the form of universality and is contained in the concrete reality of the State, is the *spirit of the people.* The true State is animated by this spirit in all its affairs, wars, institutions, etc. But man must himself know of this—his own—spirit and essence and give himself the consciousness of his original union with it. For we said that all morality is the unity of subjective and general will. The spirit, then, must give itself an express consciousness of this unity, and the center of this knowledge is religion. Art and science are only different aspects of this very same content.

In discussing religion it is important to ask whether it recognizes truth, or the Idea, only in its separation or in its true unity. In its separation: when God is conceived as the abstract highest Being, Lord of Heaven and Earth, transcending the world, beyond, and excluded from, human reality—or in its unity: God as unity of the universal and particular, in Whom even the particular is positively regarded, in the idea of incarnation. Religion is the sphere where a people gives itself the definition of what it regards as the True. Such a definition contains everything which belongs to the essence of the object, reducing its nature to a simple fundamental characteristic as focus for all other characteristics—the universal soul of all particulars. The idea of God thus is the general fundament of a people.

In this respect religion stands in closest connection with the principle of the State. Freedom can only exist where individuality is known as positive in the divine Being. There is a further connection between religion and the state: secular existence is temporal and moves within private interest. Hence it is relative and unjustified. Its justification can only be derived from the absolute justification of its universal soul, its principle. And this is justified only as determination and existence of the essence of God. For this reason the State is based on religion. We hear this often repeated in our time. But mostly nothing more is meant than that individuals should be pious in order to be more willing and prepared to do their duty; for obedience to prince and law is so easily connected with reverence toward God. It is true that reverence toward God, in elevating the universal over the particular, can turn against the particular in fanaticism, and work against the State, burning and destroying its buildings and institutions. Hence reverence for God, it is believed, should be temperate and kept in a certain degree of coolness, lest it storm against and destroy that which ought to be protected and preserved by it. The possibility of such disaster is at least latent in it.

The correct conviction that the State rests on religion may give religion a position which presupposes the existence of the State. Then, in order to preserve the State, religion must be carried into it, in buckets and bushels, in order to impress it upon people's minds. It is quite correct that man must be educated to religion, but not as to something which does not yet exist. For, when we say that the State is based on religion and that it has its roots in it, we mean essentially that it has arisen from it and now and always continues to arise out of it. That is, the principles of the State must be regarded as valid in and for themselves, which they can only insofar as they are known to be determinations of divine nature itself. The nature of its religion, therefore, determines that of the State and its constitution. It actually has originated from it: the Athenian and the Roman states were possible only through the specific paganism of these peoples, just as a Catholic state has a spirit and constitution different from a Protestant one.

It would be bad if this appeal, this urge and drive to implant religion, were a call of anguish and distress, as it looks so often—as if it expressed the danger that religion were about to disappear or already had disappeared from the State. Indeed, it would be worse than this appeal assumes; for it assumes it can still implant and inculcate religion as a means against this evil. But religion is not such an artifact. Its self-production is a much more profound process. Another and opposite folly which we meet in our time is the tendency to invent and institute constitutions independently from religion. The Catholic religion, although, like the Protestant, part of Christianity, does not concede to the State the inner justice and morality which follows from the inwardness of the Protestant principle. This separation of constitutional law and of constitutions themselves from morality is necessary because of the peculiarity of that religion; it does not regard law and morality as independent and substantial. But thus torn away from inwardness, from the last sanctuary of conscience, from the quiet corner where religion has its abode, the constitutional principles and institutions lack a real center and remain abstract and indeterminate.

In summary, the vitality of the State in individuals is what we call Morality. The State, its laws, its institutions are the rights of the citizens; its nature, its soil, its mountains, air, and waters are their land, their country, their external property. The history of the State are their deeds, and what their ancestors have accomplished belongs to them and lives in their memory. Everything is their possession just as they are possessed by it, for it constitutes their substance and being.

Their minds are full of it and their wills are their willing of these laws and of their country. It is this temporal totality which is One Being, the spirit of One People.

To it the individuals belong; each individual is the son of his people and, at the same time, insofar as his state is in development, the son of his age. No one remains behind it, no one can leap ahead of it. This spiritual being is his—he is one of its representatives—it is that from which he arises and wherein he stands. For the Athenians Athens had a double meaning, the totality of their institutions as well as the goddess which represented the spirit and the unity of the people.

This spirit of a people is a *definite* spirit and, as was just said, is also determined according to the historical state of its development. This spirit, then, is the basis and content of the other forms of consciousness which have been mentioned. For the spirit in its consciousness of itself must be concrete to itself. Its objectivity immediately contains the origin of differences, which in their totality are the various spheres of the objective spirit itself—just as the soul exists only as the organization of its members which constitute it by combining themselves into simple unity. Thus it is one individuality. Its essence is represented, revered, and enjoyed as God, in religion; presented as image and intuition, in art; apprehended cognitively and conceived as thought, in philosophy. Because of the original identity of their substance, their content, and their subject matter with that of the State these products are inseparably united with the spirit of the State. Only with such a religion can there be such a form of the State, and only with such a State such art and such philosophy.

Furthermore, the definite national spirit itself is only one individual in the course of world history. For world history is the manifestation of the Divine, the absolute process of Spirit in its highest forms. It is this development wherein it achieves its truth and the consciousness of itself. The products of its stages are the world-historical national spirits, the definiteness of their moral life, their constitution, art, religion, and science. To realize these stages is the infinite élan of the World Spirit, its irresistible urge; for this differentiation and its realization constitute its concept. World history only shows how the World Spirit gradually attains the consciousness and willing of truth. Dawn rises in the Spirit; it discovers focal points; and finally, it attains full consciousness.

LECTURES ON THE HISTORY OF PHILOSOPHY (in part)

THE FINAL RESULT

The present standpoint of philosophy is that the Idea is known in its necessity; the sides of its diremption, nature and spirit, are each recognized as representing the totality of the Idea, and not only as being in themselves identical, but as producing this one identity from themselves; and thus the identity is recognized as necessary. Nature, and the spiritual world, history, are the two actualities; what exists as actual nature is an

From the Second (1840) Edition of *Lectures on the History of Philosophy,* translated by E.S. Haldane and F.H. Simson (1892–1896), with revisions by M.J. Inwood. Reprinted from *Hegel: Selections,* edited by M.J. Inwood, *The Great Philosophers Series,* Paul Edwards, general ed. (New York: Macmillan, 1989).

image of divine reason; the forms of self-conscious reason are also forms of nature. The ultimate aim and concern of philosophy is to reconcile thought or the concept with actuality. It is easy to adopt subordinate standpoints, to find satisfaction in modes of intuition and of feeling. But the deeper the spirit goes within itself, the stronger the opposition, the more abundant the wealth without; depth is to be measured by the greatness of the need with which spirit seeks to find itself in what lies outside of itself. We saw the thought which apprehends itself emerge; it strove to make itself concrete within itself. Its first activity is formal; Aristotle was the first to say that *nous* is the thinking of thinking. The result is the thought which is at home with itself, and at the same time embraces the universe, and transforms it into an intelligent world. In conceptualisation the spiritual and the natural universe interpenetrate as one harmonious universe, which flees from itself into itself, and in its aspects develops the absolute into a totality, to become thereby conscious of itself in its unity, in thought. Philosophy is thus the true theodicy, as contrasted with art and religion and the feelings which these call up—a reconciliation of spirit, of the spirit which has apprehended itself in its freedom and in the riches of its actuality.

To this point the world-spirit has come, and each stage has its own form in the true system of philosophy; nothing is lost, all principles are preserved, since philosophy in its final aspect is the totality of forms. This concrete Idea is the result of the strivings of spirit during almost twenty-five centuries of earnest work to become objective to itself, to know itself:

Tantae molis erat, se ipsam cognoscere mentem.

All this time was required to produce the philosophy of our day; so tardily and slowly did the world-spirit work to reach this goal. What we pass in rapid review when we recall it, stretched itself out in actuality to this great length of time. For in this period, the concept of spirit, invested with its entire concrete development, external subsistence, wealth, strives to bring spirit to perfection, to make progress itself and to emerge from spirit. It goes ever on and on, because spirit is progress alone. Spirit often seems to have forgotten and lost itself, but inwardly opposed to itself, it is inwardly working ever forward (as Hamlet says of the ghost of his father, "Well said, old mole! canst work i' the ground so fast?"), until grown strong in itself it bursts asunder the crust of earth which divided it from the sun, its concept, so that the earth crumbles away. At such a time, when the encircling crust, like a soulless decaying tenement, crumbles away, and spirit displays itself arrayed in new youth, the seven league boots are put on. This work of the spirit to know itself, this activity to find itself, is the life of the spirit and the spirit itself. Its result is the concept which it takes up of itself; the history of philosophy is a revelation of what has been the aim of spirit in its history; it is therefore the world's history in its innermost signification. This work of the human spirit in inner thinking is parallel with all the stages of actuality. No philosophy oversteps its own time. The importance of the determinations of thought is another matter, which does not belong to the history of philosophy. These concepts are the simplest revelation of the world spirit: in their more concrete form they are history.

We must, therefore, firstly, not esteem lightly what spirit has won, and won now. Older philosophy is to be reverenced as necessary, and as a link in this sacred chain, but all the same only a link. The present is the highest stage. Secondly, all the various philosophies are no mere fashions or the like; they are neither chance products nor the blaze of a fire of straw, nor casual eruptions here and there, but a spiritual, rational, forward advance; they are of necessity one philosophy in its development, the revelation of God, as He knows Himself to be. Where several philosophies appear at the same time, they are different sides which make up one totality forming their basis; and on account of their one-sidedness we see the refutation of the one by the other. Thirdly, we do not find here feeble little efforts to establish or to criticize this or that particular point; each philosophy sets up a *principle* of its own, and this must be recognized.

If we glance at the main epochs in the whole history of philosophy, and grasp the necessary succession of stages in the leading moments, each of which expresses a determinate Idea, we find that after the Oriental whirl of subjectivity, which attains to no understanding and therefore to no subsistence, the light of thought dawned among the Greeks.

1. The philosophy of the ancients had the absolute Idea as its thought; and the realization or reality of it consisted in comprehending the existing present world, and regarding it as it is in and for itself. This philosophy did not start from the Idea itself, but from the objective as something given, and transformed it into the Idea: the being of Parmenides.

2. Abstract thought, *nous,* became known to itself as universal essence, not as subjective thinking: the universal of Plato.

3. In Aristotle the concept emerges, free and unconstrained, as conceptual thinking, permeating and spiritualizing all the formations of the universe.

4. The concept as subject, its becoming for itself, its inwardness, abstract separation, is represented by the Stoics, Epicureans and Sceptics: not the free concrete form, but universality abstract and in itself formal.

5. The thought of totality, the intelligible world, is the concrete Idea as we have seen it in the Neo-Platonists. This principle is ideality in general in all reality, the Idea as totality, but not the Idea which knows itself: this is not reached until the principle of subjectivity, individuality, found a place in it, and God as spirit became actual to Himself in self-consciousness.

6. But it is the work of modern times to grasp this Idea as spirit, as the Idea that knows itself. In order to proceed from the knowing Idea to the self-knowing, we must have the infinite opposition, the Idea must have come to the consciousness of its bifurcation. As spirit had the thought of objective essence, philosophy thus perfected the intellectuality of the world, and produced this spiritual world as an object existing beyond present actuality, like a nature—the first creation of spirit. The work of the spirit now consisted in bringing this Beyond back to actuality and into self-consciousness. This is accomplished by self-consciousness thinking itself, and recognizing the absolute essence to be the self-consciousness that thinks itself. With Descartes pure thought directed itself on that bifurcation. Self-consciousness, first, thinks of itself as consciousness; therein is contained all objective actuality and the positive, intuitive connexion of its actuality with the other. With Spinoza thought and being are opposed and yet identical; he has the intuition of substance, but the knowledge of substance in his case is external. We have here the principle of reconciliation taking its rise from thought as such, in order to sublimate the subjectivity of thought: this is the ease in Leibniz's monad, which possesses the power of representation.

7. Secondly, self-consciousness thinks of itself as being self-consciousness; in being self-conscious it is for itself, but still for itself it has a negative connexion with another. This is infinite subjectivity, which appears at one time as the critique of thought in Kant, and at another time, in Fichte, as the impulse towards the concrete. Absolutely pure, infinite form is expressed as self-consciousness, the ego.

8. This is a light that breaks forth on spiritual substance, and shows absolute content and absolute form to be identical; substance is in itself identical with knowledge.

Self-consciousness thus, thirdly, recognizes its positive connexion as its negative, and its negative as its positive,—or it recognizes these opposite activities as the same, i.e. it recognizes pure thought or being as self-equality, and this again as bifurcation. This is intellectual intuition; but it is requisite in order that it be in truth intellectual, that it should not be that merely immediate intuition of the eternal and the divine which we hear of, but absolute knowledge. This intuition which does not cognize itself is taken as starting-point as if it were absolutely presupposed; it has in itself intuition only as immediate knowledge, not as self-knowledge: or it knows nothing, and what it intuits it does not really know,—for, at its best, it consists of beautiful thoughts, but not knowledge.

But intellectual intuition is known, since firstly, in spite of the separation of each of the opposed sides from the other, all external reality is known as internal. If it is known according to its essence, as it is, it shows itself as not existing of itself, but as essentially consisting in the movement of transition. This Heraclitean or sceptical principle, that nothing is at rest, must be demonstrated of each individual thing; and thus in this consciousness—that the essence of each thing lies in determinacy, in the opposite of itself—there appears the comprehended unity with its opposite. Similarly this unity is, secondly, to be cognized even in its essence; its essence as this identity is likewise to pass over into its opposite, or to realize itself, to become something different; and thus the opposition in it is brought about by itself. Again, it may be said of the opposition, thirdly, that it is not in the absolute; this absolute is the essence, the eternal, etc. This is however itself an abstraction in which the absolute is apprehended in a one-sided manner only and the opposition is only ideal; but in fact it is form, as the essential moment of the movement of the absolute. This absolute is not at rest, and that opposition is not the unresting concept; for the Idea, unresting though it is, is yet at rest and satisfied in itself. Pure thought has advanced to the opposition of the subjective and objective; the true reconciliation of the opposition is the perception that this opposition, when pushed to its absolute extreme, resolves itself; as Schelling says, the opposites are in themselves identical—and not only in themselves, but eternal life consists in the very process of eternally producing the opposition and eternally reconciling it. To know opposition in unity, and unity in opposition—this is absolute knowledge; and science is the knowledge of this unity in its whole development by means of itself.

This is now the need of the time in general and of philosophy. A new epoch has arisen in the world. It would appear as if the world-spirit had at last succeeded in stripping off from itself all alien objective being, and apprehending itself at last as absolute spirit, in developing from itself what for it is objective, and keeping it in its power, yet remaining at rest. The strife of the finite self-consciousness with the absolute self-consciousness, which seemed to the former to lie outside itself, now ceases. Finite self-consciousness has ceased to be finite; and in this way absolute self-consciousness has, on the other hand, acquired the actuality which it lacked before. This is the whole history of the world in general up to the present, and the history of philosophy in particular, which only depicts this strife. Now it seems to have reached its goal, when this absolute self-consciousness, which it had the work of representing, has ceased to be alien, and when spirit is thus actualized as spirit. For it becomes such only by knowing itself to be absolute spirit, and this it knows in science. Spirit produces itself as nature, as the state; nature is its unconscious work, in which it appears to itself something different, not spirit; but in the deeds and life of history, as also of art, it brings itself to pass with consciousness; it knows very various modes of its actuality, yet they are only modes. In science alone it knows itself as absolute spirit; and this knowledge, or spirit, is its only true existence. This then is the standpoint of the present day, and the series of spiritual forms is with it for now concluded.

At this point I bring this history of philosophy to a close. It has been my desire that you should learn from it that the history of philosophy is not a blind collection of brain-waves, nor a fortuitous progression. I have rather sought to show the necessary development of the successive philosophies from one another, so that the one of necessity presupposes the preceding. The general result of the history of philosophy is this: (1) at all times there has been only one philosophy, the contemporary differences of which constitute the necessary aspects of the one principle; (2) the succession of philosophic systems is not due to chance, but the necessary succession of stages in the development of this science; (3) the final philosophy of a period is the result of this development, and is truth in the highest form which the self-consciousness of spirit affords of itself. The latest philosophy contains therefore those which went before; it embraces in itself all the stages; it is the product and result of those that preceded it. We can now be Platonists no longer. We must rise above the pettinesses of individual opinions, thoughts, objections, and difficulties; and also above our own vanity, as if our own thoughts were of particular value. For to apprehend the inward substantial spirit is the standpoint of the individual; within the whole, individuals are like blind men, driven forward by the inner spirit. Our standpoint now is accordingly the knowledge of this Idea as spirit, as absolute spirit, which in this way opposes another spirit, the finite, the principle of which is to know absolute spirit, so that absolute spirit is for it. I have tried to develop and bring before your thoughts this series of spiritual forms of philosophy in its progress, and to indicate the connection between them. This series is the true kingdom of spirits, the only kindgom of spirits that there is—it is a series which is not a multiplicity, nor does it even remain a series or succession, but in the very process of coming to knowledge of itself it is transformed into the moments of the one spirit, of the one self-present spirit. This long procession of spirits is formed by the individual pulses which beat in its life; they are the organism of our substance, an absolutely necessary progression, which expresses nothing less than the nature of spirit itself, and which lives in us all. We have to give ear to its urgency—when the mole within forces its way on—and we have to give it actuality. It is my desire that this history of philosophy should contain for you a summons to grasp the spirit of the time, which is in us by nature, and—each in his own place—consciously to bring it from its natural condition, from its lifeless seclusion, into the light of day.

I have to express my thanks to you for the attention with which you have listened to me while I have been making this attempt; it is also due to you that my efforts have met with so great a measure of success. And it has been a source of pleasure to myself to have been associated with you in this spiritual community; I ought not to speak of it as if it were a thing of the past, for I hope that a spiritual bond has been knit between us which will prove permanent. I bid you a most hearty farewell.

ARTHUR SCHOPENHAUER
1788–1860

Arthur Schopenhauer was described by his contemporaries as egoistic, vain, arrogant, overbearing, and cynical. He was known to be so anxious that as an adult he always slept with a loaded pistol. His derogatory remarks about women are legendary.* His attacks on the noted professors of his time, especially Hegel, were equally vindictive.** In short, his approach to life and the people around him was as pessimistic as his philosophy. Yet he was a man of strong character and uncompromising honesty, who took great pleasure in the theater, in music, and in good food and wine. And ironically, he came to hold that only in sympathy for the sufferings of others and in ascetic holiness can one find release from overwhelming desire. As he was later to say, "I have taught what sainthood is, but I myself am no saint."

Schopenhauer was born in Danzig, the son of a wealthy merchant father and a noted novelist mother. As a boy, Schopenhauer traveled extensively and attended schools in Germany, France, and England. By the age of sixteen, he had visited most of the countries of Europe and was fluent in at least four languages.

---

*For example, "[women] are childish, frivolous and short-sighted; in a word, they are big children all their life long . . . defective in the powers of reasoning and deliberation." From "Of Women," in *Essays of Schopenhauer*, translated by T. Bailey Saunders (New York: Wiley, n.d.), pp. 73 and 76.

**He referred to Hegel as "a philosophical creature of ministers . . . manufactured from above with a political but miscalculated purpose; a flat, commonplace, repulsive, ignorant charlatan, who, with unparalleled presumption, conceit, and absurdity, pasted together a system which was trumpeted by his venal adherents as immortal wisdom." From "The History of Philosophy" in *The Wisdom of Life and Other Essays*, translated by T. Bailey Saunders and Ernest Belfort Bax (New York: M. Walter Dunne, 1901), p. 196.

In 1804, Schopenhauer's father insisted that his son give up travel and school and join him in the family business. Schopenhauer grudgingly agreed—though he continued to study "on the sly." His father's sudden death (apparently by suicide) in 1805 freed Schopenhauer from the drudgery of his father's work, and he resumed his studies. He studied at the universities in Göttingen and Berlin before receiving his doctorate from the University of Jena.

Following a period of travel, Schopenhauer moved to Dresden, where he wrote his most important work, *The World as Will and Idea* (1818). Given that he believed this work contained the meaning of life, he was sorely disappointed when it received no recognition and sold few copies. He moved to Berlin where he could expound his views verbally in lectures. Receiving a position as *Privatdozent,* he purposely scheduled his lectures at the same time as those of his nemesis, Hegel, who was then at the height of his fame. Not surprisingly, Schopenhauer's lectures were a failure—no one attended. Within a year, he bitterly left Berlin and gave up any aspirations to an academic career.

After more travels in Europe, Schopenhauer eventually settled in Frankfurt am Main. There he published *On the Will in Nature* (1836) as well as a revised and expanded edition of his major work (in 1844). In 1848, a series of democratic revolutions swept Europe. Schopenhauer had no sympathy for the revolutionaries—he even allowed Austrian soldiers to use the windows in his Frankfurt home to shoot at demonstrators below—and asked only that the state preserve law and order. In the aftermath of the failed revolutions, the optimistic philosophy of Hegel passed out of vogue and the pessimism of Schopenhauer came into style. In 1851, Schopenhauer produced a collection of diverse essays, *Parerga and Paralipomena,* which proved quite successful. In the last years of his life, Schopenhauer finally received the fame that he believed he deserved. His final years were spent editing his *magnum opus* for one final edition and receiving and entertaining admirers.

*   *   *

The World as Will and Idea begins with the provocative assertion that "The world is my idea." Taking seriously Kant's claim that the mind structures the world as it is experienced, Schopenhauer held that the existence of the phenomenal world depends upon my consciousness of it. But whereas Kant had maintained that the *Ding-an-sich* (the "thing-in-itself" apart from my experience) could not be known, Schopenhauer declared that it is intuitively knowable, and he identified it as *Will*. The world as it is projected outward by me, the diversity of phenomena, is idea, whereas the unity that underlies those phenomena is Will.

The Will is a nonrational force, a blind, meaningless striving after existence, and all of life is a struggle to fulfill its desires. Happiness and pleasure can only be temporary as Will is never satisfied and always wants "more"—more of what it does not know, but it wants more anyway. In the chapter entitled "The Primacy of the Will in Self-Consciousness," reprinted here in the R.B. Haldane and John Kemp translation, Schopenhauer argues that intellect is merely another tool of Will: "The *will* is what is real and essential in man, and the *intellect* only subordinate, conditioned, and produced." The Will, not intellect or memory, is the essential identity of the person. Even our bodies are simply the "objectification" of our wills. Given the nature of this Will, it follows that, as Schopenhauer said elsewhere,

> Man is at bottom a wild, horrible creature. We know him merely as broken and
> tamed by what we call civilization, and hence the occasional outbreaks of his na-
> ture shock us. But where and when the padlock and chain of legal order fall off and
> anarchy enters, then he shows himself what he is.*

This means, contrary to Hegel, that human history has no purpose, that there is
no progressive manifestation of Spirit. Borrowing words from Shakespeare's
Macbeth, history is no more than "a tale told by an idiot, full of sound and fury,
signifying nothing."

How then can we escape the suffering and misery that Will invariably brings
us? Although the Will becomes "objective" through diverse particular objects
that are known in the phenomenal world, it is *immediately* objectified in Platonic
Ideas that are expressed in art. We can momentarily overcome the Will by losing
ourselves in the aesthetic enjoyment of these Ideas. But in formal, dispassionate
music we encounter "the universal imageless language of the heart," which goes
beyond Platonic Ideas and reveals the Will as the *Ding-an-sich*. At this point we
can experience "pure knowing free from will, which . . . is the only pure happiness."

But for a permanent salvation from desire, we must move beyond aesthetics
to ethics and finally to religion. Because the Will is objectified in each of us, we
tend to see ourselves as a self-sufficient entity. Borrowing from Hindu thought,
Schopenhauer pointed out that perceived individual identity is merely phenomenal, that on the noumenal level all is one. This means that if you suffer, I suffer,
which, in turn, leads me to a position of compassionate sympathy as I become
one in suffering with you. Yet even such a state of sympathy, which Schopenhauer called "love," is only temporary. What is needed is a "transition from
virtue to asceticism," in which the individual ceases to feel any concern for
earthly things: a "state of voluntary renunciation, resignation, true indifference,
and perfect will-lessness." Only when we have reached a mystical state of "denial of the will to live," only when we have become "saints," will we find release
from insatiable Will.

Although Schopenhauer may not have made the impact his enemy Hegel did,
it is difficult to read thinkers such as Nietzsche or Freud and not think of him.
Schopenhauer's insistence upon irrational Will as the ground of all human activity is clearly mirrored in Nietzsche's "will to power," and the indeterminacy of
the Will's object of desire is the archetype for Freud's "id." Freud himself stated
years later that "We have unwittingly steered our course into the harbor of
Schopenhauer's philosophy."

*   *   *

For selections from Schopenhauer's work, see *The Works of Schopenhauer,*
abridged and edited by Will Durant (New York: Simon & Schuster, 1928).
Richard Taylor, "Schopenhauer," in D.J. O'Connor, ed., *A Critical History of
Western Philosophy* (New York: The Free Press, 1964) provides an excellent
short introduction to Schopenhauer's thought. For book-length studies, see

---

*"On Ethics" in *Wisdom of Life*, op. cit., p. 276

Patrick Gardiner, *Schopenhauer* (Baltimore, MD: Penguin Books, 1963); V.J. McGill, *Schopenhauer* (New York: Haskell, 1971); David W. Hamlyn, *Schopenhauer* (London: Routledge & Kegan Paul, 1980); Bryan Magee, *The Philosophy of Schopenhauer* (1983; reprinted Oxford: Oxford University Press, 1997); Rudiger Safranski, *Schopenhauer and the Wild Years of Philosophy* (Cambridge, MA: Harvard University Press, 1990); and Christopher Janaway, *Schopenhauer* (Oxford: Oxford University Press, 1994). For an interesting interpretation from a Catholic viewpoint, see Frederick C. Copleston, *Arthur Schopenhauer: Philosopher of Pessimism* (1946; reprinted New York: Barnes & Noble, 1975). For specialized studies, see Georg Simmel, *Schopenhauer and Nietzsche,* translated by Helmut Loiskandl, Deena Weinstein, and Michael Weinstein (Amherst: University of Massachusetts Press, 1986), and Christopher Janaway, *Self and World in Schopenhauer's Philosophy* (Oxford: Oxford University Press, 1989). For a collection of critical essays, see Michael Fox, ed., *Schopenhauer: His Philosophical Achievement* (Totowa, NJ: Barnes & Noble, 1980).

THE WORLD AS WILL AND IDEA
(in part)

CHAPTER 19

ON THE PRIMACY OF THE WILL IN SELF-CONSCIOUSNESS

The will, as the thing in itself, constitutes the inner, true, and indestructible nature of man; in itself, however, it is unconscious. For consciousness is conditioned by the intellect, and the intellect is a mere accident of our being; for it is a function of the brain, which, together with the nerves and spinal cord connected with it, is a mere fruit, a product, nay, so far, a parasite of the rest of the organism; for it does not directly enter into its inner constitution, but merely serves the end of self-preservation by regulating the relations of the organism to the external world. The organism itself, on the other hand, is the visibility, the objectivity, of the individual will, the image of it as it presents itself in that very brain (which in the first book we learned to recognize as the condition of the objective world in general), therefore also brought about by its forms of knowledge, space, time, and causality, and consequently presenting itself as extended, successively acting, and material, *i.e.,* as something operative or efficient. The members are both directly felt and also perceived by means of the senses only in the brain. According to this one may say: The intellect is the secondary phenomenon; the organism the primary phenomenon, that is, the immediate manifestation of the will; the will is metaphysical, the intellect physical;—the intellect, like its objects, is merely phenomenal appearance; the will alone is the thing in itself. Then, in a more and more *figurative sense,* thus by way of simile: The will is the substance of man, the intellect the accident; the will is the matter, the intellect is the form; the will is warmth, the intellect is light.

We shall now first of all verify and also elucidate this thesis by the following facts connected with the inner life of man; and on this opportunity perhaps more will be done for the knowledge of the inner man than is to be found in many systematic psychologies.

1. Not only the consciousness of other things, *i.e.,* the apprehension of the external world, but also *self-consciousness,* contains, as was mentioned already above, a knower and a known; otherwise it would not be *consciousness.* For *consciousness* consists in knowing; but knowing requires a knower and a known; therefore there could be no self-consciousness if there were not in it also a known opposed to the knower and different from it. As there can be no object without a subject, so also there can be no subject without an object, *i.e.,* no knower without something different from it which is known. Therefore a consciousness which is through and through pure intelligence is impossible. The intelligence is like the sun, which does not illuminate space if there is no object from which its rays are reflected. The knower himself, as such, cannot be known; otherwise he would be the known of another knower. But now, as the *known* in self-consciousness we find exclusively the *will.* For not merely willing and purposing in the narrowest sense, but also all striving, wishing, shunning, hoping, fearing, loving, hating, in short, all that directly constitutes our own weal and woe, desire and aversion, is clearly only affection of the will, is a moving, a modification of willing and not-willing, is just that which, if it takes outward effect, exhibits itself as an act of will proper. In all knowledge, however, the known is first and essential, not the knower. Therefore in self-consciousness also the known, thus the will, must be what is first and original; the knower, on the other hand, only what is secondary, that which has been added, the mirror. They are related very much as the luminous to the reflecting body; or, again, as the vibrating strings to the resounding-board, in which case the note produced would be consciousness.

2. But in order not merely to describe consciousness figuratively, but to know it thoroughly, we have first of all to find out what appears in the same way in every consciousness, and therefore, as the common and constant element, will also be the essential. Then we shall consider what distinguishes *one* consciousness from an other, which accordingly will be the adventitious and secondary element.

Consciousness is positively only known to us as a property of animal nature; therefore we must not, and indeed cannot, think of it otherwise than as *animal consciousness,* so that this expression is tautological. Now, that which in every animal consciousness, even the most imperfect and the weakest, is always present, nay, lies at its foundation, is an immediate sense of *longing,* and of the alternate satisfaction and non-satisfaction of it, in very different degrees. This we know to a certain extent *a priori.* For marvellously different as the innumerable species of animals are, and strange as some new form, never seen before, appears to us, we yet assume beforehand its inmost nature, with perfect certainty, as well known, and indeed fully confided to us. We know that the animal *wills,* indeed also *what* it wills, existence, well-being, life, and propagation; and since in this we presuppose with perfect certainty identity with us, we do not hesitate to attribute to it unchanged all the affections of will which we know in ourselves, and speak at once of its desire, aversion, fear, anger, hatred, love, joy, sorrow, longing, &c. On the other hand, whenever phenomena of mere knowledge come to be spoken of we fall at once into uncertainty. We do not venture to say that the animal conceives, thinks, judges, knows: we only attribute to it with certainty ideas in general; because without them its *will* could not have those emotions referred to above. But with regard to the definite manner of knowing of the brutes and the precise limits of it in a given species, we have only indefinite conceptions, and make conjectures.

Hence our understanding with them is also often difficult, and is only brought about by skill, in consequence of experience and practice. Here then lie distinctions of consciousness. On the other hand, a longing, desiring, wishing, or a detesting, shunning, and not wishing, is proper to every consciousness: man has it in common with the polyp. This is accordingly the essential element in and the basis of every consciousness. The difference of the manifestations of this in the different species of animal beings depends upon the various extension of their sphere of knowledge, in which the motives of those manifestations lie. We understand directly from our own nature all actions and behaviour of the brutes which express movements of the will; therefore, so far, we sympathize with them in various ways. On the other hand, the gulf between us and them results simply and solely from the difference of intellect. The gulf which lies between a very sagacious brute and a man of very limited capacity is perhaps not much greater than that which exists between a blockhead and a man of genius; therefore here also the resemblance between them in another aspect, which springs from the likeness of their inclinations and emotions, and assimilates them again to each other, sometimes appears with surprising prominence, and excites astonishment. This consideration makes it clear that in all animal natures the *will* is what is primary and substantial, the *intellect* again is secondary, adventitious, indeed a mere tool for the service of the former, and is more or less complete and complicated, according to the demands of this service. As a species of animals is furnished with hoofs, claws, hands, wings, horns, or teeth according to the aims of its will, so also is it furnished with a more or less developed brain, whose function is the intelligence necessary for its endurance. The more complicated the organization becomes, in the ascending series of animals, the more numerous also are its wants, and the more varied and specially determined the objects which are capable of satisfying them; hence the more complicated and distant the paths by which these are to be obtained, which must now be all known and found: therefore in the same proportion the ideas of the animal must be more versatile, accurate, definite, and connected, and also its attention must be more highly strung, more sustained, and more easily roused, consequently its intellect must be more developed and perfected. Accordingly we see the organ of intelligence, the cerebral system, together with all the organs of sense, keep pace with the increasing wants and the complication of the organism; and the increase of the part of consciousness that has to do with ideas (as opposed to the willing part) exhibits itself in a bodily form in the ever-increasing proportion of the brain in general to the rest of the nervous system, and of the cerebrum to the cerebellum; for (according to Flourens) the former is the workshop of ideas, while the latter is the disposer and orderer of movements. The last step which nature has taken in this respect is, however, disproportionately great. For in man not only does the faculty of ideas of *perception,* which alone existed hitherto, reach the highest degree of perfection, but the *abstract* idea, thought, *i.e., reason*, and with it reflection, is added. Through this important advance of the intellect, thus of the secondary part of consciousness, it now gains a preponderance over the primary part, in so far as it becomes henceforward the predominantly active part. While in the brute the immediate sense of its satisfied or unsatisfied desire constitutes by far the most important part of its consciousness, and the more so indeed the lower the grade of the animal, so that the lowest animals are distinguished from plants only by the addition of a dull idea, in man the opposite is the case. Vehement as are his desires, even more vehement than those of any brute, rising to the level of passions, yet his consciousness remains continuously and predominantly occupied and filled with ideas and thoughts. Without doubt this has been the principal occasion of that fundamental error of all philosophers on account of which they make thought that which is essential and primary in the so-called soul, *i.e.*

in the inner or spiritual life of man, always placing it first, but will, as a mere product of thought, they regard as only a subordinate addition and consequence of it. But if willing merely proceeded from knowing, how could the brutes, even the lower grades of them, with so very little knowledge, often show such an unconquerable and vehement will? Accordingly, since that fundamental error of the philosophers makes, as it were, the accident the substance, it leads them into mistaken paths, which there is afterwards no way of getting out of. Now this relative predominance of the *knowing* consciousness over the *desiring,* consequently of the secondary part over the primary, which appears in man, may, in particular exceptionally favoured individuals, go so far that at the moments of its highest ascendancy, the secondary or knowing part of consciousness detaches itself altogether from the willing part, and passes into free activity for itself, *i.e.*, untouched by the will, and consequently no longer serving it. Thus it becomes purely objective, and the clear mirror of the world, and from it the conceptions of genius then arise, which are the subject of our third book.

3. If we run through the series of grades of animals downwards, we see the intellect always becoming weaker and less perfect, but we by no means observe a corresponding degradation of the will. Rather it retains everywhere its identical nature and shows itself in the form of great attachment to life, care for the individual and the species, egoism and regardlessness of all others, together with the emotions that spring from these. Even in the smallest insect the will is present, complete and entire; it wills what it wills as decidedly and completely as the man. The difference lies merely in *what* it wills, *i.e.,* in the motives, which, however, are the affair of the intellect. It indeed, as the secondary part of consciousness, and bound to the bodily organism, has innumerable degrees of completeness, and is in general essentially limited and imperfect. The *will,* on the contrary, as original and the thing in itself, can never be imperfect, but every act of will is all that it can be. On account of the simplicity which belongs to the will as the thing in itself, the metaphysical in the phenomenon, its nature admits of no degrees, but is always completely itself. Only its *excitement* has degrees, from the weakest inclination to the passion, and also its susceptibility to excitement, thus its vehemence from the phlegmatic to the choleric temperament. The *intellect,* on the other hand, has not merely degrees of *excitement,* from sleepiness to being in the vein, and inspiration, but also degrees of its nature, of the completeness of this, which accordingly rises gradually from the lowest animals, which can only obscurely apprehend, up to man, and here again from the fool to the genius. The *will* alone is everywhere completely itself. For its function is of the utmost simplicity; it consists in willing and not willing, which goes on with the greatest ease, without effort, and requires no practice. Knowing, on the contrary, has multifarious functions, and never takes place entirely without effort, which is required to fix the attention and to make clear the object, and at a higher stage is certainly needed for thinking and deliberation; therefore it is also capable of great improvement through exercise and education. If the intellect presents a simple, perceptible object to the will, the latter expresses at once its approval or disapproval of it, and this even if the intellect has laboriously inquired and pondered, in order from numerous data, by means of difficult combinations, ultimately to arrive at the conclusion as to which of the two seems to be most in conformity with the interests of the will. The latter has meanwhile been idly resting, and when the conclusion is arrived at it enters, as the Sultan enters the Divan, merely to express again its monotonous approval or disapproval, which certainly may vary in degree, but in its nature remains always the same.

This fundamentally different nature of the will and the intellect, the essential simplicity and originality of the former, in contrast to the complicated and secondary character of the latter, becomes still more clear to us if we observe their remarkable interaction within us, and now consider in the particular case, how the images and thoughts which arise in the intellect move the will, and how entirely separated and different are the parts which the two play. We can indeed perceive this even in actual events which excite the will in a lively manner, while primarily and in themselves they are merely objects of the intellect. But, on the one hand, it is here not so evident that this reality primarily existed only in the intellect; and, on the other hand, the change does not generally take place so rapidly as is necessary if the thing is to be easily surveyed, and thereby becomes thoroughly comprehensible. Both of these conditions, however, are fulfilled if it is merely thoughts and phantasies which we allow to act on the will. If, for example, alone with ourselves, we think over our personal circumstances, and now perhaps vividly present to ourselves the menace of an actually present danger and the possibility of an unfortunate issue, anxiety at once compresses the heart, and the blood ceases to circulate in the veins. But if then the intellect passes to the possibility of an opposite issue, and lets the imagination picture the long-hoped-for happiness thereby attained, all the pulses quicken at once with joy and the heart feels light as a feather, till the intellect awakes from its dream. Thereupon, suppose that an occasion should lead the memory to an insult or injury once suffered long ago, at once anger and bitterness pour into the breast that was but now at peace. But then arises, called up by accident, the image of a long-lost love, with which the whole romance and its magic scenes is connected; then that anger will at once give place to profound longing and sadness. Finally, if there occurs to us some former humiliating incident, we shrink together, would like to sink out of sight, blush with shame, and often try forcibly to distract and divert our thoughts by some loud exclamation, as if to scare some evil spirit. One sees, the intellect plays, and the will must dance to it. Indeed the intellect makes the will play the part of a child which is alternately thrown at pleasure into joyful or sad moods by the chatter and tales of its nurse. This depends upon the fact that the will is itself without knowledge, and the understanding which is given to it is without will. Therefore the former is like a body which is moved, the latter like the causes which set it in motion, for it is the medium of motives. Yet in all this the primacy of the will becomes clear again, if this will, which, as we have shown, becomes the sport of the intellect as soon as it allows the latter to control it, once makes its supremacy in the last instance felt by prohibiting the intellect from entertaining certain ideas, absolutely preventing certain trains of thought from arising, because it knows, *i.e.,* learns from that very intellect, that they would awaken in it some one of the emotions set forth above. It now bridles the intellect, and compels it to turn to other things. Hard as this often may be, it must yet be accomplished as soon as the will is in earnest about it, for the resisting in this case does not proceed from the intellect, which always remains indifferent, but from the will itself, which in one respect has an inclination towards an idea that in another respect it abhors. It is in itself interesting to the will simply because it excites it, but at the same time abstract knowledge tells it that this idea will aimlessly cause it a shock of painful or unworthy emotion: it now decides in conformity with this abstract knowledge, and compels the obedience of the intellect. This is called "being master of oneself." Clearly the master here is the will, the servant the intellect, for in the last instance the will always keeps the upper hand, and therefore constitutes the true core, the inner being of man. In this respect the title ⟨*Agemonikon*⟩ would belong to the *will;* yet it seems, on the other hand, to apply to the *intellect,* because it is the leader and guide, like the *valet de place* who conducts a stranger. In truth, however, the happiest figure of the relation of the two is the strong blind man who carries on his shoulders the lame man who can see.

The relation of the will to the intellect here explained may also be further recognized in the fact that the intellect is originally entirely a stranger to the purposes of the will. It supplies the motives to the will, but it only learns afterwards, completely *a posteriori,* how they have affected it, as one who makes a chemical experiment applies the reagents and awaits the result. Indeed the intellect remains so completely excluded from the real decisions and secret purposes of its own will that sometimes it can only learn them like those of a stranger, by spying upon them and surprising them, and must catch the will in the act of expressing itself in order to get at its real intentions. For example, I have conceived a plan, about which, however, I have still some scruple, but the feasibleness of which, as regards its possibility, is completely uncertain, for it depends upon external and still undecided circumstances. It would therefore certainly be unnecessary to come to a decision about it at present, and so for the time I leave the matter as it is. Now in such a case I often do not know how firmly I am already attached to that plan in secret, and how much, in spite of the scruple, I wish to carry it out: that is, my intellect does not know. But now only let me receive news that it is practicable, at once there rises within me a jubilant, irresistible gladness, that passes through my whole being and takes permanent possession of it, to my own astonishment. For now my intellect learns for the first time how firmly my will had laid hold of that plan, and how thoroughly the plan suited it, while the intellect had regarded it as entirely problematical, and had with difficulty been able to overcome that scruple. Or in another case, I have entered eagerly into a contract which I believed to be very much in accordance with my wishes. But as the matter progresses the disadvantages and burdens of it are felt, and I begin to suspect that I even repent of what I so eagerly pursued; yet I rid myself of this feeling by assuring myself that even if I were not bound I would follow the same course. Now, however, the contract is unexpectedly broken by the other side, and I perceive with astonishment that this happens to my great satisfaction and relief. Often we don't know what we wish or what we fear. We may entertain a wish for years without even confessing it to ourselves, or even allowing it to come to clear consciousness; for the intellect must know nothing about it, because the good opinion which we have of ourselves might thereby suffer. But if it is fulfilled we learn from our joy, not without shame, that we have wished this. For example, the death of a near relation whose heir we are. And sometimes we do not know what we really fear, because we lack the courage to bring it to distinct consciousness. Indeed we are often in error as to the real motive from which we have done something or left it undone, till at last perhaps an accident discovers to us the secret, and we know that what we have held to be the motive was not the true one, but another which we had not wished to confess to ourselves, because it by no means accorded with the good opinion we entertained of ourselves. For example, we refrain from doing something on purely moral grounds, as we believe, but afterwards we discover that we were only restrained by fear, for as soon as all danger is removed we do it. In particular cases this may go so far that a man does not even guess the true motive of his action, nay, does not believe himself capable of being influenced by such a motive; and yet it is the true motive of his action. We may remark in passing that in all this we have a confirmation and explanation of the rule of La Rochefoucauld: "*L'amour-propre est plus habile que le plus habile homme du monde*" ["Self-love is cleverer than the cleverest man in the world."]; nay, even a commentary on the Delphic ⟨*gnosi oeauton*⟩ ["Know thyself"] and its difficulty. If now, on the contrary, as all philosophers imagine, the intellect constituted our true nature and the purposes of the will were a mere result of knowledge, then only the motive from which we imagined that we acted would be decisive of our moral worth; in analogy with the fact that the intention, not the result, is in this respect decisive. But really then the distinction between imagined and true motive would be impossible. Thus all cases here set forth, to which every one who pays attention may observe analogous cases in himself, show us how the intellect is so strange to the will that it is sometimes even mystified by it: for it indeed supplies it with motives, but does not penetrate into the secret workshop of its purposes. It is indeed a confidant of the will, but a confidant that is not told everything. This is also further confirmed by the fact, which almost every one will some time have the opportunity of observing in himself, that sometimes the intellect does not thoroughly trust the will. If we have formed some great and bold purpose, which as such is yet really only a promise made by the will to the intellect, there often remains within us a slight unconfessed doubt whether we are quite in earnest about it, whether in carrying it out we will not waver or draw back, but will have sufficient firmness and persistency to fulfil it. It therefore requires the deed to convince us ourselves of the sincerity of the purpose.

All these facts prove the absolute difference of the will and the intellect, the primacy of the former and the subordinate position of the latter.

4. The *intellect* becomes tired; the *will* is never tired. After sustained work with the head we feel the tiredness of the brain, just like that of the arm after sustained bodily work. All *knowing* is accompanied with effort; *willing,* on the contrary, is our very nature, whose manifestations take place without any weariness and entirely of their own accord. Therefore, if our will is strongly excited, as in all emotions, thus in anger, fear, desire, grief, &c., and we are now called upon to know, perhaps with the view of correcting the motives of that emotion, the violence which we must do ourselves for this purpose is evidence of the transition from the original natural activity proper to ourselves to the derived, indirect, and formed activity. For the will alone is . . . active without being called upon, and therefore often too early and too much, and it knows no weariness. Infants who scarcely show the first weak trace of intelligence are already full of self-will: through unlimited, aimless roaring and shrieking they show the pressure of will with which they swell, while their willing has yet no object, *i.e.,* they will without knowing what they will. What Cabanis has observed is also in point here: ["All these passions, which follow one another so quickly, picture themselves naively on the mobile faces of infants. While their feeble muscles, arms and legs hardly know yet how to make the vaguest movements, the muscles of the face already express, by distinct movements, all the principal emotions proper to human nature; and the attentive observer easily recognizes in this picture the characteristic traits of the future man."]* The intellect, on the contrary, develops slowly, following the completion of the brain and the maturity of the whole organism, which are its conditions, just because it is merely a somatic function. It is because the brain attains its full size in the seventh year that from that time forward children become so remarkably intelligent, inquisitive, and reasonable. But then comes puberty; to a certain extent it affords a support to the brain, or a resounding-board, and raises the intellect at once by a large step, as it were by an octave, corresponding to the lowering of the voice by that amount. But at once the animal desires and passions that now appear resist the reasonableness that has hitherto prevailed and to which they have been added. Further evidence is given of the indefatigable nature of the will by the fault which is, more or less, peculiar to all men by nature, and is only overcome by education—*precipitation*. It consists in this, that the will hurries to its work before the time. This work is the purely active and execu-

---

*"On Ethics" in *Wisdom of Life,* op. cit., p. 276.

tive part, which ought only to begin when the explorative and deliberative part, thus the work of knowing, has been completely and thoroughly carried out. But this time is seldom waited for. Scarcely are a few data concerning the circumstances before us, or the event that has occurred, or the opinion of others conveyed to us, superficially comprehended and hastily gathered together by knowledge, than from the depths of our being the will, always ready and never weary, comes forth unasked, and shows itself as terror, fear, hope, joy, desire, envy, grief, zeal, anger, or courage, and leads to rash words and deeds, which are generally followed by repentance when time has taught us that the hegemonicon, the intellect, has not been able to finish half its work of comprehending the circumstances, reflecting on their connection, and deciding what is prudent, because the will did not wait for it, but sprang forward long before its time with "Now it is my turn!" and at once began the active work, without the intellect being able to resist, as it is a mere slave and bondman of the will, and not, like it, ⟨automatos⟩, nor active from its own power and its own impulse; therefore it is easily pushed aside and silenced by a nod of the will, while on its part it is scarcely able, with the greatest efforts, to bring the will even to a brief pause, in order to speak. This is why the people are so rare, and are found almost only among Spaniards, Turks, and perhaps Englishmen, who even under circumstances of provocation *keep the head uppermost,* imperturbably proceed to comprehend and investigate the state of affairs, and when others would already be beside themselves, still ask further questions, which is something quite different from the indifference founded upon apathy and stupidity of many Germans and Dutchmen. Iffland used to give an excellent representation of this admirable quality, as Hetmann of the Cossacks, in Benjowski, when the conspirators have enticed him into their tent and hold a rifle to his head, with the warning that they will fire it if he utters a cry, Iffland blew into the mouth of the rifle to try whether it was loaded. Of ten things that annoy us, nine would not be able to do so if we understood them thoroughly in their causes, and therefore knew their necessity and true nature; but we would do this much oftener if we made them the object of reflection before making them the object of wrath and indignation. For what bridle and bit are to an unmanageable horse the intellect is for the will in man; by this bridle it must be controlled by means of instruction, exhortation, culture, &c., for in itself it is as wild and impetuous an impulse as the force that appears in the descending waterfall, nay, as we know, it is at bottom identical with this. In the height of anger, in intoxication, in despair, it has taken the bit between its teeth, has run away, and follows its original nature. In the *Mania sine delirio* it has lost bridle and bit altogether, and shows now most distinctly its original nature, and that the intellect is as different from it as the bridle from the horse. In this condition it may also be compared to a clock which, when a certain screw is taken away, runs down without stopping.

Thus this consideration also shows us the will as that which is original, and therefore metaphysical; the intellect, on the other hand, as something subordinate and physical. For as such the latter is, like everything physical, subject to *vis inertiæ,* consequently only active if it is set agoing by something else, the will, which rules it, manages it, rouses it to effort, in short, imparts to it the activity which does not originally reside in it. Therefore it willingly rests whenever it is permitted to do so, often declares itself lazy and disinclined to activity; through continued effort it becomes weary to the point of complete stupefaction, is exhausted, like the voltaic pile, through repeated shocks. Hence all continuous mental work demands pauses and rest, otherwise stupidity and incapacity ensue, at first of course only temporarily; but if this rest is persistently denied to the intellect it will become excessively and continuously fatigued, and the consequence is a permanent deterioration of it, which in an old man may pass into complete incapacity, into childishness, imbecility, and madness. It is not to be attributed to age in and for itself, but to long-continued tyrannical overexertion of the intellect or brain, if this misfortune appears in the last years of life. This is the explanation of the fact that Swift became mad, Kant became childish, Walter Scott, and also Wordsworth, Southey, and many *minorum gentium* ["lesser gentry"] became dull and incapable. Goethe remained to the end clear, strong, and active-minded, because he, who was always a man of the world and a courtier, never carried on his mental occupations with self-compulsion. The same holds good of Wieland and of Knebel, who lived to the age of ninety-one, and also of Voltaire. Now all this proves how very subordinate and physical and what a mere tool the intellect is. Just on this account it requires, during almost a third part of its lifetime, the entire suspension of its activity in sleep, *i.e.,* the rest of the brain, of which it is the mere function, and which therefore just as truly precedes it as the stomach precedes digestion, or as a body precedes its impulsion, and with which in old age it flags and decays. The will, on the contrary, as the thing in itself, is never lazy, is absolutely untiring, its activity is its essence, it never ceases willing, and when, during deep sleep, it is forsaken of the intellect, and therefore cannot act outwardly in accordance with motives, it is active as the vital force, cares the more uninterruptedly for the inner economy of the organism, and as *vis naturæ medicatrix* ["nature's healing power"] sets in order again the irregularities that have crept into it. For it is not, like the intellect, a function of the body; *but the body is its function*; therefore it is, *ordine rerum* ["in the order of things"], prior to the body, as its metaphysical substratum, as the in-itself of its phenomenal appearance. It shares its unwearying nature, for the time that life lasts, with the heart, that *primum mobile* of the organism, which has therefore become its symbol and synonym. Moreover, it does not disappear in the old man, but still continues to will what it has willed, and indeed becomes firmer, more inflexible, than it was in youth, more implacable, self-willed, and unmanageable, because the intellect has become less susceptible: therefore in old age the man can perhaps only be matched by taking advantage of the weakness of his intellect.

Moreover, the prevailing *weakness* and *imperfection* of the intellect, as it is shown in the want of judgment, narrow-mindedness, perversity, and folly of the great majority of men, would be quite inexplicable if the intellect were not subordinate, adventitious, and merely instrumental, but the immediate and original nature of the so-called soul, or in general of the inner man: as all philosophers have hitherto assumed it to be. For how could the original nature in its immediate and peculiar function so constantly err and fail? The *truly* original in human consciousness, the *willing*, always goes on with perfect success; every being wills unceasingly, capably, and decidedly. To regard the immorality in the will as an imperfection of it would be a fundamentally false point of view. For morality has rather a source which really lies above nature, and therefore its utterances are in contradiction with it. Therefore morality is in direct opposition to the natural will, which in itself is completely egoistic; indeed the pursuit of the path of morality leads to the abolition of the will.

5. That the *will* is what is real and essential in man, and the *intellect* only subordinate, conditioned, and produced, is also to be seen in the fact that the latter can carry on its function with perfect purity and correctness only so long as the will is silent and pauses. On the other hand, the function of the intellect is disturbed by every observable excitement of the will, and its result is falsified by the intermixture of the latter; but the converse does not hold, that the intellect should in the same way be a hindrance to the will. Thus the moon cannot shine when the sun is in the heavens, but when the moon is in the heavens it does not prevent the sun from shining.

The Sleep of Reason Produces Monsters, 1796-1798, By Francisco de Goya (1746-1828).
Rosenwald Collection, (c) 1999 Board of Trustees, National Gallery of Art, Washington, published
1799, etching and acquatint, plate 43 of 80 from 'Los Caprichos' (Harris 1964 78.iii (1st ed). In his Los
Caprichos etching series, Goya questions his own Enlightenment faith in the power of reason to solve
the problems of the human condition. In this etching from the frontispiece to the collection, he depicts
the nightmarish chaos released when reason sleeps. Goya's work anticipates Schopenhauer's questioning of the intellect's primacy. (*National Gallery of Art, Washington, D.C.*)

A great *fright* often deprives us of our senses to such an extent that we are petrified, or else do the most absurd things; for example, when fire has broken out run right into the flames. *Anger* makes us no longer know what we do, still less what we say. *Zeal,* therefore called blind, makes us incapable of weighing the arguments of others, or even of seeking out and setting in order our own. *Joy* makes us inconsiderate, reckless, and foolhardy, and *desire* acts almost in the same way. *Fear* prevents us from seeing, and laying hold of the resources that are still present, and often lie close beside us. Therefore for overcoming sudden dangers, and also for fighting with opponents and enemies, the most essential qualifications are *coolness and presence of mind.* The former consists in the silence of the will so that the intellect can act; the latter in the undisturbed activity of the intellect under the pressure of events acting on the will; therefore the former is the condition of the latter, and the two are nearly related; they are seldom to be found, and always only in a limited degree. But they are of inestimable advantage, because they permit the use of the intellect just at those times when we stand most in need of it, and therefore confer decided superiority. He who is without them knows only what he should have done or said when the opportunity has passed. It is very appropriately said of him who is violently moved, *i.e.,* whose will is so strongly excited that it destroys the purity of the function of the intellect, he is *disarmed;* for the correct knowledge of the circumstances and relations is our defense and weapon in the conflict with things and with men. In this sense Balthazar Gracian says: *"Es la passion enemiga declarada de la cordura"* ["Passion is the declared enemy of prudence"]. If now the intellect were not something completely different from the will, but, as has been hitherto supposed, knowing and willing had the same root, and were equally original functions of an absolutely simple nature, then with the rousing and heightening of the will, in which the emotion consists, the intellect would necessarily also be heightened; but, as we have seen, it is rather hindered and depressed by this; whence the ancients called emotion *animi perturbatio.* The intellect is really like the reflecting surface of water, but the water itself is like the will, whose disturbance therefore at once destroys the clearness of that mirror and the distinctness of its images. The *organism* is the will itself, is embodied will, *i.e.,* will objectively perceived in the brain. Therefore many of its functions, such as respiration, circulation, secretion of bile, and muscular power, are heightened and accelerated by the pleasurable, and in general the healthy, emotions. The *intellect,* on the other hand, is the mere function of the brain, which is only nourished and supported by the organism as a parasite. Therefore every perturbation of the *will,* and with it of the *organism,* must disturb and paralyse the function of the brain, which exists for itself and for no other wants than its own, which are simply rest and nourishment.

But this disturbing influence of the activity of the will upon the intellect can be shown, not only in the perturbations brought about by emotions, but also in many other, more gradual, and therefore more lasting falsifications of thought by our inclinations. *Hope* makes us regard what we wish, and fear what we are apprehensive of, as probable and near, and both exaggerate their object. Plato (according to Ælian, V. H., 13, 28) very beautifully called hope the dream of the waking. Its nature lies in this, that the will, when its servant the intellect is not able to produce what it wishes, obliges it at least to picture it before it, in general to undertake the rôle of comforter, to appease its lord with fables, as a nurse a child, and so to dress these out that they gain an appearance of likelihood. Now in this the intellect must do violence to its own nature, which aims at the truth, for it compels it, contrary to its own laws, to regard as true things which are neither true nor probable, and often scarcely possible, only in order to appease, quiet, and send to sleep for a while the restless and unmanageable *will.* Here we see clearly who is master and who is servant. Many may well have observed that if a matter which is of importance to them may turn out in several different ways, and they have brought all of these into one disjunctive judgment which in their opinion is complete, the actual result is yet quite another, and one wholly unexpected by them: but perhaps they will not have considered this, that this result was then almost always the one which was unfavourable to them. The explanation of this is, that while their *intellect* intended to survey the possibilities completely, the worst of all remained quite invisible to it; because the *will,* as it were, covered it with its hand, that is, it so mastered the intellect that it was quite incapable of glancing at the worst case of all, although, since it actually came to pass, this was also the most probable case. Yet in very melancholy dispositions, or in those that have become prudent through experience like this, the process is reversed, for here apprehension plays the part which was formerly played by hope. The first appearance of danger throws them into groundless anxiety. If the intellect begins to investigate the matter it is rejected as incompetent, nay, as a deceitful sophist, because the heart is to be believed, whose fears are now actually allowed to pass for arguments as to the reality and greatness of the danger. So then the intellect dare make no search for good reasons on the other side, which, if left to itself, it would soon recognize, but is obliged at once to picture to them the most unfortunate issue, even if it itself can scarcely think this issue possible:

> "Such as we know is false, yet dread in sooth,
>   Because the worst is ever nearest truth."
>
> —Byron (*Lara,* c, I).

Love and *hate* falsify our judgment entirely. In our enemies we see nothing but faults—in our loved ones nothing but excellences, and even their faults appear to us amiable. Our *interest,* of whatever kind it may be, exercises a like secret power over our judgment; what is in conformity with it at once seems to us fair, just, and reasonable; what runs contrary to it presents itself to us, in perfect seriousness, as unjust and outrageous, or injudicious and absurd. Hence so many prejudices of position, profession, nationality, sect, and religion. A conceived hypothesis gives us lynx-eyes for all that confirms it, and makes us blind to all that contradicts it. What is opposed to our party, our plan, our wish, our hope, we often cannot comprehend and grasp at all, while it is clear to every one else; but what is favourable to these, on the other hand, strikes our eye from afar. What the heart opposes the head will not admit. We firmly retain many errors all through life, and take care never to examine their ground, merely from a fear, of which we ourselves are conscious, that we might make the discovery that we had so long believed and so often asserted what is false. Thus then is the intellect daily befooled and corrupted by the impositions of inclination. This has been very beautifully expressed by Bacon of Verulam in the words: *Intellectus LUMINIS SICCI non est; sed recipit infusionem a voluntate et affectibus: id quod generat ad quod vult scientias: quod enim mavult homo, id potius credit.* ["The intellect is not a dry light, but receives an infusion from the will and the emotions, which results in sciences-as-we-wish; for what a man prefers he will rather believe."] (*Org. Nov.,* i., 14). Clearly it is also this that opposes all new fundamental opinions in the sciences and all refutations of sanctioned errors, for one will not easily see the truth of that which convicts one of incredible want of thought. It is explicable, on this ground alone, that the truths of Goethe's doctrine of colours, which are so clear and simple, are still denied by the physicists; and thus Goethe himself has had to learn what a much harder position one has if one promises men instruction than if one promises them amusement. Hence it is much more fortunate to be born a poet than a philosopher. But the more obstinately an error was held by the other side, the more shameful does the conviction afterwards become. In the case of an overthrown system, as in the case of a conquered army, the most prudent is he who first runs away from it.

A trifling and absurd, but striking, example of that mysterious and immediate power which the will exercises over the intellect, is the fact that in doing accounts we make mistakes much oftener in our own favour than to our disadvantage, and this without the slightest dishonest intention, merely from the unconscious tendency to diminish our *Debit* and increase our *Credit*.

Lastly, the fact is also in point here, that when advice is given the slightest aim or purpose of the adviser generally outweighs his insight, however great it may be; therefore we dare not assume that he speaks from the latter when we suspect the existence of the former. How little perfect sincerity is to be expected even from otherwise honest persons whenever their interests are in any way concerned we can gather from the fact that we so often deceive ourselves when hope bribes us, or fear befools us, or suspicion torments us, or vanity flatters us, or any hypothesis blinds us, or a small aim which is close at hand injures a greater but more distant one; for in this we see the direct and unconscious disadvantageous influence of the will upon knowledge. Accordingly it ought not to surprise us if in asking advice the will of the person asked directly dictates the answer even before the question could penetrate to the forum of his judgment.

I wish in a single word to point out here what will be fully explained in the following book, that the most perfect knowledge, thus the purely objective comprehension of the world, *i.e.,* the comprehension of genius, is conditioned by a silence of the will so profound that while it lasts even the individuality vanishes from consciousness and the man remains as the *pure subject of knowing,* which is the correlative of the *Idea.*

The disturbing influence of the will upon the intellect, which is proved by all these phenomena, and, on the other hand, the weakness and frailty of the latter, on account of which it is incapable of working rightly whenever the will is in any way moved, gives us then another proof that the will is the radical part of our nature, and acts with original power, while the intellect, as adventitious and in many ways conditioned, can only act in a subordinate and conditional manner.

There is no direct disturbance of the will by the intellect corresponding to the disturbance and clouding of knowledge by the will that has been shown. Indeed we cannot well conceive such a thing. No one will wish to construe as such the fact that motives wrongly taken up lead the will astray, for this is a fault of the intellect in its own function, which is committed quite within its own province, and the influence of which upon the will is entirely indirect. It would be plausible to attribute *irresolution* to this, for in its case, through the conflict of the motives which the intellect presents to the will, the latter is brought to a standstill, thus is hindered. But when we consider it more closely, it becomes very clear that the cause of this hindrance does not lie in the activity of the *intellect* as such, but entirely in *external objects* which are brought about by it, for in this case they stand in precisely such a relation to the will, which is here interested, that they draw it with nearly equal strength in different directions. This real cause merely acts *through* the intellect as the medium of motives, though certainly under the assumption that it is keen enough to comprehend the objects in their manifold relations. Irresolution, as a trait of character, is just as much conditioned by qualities of the will as of the intellect. It is certainly not peculiar to exceedingly limited minds, for their weak understanding does not allow them to discover such manifold qualities and relations in things, and moreover is so little fitted for the exertion of reflection and pondering these, and then the probable consequences of each step, that they rather decide at once according to the first impression, or according to some simple rule of conduct. The converse of this occurs in the case of persons of considerable understanding. Therefore, whenever such persons also possess a tender care for their own well-being, *i.e.,* a very sensitive egoism, which constantly desires to come off well and always to be safe, this introduces a certain anxiety at every step, and thereby irresolution. This quality therefore indicates throughout not a want of understanding but a want of courage. Yet very eminent minds survey the relations and their probable developments with such rapidity and certainty, that if they are only supported by some courage they thereby acquire that quick decision and resolution that fits them to play an important part in the affairs of the world, if time and circumstances afford them the opportunity.

The only decided, direct restriction and disturbance which the will can suffer from the intellect as such may indeed be the quite exceptional one, which is the consequence of an abnormally preponderating development of the intellect, thus of that high endowment which has been defined as genius. This is decidedly a hindrance to the energy of the character, and consequently to the power of action. Hence it is not the really great minds that make historical characters, because they are capable of bridling and ruling the mass of men and carrying out the affairs of the world; but for this persons of much less capacity of mind are qualified when they have great firmness, decision, and persistency of will, such as is quite inconsistent with very high intelligence. Accordingly, where this very high intelligence exists we actually have a case in which the intellect directly restricts the will.

6. In opposition to the hindrances and restrictions which it has been shown the intellect suffers from the will, I wish now to show, in a few examples, how, conversely, the functions of the intellect are sometimes aided and heightened by the incitement and spur of the will; so that in this also we may recognize the primary nature of the one and the secondary nature of the other, and it may become clear that the intellect stands to the will in the relation of a tool.

A motive which affects us strongly, such as a yearning desire or a pressing need, sometimes raises the intellect to a degree of which we had not previously believed it capable. Difficult circumstances, which impose upon us the necessity of certain achievements, develop entirely new talents in us, the germs of which were hidden from us, and for which we did not credit ourselves with any capacity. The understanding of the stupidest man becomes keen when objects are in question that closely concern his wishes; he now observes, weighs, and distinguishes with the greatest delicacy even the smallest circumstances that have reference to his wishes or fears. This has much to do with the cunning of half-witted persons, which is often remarked with surprise. On this account Isaiah rightly says, *vexatio dat intellectum,* which is therefore also used as a proverb. Akin to it is the German proverb, *"Die Noth ist die Mutter der Künste"* ["Necessity is the mother of the arts"]; when, however, the fine arts are to be excepted, because the heart of every one of their works, that is, the conception, must proceed from a perfectly will-less, and only thereby purely objective, perception, if they are to be genuine. Even the understanding of the brutes is increased considerably by necessity, so that in cases of difficulty they accomplish things at which we are astonished. For example, they almost all calculate that it is safer not to run away when they believe they are not seen; therefore the hare lies still in the furrow of the field and lets the sportsman pass close to it; insects, when they cannot escape, pretend to be dead, &c. We may obtain a fuller knowledge of this influence from the special history of the self-education of the wolf, under the spur of the great difficulty of its position in civilized Europe; it is to be found in the second letter of Leroy's excellent book, *"Lettres sur l'intelligence et la perfectibilité des animaux."* Immediately afterwards, in the third letter, there follows the high school of the fox, which in an equally difficult position has far less physical strength. In its case, however, this is made up for by great understanding; yet only through the constant struggle with want on the one hand and danger on the other, thus under the spur of the will, does it attain that high degree of cunning which distinguishes it especially in old age. In all these enhancements of the intellect the will plays the part of a rider who with the spur urges the horse beyond the natural measure of its strength.

In the same way the memory is enhanced through the pressure of the will. Even if it is otherwise weak, it preserves perfectly what has value for the ruling passion. The lover forgets no opportunity favourable to him, the ambitious man forgets no circumstance that can forward his plans, the avaricious man never forgets the loss he has suffered, the proud man never forgets an injury to his honour, the vain man remembers every word of praise and the most trifling distinction that falls to his lot. And this also extends to the brutes: the horse stops at the inn where once long ago it was fed; dogs have an excellent memory for all occasions, times, and places that have afforded them choice morsels; and foxes for the different hiding-places in which they have stored their plunder.

Self-consideration affords opportunity for finer observations in this regard. Sometimes, through an interruption, it has entirely escaped me what I have just been thinking about, or even what news I have just heard. Now if the matter had in any way even the most distant personal interest, the after-feeling of the impression which it made upon the *will* has remained. I am still quite conscious how far it affected me agreeably or disagreeably, and also of the special manner in which this happened, whether, even in the slightest degree, it vexed me, or made me anxious, or irritated me, or depressed me, or produced the opposite of these affections. Thus the mere relation of the thing to my will is retained in the memory after the thing itself has vanished, and this often becomes the clue to lead us back to the thing itself. The sight of a man sometimes affects us in an analogous manner, for we remember merely in general that we have had something to do with him, yet without knowing where, when, or what it was, or who he is. But the sight of him still recalls pretty accurately the feeling which our dealings with him excited in us, whether it was agreeable or disagreeable, and also in what degree and in what way. Thus our memory has preserved only the response of the will, and not that which called it forth. We might call what lies at the foundation of this process the memory of the heart; it is much more intimate than that of the head. Yet at bottom the connection of the two is so far-reaching that if we reflect deeply upon the matter we will arrive at the conclusion that memory in general requires the support of a will as a connecting point, or rather as a thread upon which the memories can range themselves, and which holds them firmly together, or that the will is, as it were, the ground to which the individual memories cleave, and without which they could not last; and that therefore in a pure intelligence, *i.e.*, in a merely knowing and absolutely will-less being, a memory cannot well be conceived. Accordingly the improvement of the memory under the spur of the ruling passion, which has been shown above, is only the higher degree of that which takes place in all retention and recollection; for its basis and condition is always the will. Thus in all this also it becomes clear how very much more essential to us the will is than the intellect. The following facts may also serve to confirm this.

The intellect often obeys the will; for example, if we wish to remember something, and after some effort succeed; so also if we wish now to ponder something carefully and deliberately, and in many such cases. Sometimes, again, the intellect refuses to obey the will; for example, if we try in vain to fix our minds upon something, or if we call in vain upon the memory for something that was intrusted to it. The anger of the will against the intellect on such occasions makes its relation to it and the difference of the two very plain. Indeed the intellect, vexed by this anger, sometimes officiously brings what was asked of it hours afterwards, or even the following morning, quite unexpectedly and unseasonably. On the other hand, the will never really obeys the intellect; but the latter is only the ministerial council of that sovereign; it presents all kinds of things to the will, which then selects what is in conformity with its nature, though in doing so it determines itself with necessity, because this nature is unchangeable and the motives now lie before it. Hence no system of ethics is possible which moulds and improves the will itself. For all teaching only affects *knowledge,* and knowledge never determines the will itself, *i.e.,* the *fundamental character* of willing, only its application to the circumstances present. Rectified knowledge can only modify conduct so far as it proves more exactly and judges more correctly what objects of the will's choice are within its reach; so that the will now measures its relation to things more correctly, sees more clearly what it desires, and consequently is less subject to error in its choice. But over the will itself, over the main tendency or fundamental maxim of it, the intellect has no power. To believe that knowledge really and fundamentally determines the will is like believing that the lantern which a man carries by night is the *primum mobile* of his steps. Whoever, taught by experience or the admonitions of others, knows and laments a fundamental fault of his character, firmly and honestly forms the intention to reform and give it up; but in spite of this, on the first opportunity, the fault receives free course. New repentance, new intentions, new transgressions. When this has been gone through several times he becomes conscious that he cannot improve himself, that the fault lies in his nature and personality, indeed is one with this. Now he will blame and curse his nature and personality, will have a painful feeling, which may rise to anguish of consciousness, but to change these he is not able. Here we see that which condemns and that which is condemned distinctly separate: we see the former as a merely theoretical faculty, picturing and presenting the praiseworthy, and therefore desirable, course of life, but the other as something real and unchangeably present, going quite a different way in spite of the former: and then again the first remaining behind with impotent lamentations over the nature of the other, with which, through this very distress, it again identifies itself. Will and intellect here separate very distinctly. But here the will shows itself as the stronger, the invincible, unchangeable, primitive, and at the same time as the essential thing in question, for the intellect deplores its errors, and finds no comfort in the correctness of the *knowledge,* as its own function. Thus the intellect shows itself entirely secondary, as the spectator of the deeds of another, which it accompanies with impotent praise and blame, and also as determinable from without, because it learns from experience, weighs and alters its precepts. Accordingly, a comparison of our manner of thinking at different periods of our life will present a strange mixture of permanence and changeableness. On the one hand, the moral tendency of the man in his prime and the old man is still the same as was that of the boy; on the other hand, much has become so strange to him that he no longer knows himself, and wonders how he ever could have done or said this and that. In the first half of life to-day for the most part laughs at yesterday, indeed looks down on it with contempt; in the second half, on the contrary, it more and more looks back at it with envy. But on closer examination it will be found that the changeable element was the *intellect,* with its functions of insight and knowledge, which, daily appropriating new material from without, presents a constantly changing system of thought, while, besides this, it itself rises and sinks with the growth and decay of the organism. The will on the contrary, the basis of this, thus the inclinations, passions, and emotions, the character, shows itself as what is unalterable in consciousness. Yet we have to take account of the modifications that depend upon physical capacities for enjoyment, and hence upon age. Thus, for example, the eagerness for sensuous pleasure will show itself in childhood as a love of dainties, in youth and manhood as the tendency to sensuality, and in old age again as a love of dainties.

7. If, as is generally assumed, the will proceeded from knowledge, as its result or product, then where there is much will there would necessarily also be much knowledge, insight, and understanding. This, however, is absolutely not the case; rather, we find in many men a strong, *i.e.,* decided, resolute, persistent, unbending, wayward, and vehement will, combined with a very weak and incapable understanding, so that every one who has to do with them is thrown into despair, for their will remains inaccessible to all reasons and ideas, and is not to be got at, so that it is hidden, as it were, in a sack, out of which it wills blindly. Brutes have often violent, often stubborn wills, but yet very little understanding. Finally, plants will only without any knowledge at all.

If willing sprang merely from knowledge, our *anger* would necessarily be in every case exactly proportionate to the occasion, or at least to our relation to it, for it would be nothing more than the result of the present knowledge. This, however, is rarely the case; rather, anger generally goes far beyond the occasion. Our fury and rage, the *furor brevis,* often upon small occasions, and without error regarding them, is like the raging of an evil spirit which, having been shut up, only waits its opportunity to dare to break loose, and now rejoices that it has found it. This could not be the case if the foundation of our nature were a *knower,* and willing were merely a result of *knowledge;* for how came there into the result what did not lie in the elements? The conclusion cannot contain more than the premises. Thus here also the will shows itself as of a nature quite different from knowledge, which only serves it for communication with the external world, but then the will follows the laws of its own nature without taking from the intellect anything but the occasion.

The intellect, as the mere tool of the will, is as different from it as the hammer from the smith. So long as in a conversation the intellect alone is active it remains *cold.* It is almost as if the man himself were not present. Moreover, he cannot then, properly speaking, compromise himself, but at the most can make himself ridiculous. Only when the will comes into play is the man really present: now he becomes warm, nay, it often happens, *hot.* It is always the will to which we ascribe the warmth of life; on the other hand, we say the *cold* understanding, or to investigate a thing *coolly, i.e.,* to think without being influenced by the will. If we attempt to reverse the relation, and to regard the will as the tool of the intellect, it is as if we made the smith the tool of the hammer.

Nothing is more provoking, when we are arguing against a man with reasons and explanation, and taking all pains to convince him, under the impression that we have only to do with his *understanding,* than to discover at last that he *will* not understand; that thus we had to do with his *will,* which shuts itself up against the truth and brings into the field wilful misunderstandings, chicaneries, and sophisms in order to intrench itself behind its understanding and its pretended want of insight. Then he is certainly not to be got at, for reasons and proofs applied against the will are like the blows of a phantom produced by mirrors against a solid body. Hence the saying so often repeated, "*Stat pro ratione voluntas*" ["The will takes the place of reason"]. Sufficient evidence of what has been said is afforded by ordinary life. But unfortunately proofs of it are also to be found on the path of the sciences. The recognition of the most important truths, of the rarest achievements, will be looked for in vain from those who have an interest in preventing them from being accepted, an interest which either springs from the fact that such truths contradict what they themselves daily teach, or else from this, that they dare not make use of them and teach them; or if all this be not the case they will not accept them, because the watchword of mediocrity will always be, *Si quelqu'un excelle parmi nous, qu'il aille exceller ailleurs* ["If anyone excels among us, let him go and excel elsewhere"], as Helvetius has admirably rendered the saying of the Ephesian in the fifth book of Cicero's "*Tusculanæ*" (c. 36), or as a saying of the Abyssinian Fit Arari puts it, "Among quartzes adamant is outlawed." Thus whoever expects from this always numerous band a just estimation of what he has done will find himself very much deceived, and perhaps for a while he will not be able to understand their behaviour, till at last he finds out that while he applied himself to *knowledge* he had to do with the *will,* thus is precisely in the position described above, nay, is really like a man who brings his case before a court the judges of which have all been bribed. Yet in particular cases he will receive the fullest proof that their will and not their insight opposed him, when one or other of them makes up his mind to plagiarism. Then he will see with astonishment what good judges they are, what correct perception of the merit of others they have, and how well they know how to find out the best, like the sparrows, who never miss the ripest cherries.

The counterpart of the victorious resistance of the will to knowledge here set forth appears if in expounding our reasons and proofs we have the will of those addressed with us. Then all are at once convinced, all arguments are telling, and the matter is at once clear as the day. This is well known to popular speakers. In the one case, as in the other, the will shows itself as that which has original power, against which the intellect can do nothing.

8. But now we shall take into consideration the individual qualities, thus excellences and faults of the will and character on the one hand, and of the intellect on the other, in order to make clear, in their relation to each other, and their relative worth, the complete difference of the two fundamental faculties. History and experience teach that the two appear quite independent of each other. That the greatest excellence of mind will not easily be found combined with equal excellence of character is sufficiently explained by the extraordinary rarity of both, while their opposites are everywhere the order of the day; hence we also daily find the latter in union. However, we never infer a good will from a superior mind, nor the latter from the former, nor the opposite from the opposite, but every unprejudiced person accepts them as perfectly distinct qualities, the presence of which each for itself has to be learned from experience. Great narrowness of mind may coexist with great goodness of heart, and I do not believe Balthazar Gracian was right in saying (*Discreto*, p. 406), "*No ay simple, que no sea malicioso*" ["There is no simpleton who would not be malicious"], though he has the Spanish proverb in his favour, "*Nunca la necedad anduvo sin malicia*" ["Stupidity is never without malice"]. Yet it may be that many stupid persons become malicious for the same reason as many hunchbacks, from bitterness on account of the neglect they have suffered from nature, and because they think they can occasionally make up for what they lack in understanding through malicious cunning, seeking in this a brief triumph. From this, by the way, it is also comprehensible why almost every one easily becomes malicious in the presence of a very superior mind. On the other hand, again, stupid people have very often the reputation of special good-heartedness, which yet so seldom proves to be the case that I could not help wondering how they had gained it, till I was able to flatter myself that I had found the key to it in what follows. Moved by a secret inclination, every one likes best to choose for his more intimate intercourse some one to whom he is a little superior in understanding, for only in this case does he find himself at his ease, because, according to

Hobbes, "*Omnis animi voluptas, omnisque alacritas in eo sita est, quod quis habeat quibuscum conferens se, possit magnifice sentire de se ipso*" ["Every pleasure and vivacity of the mind lies in this, that one has something wherein, comparing himself with others, he can think himself magnificent"] (De Cive, i., 5). For the same reason every one avoids him who is superior to himself; wherefore Lichtenberg quite rightly observes: "To certain men a man of mind is a more odious production than the most pronounced rogue." And similarly Helvetius says: "*Les gens médiocres ont un instinct sür et prompt, pour connaître et fuir les gens d'esprit*" ["Mediocre people have a sure and ready instinct to know and fly from men of genius"]. And Dr. Johnson assures us that "there is nothing by which a man exasperates most people more than by displaying a superior ability of brilliancy in conversation. They seem pleased at the time, but their envy makes them curse him in their hearts" (Boswell; aet. anno 74). In order to bring this truth, so universal and so carefully concealed, more relentlessly to light, I add the expression of it by Merck, the celebrated friend of Goethe's youth, from his story "*Lindor*": "He possessed talents which were given him by nature and acquired by himself through learning; and thus it happened that in most society he left the worthy members of it far behind." If, in the moment of delight at the sight of an extraordinary man, the public swallows these superiorities also, without actually at once putting a bad construction upon them, yet a certain impression of this phenomenon remains behind, which, if it is often repeated, may on serious occasions have disagreeable future consequences for him who is guilty of it. Without any one consciously noting that on this occasion he was insulted, no one is sorry to place himself tacitly in the way of the advancement of this man. Thus on this account great mental superiority isolates more than anything else, and makes one, at least silently, hated. Now it is the opposite of this that makes stupid people so generally liked; especially since many can only find in them what, according to the law of their nature referred to above, they must seek. Yet this the true reason of such an inclination no one will confess to himself, still less to others; and therefore, as a plausible pretext for it, will impute to those he has selected a special goodness of heart, which, as we have said, is in reality only very rarely and accidentally found in combination with mental incapacity. Want of understanding is accordingly by no means favourable or akin to goodness of character. But, on the other hand, it cannot be asserted that great understanding is so; nay, rather, no scoundrel has in general been without it. Indeed even the highest intellectual eminence can coexist with the worst moral depravity.

If now it is said of one man, "He has a good heart, though a bad head," but of another, "He has a very good head, yet a bad heart," every one feels that in the first case the praise far outweighs the blame—in the other case the reverse. Answering to this, we see that if some one has done a bad deed his friends and he himself try to remove the guilt from the *will* to the *intellect,* and to give out that faults of the heart were faults of the head; roguish tricks they will call errors, will say they were merely want of understanding, want of reflection, light-mindedness, folly; nay, if need be, they will plead a paroxysm, momentary mental aberration, and if a heavy crime is in question, even madness, only in order to free the *will* from the guilt. And in the same way, we ourselves, if we have caused a misfortune or injury, will before others and ourselves willingly impeach our *stultitia,* simply in order to escape the reproach of *malitia.* In the same way, in the case of the equally unjust decision of the judge, the difference, whether he has erred or been bribed, is so infinitely great. All this sufficiently proves that the *will* alone is the real and essential, the kernel of the man, and the *intellect* is merely its tool, which may be constantly faulty without the will being concerned. The accusation of want of understanding is, at the moral judgment-seat, no accusation at all; on the contrary, it even gives privileges. And so also, before the courts of the world, it is everywhere sufficient to deliver a criminal from all punishment that his guilt should be transferred from his will to his intellect, by proving either unavoidable error or mental derangement, for then it is of no more consequence than if hand or foot had slipped against the will.

Everywhere those who are responsible for any piece of work appeal, in the event of its turning out unsatisfactorily, to their good intentions, of which there was no lack. Hereby they believe that they secure the essential, that for which they are properly answerable, and their true self; the inadequacy of their faculties, on the other hand, they regard as the want of a suitable tool.

If a man is *stupid,* we excuse him by saying that he cannot help it; but if we were to excuse a *bad* man on the same grounds we would be laughed at. And yet the one, like the other, is innate. This proves that the will is the man proper, the intellect merely its tool.

Thus it is always only our *willing* that is regarded as depending upon ourselves, *i.e.,* as the expression of our true nature, and for which we are therefore made responsible. Therefore it is absurd and unjust if we are taken to task for our beliefs, thus for our knowledge: for we are obliged to regard this as something which, although it changes in us, is as little in our power as the events of the external world. And here, also, it is clear that the *will* alone is the inner and true nature of man; the *intellect,* on the contrary, with its operations, which go on as regularly as the external world, stands to the will in the relation of something external to it, a mere tool.

9. High mental capacities have always been regarded as the gift of nature or the gods; and on that account they have been called *Gaben, Begabung, ingenii dotes,* gifts (a man highly gifted), regarding them as something different from the man himself, something that has fallen to his lot through favour. No one, on the contrary, has even taken this view of moral excellences, although they also are innate; they have rather always been regarded as something proceeding from the man himself, essentially belonging to him, nay, constituting his very self. But it follows now from this that the will is the true nature of man; the intellect, on the other hand, is secondary, a tool, a gift.

Answering to this, all religions promise a reward beyond life, in eternity, for excellences of the *will* or heart, but none for excellences of the head or understanding. Virtue expects its reward in that world; prudence hopes for it in this; genius, again, neither in this world nor in that; it is its own reward. Accordingly the will is the eternal part, the intellect the temporal.

Connection, communion, intercourse among men is based, as a rule, upon relations which concern the *will,* not upon such as concern the *intellect.* The first kind of communion may be called the *material,* the other the *formal.* Of the former kind are the bonds of family and relationship, and further, all connections that rest upon any common aim or interest, such as that of trade or profession, of the corporation, the party, the faction, &c. In these it merely amounts to a question of views, of aims; along with which there may be the greatest diversity of intellectual capacity and culture. Therefore not only can any one live in peace and unity with any one else, but can act with him and be allied to him for the common good of both. Marriage also is a bond of the heart, not of the head. It is different, however, with merely formal communion, which aims only at an exchange of thought; this demands a certain equality of intellectual capacity and culture. Great differences in this respect place between man and man an impassable gulf: such lies, for example, between a man of great mind and a fool, between a scholar and a peasant, between a courtier and a sailor. Natures as heterogeneous as this have therefore trouble in making themselves intelligible so long as it is a question of exchanging thoughts, ideas, and views. Nevertheless close *material* friendship may exist between them, and they may be faithful allies, conspirators, or men under mutual pledges. For in all that concerns the will alone, which includes friendship, enmity, honesty, fidelity, falseness, and treachery, they are perfectly homogeneous, formed of the same clay, and neither mind nor culture make any difference here; indeed here the ignorant man often shames the scholar, the sailor the courtier. For at the different grades of culture there are the same virtues and vices, emotions and passions; and although somewhat modified in their expression, they very soon mutually recognize each other even in the most heterogeneous individuals, upon which the similarly disposed agree and the opposed are at enmity.

Brilliant qualities of mind win admiration, but never affection; this is reserved for the moral, the qualities of the character. Every one will choose as his friend the honest, the good-natured, and even the agreeable, complaisant man, who easily concurs, rather than the merely able man. Indeed many will be preferred to the latter, on account of insignificant, accidental, outward qualities which just suit the inclination of another. Only the man who has much mind himself will wish able men for his society; his friendship, on the other hand, he will bestow with reference to moral qualities; for upon this depends his really high appreciation of a man in whom a single good trait of character conceals and expiates great want of understanding. The known goodness of a character makes us patient and yielding towards weaknesses of understanding, as also towards the dullness and childishness of age. A distinctly noble character along with the entire absence of intellectual excellence and culture presents itself as lacking nothing; while, on the contrary, even the greatest mind, if affected with important moral faults, will always appear blamable. For as torches and fireworks become pale and insignificant in the presence of the sun, so intellect, nay, genius, and also beauty, are outshone and eclipsed by the goodness of the heart. When this appears in a high degree it can make up for the want of those qualities to such an extent that one is ashamed of having missed them. Even the most limited understanding, and also grotesque ugliness, whenever extraordinary goodness of heart declares itself as accompanying them, become as it were transfigured, outshone by a beauty of a higher kind, for now a wisdom speaks out of them before which all other wisdom must be dumb. For goodness of heart is a transcendent quality; it belongs to an order of things that reaches beyond this life, and is incommensurable with any other perfection. When it is present in a high degree it makes the heart so large that it embraces the world, so that now everything lies within it, no longer without; for it identifies all natures with its own. It then extends to others also that boundless indulgence which otherwise each one only bestows on himself. Such a man is incapable of becoming angry; even if the malicious mockery and sneers of others have drawn attention to his own intellectual or physical faults, he only reproaches himself in his heart for having been the occasion of such expressions, and therefore, without doing violence to his own feelings, proceeds to treat those persons in the kindest manner, confidently hoping that they will turn from their error with regard to him, and recognize themselves in him also. What is wit and genius against this?— what is Bacon of Verulam?

Our estimation of our own selves leads to the same result as we have here obtained by considering our estimation of others. How different is the self-satisfaction which we experience in a moral regard from that which we experience in an intellectual regard! The former arises when, looking back on our conduct, we see that with great sacrifices we have practiced fidelity and honesty, that we have helped many, forgiven many, have behaved better to others than they have behaved to us; so that we can say with King Lear, "I am a man more sinned against than sinning"; and to its fullest extent if perhaps some noble deed shines in our memory. A deep seriousness will accompany the still peace which such a review affords us; and if we see that others are inferior to us here, this will not cause us any joy, but we will rather deplore it, and sincerely wish that they were as we are. How entirely differently does the knowledge of our intellectual superiority affect us! Its ground base is really the saying of Hobbes quoted above: *Omnis animi voluptas, omnisque alacritas in eo sita est, quod quis habeat, quibuscum conferens se, possit magnifice sentire de se ipso* ["Every pleasure and vivacity of the mind lies in this, that one has something wherein, comparing himself with others, he can think himself magnificent"]. Arrogant, triumphant vanity, proud, contemptuous looking down on others, inordinate delight in the consciousness of decided and considerable superiority, akin to pride of physical advantages,—that is the result here. This opposition between the two kinds of self-satisfaction shows that the one concerns our true inner and eternal nature, the other a more external, merely temporal, and indeed scarcely more than a mere physical excellence. The *intellect* is in fact simply the function of the brain; the will, on the contrary, is that whose function is the whole man, according to his being and nature.

10. Upon what depends the *identity of the person*? Not upon the matter of the body; it is different after a few years. Not upon its form, which changes as a whole and in all its parts; all but the expression of the glance, by which, therefore, we still know a man even after many years; which proves that in spite of all changes time produces in him something in him remains quite untouched by it. It is just this by which we recognize him even after the longest intervals of time, and find the former man entire. It is the same with ourselves, for, however old we become, we yet feel within that we are entirely the same as we were when we were young, nay, when we were still children. This, which unaltered always remains quite the same, and does not grow old along with us, is really the kernel of our nature, which does not lie in time. It is assumed that the identity of the person rests upon that of consciousness. But by this is understood merely the connected recollection of the course of life; hence it is not sufficient. We certainly know something more of our life than of a novel we have formerly read, yet only very little. The principal events, the interesting scenes, have impressed themselves upon us; in the remainder a thousand events are forgotten for one has been retained. The older we become the more do things pass by us without leaving any trace. Great age, illness, injury of the brain, madness, may deprive us of memory altogether, but the identity of the person is not thereby lost. It rests upon the identical *will* and the unalterable character of the person. It is it also which makes the expression of the glance unchangeable. In the *heart* is the man, not in the head. It is true that, in consequence of our relation to the external world, we are accustomed to regard as our real self the subject of knowledge, the knowing I, which wearies in the evening, vanishes in sleep, and in the morning shines brighter with renewed strength. This is, however, the mere function of the brain, and not our own self. Our true self, the kernel of our nature, is what is behind that, and really knows nothing but willing and not willing, being content and not content, with all the modifications of this, which are called feelings, emotions, and passions. This is that which produces the other, does not sleep with it when it sleeps, and in the same way when it sinks in death remains uninjured. Everything, on the contrary, that belongs to *knowledge* is exposed to oblivion; even actions of moral significance can sometimes, after years, be only imperfectly recalled, and we no longer know accurately and in detail how we acted on a critical occasion. But the *character itself,* to which the actions only testify, cannot be forgotten by us; it is now still quite the same as then. The will itself, alone and for itself, is permanent, for it alone is unchangeable, indestructible, not growing old, not physical, but metaphysical, not be-

longing to the phenomenal appearance, but to that itself which so appears. How the identity of consciousness also, so far as it goes, depends upon it I have shown above, so I need not dwell upon it further here.

11. Aristotle says in passing, in his book on the comparison of the desirable, "To live well is better than to live" (⟨*beltion tou zan to en zan*⟩, *Top.* iii., 2). From this we might infer, by double contraposition, not to live is better than to live badly. This is also evident to the intellect; yet the great majority live very badly rather than not at all. This clinging to life cannot therefore have its ground in the *object* of life, since life, as was shown in the fourth book, is really a constant suffering, or at the least, as will be shown further on, a business which does not cover its expenses; thus that clinging to life can only be founded in the *subject* of it. But it is not founded in the *intellect,* it is no result of reflection, and in general is not a matter of choice; but this willing of life is something that is taken for granted: it is a *prius* of the intellect itself. We ourselves are the will to live, and therefore we must live, well or ill. Only from the fact that this clinging to a life which is so little worth to them is entirely *a priori* and not *a posteriori* can we explain the excessive fear of death that dwells in every living thing, which Rochefoucauld has expressed in his last reflection, with rare frankness and naïveté, and upon which the effect of all tragedies and heroic actions ultimately rests, for it would be lost if we prized life only according to its objective worth. Upon this inexpressible *horror mortis* ["horror of death"] is also founded the favourite principle of all ordinary minds, that whosoever takes his own life must be mad; yet not less the astonishment, mingled with a certain admiration, which this action always excites even in thinking minds, because it is so opposed to the nature of all living beings that in a certain sense we are forced to admire him who is able to perform it. For suicide proceeds from a purpose of the intellect, but our will to live is a *prius* of the intellect. Thus this consideration also confirms the primacy of the will in self-consciousness.

12. On the other hand, nothing proves more clearly the secondary, dependent, conditioned nature of the *intellect* than its periodical intermittence. In deep sleep all knowing and forming of ideas ceases. But the kernel of our nature, the metaphysical part of it which the organic functions necessarily presuppose as their *primum mobile,* must never pause if life is not to cease, and, moreover, as something metaphysical and therefore incorporeal, it requires no rest. Therefore the philosophers who set up a soul as this metaphysical kernel, *i.e.,* an originally and essentially *knowing* being, see themselves forced to the assertion that this soul is quite untiring in its perceiving and knowing, therefore continues these even in deep sleep; only that we have no recollection of this when we awake. The falseness of this assertion, however, was easy to see whenever one had rejected that soul in consequence of Kant's teaching. For sleep and waking prove to the unprejudiced mind in the clearest manner that knowing is a secondary function and conditioned by the organism, just like any other. Only the *heart* is untiring, because its beating and the circulation of the blood are not directly conditioned by nerves, but are just the original manifestation of the will. Also all other physiological functions governed merely by ganglionic nerves, which have only a very indirect and distant connection with the brain, are carried on during sleep, although the secretions take place more slowly; the beating of the heart itself, on account of its dependence upon respiration, which is conditioned by the cerebral system (*medulla oblongata*), becomes with it a little slower. The stomach is perhaps most active in sleep, which is to be attributed to its special consensus with the now resting brain, which occasions mutual disturbances. The *brain* alone, and with it knowing, pauses entirely in deep sleep. For it is merely the minister of foreign affairs, as the ganglion system is the minister of the interior. The brain, with its function of knowing, is only a *vedette* established by

the will for its external ends, which, up in the watch-tower of the head, looks round through the windows of the senses and marks where mischief threatens and where advantages are to be looked for, and in accordance with whose report the will decides. This *vedette,* like every one engaged on active service, is then in a condition of strain and effort, and therefore it is glad when, after its watch is completed, it is again withdrawn, as every watch gladly retires from its post. This withdrawal is going to sleep, which is therefore so sweet and agreeable, and to which we are so glad to yield—on the other hand, being roused from sleep is unwelcome, because it recalls the *vedette* suddenly to its post. One generally feels also after the beneficent systole the reappearance of the difficult diastole, the reseparation of the intellect from the will. A so-called soul, which was originally and radically a *knowing being,* would, on the contrary, necessarily feel on awaking like a fish put back into water. In sleep, when merely the vegetative life is carried on, the will works only according to its original and essential nature, undisturbed from without, with no diminution of its power through the activity of the brain and the exertion of knowing, which is the heaviest organic function, yet for the organism merely a means, not an end; therefore, in sleep the whole power of the will is directed to the maintenance and, where it is necessary, the improvement of the organism. Hence all healing, all favourable crises, take place in sleep; for the *vis naturæ medicatrix* has free play only when it is delivered from the burden of the function of knowledge. The embryo which has still to form the body therefore sleeps continuously, and the new-born child the greater part of its time. In this sense Burdach (*Physiologie,* vol. iii., p. 484) quite rightly declares sleep to be the *original* state.

With reference to the brain itself, I account to myself for the necessity of sleep more fully through an hypothesis which appears to have been first set up in Neumann's book, "*Von den Krankheiten des Menschen,*" 1834, vol. 4, § 216. It is this, that the nutrition of the brain, thus the renewal of its substance from the blood, cannot go on while we are awake, because the very eminent organic function of knowing and thinking would be disturbed or put an end to by the low and material function of nutrition. This explains the fact that sleep is not a purely negative condition, a merely pausing of the activity of the brain, but also shows a positive character. This makes itself known through the circumstance that between sleep and waking there is no mere difference of degree, but a fixed boundary, which, as soon as sleep intervenes, declares itself in dreams which are completely different from our immediately preceding thoughts. A further proof of this is that when we have dreams which frighten us we try in vain to cry out, or to ward off attacks, or to shake off sleep; so that it is as if the connecting-link between the brain and the motor nerves, or between the cerebrum and the cerebullum (as the regulator of movements) were abolished; for the brain remains in its isolation and sleep holds us fast as with brazen claws. Finally, the positive character of sleep can be seen in the fact that a certain degree of strength is required for sleeping. Therefore too great fatigue or natural weakness prevents us from seizing it, *capere somnum.* This may be explained from the fact that the process of nutrition must be introduced if sleep is to ensue: the brain must, as it were, begin to feed. Moreover, the increased flow of blood into the brain during sleep is explicable from the nutritive process; and also the position of the arms laid together above the head, which is instinctively assumed because it furthers this process: also why children, so long as their brain is still growing, require a great deal of sleep, while in old age, on the other hand, when a certain atrophy of the brain, as of all the parts, takes place, sleep is short; and finally why excessive sleep produces a certain dullness of consciousness, the consequence of a certain hypertrophy of the brain, which in the case of habitual excess of sleep may become permanent and produce imbecility: ⟨*ania kai polus hypnos*⟩ (*noxæ* est etiam multus somnus) ["much sleep is injurious"], Od. 15, 394. The need of sleep is therefore directly proportionate to the intensity of the brain-life, thus to the clearness of the consciousness. Those animals whose brain-life is weak and dull sleep little and lightly; for example, reptiles and fishes: and here I must remind the reader that the winter sleep is sleep only in name, for it is not an inaction of the brain alone, but of the whole organism, thus a kind of apparent death. Animals of considerable intelligence sleep deeply and long. Men also require more sleep the more developed, both as regards quantity and quality, and the more active their brain is. Montaigne relates of himself that he had always been a long sleeper, that he had passed a large part of his life sleeping, and at an advanced age still slept from eight to nine hours at a time (Liv. iii., chap. 13). Descartes also is reported to have slept a great deal (Baillet, *Vie de Descartes,* 1693, p. 288). Kant allowed himself seven hours for sleep, but it was so hard for him to do with this that he ordered his servant to force him against his will, and without listening to his remonstrances, to get up at the set time (Jachmann, *Immanuel Kant,* p. 162). For the more completely awake a man is, *i.e.,* the clearer and more lively his consciousness, the greater for him is the necessity of sleep, thus the deeper and longer he sleeps. Accordingly much thinking or hard brain-work increases the need of sleep. That sustained muscular exertion also makes us sleepy is to be explained from the fact that in this the brain continuously, by means of the *medulla oblongata,* the spinal marrow, and the motor nerves, imparts the stimulus to the muscles which affects their irritability, and in this way it exhausts its strength. The fatigue which we observe in the arms and legs has accordingly its real seat in the brain; just as the pain which these parts feel is really experienced in the brain; for it is connected with the motor nerves, as with the nerves of sense. The muscles which are not actuated from the brain—for example, those of the heart—accordingly never tire. The same grounds explain the fact that both during and after great muscular exertion we cannot think acutely. That one has far less energy in mind in summer than in winter is partly explicable from the fact that in summer one sleeps less; for the deeper one has slept, the more completely awake, the more lively, is one afterwards. This, however, must not mislead us into extending sleep unduly, for then it loses in intension, *i.e.,* in deepness and soundness, what it gains in extension; whereby it becomes mere loss of time. This is what Goethe means when he says (in the second part of "Faust") of morning slumber: "Sleep is husk: throw it off." Thus in general the phenomenon of sleep most specially confirms the assertion that consciousness, apprehension, knowing, thinking, is nothing original in us, but a conditioned and secondary state. It is a luxury of nature, and indeed its highest, which it can therefore the less afford to pursue without interruption the higher the pitch to which it has been brought. It is the product, the efflorescence of the cerebral nerve-system, which is itself nourished like a parasite by the rest of the organism. This also agrees with what is shown in our third book, that knowing is so much the purer and more perfect the more it has freed and severed itself from the will, whereby the purely objective, the aesthetic comprehension, appears. Just as an extract is so much the purer the more it has been separated from that out of which it is extracted and been cleared of all sediment. The opposite is shown by the *will,* whose most immediate manifestation is the whole organic life, and primarily the untiring heart.

This last consideration is related to the theme of the following chapter, to which it therefore makes the transition: yet the following observation belongs to it: In magnetic somnambulism the consciousness is doubled: two trains of knowledge, each connected in itself, but quite different from each other, arise; the waking consciousness knows nothing of the somnambulent. But the will retains in both the same character, and remains throughout identical; it expresses in both the same inclinations and aversions. For the function may be doubled, but not the true nature.

AUGUSTE COMTE
1798–1857

When he was twenty-seven years old, Auguste Comte said of himself, "The essence of my life is a novel, and an intense novel, which would appear truly extraordinary if I ever published it under some assumed names." Little did he know at the time that the chapters yet to come in his life would indeed befit a novel.

Nothing in Comte's background gave any hint of the extraordinary life he would lead. Born Isidore-Auguste-Marie-François-Xavier Comte, the eldest of four children, Auguste was raised in a conservative Catholic home in Montpellier, France. His father, Louis-Auguste Comte, was a stern, hard-working official in the local tax office, who apparently had little influence on his son. His mother, Félicité-Rosalie Boyer, was twelve years older than her husband and was the major influence in the household. She devoted her life to the emotional and religious needs of her children.

At the age of nine, *Le Comtou,* as Comte was known because of his small stature, entered the Lycée Impérial at Montpellier. He did quite well at the school and was able to pass the entrance examination for the École Polytechnique when only fifteen, a year before the age of enrollment. By this time he had "naturally ceased believing in God," despite his mother's influence.

In 1814, Comte entered the exclusive school and again excelled academically. The fortunes of the École had long been tied to the spirit of the French Revolution, but this spirit was no longer in social favor. In 1816, Comte led a student drive against a condescending teacher. Royalists, who had always distrusted the institution's republicanism, used this incident as a pretext for closing the entire school. Though it reopened the same year, Comte never resumed formal studies.

Comte then took a series of jobs before becoming the secretary to the socialist philosopher and political theorist Claude Henri Saint-Simon in 1817. At first, Comte worked with Saint-Simon on a series of articles announcing a new "science of society." But, as the relationship developed, Comte found it difficult to remain in a subservient role. The conflict came to a head over an article they were preparing for publication. Comte objected to the introduction, which stated that Comte was still Saint-Simon's "student."

While working with Saint-Simon, Comte met Caroline Massin, a prostitute and kept woman of a Parisian lawyer. Comte set up an apartment with her, and in 1825, over the objections of his parents, married her in a civil ceremony. The lawyer who had been her paramour was a witness at the wedding, had her listing as a prostitute erased from police records, and periodically assisted the couple financially.

In 1826, Comte announced he would give a series of seventy-two lectures explaining his new philosophy. His fevered preparation for these lectures left him exhausted, and after three lectures, he suffered a complete mental breakdown and was hospitalized in a private clinic. Though officially designated as "uncured," Comte was discharged to the care of his wife after eight months. His mother believed the illness came from living in sin, in a marriage without the sanction of the church, and so she arranged for a religious wedding ceremony. (The effectiveness of this ceremony is questionable: Comte harangued the priest throughout the ritual and signed the wedding certificate "Brutus Bonaparte Comte.")

Though he continued to have episodes of violent behavior and depression, including a suicide attempt in the Seine River, Comte slowly regained his health. By 1832, he was able to secure a position at his alma mater, the École Polytechnique, as a part-time lecturer. He became the entrance examiner five years later. During this period, he completed his series of seventy-two lectures, published in 1842 as the *Cours de philosophie positive (Course in Positive Philosophy).* Immediately following the publication of his *magnum opus,* Caroline left him, ending seventeen difficult and often violent years of marriage. Two years later, Comte lost his position at the École as a result of intemperate attacks on the institution and its resistance to his new ideas. John Stuart Mill in England and Emile Littré in France then gave him financial support.

In 1844, Comte met and fell passionately in love with Mme. Clotilde de Vaux, the wife of a convicted felon. Unable to make her his mistress, Comte venerated her as his Beatrice, his saint. When she died of tuberculosis less than two years later, Comte's mental stability was severely tested. He successfully fought off depression and went on to found both the Positivist Society and the Universal Church of the Religion of Humanity. Thomas Huxley later remarked that Comte's Religion of Humanity represented "a Catholic organization without Catholic doctrine, or, in other words, Catholicism *minus* Christianity."* Comte envisioned a new Positivist calendar, secular saints, and sacramental rituals drawn from reason and science.

Comte's later years were devoted to writing and to his new Religion of Humanity. Comte spent hours in prayer and in commemoration of Clotilde, the per-

---

*Thomas Henry Huxley, "The Scientific Aspects of Positivism" (1871) as quoted in Mary Pickering, *Auguste Comte: An Intellectual Biography,* Vol. I (Cambridge: Cambridge University Press, 1993), pp. 16–17.

fect representative of the great Being, Humanity. His obsession with Clotilde, his demand for complete acceptance of his ideas, and his reactionary political support for Louis Napoleon split the Positivist movement. When former disciples, such as Littré, and supporters, such as Mill, objected, they were summarily excommunicated by Comte.

Concerned with this dissension, Comte suggested to the Jesuits that Catholics join his Religion of Humanity to fight liberals and all forces of "Protestantism, Deism, and Skepticism." Comte proposed a series of books that would develop and apply Positivism and the Religion of Humanity to social problems. Though he finished his political treatise, *Systéme de politique positive* (1851–1854), and the first section of his proposed compendium, the *Synthèse subjective* (1856), Comte died in 1857 before he could complete the series.

*   *   *

No less an admirer than E.E. Evans-Pritchard has called Comte's *Cours* "a monstrosity of 2,582 pages and probably near a million words, and stylistically repellent, which makes its prolixity and didacticism an added aggravation to a test of endurance." Yet Evans-Pritchard goes on to affirm that "this analysis of social evolution will continue to be regarded as one of the great achievements of human intellect."* In this massive work, Comte sets himself two interrelated goals. The first "special" goal is to ground the study of society on a "positive" foundation. The second "general" goal is to review the natural sciences to show how they depend on one another.

In the introduction to this work, reprinted here as the *Introduction to Positive Philosophy,* translated by Frederick Ferré, Comte discusses the first of his two goals. He explains the "great fundamental law, to which the mind is subjected by an invariable necessity": that every conception, every branch of knowledge, in fact, all human history, passes through "three different theoretical states: the theological or fictitious state, the metaphysical or abstract state, and the scientific or positive state." In the past, humans, by necessity, explained the world and themselves in terms of gods. Slowly they began to develop the idea of a single God whose providential actions were responsible for the world of experience. But, says Comte, such theological explanations ultimately proved unsatisfactory as the intellect replaced divinity with first principles and essences. In fact, such a theological method of explanation had been discarded by many, if not most, philosophers and scientists in Comte's day. These thinkers had moved to "metaphysical methods and doctrines as a transitional form of philosophy." At this second stage, the intellect makes itself a god and claims allegiance only to the truths of reason. But this explanation will lead to a breakdown in authority and to social strife.

Comte calls on thinkers to move beyond both stages and to develop a truly "positive" philosophy based entirely on "observed facts." Comte points out that in the field of astronomy, movement from theological to metaphysical to positivistic explanation had long since taken place. Physics, chemistry, and physiology had, for the most part, also moved through the three stages. Yet in the realm

---

*E.E. Evans-Pritchard, *The Sociology of Comte: An Appreciation* (Manchester: Manchester University Press, 1970), pp. 3, 19.

of social phenomena, humankind had not yet moved to positive explanation. Comte argues that only by using positive philosophy to study the human mind and social interactions could there be real social progress. No longer would society be built on the sand of beliefs, but on the rock of facts. Society's problems can never be solved by theological or metaphysical methods. Instead, Comte proposes to "complete the vast intellectual operation commenced by Bacon, Descartes, and Galileo, by furnishing the positive philosophy with the system of general ideas that is destined to prevail henceforth, and for an indefinite future, among the human race. The revolutionary crisis which harasses civilized peoples will then be at an end."

Critics of Comte have been legion. Some have argued that Comte has a mistaken or inconsistent conception of the scientific process. (For example, on the one hand, he acknowledges that science must constantly redefine its "laws," yet he seems to treat these laws as fixed and stable when applied to society.) Others have argued that his approach leaves little room for ethics, while making several illegitimate ethical assumptions. Still others have charged him with errors of fact and have claimed that his anti-Protestant sentiment colored his research. Yet it would be difficult to overstate the importance of this relatively unknown man. Comte is generally acknowledged as the founder of sociology. In addition, his positivism has had followers in every subsequent generation. In this century, for example, the Logical Positivists applied Comte's insights to the study of language. Comte's rejection of metaphysics, his historical understanding of the development of human reason, his denial of traditional religious beliefs, and even, in a modified form, his Religion of Humanity have all had proponents over the years. And echoes of his writings are heard in many contemporary philosophical debates.

*   *   *

For further study of Comte, E.E. Evans-Pritchard's short work, *The Sociology of Comte: An Appreciation* (Manchester: Manchester University Press, 1970), is a good place to begin. Jane M. Style, *Auguste Comte: Thinker and Lover* (London: Kegan Paul, 1928) is the classic biography, whereas Mary Pickering, *Auguste Comte: An Intellectual Biography,* Vol. I (Cambridge: Cambridge University Press, 1993) provides an exhaustive recent work. For general introductions, see F.S. Martin, *Comte: The Founder of Sociology* (New York: Russell & Russell, 1965); George Simpson, *Auguste Comte: Sire of Sociology* (New York: Thomas Y. Crowell, 1969); Arline Reilein Standley, *Auguste Comte* (Boston: Twayne, 1981); and Robert C. Scharff, *Comte After Positivism* (Cambridge: Cambridge University Press, 1995). Studies of Comte's influence include Richard Laurin Hawkings, *Positivism in the United States (1853–1861)* (Cambridge, MA: Harvard University Press, 1938); W.M. Simon, *European Positivism in the Nineteenth Century* (Ithaca, NY: Cornell University Press, 1963); Christopher G.A. Bryant, *Positivism in Social Theory and Research* (London: Macmillan, 1985); and Gillis J. Harp, *The Positivist Republic: Auguste Comte and the Reconstruction of American Liberalism, 1865–1920* (University Park: Pennsylvania State University Press, 1995).

INTRODUCTION TO POSITIVE PHILOSOPHY (in part)

THE NATURE AND IMPORTANCE OF THE POSITIVE PHILOSOPHY

In order to explain properly the true nature and peculiar character of the positive philosophy, it is indispensable that we should first take a brief survey of the progressive growth of the human mind viewed as a whole; for no idea can be properly understood apart from its history.

In thus studying the total development of human intelligence in its different spheres of activity, from its first and simplest beginning up to our own time, I believe that I have discovered a great fundamental law, to which the mind is subjected by an invariable necessity. The truth of this law can, I think, be demonstrated both by reasoned proofs furnished by a knowledge of our mental organization, and by historical verification due to an attentive study of the past. This law consists in the fact that each of our principal conceptions, each branch of our knowledge, passes in succession through three different theoretical states: the theological or fictitious state, the metaphysical or abstract state, and the scientific or positive state. In other words, the human mind—by its very nature—makes use successively in each of its researches of three methods of philosophizing, whose characters are essentially different and even radically opposed to each other. We have first the theological method, then the metaphysical method, and finally the positive method. Hence, there are three kinds of philosophy or general systems of conceptions on the aggregate of phenomena which are mutually exclusive of each other. The first is the necessary starting point of human intelligence; the third represents its fixed and definitive state; the second is destined to serve only as a transitional method.

In the theological state, the human mind directs its researches mainly toward the inner nature of beings, and toward the first and final causes of all the phenomena that it observes—in a word, toward absolute knowledge. It therefore represents these phenomena as being produced by the direct and continuous action of more or less numerous supernatural agents, whose arbitrary intervention explains all the apparent anomalies of the universe.

In the metaphysical state, which is in reality only a simple general modification of the first state, the supernatural agents are replaced by abstract forces, real entities or personified abstractions, inherent in the different beings of the world. These entities are looked upon as capable of giving rise by themselves to all the phenomena observed, each phenomenon being explained by assigning it to its corresponding entity.

Finally, in the positive state, the human mind, recognizing the impossibility of obtaining absolute truth, gives up the search after the origin and hidden causes of the universe and a knowledge of the final causes of phenomena. It endeavours now only to discover, by a well-combined use of reasoning and observation, the actual laws of phenomena—that is to say, their invariable relations of succession and likeness. The ex-

Auguste Comte, *Introduction to Positive Philosophy,* edited with revised translation by Frederick Ferré (New York: Macmillan/Library of the Liberal Arts, 1970).

planation of facts, thus reduced to its real terms, consists henceforth only in the connection established between different particular phenomena and some general facts, the number of which the progress of science tends more and more to diminish.

The theological system arrived at its highest form of perfection when it substituted the providential action of a single being for the varied play of the numerous independent gods which had been imagined by the primitive mind. In the same way, the last stage of the metaphysical system consisted in replacing the different special entities by the idea of a single great general entity—nature—looked upon as the sole source of all phenomena. Similarly, the ideal of the positive system, toward which it constantly tends, although in all probability it will never attain such a stage, would be reached if we could look upon all the different phenomena observable as so many particular cases of a single general fact, such as that of gravitation, for example.

This is not the place to give a special demonstration of this fundamental law of mental development, and to deduce from it its most important consequences. We shall make a direct study of it, with all the necessary details, in the part of this work relating to social phenomena. I am considering it now only in order to determine precisely the true character of the positive philosophy, as opposed to the two other philosophies which have successively dominated our whole intellectual system up to these latter centuries. For the present, to avoid leaving entirely undemonstrated so important a law, the applications of which frequently occur throughout this work, I must confine myself to a rapid enumeration of the most evident general reasons that prove its exactitude.

In the first place, it is, I think, sufficient merely to enunciate such a law for its accuracy to be immediately verified by all those who are fairly well acquainted with the general history of the sciences. For there is not a single science that has today reached the positive stage, which was not in the past—as each can easily see for himself—composed mainly of metaphysical abstractions, and, going back further still, it was altogether under the sway of theological conceptions. Unfortunately, we shall have to recognize on more than one occasion in the different parts of this course, that even the most perfect sciences retain today some very evident traces of these two primitive states.

This general revolution of the human mind can, moreover, be easily verified today in a very obvious, although indirect, manner, if we consider the development of the individual intelligence. The starting point being necessarily the same in the education of the individual as in that of the race, the various principal phases of the former must reproduce the fundamental epochs of the latter. Now, does not each of us in contemplating his own history recollect that he has been successively—as regards the most important ideas—a theologian in childhood, a metaphysician in youth, and a natural philosopher in manhood? This verification of the law can easily be made by all who are on a level with their era.

But in addition to the proofs of the truth of this law furnished by direct observation of the race or the individual, I must, above all, mention in this brief summary the theoretical considerations that show its necessity.

The most important of these considerations arises from the very nature of the subject itself. It consists in the need at every epoch of having some theory to connect the facts, while, on the other hand, it was clearly impossible for the primitive human mind to form theories based on observation.

All competent thinkers agree with Bacon* that there can be no real knowledge except that which rests upon observed facts. This fundamental maxim is evidently indis-

---

*[Francis Bacon (1561–1626), English philosopher largely responsible for laying the modern foundations of experimentalism in science and resolute empiricism in philosophy.]

putable if it is applied, as it ought to be, to the mature state of our intelligence. But, if we consider the origin of our knowledge, it is no less certain that the primitive human mind could not and, indeed, ought not to have thought in that way. For if, on the one hand, every positive theory must necessarily be founded upon observations, it is, on the other hand, no less true that, in order to observe, our mind has need of some theory or other. If in contemplating phenomena we did not immediately connect them with some principles, not only would it be impossible for us to combine these isolated observations and, therefore, to derive any profit from them, but we should even be entirely incapable of remembering the facts, which would for the most part remain unnoted by us.

Thus, there were two difficulties to be overcome: the human mind had to observe in order to form real theories; and yet it had to form theories of some sort before it could apply itself to a connected series of observations. The primitive human mind, therefore, found itself involved in a vicious circle, from which it would never have had any means of escaping if a natural way out of the difficulty had not fortunately been found by the spontaneous development of theological conceptions. These presented a rallying point for the efforts of the mind, and furnished materials for its activity. This is the fundamental motive which demonstrates the logical necessity for the purely theo-logical character of primitive philosophy, apart from those important social considera-tions relating to the matter which I cannot even indicate now.

This necessity becomes still more evident when we regard the perfect congruity of theological philosophy with the peculiar nature of the researches on which the human mind in its infancy concentrated to so high a degree all its efforts. It is, indeed, very noticeable that the most insoluble questions such as the inner nature of objects, or the origin and purpose of all phenomena, are precisely those which the human mind proposes to itself, in preference to all others, in its primitive state, all really soluble problems being looked upon as hardly worthy of serious thought. The reason for this is very obvious, since it is experience alone that has enabled us to estimate our abilities rightly, and, if man had not commenced by overestimating his forces, these would never have been able to acquire all the development of which they are capable. This fact is a necessity of our organization. But, be that as it may, let us picture to ourselves as far as we are able this [early] mental disposition, so universal and so prominent, and let us ask ourselves what kind of reception would have been accorded at such an epoch to the positive philosophy, supposing it to have been then formed. The highest ambi-tion of this philosophy is to discover the laws of phenomena, and its main characteris-tic is precisely that of regarding as necessarily interdicted to the human reason all those sublime mysteries which theological philosophy, on the contrary, explains with such admirable facility, even to the smallest detail. [Under such circumstances, it is easy to see what the choice of primitive man would be.]

The same thing is true when we consider from a practical standpoint the nature of the pursuits with which the human mind first occupies itself. Under that aspect they offer to man the strong attraction of an unlimited control over the exterior world, which is regarded as being entirely destined for our use, while all its phenomena seem to have close and continuous relations with our existence. These chimerical hopes, these exaggerated ideas of man's importance in the universe, to which the theological philosophy gives rise, are destroyed irrevocably by the first fruits of the positive phi-losophy. But at the beginning they afforded an indispensable stimulus without the aid of which we cannot, indeed, conceive how the primitive human mind would have been induced to undertake any arduous labors.

We are at the present time so far removed from that early state of mind—at least as regards the majority of phenomena—that it is difficult for us to appreciate properly the force and necessity of such considerations. Human reason is now so mature that we are able to undertake laborious scientific researches without having in view any extraneous goal capable of strongly exciting the imagination, such as that which the astrologers or alchemists proposed to themselves. Our intellectual activity is sufficiently excited by the mere hope of discovering the laws of phenomena, by the simple desire of verifying or disproving a theory. This, however, could not be the case in the infancy of the human mind. Without the attractive chimeras of astrology, or the powerful deceptions of alchemy, for example, where should we have found the perseverance and ardor necessary for collecting the long series of observations and experiments which later on served as a basis for the first positive theories of these two classes of phenomena?

The need for such a stimulus to our intellectual development was keenly felt long ago by Kepler* in the case of astronomy, and has been justly appreciated in our own time by Berthollet** in chemistry.

The above considerations show us that, although the positive philosophy represents the true final state of human intelligence—that to which it has always tended more and more—it was nonetheless necessary to employ the theological philosophy at first and during many centuries, both as a method and as furnishing provisional doctrines. Because the theological philosophy was spontaneous in its character, it was the only one possible in the beginning; it was also the only one to offer a sufficient interest to our budding intelligence. It is now very easy to see that, in order to pass from this provisional form of philosophy to the final stage, the human mind was naturally obliged to adopt metaphysical methods and doctrines as a transitional form of philosophy. This last consideration is indispensable in order to complete the general sketch of the great law which I have pointed out.

It is easily seen that our understanding, [which was] compelled to progress by almost insensible steps, could not pass suddenly and without any intermediate stages from theological to positive philosophy. Theology and physics are so profoundly incompatible, their conceptions are so radically opposed in character, that, before giving up the one in order to employ the other exclusively, the human intelligence had to make use of intermediate conceptions, which, being of a hybrid character, were eminently fitted to bring about a gradual transition. That is the part played by metaphysical conceptions, and they have no other real use. By substituting, in the study of phenomena, a corresponding inseparable entity for a direct supernatural agency—although at first the former was only held to be an offshoot of the latter—man gradually accustomed himself to consider only the facts themselves. This development was caused by the concepts of metaphysical agents gradually becoming so empty through oversubtle qualification that all right-minded persons considered them to be only the abstract names of the phenomena in question. It is impossible to imagine by what other method our understanding could have passed from frankly supernatural to purely natural considerations, or, in other words, from the theological to the positive regime.

I have thus established, insofar as it is possible without entering into a special discussion, which would be out of place at the present moment, that which I conceive to be the general law of mental development. It will now be easy for us to determine

---

*[Johann Kepler (1571–1630), German astronomer and mathematician; one of the principal founders of modern astronomy through the mathematical formulation of the laws of planetary motion.]

**[Claude Louis Berthollet (1748–1822), French chemist who, with Antoine Lavoisier (1743–1794), reformed modern chemical nomenclature and thus helped to found the modern science of chemistry.]

precisely the exact nature of the positive philosophy. To do that is the special object of this chapter.

We have seen that the fundamental character of the positive philosophy is to consider all phenomena as subject to invariable natural laws. The exact discovery of these laws and their reduction to the least possible number constitute the goal of all our efforts; for we regard the search after what are called causes, whether first or final, as absolutely inaccessible and unmeaning. It is unnecessary to dwell much on a principle that has now become so familiar to all who have made anything like a serious study of the observational sciences. Everybody, indeed, knows that in our positive explanations, even when they are most complete, we do not pretend to explain the real causes of phenomena, as this would merely throw the difficulty further back; we try only to analyze correctly the circumstances of their production, and to connect them by normal relations of succession and similarity.

Thus, to cite the best example, we say that the general phenomena of the universe are explained—as far as they can be—by the Newtonian law of gravitation. On the one hand, this admirable theory shows us all the immense variety of astronomical facts as only a single fact looked at from different points of view, that fact being the constant tendency of all molecules towards each other in direct proportion to their masses and inversely as the squares of their distances. On the other hand, this general fact is shown to be the simple extension of an extremely familiar and, therefore, well-known phenomenon—the weight of a body at the earth's surface. As to determining what attraction and weight are in themselves, or what their causes are—these are questions which we regard as insoluble and outside the domain of the positive philosophy; we, therefore, rightly abandon them to the imagination of the theologians or the subtleties of the metaphysicians. That it is clearly impossible to solve such questions is shown by the fact that, whenever an attempt has been made to give a rational explanation of the matter, the greatest thinkers have only been able to define one of these principles by the other. Attraction is defined as nothing but universal weight, and weight is said to consist simply in terrestrial attraction. Explanations of this kind raise a smile, if put forward as furnishing us with a knowledge of "things-in-themselves" and the mode of causation of phenomena. They are, however, the only satisfactory results obtainable, for they present as identical two orders of phenomena which for so long a time were regarded as unconnected. No sensible person would nowadays seek to go beyond this.

It would be easy to multiply these examples, which will occur very frequently throughout this treatise, for at the present day all great intellectual operations are conducted in this spirit. To take a single example of this from contemporary works, I will choose the fine series of researches made by Fourier* on the theory of heat. This affords us an excellent verification of the preceding general remarks. In this work, the philosophical character of which is so eminently positive, the most important and most precise laws of thermal phenomena are disclosed; but the author has not once inquired into the intimate nature of heat itself, nor has he mentioned, except to point out its uselessness, the vigorous controversy between the partisans of heat as a material substance and those who make it consist in the vibrations of a universal ether. Yet, that work treats of the most important questions, several of which had never been raised—a clear proof that the human mind, by simply confining itself to researches of an entirely positive order, can find therein inexhaustible food for its highest form of activity without attacking inaccessible problems.

*[Jean Baptiste Joseph Fourier (1768–1830), French mathematician and physicist.]

Having thus indicated, insofar as it was possible in this general sketch, the spirit of the positive philosophy, which the whole of this course is intended to develop, we must next consider what stage in the formation of that philosophy has now been reached and what remains to be done in order to constitute it fully.

For this purpose, we must in the first place remember that the different branches of our knowledge were not able to pass at the same rate through the three great phases of their development indicated above, and that consequently they did not arrive simultaneously at the positive state. There exists in this respect an invariable and necessary order that our various classes of conceptions have followed, and were bound to follow, in their progressive course; and the exact consideration of this order is the indispensable complement of the fundamental mental law previously enunciated. That order will form the special subject of the next chapter. At present it is sufficient to know that it conforms to the diverse nature of the phenomena, and that it is determined by their degree of generality, of simplicity, and of reciprocal independence—three considerations which, although quite distinct, lead to the same result. Thus, astronomical phenomena, being the most general, the simplest, and the most independent of all others, were the first to be subjected to positive theories; then followed in succession and for the same reasons the phenomena of terrestrial physics, properly so called, those of chemistry, and, finally, those of physiology.

It is impossible to fix the precise date of this mental revolution; we can say only that, like all other great human events, it took place continuously and at an increasing rate, especially since the labors of Aristotle and the Alexandrian school, and afterward from the introduction of natural science into the west of Europe by the Arabs. However, as it is better to fix an epoch in order to give greater precision to our ideas, I would select that of the great movement imparted to the human intellect two centuries ago by the combined influence of the precepts of Bacon, the conceptions of Descartes,* and the discoveries of Galileo.** It was then that the spirit of the positive philosophy began to assert itself in the world, in evident opposition to the theological and metaphysical spirit; for it was then that positive conceptions disengaged themselves clearly from the superstitious and scholastic alloy, which had more or less disguised the true character of all the previous scientific work.

Since that memorable epoch, the increasing influence of the positive philosophy and the decadent movement of theological and metaphysical philosophy have been extremely marked. These movements have at last become so pronounced that at the present day it is impossible for any observer acquainted with the spirit of his age to fail to recognize the final bent of the human mind toward positive studies, and the irrevocable break henceforth from those fruitless doctrines and provisional methods that were suited only to its first flight. This fundamental mental revolution will, therefore, necessarily be carried out to the fullest extent. If, then, there still remains some great conquest to be made, some important division of the intellectual domain to be invaded, we can be certain that the transformation will take place there also, as it has been carried

---

*[René Descartes (1596–1650), French philosopher and mathematician, largely responsible for shaping the problems of modern philosophy and for emphasizing the rational, mathematical, and theoretical aspects of science and philosophy.]

**[Galileo Galilei (1564–1642), Italian physicist and astronomer, whose combination of inductive with deductive ways of thinking (uniting Bacon and Descartes, as it were) founded the methodology of modern science, and whose discoveries in various fields provided tremendous impetus to early modern science.]

out in all the other branches of science. It would evidently be absurd to suppose that the human mind, which is so disposed to unity of method, would yet preserve indefinitely, in the case of a single class of phenomena, its primitive mode of philosophizing, when it has once adopted for the other classes a new philosophic path of an entirely opposite character.

The whole thing reduces itself, therefore, to a simple question of fact: Does the positive philosophy, which during the last two centuries has gradually acquired so great an extension, embrace at the present day all classes of phenomena? It is evident that it does not; therefore, a great scientific work still remains to be executed in order to give the positive philosophy that universal character indispensable for its final constitution.

In the four principal categories of natural phenomena enumerated above—astronomical, physical, chemical, and physiological—we notice an important omission relating to social phenomena. Although these are implicitly comprised among physiological phenomena, yet, owing to their importance and the inherent difficulties of their study, they deserve to form a distinct class. This last order of ideas is concerned with the most special, most complicated, and most dependent of all phenomena; it has, therefore, necessarily progressed more slowly than all the preceding orders, even if we do not take into account the more special obstacles to its study which we shall consider later on. However that may be, it is evident that it has not yet been included within the domain of positive philosophy. Theological and metaphysical methods are never used now by anyone in dealing with all the other kinds of phenomena, either as a means of investigation or even as a mode of reasoning. But these discarded methods are, on the contrary, still used exclusively for both purposes in everything that concerns social phenomena, although their insufficiency in this respect has been fully felt already by all good minds, such men being tired of these empty and endless discussions between, e.g., divine right and the sovereignty of the people.

Here, then, is the great, but evidently the only, gap that has to be filled in order to finish the construction of the positive philosophy. Now that the human mind has founded celestial physics, terrestrial physics (mechanical and chemical), and organic physics (vegetable and animal), it only remains to complete the system of observational sciences by the foundation of social physics. This is at the present time, under several important aspects, the greatest and most pressing of our cognitive needs, and to meet this need is, I make bold to say, the first purpose of this work, its special object.

The conceptions which I shall endeavor to present relating to the study of social phenomena, and of which I hope the present chapter has already enabled us to see the germ, cannot be expected to raise social physics at once to the degree of perfection that has been reached by the earlier branches of natural philosophy. Such a hope would be evidently chimerical, seeing that these branches still differ widely from one another in perfectness, as was, indeed, inevitable. But I aim at impressing upon this last branch of our knowledge the same positive character that already marks all the other branches. If this condition is once really fulfilled, the philosophical system of the modern world will be founded at last in its entirety; for there is no observable fact that would not then be included in one or another of the five great categories of astronomical, physical, chemical, physiological, and social phenomena. All our fundamental conceptions having thus been rendered homogeneous, philosophy will be constituted finally in the positive state. Its character will be henceforth unchangeable, and it will then have only to develop itself indefinitely, by incorporating the constantly increasing knowledge that inevitably results from new observations or more profound meditations. Having by this means acquired the character of universality which as yet it lacks, the positive philosophy, with all its natural superiority, will be able to displace entirely the theological and metaphysical philosophies. The only real property possessed by theology and metaphysics at the present day is their character of universality, and when deprived of this motive for preference they will have for our successors only a historical interest.

The first and special object of this course having been thus set forth, it is easy to comprehend its second and general aim, that which constitutes it a course of positive philosophy, and not merely a course on social physics.

The formation of social physics at last completes the system of natural sciences. It, therefore, becomes possible and even necessary to summarize these different sciences, so that they may be coordinated by presenting them as so many branches of a single trunk, instead of continuing to look upon them as only so many isolated groups. Therefore, before proceeding to the study of social phenomena, I shall successively consider, in the encyclopedic order given above, the different positive sciences already formed.

It is, I think, unnecessary to warn the reader that I do not claim to give here a series of special courses of lectures on each of the principal branches of natural philosophy. Not to speak of the enormous time that such an enterprise would take, it is clear that I cannot claim to be equipped for it, nor, I think I may add, can anyone else in the present state of human education. On the contrary, a course of the kind contemplated here requires, if it is to be understood properly, a previous series of special studies on the different sciences which will be treated therein. In the absence of this condition, it is very difficult to realize, and impossible to estimate, the philosophical reflections that will be made upon these sciences. In one word, it is a course on positive philosophy, and not on the positive sciences, that I propose to give. We shall have to consider here only each fundamental science in its relations with the whole positive system and the spirit characterizing it; that is to say, under the twofold aspect of its essential methods and its principal achievements. As to the achievements, indeed, I shall often do no more than mention them as known to specialists, though I shall try to estimate their importance.

In order to sum up the ideas relating to the twofold purpose of this course, I must call attention to the two objects—the one special, the other general—that I have in view and that, although distinct in themselves, are necessarily inseparable. On the one hand, it would be impossible to conceive of a course of positive philosophy unless social physics had been founded first, since an essential element would then be lacking; consequently, the conceptions of such a course would not have that character of generality that ought to be their principal attribute and that distinguishes our present study from any series of special studies. On the other hand, how can we proceed with sure step to the positive study of social phenomena if the mind has not been prepared first by the thorough consideration of positive methods in the case of less complex phenomena, and furnished in addition with a knowledge of the principal laws of earlier phenomena, all of which have a more or less direct influence upon social facts?

Although all the fundamental sciences do not inspire ordinary minds with an equal interest, there is not one of them that should be neglected in such a study as we are about to undertake. As regards the welfare of the human race, all of them are certainly of equal importance when we examine them thoroughly. Besides, those whose results seem at first sight to offer only a minor practical interest are yet of the greatest importance, owing to either the greater perfection of their methods or the indispensable foundation of all the others. This is a consideration to which I shall have special occasion to refer in the next chapter.

To guard as far as possible against the misconceptions likely to arise respecting a work as novel as this, I must add a few remarks to the explanations already given. I refer especially to that universal predominance of specialism, which hasty readers might think was the tendency of this course, and which is so rightly looked upon as wholly contrary to the true spirit of the positive philosophy. These remarks, moreover, will have the more important advantage of exhibiting this spirit under a new aspect, calculated to make its general idea clearer.

In the primitive state of our knowledge, no regular division exists among intellectual labors; all the sciences are cultivated simultaneously by the same minds. This method of organizing human studies is at first inevitable and even indispensable, as I shall have occasion to show later on; but it gradually changes in proportion as the different orders of conceptions develop themselves. By a law whose necessity is evident, each branch of the scientific system gradually separates from the trunk when it has developed far enough to admit of separate cultivation—that is to say, when it has arrived at a stage in which it is capable of constituting the sole pursuit of certain minds. It is to this division of the various kinds of research among different orders of scientists that we evidently owe the development which each distinct class of human knowledge has attained in our time; but this very division renders it impossible for modern scientists to practice that simultaneous cultivation of all the sciences which was so easy and so common in antiquity. In a word, the division of intellectual labor, carried out further and further, is one of the most important and characteristic attributes of the positive philosophy.

But, while recognizing the prodigious results due to this division, and while seeing that it henceforth constitutes the true fundamental basis of the general organization of the scientific world, it is, on the other hand, impossible not to be struck by the great inconveniences which it at present produces, because of the excessive specialization of the ideas that exclusively occupy each mind. This unfortunate result, being inherent in the very principle of the division of labor, is no doubt inevitable up to a certain point. Do what we will, therefore, we shall never be able to equal the ancients in this respect, for their general superiority was due to the slight degree of development of their knowledge. Yet, I think we can, by proper means, avoid the most pernicious effects of an exaggerated specialism without doing injury to the fruitful influence of the division of labor in research. There is an urgent need to consider this question seriously, for these inconveniences, which by their very nature tend constantly to increase, are now becoming very apparent. Everyone agrees that the divisions which we establish between the various branches of natural philosophy, in order to make our labors more perfect, are at bottom artificial. In spite of this admission, we must not forget that the number of scientists who study the whole of even a single science is already very small, although such a science is, in its turn, only a part of a greater whole. The majority of scientists already confine themselves entirely to the isolated consideration of a more or less extensive section of a particular science, without concerning themselves much about the relationship between their special work and the general system of positive knowledge. Let us hasten to remedy this evil before it becomes more serious. Let us take care that the human mind does not lose its way in a mass of detail. We must not conceal from ourselves that this is the essentially weak side of our system, and that this is the point on which the partisans of theological and metaphysical philosophy may still attack the positive philosophy with some hope of success.

The true means of arresting the pernicious influence that seems to threaten the intellectual future of mankind, because of too great a specialization of individual researches, is clearly not to return to the ancient confusion of labors. This would tend to put the human mind back; and, besides, such a return has happily become impossible now. The true remedy consists, on the contrary, in perfecting the division of labor itself. All that is necessary is to create one more great speciality, consisting in the study of general scientific traits. We need a new class of properly trained scientists who, instead of devoting themselves to the special study of any particular branch of science, shall employ themselves solely in the consideration of the different positive sciences in their present state. It would be their function to determine exactly the character of each science, to discover the relations and concatenation of the sciences, and to reduce, if possible, all their chief principles to the smallest number of common principles, while always conforming to the fundamental maxims of the positive method. At the same time the other scientists, before devoting themselves to their respective specialities, should have received a previous training embracing all the general principles of positive knowledge. This would enable them henceforth to make immediate use of the light thrown on their work by the scientists devoted to the study of the sciences in general, whose results the specialists would in turn be able to rectify. That is a state of things to which the existing scientists are drawing nearer every day. If these two great conditions were once fulfilled, as they evidently can be, then the division of labor in the sciences could be carried on without any danger as far as the development of the different kinds of knowledge required. There would be a distinct class of men [always open to the critical discipline of all the other classes], whose special and permanent function would consist in connecting each new special discovery with the general system; and we should then have no cause to fear that too great an attention bestowed upon the details would ever prevent us from perceiving the whole. In a word, the modern organization of the scientific world would then be accomplished, and would be susceptible of indefinite development, while always preserving the same character.

To make the study of the universal characteristics of the sciences a distinct department of intellectual labor is merely a further extension of the same principle of division that led to the successive separation of the different sciences. As long as the different positive sciences were only slightly developed, their mutual relations were not important enough to give rise (at all events permanently) to a special discipline, nor was the need of this new study nearly as urgent as it is now. But at the present day each of the sciences has developed on its own lines to such an extent that the examination of a mutual relationship affords material for systematic and continued labor, while at the same time this new order of studies becomes indispensable to prevent the dispersion of human ideas.

Such, in my view, is the office of the positive philosophy in relation to the positive sciences, properly so called. Such, at all events, is the aim of the present work.

*   *   *

To sum up the matter: the theological and metaphysical philosophies are now disputing with each other the task of reorganizing society, although the task is really too hard for their united efforts; it is between these schools only that any struggle still exists in this respect. The positive philosophy has, up to the present, intervened in the contest only in order to criticize both schools; and it has accomplished this task so well as to discredit them entirely. Let us put it in a condition to play an active part, without paying any further attention to debates that have become useless. We must complete the vast intellectual operation commenced by Bacon, Descartes, and Galileo, by furnishing the positive philosophy with the system of general ideas that is destined to prevail henceforth, and for an indefinite future, among the human race. The revolutionary crisis which harasses civilized peoples will then be at an end.

Ludwig Feuerbach
1804–1872

Ludwig Andreas Feuerbach was born into a distinguished family of legal scholars in Landshut, Bavaria. Following primary school in Munich, Feuerbach attended the *Gymnasium* (high school) in Ansbach. As a teenager he showed such interest in religion that at the University of Heidelberg in 1822 he matriculated in theology. Heidelberg religion was heavily influenced by Hegel, and Feuerback soon began to wonder if Hegelian philosophy might be more useful than theology. Feuerbach decided to eliminate the middle-man and go to Berlin to study with Hegel himself. There he gave up theology, determined to become a Hegelian philosopher instead. As he later wrote: "The theological mishmash of freedom and dependence, reason and faith, was completely repellent to my soul with its demand for truth, i.e., [for] unity, decisiveness, absoluteness.*

Following a move to the University of Erlangen for financial reasons, Feuerbach completed his studies in 1828 and became a *docent* in philosophy. Two years later, he published anonymously the book *Thoughts on Death and Immortality,* where he denied an afterlife and argued that the only "immortality" was the transmission of culture. The book was such a scandal that it effectively cut off any possibility of Feuerbach obtaining a chair of philosophy. In 1837 Feuerbach married Bertha Löw, who owned a share of a porcelain factory in Bruckberg. Feuerbach abandoned the attempt to secure a university post and spent the rest of his life as an independent scholar, living off his writings and the factory profits.

For a time Feuerbach reveled in his independence. His early writings sold well as he slowly moved away from Hegel into his own philosophy. In 1841 he

*Letter of 1846 as quoted in Eugene Kamenka, *The Philosophy of Ludwig Feuerbach* (New York: Praeger, 1970), p. 23.

published his most important and controversial work, *The Essence of Christianity*. Those disillusioned with Hegel's conservatism were drawn to Feuerbach's alternative. Karl Marx, among others, found in Feuerbach's emphasis on a this-worldly materialism an effective antidote to Hegel's Idealism.

The revolutions of 1848 changed Feuerbach's fortunes. Radical students at Heidelberg demanded he be given a chair of philosophy. Others called on Feuerbach to stand for the new National Assembly. But with the failure of the revolution and the subsequent conservative backlash, Feuerbach's thought was pushed aside. His books no longer sold and even the porcelain factory began to lose money. By 1860 the business completely failed. Feuerbach and his wife were forced to live off donations from long-time admirers. Feuerbach spent his final years editing his earlier works and fending off creditors. After a stroke in 1870, he died in 1872 in Nuremberg.

* * *

Where Hegel proclaimed that the "real is rational and the rational is real," Feuerbach held that the real is material and the material is real. There is nothing beyond the empirical world of space and time—no eternity, no God, no "other world." Yet Feuerbach denied he was espousing atheism. The philosophers of the Enlightenment had already shown there is no God. The question that remained was this: why is religion so important? Feuerbach wanted to explain the power of religion, to show what it was *really* about.

In our selection from *The Essence of Christianity* (translated by the English novelist, George Eliot), Feuerbach begins by arguing that religion is identical with the self-consciousness of our own nature. Human nature is distinguished by reason, will, and affection. All three propel us towards an object—but, says Feuerbach, "the object to which a subject essentially, necessarily relates, is nothing else than this subject's own, but objective, nature." In religion, we simply take our own human nature, objectify it, and call it "God." So, for example, where *we* are inclined by affection to love, we identify that inclination with an object and declare that "*God* is love." As Feuerbach put it,

> The divine being is nothing else than the human being, or, rather, the human nature purified, freed from the limits of the individual man, made objective—*i.e.*, contemplated and revered as another, a distinct being. All the attributes of the divine nature are, therefore, attributes of the human nature.

Hegel had seen God and humanity as essentially linked, but with humans secondary to God, who alone is the true object. Feuerbach reverses this and says God is an instantiation of the ideals of humanity, and that humans are the only real subject.

Religion, then, is a kind of fantasy—a fantasy that expresses our dependent situation as humans, yet also includes the means for overcoming our limitations. In essence, Feuerbach says, "Man wants to be God, that is the secret source of God; man shall be God, that is [religion's] frank and clearly-expressed ultimate purpose." So religion has the practical purpose of allowing us to overcome ourselves—though it does so through story and through wish-projection. When humanity becomes wiser and more technologically able, it will no longer need this artificial construct of objectified ideals. Religion will quietly die away.

Feuerbach's thought had a profound impact. By attempting to explain *why* religion is influential, without acknowledging anything supernatural, Feuerbach set the stage for Marx and Sigmund Freud. Feuerbach has also been influential on those who believe in a supernatural God. Theologians such as Karl Barth and Martin Buber have accepted much of Feuerbach's critique of "religion" as a social and cultural phenomenon. Barth even recommended Feuerbach to theology students as a prime example of what happens when theology becomes anthropology, when theology "uses" God to promote human projects.

*   *   *

For introductions to Feuerbach's life and thought see Eugene Kamenka, *The Philosophy of Ludwig Feuerbach* (New York: Praeger, 1970) and Marx Wartofsky, *Feuerbach* (Cambridge: Cambridge University Press, 1977). Friedrich Albert Lange, *The History of Materialism* (London: Routledge & Kegan Paul, 1950) and Karl Löwith, *From Hegel to Nietzsche: The Revolution in Nineteenth Century Thought,* translated by David E. Green (New York: Holt, Rinehart & Winston, 1964) are general studies that include significant sections on Feuerbach. Works on the connections between Feuerbach, Hegel, and Marx include Friedrich Engels, *Ludwig Feuerbach and the Outcome of Classical German Philosophy* (London: Lawrence, 1934); Sidney Hook, *From Hegel to Marx: Studies in the Intellectual Development of Karl Marx* (Ann Arbor, MI: University of Michigan Press, 1962); David McLellan, *The Young Hegelians and Karl Marx* (New York: Praeger, 1969); and William J. Brazill, *The Young Hegelians* (New Haven, CT: Yale University Press, 1970). Finally, for a study of Feuerbach's *The Interpretation of Christianity,* see Van A. Harvey, *Feuerbach and the Interpretation of Religion* (Cambridge: Cambridge University Press, 1995).

THE ESSENCE OF CHRISTIANITY

Chapter 1: Introduction.

§ 1. The Essential Nature of Man.

Religion has its basis in the essential difference between man and the brute—the brutes have no religion . . . But what is this essential difference between man and the brute? The most simple, general, and also the most popular answer to this question is—consciousness:—but consciousness in the strict sense; for the consciousness implied in the feeling of self as an individual, in discrimination by the senses, in the perception and even judgment of outward things according to definite sensible signs, cannot be denied to the brutes. Consciousness in the strictest sense is present only in a being to whom his species, his essential nature, is an object of thought. The brute is indeed conscious of himself as an individual—and he has accordingly the feeling of self as the common centre of successive sensations—but not as a species: hence, he is without that consciousness which in its nature, as in its name, is akin to science. Where there is this higher consciousness there is a capability of science. Science is the cognisance of species. In practical life we have to do with individuals; in science, with species. But only a being to whom his own species, his own nature, is an object of thought, can make the essential nature of other things or beings an object of thought.

Hence the brute has only a simple, man a twofold life: in the brute, the inner life is one with the outer; man has both an inner and an outer life. The inner life of man is the life which has relation to his species, to his general, as distinguished from his individual, nature. Man thinks—that is, he converses with himself. The brute can exercise no function which has relation to its species without another individual external to itself; but man can perform the functions of thought and speech, which strictly imply such a relation, apart from another individual. Man is himself at once I and thou; he can put himself in the place of another, for this reason, that to him his species, his essential nature, and not merely his individuality, is an object of thought.

Religion being identical with the distinctive characteristic of man, is then identical with self-consciousness—with the consciousness which man has of his nature. But religion, expressed generally, is consciousness of the infinite; thus it is and can be nothing else than the consciousness which man has of his own—not finite and limited, but infinite nature. A really finite being has not even the faintest adumbration, still less consciousness, of an infinite for the limit of the nature is also the limit of the consciousness. The consciousness of the caterpillar, whose life is confined to a particular species of plant, does not extend itself beyond this narrow domain. It does, indeed, discriminate between this plant and other plants, but more it knows not. A consciousness so limited, but on account of that very limitation so infallible, we do not call consciousness, but instinct. Consciousness, in the strict or proper sense, is identical with consciousness of the infinite; a limited consciousness is no consciousness; consciousness is essentially infinite in its nature. The consciousness of the infinite is nothing else than the consciousness of the infinity of the consciousness; or, in the consciousness of the infinite, the conscious subject has for his object the infinity of his own nature.

What, then, *is* the nature of man, of which he is conscious, or what constitutes the specific distinction, the proper humanity of man?* Reason, Will, Affection. To a complete man belong the power of thought, the power of will, the power of affection. The power of thought is the light of the intellect, the power of will is energy of character, the power of affection is love. Reason, love, force, of will, are perfections—the perfections of the human being—nay, more, they are absolute perfections of being. To will, to love, to think, are the highest powers, are the absolute nature of man as man, and the basis of his existence. Man exists to think, to love, to will. Now that which is the end, the ultimate aim, is also the true basis and principle of a being. But what is the end of reason? Reason. Of love? Love. Of will? Freedom of the will. We think for the sake of thinking; love for the sake of loving; will for the sake of willing—*i.e.*, that we may be free. True existence is thinking, loving, willing existence. That alone is true, perfect, divine, which exists for its own sake. But such is love, such is reason, such is will. The divine trinity in man, above the individual man, is the unity of reason, love, will. Reason, Will, Love, are not powers which man possesses, for he is nothing without them, he is what he is only by them; they are the constituent elements of his nature, which he neither has nor makes, the animating, determining, governing powers—divine, absolute powers—to which he can oppose no resistance.

How can the feeling man resist feeling, the loving one love, the rational one reason? Who has not experienced the overwhelming power of melody? And what else is the power of melody but the power of feeling? Music is the language of feeling; melody is audible feeling—feeling communicating itself. Who has not experienced the power of love, or at least heard of it? Which is the stronger—love or the individual man? Is it man that possesses love, or is it not much rather love that possesses man? When love impels a man to suffer death even joyfully for the beloved one, is this death-conquering power his own individual power, or is it not rather the power of love? And who that ever truly thought has not experienced that quiet, subtle power—the power of thought? When thou sinkest into deep reflection, forgetting thyself and what is around thee, dost thou govern reason, or is it not reason which governs and absorbs thee? Scientific enthusiasm—is it not the most glorious triumph of intellect over thee? The desire of knowledge—is it not a simply irresistible, and all-conquering power? And when thou suppressest a passion, renouncest a habit, in short, achievest a victory over thyself, is this victorious power thy own personal power, or is it not rather the energy of will, the force of morality, which seizes the mastery of thee, and fills thee with indignation against thyself and thy individual weaknesses?

Man is nothing without an object. The great models of humanity, such men as reveal to us what man is capable of, have attested the truth of this proposition by their lives. They had only one dominant passion—the realisation of the aim which was the essential object of their activity. But the object to which a subject essentially, necessarily relates, is nothing else than this subject's own, but objective, nature. If it be an object common to several individuals of the same species, but under various conditions, it is still, at least as to the form tinder which it presents itself to each of them according to their respective modifications, their own, but objective, nature.

Thus the Sun is the common object of the planets, but it is an object to Mercury, to Venus, to Saturn, to Uranus, under other conditions than to the Earth. Each planet

*The obtuse Materialist says: "Man is distinguished from the brute *only* by consciousness—he is an animal with consciousness superadded" not reflecting, that in a being which awakes to consciousness, there takes place a qualitative change, a differentiation of the entire nature. For the rest, our words are by no means intended to depreciate the nature of the lower animals. This is not the place to enter further into that question.

has its own sun. The Sun which lights and warms Uranus has no physical (only an astronomical, scientific) existence for the Earth; and not only does the Sun appear different, but it really is another sun on Uranus than on the Earth. The relation of the Sun to the Earth is therefore at the same time a relation of the Earth to itself, or to its own nature, for the measure of the size and of the intensity of light which the Sun possesses as the object of the Earth is the measure of the distance which determines the peculiar nature of the Earth. Hence each planet has in its sun the mirror of its own nature.

In the object which he contemplates, therefore, man becomes acquainted with himself; consciousness of the objective is the self-consciousness of man. We know the man by the object, by his conception of what is external to himself; in it his nature becomes evident; this object is his manifested nature, his true objective *ego*. And this is true not merely of spiritual, but also of sensuous objects. Even the objects which are the most remote from man, because they are objects to him, and to the extent to which they are so, are revelations of human nature. Even the moon, the sun, the stars, call to man ⟨*Gnosi seautov*⟩ ["Know yourself"]. That he sees them, and so sees them, is an evidence of his own nature. The animal is sensible only of the beam which immediately affects life; while man perceives the ray, to him physically indifferent, of the remotest star. Man alone has purely intellectual, disinterested joys and passions; the eye of man alone keeps theoretic festivals. The eye which looks into the starry heavens, which gazes at that light, alike useless and harmless, having nothing in common with the earth and its necessities—this eye sees in that light its own nature, its own origin. The eye is heavenly in its nature. Hence man elevates himself above the earth only with the eye; hence theory begins with the contemplation of the heavens. The first philosophers were astronomers. It is the heavens that admonish man of his destination, and remind him that he is destined not merely to action, but also to contemplation.

The *absolute* to man is his own nature. The power of the object over him is therefore the power of his own nature. Thus the power of the object of feeling is the power of feeling itself; the power of the object of the intellect is the power of the intellect itself; the power of the object of the will is the power of the will itself. The man who is affected by musical sounds is governed by feeling; by the feeling, that is, which finds its corresponding element in musical sounds. But it is not melody as such, it is only melody pregnant with meaning and emotion, which has power over feeling. Feeling is only acted on by that which conveys feeling, *i.e.,* by itself, its own nature. Thus also the will; thus, and infinitely more, the intellect. Whatever kind of object, therefore, we are at any time conscious of, we are always at the same time conscious of our own nature; we can affirm nothing without affirming ourselves. And since to will, to feel, to think, are perfections, essences, realities, it is impossible that intellect, feeling, and will should feel or perceive themselves as limited, finite powers, *i.e.,* as worthless, as nothing. For finiteness and nothingness are identical; finiteness is only a euphemism for nothingness. Finiteness is the metaphysical, the theoretical—nothingness the pathological, practical expression. What is finite to the understanding is nothing to the heart. But it is impossible that we should be conscious of will, feeling, and intellect, as finite powers, because every perfect existence, every original power, and essence, is the immediate verification and affirmation of itself. It is impossible to love, will, or think, without perceiving these activities to be perfections—impossible to feel that one is a loving, willing, thinking being, without experiencing an infinite joy therein. Consciousness consists in a being becoming objective to itself; hence it is nothing apart, nothing distinct from the being which is conscious of itself. How could it otherwise become conscious of itself? It is therefore impossible to be conscious of a perfection as an imperfection, impossible to feel feeling limited, to think thought limited.

Consciousness is self-verification, self-affirmation, self-love, joy in one's own perfection. Consciousness is the characteristic mark of a perfect nature; it exists only in a self-sufficing, complete being. Even human vanity attests this truth. A man looks in the glass—he has complacency in his appearance. This complacency is a necessary, involuntary consequence of the completeness, the beauty of his form. A beautiful form is satisfied in itself; it has necessarily joy in itself—in self-contemplation. This complacency becomes vanity only when a man piques himself on his form as being his individual form, not when he admires it as a specimen of human beauty in general. It is fitting that he should admire it thus: he can conceive no form more beautiful, more sublime than the human. Assuredly every being loves itself, its existence—and fitly so. To exist is a good . . . Everything that exists has value, is a being of distinction—at least this is true of the species: hence it asserts, maintains itself. But the highest form of self-assertion, the form which is itself a superiority, a perfection, a bliss, a good, is consciousness.

Every limitation of the reason, or in general of the nature of man, rests on a delusion, an error. It is true that the human being, as an individual, can and must—herein consists his distinction from the brute—feel and recognise himself to be limited; but he can become conscious of his limits) his finiteness, only because the perfection, the infinitude of his species, is perceived by him, whether as an object of feeling of conscience, or of the thinking consciousness. If he makes his own limitations the limitations of the species, this arises from the mistake that he identifies himself immediately with the species—a mistake which is intimately connected with the individual's love of ease, sloth, vanity, and egoism. For a limitation which I know to be merely mine humiliates, shames, and perturbs me. Hence to free myself from this feeling of shame, from this state of dissatisfaction, I convert the limits of my individuality into the limits of human nature in general. What is incomprehensible to me is incomprehensible to others; why should I trouble myself further? It is no fault of mine; my understanding is not to blame, but the understanding of the race. But it is a ludicrous and even culpable error to define as finite and limited what constitutes the essence of man, the nature of the species, which is the absolute nature of the individual. Every being is sufficient to itself. No being can deny itself, *i.e.,* its own nature; no being is a limited one to itself. Rather, every being is in and by itself infinite—has its God, its highest conceivable being, in itself. Every limit of a being is cognisable only by another being out of and above him. The life of the ephemera is extraordinarily short in comparison with that of longer-lived creatures; but nevertheless, for the ephemera this short life is as long as a life of years to others. The leaf on which the caterpillar lives is for it a world, an infinite space.

That which makes a being what it is, is its talent, its power, its wealth, its adornment. How can it possibly hold its existence non-existence, its wealth poverty, its talent incapacity? If the plants had eyes, taste, and judgment, each plant would declare its own flower the most beautiful; for its comprehension, its taste, would reach no farther than its natural power of production. What the productive power of its nature has brought forth as the highest, that must also its taste, its judgment, recognise and affirm as the highest. What the nature affirms, the understanding, the taste, the judgment, cannot deny; otherwise the understanding, the judgment, would no longer be the understanding and judgment of this particular being, but of some other. The measure of the nature is also the measure of the understanding. If the nature is limited, so also is the feeling, so also is the understanding. But to a limited being its limited understanding is not felt to be a limitation; on the contrary, it is perfectly happy and contented with this understanding; it regards it, praises and values it, as a glorious, divine power; and the limited understanding, on its part, values the limited nature whose understanding it is. Each is exactly adapted to the other; how should they be at issue with each other? A being's understanding is its sphere of vision. As far as thou seest, so far extends thy nature; and conversely. The eye of the brute reaches no farther than its needs, and its nature no farther than its needs. And so far as thy nature reaches, so far reaches thy unlimited self-consciousness, so far art thou God. The discrepancy between the understanding and the nature, between the power of conception and the power of production in the human consciousness, on the one hand, is merely of individual significance and has not a universal application; and, on the other hand, it is Only apparent. He who, having written a bad poem, knows it to be bad, is in his intelligence, and therefore in his nature, not so limited as he who, having written a bad poem, admires it and thinks it good.

It follows that if thou thinkest the infinite, thou perceivest and affirmest the infinitude of the power of thought; if thou feelest the infinite, thou feelest and affirmest the infinitude of the power of feeling. The object of the intellect is intellect objective to itself; the object of feeling is feeling objective to itself. If thou hast no sensibility, no feeling for music, thou perceivest in the finest music nothing more than in the wind that whistles by thy ear, or than in the brook which rushes past thy feet. What, then, is it which acts on thee when thou art affected by melody? What dost thou perceive in it? What else than the voice of thy own heart? Feeling speaks only to feeling; feeling is comprehensible only by feeling, that is, by itself—for this reason, that the object of feeling is nothing else than feeling. Music is a monologue of emotion. But the dialogue of philosophy also is in truth only a monologue of the intellect; thought speaks only to thought. The splendours of the crystal charm the sense, but the intellect is interested only in the laws of crystallisation. The intellectual only is the object of the intellect.*

All therefore which, in the point of view of metaphysical, transcendental speculation and religion, has the significance only of the secondary, the subjective, the medium, the organ—has in truth the significance of the primary, of the essence, of the object itself. If, for example, feeling is the essential organ of religion, the nature of God is nothing else than an expression of the nature of feeling. The true but latent sense of the phrase, "Feeling is the organ of the divine," is, feeling is the noblest, the most excellent, *i.e.,* the divine, in man. How couldst thou perceive the divine by feeling, if feeling were not itself divine in its nature? The divine assuredly is known only by means of the divine—God is known only by himself. The divine nature which is discerned by feeling is in truth nothing else than feeling enraptured, in ecstasy with itself—feeling intoxicated with joy, blissful in its own plenitude.

It is already clear from this that where feeling is held to be the organ of the infinite, the subjective essence of religion,—the external data of religion lose their objective value. And thus, since feeling has been held the cardinal principle in religion, the doctrines of Christianity, formerly so sacred, have lost their importance. If, from this point of view, some value is still conceded to Christian ideas, it is a value springing entirely from the relation they bear to feeling; if another object would excite the same emotions, it would be just as welcome. But the object of religious feeling is become a matter of indifference, only because when once feeling has been pronounced to be the subjective essence of religion, it in fact is also the objective essence of religion, though it may not be declared, at least directly, to be such. I say directly; for indirectly this is certainly admitted, when it is declared that feeling, as such, is religious, and thus the distinction between specifically religious and irreligious, or at least non-religious, feel-

---

*"The understanding is percipient only of understanding, and what proceeds thence."—Reimarus (*Wahrh. der Naturl. Religion*, iv. Abth. § 8).

ings is abolished—a necessary consequence of the point of view in which feeling only is regarded as the organ of the divine. For on what other ground than that of its essence, its nature, dost thou hold feeling to be the organ of the infinite, the divine being? And is not the nature of feeling in general also the nature of every special feeling, be its object what it may? What, then, makes this feeling religious? A given object? Not at all; for this object is itself a religious one only when it is not an object of the cold understanding or memory, but of feeling. What then? The nature of feeling—a nature of which every special feeling, without distinction of objects, partakes. Thus, feeling is pronounced to be religious, simply because it is feeling; the ground of its religiousness is its own nature—lies in itself. But is not feeling thereby declared to be itself the absolute, the divine? If feeling in itself is good, religious, *i.e.*, holy, divine, has not feeling its God in itself?

But if, notwithstanding thou wilt posit an object of feeling, but at the same time seekest to express thy feeling truly, without introducing by thy reflection any foreign element, what remains to thee but to distinguish between thy individual feeling and the general nature of feeling;—to separate the universal in feeling from the disturbing, thy adulterating influences with which feeling is bound up in thee, under thy individual conditions? Hence what thou canned alone contemplate, declare to be the infinite, and define as its essence, is merely the nature of feeling. Thou hast thus no other definition of God than this: God is pure, unlimited, free Feeling. Every other God, whom thou supposest, is a God thrust upon thy feeling from without. Feeling is atheistic in the sense of the orthodox belief, which attaches religion to an external object; it denies an objective God—it is itself God. In this point of view only the negation of feeling is the negation of God. Thou art simply too cowardly or too narrow to confess in words what thy feeling tacitly affirms. Fettered by outward considerations, still in bondage to vulgar empiricism, incapable of comprehending the spiritual grandeur of feeling thou art terrified before the religious atheism of thy heart. By this fear thou destroyest the unity of thy feeling with itself, in imagining to thyself an objective being distinct from thy feeling, and thus necessarily sinking back into the old questions and doubts—is there a God or not?—questions and doubts which vanish, nay, are impossible, where feeling is defined as the essence of religion. Feeling is thy own inward power, but at the same time a power distinct from thee, and independent of thee; it is in thee, above thee; it is itself that which constitutes the objective in thee—thy own which impresses thee as another being; in short, thy God. How wilt thou, then, distinguish from this objective being within thee another objective being? how wilt thou get beyond thy feeling?

But feeling has here been adduced only as an example. It is the same with every other power, faculty, potentiality, reality, activity—the name is indifferent—which is defined as the essential organ of any object. Whatever is a subjective expression of a nature is simultaneously also its objective expression. Man cannot get beyond his true nature. He may indeed by means of the imagination conceive individuals of another so-called higher kind, but he can never get loose from his species, his nature; the conditions of being the positive final predicates which he gives to these other individuals, are always determinations or qualities drawn from his own nature—qualities in which he in truth only images and projects himself. There may certainly be thinking beings besides men on the other planets of our solar system. But by the supposition of such beings we do not change our standing point—we extend our conceptions *quantitatively* not *qualitatively*. For as surely as all the other planets there are the same laws of motion, so surely are there the same laws of perception and thought as here. In fact, we people the other planets, not that we may place there different beings from ourselves, but more beings of our own or of a similar nature.

JOHN STUART MILL
1806–1873

John Stuart Mill was born in London, the eldest of James and Harriet Burrow Mill's nine children. His father, a well-known philosopher and follower of Jeremy Bentham, educated young John at home. Beginning with Greek at age three and Latin at age eight, the younger Mill had read six of Plato's dialogues by the age of ten. John spent most of the day in the study with his father, who was writing a history of India. Each morning, they would go on a walk and James would quiz his son on what he had learned the previous day. During these walks, James would often discourse on various topics and then expect his son to prepare a summary of his points for the following day. Given the severity of this schooling—and the fact that his father showed no "signs of feeling"—it is not surprising that John later concluded, "I never was a boy."

The publication of the elder Mill's work on India in 1818 resulted in his receiving a government post as an Assistant Examiner at the East India House. Five years later, James managed to arrange a similar position for his seventeen-year-old son. John worked for the East India House for the next thirty-four years, eventually becoming chief of his department. In his early years as a clerk, John was, like his father, a disciple of Bentham's utilitarianism. John established the Utilitarian Society, contributed articles to the *Westminster Review,* and was active in the London Debating Society. He was developing a reputation as a polemicist for the "philosophic radicals"—those who sought social changes along the lines of Bentham's theories.

But in 1826, at age twenty, Mill suffered a breakdown and went through a period of severe depression. He discovered to his horror that even if all the social changes he advocated were enacted and all the ideas he was taught about happiness were proven correct, it would not make *him* happy. As he later wrote in his *Autobiography*, "All my happiness was to have been found in the continual pursuit of this end. The end had ceased to charm, and how could there ever again be any interest in the means? I seemed to have nothing left to live for." He eventually came to the conclusion that his rigorous intellectual training had weakened his ability to feel emotion. Reading such writers as Wordsworth and Coleridge, he began to teach himself to feel as his father had taught him to think. During this period, he encountered divergent philosophies, such as those of socialist philosopher Claude-Henry Saint-Simon and positivist thinker Auguste Comte, and he began to see some of the inadequacies of the strict quantificational method of Bentham.

In 1831, Mill was introduced to Harriet Taylor, the wife of a successful merchant. They quickly developed a strong friendship and collaborated on a number of works, including *Principles of Political Economy, On Liberty,* and *The Subjection of Women.* Mill attributed to Taylor a number of his most important ideas, including his liberal feminism, and claimed that next to his father, she was the chief intellectual influence on his life. He even claimed she was the inspiration for his major epistemological work, *A System of Logic* (1843). Following her husband's death in 1849, they were finally married in 1851.

John and Harriet Mill moved to Avignon, France, in 1858, with neither of them in good health. Shortly after arriving, Harriet Taylor Mill died, and her daughter came to take care of her stepfather. Over the next seven years, Mill published *On Liberty* (1859), *Utilitarianism* (1861), *Considerations on Representative Government* (1861), *Auguste Comte and Positivism* (1865), and *The Subjection of Women* (written 1861, published 1869). In 1865, Mill was surprised by an offer to run for Parliament. Without campaigning he was elected and spent two years working on behalf of women's suffrage, Irish land reform, and the rights of blacks in Jamaica. Returning once again to the south of France, he wrote his *Autobiography* just before dying in 1873.

*   *   *

Although Mill wrote on a variety of topics and his work in induction is still used today, he is best known for his modification of Bentham's utilitarianism and his defense of individual liberty. Bentham had taught that ethics should be grounded on maximizing pleasure and minimizing pain, rather than on such abstractions as Kant's "duty" or conscience. Accordingly, Bentham developed a "hedonistic calculus," a mathematical method of determining which actions would most likely provide a greater quantity of pleasure over pain and hence yield happiness. Whereas this system might seem egoistic and individualistic, Bentham claimed that it would be to each individual person's advantage to seek the "greatest happiness of the greatest number."

In his *Utilitarianism,* given here (complete), Mill accepts Bentham's quantitative hedonism and argues that happiness, or pleasure, is the one thing that all people seek. But whereas Bentham's system merely measured quantities of pleasure and pain, Mill maintains that the *quality* of a given pleasure or pain has to be considered as well. Even though a pig might gain a great *quantity* of pleasure from wallowing in the mud, it would be a very low *quality* pleasure; and "It is better to be a human being dissatisfied than a pig satisfied; better to be Socrates dissatisfied than a fool satisfied." According to Mill, the person best able to make a qualitative determination between rival pleasures is the one who has experienced both. Presumably anyone who has both wallowed in the mud *and* studied philosophy would prefer the difficult but fulfilling pleasures of the latter.

In *On Liberty,* Mill asserts that society should maximize individual liberty. In fact, he claims that "the only purpose for which power can be rightfully exercised over any member of a civilized community, against his will, is to prevent harm to others." What an individual does in private does not concern society—even if such actions are not to that individual's own best interests. "Over himself, over his own body and mind, the individual is sovereign," and society should make no paternalistic rules.

On the Subjection of Women (portions of the first chapter are reprinted here) applies this liberal theory to women. This work points out that for centuries women have been subordinated to men and hence excluded from the kinds of individual choices that *On Liberty* extols. Such subjection is "one of the chief hindrances to human improvement" and only "a principle of perfect equality" will rectify the situation. This work was written in collaboration with Harriet Taylor Mill. Scholars are divided as to how much Mill relied on Taylor—some go so far as to suggest that the work was actually "ghost-written" by her. Whether or not one accepts that assertion, there is no question that her ideas greatly influenced Mill's version of feminism. Yet Mill never did accept her contention that women should be able to work outside the home after marriage.

Mill's contemporary critics pointed out that there seem to be discrepancies between the philosophy of *Utilitarianism* and that of *On Liberty* and *On the Subjection of Women*. For example, following the greatest happiness principle of *Utilitarianism,* wouldn't it make sense for society to increase general happiness by intruding on an individual's liberty? Mill countered this objection by arguing that on balance *laissez-faire* individualism will ultimately benefit society, that the diversity of individual choices is more conducive to general happiness than any socially imposed standard.

More recent critics have questioned Mill's distinction between private and public—for example, what you choose to do to yourself in the privacy of your home may cost the public money if you end up in a tax-supported hospital. Feminist critics have pointed out the potential oppression of the private/public distinction, questioned the possibility of "perfect equality" if paternalistic structures continue, and assailed Mill's "equal opportunity until marriage" doctrine. But there is no question that as a reforming impulse, Mill's beliefs—about the rights of the individual, the rights of women and minorities, freedom from societal intrusion into personal affairs, and utility rather than tradition—have had an enormous influence.

*   *   *

There are several good overviews of Mill's life and thought, including R.P. Anschutz, *The Philosophy of John Stuart Mill* (Oxford: Oxford University Press, 1953); Karl Britton, *John Stuart Mill* (1953; reprinted New York: Dover, 1969); Alan Ryan, *J.S. Mill* (London: Routledge & Kegan Paul, 1974); and William Thomas, *Mill* (Oxford: Oxford University Press, 1985). F.A. Hayek, *John Stuart Mill and Harriet Taylor* (Chicago: University of Chicago Press, 1951) presents a study of Mill's relationship with Harriet Taylor. For a critical evaluation of his work, see H.J. McCloskey, *John Stuart Mill: A Critical Study* (London: Macmillan, 1971). Guides to specific works of Mill include John Gray and G.W. Smith, eds., *J.S. Mill's "On Liberty" in Focus* (London: Routledge, 1991); and Roger Crisp, *Routledge Philosophy Guidebook to Mill's Utilitarianism* (London: Routledge, 1997). For more specialized studies, see Dennis F. Thompson, *John Stuart Mill and Representative Government* (Princeton, NJ: Princeton University Press, 1976); Gertrude Himmelfarb, *On Liberty and Liberalism: The Case of John Stuart Mill* (New York: Knopf, 1974); and Andrew Pyle's pair of books, *Liberty: Contemporary Responses to John Stuart Mill* and *The Subjection of Women: Contemporary Responses to John Stuart Mill* (both Bristol, UK: Thoemmes Press, 1994 and 1995). For collections of essays, see J.B. Schneewind, ed., *Mill: A Collection of Critical Essays* (Garden City, NY: Anchor Doubleday, 1968), J.M. Smith and E. Sosa, eds., *Mill's Utilitarianism* (Belmont, CA: Wadsworth, 1969); John Skorupski, ed., *The Cambridge Companion to Mill* (Cambridge: Cambridge University Press, 1997) and G. W. Smith, ed., *John Stuart Mill's Social and Political Thought: Critical Assessments;* four volumes (London: Routledge, 1998).

UTILITARIANISM

CHAPTER 1: GENERAL REMARKS

There are few circumstances among those which make up the present condition of human knowledge, more unlike what might have been expected, or more significant of the backward state in which speculation on the most important subjects still lingers, than the little progress which has been made in the decision of the controversy respecting the criterion of right and wrong. From the dawn of philosophy, the question concerning the *summum bonum,* or, what is the same thing, concerning the foundation of morality, has been accounted the main problem in speculative thought, has occupied the most gifted intellects, and divided them into sects and schools, carrying on a vigorous warfare against one another. And after more than two thousand years the same discussions continue, philosophers are still ranged under the same contending banners, and neither thinkers nor mankind at large seem nearer to being unanimous on the subject, than when the youth Socrates listened to the old Protagoras, and asserted (if Plato's dialogue be grounded on a real conversation) the theory of utilitarianism against the popular morality of the so-called sophist.

It is true that similar confusion and uncertainty, and in some cases similar discordance, exist respecting the first principles of all the sciences, not excepting that which is deemed the most certain of them, mathematics; without much impairing, generally indeed without impairing at all, the trustworthiness of the conclusions of those sciences. An apparent anomaly, the explanation of which is, that the detailed doctrines of a science are not usually deduced from, nor depend for their evidence upon, what are called its first principles. Were it not so, there would be no science more precarious, or whose conclusions were more insufficiently made out, than algebra; which derives none of its certainty from what are commonly taught to learners as its elements, since these, as laid down by some of its most eminent teachers, are as full of fictions as English law, and of mysteries as theology. The truths which are ultimately accepted as the first principles of a science, are really the last results of metaphysical analysis, practised on the elementary notions with which the science is conversant; and their relation to the science is not that of foundations to an edifice, but of roots to a tree, which may perform their office equally well though they be never dug down to and exposed to light. But though in science the particular truths precede the general theory, the contrary might be expected to be the case with a practical art, such as morals or legislation. All action is for the sake of some end, and rules of action, it seems natural to suppose, must take their whole character and colour from the end to which they are subservient. When we engage in a pursuit, a clear and precise conception of what we are pursuing would seem to be the first thing we need, instead of the last we are to look forward to. A test of right and wrong must be the means, one would think, of ascertaining what is right or wrong, and not a consequence of having already ascertained it.

The difficulty is not avoided by having recourse to the popular theory of a natural faculty, a sense or instinct, informing us of right and wrong. For—besides that the existence of such a moral instinct is itself one of the matters in dispute—those believers in it who have any pretensions to philosophy, have been obliged to abandon the idea that it discerns what is right or wrong in the particular case in hand, as our other senses discern the sight or sound actually present. Our moral faculty, according to all those of its interpreters who are entitled to the name of thinkers, supplies us only with the general principles of moral judgments; it is a branch of our reason, not of our sensitive faculty; and must be looked to for the abstract doctrines of morality, not for perception of it in the concrete. The intuitive, no less than what may be termed the inductive, school of ethics, insists on the necessity of general laws. They both agree that the morality of an individual action is not a question of direct perception, but of the application of a law to an individual case. They recognise also, to a great extent, the same moral laws; but differ as to their evidence, and the source from which they derive their authority. According to the one opinion, the principles of morals are evident *a priori,* requiring nothing to command assent, except that the meaning of the terms be understood. According to the other doctrine, right and wrong, as well as truth and falsehood, are questions of observation and experience. But both hold equally that morality must be deduced from principles; and the intuitive school affirm as strongly as the inductive, that there is a science of morals. Yet they seldom attempt to make out a list of the *a priori* principles which are to serve as the premises of the science; still more rarely do they make any effort to reduce those various principles to one first principle, or common ground of obligation. They either assume the ordinary precepts of morals as of *a priori* authority, or they lay down as the common groundwork of those maxims, some generality much less obviously authoritative than the maxims themselves, and which has never succeeded in gaining popular acceptance. Yet to support their pretensions there ought either to be some one fundamental principle or law, at the root of all morality, or if there be several, there should be a determinate order of precedence among them; and the one principle, or the rule for deciding between the various principles when they conflict, ought to be self-evident.

To inquire how far the bad effects of this deficiency have been mitigated in practice, or to what extent the moral beliefs of mankind have been vitiated or made uncertain by the absence of any distinct recognition of an ultimate standard, would imply a complete survey and criticism of past and present ethical doctrine. It would, however, be easy to show that whatever steadiness or consistency these moral beliefs have attained, has been mainly due to the tacit influence of a standard not recognised. Although the non-existence of an acknowledged first principle has made ethics not so much a guide as a consecration of men's actual sentiments, still, as men's sentiments, both of favour and of aversion, are greatly influenced by what they suppose to be the effects of things upon their happiness, the principle of utility, or as Bentham latterly called it, the Greatest Happiness Principle, has had a large share in forming the moral doctrines even of those who most scornfully reject its authority. Nor is there any school of thought which refuses to admit that the influence of actions on happiness is a most material and even predominant consideration in many of the details of morals, however unwilling to acknowledge it as the fundamental principle of morality, and the source of moral obligation. I might go much further, and say that to all those *a priori* moralists who deem it necessary to argue at all, utilitarian arguments are indispensable. It is not my present purpose to criticise these thinkers; but I cannot help referring, for illustration, to a systematic treatise by one of the most illustrious of them, the *Metaphysics of Ethics* by Kant. This remarkable man, whose system of thought will long remain one of the landmarks in the history of philosophical speculation, does, in the treatise in question, lay down a universal first principle as the origin and ground of moral obligation; it is this:—"So act, that the rule on which thou actest would admit of being adopted as a law by all rational beings." But when he begins to deduce from this precept any of the actual duties of morality, he fails, almost grotesquely, to show that there would be any contradiction, any logical (not to say physical) impossibility, in the adoption by all rational beings of the most outrageously immoral rules of conduct. All he shows is that the *consequences* of their universal adoption would be such as no one would choose to incur.

On the present occasion, I shall, without further discussion of the other theories, attempt to contribute something towards the understanding and appreciation of the Utilitarian or Happiness theory, and towards such proof as it is susceptible of. It is evident that this cannot be proof in the ordinary and popular meaning of the term. Questions of ultimate ends are not amenable to direct proof. Whatever can be proved to be good, must be so by being shown to be a means to something admitted to be good without proof. The medical art is proved to be good by its conducing to health; but how is it possible to prove that health is good? The art of music is good, for the reason, among others, that it produces pleasure; but what proof is it possible to give that pleasure is good? If, then, it is asserted that there is a comprehensive formula, including all things which are in themselves good, and that whatever else is good, is not so as an end, but as a mean, the formula may be accepted or rejected, but is not a subject of what is commonly understood by proof. We are not, however, to infer that its acceptance or rejection must depend on blind impulse, or arbitrary choice. There is a larger meaning of the word proof, in which this question is as amenable to it as any other of the disputed questions of philosophy. The subject is within the cognisance of the rational faculty; and neither does that faculty deal with it solely in the way of intuition. Considerations may be presented capable of determining the intellect either to give or withhold its assent to the doctrine; and this is equivalent to proof.

We shall examine presently of what nature are these considerations; in what manner they apply to the case, and what rational grounds, therefore, can be given for accepting or rejecting the utilitarian formula. But it is a preliminary condition of rational acceptance or rejection, that the formula should be correctly understood. I believe that the very imperfect notion ordinarily formed of its meaning, is the chief obstacle which impedes its reception; and that could it be cleared, even from only the grosser misconceptions, the question would be greatly simplified, and a large proportion of its difficulties removed. Before, therefore, I attempt to enter into the philosophical grounds which can be given for assenting to the utilitarian standard, I shall offer some illustrations of the doctrine itself; with the view of showing more clearly what it is, distinguishing it from what it is not, and disposing of such of the practical objections to it as either originate in, or are closely connected with, mistaken interpretations of its meaning. Having thus prepared the ground, I shall afterwards endeavour to throw such light as I can upon the question, considered as one of philosophical theory.

Chapter 2: What Utilitarianism Is

A passing remark is all that needs be given to the ignorant blunder of supposing that those who stand up for utility as the test of right and wrong, use the term in that restricted and merely colloquial sense in which utility is opposed to pleasure. An apology is due to the philosophical opponents of utilitarianism, for even the momentary appearance of confounding them with any one capable of so absurd a misconception; which is the more extraordinary, inasmuch as the contrary accusation, of referring everything to pleasure, and that too in its grossest form, is another of the common charges against utilitarianism: and, as has been pointedly remarked by an able writer, the same sort of persons, and often the very same persons, denounce the theory "as impracticably dry when the word 'utility' precedes the word 'pleasure,' and as too practicably voluptuous when the word 'pleasure' precedes the word 'utility.'" Those who know anything about the matter are aware that every writer, from Epicurus to Bentham, who maintained the theory of utility, meant by it, not something to be contradistinguished from pleasure, but pleasure itself, together with exemption from pain; and instead of opposing the useful to the agreeable or the ornamental, have always declared that the useful means these, among other things. Yet the common herd, including the herd of writers, not only in newspapers and periodicals, but in books of weight and pretension, are perpetually falling into this shallow mistake. Having caught up the word Utilitarian, while knowing nothing whatever about it but its sound, they habitually express by it the rejection, or the neglect, of pleasure in some of its forms; of beauty, of ornament, or of amusement. Nor is the term thus ignorantly misapplied solely in disparagement, but occasionally in compliment; as though it implied superiority to frivolity and the mere pleasures of the moment. And this perverted use is the only one in which the word is popularly known, and the one from which the new generation are acquiring their sole notion of its meaning. Those who introduced the word, but who had for many years discontinued it as a distinctive appellation, may well feel themselves called upon to resume it, if by doing so they can hope to contribute anything towards rescuing it from this utter degradation.*

The creed which accepts as the foundation of morals Utility or the Greatest Happiness Principle holds that actions are right in proportion as they tend to promote happiness, wrong as they tend to produce the reverse of happiness. By happiness is intended pleasure, and the absence of pain; by unhappiness, pain, and the privation of pleasure. To give a clear view of the moral standard set up by the theory, much more requires to be said; in particular, what things it includes in the ideas of pain and plea-

*The author of this essay has reason for believing himself to be the first person who brought the word "utilitarian" into use. He did not Invent it, but adopted It from a passing expression in Mr. Galt's *Annals of the Parish*. After using it as a designation for several years, he and others abandoned it from a growing dislike to anything resembling a badge or watchword of sectarian distinction. But as a name for one single opinion, not a set of opinions—to denote the recognition of utility as a standard not any particular way of applying it—the term supplies a want in the language, and offers, in many cases, a convenient mode of avoiding tiresome circumlocution.

sure; and to what extent this is left an open question. But these supplementary explanations do not affect the theory of life on which this theory of morality is grounded—namely, that pleasure, and freedom from pain, are the only things desirable as ends; and that all desirable things (which are as numerous in the utilitarian as in any other scheme) are desirable either for the pleasure inherent in themselves, or as means to the promotion of pleasure and the prevention of pain.

Now, such a theory of life excites in many minds, and among them in some of the most estimable in feeling and purpose, inveterate dislike. To suppose that life has (as they express it) no higher end than pleasure—no better and nobler object of desire and pursuit—they designate as utterly mean and grovelling; as a doctrine worthy only of swine, to whom the followers of Epicurus were, at a very early period, contemptuously likened; and modern holders of the doctrine are occasionally made the subject of equally polite comparisons by its German, French, and English assailants.

When thus attacked, the Epicureans have always answered, that it is not they; but their accusers, who represent human nature in a degrading light; since the accusation supposes human beings to be capable of no pleasures except those of which swine are capable. If this supposition were true, the charge could not be gainsaid, but would then be no longer an imputation; for if the sources of pleasure were precisely the same to human beings and to swine, the rule of life which is good enough for the one would be good enough for the other. The comparison of the Epicurean life to that of beasts is felt as degrading, precisely because a beast's pleasures do not satisfy a human being's conceptions of happiness. Human beings have faculties more elevated than the animal appetites, and when once made conscious of them, do not regard anything as happiness which does not include their gratification. I do not, indeed, consider the Epicureans to have been by any means faultless in drawing out their scheme of consequences from the utilitarian principle. To do this in any sufficient manner, many Stoic, as well as Christian elements require to be included. But there is no known Epicurean theory of life which does not assign to the pleasures of the intellect, of the feelings and imagination, and of the moral sentiments, a much higher value as pleasures than to those of mere sensation. It must be admitted, however, that utilitarian writers in general have placed the superiority of mental over bodily pleasures chiefly in the greater permanency, safety, uncostliness, etc., of the former—that is, in their circumstantial advantages rather than in their intrinsic nature. And on all these points utilitarians have fully proved their case; but they might have taken the other, and, as it may be called, higher ground, with entire consistency. It is quite compatible with the principle of utility to recognise the fact, that some kinds of pleasure are more desirable and more valuable than others. It would be absurd that while, in estimating all other things, quality is considered as well as quantity, the estimation of pleasures should be supposed to depend on quantity alone.

If I am asked, what I mean by difference of quality in pleasures, or what makes one pleasure more valuable than another, merely as a pleasure, except its being greater in amount, there is but one possible answer. Of two pleasures, if there be one to which all or almost all who have experience of both give a decided preference, irrespective of any feeling of moral obligation to prefer it, that is the more desirable pleasure. If one of the two is, by those who are competently acquainted with both, placed so far above the other that they prefer it, even though knowing it to be attended with a greater amount of discontent, and would not resign it for any quantity of the other pleasure which their nature is capable of, we are justified in ascribing to the preferred enjoyment a superiority in quality, so far outweighing quantity as to render it, in comparison, of small account.

Now it is an unquestionable fact that those who are equally acquainted with, and equally capable of appreciating and enjoying, both, do give almost marked preference to the manner of existence which employs their higher faculties. Few human creatures would consent to be changed into any of the lower animals, for a promise of the fullest allowance of a beast's pleasures; no intelligent human being would consent to be a fool, no instructed person would be an ignoramus, no person of feeling and conscience would be selfish and base, even though they should be persuaded that the fool, the dunce, or the rascal is better satisfied with his lot than they are with theirs. They would not resign what they possess more than he for the most complete satisfaction of all the desires which they have in common with him. If they ever fancy they would, it is only in cases of unhappiness so extreme, that to escape from it they would exchange their lot for almost any other, however undesirable in their own eyes. A being of higher faculties requires more to make him happy, is capable probably of more acute suffering, and certainly accessible to it at more points, than one of an inferior type; but in spite of these liabilities, he can never really wish to sink into what he feels to be a lower grade of existence. We may give what explanation we please of this unwillingness; we may attribute it to pride, a name which is given indiscriminately to some of the most and to some of the least estimable feelings of which mankind are capable: we may refer it to the love of liberty and personal independence, an appeal to which was with the Stoics one of the most effective means for the inculcation of it; to the love of power, or to the love of excitement, both of which do really enter into and contribute to it: but its most appropriate appellation is a sense of dignity, which all human beings possess in one form or other, and in some, though by no means in exact, proportion to their higher faculties, and which is so essential a part of the happiness of those in whom it is strong, that nothing which conflicts with it could be, otherwise than momentarily, an object of desire to them. Whoever supposes that this preference takes place at a sacrifice of happiness—that the superior being, in anything like equal circumstances, is not happier than the inferior—confounds the two very different ideas, of happiness, and content. It is indisputable that the being whose capacities of enjoyment are low, has the greatest chance of having them fully satisfied; and a highly endowed being will always feel that any happiness which he can look for, as the world is constituted, is imperfect. But he can learn to bear its imperfections, if they are at all bearable; and they will not make him envy the being who is indeed unconscious of the imperfections, but only because he feels not at all the good which those imperfections qualify. It is better to be a human being dissatisfied than a pig satisfied; better to be Socrates dissatisfied than a fool satisfied. And if the fool, or the pig, are of a different opinion, it is because they only know their own side of the question. The other party to the comparison knows both sides.

It may be objected, that many who are capable of the higher pleasures, occasionally, under the influence of temptation, postpone them to the lower. But this is quite compatible with a full appreciation of the intrinsic superiority of the higher. Men often, from infirmity of character, make their election for the nearer good, though they know it to be the less valuable; and this no less when the choice is between two bodily pleasures, than when it is between bodily and mental. They pursue sensual indulgences to the injury of health, though perfectly aware that health is the greater good. It may be further objected, that many who begin with youthful enthusiasm for everything noble, as they advance in years sink into indolence and selfishness. But I do not believe that those who undergo this very common change, voluntarily choose the lower description of pleasures in preference to the higher. I believe that before they devote themselves exclusively to the one, they have already become incapable of the other. Capacity for the nobler feelings is in most natures a very tender plant, easily killed, not only by hostile influences, but by mere want of sustenance; and in the majority of young persons it speedily dies away if the occupations to which their position in life has devoted them, and the society into which it has thrown them, are not favourable to keeping that higher capacity in exercise. Men lose their high aspirations as they lose their intellectual tastes, because they have not time or opportunity for indulging them; and they addict themselves to inferior pleasures, not because they deliberately prefer them, but because they are either the only ones to which they have access, or the only ones which they are any longer capable of enjoying. It may be questioned whether any one who has remained equally susceptible to both classes of pleasures, ever knowingly and calmly preferred the lower; though many, in all ages, have broken down in an ineffectual attempt to combine both.

From this verdict of the only competent judges, I apprehend there can be no appeal. On a question which is the best worth having of two pleasures, or which of two modes of existence is the most grateful to the feelings, apart from its moral attributes and from its consequences, the judgment of those who are qualified by knowledge of both, or, if they differ, that of the majority among them, must be admitted as final. And there needs be the less hesitation to accept this judgment respecting the quality of pleasures, since there is no other tribunal to be referred to even on the question of quantity. What means are there of determining which is the acutest of two pains, or the intensest of two pleasurable sensations, except the general suffrage of those who are familiar with both? Neither pains nor pleasures are homogeneous, and pain is always heterogeneous with pleasure. What is there to decide whether a particular pleasure is worth purchasing at the cost of a particular pain, except the feelings and judgment of the experienced? When, therefore, those feelings and judgment declare the pleasures derived from the higher faculties to be preferable in kind, apart from the question of intensity, to those of which the animal nature, disjoined from the higher faculties, is susceptible, they are entitled on this subject to the same regard.

I have dwelt on this point, as being a necessary part of a perfectly just conception of Utility or Happiness, considered as the directive rule of human conduct. But it is by no means an indispensable condition to the acceptance of the utilitarian standard; for that standard is not the agent's own greatest happiness, but the greatest amount of happiness altogether; and if it may possibly be doubted whether a noble character is always the happier for its nobleness, there can be no doubt that it makes other people happier, and that the world in general is immensely a gainer by it. Utilitarianism, therefore, could only attain its end by the general cultivation of nobleness of character, even if each individual were only benefited by the nobleness of others, and his own, so far as happiness is concerned, were a sheer deduction from the benefit. But the bare enunciation of such an absurdity as this last, renders refutation superfluous.

According to the Greatest Happiness Principle, as above explained, the ultimate end, with reference to and for the sake of which all other things are desirable (whether we are considering our own good or that of other people), is an existence exempt as far as possible from pain, and as rich as possible in enjoyments, both in point of quantity and quality; the test of quality, and the rule for measuring it against quantity, being the preference felt by those who in their opportunities of experience, to which must be added their habits of self-consciousness and self-observation, are best furnished with the means of comparison. This, being, according to the utilitarian opinion, the end of human action, is necessarily also the standard of morality; which may accordingly be defined "the rules and precepts for human conduct" by the observance of which an existence such as has been described might be, to the greatest extent possible, secured to all mankind; and not to them only, but, so far as the nature of things admits, to the whole sentient creation.

Against this doctrine, however, arises another class of objectors, who say that happiness, in any form, cannot be the rational purpose of human life and action; because, in the first place, it is unattainable: and they contemptuously ask, what right hast thou to be happy? a question which Mr. Carlyle clenches by the addition, What right, a short time ago, hadst thou even to be? Next, they say, that men can do without happiness; that all noble human beings have felt this, and could not have become noble but by learning the lesson of Entsagen, or renunciation; which lesson, thoroughly learnt and submitted to, they affirm to be the beginning and necessary condition of all virtue.

The first of these objections would go to the root of the matter were it well founded; for if no happiness is to be had at all by human beings, the attainment of it cannot be the end of morality, or of any rational conduct. Though, even in that case, something might still be said for the utilitarian theory; since utility includes not solely the pursuit of happiness, but the prevention or mitigation of unhappiness; and if the former aim be chimerical, there will be all the greater scope and more imperative need for the latter, so long at least as mankind think fit to live, and do not take refuge in the simultaneous act of suicide recommended under certain conditions by Novalis.* When, however, it is thus positively asserted to be impossible that human life should be happy, the assertion, if not something like a verbal quibble, is at least an exaggeration. If by happiness be meant a continuity of highly pleasurable excitement, it is evident enough that this is impossible. A state of exalted pleasure lasts only moments, or in some cases, and with some intermissions, hours or days, and is the occasional brilliant flash of enjoyment, not its permanent and steady flame. Of this the philosophers who have taught that happiness is the end of life were as fully aware as those who taunt them. The happiness which they meant was not a life of rapture; but moments of such, in an existence made up of few and transitory pains, many and various pleasures, with a decided predominance of the active over the passive, and having as the foundation of the whole, not to expect more from life than it is capable of bestowing. A life thus composed, to those who have been fortunate enough to obtain it, has always appeared worthy of the name of happiness. And such an existence is even now the lot of many, during some considerable portion of their lives. The present wretched education, and wretched social arrangements, are the only real hindrance to its being attainable by almost all.

The objectors perhaps may doubt whether human beings, if taught to consider happiness as the end of life, would be satisfied with such a moderate share of it. But great numbers of mankind have been satisfied with much less. The main constituents of a satisfied life appear to be two, either of which by itself is often found sufficient for the purpose: tranquillity, and excitement. With much tranquillity, many find that they can be content with very little pleasure: with much excitement, many can reconcile themselves to a considerable quantity of pain. There is assuredly no inherent impossibility in enabling even the mass of mankind to unite both; since the two are so far from being incompatible that they are in natural alliance, the prolongation of either being a preparation for, and exciting a wish for, the other. It is only those in whom indolence amounts to a vice, that do not desire excitement after an interval of repose: it is only those in whom the need of excitement is a disease, that feel the tranquillity which follows excitement dull and insipid, instead of pleasurable in direct proportion to the excitement which preceded it. When people who are tolerably fortunate in their outward

*[The German poet Friedrich Leopold Freiherr von Hardenberg (1772–1801).]

lot do not find in life sufficient enjoyment to make it valuable to them, the cause generally is, caring for nobody but themselves. To those who have neither public nor private affections, the excitements of life are much curtailed, and in any case dwindle in value as the time approaches when all selfish interests must be terminated by death: while those who leave after them objects of personal affection, and especially those who have also cultivated a fellow-feeling with the collective interests of mankind, retain as lively an interest in life on the eve of death as in the vigour of youth and health. Next to selfishness, the principal cause which makes life unsatisfactory is want of mental cultivation. A cultivated mind—I do not mean that of a philosopher, but any mind to which the fountains of knowledge have been opened, and which has been taught, in any tolerable degree, to exercise its faculties—finds sources of inexhaustible interest in all that surrounds it; in the objects of nature, the achievements of art, the imaginations of poetry, the incidents of history, the ways of mankind, past and present, and their prospects in the future. It is possible, indeed, to become indifferent to all this, and that too without having exhausted a thousandth part of it; but only when one has had from the beginning no moral or human interest in these things, and has sought in them only the gratification of curiosity.

Now there is absolutely no reason in the nature of things why an amount of mental culture sufficient to give an intelligent interest in these objects of contemplation, should not be the inheritance of every one born in a civilised country. As little is there an inherent necessity that any human being should be a selfish egotist, devoid of every feeling or care but those which centre in his own miserable individuality. Something far superior to this is sufficiently common even now, to give ample earnest of what the human species may be made. Genuine private affections, and a sincere interest in the public good, are possible, though in unequal degrees, to every rightly brought up human being. In a world in which there is so much to interest, so much to enjoy, and so much also to correct and improve, every one who has this moderate amount of moral and intellectual requisites is capable of an existence which may be called enviable; and unless such a person, through bad laws, or subjection to the will of others, is denied the liberty to use the sources of happiness within his reach, he will not fail to find this enviable existence, if he escape the positive evils of life, the great sources of physical and mental suffering—such as indigence, disease, and the unkindness, worthlessness, or premature loss of objects of affection. The main stress of the problem lies, therefore, in the contest with these calamities, from which it is a rare good fortune entirely to escape; which, as things now are, cannot be obviated, and often cannot be in any material degree mitigated. Yet no one whose opinion deserves a moment's consideration can doubt that most of the great positive evils of the world are in themselves removable, and will, if human affairs continue to improve, be in the end reduced within narrow limits. Poverty, in any sense implying suffering, may be completely extinguished by the wisdom of society, combined with the good sense and providence of individuals. Even that most intractable of enemies, disease, may be indefinitely reduced in dimensions by good physical and moral education, and proper control of noxious influences; while the progress of science holds out a promise for the future of still more direct conquests over this detestable foe. And every advance in that direction relieves us from some, not only of the chances which cut short our own lives, but, what concerns us still more, which deprive us of those in whom our happiness is wrapt up. As for vicissitudes of fortune, and other disappointments connected with worldly circumstances, these are principally the effect either of gross imprudence, of ill-regulated desires, or of bad or imperfect social institutions. All the grand sources, in short, of human suffering are in a great degree, many of them almost entirely, conquerable by human care and ef-

Crystal Palace, London, 1851, designed by Joseph Paxton (1801–1865). Built for the Works of Industry of All Nations exhibit, the building covered nineteen acres and enclosed over thirty million cubic feet. *(The Bettman Archive)*

fort; and though their removal is grievously slow—though a long succession of generations will perish in the breach before the conquest is completed, and this world becomes all that, if will and knowledge were not wanting, it might easily be made—yet every mind sufficiently intelligent and generous to bear a part, however small and unconspicuous, in the endeavour, will draw a noble enjoyment from the contest itself, which he would not for any bribe in the form of selfish indulgence consent to be without.

And this leads to the true estimation of what is said by the objectors concerning the possibility, and the obligation, of learning to do without happiness. Unquestionably it is possible to do without happiness; it is done involuntarily by nineteen-twentieths of mankind, even in those parts of our present world which are least deep in barbarism; and it often has to be done voluntarily by the hero or the martyr, for the sake of something which he prizes more than his individual happiness. But this something, what is it, unless the happiness of others, or some of the requisites of happiness? It is noble to be capable of resigning entirely one's own portion of happiness, or chances of it: but, after all, this self-sacrifice must be for some end; it is not its own end; and if we are told that its end is not happiness, but virtue, which is better than happiness, I ask, would the sacrifice be made if the hero or martyr did not believe that it would earn for others immunity from similar sacrifices? Would it be made if he thought that his renunciation of happiness for himself would produce no fruit for any of his fellow creatures, but to make their lot like his, and place them also in the condition of persons who have renounced happiness? All honour to those who can abnegate for themselves

Interior, Crystal Palace. The palace was a shrine to science, industrialization, and progress. This architectural marvel represented in concrete form Mill's optimism when he spoke of the "wisdom of society" and the "progress of science [which] holds out a promise for the future." (*Victoria and Albert Museum, London*) V&A Picture Library

the personal enjoyment of life, when by such renunciation they contribute worthily to increase the amount of happiness in the world; but he who does it, or professes to do it, for any other purpose, is no more deserving of admiration than the ascetic mounted on his pillar. He may be an inspiriting proof of what men *can* do, but assuredly not an example of what they *should*.

Though it is only in a very imperfect state of the world's arrangements that any one can best serve the happiness of others by the absolute sacrifice of his own, yet so long as the world is in that imperfect state, I fully acknowledge that the readiness to make such a sacrifice is the highest virtue which can be found in man. I will add, that in this condition of the world, paradoxical as the assertion may be, the conscious ability to do without happiness gives the best prospect of realising such happiness as is attainable. For nothing except that consciousness can raise a person above the chances of life, by making him feel that, let fate and fortune do their worst, they have not power to subdue him: which, once felt, frees him from excess of anxiety concerning the evils of life, and enables him, like many a Stoic in the worst times of the Roman Empire, to cultivate in tranquillity the sources of satisfaction accessible to him, without concerning himself about the uncertainty of their duration, any more than about their inevitable end.

Meanwhile, let utilitarians never cease to claim the morality of self devotion as a possession which belongs by as good a right to them, as either to the Stoic or to the

Transcendentalist. The utilitarian morality does recognise in human beings the power of sacrificing their own greatest good for the good of others. It only refuses to admit that the sacrifice is itself a good. A sacrifice which does not increase, or tend to increase, the sum total of happiness, it considers as wasted. The only self-renunciation which it applauds, is devotion to the happiness, or to some of the means of happiness, of others; either of mankind collectively, or of individuals within the limits imposed by the collective interests of mankind.

I must again repeat, what the assailants of utilitarianism seldom have the justice to acknowledge, that the happiness which forms the utilitarian standard of what is right in conduct, is not the agent's own happiness, but that of all concerned. As between his own happiness and that of others, utilitarianism requires him to be as strictly impartial as a disinterested and benevolent spectator. In the golden rule of Jesus of Nazareth, we read the complete spirit of the ethics of utility. "To do as you would be done by," and "to love your neighbour as yourself," constitute the ideal perfection of utilitarian morality. As the means of making the nearest approach to this ideal, utility would enjoin, first, that laws and social arrangements should place the happiness, or (as speaking practically it may be called) the interest, of every individual, as nearly as possible in harmony with the interest of the whole; and secondly, that education and opinion, which have so vast a power over human character, should so use that power as to establish in the mind of every individual an indissoluble association between his own happiness and the good of the whole; especially between his own happiness and the practice of such modes of conduct, negative and positive, as regard for the universal happiness prescribes; so that not only he may be unable to conceive the possibility of happiness to himself, consistently with conduct opposed to the general good, but also that a direct impulse to promote the general good may be in every individual one of the habitual motives of action, and the sentiments connected therewith may fill a large and prominent place in every human being's sentient existence. If the impugners of the utilitarian morality represented it to their own minds in this its true character, I know not what recommendation possessed by any other morality they could possibly affirm to be wanting to it; what more beautiful or more exalted developments of human nature any other ethical system can be supposed to foster, or what springs of action, not accessible to the utilitarian, such systems rely on for giving effect to their mandates.

The objectors to utilitarianism cannot always be charged with representing it in a discreditable light. On the contrary, those among them who entertain anything like a just idea of its disinterested character, sometimes find fault with its standard as being too high for humanity. They say it is exacting too much to require that people shall always act from the inducement of promoting the general interests of society. But this is to mistake the very meaning of a standard of morals, and confound the rule of action with the motive of it. It is the business of ethics to tell us what are our duties, or by what test we may know them; but no system of ethics requires that the sole motive of all we do shall be a feeling of duty; on the contrary, ninety-nine hundredths of all our actions are done from other motives, and rightly so done, if the rule of duty does not condemn them. It is the more unjust to utilitarianism that this particular misapprehension should be made a ground of objection to it, inasmuch as utilitarian moralists have gone beyond almost all others in affirming that the motive has nothing to do with the morality of the action, though much with the worth of the agent. He who saves a fellow creature from drowning does what is morally right, whether his motive be duty, or the hope of being paid for his trouble; he who betrays the friend that trusts him, is guilty of a crime, even if his object be to serve another friend to whom he is under greater obligations. But to speak only of actions done from the motive of duty, and in direct obedience to principle: it is a misapprehension of the utilitarian mode of thought, to conceive it as implying that people should fix their minds upon so wide a generality as the world, or society at large. The great majority of good actions are intended not for the benefit of the world, but for that of individuals, of which the good of the world is made up; and the thoughts of the most virtuous man need not on these occasions travel beyond the particular persons concerned, except so far as is necessary to assure himself that in benefiting them he is not violating the rights, that is, the legitimate and authorised expectations, of any one else. The multiplication of happiness is, according to the utilitarian ethics, the object of virtue: the occasions on which any person (except one in a thousand) has it in his power to do this on an extended scale, in other words to be a public benefactor, are but exceptional; and on these occasions alone is he called on to consider public utility; in every other case, private utility, the interest or happiness of some few persons, is all he has to attend to. Those alone the influence of whose actions extends to society in general, need concern themselves habitually about so large an object. In the case of abstinences indeed—of things which people forbear to do from moral considerations, though the consequences in the particular case might be beneficial—it would be unworthy of an intelligent agent not to be consciously aware that the action is of a class which, if practised generally, would be generally injurious, and that this is the ground of the obligation to abstain from it. The amount of regard for the public interest implied in this recognition, is no greater than is demanded by every system of morals, for they all enjoin to abstain from whatever is manifestly pernicious to society.

The same considerations dispose of another reproach against the doctrine of utility, founded on a still grosser misconception of the purpose of a standard of morality, and of the very meaning of the words "right" and "wrong." It is often affirmed that utilitarianism renders men cold and unsympathising; that it chills their moral feelings towards individuals; that it makes them regard only the dry and hard consideration of the consequences of actions, not taking into their moral estimate the qualities from which those actions emanate. If the assertion means that they do not allow their judgment respecting the rightness or wrongness of an action to be influenced by their opinion of the qualities of the person who does it, this is a complaint not against utilitarianism, but against having any standard of morality at all; for certainly no known ethical standard decides an action to be good or bad because it is done by a good or a bad man, still less because done by an amiable, a brave, or a benevolent man, or the contrary. These considerations are relevant, not to the estimation of actions, but of persons; and there is nothing in the utilitarian theory inconsistent with the fact that there are other things which interest us in persons besides the rightness and wrongness of their actions. The Stoics, indeed, with the paradoxical misuse of language which was part of their system, and by which they strove to raise themselves above all concern about anything but virtue, were fond of saying that he who has that has everything; that he, and only he, is rich, is beautiful, is a king. But no claim of this description is made for the virtuous man by the utilitarian doctrine. Utilitarians are quite aware that there are other desirable possessions and qualities besides virtue, and are perfectly willing to allow to all of them their full worth. They are also aware that a right action does not necessarily indicate a virtuous character, and that actions which are blamable, often proceed from qualities entitled to praise. When this is apparent in any particular case, it modifies their estimation, not certainly of the act, but of the agent. I grant that they are, notwithstanding, of opinion, that in the long run the best proof of a good character is good actions; and resolutely refuse to consider any mental disposition as good, of which the predominant tendency is to produce bad conduct. This makes them unpopular with many people; but it is an unpopularity which they must share with every one who regards the distinction between right and wrong in a serious light; and the reproach is not one which a conscientious utilitarian need be anxious to repel.

If no more be meant by the objection than that many utilitarians look on the morality of actions, as measured by the utilitarian standard, with too exclusive a regard, and do not lay sufficient stress upon the other beauties of character which go towards making a human being lovable or admirable, this may be admitted. Utilitarians who have cultivated their moral feelings, but not their sympathies nor their artistic perceptions, do fall into this mistake; and so do all other moralists under the same conditions. What can be said in excuse for other moralists is equally available for them, namely, that, if there is to be any error, it is better that it should be on that side. As a matter of fact, we may affirm that among utilitarians as among adherents of other systems, there is every imaginable degree of rigidity and of laxity in the application of their standard: some are even puritanically rigorous, while others are as indulgent as can possibly be desired by sinner or by sentimentalist. But on the whole, a doctrine which brings prominently forward the interest that mankind have in the repression and prevention of conduct which violates the moral law, is likely to be inferior to no other in turning the sanctions of opinion again such violations. It is true, the question, "What does violate the moral law?" is one on which those who recognise different standards of morality are likely now and then to differ. But difference of opinion on moral questions was not first introduced into the world by utilitarianism, while that doctrine does supply, if not always an easy, at all events a tangible and intelligible mode of deciding such differences.

It may not be superfluous to notice a few more of the common misapprehensions of utilitarian ethics, even those which are so obvious and gross that it might appear impossible for any person of candour and intelligence to fall into them; since persons, even of considerable mental endowments, often give themselves so little trouble to understand the bearings of any opinion against which they entertain a prejudice, and men are in general so little conscious of this voluntary ignorance as a defect, that the vulgarest misunderstandings of ethical doctrines are continually met with in the deliberate writings of persons of the greatest pretensions both to high principle and to philosophy. We not uncommonly hear the doctrine of utility inveighed against as a godless doctrine. If it be necessary to say anything at all against so mere an assumption, we may say that the question depends upon what idea we have formed of the moral character of the Deity. If it be a true belief that God desires, above all things, the happiness of his creatures, and that this was his purpose in their creation, utility is not only not a godless doctrine, but more profoundly religious than any other. If it be meant that utilitarianism does not recognise the revealed will of God as the supreme law of morals, I answer, that a utilitarian who believes in the perfect goodness and wisdom of God, necessarily believes that whatever God has thought fit to reveal on the subject of morals, must fulfil the requirements of utility in a supreme degree. But others besides utilitarians have been of opinion that the Christian revelation was intended, and is fitted, to inform the hearts and minds of mankind with a spirit which should enable them to find for themselves what is right, and incline them to do it when found, rather than to tell them, except in a very general way, what it is; and that we need a doctrine of ethics, carefully followed out, to *interpret* to us the will of God. Whether this opinion is correct or not, it is superfluous here to discuss; since whatever aid religion, either natural or revealed, can afford to ethical investigation, is as open to the utilitarian moralist as to any other. He can use it as the testimony of God to the usefulness or hurtfulness of any given course of action, by as good a right as others can use it for the indication of a transcendental law, having no connection with usefulness or with happiness.

Again, Utility is often summarily stigmatised as an immoral doctrine by giving it the name of "expediency," and taking advantage of the popular use of that term to contrast it with Principle. But the Expedient, in the sense in which it is opposed to the Right, generally means that which is expedient for the particular interest of the agent himself; as when a minister sacrifices the interests of his country to keep himself in place. When it means anything better than this, it means that which is expedient for some immediate object, some temporary purpose, but which violates a rule whose observance is expedient in a much higher degree. The Expedient, in this sense, instead of being the same thing with the useful, is a branch of the hurtful. Thus, it would often be expedient, for the purpose of getting over some momentary embarrassment, or attaining some object immediately useful to ourselves or others, to tell a lie. But inasmuch as the cultivation in ourselves of a sensitive feeling on the subject of veracity, is one of the most useful, and the enfeeblement of that feeling one of the most hurtful, things to which our conduct can be instrumental; and inasmuch as any, even unintentional, deviation from truth, does that much towards weakening the trustworthiness of human assertion, which is not only the principal support of all present social well-being, but the insufficiency of which does more than any one thing that can be named to keep back civilisation, virtue, everything on which human happiness on the largest scale depends; we feel that the violation, for a present advantage, of a rule of such transcendant expediency, is not expedient, and that he who, for the sake of a convenience to himself or to some other individual, does what depends on him to deprive mankind of the good, and inflict upon them the evil, involved in the greater or less reliance which they can place in each other's word, acts the part of one of their worst enemies. Yet that even this rule, sacred as it is, admits of possible exceptions, is acknowledged by all moralists; the chief of which is when the withholding of some fact (as of information from a malefactor, or of bad news from a person dangerously ill) would save an individual (especially an individual other than oneself) from great and unmerited evil, and when the withholding can only be effected by denial. But in order that the exception may not extend itself beyond the need, and may have the least possible effect in weakening reliance on veracity, it ought to be recognised, and, if possible, its limits defined; and if the principle of utility is good for anything, it must be good for weighing these conflicting utilities against one another, and marking out the region within which one or the other preponderates.

Again, defenders of utility often find themselves called upon to reply to such objections as this—that there is not time, previous to action, for calculating and weighing the effects of any line of conduct on the general happiness. This is exactly as if any one were to say that it is impossible to guide our conduct by Christianity, because there is not time, on every occasion on which anything has to be done, to read through the Old and New Testaments. The answer to the objection is, that there has been ample time, namely, the whole past duration of the human species. During all that time, mankind have been learning by experience the tendencies of actions; on which experience all the prudence, as well as all the morality of life, are dependent. People talk as if the commencement of this course of experience had hitherto been put off, and as if, at the moment when some man feels tempted to meddle with the property or life of another, he had to begin considering for the first time whether murder and theft are injurious to human happiness. Even then I do not think that he would find the question very puzzling; but, at all events, the matter is now done to his hand. It is truly a whimsical supposition that, if mankind were agreed in considering utility to be the test of morality, they would remain without any agreement as to what is useful, and would take no measures for having their notions on the subject taught to the young, and enforced by law and opinion. There is no difficulty in proving any ethical standard whatever to work ill, if we suppose universal idiocy to be conjoined with it; but on any hypothesis short of that, mankind must by this time have acquired positive beliefs as to the effects of some actions on their happiness; and the beliefs which have thus come down are the rules of morality for the multitude, and for the philosopher until he has succeeded in finding better. That philosophers might easily do this, even now, on many subjects; that the received code of ethics is by no means of divine right; and that mankind have still much to learn as to the effects of actions on the general happiness, I admit, or rather, earnestly maintain. The corollaries from the principle of utility, like the precepts of every practical art, admit of indefinite improvement, and, in a progressive state of the human mind, their improvement is perpetually going on. But to consider the rules of morality as improvable, is one thing; to pass over the intermediate generalisations entirely, and endeavour to test each individual action directly by the first principle, is another. It is a strange notion that the acknowledgment of a first principle is inconsistent with the admission of secondary ones. To inform a traveller respecting the place of his ultimate destination, is not to forbid the use of landmarks and direction-posts on the way. The proposition that happiness is the end and aim of morality, does not mean that no road ought to be laid down to that goal, or that persons going thither should not be advised to take one direction rather than another. Men really ought to leave off talking a kind of nonsense on this subject, which they would neither talk nor listen to on other matters of practical concernment. Nobody argues that the art of navigation is not founded on astronomy, because sailors cannot wait to calculate the *Nautical Almanac*. Being rational creatures, they go to sea with it ready calculated; and all rational creatures go out upon the sea of life with their minds made up on the common questions of right and wrong, as well as on many of the far more difficult questions of wise and foolish. And this, as long as foresight is a human quality, it is to be presumed they will continue to do. Whatever we adopt as the fundamental principle of morality, we require subordinate principles to apply it by; the impossibility of doing without them, being common to all systems, can afford no argument against any one in particular; but gravely to argue as if no such secondary principles could be had, and as if mankind had remained till no, and always must remain, without drawing any general conclusions from the experience of human life, is as high a pitch, I think, as absurdity has ever reached in philosophical controversy.

The remainder of the stock arguments against utilitarianism mostly consist in laying to its charge the common infirmities of human nature, and the general difficulties which embarrass conscientious persons in shaping their course through life. We are told that a utilitarian will be apt to make his own particular case an exception to moral rules, and, when under temptation, will see a utility in the breach of a rule, greater than he will see in its observance. But is utility the only creed which is able to furnish us with excuses for evil doing, and means of cheating our own conscience? They are afforded in abundance by all doctrines which recognise as a fact in morals the existence of conflicting considerations; which all doctrines do, that have been believed by sane persons. It is not the fault of any creed, but of the complicated nature of human affairs, that rules of conduct cannot be so framed as to require no exceptions, and that hardly any kind of action can safely be laid down as either always obligatory or always condemnable. There is no ethical creed which does not temper the rigidity of its laws, by giving a certain latitude, under the moral responsibility of the agent, for accommodation to peculiarities of circumstances; and under every creed, at the opening thus made, self-deception and dishonest casuistry get in. There exists no moral system under which there do not arise unequivocal cases of conflicting obligation. These are the real difficulties, the knotty points both in the theory of ethics, and in the conscientious guidance of personal conduct. They are overcome practically, with greater or with less success, according to the intellect and virtue of the individual; but it can hardly be pretended that any one will be the less qualified for dealing with them, from possessing an ultimate standard to which conflicting rights and duties can be referred. If utility is the ultimate source of moral obligations, utility may be invoked to decide between them when their demands are incompatible. Though the application of the standard may be difficult, it is better than none at all: while in other systems, the moral laws all claiming independent authority, there is no common umpire entitled to interfere between them; their claims to precedence one over another rest on little better than sophistry, and unless determined, as they generally are, by the unacknowledged influence of considerations of utility, afford a free scope for the action of personal desires and partialities. We must remember that only in these cases of conflict between secondary principles is it requisite that first principles should be appealed to. There is no case of moral obligation in which some secondary principle is not involved; and if only one, there can seldom be any real doubt which one it is, in the mind of any person by whom the principle itself is recognised.

CHAPTER 3: OF THE ULTIMATE SANCTION OF THE PRINCIPLE OF UTILITY

The question is often asked, and properly so, in regard to any supposed moral standard—What is its sanction? what are the motives to obey it? or more specifically, what is the source of its obligation? whence does it derive its binding force? It is a necessary part of moral philosophy to provide the answer to this question; which, though frequently assuming the shape of an objection to the utilitarian morality, as if it had some special applicability to that above others, really arises in regard to all standards. It arises, in fact, whenever a person is called on to *adopt* a standard, or refer morality to any basis on which he has not been accustomed to rest it. For the customary morality, that which education and opinion have consecrated, is the only one which presents itself to the mind with the feeling of being *in itself* obligatory; and when a person is asked to believe that this morality *derives* its obligation from some general principle round which custom has not thrown the same halo, the assertion is to him a paradox; the supposed corollaries seem to have a more binding force than the original theorem; the superstructure seems to stand better without, than with, what is represented as its foundation. He says to himself, I feel that I am bound not to rob or murder, betray or deceive; but why am I bound to promote the general happiness? If my own happiness lies in something else, why may I not give that the preference?

If the view adopted by the utilitarian philosophy of the nature of the moral sense be correct, this difficulty will always present itself, until the influences which form moral character have taken the same hold of the principle which they have taken of some of the consequences—until, by the improvement of education, the feeling of unity with our fellow-creatures shall be (what it cannot be denied that Christ intended it to be) as deeply rooted in our character, and to our own consciousness as completely a part of our nature, as the horror of crime is in an ordinarily well brought up young person. In the meantime, however, the difficulty has no peculiar application to the doctrine of utility, but is inherent in every attempt to analyse morality and reduce it to principles; which, unless the principle is already in men's minds invested with as much sacredness as any of its applications, always seems to divest them of a part of their sanctity.

The principle of utility either has, or there is no reason why it might not have, all the sanctions which belong to any other system of morals. Those sanctions are either external or internal. Of the external sanctions it is not necessary to speak at any length. They are, the hope of favour and the fear of displeasure, from our fellow-creatures or from the Ruler of the Universe, along with whatever we may have of sympathy or affection for them, or of love and awe of Him, inclining us to do his will independently of selfish consequences. There is evidently no reason why all these motives for observance should not attach themselves to the utilitarian morality, as completely and as powerfully as to any other. Indeed, those of them which refer to our fellow-creatures are sure to do so, in proportion to the amount of general intelligence; for whether there be any other ground of moral obligation than the general happiness or not, men do desire happiness; and however imperfect may be their own practice, they desire and commend all conduct in others towards themselves, by which they think their happiness is promoted. With regard to the religious motive, if men believe, as most profess to do, in the goodness of God, those who think that conduciveness to the general happiness is the essence, or even only the criterion of good, must necessarily believe that it is also that which God approves. The whole force therefore of external reward and punishment, whether physical or moral, and whether proceeding from God or from our fellow men, together with all that the capacities of human nature admit of disinterested devotion to either, become available to enforce the utilitarian morality, in proportion as that morality is recognised; and the more powerfully, the more the appliances of education and general cultivation are bent to the purpose.

So far as to external sanctions. The internal sanction of duty, whatever our standard of duty may be, is one and the same—a feeling in our own mind; a pain, more or less intense, attendant on violation of duty, which in properly cultivated moral natures rises, in the more serious cases, into shrinking from it as an impossibility. This feeling, when disinterested, and connecting itself with the pure idea of duty, and not with some particular form of it, or with any of the merely accessory circumstances, is the essence of Conscience; though in that complex phenomenon as it actually exists, the simple fact is in general all encrusted over with collateral associations, derived from sympathy, from love, and still more from fear; from all the forms of religious feeling; from the recollections of childhood and of all our past life; from self-esteem, desire of the esteem of others, and occasionally even self-abasement. This extreme complication is, I apprehend, the origin of the sort of mystical character which, by a tendency of the human mind of which there are many other examples, is apt to be attributed to the idea of moral obligation, and which leads people to believe that the idea cannot possibly attach itself to any other objects than those which, by a supposed mysterious law, are found in our present experience to excite it. Its binding force, however, consists in the existence of a mass of feeling which must be broken through in order to do what violates our standard of right, and which, if we do nevertheless violate that standard, will probably have to be encountered afterwards in the form of remorse. Whatever theory we have of the nature or origin of conscience, this is what essentially constitutes it.

The ultimate sanction, therefore, of all morality (external motives apart) being a subjective feeling in our own minds, I see nothing embarrassing to those whose standard is utility, in the question, "What is the sanction of that particular standard?" We may answer, the same as of all other moral standards—the conscientious feelings of mankind. Undoubtedly this sanction has no binding efficacy on those who do not possess the feelings it appeals to; but neither will these persons be more obedient to any other moral principle than to the utilitarian one. On them morality of any kind has no hold but through the external sanctions. Meanwhile the feelings exist, a fact in human nature, the reality of which, and the great power with which they are capable of acting on those in whom they have been duly cultivated, are proved by experience. No reason has ever been shown why they may not be cultivated to as great intensity in connection with the utilitarian, as with any other rule of morals.

There is, I am aware, a disposition to believe that a person who sees in moral obligation a transcendental fact, an objective reality belonging to the province of "things in themselves," is likely to be more obedient to it than one who believes it to be entirely subjective, having its seat in human consciousness only. But whatever a person's opinion may be on this point of Ontology, the force he is really urged by is his own subjective feeling, and is exactly measured by its strength. No one's belief that duty is an objective reality is stronger than the belief that God is so; yet the belief in God, apart from the expectation of actual reward and punishment, only operates on conduct through, and in proportion to, the subjective religious feeling. The sanction, so far as it is disinterested, is always in the mind itself; and the notion therefore of the transcendental moralists must be, that this sanction will not exist *in* the mind unless it is believed to have its root out of the mind; and that if a person is able to say to himself, "This which is restraining me, and which is called my conscience, is only a feeling in my own mind," he may possibly draw the conclusion that when the feeling ceases the obligation ceases, and that if he find the feeling inconvenient, he may disregard it, and endeavour to get rid of it. But is this danger confined to the utilitarian morality? Does the belief that moral obligation has its seat outside the mind make the feeling of it too strong to be got rid of? The fact is so far otherwise, that all moralists admit and lament the ease with which, in the generality of minds, conscience can be silenced or stifled. The question, "Need I obey my conscience?" is quite as often put to themselves by persons who never heard of the principle of utility, as by its adherents. Those whose conscientious feelings are so weak as to allow of their asking this question, if they answer it affirmatively, will not do so because they believe in the transcendental theory, but because of the external sanctions.

It is not necessary, for the present purpose, to decide whether the feeling of duty is innate or implanted. Assuming it to be innate, it is an open question to what objects it naturally attaches itself; for the philosophic supporters of that theory are now agreed that the intuitive perception is of principles of morality and not of the details. If there be anything innate in the matter, I see no reason why the feeling which is innate should not be that of regard to the pleasures and pains of others. If there is any principle of morals which is intuitively obligatory, I should say it must be that. If so, the intuitive ethics would coincide with the utilitarian, and there would be no further quarrel between them. Even as it is, the intuitive moralists, though they believe that there are other intuitive moral obligations, do already believe this to be one; for they unanimously hold that a large *portion* of morality turns upon the consideration due to the interests of our fellow-creatures. Therefore, if the belief in the transcendental origin of moral obligation gives any additional efficacy to the internal sanction, it appears to me that the utilitarian principle has already the benefit of it.

On the other hand, if, as is my own belief, the moral feelings are not innate, but acquired, they are not for that reason the less natural. It is natural to man to speak, to reason, to build cities, to cultivate the ground, though these are acquired faculties. The moral feelings are not indeed a part of our nature, in the sense of being in any perceptible degree present in all of us; but this, unhappily, is a fact admitted by those who believe the most strenuously in their transcendental origin. Like the other acquired capacities above referred to, the moral faculty, if not a part of our nature, is a natural outgrowth from it; capable, like them, in a certain small degree, of springing up spontaneously; and susceptible of being brought by cultivation to a high degree of development. Unhappily it is also susceptible, by a sufficient use of the external sanctions and of the force of early impressions, of being cultivated in almost any direction: so that there is hardly anything so absurd or so mischievous that it may not, by means of these influences, be made to act on the human mind with all the authority of conscience. To doubt that the same potency might be given by the same means to the principle of utility, even if it had no foundation in human nature, would be flying in the face of all experience.

But moral associations which are wholly of artificial creation, when intellectual culture goes on, yield by degrees to the dissolving force of analysis: and if the feeling of duty, when associated with utility, would appear equally arbitrary; if there were no leading department of our nature, no powerful class of sentiments, with which that association would harmonise, which would make us feel it congenial, and incline us not only to foster it in others (for which we have abundant interested motives), but also to cherish it in ourselves; if there were not, in short, a natural basis of sentiment for utilitarian morality, it might well happen that this association also, even after it had been implanted by education, might be analysed away.

But there *is* this basis of powerful natural sentiment; and this it is which, when once the general happiness is recognised as the ethical standard, will constitute the strength of the utilitarian morality. This firm foundation is that of the social feelings of mankind; the desire to be in unity with our fellow creatures, which is already a powerful principle in human nature, and happily one of those which tend to become stronger, even without express inculcation, from the influences of advancing civilisation. The social state is at once so natural, so necessary, and so habitual to man, that, except in some unusual circumstances or by an effort of voluntary abstraction, he never conceives himself otherwise than as a member of a body; and this association is riveted more and more, as mankind are further removed from the state of savage independence. Any condition, therefore, which is essential to a state of society, becomes more and more an inseparable part of every person's conception of the state of things which he is born into, and which is the destiny of a human being. Now, society between human beings, except in the relation of master and slave, is manifestly impossible on any other footing than that the interests of all are to be consulted. Society between equals can only exist on the understanding that the interests of all are to be regarded equally. And since in all states of civilisation, every person, except an absolute monarch, has equals, every one is obliged to live on these terms with somebody; and in every age some advance is made towards a state in which it will be impossible to live permanently on other terms with anybody. In this way people grow up unable to conceive as possible to them a state of total disregard of other people's interests. They are under a necessity of conceiving themselves as at least abstaining from all the grosser injuries, and (if only for their own protection) living in a state of constant protest against them. They are also familiar with the fact of cooperating with others and proposing to themselves a collective, not an individual interest as the aim (at least for the time being) of their actions. So long as they are cooperating, their ends are identified with those of others; there is at least a temporary feeling that the interests of others are their own interests. Not only does all strengthening of social ties, and all healthy growth of society, give to each individual a stronger personal interest in practically consulting the welfare of others; it also leads him to identify his *feelings* more and more with their good, or at least with an even greater degree of practical consideration for it. He comes, as though instinctively, to be conscious of himself as a being who *of course* pays regard to others. The good of others becomes to him a thing naturally and necessarily to be attended to, like any of the physical conditions of our existence. Now, whatever amount of this feeling a person has, he is urged by the strongest motives both of interest and of sympathy to demonstrate it, and to the utmost of his power encourage it in others; and even if he has none of it himself, he is as greatly interested as any one else that others should have it. Consequently the smallest germs of the feeling are laid hold of and nourished by the contagion of sympathy and the influences of education; and a complete web of corroborative association is woven round it, by the powerful agency of the external sanctions. This mode of conceiving ourselves and human life, as civilisation goes on, is felt to be more and more natural. Every step in political improvement renders it more so, by removing the sources of opposition of interest, and levelling those inequalities of legal privilege between individuals or classes, owing to which there are large portions of mankind whose happiness it is still practicable to disregard. In an improving state of the human mind, the influences are constantly on the increase, which tend to generate in each individual a feeling of unity with all the rest; which, if perfect, would make him never think of, or desire, any beneficial condition for himself, in the benefits of which they are not included. If we now suppose this feeling of unity to be taught as a religion, and the whole force of education, of institutions, and of opinion, directed, as it once was in the case of religion, to make every person grow up from infancy surrounded on all sides both by the profession and the practice of it, I think that no one, who can realise this conception, will feel any misgiving about the sufficiency of the ultimate sanction for the Happiness morality. To any ethical student who finds the realisation difficult, I recommend, as a means of facilitating it, the second of M. Comte's two principal works, the *Traité de Politique Positive*. I entertain the strongest objections to the system of politics and morals set forth in that treatise; but I think it has superabundantly shown the possibility of giving to the service of humanity, even without the aid of belief in a Providence, both the psychological power and the social efficacy of a religion; making it take hold of human life, and colour all thought, feeling, and action, in a manner of which the greatest ascendancy ever exercised by any religion may be but a type and foretaste; and of which the danger is, not that it should be insufficient, but that it should be so excessive as to interfere unduly with human freedom and individuality.

Neither is it necessary to the feeling which constitutes the binding force of the utilitarian morality on those who recognise it, to wait for those social influences which would make its obligation felt by mankind at large. In the comparatively early state of human advancement in which we now live, a person cannot indeed feel that entireness of sympathy with all others, which would make any real discordance in the general direction of their conduct in life impossible; but already a person in whom the social feeling is at all developed, cannot bring himself to think of the rest of his fellow-creatures as struggling rivals with him for the means of happiness, whom he must desire to see defeated in their object in order that he may succeed in his. The deeply rooted conception which every individual even now has of himself as a social being, tends to make him feel it one of his natural wants that there should be harmony between his feelings and aims and those of his fellow-creatures. If differences of opinion and of mental culture make it impossible for him to share many of their actual feelings—perhaps make him denounce and defy those feelings—he still needs to be conscious that his real aim and theirs do not conflict; that he is not opposing himself to what they really wish for, namely their own good, but is, on the contrary, promoting it. This feeling in most individuals is much inferior in strength to their selfish feelings, and is often wanting altogether. But to those who have it, it possesses all the characters of a natural feeling. It does not present itself to their minds as a superstition of education, or a law despotically imposed by the power of society, but as an attribute which it would not be well for them to be without. This conviction is the ultimate sanction of the greatest happiness morality. This it is which makes any mind, of well-developed feelings, work with, and not against, the outward motives to care for others, afforded by what I have called the external sanctions; and when those sanctions are wanting, or act in an opposite direction, constitutes in itself a powerful internal binding force, in proportion to the sensitiveness and thoughtfulness of the character; since few but those whose mind is a moral blank, could bear to lay out their course of life on the plan of paying no regard to others except so far as their own private interest compels.

CHAPTER 4: OF WHAT SORT OF PROOF THE PRINCIPLE OF UTILITY IS SUSCEPTIBLE

It has already been remarked, that questions of ultimate ends do not admit of proof, in the ordinary acceptation of the term. To be incapable of proof by reasoning is common to all first principles; to the first premises of our knowledge, as well as to those of our conduct. But the former, being matters of fact, may be the subject of a direct appeal to the faculties which judge of fact—namely, our senses, and our internal consciousness. Can an appeal be made to the same faculties on questions of practical ends? Or by what other faculty is cognisance taken of them?

Questions about ends are, in other words, questions what things are desirable. The utilitarian doctrine is, that happiness is desirable, and the only thing desirable, as an end; all other things being only desirable as means to that end. What ought to be required of this doctrine—what conditions is it requisite that the doctrine should fulfil—to make good its claim to be believed?

The only proof capable of being given that an object is visible, is that people actually see it. The only proof that a sound is audible, is that people hear it: and so of the other sources of our experience. In like manner, I apprehend, the sole evidence it is possible to produce that anything is desirable, is that people do actually desire it. If the end which the utilitarian doctrine proposes to itself were not, in theory and in practice, acknowledged to be an end, nothing could ever convince any person that it was so. No reason can be given why the general happiness is desirable, except that each person, so far as he believes it to be attainable, desires his own happiness. This, however, being a fact, we have not only all the proof which the case admits of, but all which it is possible to require, that happiness is a good: that each person's happiness is a good to that person, and the general happiness, therefore, a good to the aggregate of all persons. Happiness has made out its title as one of the ends of conduct, and consequently one of the criteria of morality.

But it has not, by this alone, proved itself to be the sole criterion. To do that, it would seem, by the same rule, necessary to show, not only that people desire happiness, but that they never desire anything else. Now it is palpable that they do desire things which, in common language, are decidedly distinguished from happiness. They desire, for example, virtue, and the absence of vice, no less really than pleasure and the absence of pain. The desire of virtue is not as universal, but it is as authentic a fact, as the desire of happiness. And hence the opponents of the utilitarian standard deem that they have a right to infer that there are other ends of human action besides happiness, and that happiness is not the standard of approbation and disapprobation.

But does the utilitarian doctrine deny that people desire virtue, or maintain that virtue is not a thing to be desired? The very reverse. It maintains not only that virtue is to be desired, but that it is to be desired disinterestedly, for itself. Whatever may be the opinion of utilitarian moralists as to the original conditions by which virtue is made virtue; however they may believe (as they do) that actions and dispositions are only virtuous because they promote another end than virtue; yet this being granted, and it having been decided, from considerations of this description, what is virtuous, they not only place virtue at the very head of the things which are good as means to the ultimate end, but they also recognise as a psychological fact the possibility of its being, to the individual, a good in itself, without looking to any end beyond it; and hold, that the mind is not in a right state, not in a state conformable to Utility, not in the state most conducive to the general happiness, unless it does love virtue in this manner—as a thing desirable in itself, even although, in the individual instance, it should not produce those other desirable consequences which it tends to produce, and on account of which it is held to be virtue. This opinion is not, in the smallest degree, a departure from the Happiness principle. The ingredients of happiness are very various, and each of them is desirable in itself, and not merely when considered as swelling an aggregate. The principle of utility does not mean that any given pleasure, as music, for instance, or any given exemption from pain, as for example health, is to be looked upon as means to a collective something termed happiness, and to be desired on that account. They are desired and desirable in and for themselves; besides being means, they are a part of the end. Virtue, according to the utilitarian doctrine, is not naturally and originally part of the end, but it is capable of becoming so; and in those who love it disinterestedly it has become so, and is desired and cherished, not as a means to happiness, but as a part of their happiness.

To illustrate this farther, we may remember that virtue is not the only thing, originally a means, and which if it were not a means to anything else, would be and remain indifferent, but which by association with what it is a means to, comes to be desired for itself, and that too with the utmost intensity. What, for example, shall we say of the love of money? There is nothing originally more desirable about money than about any heap of glittering pebbles. Its worth is solely that of the things which it will buy; the desires for other things than itself, which it is a means of gratifying. Yet the love of money is not only one of the strongest moving forces of human life, but money is, in many cases, desired in and for itself; the desire to possess it is often stronger than the desire to use it, and goes on increasing when all the desires which point to ends beyond it, to be compassed by it, are falling off. It may, then, be said truly, that money is desired not for the sake of an end, but as part of the end. From being a means to happiness, it has come to be itself a principal ingredient of the individual's conception of happiness. The same may be said of the majority of the great objects of human life—power, for example, or fame; except that to each of these there is a certain amount of immediate pleasure annexed, which has at least the semblance of being naturally inherent in them; a thing which cannot be said of money. Still, however, the strongest natural attraction, both of power and of fame, is the immense aid they give to the attainment of our other wishes; and it is the strong association thus generated between them and all our objects of desire, which gives to the direct desire of them the intensity it often assumes, so as in some characters to surpass in strength all other desires. In these cases the means have become a part of the end, and a more important part of it than any of the things which they are means to. What was once desired as an instrument for the attainment of happiness, has come to be desired for its own sake. In being desired for its own sake it is, however, desired as *part* of happiness. The person is made, or thinks he would be made, happy by its mere possession; and is made unhappy by failure to obtain it. The desire of it is not a different thing from the desire of happiness, any more than the love of music, or the desire of health. They are included in happiness. They are some of the elements of which the desire of happiness is made up. Happiness is not an abstract idea, but a concrete whole; and these are some of its parts. And the utilitarian standard sanctions and approves their being so. Life would be a poor thing, very ill provided with sources of happiness, if there were not this provision of nature, by which things originally indifferent, but conducive to, or otherwise associated with, the satisfaction of our primitive desires, become in themselves sources of pleasure more valuable than the primitive pleasures, both in permanency, in the space of human existence that they are capable of covering, and even in intensity.

Virtue, according to the utilitarian conception, is a good of this description. There was no original desire of it, or motive to it, save its conduciveness to pleasure, and especially to protection from pain. But through the association thus formed, it may be felt a good in itself, and desired as such with as great intensity as any other good; and with this difference between it and the love of money, of power, or of fame, that all of these may, and often do, render the individual noxious to the other members of the society to which he belongs, whereas there is nothing which makes him so much a blessing to them as the cultivation of the disinterested love of virtue. And consequently, the utilitarian standard, while it tolerates and approves those other acquired desires, up to the point beyond which they would be more injurious to the general happiness than promotive of it, enjoins and requires the cultivation of the love of virtue up to the greatest strength possible, as being above all things important to the general happiness.

It results from the preceding considerations, that there is in reality nothing desired except happiness. Whatever is desired otherwise than as a means to some end beyond itself, and ultimately to happiness, is desired as itself a part of happiness, and is not desired for itself until it has become so. Those who desire virtue for its own sake, desire it either because the consciousness of it is a pleasure, or because the consciousness of being without it is a pain, or for both reasons united; as in truth the pleasure and pain seldom exist separately, but almost always together, the same person feeling pleasure in the degree of virtue attained, and pain in not having attained more. If one of these gave him no pleasure, and the other no pain, he would not love or desire virtue, or would desire it only for the other benefits which it might produce to himself or to persons whom he cared for.

We have now, then, an answer to the question, of what sort of proof the principle of utility is susceptible. If the opinion which I have now stated is psychologically true—if human nature is so constituted as to desire nothing which is not either a part of happiness or a means of happiness—we can have no other proof, and we require no other, that these are the only things desirable. If so, happiness is the sole end of human action, and the promotion of it the test by which to judge of all human conduct; from whence it necessarily follows that it must be the criterion of morality, since a part is included in the whole.

And now to decide whether this is really so; whether mankind do desire nothing for itself but that which is a pleasure to them, or of which the absence is a pain; we have evidently arrived at a question of fact and experience, dependent, like all similar questions, upon evidence. It can only be determined by practised self-consciousness and self-observation, assisted by observation of others. I believe that these sources of evidence, impartially consulted, will declare that desiring a thing and finding it pleasant, aversion to it and thinking of it as painful, are phenomena entirely inseparable, or rather two parts of the same phenomenon—in strictness of language, two different modes of naming the same psychological fact: that to think of an object as desirable (unless for the sake of its consequences), and to think of it as pleasant, are one and the same thing; and that to desire anything, except in proportion as the idea of it is pleasant, is a physical and metaphysical impossibility.

So obvious does this appear to me, that I expect it will hardly be disputed: and the objection made will be, not that desire can possibly be directed to anything ultimately except pleasure and exemption from pain, but that the will is a different thing from desire; that a person of confirmed virtue, or any other person whose purposes are fixed, carries out his purposes without any thought of the pleasure he has in contemplating them, or expects to derive from their fulfilment; and persists in acting on them, even though these pleasures are much diminished, by changes in his character or decay of his passive sensibilities, or are out weighed by the pains which the pursuit of the purposes may bring upon him. All this I fully admit, and have stated it elsewhere, as positively and emphatically as any one. Will, the active phenomenon, is a different thing from desire, the state of passive sensibility, and though originally an offshoot from it, may in time take root and detach itself from the parent stock; so much so, that in the case of an habitual purpose, instead of willing the thing because we desire it, we often desire it only because we will it. This, however, is but an instance of that familiar fact, the power of habit, and is no wise confined to the case of virtuous actions. Many indifferent things, which men originally did from a motive of some sort, they continue to do from habit. Sometimes this is done unconsciously, the consciousness coming only after the action: at other times with conscious volition, but volition which has become habitual, and is put in operation by the force of habit, in opposition perhaps to the deliberate preference, as often happens with those who have contracted habits of vicious or hurtful indulgence. Third and last comes the case in which the habitual act of will in the individual instance is not in contradiction to the general intention prevailing at other times, but in fulfilment of it; as in the case of the person of confirmed virtue, and of all who pursue deliberately and consistently any determinate end. The distinction between will and desire thus understood is an authentic and highly important psychological fact; but the fact consists solely in this—that will, like all other parts of our constitution, is amenable to habit, and that we may will from habit what we no longer desire for itself, or desire only because we will it. It is not the less true that will, in the beginning, is entirely produced by desire; including in that term the repelling influence of pain as well as the attractive one of pleasure. Let us take into consideration, no longer the person who has a confirmed will to do right, but him in whom that virtuous will is still feeble, conquerable by temptation, and not to be fully relied on; by what means can it be strengthened? How can the will to be virtuous, where it does not exist in sufficient force, be implanted or awakened? Only by making the person *desire* virtue—by making him think of it in a pleasurable light, or of its absence in a painful one. It is by associating the doing right with pleasure, or the doing wrong with pain, or by eliciting and impressing and bringing home to the person's experience the pleasure naturally involved in the one or the pain in the other, that it is possible to call forth that will to be virtuous, which, when confirmed, acts without any thought of either pleasure or pain. Will is the child of desire, and passes out of the dominion of its parent only to come under that of habit. That which is the result of habit affords no presumption of being intrinsically good; and there would be no reason for wishing that the purpose of virtue should become independent of pleasure and pain, were it not that the influence of the pleasurable and painful associations which prompt to virtue is not sufficiently to be depended on for unerring constancy of action until it has acquired the support of habit. Both in feeling and in conduct, habit is the only thing which imparts certainty; and it is because of the importance to others of being able to rely absolutely on one's feelings and conduct, and to oneself of being able to rely on one's own, that the will to do right ought to be cultivated into this habitual independence. In other words, this state of the will is a means to good, not intrinsically a good; and does not contradict the doctrine that nothing is a good to human beings but in so far as it is either itself pleasurable, or a means of attaining pleasure or averting pain.

But if this doctrine be true, the principle of utility is proved. Whether it is so or not, must now be left to the consideration of the thoughtful reader.

CHAPTER 5: ON THE CONNECTION BETWEEN JUSTICE AND UTILITY

In all ages of speculation, one of the strongest obstacles to the reception of the doctrine that Utility or Happiness is the criterion of right and wrong, has been drawn from the idea of Justice. The powerful sentiment, and apparently clear perception, which that word recalls with a rapidity and certainty resembling an instinct, have seemed to the majority of thinkers to point to an inherent quality in things; to show that the Just must have an existence in Nature as something absolute, generically distinct from every variety of the Expedient, and, in idea, opposed to it, though (as is commonly acknowledged) never, in the long run, disjoined from it in fact.

In the case of this, as of our other moral sentiments, there is no necessary connection between the question of its origin, and that of its binding force. That a feeling is bestowed on us by Nature, does not necessarily legitimate all its promptings. The feeling of justice might be a peculiar instinct, and might yet require, like our other instincts, to be controlled and enlightened by a higher reason. If we have intellectual instincts, leading us to judge in a particular way, as well as animal instincts that prompt us to act in a particular way, there is no necessity that the former should be more infallible in their sphere than the latter in theirs: it may as well happen that wrong judgments are occasionally suggested by those, as wrong actions by these. But though it is one thing to believe that we have natural feelings of justice, and another to acknowledge them as an ultimate criterion of conduct, these two opinions are very closely connected in point of fact. Mankind are always predisposed to believe that any subjective feeling, not otherwise accounted for, is a revelation of some objective reality. Our present object is to determine whether the reality, to which the feeling of justice corresponds, is one which needs any such special revelation; whether the justice or injustice of an action is a thing intrinsically peculiar, and distinct from all its other qualities, or only a combination of certain of those qualities, presented under a peculiar aspect. For the purpose of this inquiry it is practically important to consider whether the feeling itself, of justice and injustice, is *sui generis* like our sensations of colour and taste, or a derivative feeling, formed by a combination of others. And this it is the more essential to examine, as people are in general willing enough to allow, that objectively the dictates of Justice coincide with a part of the field of General Expediency; but inasmuch as the subjective mental feeling of Justice is different from that which commonly attaches to simple expediency, and, except in the extreme cases of the latter, is far more imperative in its demands, people find it difficult to see, in Justice, only a particular kind or branch of general utility, and think that its superior binding force requires a totally different origin.

To throw light upon this question, it is necessary to attempt to ascertain what is the distinguishing character of justice, or of injustice: what is the quality, or whether there is any quality, attributed in common to all modes of conduct designated as unjust (for justice, like many other moral attributes, is best defined by its opposite), and distinguishing them from such modes of conduct as are disapproved, but without having that particular epithet of disapprobation applied to them. If in everything which men are accustomed to characterise as just or unjust, some one common attribute or collection of attributes is always present, we may judge whether this particular attribute or combination of attributes would be capable of gathering round it a sentiment of that peculiar character and intensity by virtue of the general laws of our emotional constitution, or whether the sentiment is inexplicable, and requires to be regarded as a special provision of Nature. If we find the former to be the case, we shall, in resolving this question, have resolved also the main problem: if the latter, we shall have to seek for some other mode of investigating it.

To find the common attributes of a variety of objects, it is necessary to begin by surveying the objects themselves in the concrete. Let us therefore advert successively to the various modes of action, and arrangements of human affairs, which are classed, by universal or widely spread opinion, as Just or as Unjust. The things well known to excite the sentiments associated with those names are of a very multifarious character. I shall pass them rapidly in review, without studying any particular arrangement.

In the first place, it is mostly considered unjust to deprive any one of his personal liberty, his property, or any other thing which belongs to him by law. Here, therefore, is one instance of the application of the terms "just" and "unjust" in a perfectly definite sense, namely, that it is just to respect, unjust to violate, the *legal rights* of any one. But this judgment admits of several exceptions, arising from the other forms in which the notions of justice and injustice present themselves. For example, the person who suffers the deprivation may (as the phrase is) have *forfeited* the rights which he is so deprived of: a case to which we shall return presently. But also—

Secondly; the legal rights of which he is deprived, may be rights which *ought* not to have belonged to him; in other words, the law which confers on him these rights, may be a bad law. When it is so, or when (which is the same thing for our purpose) it is supposed to be so, opinions will differ as to the justice or injustice of infringing it. Some maintain that no law, however bad, ought to be disobeyed by an individual citizen; that his opposition to it, if shown at all, should only be shown in endeavouring to get it altered by competent authority. This opinion (which condemns many of the most illustrious benefactors of mankind, and would often protect pernicious institutions against the only weapons which, in the state of things existing at the time, have any chance of succeeding against them) is defended, by those who hold it, on grounds of expediency; principally on that of the importance, to the common interest of mankind, of maintaining inviolate the sentiment of submission to law. Other persons, again, hold the directly contrary opinion, that any law, judged to be bad, may blamelessly be disobeyed, even though it be not judged to be unjust, but only inexpedient; while others would confine the licence of disobedience to the case of unjust laws: but again, some say, that all laws which are inexpedient are unjust; since every law imposes some restriction on the natural liberty of mankind, which restriction is an injustice, unless legitimated by tending to their good. Among these diversities of opinion, it seems to be universally admitted that there may be unjust laws, and that law, consequently, is not the ultimate criterion of justice, but may give to one person a benefit, or impose on another an evil, which justice condemns. When, however, a law is thought to be unjust, it seems always to be regarded as being so in the same way in which a breach of law is unjust, namely, by infringing somebody's right; which, as it cannot in this case be a legal right, receives a different appellation, and is called a moral right. We may say, therefore, that a second case of injustice consists in taking or withholding from any person that to which he has a *moral right*.

Thirdly, it is universally considered just that each person should obtain that (whether good or evil) which he *deserves* and unjust that he should obtain a good, or be made to undergo an evil, which he does not deserve. This is, perhaps, the clearest and most emphatic form in which the idea of justice is conceived by the general mind. As it involves the notion of desert, the question arises, what constitutes desert? Speaking in a general way, a person is understood to deserve good if he does right, evil if he does wrong; and in a more particular sense, to deserve good from those to whom he does or has done good, and evil from those to whom he does or has done evil. The precept of re-turning good for evil has never been regarded as a case of the fulfilment of justice, but as one in which the claims of justice are waived, in obedience to other considerations.

Fourthly, it is confessedly unjust to *break faith* with any one: to violate an engage-ment, either express or implied, or disappoint expectations raised by our own conduct, at least if we have raised those expectations knowingly and voluntarily. Like the other obligations of justice already spoken of, this one is not regarded as absolute, but as capa-ble of being overruled by a stronger obligation of justice on the other side; or by such con-duct on the part of the person concerned as is deemed to absolve us from our obligation to him, and to constitute a *forfeiture* of the benefit which he has been led to expect.

Fifthly, it is, by universal admission, inconsistent with justice to be *partial*—to show favour or preference to one person over another, in matters to which favour and preference do not properly apply. Impartiality, however, does not seem to be regarded as a duty in itself, but rather as instrumental to some other duty; for it is admitted that favour and preference are not always censurable, and indeed the cases in which they are condemned are rather the exception than the rule. A person would be more likely to be blamed than applauded for giving his family or friends no superiority in good of-fices over strangers, when he could do so without violating any other duty; and no one thinks it unjust to seek one person in preference to another as a friend, connection, or companion. Impartiality where rights are concerned is of course obligatory, but this is involved in the more general obligation of giving to every one his right. A tribunal, for example, must be impartial, because it is bound to award, without regard to any other consideration, a disputed object to the one of two parties who has the right to it. There are other cases in which impartiality means, being solely influenced by desert; as with those who, in the capacity of judges, preceptors, or parents, administer reward and punishment as such. There are cases, again, in which it means, being solely influenced by consideration for the public interest; as in making a selection among candidates for a government employment. Impartiality, in short, as an obligation of justice, may be said to mean, being exclusively influenced by the considerations which it is supposed ought to influence the particular case in hand; and resisting the solicitation of any mo-tives which prompt to conduct different from what those considerations would dictate.

Nearly allied to the idea of impartiality is that of *equality,* which often enters as a component part both into the conception of justice and into the practice of it, and, in the eyes of many persons, constitutes its essence. But in this, still more than in any other case, the notion of justice varies in different persons, and always conforms in its variations to their notion of utility. Each person maintains that equality is the dictate of justice, except where he thinks that expediency requires inequality. The justice of giv-ing equal protection to the rights of all, is maintained by those who support the most outrageous inequality in the rights themselves. Even in slave countries it is theoreti-cally admitted that the rights of the slave, such as they are, ought to be as sacred as those of the master; and that a tribunal which fails to enforce them with equal strictness is wanting in justice; while, at the same time, institutions which leave to the slave scarcely any rights to enforce, are not deemed unjust, because they are not deemed inexpedient. Those who think that utility requires distinctions of rank, do not consider it unjust that riches and social privileges should be unequally dispensed; but those who think this inequality inexpedient, think it unjust also. Whoever thinks that government is necessary, sees no injustice in as much inequality as is constituted by giving to the magistrate powers not granted to other people. Even among those who hold levelling doctrines, there are as many questions of justice as there are differences of opinion about expediency. Some Communists consider it unjust that the produce of the labour of the community should be shared on any other principle than that of exact equality; others think it just that those should receive most whose wants are greatest; while others hold that those who work harder, or who produce more, or whose services are more valuable to the community, may justly claim a larger quota in the division of the produce. And the sense of natural justice may be plausibly appealed to in behalf of every one of these opinions.

Among so many diverse applications of the term "justice," which yet is not regarded as ambiguous, it is a matter of some difficulty to seize the mental link which holds them together, and on which the moral sentiment adhering to the term essentially depends. Perhaps, in this embarrassment, some help may be derived from the history of the word, as indicated by its etymology.

In most, if not in all, languages, the etymology of the word which corresponds to "just" points distinctly to an origin connected with the ordinances of law. *Justum* is a form of *jussum,* that which has been ordered. ⟨*Dikaion*⟩ comes directly from ⟨*dike*⟩, a suit at law. *Recht,* from which came *right* and *righteous,* is synonymous with law. The courts of justice, the administration of justice, are the courts and the administration of law. *La justice,* in French, is the established term for judicature. I am not committing the fallacy imputed with some show of truth to Horne Tooke,* of assuming that a word must still continue to mean what it originally meant. Etymology is slight evidence of what the idea now signified is, but the very best evidence of how it sprang up. There can, I think, be no doubt that the *idée mère,* the primitive element, in the formation of the notion of justice, was conformity to law. It constituted the entire idea among the Hebrews, up to the birth of Christianity; as might be expected in the case of a people whose laws attempted to embrace all subjects on which precepts were required, and who believed those laws to be a direct emanation from the Supreme Being. But other nations, and in particular the Greeks and Romans, who knew that their laws had been made originally, and still continued to be made, by men, were not afraid to admit that those men might make bad laws; might do, by law, the same things, and from the same motives, which if done by individuals without the sanction of law, would be called unjust. And hence the sentiment of injustice came to be attached, not to all violations of law, but only to violations of such laws as *ought* to exist, including such as ought to exist, but do not; and to laws themselves, if supposed to be contrary to what ought to be law. In this manner the idea of law and of its injunctions was still predominant in the notion of justice, even when the laws actually in force ceased to be accepted as the standard of it.

It is true that mankind consider the idea of justice and its obligations as applicable to many things which neither are, nor is it desired that they should be, regulated by law. Nobody desires that laws should interfere with the whole detail of private life; yet every one allows that in all daily conduct a person may and does show himself to be ei-

*[John Tooke (1736–1812), a radical writer and close friend of Bentham.]

ther just or unjust. But even here, the idea of the breach of what ought to be law, still lingers in a modified shape. It would always give us pleasure, and chime in with our feelings of fitness, that acts which we deem unjust should be punished, though we do not always think it expedient that this should be done by the tribunals. We forego that gratification on account of incidental inconveniences. We should be glad to see just conduct enforced and injustice repressed, even in the minutest details, if we were not, with reason, afraid of trusting the magistrate with so unlimited an amount of power over individuals. When we think that a person is bound in justice to do a thing, it is an ordinary form of language to say, that he ought to be compelled to do it. We should be gratified to see the obligation enforced by anybody who had the power. If we see that its enforcement by law would be inexpedient, we lament the impossibility, we consider the impunity given to injustice as an evil, and strive to make amends for it by bringing a strong expression of our own and the public disapprobation to bear upon the offender. Thus the idea of legal constraint is still the generating idea of the notion of justice, though undergoing several transformations before that notion, as it exists in an advanced state of society, becomes complete.

The above is, I think, a true account, as far as it goes, of the origin and progressive growth of the idea of justice. But we must observe, that it contains, as yet, nothing to distinguish that obligation from moral obligation in general. For the truth is, that the idea of penal sanction, which is the essence of law, enters not only into the conception of injustice, but into that of any kind of wrong. We do not call anything wrong, unless we mean to imply that a person ought to be punished in some way or other for doing it; if not by law, by the opinion of his fellow-creatures; if not by opinion, by the reproaches of his own conscience. This seems the real turning point of the distinction between morality and simple expediency. It is a part of the notion of Duty in every one of its forms, that a person may rightfully be compelled to fulfil it. Duty is a thing which may be *exacted* from a person, as one exacts a debt. Unless we think that it may be exacted from him, we do not call it his duty. Reasons of prudence, or the interest of other people, may militate against actually exacting it; but the person himself, it is clearly understood, would not be entitled to complain. There are other things, on the contrary, which we wish that people should do, which we like or admire them for doing, perhaps dislike or despise them for not doing, but yet admit that they are not bound to do; it is not a case of moral obligation; we do not blame them, that is, we do not think that they are proper objects of punishment. How we come by these ideas of deserving and not deserving punishment, will appear, perhaps, in the sequel; but I think there is no doubt that this distinction lies at the bottom of the notions of right and wrong; that we call any conduct wrong, or employ, instead, some other term of dislike or disparagement, according as we think that the person ought, or ought not, to be punished for it; and we say, it would be right to do so and so, or merely that it would be desirable or laudable, according as we would wish to see the person whom it concerns, compelled, or only persuaded and exhorted, to act in that manner.*

This, therefore, being the characteristic difference which marks off, not justice, but morality in general, from the remaining provinces of Expediency and Worthiness; the character is still to be sought which distinguishes justice from other branches of morality. Now it is known that ethical writers divide moral duties into two classes, denoted by the ill-chosen expressions, duties of perfect and of imperfect obligation; the latter being

*I see this point enforced and illustrated by Professor Bain, in an admirable chapter (entitled "The Ethical Emotions, or the Moral Sense"), of the second of the two treatises composing his elaborate and profound work on the Mind.

those in which, though the act is obligatory, the particular occasions of performing it are left to our choice; as in the case of charity or beneficence, which we are indeed bound to practise, but not towards any definite person, nor at any prescribed time. In the more precise language of philosophic jurists, duties of perfect obligation are those duties in virtue of which a correlative *right* resides in some person or persons; duties of imperfect obligation are those moral obligations which do not give birth to any right. I think it will be found that this distinction exactly coincides with that which exists between justice and the other obligations of morality. In our survey of the various popular acceptations of justice, the term appeared generally to involve the idea of a personal right—a claim on the part of one or more individuals, like that which the law gives when it confers a proprietary or other legal right. Whether the injustice consists in depriving a person of a possession, or in breaking faith with him, or in treating him worse than he deserves, or worse than other people who have no greater claims, in each case the supposition implies two things—a wrong done, and some assignable person who is wronged. Injustice may also be done by treating a person better than others; but the wrong in this case is to his competitors, who are also assignable persons. It seems to me that this feature in the case—a right in some person, correlative to the moral obligation—constitutes the specific difference between justice, and generosity or beneficence. Justice implies something which it is not only right to do, and wrong not to do, but which some individual person can claim from us as his moral right. No one has a moral right to our generosity or beneficence, because we are not morally bound to practise those virtues towards any given individual. And it will be found with respect to this as to every correct definition, that the instances which seem to conflict with it are those which most confirm it. For if a moralist attempts, as some have done, to make out that mankind generally, though not any given individual, have a right to all the good we can do them, he at once, by that thesis, includes generosity and beneficence within the category of justice. He is obliged to say, that our utmost exertions are due to our fellow-creatures, thus assimilating them to a debt; or that nothing less can be a sufficient return for what society does for us, thus classing the case as one of gratitude; both of which are acknowledged cases of justice. Wherever there is a right, the case is one of justice, and not of the virtue of beneficence: and whoever does not place the distinction between justice and morality in general, where we have now placed it, will be found to make no distinction between them at all, but to merge all morality in justice.

Having thus endeavoured to determine the distinctive elements which enter into the composition of the idea of justice, we are ready to enter on the inquiry, whether the feeling, which accompanies the idea, is attached to it by a special dispensation of nature, or whether it could have grown up, by any known laws, out of the idea itself; and in particular, whether it can have originated in considerations of general expediency.

I conceive that the sentiment itself does not arise from anything which would commonly, or correctly, be termed an idea of expediency; but that though the sentiment does not, whatever is moral in it does.

We have seen that the two essential ingredients in the sentiment of justice are, the desire to punish a person who has done harm and the knowledge or belief that there is some definite individual or individuals to whom harm has been done.

Now it appears to me, that the desire to punish a person who has done harm to some individual is a spontaneous outgrowth from two sentiments, both in the highest degree natural, and which either are or resemble instincts; the impulse of self-defence, and the feeling of sympathy.

It is natural to resent, and to repel or retaliate, any harm done or attempted against ourselves, or against those with whom we sympathise. The origin of this sentiment it is not necessary here to discuss. Whether it be an instinct or a result of intelligence, it is, we know, common to all animal nature; for every animal tries to hurt those who have hurt, or who it thinks are about to hurt, itself or its young. Human beings, on this point, only differ from other animals in two particulars. First, in being capable of sympathising, not solely with their offspring, or, like some of the more noble animals, with some superior animal who is kind to them, but with all human, and even with all sentient, beings. Secondly, in having a more developed intelligence, which gives a wider range to the whole of their sentiments, whether self-regarding or sympathetic. By virtue of his superior intelligence, even apart from his superior range of sympathy, a human being is capable of apprehending a community of interest between himself and the human society of which he forms a part, such that any conduct which threatens the security of the society generally, is threatening to his own, and calls forth his instinct (if instinct it be) of self-defence. The same superiority of intelligence, joined to the power of sympathising with human beings generally, enables him to attach himself to the collective idea of his tribe, his country, or mankind, in such a manner that any act hurtful to them, raises his instinct of sympathy, and urges him to resistance.

The sentiment of justice, in that one of its elements which consists of the desire to punish, is thus, I conceive, the natural feeling of retaliation or vengeance, rendered by intellect and sympathy applicable to those injuries, that is, to those hurts, which wound us through, or in common with, society at large. This sentiment, in itself, has nothing moral in it; what is moral is, the exclusive subordination of it to the social sympathies, so as to wait on and obey their call. For the natural feeling would make us resent indiscriminately whatever any one does that is disagreeable to us; but when moralised by the social feeling, it only acts in the directions conformable to the general good: just persons resenting a hurt to society, though not otherwise a hurt to themselves, and not resenting a hurt to themselves, however painful, unless it be of the kind which society has a common interest with them in the repression of.

It is no objection against this doctrine to say, that when we feel our sentiment of justice outraged, we are not thinking of society at large, or of any collective interest, but only of the individual case. It is common enough certainly, though the reverse of commendable, to feel resentment merely because we have suffered pain; but a person whose resentment is really a moral feeling, that is, who considers whether an act is blamable before he allows himself to resent it—such a person, though he may not say expressly to himself that he is standing up for the interest of society, certainly does feel that he is asserting a rule which is for the benefit of others as well as for his own. If he is not feeling this—if he is regarding the act solely as it affects him individually—he is not consciously just; he is not concerning himself about the justice of his actions. This is admitted even by anti-utilitarian moralists. When Kant (as before remarked) propounds as the fundamental principle of morals, "So act, that thy rule of conduct might be adopted as a law by all rational beings," he virtually acknowledges that the interest of mankind collectively, or at least of mankind indiscriminately, must be in the mind of the agent when conscientiously deciding on the morality of the act. Otherwise he uses words without a meaning: for, that a rule even of utter selfishness could not *possibly* be adopted by all rational beings—that there is any insuperable obstacle in the nature of things to its adoption—cannot be even plausibly maintained. To give any meaning to Kant's principle, the sense put upon it must be, that we ought to shape our conduct by a rule which all rational beings might adopt *with benefit to their collective interest.*

To recapitulate: the idea of justice supposes two things—a rule of conduct, and a sentiment which sanctions the rule. The first must be supposed common to all mankind, and intended for their good. The other (the sentiment) is a desire that punishment may be suffered by those who infringe the rule. There is involved, in addition, the conception of some definite person who suffers by the infringement; whose rights (to use the expression appropriated to the case) are violated by it. And the sentiment of justice appears to me to be, the animal desire to repel or retaliate a hurt or damage to oneself, or to those with whom one sympathises, widened so as to include all persons, by the human capacity of enlarged sympathy, and the human conception of intelligent self-interest. From the latter elements, the feeling derives its morality; from the former, its peculiar impressiveness, and energy of self-assertion.

I have, throughout, treated the idea of a *right* residing in the injured person, and violated by the injury, not as a separate element in the composition of the idea and sentiment, but as one of the forms in which the other two elements clothe themselves. These elements are, a hurt to some assignable person or persons on the one hand, and a demand for punishment on the other. An examination of our own minds, I think, will show, that these two things include all that we mean when we speak of violation of a right. When we call anything a person's right, we mean that he has a valid claim on society to protect him in the possession of it, either by the force of law, or by that of education and opinion. If he has what we consider a sufficient claim, on whatever account, to have something guaranteed to him by society, we say that he has a right to it. If we desire to prove that anything does not belong to him by right, we think this done as soon as it is admitted that society ought not to take measures for securing it to him, but should leave him to chance, or to his own exertions. Thus, a person is said to have a right to what he can earn in fair professional competition; because society ought not to allow any other person to hinder him from endeavouring to earn in that manner as much as he can. But he has not a right to three hundred a year, though he may happen to be earning it; because society is not called on to provide that he shall earn that sum. On the contrary, if he owns ten thousand pounds three percent stock, he *has* a right to three hundred a year because society has come under an obligation to provide him with an income of that amount.

To have a right, then, is, I conceive, to have something which society ought to defend me in the possession of. If the objector goes on to ask, why it ought? I can give him no other reason than general utility. If that expression does not seem to convey a sufficient feeling of the strength of the obligation, nor to account for the peculiar energy of the feeling, it is because there goes to the composition of the sentiment, not a rational only, but also an animal element, the thirst for retaliation; and this thirst derives its intensity, as well as its moral justification, from the extraordinarily important and impressive kind of utility which is concerned. The interest involved is that of security, to every one's feelings the most vital of all interests. All other earthly benefits are needed by one person, not needed by another; and many of them can, if necessary, be cheerfully foregone, or replaced by something else; but security no human being can possibly do without; on it we depend for all our immunity from evil, and for the whole value of all and every good, beyond the passing moment; since nothing but the gratification of the instant could be of any worth to us, if we could be deprived of anything the next instant by whoever was momentarily stronger than ourselves. Now this most indispensable of all necessaries, after physical nutriment, cannot be had, unless the machinery for providing it is kept unintermittedly in active play. Our notion, therefore, of the claim we have on our fellow-creatures to join in making safe for us the very groundwork of our existence, gathers feelings around it so much more intense than those concerned in any of the more common cases of utility, that the difference in degree (as is often the case in psychology) becomes a real difference in kind. The claim assumes that character of absoluteness, that apparent infinity, and incommensurability with all other considerations, which constitute the distinction between the feeling of right and wrong and that of ordinary expediency and inexpediency. The feelings concerned are so powerful, and we count so positively on finding a responsive feeling in others (all being alike interested), that *ought* and *should* grow into *must*, and recognised indispensability becomes a moral necessity, analogous to physical, and often not inferior to it in binding force.

If the preceding analysis, or something resembling it, be not the correct account of the notion of justice; if justice be totally independent of utility, and be a standard per se, which the mind can recognise by simple introspection of itself; it is hard to understand why that internal oracle is so ambiguous, and why so many things appear either just or unjust, according to the light in which they are regarded.

We are continually informed that Utility is an uncertain standard, which every different person interprets differently, and that there is no safety but in the immutable, ineffaceable, and unmistakable dictates of Justice, which carry their evidence in themselves, and are independent of the fluctuations of opinion. One would suppose from this that on questions of justice there could be no controversy; that if we take that for our rule, its application to any given case could leave us in as little doubt as a mathematical demonstration. So far is this from being the fact, that there is as much difference of opinion, and as much discussion, about what is just, as about what is useful to society. Not only have different nations and individuals different notions of justice, but in the mind of one and the same individual, justice is not some one rule, principle, or maxim, but many, which do not always coincide in their dictates, and in choosing between which, he is guided either by some extraneous standard, or by his own personal predilections.

For instance, there are some who say, that it is unjust to punish any one for the sake of example to others; that punishment is just, only when intended for the good of the sufferer himself. Others maintain the extreme reverse, contending that to punish persons who have attained years of discretion, for their own benefit, is despotism and injustice, since if the matter at issue is solely their own good, no one has a right to control their own judgment of it; but that they may justly be punished to prevent evil to others, this being the exercise of the legitimate right of self-defence. Mr. Owen,* again, affirms that it is unjust to punish at all; for the criminal did not make his own character; his education, and the circumstances which surrounded him, have made him a criminal, and for these he is not responsible. All these opinions are extremely plausible; and so long as the question is argued as one of justice simply, without going down to the principles which lie under justice and are the source of its authority, I am unable to see how any of these reasoners can be refuted. For in truth every one of the three builds upon rules of justice confessedly true. The first appeals to the acknowledged injustice of singling out an individual, and making him a sacrifice, without his consent, for other people's benefit. The second relies on the acknowledged justice of self-defence, and the admitted injustice of forcing one person to conform to another's notions of what constitutes his good. The Owenite invokes the admitted principle, that it is unjust to punish any one for what he cannot help. Each is triumphant so long as he is not compelled to take into consideration any other maxims of justice than the one he has selected; but as soon as their several maxims are brought face to face, each disputant seems to have exactly as much to say for himself as the others. No one of them can carry out his own notion of justice without trampling upon another equally binding. These are difficulties; they have always been felt to be such; and many devices have been invented to turn rather than to overcome them. As a refuge from the last of the three, men imagined what they called the freedom of the will; fancying that they could not justify punishing a man whose will is in a thoroughly hateful state, unless it be supposed to have come into that state through no influence of anterior circum-

*[Robert Owen (1771–1858), a British reformer who argued for environmental determinism.]

stances. To escape from the other difficulties, a favourite contrivance has been the fiction of a contract, whereby at some unknown period all the members of society engaged to obey the laws, and consented to be punished for any disobedience to them; thereby giving to their legislators the right, which it is assumed they would not otherwise have had, of punishing them, either for their own good or for that of society. This happy thought was considered to get rid of the whole difficulty, and to legitimate the infliction of punishment, in virtue of another received maxim of justice, *volenti non fit injuria;* that is not unjust which is done with the consent of the person who is supposed to be hurt by it. I need hardly remark, that even if the consent were not a mere fiction, this maxim is not superior in authority to the others which it is brought in to supersede. It is, on the contrary, an instructive specimen of the loose and irregular manner in which supposed principles of justice grow up. This particular one evidently came into use as a help to the coarse exigencies of courts of law, which are sometimes obliged to be content with very uncertain presumptions, on account of the greater evils which would often arise from any attempt on their part to cut finer. But even courts of law are not able to adhere consistently to the maxim, for they allow voluntary engagements to be set aside on the ground of fraud, and sometimes on that of mere mistake or misinformation.

Again, when the legitimacy of inflicting punishment is admitted, how many conflicting conceptions of justice come to light in discussing the proper apportionment of punishments to offences. No rule on the subject recommends itself so strongly to the primitive and spontaneous sentiment of justice, as the *lex talionis,* an eye for an eye and a tooth for a tooth. Though this principle of the Jewish and of the Mohammedan law has been generally abandoned in Europe as a practical maxim, there is, I suspect, in most minds, a secret hankering after it; and when retribution accidentally falls on an offender in that precise shape, the general feeling of satisfaction evinced bears witness how natural is the sentiment to which this repayment in kind is acceptable. With many, the test of justice in penal infliction is that the punishment should be proportioned to the offence; meaning that it should be exactly measured by the moral guilt of the culprit (whatever be their standard for measuring moral guilt): the consideration, what amount of punishment is necessary to deter from the offence, having nothing to do with the question of justice, in their estimation: while there are others to whom that consideration is all in all; who maintain that it is not just, at least for man, to inflict on a fellow-creature, whatever may be his offences, any amount of suffering beyond the least that will suffice to prevent him from repeating, and others from imitating, his misconduct.

To take another example from a subject already once referred to. In a co-operative industrial association, is it just or not that talent or skill should give a title to superior remuneration? On the negative side of the question it is argued, that whoever does the best he can, deserves equally well, and ought not in justice to be put in a position of inferiority for no fault of his own; that superior abilities have already advantages more than enough, in the admiration they excite, the personal influence they command, and the internal sources of satisfaction attending them, without adding to these a superior share of the world's goods; and that society is bound in justice rather to make compensation to the less favoured, for this unmerited inequality of advantages, than to aggravate it. On the contrary side it is contended, that society receives more from the more efficient labourer; that his services being more useful, society owes him a larger return for them; that a greater share of the joint result is actually his work, and not to allow his claim to it is a kind of robbery; that if he is only to receive as much as others, he can only be justly required to produce as much, and to give a smaller amount of time and exertion, proportioned to his superior efficiency. Who shall decide between these appeals to conflicting principles of justice? Justice has in this case two sides to it, which it is impossible to bring into harmony, and the two disputants have chosen opposite sides; the one looks to what it is just that the individual should receive, the other to what it is just that the community should give. Each, from his own point of view, is unanswerable; and any choice between them, on grounds of justice, must be perfectly arbitrary. Social utility alone can decide the preference.

How many, again, and how irreconcilable, are the standards of justice to which reference is made in discussing the repartition of taxation. One opinion is, that payment to the State should be in numerical proportion to pecuniary means. Others think that justice dictates what they term graduated taxation; taking a higher percentage from those who have more to spare. In point of natural justice a strong case might be made for disregarding means altogether, and taking the same absolute sum (whenever it could be got) from every one: as the subscribers to a mess, or to a club, all pay the same sum for the same privileges, whether they can all equally afford it or not. Since the protection (it might be said) of law and government is afforded to, and is equally required by all, there is no injustice in making all buy it at the same price. It is reckoned justice, not injustice, that a dealer should charge to all customers the same price for the same article, not a price varying according to their means of payment. This doctrine, as applied to taxation, finds no advocates, because it conflicts so strongly with man's feelings of humanity and of social expediency; but the principle of justice which it invokes is as true and as binding as those which can be appealed to against it. Accordingly it exerts a tacit influence on the line of defence employed for other modes of assessing taxation. People feel obliged to argue that the State does more for the rich than for the poor, as a justification for its taking more from them: though this is in reality not true, for the rich would be far better able to protect themselves, in the absence of law or government, than the poor, and indeed would probably be successful in converting the poor into their slaves. Others, again, so far defer to the same conception of justice, as to maintain that all should pay an equal capitation tax for the protection of their persons (these being of equal value to all), and an unequal tax for the protection of their property, which is unequal. To this others reply, that the all of one man is as valuable to him as the all of another. From these confusions there is no other mode of extrication than the utilitarian.

Is, then, the difference between the Just and the Expedient a merely imaginary distinction? Have mankind been under a delusion in thinking that justice is a more sacred thing than policy, and that the latter ought only to be listened to after the former has been satisfied? By no means. The exposition we have given of the nature and origin of the sentiment, recognises a real distinction; and no one of those who profess the most sublime contempt for the consequences of actions as an element in their morality, attaches more importance to the distinction than I do. While I dispute the pretensions of any theory which sets up an imaginary standard of justice not grounded on utility, I account the justice which is grounded on utility to be the chief part, and incomparably the most sacred and binding part, of all morality. Justice is a name for certain classes of moral rules, which concern the essentials of human well-being more nearly, and are therefore of more absolute obligation, than any other rules for the guidance of life; and the notion which we have found to be of the essence of the idea of justice, that of a right residing in an individual, implies and testifies to this more binding obligation.

The moral rules which forbid mankind to hurt one another (in which we must never forget to include wrongful interference with each other's freedom) are more vital to human well-being than any maxims, however important, which only point out the best mode of managing some department of human affairs. They have also the peculiarity, that they are the main element in determining the whole of the social feelings of mankind. It is their observance which alone preserves peace among human beings: if obedience to them were not the rule, and disobedience the exception, every one would see in every one else an enemy, against whom he must be perpetually guarding himself. What is hardly less important, these are the precepts which mankind have the strongest and the most direct inducements for impressing upon one another. By merely giving to each other prudential instruction or exhortation, they may gain, or think they gain, nothing: in inculcating on each other the duty of positive beneficence they have an unmistakable interest, but far less in degree: a person may possibly not need the benefits of others; but he always needs that they should not do him hurt. Thus the moralities which protect every individual from being harmed by others, either directly or by being hindered in his freedom of pursuing his own good, are at once those which he himself has most at heart, and those which he has the strongest interest in publishing and enforcing by word and deed. It is by a person's observance of these that his fitness to exist as one of the fellowship of human beings is tested and decided; for on that depends his being a nuisance or not to those with whom he is in contact. Now it is these moralities primarily which compose the obligations of justice. The most marked cases of injustice, and those which give the tone to the feeling of repugnance which characterises the sentiment, are acts of wrongful aggression, or wrongful exercise of power over some one; the next are those which consist in wrongfully withholding from him something which is his due; in both cases, inflicting on him a positive hurt, either in the form of direct suffering, or of the privation of some good which he had reasonable ground, either of a physical or of a social kind, for counting upon.

The same powerful motives which command the observance of these primary moralities, enjoin the punishment of those who violate them; and as the impulses of self-defence, of defence of others, and of vengeance, are all called forth against such persons, retribution, or evil for evil, becomes closely connected with the sentiment of justice, and is universally included in the idea. Good for good is also one of the dictates of justice; and this, though its social utility is evident, and though it carries with it a natural human feeling, has not at first sight that obvious connection with hurt or injury, which, existing in the most elementary cases of just and un-just, is the source of the characteristic intensity of the sentiment. But the connection, though less obvious, is not less real. He who accepts benefits, and denies a return of them when needed, inflicts a real hurt, by disappointing one of the most natural and reasonable of expectations, and one which he must at least tacitly have encouraged, otherwise the benefits would seldom have been conferred. The important rank, among human evils and wrongs, of the disappointment of expectation, is shown in the fact that it constitutes the principal criminality of two such highly immoral acts as a breach of friendship and a breach of promise. Few hurts which human beings can sustain are greater, and none wound more, than when that on which they habitually and with full assurance relied, fails them in the hour of need; and few wrongs are greater than this mere withholding of good; none excite more resentment, either in the person suffering, or in a sympathising spectator. The principle, therefore, of giving to each what they deserve, that is, good for good as well as evil for evil, is not only included within the idea of Justice as we have defined it, but is a proper object of that intensity of sentiment, which places the Just, in human estimation, above the simply Expedient.

Most of the maxims of justice current in the world, and commonly appealed to in its transactions, are simply instrumental to carrying into effect the principles of justice which we have now spoken of. That a person is only responsible for what he has done voluntarily, or could voluntarily have avoided; that it is unjust to condemn any person unheard; that the punishment ought to be proportioned to the offence, and the like, are maxims intended to prevent the just principle of evil for evil from being perverted to the infliction of evil without that justification. The greater part of these common maxims have come into use from the practice of courts of justice, which have been naturally led to a more complete recognition and elaboration than was likely to suggest itself to others, of the rules necessary to enable them to fulfil their double function, of inflicting punishment when due, and of awarding to each person his right.

That first of judicial virtues, impartiality, is an obligation of justice, partly for the reason last mentioned; as being a necessary condition of the fulfilment of the other obligations of justice. But this is not the only source of the exalted rank, among human obligations, of those maxims of equality and impartiality, which, both in popular estimation and in that of the most enlightened, are included among the precepts of justice. In one point of view, they may be considered as corollaries from the principles already laid down. If it is a duty to do to each according to his deserts, returning good for good as well as repressing evil by evil, it necessarily follows that we should treat all equally well (when no higher duty forbids) who have deserved equally well of *us,* and that society should treat all equally well who have deserved equally well of *it,* that is, who have deserved equally well absolutely. This is the highest abstract standard of social and distributive justice; towards which all institutions, and the efforts of all virtuous citizens, should be made in the utmost possible degree to converge. But this great moral duty rests upon a still deeper foundation, being a direct emanation from the first principle of morals, and not a mere logical corollary from secondary or derivative doctrines. It is involved in the very meaning of Utility, or the Greatest Happiness Principle. That principle is a mere form of words without rational signification, unless one person's happiness, supposed equal in degree (with the proper allowance made for kind), is counted for exactly as much as another's. Those conditions being supplied, Bentham's dictum, "everybody to count for one, nobody for more than one," might be written under the principle of utility as an explanatory commentary.* The equal claim of everybody to happiness in

---

*This implication, in the first principle of the utilitarian scheme, of perfect impartiality between persons, is regarded by Mr. Herbert Spencer (in his *Social Statics*) as a disproof of the pretensions of utility to be a sufficient guide to right, since (he says) the principle of utility presupposes the anterior principle that everybody has an equal right to happiness. It may be more correctly described as supposing that equal amounts of happiness are equally desirable whether felt by the same or by different persons. This, however, is not a pre-supposition; not a premise needful to support the principle of utility, but the very principle itself; for what is the principle of utility, if it be not that "happiness" and "desirable" are synonymous terms? If there Is any anterior principle Implied, it can be no other than this, that the truths of arithmetic are applicable to the valuation of happiness, as of all other measurable quantities.

(Mr. Herbert Spencer in a private communication on the subject of the preceding note, objects to being considered an opponent of utilitarianism, and states that he regards happiness as the ultimate end of morality; but deems that end only partially attainable by empirical generalisations from the observed results of conduct, and completely attainable only by deducing, from the laws of life and the conditions of existence, what kinds of action necessarily tend to produce happiness, and what kinds to produce unhappiness. With the exception of the word "necessarily," I have no dissent to express from this doctrine; and (omitting that word) I am not aware that any modern advocate of utilitarianism is of a different opinion. Bentham, certainly, to whom in the *Social Statics* Mr. Spencer particularly referred, is, least of all writers, chargeable with unwillingness to deduce the effect of actions on happiness from the laws of human nature and the universal conditions of human life. The common charge against him is of relying too exclusively upon such deductions, and declining altogether to be bound by the generalisations from specific experience which Mr. Spencer thinks that utilitarians generally confine themselves to. My own opinion (and, as I collect, Mr. Spencer's) is, that in ethics, as in all other branches of scientific study, the consilience of the results of both these processes, each corroborating and verifying the other, is requisite to give to any general proposition the kind and degree of evidence which constitutes scientific proof.)

the estimation of the moralist and of the legislator, involves an equal claim to all the means of happiness, except in so far as the inevitable conditions of human life, and the general interest, in which that of every individual is included, set limits to the maxim; and those limits ought to be strictly construed. As every other maxim of justice, so this is by no means applied or held applicable universally; on the contrary, as I have already remarked, it bends to every person's ideas of social expediency. But in whatever case it is deemed applicable at all, it is held to be the dictate of justice. All persons are deemed to have a *right* to equality of treatment, except when some recognised social expediency requires the reverse. And hence all social inequalities which have ceased to be considered expedient, assume the character not of simple inexpediency, but of injustice, and appear so tyrannical, that people are apt to wonder how they ever could have been tolerated; forgetful that they themselves perhaps tolerate other inequalities under an equally mistaken notion of expediency, the correction of which would make that which they approve seem quite as monstrous as what they have at last learnt to condemn. The entire history of social improvement has been a series of transitions, by which one custom or institution after another, from being a supposed primary necessity of social existence, has passed into the rank of a universally stigmatised injustice and tyranny. So it has been with the distinctions of slaves and freemen, nobles and serfs, patricians and plebeians; and so it will be, and in part already is, with the aristocracies of colour, race, and sex.

It appears from what has been said, that justice is a name for certain moral requirements, which, regarded collectively, stand higher in the scale of social utility, and are therefore of more paramount obligation, than any others; though particular cases may occur in which some other social duty is so important, as to overrule any one of the general maxims of justice. Thus, to save a life, it may not only be allowable, but a duty, to steal, or take by force, the necessary food or medicine, or to kidnap, and compel to officiate, the only qualified medical practitioner. In such cases, as we do not call anything justice which is not a virtue, we usually say, not that justice must give way to some other moral principle, but that what is just in ordinary cases is, by reason of that other principle, not just in the particular case. By this useful accommodation of language, the character of indefeasibility attributed to justice is kept up, and we are saved from the necessity of maintaining that there can be laudable injustice.

The considerations which have now been adduced resolve, I conceive, the only real difficulty in the utilitarian theory of morals. It has always been evident that all cases of justice are also cases of expediency: the difference is in the peculiar sentiment which attaches to the former, as contradistinguished from the latter. If this characteristic sentiment has been sufficiently accounted for; if there is no necessity to assume for it any peculiarity of origin; if it is simply the natural feeling of resentment, moralised by being made coextensive with the demands of social good; and if this feeling not only does but ought to exist in all the classes of cases to which the idea of justice corresponds; that idea no longer presents itself as a stumbling-block to the utilitarian ethics. Justice remains the appropriate name for certain social utilities which are vastly more important, and therefore more absolute and imperative, than any others are as a class (though not more so than others may be in particular cases); and which, therefore, ought to be, as well as naturally are, guarded by a sentiment not only different in degree, but also in kind; distinguished from the milder feeling which attaches to the mere idea of promoting human pleasure or convenience, at once by the more definite nature of its commands, and by the sterner character of its sanctions.

ON LIBERTY

> The Grand, Leading Principle, towards which every argument unfolded in these pages directly converges, is the absolute and essential importance of human development in its richest diversity.
>
> —Wilhem von Humbodt, *Sphere and Duties of Government.*

To the beloved and deplored memory of her who was the inspirer, and in part the author, of all that is best in my writings—the friend and wife whose exalted sense of truth and right was my strongest incitement, and whose approbation was my chief reward— I dedicate this volume. Like all that I have written for many years, it belongs as much to her as to me; but the work as it stands has had, in a very insufficient degree, the inestimable advantage of her revision; some of the most important portions having been reserved for a more careful re-examination, which they are now never destined to receive. Were I but capable of interpreting to the world one half the great thoughts and noble feelings which are buried in her grave, I should be the medium of a greater benefit to it, than is ever likely to arise from anything that I can write, unprompted and unassisted by her all but unrivaled wisdom.

CHAPTER 1: INTRODUCTORY

The subject of this essay is not the so-called "liberty of the will," so unfortunately opposed to the misnamed doctrine of philosophical necessity; but civil, or social liberty: the nature and limits of the power which can be legitimately exercised by society over the individual. A question seldom stated, and hardly ever discussed in general terms, but which profoundly influences the practical controversies of the age by its latent presence, and is likely soon to make itself recognized as the vital question of the future. It is so far from being new that, in a certain sense, it has divided mankind almost from the remotest ages; but in the stage of progress into which the more civilized portions of the species have now entered, it presents itself under new conditions and requires a different and more fundamental treatment.

The struggle between liberty and authority is the most conspicuous feature in the portions of history with which we are earliest familiar, particularly in that of Greece, Rome, and England. But in old times this contest was between subjects, or some classes of subjects, and the government. By liberty was meant protection against the tyranny of the political rulers. The rulers were conceived (except in some of the popular governments of Greece) as in a necessarily antagonistic position to the people whom they ruled. They consisted of a governing One, or a governing tribe or caste, who derived their authority from inheritance or conquest, who, at all events, did not hold it at the pleasure of the governed, and whose supremacy men did not venture, perhaps did not desire, to contest, whatever precautions might be taken against its oppressive exercise. Their power was regarded as necessary, but also as highly dangerous; as a weapon which they would attempt to use against their subjects, no less than against external enemies. To prevent the weaker members of the community from being preyed upon by innumerable vultures, it was needful that there should be an animal of prey stronger than the rest, commissioned to keep them down. But as the king of the vultures would be no less bent upon preying on the flock than any of the minor harpies, it was indispensable to be in a perpetual attitude of defense against his beak and claws. The aim, therefore, of patriots was to set limits to the power which the ruler should be suffered to exercise over the community; and this limitation was what they meant by liberty. It was attempted in two ways. First, by obtaining a recognition of certain immunities, called political liberties or rights, which it was to be regarded as a breach of duty in the ruler to infringe, and which if he did infringe, specific resistance or general rebellion was held to be justifiable. A second, and generally a later, expedient was the establishment of constitutional checks by which the consent of the community, or of a body of some sort, supposed to represent its interests, was made a necessary condition to some of the more important acts of the governing power. To the first of these modes of limitation, the ruling power, in most European countries, was compelled, more or less, to submit. It was not so with the second; and, to attain this, or, when already in some degree possessed, to attain it more completely, became everywhere the principal object of the lovers of liberty. And so long as mankind were content to combat one enemy by another, and to be ruled by a master on condition of being guaranteed more or less efficaciously against his tyranny, they did not carry their aspirations beyond this point.

A time, however, came, in the progress of human affairs, when men ceased to think it a necessity of nature that their governors should be an independent power opposed in interest to themselves. It appeared to them much better that the various magistrates of the state should be their tenants or delegates, revocable at their pleasure. In that way alone, it seemed, could they have complete security that the powers of government would never be abused to their disadvantage. By degrees this new demand for elective and temporary rulers became the prominent object of the exertions of the popular party wherever any such party existed, and superseded, to a considerable extent, the previous efforts to limit the power of rulers. As the struggle proceeded for making the ruling power emanate from the periodical choice of the ruled, some persons began to think that too much importance had been attached to the limitation of the power itself. *That* (it might seem) was a resource against rulers whose interests were habitually opposed to those of the people. What was now wanted was that the rulers should be identified with the people, that their interest and will should be the interest and will of the nation. The nation did not need to be protected against its own will. There was no fear of its tyrannizing over itself. Let the rulers be effectually responsible to it, promptly removable by it, and it could afford to trust them with power of which it could itself dictate the use to be made. Their power was but the nation's own power, concentrated and in a form convenient for exercise. This mode of thought, or rather perhaps of feeling, was common among the last generation of European liberalism, in the Continental section of which it still apparently predominates. Those who admit any limit to what a government may do, except in the case of such governments as they think ought not to exist, stand out as brilliant exceptions among the political thinkers of the Continent. A similar tone of sentiment might by this time have been prevalent in our own country if the circumstances which for a time encouraged it had continued unaltered.

But, in political and philosophical theories as well as in persons, success discloses faults and infirmities which failure might have concealed from observation. The notion that the people have no need to limit their power over themselves might seem axiomatic, when popular government was a thing only dreamed about, or read of as having existed at some distant period of the past. Neither was that notion necessarily disturbed by such temporary aberrations as those of the French Revolution, the worst of which were the work of a usurping few, and which, in any case, belonged, not to the permanent working of popular institutions, but to a sudden and convulsive outbreak against monarchical and aristocratic despotism. In time, however, a democratic republic came to occupy a large portion of the earth's surface and made itself felt as one of the most powerful members of the community of nations;* and elective and responsible government became subject to the observations and criticisms which wait upon a great existing fact. It was now perceived that such phrases as "self-government," and "the power of the people over themselves," do not express the true state of the case. The "people" who exercise the power are not always the same people with those over whom it is exercised; and the "self-government" spoken of is not the government of each by himself, but of each by all the rest. The will of the people, moreover, practically means the will of the most numerous or the most active *part* of the people—the majority, or those who succeed in making themselves accepted as the majority; the people, consequently, may desire to oppress a part of their number, and precautions are as much needed against this as against any other abuse of power. The limitation, therefore, of the power of government over individuals loses none of its importance when the holders of power are regularly accountable to the community, that is, to the strongest party therein. This view of things, recommending itself equally to the intelligence of thinkers and to the inclination of those important classes in European society to whose real or supposed interests democracy is adverse, has had no difficulty in establishing itself; and in political speculations "the tyranny of the majority" is now generally included among the evils against which society requires to be on its guard.

Like other tyrannies, the tyranny of the majority was at first, and is still vulgarly, held in dread, chiefly as operating through the acts of the public authorities. But reflecting persons perceived that when society is itself the tyrant—society collectively over the separate individuals who compose it—its means of tyrannizing are not restricted to the acts which it may do by the hands of its political functionaries. Society can and does execute its own mandates; and if it issues wrong mandates instead of right, or any mandates at all in things with which it ought not to meddle, it practices a social tyranny more formidable than many kinds of political oppression, since, though not usually upheld by such extreme penalties, it leaves fewer means of escape, penetrating much more deeply into the details of life, and enslaving the soul itself. Protection, therefore, against the tyranny of the magistrate is not enough; there needs protection also against the tyranny of the prevailing opinion and feeling, against the tendency of society to impose, by other means than civil penalties, its own ideas and practices as rules of conduct on those who dissent from them; to fetter the development and, if possible, prevent the formation of any individuality not in harmony with its ways, and compel all characters to fashion themselves upon the model of its own. There is a limit to the legitimate interference of collective opinion with individual independence; and to find that limit, and maintain it against encroachment, is as indispensable to a good condition of human affairs as protection against political despotism.

But though this proposition is not likely to be contested in general terms, the practical question where to place the limit—how to make the fitting adjustment between individual independence and social control—is a subject on which nearly everything remains to be done. All that makes existence valuable to anyone depends on the enforcement of restraints upon the actions of other people. Some rules of conduct,

---

*[Referring to the United States of America.]

therefore, must be imposed—by law in the first place, and by opinion on many things which are not fit subjects for the operation of law. What these rules should be is the principal question in human affairs; but if we except a few of the most obvious cases, it is one of those which least progress has been made in resolving. No two ages, and scarcely any two countries, have decided it alike; and the decision of one age or country is a wonder to another. Yet the people of any given age and country no more suspect any difficulty in it than if it were a subject on which mankind had always been agreed. The rules which obtain among themselves appear to them self-evident and self-justifying. This all but universal illusion is one of the examples of the magical influence of custom, which is not only, as the proverb says, a second nature but is continually mistaken for the first. The effect of custom, in preventing any misgiving respecting the rules of conduct which mankind impose on one another, is all the more complete because the subject is one on which it is not generally considered necessary that reasons should be given, either by one person to others or by each to himself. People are accustomed to believe, and have been encouraged in the belief by some who aspire to the character of philosophers, that their feelings on subjects of this nature are better than reasons and render reasons unnecessary. The practical principle which guides them to their opinions on the regulation of human conduct is the feeling in each person's mind that everybody should be required to act as he, and those with whom he sympathizes, would like them to act. No one, indeed, acknowledges to himself that his standard of judgment is his own liking; but an opinion on a point of conduct, not supported by reasons, can only count as one person's preference; and if the reasons, when given, are a mere appeal to a similar preference felt by other people, it is still only many people's liking instead of one. To an ordinary man, however, his own preference, thus supported, is not only a perfectly satisfactory reason but the only one he generally has for any of his notions of morality, taste, or propriety, which are not expressly written in his religious creed, and his chief guide in the interpretation even of that. Men's opinions, accordingly, on what is laudable or blamable are affected by all the multifarious causes which influence their wishes in regard to the conduct of others, and which are as numerous as those which determine their wishes on any other subject. Sometimes their reason; at other times their prejudices or superstitions; often their social affections, not seldom their antisocial ones, their envy or jealousy, their arrogance or contemptuousness; but most commonly their desires or fears for themselves—their legitimate or illegitimate self-interest. Wherever there is an ascendant class, a large portion of the morality of the country emanates from its class interests and its feelings of class superiority. The morality between Spartans and Helots [serfs], between planters and Negroes, between princes and subjects, between nobles and roturiers [freemen holding land through payment of rent], between men and women has been for the most part the creation of these class interests and feelings; and the sentiments thus generated react in turn upon the moral feelings of the members of the ascendant class, in their relations among themselves. Where, on the other hand, a class, formerly ascendant, has lost its ascendancy, or where its ascendancy is unpopular, the prevailing moral sentiments frequently bear the impress of an impatient dislike of superiority. Another grand determining principle of the rules of conduct, both in act and forbearance, which have been enforced by law or opinion, has been the servility of mankind toward the supposed preferences or aversions of their temporal masters or of their gods. This servility, though essentially selfish, is not hypocrisy; it gives rise to perfectly genuine sentiments of abhorrence; it made men burn magicians and heretics. Among so many baser influences, the general and obvious interests of society have, of course, had a share, and a large one, in the direction of the moral sentiments; less, however, as a matter of reason, and on their own account, than as a consequence of the sympathies and antipathies which grew out of them; and sympathies and antipathies which had little or nothing to do with the interests of society have made themselves felt in the establishment of moralities with quite as great force.

The likings and dislikings of society, or of some powerful portion of it, are thus the main thing which has practically determined the rules laid down for general observance, under the penalties of law or opinion. And in general, those who have been in advance of society in thought and feeling have left this condition of things unassailed in principle, however they may have come into conflict with it in some of its details. They have occupied themselves rather in inquiring what things society ought to like or dislike than in questioning whether its likings or dislikings should be a law to individuals. They preferred endeavoring to alter the feelings of mankind on the particular points on which they were themselves heretical rather than make common cause in defense of freedom with heretics generally. The only case in which the higher ground has been taken on principle and maintained with consistency, by any but an individual here and there, is that of religious belief: a case instructive in many ways, and not least so as forming a most striking instance of the fallibility of what is called the moral sense; for the *odium theologicum* [theologically-based hatred], in a sincere bigot, is one of the most unequivocal cases of moral feeling. Those who first broke the yoke of what called itself the Universal Church were in general as little willing to permit difference of religious opinion as that church itself. But when the heat of the conflict was over, without giving a complete victory to any party, and each church or sect was reduced to limit its hopes to retaining possession of the ground it already occupied, minorities, seeing that they had no chance of becoming majorities, were under the necessity of pleading to those whom they could not convert for permission to differ. It is accordingly on this battlefield, almost solely, that the rights of the individual against society have been asserted on broad grounds of principle, and the claim of society to exercise authority over dissentients openly controverted. The great writers to whom the world owes what religious liberty it possesses have mostly asserted freedom of conscience as an indefeasible right, and denied absolutely that a human being is accountable to others for his religious belief. Yet so natural to mankind is intolerance in whatever they really care about that religious freedom has hardly anywhere been practically realized, except where religious indifference, which dislikes to have its peace disturbed by theological quarrels, has added its weight to the scale. In the minds of almost all religious persons, even in the most tolerant countries, the duty of toleration is admitted with tacit reserves. One person will bear with dissent in matters of church government, but not of dogma; another can tolerate everybody, short of a Papist or a Unitarian; another, everyone who believes in revealed religion; a few extend their charity a little further, but stop at the belief in a God and in a future state. Wherever the sentiment of the majority is still genuine and intense, it is found to have abated little of its claim to be obeyed.

In England, from the peculiar circumstances of our political history, though the yoke of opinion is perhaps heavier, that of law is lighter than in most other countries of Europe; and there is considerable jealousy of direct interference by the legislative or the executive power with private conduct, not so much from any just regard for the independence of the individual as from the still subsisting habit of looking on the government as representing an opposite interest to the public. The majority have not yet learned to feel the power of the government their power, or its opinions their opinions. When they do so, individual liberty will probably be as much exposed to invasion from the government as it already is from public opinion. But, as yet, there is a considerable amount of feeling ready to be called forth against any attempt of the law to control individuals in things in which they have not hitherto been accustomed to be controlled by it; and this with very little discrimination as to whether the matter is, or is not, within the legitimate sphere of legal control; insomuch that the feeling, highly salutary on the whole, is perhaps quite as often misplaced as well grounded in the particular instances of its application. There is, in fact, no recognized principle by which the propriety or impropriety of government interference is customarily tested. People decide according to their personal preferences. Some, whenever they see any good to be done, or evil to be remedied, would willingly instigate the government to undertake the business, while others prefer to bear almost any amount of social evil rather than add one to the departments of human interests amenable to governmental control. And men range themselves on one or the other side in any particular case, according to this general direction of their sentiments, or according to the degree of interest which they feel in the particular thing which it is proposed that the government should do, or according to the belief they entertain that the government would, or would not, do it in the manner they prefer; but very rarely on account of any opinion to which they consistently

Liberty Leading the People, 1830, by Ferdinand Victor Eugène de la Croix (1798–1863). The French painter de la Croix celebrated the spirit of revolutionary political liberty in this allegorical work. Mill argued that this spirit of liberty must extend to individuals as well. Individuals should have the liberty to do as they please, even if they choose actions that are not to their own best interests. "The only purpose for which power can be rightfully exercised over any member of a civilized community, against his will," Mill wrote, "is to prevent harm to others." *(The Louvre Museum, Paris. Copyright RMN.)*

adhere, as to what things are fit to be done by a government. And it seems to me that in consequence of this absence of rule or principle, one side is at present as often wrong as the other; the interference of government is, with about equal frequency, improperly invoked and improperly condemned.

The object of this essay is to assert one very simple principle, as entitled to govern absolutely the dealings of society with the individual in the way of compulsion and control, whether the means used be physical force in the form of legal penalties or the moral coercion of public opinion. That principle is that the sole end for which mankind are warranted, individually or collectively, in interfering with the liberty of action of any of their number is self-protection. That the only purpose for which power can be rightfully exercised over any member of a civilized community, against his will, is to prevent harm to others. His own good, either physical or moral, is not a sufficient warrant. He cannot rightfully be compelled to do or forbear because it will be better for him to do so, because it will make him happier, because, in the opinions of others, to do so would be wise or even right. These are good reasons for remonstrating with him, or reasoning with him, or persuading him, or entreating him, but not for compelling him or visiting him with any evil in case he do otherwise. To justify that, the conduct from which it is desired to deter him must be calculated to produce evil to someone else. The only part of the conduct of anyone for which he is amenable to society is that which concerns others. In the part which merely concerns himself, his independence is, of right, absolute. Over himself, over his own body and mind, the individual is sovereign.

It is, perhaps, hardly necessary to say that this doctrine is meant to apply only to human beings in the maturity of their faculties. We are not speaking of children or of young persons below the age which the law may fix as that of manhood or womanhood. Those who are still in a state to require being taken care of by others must be protected against their own actions as well as against external injury. For the same reason we may leave out of consideration those backward states of society in which the race itself may be considered as in its nonage. The early difficulties in the way of spontaneous progress are so great that there is seldom any choice of means for overcoming them; and a ruler full of the spirit of improvement is warranted in the use of any expedients that will attain an end perhaps otherwise unattainable. Despotism is a legitimate mode of government in dealing with barbarians, provided the end be their improvement and the means justified by actually effecting that end. Liberty, as a principle, has no application to any state of things anterior to the time when mankind have become capable of being improved by free and equal discussion. Until then, there is nothing for them but implicit obedience to an Akbar or a Charlemagne, if they are so fortunate as to find one. But as soon as mankind have attained the capacity of being guided to their own improvement by conviction or persuasion (a period long since reached in all nations with whom we need here concern ourselves), compulsion, either in the direct form or in that of pains and penalties for noncompliance, is no longer admissible as a means to their own good, and justifiable only for the security of others.

It is proper to state that I forego any advantage which could be derived to my argument from the idea of abstract right as a thing independent of utility. I regard utility as the ultimate appeal on all ethical questions; but it must be utility in the largest sense, grounded on the permanent interests of man as a progressive being. Those interests, I contend, authorize the subjection of individual spontaneity to external control only in respect to those actions of each which concern the interest of other people. If anyone does an act hurtful to others, there is a *prima facie* case for punishing him by law or, where legal penalties are not safely applicable, by general disapprobation. There are also many positive acts for the benefit of others which he may rightfully be compelled to perform, such as to give evidence in a court of justice, to bear his fair share in the common defense or in any other joint work necessary to the interest of the society of which he enjoys the protection, and to perform certain acts of individual beneficence, such as saving a fellow creature's life or interposing to protect the defenseless against ill usage—things which whenever it is obviously a man's duty to do he may rightfully be made responsible to society for not doing. A person may cause evil to others not only by his actions but by his inaction, and in either case he is justly accountable to them for the injury. The latter case, it is true, requires a much more cautious exercise of compulsion than the former. To make anyone answerable for doing evil to others is the rule; to make him answerable for not preventing evil is, comparatively speaking, the exception. Yet there are many cases clear enough and grave enough to justify that exception. In all things which regard the external relations of the individual, he is *de jure* amenable to those whose interests are concerned, and, if need be, to society as their protector. There are often good reasons for not holding him to the responsibility; but these reasons must arise from the special expediencies of the case: either because it is a kind of case in which he is on the whole likely to act better when left to his own discretion than when controlled in any way in which society have it in their power to control him; or because the attempt to exercise control would produce other evils, greater than those which it would prevent. When such reasons as these preclude the enforcement of responsibility, the conscience of the agent himself should step into the vacant judgment seat and protect those interests of others which have no external protection; judging himself all the more rigidly, because the case does not admit of his being made accountable to the judgment of his fellow creatures.

But there is a sphere of action in which society, as distinguished from the individual, has, if any, only an indirect interest: comprehending all that portion of a person's life and conduct which affects only himself or, if it also affects others, only with their free, voluntary, and undeceived consent and participation. When I say only himself, I mean directly and in the first instance; for whatever affects himself may affect others through himself; and the objection which may be grounded on this contingency will receive consideration in the sequel. This, then, is the appropriate region of human liberty. It comprises, first, the inward domain of consciousness, demanding liberty of conscience in the most comprehensive sense, liberty of thought and feeling, absolute freedom of opinion and sentiment on all subjects, practical or speculative, scientific, moral, or theological. The liberty of expressing and publishing opinions may seem to fall under a different principle, since it belongs to that part of the conduct of an individual which concerns other people, but, being almost of as much importance as the liberty of thought itself and resting in great part on the same reasons, is practically inseparable from it. Secondly, the principle requires liberty of tastes and pursuits, of framing the plan of our life to suit our own character, of doing as we like, subject to such consequences as may follow, without impediment from our fellow creatures, so long as what we do does not harm them, even though they should think our conduct foolish, perverse, or wrong. Thirdly, from this liberty of each individual follows the liberty, within the same limits, of combination among individuals; freedom to unite for any purpose not involving harm to others: the persons combining being supposed to be of full age and not forced or deceived.

No society in which these liberties are not, on the whole, respected is free, whatever may be its form of government; and none is completely free in which they do not exist absolute and unqualified. The only freedom which deserves the name is that of pursuing our own good in our own way, so long as we do not attempt to deprive others of theirs or impede their efforts to obtain it. Each is the proper guardian of his own health, whether bodily *or* mental and spiritual. Mankind are greater gainers by suffering each other to live as seems good to themselves than by compelling each to live as seems good to the rest.

Though this doctrine is anything but new and, to some persons, may have the air of a truism, there is no doctrine which stands more directly opposed to the general tendency of existing opinion and practice. Society has expended fully as much effort in the attempt (according to its lights) to compel people to conform to its notions of personal as of social excellence. The ancient commonwealths thought themselves entitled to practice, and the ancient philosophers countenanced, the regulation of every part of private conduct by public authority, on the ground that the State had a deep interest in the whole bodily and mental discipline of every one of its citizens—a mode of thinking which may have been admissible in small republics surrounded by powerful enemies, in constant peril of being subverted by foreign attack or internal commotion, and to which even a short interval of relaxed energy and self-command might so easily be fatal that they could not afford to wait for the salutary permanent effects of freedom. In the modern world, the greater size of political communities and, above all, the separation between spiritual and temporal authority (which placed the direction of men's consciences in other hands than those which controlled their worldly affairs) prevented so great an interference by law in the details of private life; but the engines of moral repression have been wielded more strenuously against divergence from the reigning opinion in self-regarding than even in social matters; religion, the most powerful of the elements which have entered into the formation of moral feeling, having almost always been governed either by the ambition of a hierarchy seeking control over every department of human conduct, or by the spirit of Puritanism. And some of those modern reformers who have placed themselves in strongest opposition to the religions of the past have been noway behind either churches or sects in their assertion of the right of spiritual domination: M. Comte, in particular, whose social system, as unfolded in his *Systéme de Politique Positive,* aims at establishing (though by moral more than by legal appliances) a despotism of society over the individual surpassing anything contemplated in the political ideal of the most rigid disciplinarian among the ancient philosophers.

Apart from the peculiar tenets of individual thinkers, there is also in the world at large an increasing inclination to stretch unduly the powers of society over the individual both by the force of opinion and even by that of legislation; and as tendency of all the changes taking place in the world is to strengthen the society and diminish the power of the individual, this encroachment is not one of the evils which tend spontaneously to disappear, but, on the contrary, to grow more and more formidable. The disposition of mankind, whether as rulers or as fellow citizens, to impose their own opinions and inclinations as a rule of conduct on others is so energetically supported by some of the best and by some of the worst feelings incident to human nature that it is hardly ever kept under restraint by anything but want of power; and as the power is not declining, but growing, unless a strong barrier; of moral conviction can be raised against the mischief, we must expect, in the present circumstances of the world, to see it increase.

It will be convenient for the argument if, instead of at once entering upon the general thesis, we confine ourselves in the first instance to a single branch of it on which the principle here stated is, if not fully, yet to a certain point, recognized by the current opinions. This one branch is the Liberty of Thought, from which it is impossible to separate the cognate liberty of speaking and of writing. Although these liberties, to some considerable amount, form part of the political morality of all countries which profess religious toleration and free institutions, the grounds, both philosophical and practical, on which they rest are perhaps not so familiar to the general mind, nor so thoroughly appreciated by many, even of the leaders of opinion, as might have been expected. Those grounds, when rightly understood, are of much wider application than to only one division of the subject, and a thorough consideration of this part of the question will be found the best introduction to the remainder. Those to whom nothing which I am about to say will be new may therefore, I hope, excuse me if on a subject which for now three centuries has been so often discussed I venture on one discussion more.

CHAPTER 2: OF THE LIBERTY OF THOUGHT AND DISCUSSION

The time, it is to be hoped, is gone by when any defense would be necessary of the "liberty of the press" as one of the securities against corrupt or tyrannical government. No argument, we may suppose, can now be needed against permitting a legislature or an executive, not identified in interest with the people, to prescribe opinions to them and determine what doctrines or what arguments they shall be allowed to hear. This aspect of the question, besides, has been so often and so triumphantly enforced by preceding writers that it needs not be specially insisted on in this place. Though the law of England, on the subject of the press, is as servile to this day as it was in the time of the Tudors, there is little danger of its being actually put in force against political discussion except during some temporary panic when fear of insurrection drives ministers and judges from their propriety;* and, speaking generally, it is not, in constitutional countries, to be apprehended that the government, whether completely responsible to the people or not, will often attempt to control the expression of opinion, except when in doing so it makes itself the organ of the general intolerance of the public. Let us sup-

---

*These words had scarcely been written when, as if to give them an emphatic contradiction, occurred the Government Press Prosecutions of 1858. That ill-judged interference with the liberty of public discussion has not, however, induced me to alter a single word in the text, nor has it at all weakened my conviction that, moments of panic excepted, the era of pains and penalties for political discussion has, in our own country, passed away. For, in the first place, the prosecutions were not persisted in; and, in the second, they were never, properly speaking, political prosecutions. The offense charged was not that of criticizing institutions or the acts or persons of rulers, but of circulating what was deemed an immoral doctrine, the lawfulness of tyrannicide.

If the arguments of the present chapter are of any validity, there ought to exist the fullest liberty of professing and discussing, as a matter of ethical conviction, any doctrine, however immoral it may be considered. It would, therefore, be irrelevant and out of place to examine here whether the doctrine of tyrannicide deserves that title. I shall content myself with saying that the subject has been at all times one of the open questions of morals; that the act of a private citizen in striking down a criminal who, by raising himself above the law, has placed himself beyond the reach of legal punishment or control has been accounted by whole nations, and by some of the best and wisest of men, not a crime but an act of exalted virtue; and that, right or wrong, it is not of the nature of assassination, but of civil war. As such, I hold that the instigation to it, in a specific case, may be a proper subject of punishment, but only if an overt act has followed, and at least a probable connection can be established between the act and the instigation. Even then it is not a foreign government but the very government assailed which alone, in the exercise of self-defense, can legitimately punish attacks directed against its own existence.

pose, therefore, that the government is entirely at one with the people, and never thinks of exerting any power of coercion unless in agreement with what it conceives to be their voice.

But I deny the right of the people to exercise such coercion, either by themselves or by their government. The power itself is illegitimate. The best government has no more title to it than the worst. It is as noxious, or more noxious, when exerted in accordance with public opinion than when in opposition to it. If all mankind minus one were of one opinion, mankind would be no more justified in silencing that one person than he, if he had the power, would be justified in silencing mankind. Were an opinion a personal possession of no value except to the owner, if to be obstructed in the enjoyment of it were simply a private injury, it would make some difference whether the injury was inflicted only on a few persons or on many. But the peculiar evil of silencing the expression of an opinion is that it is robbing the human race, posterity as well as the existing generation—those who dissent from the opinion, still more than those who hold it. If the opinion is right, they are deprived of the opportunity of exchanging error for truth; if wrong, they lose, what is almost as great a benefit, the clearer perception and livelier impression of truth produced by its collision with error.

It is necessary to consider separately these two hypotheses, each of which has a distinct branch of the argument corresponding to it. We can never be sure that the opinion we are endeavoring to stifle is a false opinion; and if we were sure, stifling it would be an evil still.

First, the opinion which it is attempted to suppress by authority may possibly be true. Those who desire to suppress it, of course, deny its truth; but they are not infallible. They have no authority to decide the question for all mankind and exclude every other person from the means of judging. To refuse a hearing to an opinion because they are sure that it is false is to assume that *their* certainty is the same thing as *absolute* certainty. All silencing of discussion is an assumption of infallibility. Its condemnation may be allowed to rest on this common argument, not the worse for being common.

Unfortunately for the good sense of mankind, the fact of their fallibility is far from carrying the weight in their practical judgment which is always allowed to it in theory; for while everyone well knows himself to be fallible, few think it necessary to take any precautions against their own fallibility, or admit the supposition that any opinion of which they feel very certain may be one of the examples of the error to which they acknowledge themselves to be liable. Absolute princes, or others who are accustomed to unlimited deference, usually feel this complete confidence in their own opinions on nearly all subjects. People more happily situated, who sometimes hear their opinions disputed and are not wholly unused to be set right when they are wrong, place the same unbounded reliance only on such of their opinions as are shared by all who surround them, or to whom they habitually defer; for in proportion to a man's want of confidence in his own solitary judgment does he usually repose, with implicit trust, on the infallibility of "the world" in general. And the world, to each individual, means the part of it with which he comes in contact: his party, his sect, his church, his class of society; the man may be called, by comparison, almost liberal and large-minded to whom it means anything so comprehensive as his own country or his own age. Nor is his faith in this collective authority at all shaken by his being aware that other ages, countries, sects, churches, classes, and parties have thought, and even now think, the exact reverse. He devolves upon his own world the responsibility of being in the right against the dissentient worlds of other people; and it never troubles him that mere accident has decided which of these numerous worlds is the object of his reliance, and that the same causes which make him a churchman in London would have made him a Buddhist or a Confucian in Peking. Yet it is as evident in itself, as any amount of argument can make it, that ages are no more infallible than individuals—every age having held many opinions which subsequent ages have deemed not only false but absurd; and it is as certain that many opinions, now general, will be rejected by future ages, as it is that many, once general, are rejected by the present.

The objection likely to be made to this argument would probably take some such form as the following. There is no greater assumption of infallibility in forbidding the propagation of error than in any other thing which is done by public authority on its own judgment and responsibility. Judgment is given to men that they may use it. Because it may be used erroneously, are men to be told that they ought not to use it at all? To prohibit what they think pernicious is not claiming exemption from error, but fulfilling the duty incumbent on them, although fallible, of acting on their conscientious conviction. If we were never to act on our opinions, because those opinions may be wrong, we should leave all our interests uncared for, and all our duties unperformed. An objection which applies to all conduct can be no valid objection to any conduct in particular. It is the duty of governments, and of individuals, to form the truest opinions they can; to form them carefully, and never impose them upon others unless they are quite sure of being right. But when they are sure (such reasoners may say), it is not conscientiousness but cowardice to shrink from acting on their opinions and allow doctrines which they honestly think dangerous to the welfare of mankind, either in this life or in another, to be scattered abroad without restraint, because other people, in less enlightened times, have persecuted opinions now believed to be true. Let us take care, it may be said, not to make the same mistake; but governments and nations have made mistakes in other things which are not denied to be fit subjects for the exercise of authority: they have laid on bad taxes, made unjust wars. Ought we therefore to lay on no taxes and, under whatever provocation, make no wars? Men and governments must act to the best of their ability. There is no such thing as absolute certainty, but there is assurance sufficient for the purposes of human life. We may, and must, assume our opinion to be true for the guidance of our own conduct; and it is assuming no more when we forbid bad men to pervert society by the propagation of opinions which we regard as false and pernicious.

I answer, that it is assuming very much more. There is the greatest difference between presuming an opinion to be true because, with every opportunity for contesting it, it has not been refuted, and assuming its truth for the purpose of not permitting its refutation. Complete liberty of contradicting and disproving our opinion is the very condition which justifies us in assuming its truth for purposes of action; and on no other terms can a being with human faculties have any rational assurance of being right.

When we consider either the history of opinion or the ordinary conduct of human life, to what is it to be ascribed that the one and the other are no worse than they are? Not certainly to the inherent force of the human understanding, for on any matter not self-evident there are ninety-nine persons totally incapable of judging of it for one who is capable; and the capacity of the hundredth person is only comparative, for the majority of the eminent men of every past generation held many opinions now known to be erroneous, and did or approved numerous things which no one will now justify. Why is it, then, that there is on the whole a preponderance among mankind of rational opinions and rational conduct? If there really is this preponderance—which there must be unless human affairs are, and have always been, in an almost desperate state—it is owing to a quality of the human mind, the source of everything respectable in man either as an intellectual or as a moral being, namely, that his errors are corrigible. He is capable of rectifying his mistakes by discussion and experience. Not by experience alone. There must be discussion to show how experience is to be interpreted. Wrong opinions and practices gradually yield to fact and argument; but facts and arguments, to produce any effect on the mind, must be brought before it. Very few facts are able to tell their own story, without comments to bring out their meaning. The whole strength and value, then, of human judgment depending on the one property, that it can be set right when it is wrong, reliance can be placed on it only when the means of setting it right are kept constantly at hand. In the case of any person whose judgment is really deserving of confidence, how has it become so? Because he has kept his mind open to criticism of his opinions and conduct. Because it has been his practice to listen to all that could be said against him; to profit by as much of it as was just, and to expound to himself, and upon occasion to others, the fallacy of what was fallacious. Because he has felt that the only way in which a human being can make some approach to know-ing the whole of a subject is by hearing what can be said about it by persons of every variety of opinion, and studying all modes in which it can be looked at by every char-acter of mind. No wise man ever acquired his wisdom in any mode but this; nor is it in the nature of human intellect to become wise in any other manner. The steady habit of correcting and completing his own opinion by collating it with those of others, so far from causing doubt and hesitation in carrying it into practice, is the only stable founda-tion for a just reliance on it; for, being cognizant of all that can, at least obviously, be said against him, and having taken up his position against all gainsayers knowing that he has sought for objections and difficulties instead of avoiding them, and has shut out no light which can be thrown upon the subject from any quarter—he has a right to think his judgment better than that of any person, or any multitude, who have not gone through a similar process.

It is not too much to require that what the wisest of mankind, those who are best entitled to trust their own judgment, find necessary to warrant their relying on it, should be submitted to by that miscellaneous collection of a few wise and many fool-ish individuals called the public. The most intolerant of churches, the Roman Catholic Church, even at the canonization of a saint admits, and listens patiently to, a "devil's advocate." The holiest of men, it appears, cannot be admitted to posthumous honors until all that the devil could say against him is known and weighed. If even the New-tonian philosophy were not permitted to be questioned, mankind could not feel as com-plete assurance of its truth as they now do. The beliefs which we have most warrant for have no safeguard to rest on but a standing invitation to the whole world to prove them unfounded. If the challenge is not accepted, or is accepted and the attempt fails, we are far enough from certainty still, but we have done the best that the existing state of human reason admits of: we have neglected nothing that could give the truth a chance of reaching us; if the lists are kept open, we may hope that, if there be a better truth, it will be found when the human mind is capable of receiving it; and in the meantime we may rely on having attained such approach to truth as is possible in our own day. This is the amount of certainty attainable by a fallible being, and this the sole way of attain-ing it.

Strange it is that men should admit the validity of the arguments for free discus-sion, but object to their being "pushed to an extreme," not seeing that unless the rea-sons are good for an extreme case, they are not good for any case. Strange that they should imagine that they are not assuming infallibility when they acknowledge that there should be free discussion on all subjects which can possibly be *doubtful*, but think that some particular principle or doctrine should be forbidden to be questioned because it is so *certain*, that is, because *they are certain* that it is certain. To call any proposition certain, while there is anyone who would deny its certainty if permitted, but who is not permitted, is to assume that we ourselves, and those who agree with us, are the judges of certainty, and judges without hearing the other side.

In the present age—which has been described as "destitute of faith, but terrified at skepticism"—in which people feel sure, not so much that their opinions are true as that they should not know what to do without them—the claims of an opinion to be protected from public attack are rested not so much on its truth as on its importance to society. There are, it is alleged, certain beliefs so useful, not to say indispensable, to well-being that it is as much the duty of governments to uphold those beliefs as to protect any other of the interests of society. In a case of such necessity, and so directly in the line of their duty, something less than infallibility may, it is maintained, warrant, and even bind, governments to act on their own opinion confirmed by the general opinion of mankind. It is also often argued, and still oftener thought, that none but bad men would desire to weaken these salutary beliefs; and there can be nothing wrong, it is thought, in restraining bad men and prohibiting what only such men would wish to practice. This mode of thinking makes the justification of restraints on discussion not a question of the truth of doctrines but of their usefulness, and flatters itself by that means to escape the responsibility of claiming to be an infallible judge of opinions. But those who thus satisfy themselves do not perceive that the assumption of infallibility is merely shifted from one point to another. The usefulness of an opinion is itself matter of opinion—as disputable, as open to discussion, and requiring discussion as much as the opinion itself. There is the same need of an infallible judge of opinions to decide an opinion to be noxious as to decide it to be false, unless the opinion condemned has full opportunity of defending itself. And it will not do to say that the heretic may be allowed to maintain the utility or harmlessness of his opinion, though forbidden to maintain its truth. The truth of an opinion is part of its utility. If we would know whether or not it is desirable that a proposition should be believed, is it possible to exclude the consideration of whether or not it is true? In the opinion, not of bad men, but of the best men, no belief which is contrary to truth can be really useful; and can you prevent such men from urging that plea when they are charged with culpability for denying some doctrine which they are told is useful, but which they believe to be false? Those who are on the side of received opinions never fail to take all possible advantage of this plea; you do not find them handling the question of ability as if it could be completely abstracted from that of truth; on the contrary, it is, above all, because their doctrine is "the truth" that the knowledge or the belief of it is held to be so indispensable. There can be no fair discussion of the question of usefulness when an argument so vital may be employed on one side, but not on the other. And in point of fact, when law or public feeling do not permit the truth of an opinion to be disputed, they are just as little tolerant of a denial of its usefulness. The utmost they allow is an extenuation of its absolute necessity, or of the positive guilt of rejecting it.

In order more fully to illustrate the mischief of denying a hearing to opinions because we, in our own judgment, have condemned them, it will be desirable to fix down the discussion to a concrete case; and I choose, by preference, the cases which are least favorable to me—in which the argument against freedom of opinion, both on the score of truth and on that of utility, is considered the strongest. Let the opinions impugned be the belief in a God and in a future state, or any of the commonly received doctrines of morality. To fight the battle on such ground gives a great advantage to an unfair antagonist, since he will be sure to say (and many who have no desire to be unfair will say it internally), Are these the doctrines which you do not deem sufficiently certain to be taken under the protection of law? Is the belief in a God one of the opinions to feel sure of which you hold to be assuming infallibility? But I must be permitted to observe that it is not the feeling sure of a doctrine (be it what it may) which I call an assumption of infallibility. It is the undertaking to decide that question *for others,* without allowing them to hear what can be said on the contrary side. And I denounce and reprobate this pretension not the less if put forth on the side of my most solemn convictions. However positive anyone's persuasion may be, not only of the falsity but of the pernicious consequences—not only of the pernicious consequences, but (to adopt expressions which I altogether condemn) the immorality and impiety of an opinion—yet if, in pursuance of that private judgment, though backed by the public judgment of his country or his contemporaries, he prevents the opinion from being heard in its defense, he assumes infallibility. And so far from the assumption being less objectionable or less dangerous because the opinion is called immoral or impious, this is the case of all others in which it is most fatal. These are exactly the occasions on which the men of one generation commit those dreadful mistakes which excite the astonishment and horror of posterity. It is among such that we find the instances memorable in history, when the arm of the law has been employed to root out the best men and the noblest doctrines; with deplorable success as to the men, though some of the doctrines have survived to be (as if in mockery) invoked in defense of similar conduct toward those who dissent from *them,* or from their received interpretation.

Mankind can hardly be too often reminded that there was once a man called Socrates, between whom and the legal authorities and public opinion of his time there took place a memorable collision. Born in an age and country abounding in individual greatness, this man has been handed down to us by those who best knew both him and the age as the most virtuous man in it; while we know him as the head and prototype of all subsequent teachers of virtue, the source equally of the lofty inspiration of Plato and the judicious utilitarianism of Aristotle, "*i maestri di color che sanno*" ["the master of those that know"], the two headsprings of ethical as of all other philosophy. This acknowledged master of all the eminent thinkers who have since lived—whose fame, still growing after more than two thousand years, all but outweighs the whole remainder of the names which make his native city illustrious—was put to death by his countrymen, after a judicial conviction, for impiety and immorality. Impiety, in denying the gods recognized by the State; indeed, his accuser asserted (see the *Apologia*) that he believed in no gods at all. Immorality, in being, by his doctrines and instructions, a "corruptor of youth." Of these charges the tribunal, there is every ground for believing, honestly found him guilty, and condemned the man who probably of all then born had deserved best of mankind to be put to death as a criminal.

To pass from this to the only other instance of judicial iniquity, the mention of which, after the condemnation of Socrates, would not be an anticlimax: the event which took place on Calvary rather more than eighteen hundred years ago. The man who left on the memory of those who witnessed his life and conversation such an impression of his moral grandeur that eighteen subsequent centuries have done homage to him as the Almighty in person, was ignominiously put to death, as what? As a blasphemer. Men did not merely mistake their benefactor, they mistook him for the exact contrary of what he was and treated him as that prodigy of impiety which they themselves are now held to be for their treatment of him. The feelings with which mankind now regard these lamentable transactions, especially the later of the two, render them extremely unjust in their judgment of the unhappy actors. These were, to all appearance, not bad men—not worse than men commonly are, but rather the contrary; men who possessed in a full, or somewhat more than a full measure, the religious, moral, and patriotic feelings of their time and people: the very kind of men who, in all times, our own included, have every chance of passing through life blameless and respected. The high priest who rent his garments when the words were pronounced, which, ac-

cording to all the ideas of his country, constituted the blackest guilt, was in all probability quite as sincere in his horror and indignation as the generality of respectable and
pious men now are in the religious and moral sentiments they profess; and most of
those who now shudder at his conduct, if they had lived in his time, and been born
Jews, would have acted precisely as he did. Orthodox Christians who are tempted to
think that those who stoned to death the first martyrs must have been worse men than
they themselves are ought to remember that one of those persecutors was Saint Paul.

Let us add one more example, the most striking of all, if the impressiveness of an
error is measured by the wisdom and virtue of him who falls into it. If ever anyone possessed of power had grounds for thinking himself the best and most enlightened among
his contemporaries, it was the Emperor Marcus Aurelius. Absolute monarch of the whole
civilized world, he preserved through life not only the most unblemished justice, but
what was less to be expected from his Stoical breeding, the tenderest heart. The few fail-
ings which are attributed to him were all on the side of indulgence, while his writings, the
highest ethical product of the ancient mind, differ scarcely perceptibly, if they differ at
all, from the most characteristic teachings of Christ. This man, a better Christian in all
but the dogmatic sense of the word than almost any of the ostensibly Christian sovereigns who have since reigned, persecuted Christianity. Placed at the summit of all the
previous attainments of humanity, with an open, unfettered intellect, and a character
which led him of himself to embody in his moral writings the Christian ideal, he yet
failed to see that Christianity was to be a good and not an evil to the world, with his duties to which he was so deeply penetrated. Existing society he knew to be in a deplorable
state. But such as it was, he saw, or thought he saw, that it was held together, and prevented from being worse, by belief and reverence of the received divinities. As a ruler of
mankind, he deemed it his duty not to suffer society to fall in pieces; and saw not how, if
its existing ties were removed, any others could be formed which could again knit it together. The new religion openly aimed at dissolving these ties; unless, therefore, it was
his duty to adopt that religion, it seemed to be his duty to put it down. Inasmuch then as
the theology of Christianity did not appear to him true or of divine origin, inasmuch as
this strange history of a crucified God was not credible to him, and a system which pur-
ported to rest entirely upon a foundation to him so wholly unbelievable, could not be
foreseen by him to be that renovating agency which, after all abatements, it has in fact
proved to be; the gentlest and most amiable of philosophers and rulers, under a solemn
sense of duty, authorized the persecution of Christianity. To my mind this is one of the
most tragical facts in all history. It is a bitter thought how different a thing the Christianity of the world might have been if the Christian faith had been adopted as the religion of
the empire under the auspices of Marcus Aurelius instead of those of Constantine. But it
would be equally unjust to him and false to truth to deny that no one plea which can be
urged for punishing anti-Christian teaching was wanting to Marcus Aurelius for punishing, as he did, the propagation of Christianity. No Christian more firmly believes that
atheism is false and tends to the dissolution of society than Marcus Aurelius believed the
same things of Christianity; he who, of all men then living, might have been thought the
most capable of appreciating it. Unless anyone who approves of punishment for the pro-
mulgation of opinions flatters himself that he is a wiser and better man than Marcus Aurelius—more deeply versed in the wisdom of his time, more elevated in his intellect
above it, more earnest in his search for truth, or more single-minded in his devotion to it
when found—let him abstain from that assumption of the joint infallibility of himself and
the multitude which the great Antoninus [Aurelius] made with so unfortunate a result.

Aware of the impossibility of defending the use of punishment for restraining irreligious opinions by any argument which will not justify Marcus Antoninus, the ene-

mies of religious freedom, when hard pressed, occasionally accept this consequence and say, with Dr. Johnson, that the persecutors of Christianity were in the right, that persecution is an ordeal through which truth ought to pass, and always passes successfully, legal penalties being, in the end, powerless against truth, though sometimes beneficially effective against mischievous errors. This is a form of the argument for religious intolerance sufficiently remarkable not to be passed without notice.

A theory which maintains that truth may justifiably be persecuted because persecution cannot possibly do it any harm cannot be charged with being intentionally hostile to the reception of new truths; but we cannot commend the generosity of its dealing with the persons to whom mankind are indebted for them. To discover to the world something which deeply concerns it, and of which it was previously ignorant, to prove to it that it had been mistaken on some vital point of temporal or spiritual interest, is as important a service as a human being can render to his fellow creatures, and in certain cases, as in those of the early Christians and of the Reformers, those who think with Dr. Johnson believe it to have been the most precious gift which could be bestowed on mankind. That the authors of such splendid benefits should be requited by martyrdom, that their reward should be to be dealt with as the vilest of criminals, is not, upon this theory, a deplorable error and misfortune for which humanity should mourn in sackcloth and ashes, but the normal and justifiable state of things. The propounder of a new truth, according to this doctrine, should stand, as stood, in the legislation of the Locrians,* the proposer of a new law, with a halter round his neck, to be instantly tightened if the public assembly did not, on hearing his reasons, then and there adopt his proposition. People who defend this mode of treating benefactors cannot be supposed to set much value on the benefit; and I believe this view of the subject is mostly confined to the sort of persons who think that new truths may have been desirable once, but that we have had enough of them now.

But, indeed, the dictum that truth always triumphs over persecution is one of those pleasant falsehoods which men repeat after one another till they pass into commonplaces, but which all experience refutes. History teems with instances of truth put down by persecution. If not suppressed forever, it may be thrown back for centuries. To speak only of religious opinions: the Reformation broke out at least twenty times before Luther, and was put down. Arnold of Brescia was put down. Fra Dolcino was put down. Savonarola was put down. The Albigeois were put down. The Vaudois were put down. The Lollards were put down. The Hussites were put down.** Even after the

---

*[Mill refers to the Locrian law code, which is attributed to Zaleucus (about 660 B.C.). The code was extremely severe, apparently in order to combat the lawlessness of that young community and to give it a political order. Loci was founded by the Eastern or Opuntia Locris about 683 B.C. This law code, incidentally, was the first written code among the Greeks and in Europe, and many of its principles remained in force for many centuries thereafter. Apart from the principle the author refers to, it also sanctioned in Greek social life the principle of retaliation ⟨lex talionis⟩.]

**[Arnoldo da Brescia was executed in 1155. Fra Dolcino of Novara, referred to in Dante's *Inferno* (c. XXVIII), was tortured to death in 1307. Savonarola Girolamo was hanged and burned to death in 1498. The Albigeois or Albigenses (also the Catharists) tried to establish a church independent of the Roman Catholic Church. The movement was suppressed by the Inquisition about the middle of the thirteenth century. The Vaudois, or Waldenses, sought to establish a religious society independent of the Roman Catholic Church. It was the only medieval sect that survived the pressure of the Inquisition, although it was greatly weakened. The group became affiliated with the movement of Protestantism. The Lollards, followers of John Wycliffe (1320–1384), revolted against the authority and the worldly interests of the Church. The movement was severely suppressed, but remnants survived and, to a large extent, prepared the way for Protestantism in England. The Hussites were the followers of John Huss (1369–1415). Their movement was suppressed and Huss burned at the stake, in violation of a "safe conduct" promised by the Emperor, while Huss was attending the Council of Constance.]

era of Luther, wherever persecution was persisted in, it was successful. In Spain, Italy, Flanders, the Austrian empire, Protestantism was rooted out; and, most likely, would have been so in England had Queen Mary lived or Queen Elizabeth died. Persecution has always succeeded save where the heretics were too strong a party to be effectually persecuted. No reasonable person can doubt that Christianity might have been extirpated in the Roman Empire. It spread and became predominant because the persecutions were only occasional, lasting but a short time, and separated by long intervals of almost undisturbed propagandism. It is a piece of idle sentimentality that truth, merely as truth, has any inherent power denied to error of prevailing against the dungeon and the stake. Men are not more zealous for truth than they often are for error, and a sufficient application of legal or even of social penalties will generally succeed in stopping the propagation of either. The real advantage which truth has consists in this, that when an opinion is true, it may be extinguished once, twice, or many times, but in the course of ages there will generally be found persons to rediscover it, until some one of its reappearances falls on a time when from favorable circumstances it escapes persecution until it has made such head as to withstand all subsequent attempts to suppress it.

It will be said that we do not now put to death the introducers of new opinions: we are not like our fathers who slew the prophets; we even build sepulchers to them. It is true we no longer put heretics to death; and the amount of penal infliction which modern feeling would probably tolerate, even against the most obnoxious opinions, is not sufficient to extirpate them. But let us not flatter ourselves that we are yet free from the stain even of legal persecution. Penalties for opinion, or at least for its expression, still exist by law; and their enforcement is not, even in these times, so unexampled as to make it at all incredible that they may some day be revived in full force. In the year 1857, at the summer assizes of the county of Cornwall, an unfortunate man, said to be of unexceptionable conduct in all relations of life, was sentenced to twenty-one months' imprisonment for uttering, and writing on a gate, some offensive words concerning Christianity.* Within a month of the same time, at the Old Bailey, two persons, on two separate occasions,** were rejected as jurymen, and one of them grossly insulted by the judge and by one of the counsel, because they honestly declared that they had no theological belief; and a third, a foreigner,*** for the same reason, was denied justice against a thief. This refusal of redress took place in virtue of the legal doctrine that no person can be allowed to give evidence in a court of justice who does not profess belief in a God (any god is sufficient) and in a future state, which is equivalent to declaring such persons to be outlaws, excluded from the protection of the tribunals; who may not only be robbed or assaulted with impunity, if no one but themselves, or persons of similar opinions, be present, but anyone else may be robbed or assaulted with impunity if the proof of the fact depends on their evidence. The assumption on which this is grounded is that the oath is worthless of a person who does not believe in a future state—a proposition which betokens much ignorance of history in those who assent to it (since it is historically true that a large proportion of infidels in all ages have been persons of distinguished integrity and honor), and would be maintained by no one who had the smallest conception how many of the persons in greatest repute with the world, both for virtues and attainments, are well known, at least to their intimates, to be unbelievers. The rule, besides, is suicidal and cuts away its own founda-

---

*Thomas Pooley, Bodmin Assizes, July 31, 1857. In December following, he received a free pardon from the Crown.

**George Jacob Holyoake, August 17, 1857; Edward Truelove, July 1857.

***Baron de Gleichen, Marlborough Street Police Court, August 4, 1857.

tion. Under pretense that atheists must be liars, it admits the testimony of all atheists who are willing to lie, and rejects only those who brave the obloquy of publicly confessing a detested creed rather than affirm a falsehood. A rule thus self-convicted of absurdity so far as regards its professed purpose can be kept in force only as a badge of hatred, a relic of persecution—a persecution, too, having the peculiarity that the qualification for undergoing it is the being clearly proved not to deserve it. The rule and the theory it implies are hardly less insulting to believers than to infidels. For if he who does not believe in a future state necessarily lies, it follows that they who do believe are only prevented from lying, if prevented they are, by the fear of hell. We will not do the authors and abettors of the rule the injury of supposing that the conception which they have formed of Christian virtue is drawn from their own consciousness.

These, indeed, are but rags and remnants of persecution, and may be thought to be not so much an indication of the wish to persecute, as an example of that very frequent infirmity of English minds, which makes them take a preposterous pleasure in the assertion of a bad principle, when they are no longer bad enough to desire to carry it really into practice. But unhappily there is no security in the state of the public mind that the suspension of worse forms of legal persecution, which has lasted for about the space of a generation, will continue. In this age the quiet surface of routine is as often ruffled by attempts to resuscitate past evils as to introduce new benefits. What is boasted of at the present time as the revival of religion is always, in narrow and uncultivated minds, at least as much the revival of bigotry; and where there is the strong permanent leaven of intolerance in the feelings of a people, which at all times abides in the middle classes of this country, it needs but little to provoke them into actively persecuting those whom they have never ceased to think proper objects of persecution.* For it is this—it is the opinions men entertain, and the feelings they cherish, respecting those who disown the beliefs they deem important which makes this country not a place of mental freedom. For a long time past, the chief mischief of the legal penalties is that they strengthen the social stigma. It is that stigma which is really effective, and so effective is it that the profession of opinions which are under the ban of society is much less common in England than is, in many other countries, the avowal of those which incur risk of judicial punishment. In respect to all persons but those whose pecuniary circumstances make them independent of the good will of other people, opinion, on this subject, is as efficacious as law; men might as well be imprisoned as excluded from the means of earning their bread. Those whose bread is already secured, and who

---

*Ample warning may be drawn from the large infusion of the passions of a persecutor, which mingled with the general display of the worst parts of our national character on the occasion of the Sepoy insurrection. The ravings of fanatics or charlatans from the pulpit may be unworthy of notice; but the heads of the Evangelical party have announced as their principle for the government of Hindus and Mohammedans that no schools be supported by public money in which the Bible is not taught, and by necessary consequence that no public employment be given to any but real or pretended Christians. An Undersecretary of State, in a speech delivered to his constituents on the 12th of November, 1857, is reported to have said: "Toleration of their faith" (the faith of a hundred millions of British subjects), "the superstition which they called religion, by the British Government, had had the effect of retarding the ascendancy of the British name, and preventing the salutary growth of Christianity. . . . Toleration was the great cornerstone of the religious liberties of this country; but do not let them abuse that precious word 'toleration.' As he understood it, it meant the complete liberty to all, freedom of worship, *among Christians, who worshiped upon the same foundation.* It meant toleration of all sects and denominations of *Christians who believed in the one mediation.*" I desire to call attention to the fact that a man who has been deemed fit to fill a high office in the government of this country under a liberal ministry maintains the doctrine that all who do not believe in the divinity of Christ are beyond the pale of toleration. Who, after this imbecile display, can indulge the illusion that religious persecution has passed away, never to return?

desire no favors from men in power, or from bodies of men, or from the public, have nothing to fear from the open avowal of any opinions but to be ill-thought of and ill-spoken of, and this it ought not to require a very heroic mold to enable them to bear. There is no room for any appeal *ad misericordiam* in behalf of such persons. But though we do not now inflict so much evil on those who think differently from us as it was formerly our custom to do, it may be that we do ourselves as much evil as ever by our treatment of them. Socrates was put to death, but the Socratic philosophy rose like the sun in heaven and spread its illumination over the whole intellectual firmament. Christians were cast to the lions, but the Christian church grew up a stately and spreading tree, overtopping the older and less vigorous growths, and stifling them by its shade. Our merely social intolerance kills no one, roots out no opinions, but induces men to disguise them or to abstain from any active effort for their diffusion. With us, heretical opinions do not perceptibly gain, or even lose, ground in each decade or generation; they never blaze out far and wide, but continue to smolder in the narrow circles of thinking and studious persons among whom they originate, without ever lighting up the general affairs of mankind with either a true or a deceptive light. And thus is kept up a state of things very satisfactory to some minds, because, without the unpleasant process of fining or imprisoning anybody, it maintains all prevailing opinions outwardly undisturbed, while it does not absolutely interdict the exercise of reason by dissentients afflicted with the malady of thought. A convenient plan for having peace in the intellectual world, and keeping all things going on therein very much as they do already. But the price paid for this sort of intellectual pacification is the sacrifice of the entire moral courage of the human mind. A state of things in which a large portion of the most active and inquiring intellects find it advisable to keep the general principles and grounds of their convictions within their own breasts, and attempt, in what they address to the public, to fit as much as they can of their own conclusions to premises which they have internally renounced, cannot send forth the open, fearless characters and logical, consistent intellects who once adorned the thinking world. The sort of men who can be looked for under it are either mere conformers to commonplace, or time-servers for truth, whose arguments on all great subjects are meant for their hearers, and are not those which have convinced themselves. Those who avoid this alternative do so by narrowing their thoughts and interest to things which can be spoken of without venturing within the region of principles, that is, to small practical matters which would come right of themselves, if but the minds of mankind were strengthened and enlarged, and which will never be made effectually right until then, while that which would strengthen and enlarge men's minds—free and daring speculation on the highest subjects—is abandoned.

Those in whose eyes this reticence on the part of heretics is no evil should consider, in the first place, that in consequence of it there is never any fair and thorough discussion of heretical opinions; and that such of them as could not stand such a discussion, though they may be prevented from spreading, do not disappear. But it is not the minds of heretics that are deteriorated most by the ban placed on all inquiry which does not end in the orthodox conclusions. The greatest harm done is to those who are not heretics, and whose whole mental development is cramped and their reason cowed by the fear of heresy. Who can compute what the world loses in the multitude of promising intellects combined with timid characters, who dare not follow out any bold, vigorous, independent train of thought, lest it should land them in something which would admit of being considered irreligious or immoral? Among them we may occasionally see some man of deep conscientiousness and subtle and refined understanding, who spends a life in sophisticating with an intellect which he cannot silence, and exhausts the resources of ingenuity in attempting to reconcile the promptings of his conscience and reason with orthodoxy, which yet he does not, perhaps, to the end succeed in doing. No one can be a great thinker who does not recognize that as a thinker it is his first duty to follow his intellect to whatever conclusions it may lead. Truth gains more even by the errors of one who, with due study and preparation, thinks for himself than by the true opinions of those who only hold them because they do not suffer themselves to think. Not that it is solely, or chiefly, to form great thinkers that freedom of thinking is required. On the contrary, it is as much and even more indispensable to enable average human beings to attain the mental stature which they are capable of. There have been, and may again be, great individual thinkers in a general atmosphere of mental slavery. But there never has been, nor ever will be, in that atmosphere an intellectually active people. Where any people has made a temporary approach to such a character, it has been because the dread of heterodox speculation was for a time suspended. Where there is a tacit convention that principles are not to be disputed, where the discussion of the greatest questions which can occupy humanity is considered to be closed, we cannot hope to find that generally high scale of mental activity which has made some periods of history so remarkable. Never when controversy avoided the subjects which are large and important enough to kindle enthusiasm was the mind of a people stirred up from its foundations, and the impulse given which raised even persons of the most ordinary intellect to something of the dignity of thinking beings. Of such we have had an example in the condition of Europe during the times immediately following the Reformation; another, though limited to the Continent and to a more cultivated class, in the speculative movement of the latter half of the eighteenth century; and a third, of still briefer duration, in the intellectual fermentation of Germany during the Goethian and Fichtean period. These periods differed widely in the particular opinions which they developed, but were alike in this, that during all three the yoke of authority was broken. In each, an old mental despotism had been thrown off, and no new one had yet taken its place. The impulse given at these three periods has made Europe what it now is. Every single improvement which has taken place either in the human mind or in institutions may be traced distinctly to one or other of them. Appearances have for some time indicated that all three impulses are well-nigh spent; and we can expect no fresh start until we again assert our mental freedom.

Let us now pass to the second division of the argument, and dismissing the supposition that any of the received opinions may be false, let us assume them to be true and examine into the worth of the manner in which they are likely to be held when their truth is not freely and openly canvassed. However unwillingly a person who has a strong opinion may admit the possibility that his opinion may be false, he ought to be moved by the consideration that, however true it may be, if it is not fully, frequently, and fearlessly discussed, it will be held as a dead dogma, not a living truth.

There is a class of persons (happily not quite so numerous as formerly) who think it enough if a person assents undoubtingly to what they think true, though he has no knowledge whatever of the grounds of the opinion and could not make a tenable defense of it against the most superficial objections. Such persons, if they can once get their creed taught from authority, naturally think that no good, and some harm, comes of its being allowed to be questioned. Where their influence prevails, they make it nearly impossible for the received opinion to be rejected wisely and considerately, though it may still be rejected rashly and ignorantly; for to shut out discussion entirely is seldom possible, and when it once gets in, beliefs not grounded on conviction are apt to give way before the slightest semblance of an argument. Waiving, however, this possibility—assuming that the true opinion abides in the mind, but abides as a prejudice, a belief independent of, and proof against, argument—this is not the way in which truth ought to be held by a rational being. This is not knowing the truth. Truth, thus held, is but one superstition the more, accidentally clinging to the words which enunciate a truth.

If the intellect and judgment of mankind ought to be cultivated, a thing which Protestants at least do not deny, on what can these faculties be more appropriately exercised by anyone than on the things which concern him so much that it is considered necessary for him to hold opinions on them? If the cultivation of the understanding consists in one thing more than in another, it is surely in learning the grounds of one's own opinions. Whatever people believe, on subjects on which it is of the first importance to believe rightly, they ought to be able to defend against at least the common objections. But, someone may say, "Let them be taught the grounds of their opinions. It does not follow that opinions must be merely parroted because they are never heard controverted. Persons who learn geometry do not simply commit the theorems to memory, but understand and learn likewise the demonstrations; and it would be absurd to say that they remain ignorant of the grounds of geometrical truths because they never hear anyone deny and attempt to disprove them." Undoubtedly: and such teaching suffices on a subject like mathematics, where there is nothing at all to be said on the wrong side of the question. The peculiarity of the evidence of mathematical truths is that all the argument is on one side. There are no objections, and no answers to objections. But on every subject on which difference of opinion is possible, the truth depends on a balance to be struck between two sets of conflicting reasons. Even in natural philosophy, there is always some other explanation possible of the same facts; some geocentric theory instead of heliocentric, some phlogiston instead of oxygen; and it has to be shown why that other theory cannot be the true one; and until this is shown, and until we know how it is shown, we do not understand the grounds of our opinion. But when we turn to subjects infinitely more complicated, to morals, religion, politics, social relations, and the business of life, three-fourths of the arguments for every disputed opinion consist in dispelling the appearances which favor some opinion different from it. The greatest orator, save one, of antiquity, has left it on record that he always studied his adversary's case with as great, if not still greater, intensity than even his own. What Cicero practiced as the means of forensic success requires to be imitated by all who study any subject in order to arrive at the truth. He who knows only his own side of the case knows little of that. His reasons may be good, and no one may have been able to refute them. But if he is equally unable to refute the reasons on the opposite side, if he does not so much as know what they are, he has no ground for preferring either opinion. The rational position for him would be suspension of judgment, and unless he contents himself with that, he is either led by authority or adopts, like the generality of the world, the side to which he feels most inclination. Nor is it enough that he should hear the arguments of adversaries from his own teachers, presented as they state them, and accompanied by what they offer as refutations. That is not the way to do justice to the arguments or bring them into real contact with his own mind. He must be able to hear them from persons who actually believe them, who defend them in earnest and do their very utmost for them. He must know them in their most plausible and persuasive form; he must feel the whole force of the difficulty which the true view of the subject has to encounter and dispose of, else he will never really possess himself of the portion of truth which meets and removes that difficulty. Ninety-nine in a hundred of what are called educated men are in this condition, even of those who can argue fluently for their opinions. Their conclusion may be true, but it might be false for anything they know; they have never thrown themselves into the mental position of those who think differently from them, and considered what such persons may have to say; and, consequently, they do not, in any proper sense of the word, know the doctrine which they themselves profess. They do not know those parts of it which explain and justify the remainder—the considerations which show that a fact which seemingly conflicts with another is reconcilable with it, or that, of two apparently strong reasons, one and not the other ought to be preferred. All that part of the truth which turns the scale and decides the judgment of a completely informed mind, they are strangers to; nor is it ever really known but to those who have attended equally and impartially to both sides and endeavored to see the reasons of both in the strongest light. So essential is this discipline to a real understanding of moral and human subjects that, if opponents of all-important truths do not exist, it is indispensable to imagine them and supply them with the strongest arguments which the most skillful devil's advocate can conjure up.

To abate the force of these considerations, an enemy of free discussion may be supposed to say that there is no necessity for mankind in general to know and understand all that can be said against or for their opinions by philosophers and theologians. That it is not needful for common men to be able to expose all the misstatements or fallacies of an ingenious opponent. That it is enough if there is always somebody capable of answering them, so that nothing likely to mislead uninstructed persons remains unrefuted. That simple minds, having been taught the obvious grounds of the truths inculcated in them, may trust to authority for the rest and, being aware that they have neither knowledge nor talent to resolve every difficulty which can be raised, may repose in the assurance that all those which have been raised have been or can be answered by those who are specially trained to the task.

Conceding to this view of the subject the utmost that can be claimed for it by those most easily satisfied with the amount of understanding of truth which ought to accompany the belief of it, even so, the argument for free discussion is noway weakened. For even this doctrine acknowledges that mankind ought to have a rational assurance that all objections have been satisfactorily answered; and how are they to be answered if that which requires to be answered is not spoken? Or how can the answer be known to be satisfactory if the objectors have no opportunity of showing that it is unsatisfactory? If not the public, at least the philosophers and theologians who are to resolve the difficulties must make themselves familiar with those difficulties in their most puzzling form; and this cannot be accomplished unless they are freely stated and placed in the most advantageous light which they admit of. The Catholic Church has its own way of dealing with this embarrassing problem. It makes a broad separation between those who can be permitted to receive its doctrines on conviction and those who must accept them on trust. Neither, indeed, are allowed any choice as to what they will accept; but the clergy, such at least as can be fully confided in, may admissibly and meritoriously make themselves acquainted with the arguments of opponents, in order to answer them, and may, therefore, read heretical books; the laity, not unless by special permission, hard to be obtained. This discipline recognizes a knowledge of the enemy's case as beneficial to the teachers, but finds means, consistent with this, of denying it to the rest of the world, thus giving to the *élite* more mental culture, though not more mental freedom, than it allows to the mass. By this device it succeeds in obtaining the kind of mental superiority which its purposes require; for though culture without freedom never made a large and liberal mind, it can make a clever *nisi prius* [i.e., assumed valid] advocate of a cause. But in countries professing Protestantism, this resource is denied, since Protestants hold, at least in theory, that the responsibility for the choice of a religion must be borne by each for himself and cannot be thrown off upon teachers. Besides, in the present state of the world, it is practically impossible that writings which are read by the instructed can be kept from the uninstructed. If the teachers of mankind are to be cognizant of all that they ought to know, everything must be free to be written and published without restraint.

If, however, the mischievous operation of the absence of free discussion, when the received opinions are true, were confined to leaving men ignorant of the grounds of those opinions, it might be thought that this, if an intellectual, is no moral evil and does not affect the worth of the opinions, regarded in their influence on the character. The fact, however, is that not only the grounds of the opinion are forgotten in the absence of discussion, but too often the meaning of the opinion itself. The words which convey it cease to suggest ideas, or suggest only a small portion of those they were originally employed to communicate. Instead of a vivid conception and a living belief, there remain only a few phrases retained by rote; or, if any part, the shell and husk only of the meaning is retained, the finer essence being lost. The great chapter in human history which this fact occupies and fills cannot be too earnestly studied and meditated on.

It is illustrated in the experience of almost all ethical doctrines and religious creeds. They are all full of meaning and vitality to those who originate them, and to the direct disciples of the originators. Their meaning continues to be felt in undiminished strength, and is perhaps brought out into even fuller consciousness, so long as the struggle lasts to give the doctrine or creed an ascendancy over other creeds. At last it either prevails and becomes the general opinion, or its progress stops; it keeps possession of the ground it has gained, but ceases to spread further. When either of these results has become apparent, controversy on the subject flags, and gradually dies away. The doctrine has taken its place, if not as a received opinion, as one of the admitted sects or divisions of opinion; those who hold it have generally inherited, not adopted it; and conversion from one of these doctrines to another, being now an exceptional fact, occupies little place in the thoughts of their professors. Instead of being, as at first, constantly on the alert either to defend themselves against the world or to bring the world over to them, they have subsided into acquiescence and neither listen, when they can help it, to arguments against their creed, nor trouble dissentients (if there be such) with arguments in its favor. From this time may usually be dated the decline in the living power of the doctrine. We often hear the teachers of all creeds lamenting the difficulty of keeping up in the minds of believers a lively apprehension of the truth which they nominally recognize, so that it may penetrate the feelings and acquire a real mastery over the conduct. No such difficulty is complained of while the creed is still fighting for its existence; even the weaker combatants then know and feel what they are fighting for, and the difference between it and other doctrines; and in that period of every creed's existence not a few persons may be found who have realized its fundamental principles in all the forms of thought, have weighed and considered them in all their important bearings, and have experienced the full effect on the character which belief in that creed ought to produce in a mind thoroughly imbued with it. But when it has come to be an hereditary creed, and to be received passively, not actively—when the mind is no longer compelled, in the same degree as at first, to exercise its vital powers on the questions which its belief presents to it, there is a progressive tendency to forget all of the belief except the formularies, or to give it a dull and torpid assent, as if accepting it on trust dispensed with the necessity of realizing it in consciousness, or testing it by personal experience, until it almost ceases to connect itself at all with the inner life of the human being. Then are seen the cases, so frequent in this age of the world as almost to form the majority, in which the creed remains as it were outside the mind, incrusting and petrifying it against all other influences addressed to the higher parts of our nature; manifesting its power by not suffering any fresh and living conviction to get in, but itself doing nothing for the mind or heart except standing sentinel over them to keep them vacant.

To what an extent doctrines intrinsically fitted to make the deepest impression upon the mind may remain in it as dead beliefs, without being ever realized in the imagination, the feelings, or the understanding, is exemplified by the manner in which the majority of believers hold the doctrines of Christianity. By Christianity, I here mean what is accounted such by all churches and sects—the maxims and precepts contained in the New Testament. These are considered sacred, and accepted as laws, by all professing Christians. Yet it is scarcely too much to say that not one Christian in a thousand guides or tests his individual conduct by reference to those laws. The standard to which he does refer it is the custom of his nation, his class, or his religious profession. He has thus, on the one hand, a collection of ethical maxims which he believes to have been vouchsafed to him by infallible wisdom as rules for his government; and, on the other, a set of everyday judgments and practices which go a certain length with some of those maxims, not so great a length with others, stand in direct opposition to some, and are, on the whole, a compromise between the Christian creed and the interests and suggestions of worldly life. To the first of these standards he gives his homage; to the other his real allegiance. All Christians believe that the blessed are the poor and humble, and those who are ill-used by the world; that it is easier for a camel to pass through the eye of a needle than for a rich man to enter the kingdom of heaven; that they should judge not, lest they be judged; that they should swear not at all; that they should love their neighbor as themselves; that if one take their cloak, they should give him their coat also; that they should take no thought for the morrow; that if they would be perfect they should sell all that they have and give it to the poor. They are not insincere when they say that they believe these things. They do believe them, as people believe what they have always heard lauded and never discussed. But in the sense of that living belief which regulates conduct, they believe these doctrines just up to the point to which it is usual to act upon them. The doctrines in their integrity are serviceable to pelt adversaries with; and it is understood that they are to be put forward (when possible) as the reasons for whatever people do that they think laudable. But anyone who reminded them that the maxims require an infinity of things which they never even think of doing would gain nothing but to be classed among those very unpopular characters who affect to be better than other people. The doctrines have no hold on ordinary believers—are not a power in their minds. They have an habitual respect for the sound of them, but no feeling which spreads from the words to the things signified and forces the mind to take *them* in and make them conform to the formula. Whenever conduct is concerned, they look round for Mr. A and B to direct them how far to go in obeying Christ.

Now we may be well assured that the case was not thus, but far otherwise, with the early Christians. Had it been thus, Christianity never would have expanded from an obscure sect of the despised Hebrews into the religion of the Roman empire. When their enemies said, "See how these Christians love one another" (a remark not likely to be made by anybody now), they assuredly had a much livelier feeling of the meaning of their creed than they have ever had since. And to this cause, probably, it is chiefly owing that Christianity now makes so little progress in extending its domain, and after eighteen centuries is still nearly confined to Europeans and the descendants of Europeans. Even with the strictly religious, who are much in earnest about their doctrines and attach a greater amount of meaning to many of them than people in general, it commonly happens that the part which is thus comparatively active in their minds is that which was made by Calvin, or Knox, or some such person much nearer in character to themselves. The sayings of Christ coexist passively in their minds, producing hardly any effect beyond what is caused by mere listening to words so amiable and bland. There are many reasons, doubtless, why doctrines which are the badge of a sect retain more of their vitality than those common to all recognized sects, and why more pains are taken by teachers to keep their meaning alive; but one reason certainly is that the peculiar doctrines are more questioned and have to be oftener defended against open gainsayers. Both teachers and learners go to sleep at their post as soon as there is no enemy in the field.

The same thing holds true, generally speaking, of all traditional doctrines—those of prudence and knowledge of life as well as of morals or religion. All languages and literatures are full of general observations on life, both as to what it is and how to conduct oneself in it—observations which everybody knows, which everybody repeats or hears with acquiescence, which are received as truisms, yet of which most people first truly learn the meaning when experience, generally of a painful kind, has made it a reality to them. How often, when smarting under some unforeseen misfortune or disappointment, does a person call to mind some proverb or common saying, familiar to him all his life, the meaning of which, if he had ever before felt it as he does now, would have saved him from the calamity. There are indeed reasons for this, other than the absence of discussion; there are many truths of which the full meaning cannot be realized until personal experience has brought it home. But much more of the meaning even of these would have been understood, and what was understood would have been far more deeply impressed on the mind, if the man had been accustomed to hear it argued pro and con by people who did understand it. The fatal tendency of mankind to leave off thinking about a thing when it is no longer doubtful is the cause of half their errors. A contemporary author has well spoken of "the deep slumber of a decided opinion."

But what! (it may be asked), Is the absence of unanimity an indispensable condition of true knowledge? Is it necessary that some part of mankind should persist in error to enable any to realize the truth? Does a belief cease to be real and vital as soon as it is generally received—and is a proposition never thoroughly understood and felt unless some doubt of it remains? As soon as mankind have unanimously accepted a truth, does the truth perish within them? The highest aim and best result of improved intelligence, it has hitherto been thought, is to unite mankind more and more in the acknowledgment of all-important truths; and does the intelligence only last as long as it has not achieved its object? Do the fruits of conquest perish by the very completeness of the victory?

I affirm no such thing. As mankind improve, the number of doctrines which are no longer disputed or doubted will be constantly on the increase; and the well-being of mankind may almost be measured by the number and gravity of the truths which have reached the point of being uncontested. The cessation, on one question after another, of serious controversy is one of the necessary incidents of the consolidation of opinion—a consolidation as salutary in the case of true opinions as it is dangerous and noxious when the opinions are erroneous. But though this gradual narrowing of the bounds of diversity of opinion is necessary in both senses of the term, being at once inevitable and indispensable, we are not therefore obliged to conclude that all its consequences must be beneficial. The loss of so important an aid to the intelligent and living apprehension of a truth as is afforded by the necessity of explaining it to, or defending it against, opponents, though not sufficient to outweigh, is no trifling drawback from the benefit of its universal recognition. Where this advantage can no longer be had, I confess I should like to see the teachers of mankind endeavoring to provide a substitute for it—some contrivance for making the difficulties of the question as present to the learner's consciousness as if they were pressed upon him by a dissentient champion, eager for his conversion.

But instead of seeking contrivances for this purpose, they have lost those they formerly had. The Socratic dialectics, so magnificently exemplified in the dialogues of

Plato, were a contrivance of this description. They were essentially a negative discussion of the great questions of philosophy and life, directed with consummate skill to the purpose of convincing anyone who had merely adopted the commonplaces of received opinion that he did not understand the subject—that he as yet attached no definite meaning to the doctrines he professed; in order that, becoming aware of his ignorance, he might be put in the way to obtain a stable belief, resting on a clear apprehension both of the meaning of doctrines and of their evidence. The school disputations of the Middle Ages had a somewhat similar object. They were intended to make sure that the pupil understood his own opinion, and (by necessary correlation) the opinion opposed to it, and could enforce the grounds of the one and confute those of the other. These last-mentioned contests had indeed the incurable defect that the premises appealed to were taken from authority, not from reason; and, as a discipline to the mind, they were in every respect inferior to the powerful dialectics which formed the intellects of the "*Socratici viri*" [Socrates' followers]; but the modern mind owes far more to both than it is generally willing to admit, and the present modes of education contain nothing which in the smallest degree supplies the place either of the one or of the other. A person who derives all his instruction from teachers or books, even if he escape the besetting temptation of contenting himself with cram, is under no compulsion to hear both sides; accordingly it is far from a frequent accomplishment, even among thinkers, to know both sides; and the weakest part of what everybody says in defense of his opinion is what he intends as a reply to antagonists. It is the fashion of the present time to disparage negative logic—that which points out weaknesses in theory or errors in practice without establishing positive truths. Such negative criticism would indeed be poor enough as an ultimate result, but as a means to attaining any positive knowledge or conviction worthy the name it cannot be valued too highly; and until people are again systematically trained to it, there will be few great thinkers and a low general average of intellect in any but the mathematical and physical departments of speculation. On any other subject no one's opinions deserve the name of knowledge, except so far as he has either had forced upon him by others or gone through of himself the same mental process which would have been required of him in carrying on an active controversy with opponents. That, therefore, which, when absent, it is so indispensable, but so difficult, to create, how worse than absurd it is to forego when spontaneously offering itself! If there are any persons who contest a received opinion, or who will do so if law or opinion will let them, let us thank them for it, open our minds to listen to them, and rejoice that there is someone to do for us what we otherwise ought, if we have any regard for either the certainty or the vitality of our convictions, to do with much greater labor for ourselves.

It still remains to speak of one of the principal causes which make diversity of opinion advantageous, and will continue to do so until mankind shall have entered a stage of intellectual advancement which at present seems at an incalculable distance. We have hitherto considered only two possibilities: that the received opinion may be false, and some other opinion, consequently, true; or that, the received opinion being true, a conflict with the opposite error is essential to a clear apprehension and deep feeling of its truth. But there is a commoner case than either of these: when the conflicting doctrines, instead of being one true and the other false, share the truth between them, and the nonconforming opinion is needed to supply the remainder of the truth of which the received doctrine embodies only a part. Popular opinions, on subjects not palpable to sense, are often true, but seldom or never the whole truth. They are a part of the truth, sometimes a greater, sometimes a smaller part, but exaggerated, distorted, and disjointed from the truths by which they ought to be accompanied and limited.

Heretical opinions, on the other hand, are generally some of these suppressed and neglected truths, bursting the bonds which kept them down, and either seeking reconciliation with the truth contained in the common opinion, or fronting it as enemies, and setting themselves up, with similar exclusiveness, as the whole truth. The latter case is hitherto the most frequent, as, in the human mind, one-sidedness has always been the rule, and many-sidedness the exception. Hence, even in revolutions of opinion, one part of the truth usually sets while another rises. Even progress, which ought to superadd, for the most part only substitutes one partial and incomplete truth for another; improvement consisting chiefly in this, that the new fragment of truth is more wanted, more adapted to the needs of the time than that which it displaces. Such being the partial character of prevailing opinions, even when resting on a true foundation, every opinion which embodies somewhat of the portion of truth which the common opinion omits ought to be considered precious, with whatever amount of error and confusion that truth may be blended. No sober judge of human affairs will feel bound to be indignant because those who force on our notice truths which we should otherwise have overlooked, overlook some of those which we see. Rather, he will think that so long as popular truth is one-sided, it is more desirable than otherwise that unpopular truth should have onesided assertors, too, such being usually the most energetic and the most likely to compel reluctant attention to the fragment of wisdom which they proclaim as if it were the whole.

Thus, in the eighteenth century, when nearly all the instructed, and all those of the uninstructed who were led by them, were lost in admiration of what is called civilization, and of the marvels of modern science, literature, and philosophy, and while greatly overrating the amount of unlikeness between the men of modern and those of ancient times, indulged the belief that the whole of the difference was in their own favor; with what a salutary shock did the paradoxes of Rousseau explode like bombshells in the midst, dislocating the compact mass of one-sided opinion and forcing its elements to recombine in a better form and with additional ingredients. Not that the current opinions were on the whole farther from the truth than Rousseau's were; on the contrary, they were nearer to it; they contained more of positive truth, and very much less of error. Nevertheless there lay in Rousseau's doctrine, and has floated down the stream of opinion along with it, a considerable amount of exactly those truths which the popular opinion wanted; and these are the deposit which was left behind them when the flood subsided. The superior worth of simplicity of life, the enervating and demoralizing effect of the trammels and hypocrisies of artificial society are ideas which have never been entirely absent from cultivated minds since Rousseau wrote; and they will in time produce their due effect, though at present needing to be asserted as much as ever, and to be asserted by deeds; for words, on this subject, have nearly exhausted their power.

In politics, again, it is almost a commonplace that a party of order or stability and a party of progress or reform are both necessary elements of a healthy state of political life, until the one or the other shall have so enlarged its mental grasp as to be a party equally of order and of progress, knowing and distinguishing what is fit to be preserved from what ought to be swept away. Each of these modes of thinking derives its utility from the deficiencies of the other; but it is in a great measure the opposition of the other that keeps each within the limits of reason and sanity. Unless opinions favorable to democracy and to aristocracy, to property and to equality, to cooperation and to competition, to luxury and to abstinence, to sociality and individuality, to liberty and discipline, and all the other standing antagonisms of practical life, are expressed with equal freedom and enforced and defended with equal talent and energy, there is no chance of both elements obtaining their due; one scale is sure to go up, and the other down. Truth, in the great practical concerns of life, is so much a question of the reconciling and combining of opposites that very few have minds sufficiently capacious and impartial to make the adjustment with an approach to correctness, and it has to be made by the rough process of a struggle between combatants fighting under hostile banners. On any of the great open questions just enumerated, if either of the two opinions has a better claim than the other, not merely to be tolerated, but to be encouraged and countenanced, it is the one which happens at the particular time and place to be in a minority. That is the opinion which, for the time being, represents the neglected interests, the side of human well-being which is in danger of obtaining less than its share. I am aware that there is not, in this country, any intolerance of differences of opinion on most of these topics. They are adduced to show, by admitted and multiplied examples, the universality of the fact that only through diversity of opinion is there, in the existing state of human intellect, a chance of fair play to all sides of the truth. When there are persons to be found who form an exception to the apparent unanimity of the world on any subject, even if the world is in the right, it is always probable that dissentients have something worth hearing to say for themselves, and that truth would lose something by their silence.

It may be objected, "But *some* received principles, especially on the highest and most vital subjects, are more than half-truths. The Christian morality, for instance, is the whole truth on that subject, and if anyone teaches a morality which varies from it, he is wholly in error." As this is of all cases the most important in practice, none can be fitter to test the general maxim. But before pronouncing what Christian morality is or is not, it would be desirable to decide what is meant by Christian morality. If it means the morality of the New Testament, I wonder that any one who derives his knowledge of this from the book itself can suppose that it was announced, or intended, as a complete doctrine of morals. The Gospel always refers to a pre-existing morality and confines its precepts to the particulars in which that morality was to be corrected or superseded by a wider and higher, expressing itself, moreover, in terms most general, often impossible to be interpreted literally, and possessing rather the impressiveness of poetry or eloquence than the precision of legislation. To extract from it a body of ethical doctrine has never been possible without eking it out from the Old Testament, that is, from a system elaborate indeed, but in many respects barbarous, and intended only for a barbarous people. St. Paul, a declared enemy to this Judaical mode of interpreting the doctrine and filling up the scheme of his Master, equally assumes a pre-existing morality, namely that of the Greeks and Romans; and his advice to Christians is in a great measure a system of accommodation to that, even to the extent of giving an apparent sanction to slavery. What is called Christian, but should rather be termed theological, morality was not the work of Christ or the Apostles, but is of much later origin, having been gradually built up by the Catholic Church of the first five centuries, and though not implicitly adopted by moderns and Protestants, has been much less modified by them than might have been expected. For the most part, indeed, they have contented themselves with cutting off the additions which had been made to it in the Middle Ages, each sect supplying the place by fresh additions, adapted to its own character and tendencies. That mankind owe a great debt to this morality, and to its early teachers, I should be the last person to deny, but I do not scruple to say of it that it is, in many important points, incomplete and one-sided, and that, unless ideas and feelings not sanctioned by it had contributed to the formation of European life and character, human affairs would have been in a worse condition than they now are. Christian morality (so called) has all the characters of a reaction; it is, in great part, a protest against paganism. Its ideal is negative rather than positive; passive rather than active; innocence rather than nobleness; abstinence from evil rather than energetic pursuit of good; in its precepts (as has been well said) "thou shalt not" predominates unduly over "thou shalt." In its horror of sensuality, it made an idol of asceticism which has been gradually compromised away into one of legality. It holds out the hope of heaven and the threat of hell as the appointed and appropriate motives to a virtuous life: in this falling far below the best of the ancients, and doing what lies in it to give to human morality an essentially selfish character, by disconnecting each man's feelings of duty from the interests of his fellow creatures, except so far as a self-interested inducement is offered to him for consulting them. It is essentially a doctrine of passive obedience; it inculcates submission to all authorities found established; who indeed are not to be actively obeyed when they command what religion forbids, but who are not to be re-sisted, far less rebelled against, for any amount of wrong to ourselves. And while, in the morality of the best pagan nations, duty to the State holds even a disproportionate place, infringing on the just liberty of the individual, in purely Christian ethics that grand department of duty is scarcely noticed or acknowledged. It is in the Koran, not the New Testament, that we read the maxim: "A ruler who appoints any man to an of-fice, when there is in his dominions another man better qualified for it, sins against God and against the State." What little recognition the idea of obligation to the public obtains in modern morality is derived from Greek and Roman sources, not from Chris-tian; as, even in the morality of private life, whatever exists of magnanimity, high-mindedness, personal dignity, even the sense of honor, is derived from the purely human, not the religious part of our education, and never could have grown out of a standard of ethics in which the only worth, professedly recognized, is that of obedi-ence.

I am as far as anyone from pretending that these defects are necessarily inherent in the Christian ethics in every manner in which it can be conceived, or that the many requisites of a complete moral doctrine which it does not contain do not admit of being reconciled with it. Far less would I insinuate this out of the doctrines and precepts of Christ himself. I believe that the sayings of Christ are all that I can see any evidence of their having been intended to be; that they are irreconcilable with nothing which a comprehensive morality requires; that everything which is excellent in ethics may be brought within them, with no greater violence to their language than has been done to it by all who have attempted to deduce from them any practical system of conduct whatever. But it is quite consistent with this to believe that they contain, and were meant to contain, only a part of the truth; that many essential elements of the highest morality are among the things which are not provided for, nor intended to be provided for, in the recorded deliverances of the Founder of Christianity, and which have been entirely thrown aside in the system of ethics erected on the basis of those deliverances by the Christian Church. And this being so, I think it a great error to persist in attempt-ing to find in the Christian doctrine that complete rule for our guidance which its Au-thor intended it to sanction and enforce, but only partially to provide. I believe, too, that this narrow theory is becoming a grave practical evil, detracting greatly from the moral training and instruction which so many well-meaning persons are now at length exerting themselves to promote. I much fear that by attempting to form the mind and feelings on an exclusively religious type, and discarding those secular standards (as for want of a better name they may be called) which heretofore coexisted with and supple-mented the Christian ethics, receiving some of its spirit, and infusing into it some of theirs, there will result, and is even now resulting, a low, abject, servile type of charac-ter which, submit itself as it may to what it deems the Supreme Will, is incapable of rising to or sympathizing in the conception of Supreme Goodness. I believe that other ethics than any which can be evolved from exclusively Christian sources must exist side by side with Christian ethics to produce the moral regeneration of mankind; and that the Christian system is no exception to the rule that in an imperfect state of the human mind the interests of truth require a diversity of opinions. It is not necessary that in ceasing to ignore the moral truths not contained in Christianity men should ignore any of those which it does contain. Such prejudice or oversight, when it occurs, is altogether an evil, but it is one from which we cannot hope to be always exempt, and must be regarded as the price paid for an inestimable good. The exclusive pretension made by a part of the truth to be the whole must and ought to be protested against; and if a reactionary impulse should make the protestors unjust in their turn, this one-sidedness, like the other, may be lamented but must be tolerated. If Christians would teach infidels to be just to Christianity, they should themselves be just to infidelity. It can do truth no service to blink the fact, known to all who have the most ordinary acquaintance with literary history, that a large portion of the noblest and most valuable moral teaching has been the work, not only of men who did not know, but of men who knew and rejected, the Christian faith.

I do not pretend that the most unlimited use of the freedom of enunciating all possible opinions would put an end to the evils of religious or philosophical sectarianism. Every truth which men of narrow capacity are in earnest about is sure to be asserted, inculcated, and in many ways even acted on, as if no other truth existed in the world, or at all events none that could limit or qualify the first. I acknowledge that the tendency of all opinions to become sectarian is not cured by the freest discussion, but is often heightened and exacerbated thereby; the truth which ought to have been, but was not, seen, being rejected all the more violently because proclaimed by persons regarded as opponents. But it is not on the impassioned partisan, it is on the calmer and more disinterested bystander, that this collision of opinions works its salutary effect. Not the violent conflict between parts of the truth, but the quiet suppression of half of it, is the formidable evil; there is always hope when people are forced to listen to both sides; it is when they attend only to one that errors harden into prejudices, and truth itself ceases to have the effect of truth by being exaggerated into falsehood. And since there are few mental attributes more rare than that judicial faculty which can sit in intelligent judgment between two sides of a question, of which only one is represented by an advocate before it, truth has no chance but in proportion as every side of it, every opinion which embodies any fraction of the truth, not only finds advocates, but is so advocated as to be listened to.

We have now recognized the necessity to the mental well-being of mankind (on which all their other well-being depends) of freedom of opinion, and freedom of the expression of opinion, on four distinct grounds, which we will now briefly recapitulate:

First, if any opinion is compelled to silence, that opinion may, for aught we can certainly know, be true. To deny this is to assume our own infallibility.

Secondly, though the silenced opinion be an error, it may, and very commonly does, contain a portion of truth; and since the general or prevailing opinion on any subject is rarely or never the whole truth, it is only by the collision of adverse opinions that the remainder of the truth has any chance of being supplied.

Thirdly, even if the received opinion be not only true, but the whole truth; unless it is suffered to be, and actually is, vigorously and earnestly contested, it will, by most of those who receive it, be held in the manner of a prejudice, with little comprehension or feeling of its rational grounds. And not only this, but, fourthly, the meaning of the doctrine itself will be in danger of being lost or enfeebled, and deprived of its vital effect on the character and conduct: the dogma becoming a mere formal profession, inefficacious for good, but cumbering the ground and preventing the growth of any real and heartfelt conviction from reason or personal experience.

Before quitting the subject of freedom of opinion, it is fit to take some notice of those who say that the free expression of all opinions should be permitted on condition that the manner be temperate, and do not pass the bounds of fair discussion. Much might be said on the impossibility of fixing where these supposed bounds are to be placed; for if the test be offense to those whose opinions are attacked, I think experience testifies that this offense is given whenever the attack is telling and powerful, and that every opponent who pushes them hard, and whom they find it difficult to answer, appears to them, if he shows any strong feeling on the subject, an intemperate opponent. But this, though an important consideration in a practical point of view, merges in a more fundamental objection. Undoubtedly, the manner of asserting an opinion, even though it be a true one, may be very objectionable and may justly incur severe censure. But the principal offenses of the kind are such as it is mostly impossible, unless by accidental self-betrayal, to bring home to conviction. The gravest of them is, to argue sophistically, to suppress facts or arguments, to misstate the elements of the case, or misrepresent the opposite opinion. But all this, even to the most aggravated degree, is so continually done in perfect good faith by persons who are not considered, and in many other respects may not deserve to be considered, ignorant or incompetent, that it is rarely possible, on adequate grounds, conscientiously to stamp the misrepresentation as morally culpable, and still less could law presume to interfere with this kind of controversial misconduct. With regard to what is commonly meant by intemperate discussion, namely invective, sarcasm, personality, and the like, the denunciation of these weapons would deserve more sympathy if it were ever proposed to interdict them equally to both sides; but it is only desired to restrain the employment of them against the prevailing opinion; against the unprevailing they may not only be used without general disapproval, but will be likely to obtain for him who uses them the praise of honest zeal and righteous indignation. Yet whatever mischief arises from their use is greatest when they are employed against the comparatively defenseless; and whatever unfair advantage can be derived by any opinion from this mode of asserting it accrues almost exclusively to received opinions. The worst offense of this kind which can be committed by a polemic is to stigmatize those who hold the contrary opinion as bad and immoral men. To calumny of this sort, those who hold any unpopular opinion are peculiarly exposed, because they are in general few and uninfluential, and nobody but themselves feels much interested in seeing justice done them; but this weapon is, from the nature of the case, denied to those who attack a prevailing opinion: they can neither use it with safety to themselves, nor, if they could, would it do anything but recoil on their own cause. In general, opinions contrary to those commonly received can only obtain a hearing by studied moderation of language and the most cautious avoidance of unnecessary offense, from which they hardly ever deviate even in a slight degree without losing ground, while unmeasured vituperation employed on the side of the prevailing opinion really does deter people from professing contrary opinions and from listening to those who profess them. For the interest, therefore, of truth and justice it is far more important to restrain this employment of vituperative language than the other; and, for example, if it were necessary to choose, there would be much more need to discourage offensive attacks on infidelity than on religion. It is, however, obvious that law and authority have no business with restraining either, while opinion ought, in every instance, to determine its verdict by the circumstances of the individual case—condemning everyone, on whichever side of the argument he places himself, in whose mode of advocacy either want of candor, or malignity, bigotry, or intolerance of feeling manifest themselves; but not inferring these vices from the side which a person takes, though it be the contrary side of the question to our own; and giving merited honor to everyone, whatever opinion he may hold, who has calmness to see and honesty to state what his opponents and their opinions really are, exaggerating nothing to their discredit, keeping nothing back which tells, or can be supposed to tell, in their favor. This is the real morality of public discussion; and if often violated, I am happy to think that there are many controversialists who to a great extent observe it, and a still greater number who conscientiously strive toward it.

Chapter 3: Of Individuality, as One of the Elements of Well-Being

Such being the reasons which make it imperative that human beings should be free to form opinions and to express their opinions without reserve; and such the baneful consequences to the intellectual, and through that to the moral nature of man, unless this liberty is either conceded or asserted in spite of prohibition; let us next examine whether the same reasons do not require that men should be free to act upon their opinions—to carry these out in their lives without hindrance, either physical or moral, from their fellow men, so long as it is at their own risk and peril. This last proviso is of course indispensable. No one pretends that actions should be as free as opinions. On the contrary, even opinions lose their immunity when the circumstances in which they are expressed are such as to constitute their expression a positive instigation to some mischievous act. An opinion that corn dealers are starvers of the poor, or that private property is robbery, ought to be unmolested when simply circulated through the press, but may justly incur punishment when delivered orally to an excited mob assembled before the house of a corn dealer, or when handed about among the same mob in the form of a placard. Acts, of whatever kind, which without justifiable cause do harm to others may be, and in the more important cases absolutely require to be, controlled by the unfavorable sentiments, and, when needful, by the active interference of mankind. The liberty of the individual must be thus far limited; he must not make himself a nuisance to other people. But if he refrains from molesting others in what concerns them, and merely acts according to his own inclination and judgment in things which concern himself, the same reasons which show that opinion should be free prove also that he should be allowed, without molestation, to carry his opinions into practice at his own cost. That mankind are not infallible; that their truths, for the most part, are only half-truths; that unity of opinion, unless resulting from the fullest and freest comparison of opposite opinions, is not desirable, and diversity not an evil, but a good, until mankind are much more capable than at present of recognizing all sides of the truth, are principles applicable to men's modes of action not less than to their opinions. As it is useful that while mankind are imperfect there should be different opinions, so it is that there should be different experiments of living; that free scope should be given to varieties of character, short of injury to others; and that the worth of different modes of life should be proved practically, when anyone thinks fit to try them. It is desirable, in short, that in things which do not primarily concern others individuality should assert itself. Where not the person's own character, but the traditions or customs of other people are the rule of conduct, there is wanting one of the principal ingredients of human happiness, and quite the chief ingredient of individual and social progress.

In maintaining this principle, the greatest difficulty to be encountered does not lie in the appreciation of means toward an acknowledged end, but in the indifference of persons in general to the end itself. If it were felt that the free development of individuality is one of the leading essentials of well-being; that it is not only a co-ordinate element with all that is designated by the terms civilization, instruction, education, culture, but is itself a necessary part and condition of all those things, there would be no danger that liberty should be undervalued, and the adjustment of the boundaries between it and social control would present no extraordinary difficulty. But the evil is that individual spontaneity is hardly recognized by the common modes of thinking as having any intrinsic worth, or deserving any regard on its own account. The majority being satisfied with the ways of mankind as they now are (for it is they who make them what they are), cannot comprehend why those ways should not be good enough for everybody; and what is more, spontaneity forms no part of the ideal of the majority of moral and social reformers, but is rather looked on with jealousy, as a troublesome and perhaps rebellious obstruction to the general acceptance of what these reformers, in their own judgment, think would be best for mankind. Few persons, out of Germany, even comprehend the meaning of the doctrine which Wilhelm von Humboldt, so eminent both as a *savant* and as a politician, made the text of a treatise—that "the end of man, or that which is prescribed by the eternal or immutable dictates of reason, and not suggested by vague and transient desires, is the highest and most harmonious development of his powers to a complete and consistent whole"; that, therefore, the object "toward which every human being must ceaselessly direct his efforts, and on which especially those who design to influence their fellow men must ever keep their eyes, is the individuality of power and development"; that for this there are two requisites, "freedom, and variety of situations"; and that from the union of these arise "individual vigor and manifold diversity," which combine themselves in "originality."*

Little, however, as people are accustomed to a doctrine like that of von Humboldt, and surprising as it may be to them to find so high a value attached to individuality, the question, one must nevertheless think, can only be one of degree. No one's idea of excellence in conduct is that people should do absolutely nothing but copy one another. No one would assert that people ought not to put into their mode of life, and into the conduct of their concerns, any impress whatever of their own judgment or of their own individual character. On the other hand, it would be absurd to pretend that people ought to live as if nothing whatever had been known in the world before they came into it; as if experience had as yet done nothing toward showing that one mode of existence, or of conduct, is preferable to another. Nobody denies that people should be so taught and trained in youth as to know and benefit by the ascertained results of human experience. But it is the privilege and proper condition of a human being, arrived at the maturity of his faculties, to use and interpret experience in his own way. It is for him to find out what part of recorded experience is properly applicable to his own circumstances and character. The traditions and customs of other people are, to a certain extent, evidence of what their experience has taught *them;* presumptive evidence, and as such, have a claim to his deference: but, in the first place, their experience may be too

---

*The Sphere and Duties of Government, from the German of Baron Wilhelm von Humboldt, pp. 11–13. [Wilhelm von Humboldt (1767–1835) wrote this work in 1792 to oppose Fichte's and Hegel's theories of the state. The work shows the influence of the French Revolution on von Humboldt's thinking following his visit to Paris in 1789.]

narrow, or they may have not interpreted it rightly. Secondly, their interpretation of experience may be correct, but unsuitable to him. Customs are made for customary circumstances and customary characters; and his circumstances or his character may be uncustomary. Thirdly, though the customs be both good as customs and suitable to him, yet to conform to custom merely *as* custom does not educate or develop in him any of the qualities which are the distinctive endowment of a human being. The human faculties of perception, judgment, discriminative feeling, mental activity, and even moral preference are exercised only in making a choice. He who does anything because it is the custom makes no choice. He gains no practice either in discerning or in desiring what is best. The mental and moral, like the muscular, powers are improved only by being used. The faculties are called into no exercise by doing a thing merely because others do it, no more than by believing a thing only because others believe it. If the grounds of an opinion are not conclusive to the person's own reason, his reason cannot be strengthened, but is likely to be weakened, by his adopting it: and if the inducements to an act are not such as are consentaneous to his own feelings and character (where affection, or the rights of others, are not concerned), it is so much done toward rendering his feelings and character inert and torpid instead of active and energetic.

He who lets the world, or his own portion of it, choose his plan of life for him has no need of any other faculty than the ape-like one of imitation. He who chooses his plan for himself employs all his faculties. He must use observation to see, reasoning and judgment to foresee, activity to gather materials for decision, discrimination to decide, and when he has decided, firmness and self-control to hold to his deliberate decision. And these qualities he requires and exercises exactly in proportion as the part of his conduct which he determines according to his own judgment and feelings is a large one. It is possible that he might be guided in some good path, and kept out of harm's way, without any of these things. But what will be his comparative worth as a human being? It really is of importance, not only what men do, but also what manner of men they are that do it. Among the works of man which human life is rightly employed in perfecting and beautifying, the first in importance surely is man himself. Supposing it were possible to get houses built, corn grown, battles fought, causes tried, and even churches erected and prayers said by machinery—by automatons in human form—it would be a considerable loss to exchange for these automatons even the men and women who at present inhabit the more civilized parts of the world, and who assuredly are but starved specimens of what nature can and will produce. Human nature is not a machine to be built after a model, and set to do exactly the work prescribed for it, but a tree, which requires to grow and develop itself on all sides, according to the tendency of the inward forces which make it a living thing.

It will probably be conceded that it is desirable people should exercise their understandings, and that an intelligent following of custom, or even occasionally an intelligent deviation from custom, is better than a blind and simply mechanical adhesion to it. To a certain extent it is admitted that our understanding should be our own; but there is not the same willingness to admit that our desires and impulses should be our own likewise; or that to possess impulses of our own, and of any strength, is anything but a peril and a snare. Yet desires and impulses are as much a part of a perfect human being as beliefs and restraints: and strong impulses are only perilous when not properly balanced; when one set of aims and inclinations is developed into strength, while others, which ought to coexist with them, remain weak and inactive. It is not because men's desires are strong that they act ill; it is because their consciences are weak. There is no natural connection between strong impulses and a weak conscience. The natural connextion is the other way. To say that one person's desires and feelings are stronger and more various than those of another is merely to say that he has more of the raw material of human nature and is therefore capable, perhaps of more evil, but certainly of more good. Strong impulses are but another name for energy. Energy may be turned to bad uses; but more good may always be made of an energetic nature than of an indolent and impassive one. Those who have most natural feeling are always those whose cultivated feelings may be made the strongest. The same strong susceptibilities which make the personal impulses vivid and powerful are also the source from whence are generated the most passionate love of virtue and the sternest self-control. It is through the cultivation of these that society both does its duty and protects its interests, not by rejecting the stuff of which heroes are made, because it knows not how to make them. A person whose desires and impulses are his own—are the expression of his own nature, as it has been developed and modified by his own culture—is said to have a character. One whose desires and impulses are not his own has no character, no more than a steam engine has a character. If, in addition to being his own, his impulses are strong and are under the government of a strong will, he has an energetic character. Whoever thinks that individuality of desires and impulses should not be encouraged to unfold itself must maintain that society has no need of strong natures—is not the better for containing many persons who have much character—and that a high general average of energy is not desirable.

In some early states of society, these forces might be, and were, too much ahead of the power which society then possessed of disciplining and controlling them. There has been a time when the element of spontaneity and individuality was in excess, and the social principle had a hard struggle with it. The difficulty then was to induce men of strong bodies or minds to pay obedience to any rules which required them to control their impulses. To overcome this difficulty, law and discipline, like the Popes struggling against the Emperors, asserted a power over the whole man, claiming to control all his life in order to control his character—which society had not found any other sufficient means of binding. But society has now fairly got the better of individuality; and the danger which threatens human nature is not the excess, but the deficiency, of personal impulses and preferences. Things are vastly changed since the passions of those who were strong by station or by personal endowment were in a state of habitual rebellion against laws and ordinances, and required to be rigorously chained up to enable the persons within their reach to enjoy any particle of security. In our times, from the highest class of society down to the lowest, everyone lives as under the eye of a hostile and dreaded censorship. Not only in what concerns others, but in what concerns only themselves, the individual or the family do not ask themselves—what do I prefer? or, what would suit my character and disposition? or, what would allow the best and highest in me to have fair play and enable it to grow and thrive? They ask themselves, what is suitable to my position? what is usually done by persons of my station and pecuniary circumstances? or (worse still) what is usually done by persons of a station and circumstances superior to mine? I do not mean that they choose what is customary in preference to what suits their own inclination. It does not occur to them to have any inclination except for what is customary. Thus the mind itself is bowed to the yoke: even in what people do for pleasure, conformity is the first thing thought of; they like in crowds; they exercise choice only among things commonly done; peculiarity of taste, eccentricity of conduct are shunned equally with crimes, until by dint of not following their own nature they have no nature to follow: their human capacities are withered and starved; they become incapable of any strong wishes or native pleasures, and are generally without either opinions or feelings of home growth, or properly their own. Now is this, or is it not, the desirable condition of human nature?

It is so, on the Calvinistic theory. According to that, the one great offence of man is self-will. All the good of which humanity is capable is comprised in obedience. You have no choice; thus you must do, and no otherwise: "Whatever is not a duty is a sin." Human nature being radically corrupt, there is no redemption for anyone until human nature is killed within him. To one holding this theory of life, crushing out any of the human faculties, capacities, and susceptibilities is no evil: man needs no capacity but that of surrendering himself to the will of God; and if he uses any of his faculties for any other purpose but to do that supposed will more effectually, he is better without them. This is the theory of Calvinism; and it is held, in a mitigated form, by many who do not consider themselves Calvinists; the mitigation consisting in giving a less ascetic interpretation to the alleged will of God, asserting it to be his will that mankind should gratify some of their inclinations; of course not in the manner they themselves prefer, but in the way of obedience, that is, in a way prescribed to them by authority, and, therefore, by the necessary condition of the case, the same for all.

In some such insidious form there is at present a strong tendency to this narrow theory of life, and to the pinched and hidebound type of human character which it patronizes. Many persons, no doubt, sincerely think that human beings thus cramped and dwarfed are as their Maker designed them to be, just as many have thought that trees are a much finer thing when clipped into pollards, or cut out into figures of animals, than as nature made them. But if it be any part of religion to believe that man was made by a good Being, it is more consistent with that faith to believe that this Being gave all human faculties that they might be cultivated and unfolded, not rooted out and consumed, and that he takes delight in every nearer approach made by his creatures to the ideal conception embodied in them, every increase in any of their capabilities of comprehension, of action, or of enjoyment. There is a different type of human excellence from the Calvinistic: a conception of humanity as having its nature bestowed on it for other purposes than merely to be abnegated. "Pagan self-assertion" is one of the elements of human worth, as well as "Christian self-denial."* There is a Greek ideal of self-development, which the Platonic and Christian ideal of self-government blends with, but does not supersede. It may be better to be a John Knox than an Alcibiades, but it is better to be a Pericles** than either; nor would a Pericles, if we had one in these days, be without anything good which belonged to John Knox.

It is not by wearing down into uniformity all that is individual in themselves, but by cultivating it and calling it forth, within the limits imposed by the rights and interests of others, that human beings become a noble and beautiful object of contemplation; and as the works partake the character of those who do them, by the same process human life also becomes rich, diversified, and animating, furnishing more abundant aliment [sustenance] to high thoughts and elevating feelings, and strengthening the tie which binds every individual to the race, by making the race infinitely better worth belonging to. In proportion to the development of his individuality, each person becomes more valuable to himself, and is, therefore, capable of being more valuable to others. There is a greater fullness of life about his own existence, and when there is more life

---

*Sterling's *Essays*. [John Sterling (1806–1844) was a British writer.]

**[John Knox (1505–1572) was a leader of the Reformation and the founder of the Scottish Presbyterian Church; Alcibiades (ca. 450–404 B.C.) was a disreputable Athenian general who symbolized for many the decline of Athens; Pericles (ca. 495–429 B.C.) was a famous and beloved Athenian statesman.]

in the units there is more in the mass which is composed of them. As much compression as is necessary to prevent the stronger specimens of human nature from encroaching on the rights of others cannot be dispensed with; but for this there is ample compensation even in the point of view of human development. The means of development which the individual loses by being prevented from gratifying his inclinations to the injury of others are chiefly obtained at the expense of the development of other people. And even to himself there is a full equivalent in the better development of the social part of his nature, rendered possible by the restraint put upon the selfish part. To be held to rigid rules of justice for the sake of others develops the feelings and capacities which have the good of others for their object. But to be restrained in things not affecting their good, by their mere displeasure, develops nothing valuable except such force of character as may unfold itself in resisting the restraint. If acquiesced in, it dulls and blunts the whole nature. To give any fair play to the nature of each, it is essential that different persons should be allowed to lead different lives. In proportion as this latitude has been exercised in any age has that age been noteworthy to posterity. Even despotism does not produce its worst effects so long as individuality exists under it; and whatever crushes individuality is despotism, by whatever name it may be called and whether it professes to be enforcing the will of God or the injunctions of men.

Having said that individuality is the same thing with development, and that it is only the cultivation of individuality which produces, or can produce, well-developed human beings, I might here close the argument; for what more or better can be said of any condition of human affairs than that it brings human beings themselves nearer to the best thing they can be? Or what worse can be said of any obstruction to good than that it prevents this? Doubtless, however, these considerations will not suffice to convince those who most need convincing; and it is necessary further to show that these developed human beings are of some use to the undeveloped—to point out to those who do not desire liberty, and would not avail themselves of it, that they may be in some intelligible manner rewarded for allowing other people to make use of it without hindrance.

In the first place, then, I would suggest that they might possibly learn something from them. It will not be denied by anybody that originality is a valuable element in human affairs. There is always need of persons not only to discover new truths and point out when what were once truths are true no longer, but also to commence new practices and set the example of more enlightened conduct and better taste and sense in human life. This cannot well be gainsaid by anybody who does not believe that the world has already attained perfection in all its ways and practices. It is true that this benefit is not capable of being rendered by everybody alike; there are but few persons, in comparison with the whole of mankind, whose experiments, if adopted by others, would be likely to be any improvement on established practice. But these few are the salt of the earth; without them, human life would become a stagnant pool. Not only is it they who introduce good things which did not before exist; it is they who keep the life in those which already exist. If there were nothing new to be done, would human intellect cease to be necessary? Would it be a reason why those who do the old things should forget why they are done, and do them like cattle, not like human beings? There is only too great a tendency in the best beliefs and practices to degenerate into the mechanical; and unless there were a succession of persons whose ever-recurring originality prevents the grounds of those beliefs and practices from becoming merely traditional, such dead matter would not resist the smallest shock from anything really alive, and there would be no reason why civilization should not die out, as in the Byzantine Empire. Persons of genius it is true, are, and are always likely to be, a small minority; but in order to have them, it is necessary to preserve the soil in which they grow. Genius can only breathe freely in an *atmosphere* of freedom. Persons of genius are, *ex vi termini* [by definition], more individual than any other people—less capable, consequently, of fitting themselves, without hurtful compression, into any of the small number of molds which society provides in order to save its members the trouble of forming their own character. If from timidity they consent to be forced into one of these molds, and to let all that part of themselves which cannot expand under the pressure remain unexpanded, society will be little the better for their genius. If they are of a strong character and break their fetters, they become a mark for the society which has not succeeded in reducing them to commonplace, to point out with solemn warning as "wild," "erratic," and the like, much as if one should complain of the Niagara river for not flowing smoothly between its banks like a Dutch canal.

I insist thus emphatically on the importance of genius, and the necessity of allowing it to unfold itself freely both in thought and in practice, being well aware that no one will deny the position in theory, but knowing also that almost everyone, in reality, is totally indifferent to it. People think genius a fine thing if it enables a man to write an exciting poem or paint a picture. But in its true sense, that of originality in thought and action, though no one says that it is not a thing to be admired, nearly all, at heart, think that they can do very well without it. Unhappily this is too natural to be wondered at. Originality is the one thing which unoriginal minds cannot feel the use of. They cannot see what it is to do for them: how should they? If they could see what it would do for them, it would not be originality. The first service which originality has to render them is that of opening their eyes: which being once fully done, they would have a chance of being themselves original. Meanwhile, recollecting that nothing was ever yet done which someone was not the first to do, and that all good things which exist are the fruits of originality, let them be modest enough to believe that there is something still left for it to accomplish, and assure themselves that they are more in need of originality the less they are conscious of the want.

In sober truth, whatever homage may be professed, or even paid, to real or supposed mental superiority, the general tendency of things throughout the world is to render mediocrity the ascendant power among mankind. In ancient history, in the Middle Ages, and in a diminishing degree through the long transition from feudality to the present time, the individual was a power in himself; and if he had either great talents or a high social position, he was a considerable power. At present individuals are lost in the crowd. In politics it is almost a triviality to say that public opinion now rules the world. The only power deserving the name is that of masses, and of governments while they make themselves the organ of the tendencies and instincts of masses. This is as true in the moral and social relations of private life as in public transactions. Those whose opinions go by the name of public opinion are not always the same sort of public: in America, they are the whole white population; in England, chiefly the middle class. But they are always a mass, that is to say, collective mediocrity. And what is a still greater novelty, the mass do not now take their opinions from dignitaries in Church or State, from ostensible leaders, or from books. Their thinking is done for them by men much like themselves, addressing them or speaking in their name, on the spur of the moment, through the newspapers. I am not complaining of all this. I do not assert that anything better is compatible, as a general rule, with the present low state of the human mind. But that does not hinder the government of mediocrity from being mediocre government. No government by a democracy or a numerous aristocracy, either in its political acts or in the opinions, qualities, and tone of mind which it fosters, ever did or could rise above mediocrity, except in so far as the sovereigns. Many have let themselves be guided (which in their best times they always have done) by the counsels and influence of a more highly gifted and instructed *One* or *Few*. The initiation of all wise or noble things comes and must come from individuals; generally at first from some one individual. The honor and glory of the average man is that he is capable of following that initiative; that he can respond internally to wise and noble things, and be led to them with his eyes open. I am not countenancing the sort of "hero-worship" which applauds the strong man of genius for forcibly seizing on the government of the world and making it do his bidding in spite of itself. All he can claim is freedom to point out the way. The power of compelling others into it is not only inconsistent with the freedom and development of all the rest, but corrupting to the strong man himself. It does seem, however, that when the opinions of masses of merely average men are everywhere become or becoming the dominant power, the counterpoise and corrective to that tendency would be the more and more pronounced individuality of those who stand on the higher eminences of thought. It is in these circumstances most especially that exceptional individuals, instead of being deterred, should be encouraged in acting differently from the mass. In other times there was no advantage in their doing so, unless they acted not only differently, but better. In this age, the mere example of nonconformity, the mere refusal to bend the knee to custom, is itself a service. Precisely because the tyranny of opinion is such as to make eccentricity a reproach, it is desirable, in order to break through that tyranny, that people should be eccentric. Eccentricity has always abounded when and where strength of character has abounded; and the amount of eccentricity in a society has generally been proportional to the amount of genius, mental vigor, and moral courage which it contained. That so few now dare to be eccentric marks the chief danger of the time.

I have said that it is important to give the freest scope possible to uncustomary things, in order that it may in time appear which of these are fit to be converted into customs. But independence of action and disregard of custom are not solely deserving of encouragement for the chance they afford that better modes of action, and customs more worthy of general adoption, may be struck out; nor is it only persons of decided mental superiority who have a just claim to carry on their lives in their own way. There is no reason that all human existence should be constructed on some one or some small number of patterns. If a person possesses any tolerable amount of common sense and experience, his own mode of laying out his existence is the best, not because it is the best in itself, but because it is his own mode. Human beings are not like sheep; and even sheep are not undistinguishably alike. A man cannot get a coat or a pair of boots to fit him unless they are either made to his measure or he has a whole warehouseful to choose from; and is it easier to fit him with a life than with a coat, or are human beings more like one another in their whole physical and spiritual conformation than in the shape of their feet? If it were only that people have diversities of taste, that is reason enough for not attempting to shape them all after one model. But different persons also require different conditions for their spiritual development; and can no more exist healthily in the same moral, than all the variety of plants can in the same physical, atmosphere and climate. The same things which are helps to one person toward the cultivation of his higher nature are hindrances to another. The same mode of life is a healthy excitement to one, keeping all his faculties of action and enjoyment in their best order, while to another it is a distracting burden, which suspends or crushes all internal life. Such are the differences among human beings in their sources of pleasure, their susceptibilities of pain, and the operation on them of different physical and moral agencies, that unless there is a corresponding diversity in their modes of life, they neither obtain their fair share of happiness, nor grow up to the mental, moral, and aesthetic stature of which their nature is capable. Why then should tolerance, as far as the public sentiment is concerned, extend only to tastes and modes of life which extort acquiescence by the multitude of their adherents? Nowhere (except in some monastic institutions) is diversity of taste entirely unrecognized; a person may, without blame, either like or dislike rowing, or smoking, or music, or athletic exercises, or chess, or cards, or study, because both those who like each of these things and those who dislike them are too numerous to be put down. But the man, and still more the woman, who can be accused either of doing "what nobody does," or of not doing "what everybody does," is the subject of as much depreciatory remark as if he or she had committed some grave moral delinquency. Persons require to possess a title, or some other badge of rank, or of the consideration of people of rank, to be able to indulge somewhat in the luxury of doing as they like without detriment to their estimation. To indulge somewhat, I repeat: for whoever allow themselves much of that indulgence incur the risk of something worse than disparaging speeches—they are in peril of a commission *de lunatico*, and of having their property taken from them and given to their relations.*

There is one characteristic of the present direction of public opinion peculiarly calculated to make it intolerant of any marked demonstration of individuality. The general average of mankind are not only moderate in intellect, but also moderate in inclinations; they have no tastes or wishes strong enough to incline them to do anything unusual, and they consequently do not understand those who have, and class all such with the wild and intemperate whom they are accustomed to look down upon. Now in addition to this fact which is general, we have only to suppose that a strong movement has set in toward the improvement of morals, and it is evident what we have to expect. In these days such a movement has set in; much has actually been effected in the way of increased regularity of conduct and discouragement of excesses; and there is a philanthropic spirit abroad for the exercise of which there is no more inviting field than the moral and prudential improvement of our fellow creatures. These tendencies of the times cause the public to be more disposed than at most former periods to prescribe general rules of conduct and endeavor to make everyone conform to the approved standard. And that standard, express or tacit, is to desire nothing strongly. Its ideal of character is to be without any marked character; to maim by compression, like a Chinese lady's foot, every part of human nature which stands out prominently and tends to make the person markedly dissimilar in outline to commonplace humanity.

As is usually the case with ideals which exclude one-half of what is desirable, the present standard of approbation produces only an inferior imitation of the other half. Instead of great energies guided by vigorous reason and strong feelings strongly

---

*There is something both contemptible and frightful in the sort of evidence on which, of late years, any person can be judicially declared unfit for the management of his affairs, and after his death, his disposal of his property can be set aside if there is enough of it to pay the expenses of litigation—which are charged on the property itself. All the minute details of his daily life are pried into, and whatever is found which, seen through the medium of the perceiving and describing faculties of the lowest of the low, bears an appearance unlike absolute commonplace, is laid before the jury as evidence of insanity, and often with success; the jurors being little, if at all, less vulgar and ignorant than the witnesses, while the judges, with that extraordinary want of knowledge of human nature and life which continually astonishes us in English lawyers, often help to mislead them. These trials speak volumes as to the state of feeling and opinion among the vulgar with regard to human liberty. So far from setting any value on individuality—so far from respecting the right of each individual to act, in things indifferent, as seems good to his own judgment and inclinations, judges and juries cannot even conceive that a person in a state of sanity can desire such freedom. In former days, when it was proposed to burn atheists, charitable people used to suggest putting them in a madhouse instead; it would be nothing surprising nowadays were we to see this done, and the doers applauding themselves because, instead of persecuting for religion, they had adopted so humane and Christian a mode of treating these unfortunates, not without a silent satisfaction at their having thereby obtained their desserts.

controlled by a conscientious will, its result is weak feelings and weak energies, which therefore can be kept in outward conformity to rule without any strength either of will or of reason. Already energetic characters on any large scale are becoming merely traditional. There is now scarcely any outlet for energy in this country except business. The energy expended in this may still be regarded as considerable. What little is left from that employment is expended on some hobby, which may be a useful, even a philanthropic, hobby, but is always some one thing, and generally a thing of small dimensions. The greatness of England is now all collective; individually small, we only appear capable of anything great by our habit of combining; and with this our moral and religious philanthropists are perfectly contented. But it was men of another stamp than this that made England what it has been; and men of another stamp will be needed to prevent its decline.

The despotism of custom is everywhere the standing hindrance to human advancement, being in unceasing antagonism to that disposition to aim at something better than customary, which is called, according to circumstances, the spirit of liberty, or that of progress or improvement. The spirit of improvement is not always a spirit of liberty, for it may aim at forcing improvements on an unwilling people; and the spirit of liberty, in so far as it resists such attempts, may ally itself locally and temporarily with the opponents of improvement; but the only unfailing and permanent source of improvement is liberty, since by it there are as many possible independent centers of improvement as there are individuals. The progressive principle, however, in either shape, whether as the love of liberty or of improvement, is antagonistic to the sway of custom, involving at least emancipation from that yoke; and the contest between the two constitutes the chief interest of the history of mankind. The greater part of the world has, properly speaking, no history, because the despotism of Custom is complete. This is the case over the whole East. Custom is there, in all things, the final appeal; justice and right mean conformity to custom; the argument of custom no one, unless some tyrant intoxicated with power, thinks of resisting. And we see the result. Those nations must once have had originality; they did not start out of the ground populous, lettered, and versed in many of the arts of life; they made themselves all this, and were then the greatest and most powerful nations of the world. What are they now? The subjects or dependents of tribes whose forefathers wandered in the forests when theirs had magnificent palaces and gorgeous temples, but over whom custom exercised only a divided rule with liberty and progress. A people, it appears, may be progressive for a certain length of time, and then stop: when does it stop? When it ceases to possess individuality. If a similar change should befall the nations of Europe, it will not be in exactly the same shape: the despotism of custom with which these nations are threatened is not precisely stationariness. It proscribes singularity, but it does not preclude change, provided all change together. We have discarded the fixed costumes of our forefathers; everyone must still dress like other people, but the fashion may change once or twice a year. We thus take care that when there is a change, it shall be for change's sake, and not from any idea of beauty or convenience; for the same idea of beauty or convenience would not strike all the world at the same moment, and be simultaneously thrown aside by all at another moment. But we are progressive as well as changeable: we continually make new inventions in mechanical things, and keep them until they are again superseded by better; we are eager for improvement in politics, in education, even in morals, though in this last our idea of improvement chiefly consists in persuading or forcing other people to be as good as ourselves. It is not progress that we object to; on the contrary, we flatter ourselves that we are the most progressive people who ever lived. It is individuality that we war against: we should think we had done wonders if we had made ourselves all alike, forgetting that the unlikeness of one person to another is generally the first thing which draws the attention of either to the imperfection of his own type and the superiority of another, or the possibility, by combining the advantages of both, of producing something better than either. We have a warning example in China—a nation of much talent and, in some respects, even wisdom, owing to the rare good fortune of having been provided at an early period with a particularly good set of customs, the work, in some measure, of men to whom even the most enlightened European must accord, under certain limitations, the title of sages and philosophers. They are remarkable, too, in the excellence of their apparatus for impressing, as far as possible, the best wisdom they possess upon every mind in the community, and securing that those who have appropriated most of it shall occupy the posts of honor and power. Surely the people who did this have discovered the secret of human progressiveness and must have kept themselves steadily at the head of the movement of the world. On the contrary, they have become stationary—have remained so for thousands of years; and if they are ever to be further improved, it must be by foreigners. They have succeeded beyond all hope in what English philanthropists are so industriously working at—in making a people all alike, all governing their thoughts and conduct by the same maxims and rules; and these are the fruits. The modern regime of public opinion is, in an unorganized form, what the Chinese educational and political systems are in an organized; and unless individuality shall be able successfully to assert itself against this yoke, Europe, notwithstanding its noble antecedents and its professed Christianity, will tend to become another China.

What is it that has hitherto preserved Europe from this lot? What has made the European family of nations an improving, instead of a stationary, portion of mankind? Not any superior excellence in them, which, when it exists, exists as the effect, not as the cause, but their remarkable diversity of character and culture. Individuals, classes, nations have been extremely unlike one another: they have struck out a great variety of paths, each leading to something valuable; and although at every period those who traveled in different paths have been intolerant of one another, and each would have thought it an excellent thing if all the rest could have been compelled to travel his road, their attempts to thwart each other's development have rarely had any permanent success, and each has in time endured to receive the good which the others have offered. Europe is, in my judgment, wholly indebted to this plurality of paths for its progressive and many-sided development. But it already begins to possess this benefit in a considerably less degree. It is decidedly advancing toward the Chinese ideal of making all people alike. M. de Tocqueville, in his last important work,* remarks how much more the Frenchmen of the present day resemble one another than did those even of the last generation. The same remark might be made of Englishmen in a far greater degree. In a passage already quoted from Wilhelm von Humboldt, he points out two things as necessary conditions of human development—because necessary to render people unlike one another—namely, freedom and variety of situations. The second of these two conditions is in this country every day diminishing. The circumstances which surround different classes and individuals, and shape their characters, are daily becoming more assimilated. Formerly, different ranks, different neighborhoods, different trades and professions lived in what might be called different worlds; at present, to a great degree in the same. Comparatively speaking, they now read the same things, listen to the same

*[Alexis de Tocqueville (1805–1859), *The Old Régime and the French Revolution*. De Tocqueville was a Frenchman who wrote *Democracy in America,* an insightful analysis of American culture.]

things, see the same things, go to the same places, have their hopes and fears directed to the same objects, have the same rights and liberties, and the same means of asserting them. Great as are the differences of position which remain, they are nothing to those which have ceased. And the assimilation is still proceeding. All the political changes of the age promote it, since they all tend to raise the low and to lower the high. Every extension of education promotes it, because education brings people under common influences and gives them access to the general stock of facts and sentiments. Improvement in the means of communication promotes it, by bringing the inhabitants of distant places into personal contact, and keeping up a rapid flow of changes of residence between one place and another. The increase of commerce and manufactures promotes it, by diffusing more widely the advantages of easy circumstances and opening all objects of ambition, even the highest, to general competition, whereby the desire of rising becomes no longer the character of a particular class, but of all classes. A more powerful agency than even all these, in bringing about a general similarity among mankind, is the complete establishment, in this and other free countries, of the ascendancy of public opinion in the State. As the various social eminences which enabled persons entrenched on them to disregard the opinion of the multitude gradually become leveled; as the very idea of resisting the will of the public, when it is positively known that they have a will, disappears more and more from the minds of practical politicians, there ceases to be any social support for nonconformity—any substantive power in society which, itself opposed to the ascendancy of numbers, is interested in taking under its protection opinions and tendencies at variance with those of the public.

The combination of all these causes forms so great a mass of influences hostile to individuality that it is not easy to see how it can stand its ground. It will do so with increasing difficulty unless the intelligent part of the public can be made to feel its value—to see that it is good there should be differences, even though not for the better, even though, as it may appear to them, some should be for the worse. If the claims of individuality are ever to be asserted, the time is now while much is still wanting to complete the enforced assimilation. It is only in the earlier stages that any stand can be successfully made against the encroachment. The demand that all other people shall resemble ourselves grows by what it feeds on. If resistance waits till life is reduced nearly to one uniform type, all deviations from that type will come to be considered impious, immoral, even monstrous and contrary to nature. Mankind speedily become unable to conceive diversity when they have been for some time unaccustomed to see it.

CHAPTER 4: OF THE LIMITS TO THE AUTHORITY OF SOCIETY OVER THE INDIVIDUAL

What, then, is the rightful limit to the sovereignty of the individual over himself? Where does the authority of society begin? How much of human life should be assigned to individuality, and how much to society?

Each will receive its proper share if each has that which more particularly concerns it. To individuality should belong the part of life in which it is chiefly the individual that is interested; to society, the part which chiefly interests society.

Though society is not founded on a contract, and though no good purpose is answered by inventing a contract in order to deduce social obligations from it, everyone who receives the protection of society owes a return for the benefit, and the fact of living in society renders it indispensable that each should be bound to observe a certain line of conduct toward the rest. This conduct consists, first, in not injuring the interests of one another, or rather certain interests which, either by express legal provision or by tacit understanding, ought to be considered as rights; and secondly, in each person's bearing his share (to be fixed on some equitable principle) of the labors and sacrifices incurred for defending the society or its members from injury and molestation. These conditions society is justified in enforcing at all costs to those who endeavor to withhold fulfillment. Nor is this all that society may do. The acts of an individual may be hurtful to others or wanting in due consideration for their welfare, without going to the length of violating any of their constituted rights. The offender may then be justly punished by opinion, though not by law. As soon as any part of a person's conduct affects prejudicially the interests of others, society has jurisdiction over it, and the question whether the general welfare will or will not be promoted by interfering with it becomes open to discussion. But there is no room for entertaining any such question when a person's conduct affects the interests of no persons besides himself, or needs not affect them unless they like (all the persons concerned being of full age and the ordinary amount of understanding). In all such cases, there should be perfect freedom, legal and social, to do the action and stand the consequences.

It would be a great misunderstanding of this doctrine to suppose that it is one of selfish indifference which pretends that human beings have no business with each other's conduct in life, and that they should not concern themselves about the well-doing or well-being of one another, unless their own interest is involved. Instead of any diminution, there is need of a great increase of disinterested exertion to promote the good of others. But disinterested benevolence can find other instruments to persuade people to their good than whips and scourges, either of the literal or the metaphorical sort. I am the last person to undervalue the self-regarding virtues; they are only second in importance, if even second, to the social. It is equally the business of education to cultivate both. But even education works by conviction and persuasion as well as by compulsion, and it is by the former only that, when the period of education is passed, the self-regarding virtues should be inculcated. Human beings owe to each other help to distinguish the better from the worse, and encouragement to choose the former and avoid the latter. They should be forever stimulating each other to increased exercise of their higher faculties and increased direction of their feelings and aims toward wise instead of foolish, elevating instead of degrading, objects and contemplations. But neither one person, nor any number of persons, is warranted in saying to another human creature of ripe years that he shall not do with his life for his own benefit what he chooses to do with it. He is the person most interested in his own well-being: the interest which any other person, except in cases of strong personal attachment, can have in it is trifling compared with that which he himself has; the interest which society has in him individually (except as to his conduct to others) is fractional and altogether indirect, while with respect to his own feelings and circumstances the most ordinary man or woman has means of knowledge immeasurably surpassing those that can be possessed by anyone else. The interference of society to overrule his judgment and purposes in what only regards himself must be grounded on general presumptions which may be altogether wrong and, even if right, are as likely as not to be misapplied to individual cases, by persons no better acquainted with the circumstances of such cases than those are who look at them merely from without. In this department, therefore, of human affairs, individuality has its proper field of action. In the conduct of human beings toward one another it is necessary that general rules should for the most part be observed in order that people may know what they have to expect; but in each person's own concerns his individual spontaneity is entitled to free exercise. Considerations to aid his judgment, exhortations to strengthen his will may be offered to him, even obtruded on him, by others; but he himself is the final judge. All errors which he is likely to commit against advice and warning are far outweighed by the evil of allowing others to constrain him to what they deem his good.

I do not mean that the feelings with which a person is regarded by others ought not to be in any way affected by his self-regarding qualities or deficiencies. This is neither possible nor desirable. If he is eminent in any of the qualities which conduce to his own good, he is, so far, a proper object of admiration. He is so much the nearer to the ideal perfection of human nature. If he is grossly deficient in those qualities, a sentiment the opposite of admiration will follow. There is a degree of folly, and a degree of what may be called (though the phrase is not unobjectionable) lowness or depravation of taste, which, though it cannot justify doing harm to the person who manifests it, renders him necessarily and properly a subject of distaste, or, in extreme cases, even of contempt: a person could not have the opposite qualities in due strength without entertaining these feelings. Though doing no wrong to anyone, a person may so act as to compel us to judge him, and feel to him, as a fool or as a being of an inferior order; and since this judgment and feeling are a fact which he would prefer to avoid, it is doing him a service to warn him of it beforehand, as of any other disagreeable consequence to which he exposes himself. It would be well, indeed, if this good office were much more freely rendered than the common notions of politeness at present permit, and if one person could honestly point out to another that he thinks him in fault, without being considered unmannerly or presuming. We have a right, also, in various ways, to act upon our unfavorable opinion of anyone, not to the oppression of his individuality, but in the exercise of ours. We are not bound, for example, to seek his society; we have a right to avoid it (though not to parade the avoidance), for we have a right to choose the society most acceptable to us. We have a right, and it may be our duty, to caution others against him if we think his example or conversation likely to have a pernicious effect on those with whom he associates. We may give others a preference over him in optional good offices, except those which tend to his improvement. In these various modes a person may suffer very severe penalties at the hands of others for faults which directly concern only himself; but he suffers these penalties only in so far as they are the natural and, as it were, the spontaneous consequences of the faults themselves, not because they are purposely inflicted on him for the sake of punishment. A person who shows rashness, obstinacy, self-conceit—who cannot live within moderate means; who cannot restrain himself from hurtful indulgence; who pursues animal pleasures at the expense of those of feeling and intellect—must expect to be lowered in the opinion of others, and to have a less share of their favorable sentiments; but of this he has no right to complain unless he has merited their favor by special excellence in his social relations and has thus established a title to their good offices, which is not affected by his demerits toward himself.

What I contend for is that the inconveniences which are strictly inseparable from the unfavorable judgment of others are the only ones to which a person should ever be subjected for that portion of his conduct and character which concerns his own good, but which does not affect the interest of others in their relations with him. Acts injurious to others require a totally different treatment. Encroachment on their rights; infliction on them of any loss or damage not justified by his own rights; falsehood or duplicity in dealing with them; unfair or ungenerous use of advantages over them; even selfish abstinence from defending them against injury—these are fit objects of moral reprobation and, in grave cases, of moral retribution and punishment. And not only these acts, but the dispositions which lead to them, are properly immoral and fit subjects of disapprobation which may rise to abhorrence. Cruelty of disposition; malice and ill-nature: that most antisocial and odious of all passions, envy; dissimulation and insincerity, irascibility on insufficient cause, and resentment disproportioned to the provocation; the love of domineering over others; the desire to engross more than one's share of advantages (the *pleonexia* [greed] of the Greeks); the pride which derives gratification from the abasement of others; the egotism which thinks self and its concerns more important than everything else, and decides all doubtful questions in its own favor—these are moral vices and constitute a bad and odious moral character; unlike the self-regarding faults previously mentioned, which are not properly immoralities and, to whatever pitch they may be carried, do not constitute wickedness. They may be proofs of any amount of folly or want of personal dignity and self-respect, but they are only a subject of moral reprobation when they involve a breach of duty to others, for whose sake the individual is bound to have care for himself. What are called duties to ourselves are not socially obligatory unless circumstances render them at the same time duties to others. The term duty to oneself, when it means anything more than prudence, means self-respect or self-development, and for none of these is anyone accountable to his fellow creatures, because for none of them is it for the good of mankind that he be held accountable to them.

The distinction between the loss of consideration which a person may rightly incur by defect of prudence or of personal dignity, and the reprobation which is due to him for an offense against the rights of others, is not a merely nominal distinction. It makes a vast difference both in our feelings and in our conduct toward him whether he displeases us in things in which we think we have a right to control him or in things in which we know that we have not. If he displeases us, we may express our distaste, and we may stand aloof from a person as well as from a thing that displeases us; but we shall not therefore feel called on to make his life uncomfortable. We shall reflect that he already bears, or will bear, the whole penalty of his error; if he spoils his life by mismanagement, we shall not, for that reason, desire to spoil it still further; instead of wishing to punish him, we shall rather endeavor to alleviate his punishment by showing him how he may avoid or cure the evils his conduct tends to bring upon him. He may be to us an object of pity, perhaps of dislike, but not of anger or resentment; we shall not treat him like an enemy of society; the worst we shall think ourselves justified in doing is leaving him to himself, if we do not interfere benevolently by showing interest or concern for him. It is far otherwise if he has infringed the rules necessary for the protection of his fellow creatures, individually or collectively. The evil consequences of his acts do not then fall on himself, but on others; and society, as the protector of all its members, must retaliate on him, must inflict pain on him for the express purpose of punishment, and must take care that it be sufficiently severe. In the one case, he is an offender at our bar, and we are called on not only to sit in judgment on him, but, in one shape or another, to execute our own sentence; in the other case, it is not our part to inflict any suffering on him, except what may incidentally follow from our using the same liberty in the regulation of our own affairs which we allow to him in his.

The distinction here pointed out between the part of a person's life which concerns only himself and that which concerns others, many persons will refuse to admit. How (it may be asked) can any part of the conduct of a member of society be a matter of indifference to the other members? No person is an entirely isolated being; it is impossible for a person to do anything seriously or permanently hurtful to himself without mischief reaching at least to his near connections, and often far beyond them. If he injures his property, he does harm to those who directly or indirectly derived support from it, and usually diminishes, by a greater or less amount, the general resources of the community. If he deteriorates his bodily or mental faculties, he not only brings evil upon all who depended on him for any portion of their happiness, but disqualifies himself for rendering the services which he owes to his fellow creatures generally, perhaps becomes a burden on their affection or benevolence; and if such conduct were very frequent hardly any offense that is committed would detract more from the general sum of good. Finally, if by his vices or follies a person does no direct harm to others, he is nevertheless (it may be said) injurious by his example, and ought to be compelled to control himself for the sake of those whom the sight or knowledge of his conduct might corrupt or mislead.

And even (it will be added) if the consequences of misconduct could be confined to the vicious or thoughtless individual, ought society to abandon to their own guidance those who are manifestly unfit for it? If protection against themselves is confessedly due to children and persons under age, is not society equally bound to afford it to persons of mature years who are equally incapable of self-government? If gambling, or drunkenness, or incontinence, or idleness, or uncleanliness are as injurious to happiness, and as great a hindrance to improvement, as many or most of the acts prohibited by law, why (it may be asked) should not law, so far as is consistent with practicability and social convenience, endeavor to repress these also? And as a supplement to the unavoidable imperfections of law, ought not opinion at least to organize a powerful police against these vices and visit rigidly with social penalties those who are known to practice them? There is no question here (it may be said) about restricting individuality, or impeding the trial of new and original experiments in living. The only things it is sought to prevent are things which have been tried and condemned from the beginning of the world until now—things which experience has shown not to be useful or suitable to any person's individuality. There must be some length of time and amount of experience after which a moral or prudential truth may be regarded as established; and it is merely desired to prevent generation after generation from falling over the same precipice which has been fatal to their predecessors.

I fully admit that the mischief which a person does to himself may seriously affect, both through their sympathies and their interests, those nearly connected with him and, in a minor degree, society at large. When, by conduct of this sort, a person is led to violate a distinct and assignable obligation to any other person or persons, the case is taken out of the self-regarding class and becomes amenable to moral disapprobation in the proper sense of the term. If, for example, a man, through intemperance or extravagance, becomes unable to pay his debts, or, having undertaken the moral responsibility of a family, becomes from the same cause incapable of supporting or educating them, he is deservedly reprobated and might be justly punished; but it is for the breach of duty to his family or creditors, not for the extravagance. If the resources which ought to have been devoted to them had been diverted from them for the most prudent investment, the moral culpability would have been the same. George Barnwell murdered his uncle to get money for his mistress, but if he had done it to set himself up in business, he would equally have been hanged. Again, in the frequent case of a man who causes grief to his family by addiction to bad habits, he deserves reproach for his unkindness or ingratitude; but so he may for cultivating habits not in themselves vicious, if they are painful to those with whom he passes his life, or who from personal ties are dependent on him for their comfort. Whoever fails in the consideration generally due to the interests and feelings of others, not being compelled by some more imperative duty, or justified by allowable self-preference, is a subject of moral disapprobation for that failure, but not for the cause of it, nor for the errors, merely personal to himself, which may have remotely led to it. In like manner, when a person disables himself, by conduct purely self-regarding, from the performance of some definite duty incumbent on him to the public, he is guilty of a social offense. No person ought to be punished simply for being drunk; but a soldier or a policeman should be punished for being drunk on duty. Whenever, in short, there is a definite damage, or a definite risk of damage, either to an individual or to the public, the case is taken out of the province of liberty and placed in that of morality or law.

But with regard to the merely contingent or, as it may be called, constructive injury which a person causes to society by conduct which neither violates any specific duty to the public, nor occasions perceptible hurt to any assignable individual except himself, the inconvenience is one which society can afford to bear, for the sake of the greater good of human freedom. If grown persons are to be punished for not taking proper care of themselves, I would rather it were for their own sake than under pretense of preventing them from impairing their capacity or rendering to society benefits which society does not pretend it has a right to exact. But I cannot consent to argue the point as if society had no means of bringing its weaker members up to its ordinary standard of rational conduct, except waiting till they do something irrational, and then punishing them, legally or morally, for it. Society has had absolute power over them during all the early portion of their existence; it has had the whole period of childhood and nonage in which to try whether it could make them capable of rational conduct in life. The existing generation is master both of the training and the entire circumstances of the generation to come; it cannot indeed make them perfectly wise and good, because it is itself so lamentably deficient in goodness and wisdom; and its best efforts are not always, in individual cases, its most successful ones; but it is perfectly well able to make the rising generation, as a whole, as good as, and a little better than, itself. If society lets any considerable number of its members grow up mere children, incapable of being acted on by rational consideration of distant motives, society has itself to blame for the consequences. Armed not only with all the powers of education, but with the ascendancy which the authority of a received opinion always exercises over the minds who are least fitted to judge for themselves, and aided by the natural penalties which cannot be prevented from falling on those who incur the distaste or the contempt of those who know them—let not society pretend that it needs, besides all this, the power to issue commands and enforce obedience in the personal concerns of individuals in which, on all principles of justice and policy, the decision ought to rest with those who are to abide the consequences. Nor is there anything which tends more to discredit and frustrate the better means of influencing conduct than a resort to the worse. If there be among those whom it is attempted to coerce into prudence or temperance any of the material of which vigorous and independent characters are made, they will infallibly rebel against the yoke. No such person will ever feel that others have a right to control him in his concerns, such as they have to prevent him from injuring them in theirs; and it easily comes to be considered a mark of spirit and courage to fly in the face of such usurped authority and do with ostentation the exact opposite of what it enjoins, as in the fashion of grossness which succeeded, in the time of Charles II, to the fanatical moral intolerance of the Puritans. With respect to what is said of the necessity of protecting society from the bad example set to others by the vicious or the self-indulgent, it is true that bad example may have a pernicious effect, especially the example of doing wrong to others with impunity to the wrongdoer. But we are now speaking of conduct which, while it does no wrong to others, is supposed to do great harm to the agent himself; and I do not see how those who believe this can think otherwise than that the example, on the whole, must be more salutary than hurtful, since, if it displays the misconduct, it displays also the painful or degrading consequences which, if the conduct is justly censured, must be supposed to be in all or most cases attendant on it.

But the strongest of all the arguments against the interference of the public with purely personal conduct is that, when it does interfere, the odds are that it interferes wrongly and in the wrong place. On questions of social morality, of duty to others, the opinion of the public, that is, of an overruling majority, though often wrong, is likely to be still oftener right, because on such questions they are only required to judge of their own interests, of the manner in which some mode of conduct, if allowed to be practiced, would affect themselves. But the opinion of a similar majority, imposed as a law on the minority, on questions of self-regarding conduct is quite as likely to be wrong as right, for in these cases public opinion means, at the best, some people's opinion of what is good or bad for other people, while very often it does not even mean that—the public, with the most perfect indifference, passing over the pleasure or convenience of those whose conduct they censure and considering only their own preference. There are many who consider as an injury to themselves any conduct which they have a distaste for, and resent it as an outrage to their feelings; as a religious bigot, when charged with disregarding the religious feelings of others, has been known to retort that they disregard his feelings by persisting in their abominable worship or creed. But there is no parity between the feeling of a person for his own opinion and the feeling of another who is offended at his holding it, no more than between the desire of a thief to take a purse and the desire of the right owner to keep it. And a person's taste is as much his own peculiar concern as his opinion or his purse. It is easy for anyone to imagine an ideal public which leaves the freedom and choice of individuals in all uncertain matters undisturbed and only requires them to abstain from modes of conduct which universal experience has condemned. But where has there been seen a public which set any such limit to its censorship? Or when does the public trouble itself about universal experience? In its interferences with personal conduct it is seldom thinking of anything but the enormity of acting or feeling differently from itself: and this standard of judgment, thinly disguised, is held up to mankind as the dictate of religion and philosophy by nine-tenths of all moralists and speculative writers. These teach that things are right because they are right; because we feel them to be so. They tell us to search in our own minds and hearts for laws of conduct binding on ourselves and on all others. What can the poor public do but apply these instructions and make their own personal feelings of good and evil, if they are tolerably unanimous in them, obligatory on all the world?

The evil here pointed out is not one which exists only in theory: and it may perhaps be expected that I should specify the instances in which the public of this age and country improperly invests its own preferences with the character of moral laws. I am not writing an essay on the aberrations of existing moral feeling. That is too weighty a subject to be discussed parenthetically, and by way of illustration. Yet examples are necessary to show that the principle I maintain is of serious and practical moment, and that I am not endeavoring to erect a barrier against imaginary evils. And it is not difficult to show, by abundant instances, that to extend the bounds of what may be called moral police until it encroaches on the most unquestionably legitimate liberty of the individual is one of the most universal of all human propensities.

As a first instance, consider the antipathies which men cherish on no better grounds than that persons whose religious opinions are different from theirs do not practice their religious observances, especially their religious abstinences. To cite a rather trivial example, nothing in the creed or practice of Christians does more to en-venom the hatred of Mohammedans against them than the fact of their eating pork. There are few acts which Christians and Europeans regard with more unaffected dis-gust than Mussulmans regard this particular mode of satisfying hunger. It is in the first place, an offense against their religion; but this circumstance by no means explains ei-ther the degree or the kind of their repugnance; for wine also is forbidden by their reli-gion, and to partake of it is by all Mussulmans accounted wrong, but not disgusting. Their aversion to the flesh of the "unclean beast" is, on the contrary, of that peculiar character, resembling an instinctive antipathy, which the idea of uncleanness, when once it thoroughly sinks into the feelings, seems always to excite even in those whose personal habits are anything but scrupulously cleanly, and of which the sentiment of religious impurity, so intense in the Hindus, is a remarkable example. Suppose now that in a people of whom the majority were Mussulmans, that majority should insist upon not permitting pork to be eaten within the limits of the country. This would be nothing new in Mohammedan countries.* Would it be a legitimate exercise of the moral authority of public opinion, and if not, why not? The practice is really revolting to such a public. They also sincerely think that it is forbidden and abhorred by the Deity. Neither could the prohibition be censured as religious persecution. It might be religious in its origin, but it would not be persecution for religion, since nobody's reli-gion makes it a duty to eat pork. The only tenable ground of condemnation would be that with the personal tastes and self-regarding concerns of individuals the public has no business to interfere.

To come somewhat nearer home: the majority of Spaniards consider it a gross impiety, offensive in the highest degree to the Supreme Being, to worship him in any other manner than the Roman Catholic; and no other public worship is lawful on Span-ish soil. The people of all southern Europe look upon a married clergy as not only irre-ligious, but unchaste, indecent, gross, disgusting. What do Protestants think of these perfectly sincere feelings, and of the attempt to enforce them against non-Catholics? Yet, if mankind are justified in interfering with each other's liberty in things which do not concern the interests of others, on what principle is it possible consistently to ex-clude these cases? Or who can blame people for desiring to suppress what they regard as a scandal in the sight of God and man? No stronger case can be shown for prohibit-ing anything which is regarded as a personal immorality than is made out for suppress-ing these practices in the eyes of those who regard them as impieties; and unless we are willing to adopt the logic of persecutors, and to say that we may persecute others be-cause we are right, and that they must not persecute us because they are wrong, we must beware of admitting a principle of which we should resent as a gross injustice the application to ourselves.

The preceding instances may be objected to, although unreasonably, as drawn from contingencies impossible among us—opinion, in this country, not being likely to enforce abstinence from meats or to interfere with people for worshiping and for either

---

*The case of the Bombay Parsees is a curious instance in point. When this industrious and enterpris-ing tribe, the descendants of the Persian fire-worshipers, flying from their native country before the Caliphs, arrived in western India, they were admitted to toleration by the Hindu sovereigns, on condition of not eating beef. When those regions afterward fell under the dominion of Mohammedan conquerors, the Parsees ob-tained from them a continuance of indulgence, on condition of refraining from pork. What was at first obedi-ence to authority became a second nature, and the Parsees to this day abstain both from beef and pork. Though not required by their religion, the double abstinence has had time to grow into a custom of their tribe; and custom, in the East, is a religion.

marrying or not marrying, according to their creed or inclination. The next example, however, shall be taken from an interference with liberty which we have by no means passed all danger of. Wherever the Puritans have been sufficiently powerful, as in New England, and in Great Britain at the time of the Commonwealth, they have endeavored, with considerable success, to put down all public, and nearly all private, amusements: especially music, dancing, public games, or other assemblages for purposes of diversion, and the theater. There are still in this country large bodies of persons by whose notions of morality and religion these recreations are condemned; and those persons belonging chiefly to the middle class, who are the ascendant power in the present social and political condition of the kingdom, it is by no means impossible that persons of these sentiments may at some time or other command a majority in Parliament. How will the remaining portion of the community like to have the amusements that shall be permitted to them regulated by the religious and moral sentiments of the stricter Calvinists and Methodists? Would they not, with considerable peremptoriness, desire these intrusively pious members of society to mind their own business? This is precisely what should be said to every government and every public who have the pretension that no person shall enjoy any pleasure which they think wrong. But if the principle of the pretension be admitted, no one can reasonably object to its being acted on in the sense of the majority, or other preponderating power in the country; and all persons must be ready to conform to the idea of a Christian commonwealth as understood by the early settlers in New England, if a religious profession similar to theirs should ever succeed in regaining its lost ground, as religions supposed to be declining have so often been known to do.

To imagine another contingency, perhaps more likely to be realized than the one last mentioned. There is confessedly a strong tendency in the modern world toward a democratic constitution of society, accompanied or not by popular political institutions. It is affirmed that in the country where this tendency is most completely realized—where both society and the government are most democratic: the United States—the feeling of the majority, to whom any appearance of a more showy or costly style of living than they can hope to rival is disagreeable, operates as a tolerably effectual sumptuary law, and that in many parts of the Union it is really difficult for a person possessing a very large income to find any mode of spending it which will not incur popular disapprobation. Though such statements as these are doubtless much exaggerated as a representation of existing facts, the state of things they describe is not only a conceivable and possible, but a probable result of democratic feeling combined with the notion that the public has a right to a veto on the manner in which individuals shall spend their incomes. We have only further to suppose a considerable diffusion of Socialist opinions, and it may become infamous in the eyes of the majority to possess more property than some very small amount, or any income not earned by manual labor. Opinions similar in principle to these already prevail widely among the artisan class and weigh oppressively on those who are amenable to the opinion chiefly of that class, namely, its own members. It is known that the bad workmen who form the majority of the operatives in many branches of industry are decidedly of opinion that bad workmen ought to receive the same wages as good, and that no one ought to be allowed, through piecework or otherwise, to earn by superior skill or industry more than others can without it. And they employ a moral police, which occasionally becomes a physical one, to deter skillful workmen from receiving, and employers from giving, a larger remuneration for a more useful service. If the public have any jurisdiction over private concerns, I cannot see that these people are in fault, or that any individual's particular public can be blamed for asserting the same authority over his individual conduct which the general public asserts over people in general.

But, without dwelling upon supposititious cases, there are, in our own day, gross usurpations upon the liberty of private life actually practiced, and still greater ones threatened with some expectation of success, and opinions propounded which assert an unlimited right in the public not only to prohibit by law everything which it thinks wrong, but, in order to get at what it thinks wrong, to prohibit a number of things which it admits to be innocent.

Under the name of preventing intemperance, the people of one English colony, and of nearly half the United States, have been interdicted by law from making any use whatever of fermented drinks, except for medical purposes, for prohibition of their sale is in fact, as it is intended to be, prohibition of their use. And though the impracticability of executing the law has caused its repeal in several of the States which had adopted it, including the one from which it derives its name, an attempt has notwithstanding been commenced, and is prosecuted with considerable zeal by many of the professed philanthropists, to agitate for a similar law in this country. The association, or "Alliance," as it terms itself, which has been formed for this purpose, has acquired some notoriety through the publicity given to a correspondence between its secretary and one of the very few English public men who hold that a politician's opinions ought to be founded on principles. Lord Stanley's share in this correspondence is calculated to strengthen the hopes already built on him by those who know how rare such qualities as are manifested in some of his public appearances unhappily are among those who figure in political life. The organ of the Alliance, who would "deeply deplore the recognition of any principle which could be wrested to justify bigotry and persecution," undertakes to point out the "broad and impassable barrier" which divides such principles from those of the association. "All matters relating to thought, opinion, conscience, appear to me," he says, "to be without the sphere of legislation; all pertaining to social act, habit, relation, subject only to a discretionary power vested in the State itself, and not in the individual, to be within it." No mention is made of a third class, different from either of these, viz., acts and habits which are not social, but individual; although it is to this class, surely, that the act of drinking fermented liquors belongs. Selling fermented liquors, however, is trading, and trading is a social act. But the infringement complained of is not on the liberty of the seller, but on that of the buyer and consumer; since the State might just as well forbid him to drink wine as purposely make it impossible for him to obtain it. The secretary, however, says, "I claim, as a citizen, a right to legislate whenever my social rights are invaded by the social act of another." And now for the definition of these "social rights": "If anything invades my social rights, certainly the tragic in strong drink does. It destroys my primary right of security by constantly creating and stimulating social disorder. It invades my right of equality by deriving a profit from the creation of a misery I am taxed to support. It impedes my right to free moral and intellectual development by surrounding my path with dangers and by weakening and demoralizing society, from which I have a right to claim mutual aid and intercourse." A theory of "social rights" the like of which probably never before found its way into distinct language: being nothing short of this—that it is the absolute social right of every individual that every other individual shall act in every respect exactly as he ought; that whosoever fails thereof in the smallest particular violates my social right and entitles me to demand from the legislature the removal of the grievance. So monstrous a principle is far more dangerous than any single interference with liberty; there is no violation of liberty which it would not justify; it acknowledges no right to any freedom whatever, except perhaps to that of holding opinions in secret, without ever disclosing them; for the moment an opinion which I consider noxious passes anyone's lips, it invades all the "social rights" attributed to me by the Alliance. The doctrine ascribes to all mankind a vested interest in each other's moral, intellectual, and even physical perfection, to be defined by each claimant according to his own standard.

Another important example of illegitimate interference with the rightful liberty of the individual, not simply threatened, but long since carried into triumphant effect, is Sabbatarian legislation. Without doubt, abstinence on one day in the week, so far as the exigencies of life permit, from the usual daily occupation, though in no respect religiously binding on any except Jews, is a highly beneficial custom. And inasmuch as this custom cannot be observed without a general consent to that effect among the industrious classes, therefore, in so far as some persons by working may impose the same necessity on others, it may be allowable and right that the law should guarantee to each the observance by others of the custom, by suspending the greater operations of industry on a particular day. But this justification, grounded on the direct interest which others have in each individual's observance of the practice, does not apply to the self-chosen occupations in which a person may think fit to employ his leisure, nor does it hold good, in the smallest degree, for legal restrictions on amusements. It is true that the amusement of some is the day's work of others; but the pleasure, not to say the useful recreation, of many is worth the labor of a few, provided the occupation is freely chosen and can be freely resigned. The operatives are perfectly right in thinking that if all worked on Sunday, seven days' work would have to be given for six days' wages; but so long as the great mass of employments are suspended, the small number who for the enjoyment of others must still work obtain a proportional increase of earnings; and they are not obliged to follow those occupations if they prefer leisure to emolument. If a further remedy is sought, it might be found in the establishment by custom of a holiday on some other day of the week for those particular classes of persons. The only ground, therefore, on which restrictions on Sunday amusements can be defended must be that they are religiously wrong—a motive of legislation which can never be too earnestly protested against. "*Deorum injuriae Diis curae*" ["Injustices to the gods are the gods' concern"]. It remains to be proved that society or any of its officers holds a commission from on high to avenge any supposed offense to Omnipotence which is not also a wrong to our fellow creatures. The notion that it is one man's duty that another should be religious was the foundation of all the religious persecutions ever perpetrated, and, if admitted, would fully justify them. Though the feeling which breaks out in the repeated attempts to stop railway traveling on Sunday, in the resistance to the opening of museums, and the like, has not the cruelty of the old persecutors, the state of mind indicated by it is fundamentally the same. It is a determination not to tolerate others in doing what is permitted by their religion, because it is not permitted by the persecutor's religion. It is a belief that God not only abominates the act of the misbeliever, but will not hold us guiltless if we leave him unmolested.

I cannot refrain from adding to these examples of the little account commonly made of human liberty the language of downright persecution which breaks out from the press of this country whenever it feels called on to notice the remarkable phenomenon of Mormonism. Much might be said on the unexpected and instructive fact that an alleged new revelation and a religion rounded on it—the product of palpable imposture, not even supported by the *prestige* of extraordinary qualities in its founder—is believed by hundreds of thousands, and has been made the foundation of a society in the age of newspapers, railways, and the electric telegraph. What here concerns us is that this religion, like other and better religions, has its martyrs: that its prophet and founder was, for his teaching, put to death by a mob; that others of its adherents lost their lives by the same lawless violence; that they were forcibly expelled, in a body, from the country in which they first grew up, while, now that they have been chased into a solitary recess in the midst of a desert, many in this country openly declare that it would be right (only that it is not convenient) to send an expedition against them and compel them by force to conform to the opinions of other people. The article of the Mormonite doctrine which is the chief provocative to the antipathy which thus breaks through the ordinary restraints of religious tolerance is its sanction of polygamy; which, though permitted to Mohammedans, and Hindus, and Chinese, seems to excite unquenchable animosity when practiced by persons who speak English and profess to be a kind of Christians. No one has a deeper disapprobation than I have of this Mormon institution; both for other reasons and because, far from being in any way countenanced by the principle of liberty, it is a direct infraction of that principle, being a mere riveting of the chains of one half of the community, and an emancipation of the other from reciprocity of obligation toward them. Still, it must be remembered that this relation is as much voluntary on the part of the women concerned in it, and who may be deemed the sufferers by it, as is the case with any other form of the marriage institution; and however surprising this fact may appear, it has its explanation in the common ideas and customs of the world, which, teaching women to think marriage the one thing needful, make it intelligible that many a woman should prefer being one of several wives to not being a wife at all. Other countries are not asked to recognize such unions, or release any portion of their inhabitants from their own laws on the score of Mormonite opinions. But when the dissentients have conceded to the hostile sentiments of others far more than could justly be demanded; when they have left the countries to which their doctrines were unacceptable and established themselves in a remote corner of the earth, which they have been the first to render habitable to human beings, it is difficult to see on what principles but those of tyranny they can be prevented from living there under what laws they please, provided they commit no aggression on other nations and allow perfect freedom of departure to those who are dissatisfied with their ways. A recent writer, in some respects of considerable merit, proposes (to use his own words) not a crusade, but a civilizade, against this polygamous community, to put an end to what seems to him a retrograde step in civilization. It also appears so to me, but I am not aware that any community has a right to force another to be civilized. So long as the sufferers by the bad law do not invoke assistance from other communities, I cannot admit that persons entirely unconnected with them ought to step in and require that a condition of things with which all who are directly interested appear to be satisfied should be put an end to because it is a scandal to persons some thousands of miles distant who have no part or concern in it. Let them send missionaries, if they please, to preach against it; and let them, by any fair means (of which silencing the teachers is not one), oppose the progress of similar doctrines among their own people. If civilization has got the better of barbarism when barbarism had the world to itself, it is too much to profess to be afraid lest barbarism, after having been fairly got under, should revive and conquer civilization. A civilization that can thus succumb to its vanquished enemy must first have become so degenerate that neither its appointed priests and teachers, nor anybody else, has the capacity, or will take the trouble, to stand up for it. If this be so, the sooner such a civilization receives notice to quit, the better. It can only go on from bad to worse until destroyed and regenerated (like the Western Empire) by energetic barbarians.

CHAPTER 5: APPLICATIONS

The principles asserted in these pages must be more generally admitted as the basis for discussion of details before a consistent application of them to all the various departments of government and morals can be attempted with any prospect of advantage. The few observations I propose to make on questions of detail are designed to illustrate the principles rather than to follow them out to their consequences. I offer not so much applications as specimens of application, which may serve to bring into greater clearness the meaning and limits of the two maxims which together form the entire doctrine of this essay, and to assist the judgment in holding the balance between them in the cases where it appears doubtful which of them is applicable to the case.

The maxims are, first, that the individual is not accountable to society for his actions in so far as these concern the interests of no person but himself. Advice, instruction, persuasion, and avoidance by other people, if thought necessary by them for their own good, are the only measures by which society can justifiably express its dislike or disapprobation of his conduct. Secondly, that for such actions as are prejudicial to the interests of others, the individual is accountable and may be subjected either to social or to legal punishment if society is of opinion that the one or the other is requisite for its protection.

In the first place, it must by no means be supposed, because damage, or probability of damage, to the interests of others can alone justify the interference of society, that therefore it always does justify such interference. In many cases an individual, in pursuing a legitimate object, necessarily and therefore legitimately causes pain or loss to others, or intercepts a good which they had a reasonable hope of obtaining. Such oppositions of interest between individuals often arise from bad social institutions, but are unavoidable while those institutions last; and some would be unavoidable under any institutions. Whoever succeeds in an overcrowded profession or in a competitive examination, whoever is preferred to another in any contest for an object which both desire, reaps benefit from the loss of others, from their wasted exertion and their disappointment. But it is, by common admission, better for the general interest of mankind that persons should pursue their objects undeterred by this sort of consequences. In other words, society admits no right, either legal or moral, in the disappointed competitors to immunity from this kind of suffering, and feels called on to interfere only when means of success have been employed which it is contrary to the general interest to permit—namely, fraud or treachery, and force.

Again, trade is a social act. Whoever undertakes to sell any description of goods to the public does what affects the interest of other persons, and of society in general; and thus his conduct, in principle, comes within the jurisdiction of society; accordingly, it was once held to be the duty of governments, in all cases which were considered of importance, to fix prices and regulate the processes of manufacture. But it is now recognized, though not till after a long struggle, that both the cheapness and the good quality of commodities are most effectually provided for by leaving the producers and sellers perfectly free, under the sole check of equal freedom to the buyers for supplying themselves elsewhere. This is the so-called doctrine of "free trade," which rests on grounds different from, though equally solid with, the principle of individual liberty asserted in this essay. Restrictions on trade, or on production for purposes of trade, are indeed restraints; and all restraint, *qua* restraint, is an evil; but the restraints in question affect only that part of conduct which society is competent to restrain, and are wrong solely because they do not really produce the results which it is desired to produce by them. As the principle of individual liberty is not involved in the doctrine of free trade, so neither is it in most of the questions which arise respecting the limits of that doctrine, as, for example, what amount of public control is admissible for the prevention of fraud by adulteration; how far sanitary precautions, or arrangements to protect workpeople employed in dangerous occupations, should be enforced on employers. Such questions involve considerations of liberty only in so far as leaving people to themselves is always better, *caeteris paribus,* than controlling them; but that they may be legitimately controlled for these ends is in principle undeniable. On the other hand, there are questions relating to interference with trade which are essentially questions of liberty, such as the Maine Law, already touched upon; the prohibition of the importation of opium into China; the restriction of the sale of poisons—all cases, in short, where the object of the interference is to make it impossible or difficult to obtain a particular commodity. These interferences are objectionable, not as infringements on the liberty of the producer or seller, but on that of the buyer.

One of these examples, that of the sale of poisons, opens a new question: the proper limits of what may be called the functions of police; how far liberty may legitimately be invaded for the prevention of crime, or of accident. It is one of the undisputed functions of government to take precautions against crime before it has been committed, as well as to detect and punish it afterwards. The preventive function of government, however, is far more liable to be abused, to the prejudice of liberty, than the punitory function; for there is hardly any part of the legitimate freedom of action of a human being which would not admit of being represented, and fairly, too, as increasing the facilities for some form or other of delinquency. Nevertheless, if a public authority, or even a private person, sees anyone evidently preparing to commit a crime, they are not bound to look on inactive until the crime is committed, but may interfere to prevent it. If poisons were never bought or used for any purpose except the commission of murder, it would be right to prohibit their manufacture and sale. They may, however, be wanted not only for innocent but for useful purposes, and restrictions cannot be imposed in the one case without operating in the other. Again, it is a proper office of public authority to guard against accidents. If either a public officer or anyone else saw a person attempting to cross a bridge which had been ascertained to be unsafe, and there were no time to warn him of his danger, they might seize him and turn him back, without any real infringement of his liberty; for liberty consists in doing what one desires, and he does not desire to fall into the river. Nevertheless, when there is not a certainty, but only a danger of mischief, no one but the person himself can judge of the sufficiency of the motive which may prompt him to incur the risk; in this case, therefore (unless he is a child, or delirious, or in some state of excitement or absorption incompatible with the full use of the reflecting faculty), he ought, I conceive, to be only warned of the danger; not forcibly prevented from exposing himself to it. Similar considerations, applied to such a question as the sale of poisons, may enable us to decide which among the possible modes of regulation are or are not contrary to principle. Such a precaution, for example, as that of labeling the drug with some word expressive of its dangerous character may be enforced without violation of liberty: the buyer cannot wish not to know that the thing he possesses has poisonous qualities. But to require in all cases the certificate of a medical practitioner would make it sometimes impossible, always expensive, to obtain the article for legitimate uses. The only mode apparent to me, in which difficulties may be thrown in the way of crime committed through this means, without any infringement worth taking into account upon the liberty of those who desire the poisonous substance for other purposes, consists in providing what, in the apt language of Bentham, is called "preappointed evidence." This provision is familiar to everyone in the case of contracts. It is usual and right that the law, when a contract is entered into, should require as the condition of its enforcing performance that certain formalities should be observed, such as signatures, attestation of witnesses, and the like, in order that in case of subsequent dispute there may be evidence to prove that the contract was really entered into, and that there was nothing in the circumstances to render it legally invalid, the effect being to throw great obstacles in the way of fictitious contracts, or contracts made in circumstances which, if known, would destroy their validity. Precautions of a similar nature might be enforced in the sale of articles adapted to be instruments of crime. The seller, for example, might be required to enter in a register the exact time of the transaction, the name and address of the buyer, the precise quality and quantity sold; to ask the purpose for which it was wanted, and record the answer he received. When there was no medical prescription, the presence of some third person might be required to bring home the fact to the purchaser, in case there should afterwards be reason to believe that the article had been applied to criminal purposes. Such regulations would in general be no material impediment to obtaining the article, but a very considerable one to making an improper use of it without detection.

The right inherent in society to ward off crimes against itself by antecedent precautions suggests the obvious limitations to the maxim that purely self-regarding misconduct cannot properly be meddled with in the way of prevention or punishment. Drunkenness, for example, in ordinary cases, is not a fit subject for legislative interference, but I should deem it perfectly legitimate that a person who had once been convicted of any act of violence to others under the influence of drink should be placed under a special legal restriction, personal to himself; that if he were afterwards found drunk, he should be liable to a penalty, and that if, when in that state, he committed another offense, the punishment to which he would be liable for that other offense should be increased in severity. The making himself drunk, in a person whom drunkenness excites to do harm to others, is a crime against others. So, again, idleness, except in a person receiving support from the public, or except when it constitutes a breach of contract, cannot without tyranny be made a subject of legal punishment; but if, either from idleness or from any other avoidable cause, a man fails to perform his legal duties to others, as for instance to support his children, it is no tyranny to force him to fulfill that obligation by compulsory labor if no other means are available.

Again, there are many acts which, being directly injurious only to the agents themselves, ought not to be legally interdicted, but which, if done publicly, are a violation of good manners and, coming thus within the category of offenses against others, may rightly be prohibited. Of this kind are offenses against decency; on which it is unnecessary to dwell, the rather as they are only connected indirectly with our subject, the objection to publicity being equally strong in the case of many actions not in themselves condemnable, nor supposed to be so.

There is another question to which an answer must be found, consistent with the principles which have been laid down. In cases of personal conduct supposed to be blamable, but which respect for liberty precludes society from preventing or punishing because the evil directly resulting falls wholly on the agent; what the agent is free to do, ought other persons to be equally free to counsel or instigate? This question is not free from difficulty. The case of a person who solicits another to do an act is not strictly a case of self-regarding conduct. To give advice or offer inducements to anyone is a social act and may, therefore, like actions in general which affect others, be supposed amenable to social control. But a little reflection corrects the first impression, by showing that if the case is not strictly within the definition of individual liberty, yet the reasons on which the principle of individual liberty is grounded are applicable to it. If people must be allowed, in whatever concerns only themselves, to act as seems best to themselves, at their own peril, they must equally be free to consult with one another about what is fit to be so done; to exchange opinions, and give and receive suggestions. Whatever it is permitted to do, it must be permitted to advise to do. The question is doubtful only when the instigator derives a personal benefit from his advice, when he makes it his occupation, for subsistence or pecuniary gain, to promote what society and the State consider to be an evil. Then, indeed, a new element of complication is introduced—namely, the existence of classes of persons with an interest opposed to what is considered as the public weal, and whose mode of living is grounded on the counteraction of it. Ought this to be interfered with, or not? Fornication, for example, must be tolerated, and so must gambling; but should a person be free to be a pimp, or to keep a gambling house? The case is one of those which lie on the exact boundary line between two principles, and it is not at once apparent to which of the two it properly belongs. There are arguments on both sides. On the side of toleration it may be said that the fact of following anything as an occupation, and living or profiting by the practice of it, cannot make that criminal which would otherwise be admissible; that the act should either be consistently permitted or consistently prohibited; that if the principles which we have hitherto defended are true, society has no business, as society, to decide anything to be wrong which concerns only the individual; that it cannot go beyond dissuasion, and that one person should be as free to persuade as another to dissuade. In opposition to this it may be contended that, although the public, or the State, are not warranted in authoritatively deciding, for purposes of repression or punishment, that such or such conduct affecting only the interests of the individual is good or bad, they are fully justified in assuming, if they regard it as bad, that its being so or not is at least a disputable question: that, this being supposed, they cannot be acting wrongly in endeavoring to exclude the influence of solicitations which are not disinterested, of instigators who cannot possibly be impartial—who have a direct personal interest on one side, and that side the one which the State believes to be wrong, and who confessedly promote it for personal objects only. There can surely, it may be urged, be nothing lost, no sacrifice of good, by so ordering matters that persons shall make their election, either wisely or foolishly, on their own prompting, as free as possible from the arts of persons who stimulate their inclinations for interested purposes of their own. Thus (it may be said), though the statutes respecting unlawful games are utterly indefensible—though all persons should be free to gamble in their own or each other's houses, or in any place of meeting established by their own subscriptions and open only to the members and their visitors—yet public gambling houses should not be permitted. It is true that the prohibition is never effectual, and that, whatever amount of tyrannical power may be given to the police, gambling houses can always be maintained under other pretenses; but they may be compelled to conduct their operations with a certain degree of secrecy and mystery, so that nobody knows anything about them but those who seek them; and more than this society ought not to aim at. There is considerable force in these arguments. I will not venture to decide whether they are sufficient to justify the moral anomaly of punishing the accessory when the principal is (and must be) allowed to go free; of fining or imprisoning the procurer, but not the fornicator—the gambling-house keeper, but not the gambler. Still less ought the common operations of buying and selling to be interfered with on analogous grounds. Almost every article which is bought and sold may be used in excess, and the sellers have a pecuniary interest in encouraging that excess; but no argument can be founded on this in favor, for instance, of the Maine Law; because the class of dealers in strong drinks, though interested in their abuse, are indispensably required for the sake of their legitimate use. The interest, however, of these dealers in promoting intemperance is a real evil and justifies the State in imposing restrictions and requiring guarantees which, but for that justification, would be infringements of legitimate liberty.

A further question is whether the State, while it permits, should nevertheless indirectly discourage conduct which it deems contrary to the best interests of the agent; whether, for example, it should take measures to render the means of drunkenness more costly, or add to the difficulty of procuring them by limiting the number of the places of sale. On this, as on most other practical questions, many distinctions require to be made. To tax stimulants for the sole purpose of making them more difficult to be obtained is a measure differing only in degree from their entire prohibition, and would be justifiable only if that were justifiable. Every increase of cost is a prohibition to those whose means do not come up to the augmented price; and to those who do, it is a penalty laid on them for gratifying a particular taste. Their choice of pleasures and their mode of expending their income, after satisfying their legal and moral obligations to the State and to individuals, are their own concern and must rest with their own judgment. These considerations may seem at first sight to condemn the selection of stimulants as special subjects of taxation for purposes of revenue. But it must be remembered that taxation for fiscal purposes is absolutely inevitable; that in most countries it is necessary that a considerable part of that taxation should be indirect; that the State, therefore, cannot help imposing penalties, which to some persons may be prohibitory, on the use of some articles of consumption. It is hence the duty of the State to consider, in the imposition of taxes, what commodities the consumers can best spare; and *a fortiori,* to select in preference those of which it deems the use, beyond a very moderate quantity, to be positively injurious. Taxation, therefore, of stimulants up to the point which produces the largest amount of revenue (supposing that the State needs all the revenue which it yields) is not only admissible, but to be approved of.

The question of making the sale of these commodities a more or less exclusive privilege must be answered differently, according to the purposes to which the restriction is intended to be subservient. All places of public resort require the restraint of a police, and places of this kind peculiarly, because offenses against society are especially apt to originate there. It is, therefore, fit to confine the power of selling these commodities (at least for consumption on the spot) to persons of known or vouched-for respectability of conduct; to make such regulations respecting hours of opening and closing as may be requisite for public surveillance, and to withdraw the license if breaches of the peace repeatedly take place through the connivance or incapacity of the keeper of the house, or if it becomes a rendezvous for concocting and preparing offenses against the law. Any further restriction I do not conceive to be, in principle, justifiable. The limitation in number, for instance, of beer and spirit houses, for the express purpose of rendering them more difficult of access and diminishing the occasions of temptation, not only exposes all to an inconvenience because there are some by whom the facility would be abused, but is suited only to a state of society in which the laboring classes are avowedly treated as children or savages, and placed under an education of restraint, to fit them for future admission to the privileges of freedom. This is not the principle on which the laboring classes are professedly governed in any free country; and no person who sets due value on freedom will give his adhesion to their being so governed, unless after all efforts have been exhausted to educate them for freedom and govern them as freemen, and it has been definitively proved that they can only be governed as children. The bare statement of the alternative shows the absurdity of supposing that such efforts have been made in any case which needs be considered here. It is only because the institutions of this country are a mass of inconsistencies, that things find admittance into our practice which belong to the system of despotic, or what is called paternal, government, while the general freedom of our institutions precludes the exercise of the amount of control necessary to render the restraint of any real efficacy as a moral education.

It was pointed out in an early part of this essay that the liberty of the individual, in things wherein the individual is alone concerned, implies a corresponding liberty in any number of individuals to regulate by mutual agreement such things as regard them jointly, and regard no persons but themselves. This question presents no difficulty so long as the will of all the persons implicated remains unaltered; but since that will may change, it is often necessary, even in things in which they alone are concerned, that they should enter into engagements with one another; and when they do, it is fit, as a general rule, that those engagements should be kept. Yet, in the laws, probably, of every country, this general rule has some exceptions. Not only persons are not held to engagements which violate the rights of third parties, but it is sometimes considered a sufficient reason for releasing them from an engagement that it is injurious to themselves. In this and most other civilized countries, for example, an engagement by which a person should sell himself, or allow himself to be sold, as a slave would be null and void, neither enforced by law nor by opinion. The ground for thus limiting his power of voluntarily disposing of his own lot in life is apparent, and is very clearly seen in this extreme case. The reason for not interfering, unless for the sake of others, with a person's voluntary acts is consideration for his liberty. His voluntary choice is evidence that what he so chooses is desirable, or at least endurable, to him, and his good is on the whole best provided for by allowing him to take his own means of pursuing it. But by selling himself for a slave, he abdicates his liberty; he foregoes any future use of it beyond that single act. He therefore defeats, in his own case, the very purpose which is the justification of allowing him to dispose of himself. He is no longer free, but is thenceforth in a position which has no longer the presumption in its favor that would be afforded by his voluntarily remaining in it. The principle of freedom cannot require that he should be free not to be free. It is not freedom to be allowed to alienate his freedom. These reasons, the force of which is so conspicuous in this peculiar case, are evidently of far wider application, yet a limit is everywhere set to them by the necessities of life, which continually require, not indeed that we should resign our freedom, but that we should consent to this and the other limitation of it. The principle, however, which demands uncontrolled freedom of action in all that concerns only the agents themselves requires that those who have become bound to one another, in things which concern no third party, should be able to release one another from the engagement; and even without such voluntary release there are perhaps no contracts or engagements, except those that relate to money or money's worth, of which one can venture to say that there ought to be no liberty whatever of retractation. Baron Wilhelm von Humboldt, in the excellent essay from which I have already quoted, states it as his conviction that engagements which involve personal relations or services should never be legally binding beyond a limited duration of time; and that the most important of these engagements, marriage, having the peculiarity that its objects are frustrated unless the feelings of both the parties are in harmony with it, should require nothing more than the declared will of either party to dissolve it. This subject is too important and too complicated to be discussed in a parenthesis, and I touch on it only so far as is necessary for purposes of illustration. If the conciseness and generality of Baron Humboldt's dissertation had not obliged him in this instance to content himself with enunciating his conclusion without discussing the premises, he would doubtless have recognized that the question cannot be decided on grounds so simple as those to which he confines himself. When a person, either by express promise or by conduct, has encouraged another to rely upon his continuing to act in a certain way—to build expectations and calculations, and stake any part of his plan of life upon that supposition—a new series of moral obligations arises on his part toward that person, which may possibly be overruled, but cannot be ignored. And again, if the relation between two contracting parties has been followed by consequences to others; if it has placed third parties in any peculiar position, or, as in the case of marriage, has even called third parties into existence, obligations arise on the part of both the contracting parties toward those third persons, the fulfillment of which, or at all events the mode of fulfillment, must be greatly affected by the continuance or disruption of the relation between the original parties to the contract. It does not follow, nor can I admit, that these obligations extend to requiring the fulfillment of the contract at all costs to the happiness of the reluctant party; but they are a necessary element in the question; and even if, as von Humboldt maintains, they ought to make no difference in the *legal* freedom of the parties to release themselves from the engagement (and I also hold that they ought not to make *much* difference), they necessarily make a great difference in the *moral* freedom. A person is bound to take all these circumstances into account before resolving on a step which may affect such important interests of others; and if he does not allow proper weight to those interests, he is morally responsible for the wrong. I have made these obvious remarks for the better illustration of the general principle of liberty, and not because they are at all needed on the particular question, which, on the contrary, is usually discussed as if the interest of children was everything, and that of grown persons nothing.

I have already observed that, owing to the absence of any recognized general principles, liberty is often granted where it should be withheld, as well as withheld where it should be granted; and one of the cases in which, in the modern European world, the sentiment of liberty is the strongest is a case where, in my view, it is altogether misplaced. A person should be free to do as he likes in his own concerns, but he ought not to be free to do as he likes in acting for another, under the pretext that the affairs of the other are his own affairs. The State, while it respects the liberty of each in what specially regards himself, is bound to maintain a vigilant control over his exercise of any power which it allows him to possess over others. This obligation is almost entirely disregarded in the case of the family relations—a case, in its direct influence on human happiness, more important than all others taken together. The almost despotic power of husbands over wives needs not be enlarged upon here, because nothing more is needed for the complete removal of the evil than that wives should have the same rights and should receive the protection of law in the same manner as all other persons; and because, on this subject, the defenders of established injustice do not avail themselves of the plea of liberty but stand forth openly as the champions of power. It is in the case of children that misapplied notions of liberty are a real obstacle to the fulfillment by the State of its duties. One would almost think that a man's children were supposed to be literally, and not metaphorically, a part of himself, so jealous is opinion of the smallest interference of law with his absolute and exclusive control over them, more jealous than of almost any interference with his own freedom of action: so much less do the generality of mankind value liberty than power. Consider, for example, the case of education. Is it not almost a self-evident axiom that the State should require and compel the education, up to a certain standard, of every human being who is born its citizen? Yet who is there that is not afraid to recognize and assert this truth? Hardly anyone, indeed, will deny that it is one of the most sacred duties of the parents (or, as law and usage now stand, the father), after summoning a human being into the world, to give to that being an education fitting him to perform his part well in life toward others and toward himself. But while this is unanimously declared to be the father's duty, scarcely anybody, in this country, will bear to hear of obliging him to perform it. Instead of his being required to make any exertion or sacrifice for securing education to his child, it is left to his choice to accept it or not when it is provided gratis! It still remains unrecognized that to bring a child into existence without a fair prospect of being able, not only to provide food for its body, but instruction and training for its mind is a moral crime, both against the unfortunate offspring and against society; and that if the parent does not fulfill this obligation, the State ought to see it fulfilled at the charge, as far as possible, of the parent.

Were the duty of enforcing universal education once admitted there would be an end to the difficulties about what the State should teach, and how it should teach, which now convert the subject into a mere battlefield for sects and parties, causing the time and labor which should have been spent in educating to be wasted in quarreling about education. If the government would make up its mind to require for every child a good education, it might save itself the trouble of providing one. It might leave to parents to obtain the education where and how they pleased, and content itself with helping to pay the school fees of the poorer classes of children, and defraying the entire school expenses of those who have no one else to pay for them. The objections which are urged with reason against State education do not apply to the enforcement of education by the State, but to the State's taking upon itself to direct that education; which is a totally different thing. That the whole or any large part of the education of the people should be in State hands, I go as far as anyone in deprecating. All that has been said of the importance of individuality of character, and diversity in opinions and modes of conduct, involves, as of the same unspeakable importance, diversity of education. A general State education is a mere contrivance for molding people to be exactly like one another; and as the mold in which it casts them is that which pleases the predominant power in the government—whether this be a monarch, a priesthood, an aristocracy, or the majority of the existing generation—in proportion as it is efficient and successful, it establishes a despotism over the mind, leading by natural tendency to one over the body. An education established and controlled by the State should only exist, if it exist at all, as one among many competing experiments, carried on for the purpose of example and stimulus to keep the others up to a certain standard of excellence. Unless, indeed, when society in general is in so backward a state that it could not or would not provide for itself any proper institutions of education unless the government undertook the task, then, indeed, the government may, as the less of two great evils, take upon itself the business of schools and universities, as it may that of joint stock companies when private enterprise in a shape fitted for undertaking great works of industry does not exist in the country. But in general, if the country contains a sufficient number of persons qualified to provide education under government auspices, the same persons would be able and willing to give an equally good education on the voluntary principle, under the assurance of remuneration afforded by a law rendering education compulsory, combined with State aid to those unable to defray the expense.

The instrument for enforcing the law could be no other than public examinations, extending to all children and beginning at an early age. An age might be fixed at which every child must be examined, to ascertain if he (or she) is able to read. If a child proves unable, the father, unless he has some sufficient ground of excuse, might be subjected to a moderate fine, to be worked out, if necessary, by his labor, and the child might be put to school at his expense. Once in every year the examination should be renewed, with a gradually extending range of subjects, so as to make the universal acquisition and, what is more, retention of a certain minimum of general knowledge virtually compulsory. Beyond that minimum there should be voluntary examinations on all subjects, at which all who come up to a certain standard of proficiency might claim a certificate. To prevent the State from exercising, through these arrangements, an improper influence over opinion, the knowledge required for passing an examination (beyond the merely instrumental parts of knowledge, such as languages and their use) should, even in the higher classes of examinations, be confined to facts and positive science exclusively. The examinations on religion, politics, or other disputed topics should not turn on the truth or falsehood of opinions, but on the matter of fact that such and such an opinion is held, on such grounds, by such authors, or schools, or churches. Under this system, the rising generation would be no worse off in regard to all disputed truths than they are at present; they would be brought up either churchmen or dissenters as they now are, the State merely taking care that they should be instructed churchmen, or instructed dissenters. There would be nothing to hinder them from being taught religion, if their parents chose, at the same schools where they were taught other things. All attempts by the State to bias the conclusions of its citizens on disputed subjects are evil; but it may very properly offer to ascertain and certify that a person possesses the knowledge requisite to make his conclusions on any given subject worth attending to. A student of philosophy would be the better for being able to stand an examination both in Locke and in Kant, whichever of the two he takes up with, or even if with neither: and there is no reasonable objection to examining an atheist in the evidences of Christianity, provided he is not required to profess a belief in them. The examinations, however, in the higher branches of knowledge should, I conceive, be entirely voluntary. It would be giving too dangerous a power to governments were they allowed to exclude anyone from professions, even from the profession of teacher, for alleged deficiency of qualifications; and I think, with Wilhelm von Humboldt, that degrees or other public certificates of scientific or professional acquirements should be given to all who present themselves for examination and stand the test, but that such certificates should confer no advantage over competitors other than the weight which may be attached to their testimony by public opinion.

It is not in the matter of education only that misplaced notions of liberty prevent moral obligations on the part of parents from being recognized, and legal obligations from being imposed, where there are the strongest grounds for the former always, and in many cases for the latter also. The fact itself, of causing the existence of a human being, is one of the most responsible actions in the range of human life. To undertake this responsibility—to bestow a life which may be either a curse or a blessing—unless the being on whom it is to be bestowed will have at least the ordinary chances of a desirable existence, is a crime against that being. And in a country, either overpeopled or threatened with being so, to produce children, beyond a very small number, with the effect of reducing the reward of labor by their competition is a serious offense against all who live by the remuneration of their labor. The laws which, in many countries on the Continent, forbid marriage unless the parties can show that they have the means of supporting a family do not exceed the legitimate powers of the State; and whether such laws be expedient or not (a question mainly dependent on local circumstances and feelings), they are not objectionable as violations of liberty. Such laws are interferences of the State to prohibit a mischievous act—an act injurious to others, which ought to be a subject of reprobation and social stigma, even when it is not deemed expedient to superadd legal punishment. Yet the current ideas of liberty, which bend so easily to real infringements of the freedom of the individual in things which concern only himself, would repel the attempt to put any restraint upon his inclinations when the consequence of their indulgence is a life or lives of wretchedness and depravity to the offspring, with manifold evils to those sufficiently within reach to be in any way affected by their actions. When we compare the strange respect of mankind for liberty with their strange want of respect for it, we might imagine that a man had an indispensable right to do harm to others, and no right at all to please himself without giving pain to anyone.

I have reserved for the last place a large class of questions respecting the limits of government interference, which, though closely connected with the subject of this essay, do not, in strictness, belong to it. These are cases in which the reasons against interference do not turn upon the principle of liberty: the question is not about restraining the actions of individuals, but about helping them; it is asked whether the government should do, or cause to be done, something for their benefit instead of leaving it to be done by themselves, individually or in voluntary combination.

The objections to government interference, when it is not such as to involve infringement of liberty, may be of three kinds: The first is when the thing to be done is likely to be better done by individuals than by the government. Speaking generally, there is no one so fit to conduct any business, or to determine how or by whom it shall be conducted, as those who are personally interested in it. This principle condemns the interferences, once so common, of the legislature, or the officers of government, with the ordinary processes of industry. But this part of the subject has been sufficiently enlarged upon by political economists, and is not particularly related to the principles of this essay.

The second objection is more nearly allied to our subject. In many cases, though individuals may not do the particular thing so well, on the average, as the officers of government, it is nevertheless desirable that it should be done by them, rather than by the government, as a means to their own mental education—a mode of strengthening their active faculties, exercising their judgment, and giving them a familiar knowledge of the subjects with which they are thus left to deal. This is a principal, though not the sole, recommendation of jury trial (in cases not political); of free and popular local and municipal institutions; of the conduct of industrial and philanthropic enterprises by voluntary associations. These are not questions of liberty, and are connected with that subject only by remote tendencies, but they are questions of development. It belongs to a different occasion from the present to dwell on these things as parts of national education, as being, in truth, the peculiar training of a citizen, the practical part of the political education of a free people, taking them out of the narrow circle of personal and family selfishness, and accustoming them to the comprehension of joint interests, the management of joint concerns—habituating them to act from public or semi-public motives, and guide their conduct by aims which unite instead of isolating them from one another. Without these habits and powers, a free constitution can neither be worked nor preserved, as is exemplified by the too-often transitory nature of political freedom in countries where it does not rest upon a sufficient basis of local liberties. The management of purely local business by the localities, and of the great enterprises of industry by the union of those who voluntarily supply the pecuniary means, is further recommended by all the advantages which have been set forth in this essay as belonging to individuality of development and diversity of modes of action. Government operations tend to be everywhere alike. With individuals and voluntary associations, on the contrary, there are varied experiments and endless diversity of experience. What the State can usefully do is to make itself a central depository, and active circulator and diffuser, of the experience resulting from many trials. Its business is to enable each experimentalist to benefit by the experiments of others, instead of tolerating no experiments but its own.

The third and most cogent reason for restricting the interference of government is the great evil of adding unnecessarily to its power. Every function superadded to those already exercised by the government causes its influence over hopes and fears to be more widely diffused, and converts, more and more, the active and ambitious part of the public into hangers-on of the government, or of some party which aims at becoming the government. If the roads, the railways, the banks, the insurance offices, the great joint-stock companies, the universities, and the public charities were all of them branches of the government; if, in addition, the municipal corporations and local boards, with all that now devolves on them, became departments of the central administration; if the employees of all these different enterprises were appointed and paid by the government and looked to the government for every rise in life, not all the freedom of the press and popular constitution of the legislature would make this or any other country free otherwise than in name. And the evil would be greater, the more efficiently and scientifically the administrative machinery was constructed—the more skillful the arrangements for obtaining the best qualified hands and heads with which to work it. In England it has of late been proposed that all the members of the civil service of government should be selected by competitive examination, to obtain for these employments the most intelligent and instructed persons procurable; and much has been said and written for and against this proposal. One of the arguments most insisted on by its opponents is that the occupation of a permanent official servant of the State does not hold out sufficient prospects of emolument and importance to attract the highest talents, which will always be able to find a more inviting career in the professions or in the service of companies and other public bodies. One would not have been surprised if this argument had been used by the friends of the proposition as an answer to its principal difficulty. Coming from the opponents it is strange enough. What is urged as an objection is the safety valve of the proposed system. If, indeed, all the high talent of the country *could* be drawn into the service of the government, a proposal tending to bring about that result might well inspire uneasiness. If every part of the business of society which required organized concert, or large and comprehensive views, were in the hands of the government, and if government offices were universally filled by the ablest men, all the enlarged culture and practiced intelligence in the country, except the purely speculative, would be concentrated in a numerous bureaucracy, to whom alone the rest of the community would look for all things—the multitude for direction and dictation in all they had to do; the able and aspiring for personal advancement. To be admitted into the ranks of this bureaucracy, and when admitted, to rise therein, would be the sole objects of ambition. Under this *régime* not only is the outside public ill-qualified, for want of practical experience, to criticize or check the mode of operation of the bureaucracy, but even if the accidents of despotic or the natural working of popular institutions occasionally raise to the summit a ruler or rulers of reforming inclinations, no reform can be effected which is contrary to the interest of the bureaucracy. Such is the melancholy condition of the Russian Empire, as shown in the accounts of those who have had sufficient opportunity of observation. The Czar himself is powerless against the bureaucratic body; he can send any one of them to Siberia, but he cannot govern without them, or against their will. On every decree of his they have a tacit veto, by merely refraining from carrying it into effect. In countries of more advanced civilization and of a more insurrectionary spirit, the public, accustomed to expect everything to be done for them by the State, or at least to do nothing for themselves without asking from the State not only leave to do it, but even how it is to be done, naturally hold the State responsible for all evil which befalls them, and when the evil exceeds their amount of patience, they rise against the government and make what is called a revolution; whereupon somebody else, with or without legitimate authority from the nation, vaults into the seat, issues his orders to the bureaucracy, and everything goes on much as it did before; the bureaucracy being unchanged, and nobody else being capable of taking their place.

A very different spectacle is exhibited among a people accustomed to transact their own business. In France, a large part of the people, having been engaged in military service, many of whom have held at least the rank of noncommissioned officers, there are in every popular insurrection several persons competent to take the lead and improvise some tolerable plan of action. What the French are in military affairs, the Americans are in every kind of civil business; let them be left without a government, every body of Americans is able to improvise one and to carry on that or any other public business with a sufficient amount of intelligence, order, and decision. This is what every free people ought to be; and a people capable of this is certain to be free; it will never let itself be enslaved by any man or body of men because these are able to seize and pull the reins of the central administration. No bureaucracy can hope to make such a people as this do or undergo anything that they do not like. But where everything is done through the bureaucracy, nothing to which the bureaucracy is really adverse can be done at all. The constitution of such countries is an organization of the experience and practical ability of the nation into a disciplined body for the purpose of governing the rest; and the more perfect that organization is in itself, the more successful in drawing to itself and educating for itself the persons of greatest capacity from all ranks of the community, the more complete is the bondage of all, the members of the bureaucracy included. For the governors are as much the slaves of their organization and discipline as the governed are of the governors. A Chinese mandarin is as much the tool and creature of a despotism as the humblest cultivator. An individual Jesuit is to the utmost degree of abasement the slave of his order, though the order itself exists for the collective power and importance of its members.

It is not, also, to be forgotten that the absorption of all the principal ability of the country into the governing body is fatal, sooner or later, to the mental activity and progressiveness of the body itself. Banded together as they are—working a system which, like all systems, necessarily proceeds in a great measure by fixed rules—the official body are under the constant temptation of sinking into indolent routine, or, if they now and then desert that mill-horse round, of rushing into some half-examined crudity which has struck the fancy of some leading member of the corps; and the sole check to these closely allied, though seemingly opposite, tendencies, the only stimulus which can keep the ability of the body itself up to a high standard, is liability to the watchful criticism of equal ability outside the body. It is indispensable, therefore, that the means should exist, independently of the government, of forming such ability and furnishing it with the opportunities and experience necessary for a correct judgment of great practical affairs. If we would possess permanently a skillful and efficient body of functionaries—above all a body able to originate and willing to adopt improvements—if we would not have our bureaucracy degenerate into a pedantocracy, this body must not engross all the occupations which form and cultivate the faculties required for the government of mankind.

To determine the point at which evils, so formidable to human freedom and advancement, begin, or rather at which they begin to predominate over the benefits attending the collective application of the force of society, under its recognized chiefs, for the removal of the obstacles which stand in the way of its well-being; to secure as much of the advantages of centralized power and intelligence as can be had without turning into governmental channels too great a proportion of the general activity—is one of the most difficult and complicated questions in the art of government. It is, in a great measure, a question of detail in which many and various considerations must be kept in view, and no absolute rule can be laid down. But I believe that the practical principle in which safety resides, the ideal to be kept in view, the standard by which to test all arrangements intended for overcoming the difficulty, may be conveyed in these words: the greatest dissemination of power consistent with efficiency; but the greatest possible centralization of information and diffusion of it from the center. Thus, in municipal administration, there would be, as in the New England states, a very minute division among separate officers, chosen by the localities, of all business which is not better left to the persons directly interested; but besides this, there would be, in each department of local affairs, a central superintendence, forming a branch of the general government. The organ of this superintendence would concentrate, as in a focus, the variety of information and experience derived from the conduct of that branch of public business in all the localities, from everything analogous which is done in foreign countries, and from the general principles of political science. This central organ should have a right to know all that is done, and its special duty should be that of making the knowledge acquired in one place available for others. Emancipated from the petty prejudices and narrow views of a locality by its elevated position and comprehensive sphere of observation, its advice would naturally carry much authority; but its actual power, as a permanent institution, should, I conceive, be limited to compelling the local officers to obey the laws laid down for their guidance. In all things not provided for by general rules, those officers should be left to their own judgment, under responsibility to their constituents. For the violation of rules, they should be responsible to law, and the rules themselves should be laid down by the legislature; the central administrative authority only watching over their execution and, if they were not properly carried into effect, appealing, according to the nature of the case, to the tribunals to enforce the law, or to the constituencies to dismiss the functionaries who had not executed it according to its spirit. Such, in its general conception, is the central superintendence which the Poor Law Board is intended to exercise over the administrators of the Poor Rate throughout the country. Whatever powers the Board exercises beyond this limit were right and necessary in that peculiar case, for the cure of rooted habits of maladministration in matters deeply affecting not the localities merely, but the whole community; since no locality has a moral right to make itself by mismanagement a nest of pauperism, necessarily overflowing into other localities and impairing the moral and physical condition of the whole laboring community. The powers of administrative coercion and subordinate legislation possessed by the Poor Law Board (but which, owing to the state of opinion on the subject, are very scantily exercised by them), though perfectly justifiable in a case of first-rate national interest, would be wholly out of place in the superintendence of interests purely local. But a central organ of information and instruction for all the localities would be equally valuable in all departments of administration. A government cannot have too much of the kind of activity which does not impede, but aids and stimulates, individual exertion and development. The mischief begins when, instead of calling forth the activity and powers of individuals and bodies, it substitutes its own activity for theirs; when, instead of informing, advising, and, upon occasion, denouncing, it makes them work in fetters, or bids them stand aside and does their work instead of them. The worth of a State, in the long run, is the worth of the individuals composing it; and a State which postpones the interests of their mental expansion and elevation to a little more of administrative skill, or of that semblance of it which practice gives in the details of business; a State which dwarfs its men, in order that they may be more docile instruments in its hands even for beneficial purposes—will find that with small men no great thing can really be accomplished; and that the perfection of machinery to which it has sacrificed everything will in the end avail it nothing, for want of the vital power which, in order that the machine might work more smoothly, it has preferred to banish.

THE SUBJECTION OF WOMEN (in part)

CHAPTER 1

The object of this Essay is to explain as clearly as I am able the grounds of an opinion which I have held from the very earliest period when I had formed any opinions at all on social or political matters, and which, instead of being weakened or modified, has been constantly growing stronger by the progress of reflection and the experience of life: That the principle which regulates the existing social relations between the two sexes—the legal subordination of one sex to the other—is wrong in itself, and now one of the chief hindrances to human improvement; and that it ought to be replaced by a principle of perfect equality, admitting no power or privilege on the one side, nor disability on the other. . . .

The truth is that people of the present and the last two or three generations have lost all practical sense of the primitive condition of humanity; and only the few who have studied history accurately, or have much frequented the parts of the world occupied by the living representatives of ages long past, are able to form any mental picture of what society then was. People are not aware how entirely, in former ages, the law of superior strength was the rule of life; how publicly and openly it was avowed, I do not say cynically or shamelessly—for these words imply a feeling that there was something in it to be ashamed of, and no such notion could find a place in the faculties of any person in those ages, except a philosopher or a saint. History gives a cruel experience of human nature, in showing how exactly the regard due to the life, possessions, and entire earthly happiness of any class of persons, was measured by what they had the power of enforcing; how all who made any resistance to authorities that had arms in their hands, however dreadful might be the provocation, had not only the law of force but all other laws, and all the notions of social obligation against them; and in the eyes of those whom they resisted, were not only guilty of crime, but of the worst of all crimes, deserving the most cruel chastisement which human beings could inflict. The first small vestige of a feeling of obligation in a superior to acknowledge any right in inferiors began when he had been induced, for convenience, to make some promise to them. Though these promises, even when sanctioned by the most solemn oaths, were for many ages revoked or violated on the most trifling provocation or temptation, it is probable that this, except by persons of still worse than the average morality, was seldom done without some twinges of conscience.* . . .

*[The brief history of the use of force to establish power that follows this paragraph has been deleted.]

"The Ladies' Advocate," This cartoon from *Punch* magazine ridicules John Stuart Mill for advocating women's rights. The woman informs Mill that "Prior to your speech I was unaware that women were such miserable creatures." *(Library of Congress)*

How different are these cases from that of the power of men over women! I am not now prejudging the question of its justification. I am showing how vastly more permanent it could not but be, even if not justifiable, than these other dominations which have nevertheless lasted down to our own time. Whatever gratification of pride there is in the possession of power, and whatever personal interest in its exercise, is in this case not confined to a limited class, but common to the whole male sex. Instead of being, to most of its supporters, a thing desirable chiefly in the abstract, or, like the political ends usually contended for by factious, of little private importance to any but the leaders; it comes home to the person and hearth of every male head of a family, and of every one who looks forward to being so. The clodhopper exercises, or is to exercise, his share of the power equally with the highest nobleman. And the case is that in which the desire of power is the strongest: for every one who desires power, desires it most over those who are nearest to him, with whom his life is passed, with whom he has most concerns in common, and in whom any independence of his authority is most often likely to interfere with his individual preferences. If, in the other cases specified, powers manifestly grounded only on force, and having so much less to support them, are so slowly and with so much difficulty got rid of, much more must it be so with this, even if it rests on no better foundation than those. We must consider, too, that the possessors of the power have facilities in this case, greater than in any other, to prevent any uprising against it. Every one of the subjects lives under the very eye, and almost, it may be said, in the hands, of one of the masters—in closer intimacy with him than with any of her fellow-subjects; with no means of combining against him, no power of even locally overmastering him, and, on the other hand, with the strongest motives for seeking his favour and avoiding to give him offence. In struggles for political emancipation, everybody knows how often its champions are bought off by bribes, or daunted by terrors. In the case of women, each individual of the subject-class is in a chronic state of bribery and intimidation combined. In setting up the standard of resistance, a large number of the leaders, and still more of the followers, must make an almost complete sacrifice of the pleasures or the alleviations of their own individual lot. If ever any system of privilege and enforced subjection had its yoke tightly riveted on the necks of those who are kept down by it, this has. . . .

But, it will be said, the rule of men over women differs from all these others in not being a rule of force: it is accepted voluntarily; women make no complaint, and are consenting parties to it. In the first place, a great number of women do not accept it. Ever since there have been women able to make their sentiments known by their writings (the only mode of publicity which society permits to them), an increasing number of them have recorded protests against their present social condition: and recently many thousands of them, headed by the most eminent women known to the public, have petitioned Parliament for their admission to the Parliamentary Suffrage. The claim of women to be educated as solidly, and in the same branches of knowledge, as men, is urged with growing intensity, and with a great prospect of success; while the demand for their admission into professions and occupations hitherto closed against them, becomes every year more urgent. Though there are not in this country, as there are in the United States, periodical Conventions and an organized party to agitate for the Rights of Women, there is a numerous and active Society organized and managed by women, for the more limited object of obtaining the political franchise. Nor is it only in our own country and in America that women are beginning to protest, more or less collectively, against the disabilities under which they labour. France, and Italy, and Switzerland, and Russia now afford examples of the same thing. How many more women there are who silently cherish similar aspirations, no one can possibly know; but there are abundant tokens how many *would* cherish them, were they not so strenuously taught to repress them as contrary to the proprieties of their sex. It must be remembered, also, that no enslaved class ever asked for complete liberty at once. When Simon de Montfort called the deputies of the commons to sit for the first time in Parliament, did any of them dream of demanding that an assembly, elected by their constituents, should make and destroy ministries, and dictate to the king in affairs of state?

No such thought entered into the imagination of the most ambitious of them. The nobility had already these pretensions; the commons pretended to nothing but to be exempt from arbitrary taxation, and from the gross individual oppression of the king's officers. It is a political law of nature that those who are under any power of ancient origin never begin by complaining of the power itself, but only of its oppressive exercise. There is never any want of women who complain of ill usage by their husbands. There would be infinitely more, if complaint were not the greatest of all provocatives to a repetition and increase of the ill usage. It is this which frustrates all attempts to maintain the power but protect the woman against its abuses. In no other case (except that of a child) is the person who has been proved judicially to have suffered an injury replaced under the physical power of the culprit who inflicted it. Accordingly wives, even in the most extreme and protracted cases of bodily ill usage hardly ever dare avail themselves of the laws made for their protection: and if, in a moment of irrepressible indignation, or by the interference of neighbours, they are induced to do so, their whole effort afterwards is to disclose as little as they can, and to beg off their tyrant from his merited chastisement.

All causes, social and natural, combine to make it unlikely that women should be collectively rebellious to the power of men. They are so far in a position different from all other subject classes, that their masters require something more from them than actual service. Men do not want solely the obedience of women, they want their sentiments. All men, except the most brutish, desire to have, in the woman most nearly connected with them, not a forced slave but a willing one, not a slave merely, but a favourite. They have therefore put everything in practice to enslave their minds. The masters of all other slaves rely, for maintaining obedience, on fear; either fear of themselves, or religious fears. The masters of women wanted more than simple obedience, and they turned the whole force of education to effect their purpose. All women are brought up from the very earliest years in the belief that their ideal of character is the very opposite to that of men; not self-will, and government by self-control, but submission, and yielding to the control of others. All the moralities tell them that it is the duty of women, and all the current sentimentalities that it is their nature, to live for others; to make complete abnegation of themselves, and to have no life but in their affections. And by their affections are meant the only ones they are allowed to have—those to the men with whom they are connected, or to the children who constitute an additional and indefeasible tie between them and a man. When we put together three things—first, the natural attraction between opposite sexes; secondly, the wife's entire dependence on the husband, every privilege or pleasure she has being either his gift, or depending entirely on his will; and lastly, that the principal object of human pursuit, consideration, and all objects of social ambition, can in general be sought or obtained by her only through him, it would be a miracle if the object of being attractive to men had not become the polar star of feminine education and formation of character. And, this great means of influence over the minds of women having been acquired, an instinct of selfishness made men avail themselves of it to the utmost as a means of holding women in subjection, by representing to them meekness, submissiveness, and resignation of all individual will into the hands of a man, as an essential part of sexual attractiveness. Can it be doubted that any of the other yokes which mankind have succeeded in breaking would have subsisted till now if the same means had existed, and had been as sedulously used, to bow down their minds to it? If it had been made the object of the life of every young plebeian to find personal favour in the eyes of some patrician, of every young serf with some seigneur; if domestication with him, and a share of his personal affections, had been held out as the prize which they all should look out for, the most gifted and aspiring being able to reckon on the most desirable prizes; and if, when this prize had been obtained, they had been shut out by a wall of brass from all interests not centering in him, all feelings and desires but those which he shared or inculcated; would not serfs and seigneurs, plebeians and patricians, have been as broadly distinguished at this day as men and women are? and would not all but a thinker here and there, have believed the distinction to be a fundamental and unalterable fact in human nature? . . .

At present, in the more improved countries, the disabilities of women are the only case, save one, in which laws and institutions take persons at their birth, and ordain that they shall never in all their lives be allowed to compete for certain things. The one exception is that of royalty. Persons still are born to the throne; no one, not of the reigning family, can ever occupy it, and no one even of that family can, by any means but the course of hereditary succession, attain it. All other dignities and social advantages are open to the whole male sex: many indeed are only attainable by wealth, but wealth may be striven for by any one, and is actually obtained by many men of the very humblest origin. The difficulties, to the majority, are indeed insuperable without the aid of fortunate accidents; but no male human being is under any legal ban: neither law nor opinion superadd artificial obstacles to the natural ones. Royalty, as I have said, is excepted: but in this case every one feels it to be an exception—an anomaly in the modern world, in marked opposition to its customs and principles, and to be justified only by extraordinary special expediencies, which, though individuals and nations differ in estimating their weight, unquestionably do in fact exist. But in this exceptional case, in which a high social function is, for important reasons, bestowed on birth instead of being put up to competition, all free nations contrive to adhere in substance to the principle from which they nominally derogate; for they circumscribe this high function by conditions avowedly intended to prevent the person to whom it ostensibly belongs from really performing it; while the person by whom it is performed, the responsible minister, does obtain the post by a competition from which no full-grown citizen of the male sex is legally excluded. The disabilities, therefore, to which women are subject from the mere fact of their birth are the solitary examples of the kind in modern legislation. In no instance except this, which comprehends half the human race, are the higher social functions closed against any one by a fatality of birth which no exertions, and no change of circumstances, can overcome; for even religious disabilities (besides that in England and in Europe they have practically almost ceased to exist) do not close any career to the disqualified person in case of conversion.

The social subordination of women thus stands out an isolated fact in modern social institutions; a solitary breach of what has become their fundamental law; a single relic of an old world of thought and practice exploded in everything else, but retained in the one thing of most universal interest; as if a gigantic dolmen [monument], or a vast temple of Jupiter Olympius, occupied the site of St. Paul's and received daily worship, while the surrounding Christian churches were only resorted to on fasts and festivals. This entire discrepancy between one social fact and all those which accompany it, and the radical opposition between its nature and the progressive movement which is the boast of the modern world, and which has successively swept away everything else of an analogous character, surely affords, to a conscientious observer of human tendencies, serious matter for reflection.

The preceding considerations are amply sufficient to show that custom, however universal it may be, affords in this case no presumption, and ought not to create any prejudice, in favour of the arrangements which place women in social and political subjection to men.

SØREN KIERKEGAARD
1813–1855

Søren Aabye Kierkegaard was born in Copenhagen, Denmark, the youngest child of middle-aged parents. His father, Michael, had been an impoverished serf in a bleak area of northern Denmark. While still a boy, Michael had cursed God for the dreariness of his life and from that point on considered himself and his descendants to be under God's condemnation. The external events of Michael's life gave little indication of such a curse, however, as he worked his way to great wealth as a merchant in Copenhagen. Following the death of his first wife, and before the period of mourning was over, Michael was forced to marry his first wife's maid, Anne Lund, and five months later she bore the first of their five children.

Michael was already fifty-six and retired from business when Søren was born in 1813. Like James Mill, Michael educated Søren at home and also put his son through rigorous intellectual endeavors. But unlike his predecessor, Michael also communicated to his son a strong religious sentiment and deep, though perhaps warped, emotional feelings. Michael often took Søren on "trips of fantasy" while conversing in the family library.

In 1830, at his father's urging, Kierkegaard entered the University of Copenhagen to study theology. While there, he encountered the work of Hegel and reacted strongly against it. Kierkegaard objected to the implicit optimism and the "swallowing up" of contradictions in Hegel's dialectic. But more important, Kierkegaard claimed that even though Hegel's "System" was an impressive philosophical *tour de force,* it did not relate to the lived existence of the individual—it did not give any guidance as to what a person should *do*. A famous entry from Kierkegaard's journal at this time is worth quoting at length:

What I really lack is to be clear in my mind *what I am to do,* not what I am to know, except in so far as a certain understanding must precede every action. The thing is to understand myself, to see what God really wishes *me* to do; the thing is to find a truth which is true *for me,* to find *the idea for which I can live and die.* What would be the use of discovering so-called objective truth, of working through all the systems of philosophy and of being able, if required, to review them all and show up the inconsistencies within each system;—what good would it do me to be able to develop a theory of the state and combine all the details into a single whole, and so construct a world in which I did not live, but only held up to the view of others;—what good would it do me to be able to explain the meaning of Christianity if it had *no* deeper significance *for me and for my life;*—what good would it do me if truth stood before me, cold and naked, not caring whether I recognised her or not, and producing in me a shudder of fear rather than a trusting devotion? I certainly do not deny that I still recognise an *imperative of understanding* and that through it one can work upon men, *but it must be taken up into my life, and that is what I now recognise as the most important thing.**

Kierkegaard did not find the answer for "what to do" in his studies in theology and soon began living what he would later call an "aesthetic" life as a rich merchant's son. He spent large sums of money on food, drink, and clothing. He frequented parties and appeared to be having a great time. But hedonistic indulgence did not really give an answer for "what to do" either, and he plunged into despair. Another entry from his journals makes this clear:

I have just returned from a party of which I was the life and soul; wit poured from my lips, everyone laughed and admired me—but I went away—and the dash should be as long as the earth's orbit ————————————————————————

and wanted to shoot myself.**

On his son's twenty-fifth birthday, May 15, 1838, Michael revealed to Søren his own sexual sins as well as his understanding of God's condemnation of their family. Four days later, Søren Kierkegaard underwent a religious conversion and was reconciled to his father, who died shortly afterward. Kierkegaard now had an answer for "what to do"—he would live as a penitent seeking to "become a Christian." Kierkegaard finished his theological studies, prepared to become a Lutheran pastor, and became engaged to marry seventeen-year-old Regine Olsen.

But by 1841, Kierkegaard realized that he could never live the life of a Lutheran pastor and devoted husband. He came to believe that the Danish Lutheran church had made religion a matter of intellectual assent to certain objective truths and no longer deserved to be called "Christian." For the rest of his life, Kierkegaard opposed institutional Christianity. The decision to break his engagement to Regine Olsen was a torturous one, but one he believed he had to make. He decided that a "divine veto" had been cast against this marriage, that his role as penitent was incompatible with that of husband.

___

  *Søren Kierkegaard, *The Journals of Søren Kierkegaard,* edited and translated by Alexander Dru (London: Oxford University Press, 1938), p. 15 [entry from August 1, 1835].
  ***Ibid.,* p. 27 [entry from early spring, 1836].

Kierkegaard spent the rest of his short life as a writer, publishing a number of books including *Either/Or* (1843), *Fear and Trembling* (1843), *Philosophical Fragments* (1844), *Stages on Life's Way* (1845), *Concluding Unscientific Post-script* (1846), *The Sickness unto Death* (1849), *Training in Christianity* (1850), and *The Attack upon "Christendom"* (1854–1855). All but the last of these works were written under various pseudonyms, and virtually all of them included attacks on the prevailing Hegelian philosophy of his time. In 1855, while returning from the bank with the last of his considerable inheritance, Kierkegaard collapsed on the street and died soon thereafter.

*   *   *

Kierkegaard's biography is reflected in his philosophical quest to establish what it means to be an individual. In such works as *Either/Or, Stages on Life's Way,* and *Fear and Trembling,* he describes a process of self-actualization through three stages in life: the aesthetic, the ethical, and the religious. At the aesthetic stage, an individual's life centers on either hedonistic pleasure or abstract philosophical speculation. The hedonist lives for the immediate pleasures of the moment without concern for the future. The abstract intellectual (Hegel being the prime example) lives in a theoretical world removed from concrete existence. The hedonist reduces existence to immediate pleasure whereas the abstract speculator reduces existence to thought; but in both cases the aesthete has avoided the either/or decisions of real life, and authentic selfhood has not been achieved. The result, says Kierkegaard, is a life of boredom—and the pointless pursuit of diversions to alleviate such boredom. This was the life Kierkegaard himself lived in his early years at the university.

Those who move beyond the aesthetic to the ethical level choose to accept moral standards and attempt to do their duty. By choosing decisively and accepting responsibility for that choice, an individual's life becomes centralized and unified. For example, the seducing man operates on the aesthetic level where every woman he meets is merely a general source of momentary pleasure. He has no past, no future, only the present desire for fulfillment. He is not really a complete person because he is living life as a series of disconnected "nows." On the other hand, the man who has chosen to fulfill the duties of a faithful husband operates on the ethical level. He has a memory of the past and a hope for the future based on his commitments, which give an integrated wholeness to his present.

But even though universal moral standards can become personal when chosen by an individual, the ethical stage is not sufficient to bring a person to complete self-actualization. The ethical stage leads to a point at which one realizes that one cannot entirely fulfill the moral law, that one is sinful in the presence of God. Only in the religious stage, where one "leaps" to passionate commitment to God, is one totally free from meaninglessness and dread. In the religious stage, a person must be willing to give up everything—even abstract ethical universals—to God. In the selection reprinted here from *Fear and Trembling,* in the Howard and Edna Hong translation, Kierkegaard illustrates this movement from the ethical to the religious stage by contrasting the stories of Agamemnon and Abraham. Although both were called upon by a divinity to sacrifice a child, Agamemnon's sacrifice would serve a higher ethical purpose whereas Abraham's would not. In fact, Abraham was in the odd position of being *tempted* to do the ethical: to not murder/sacrifice Isaac. Yet Abraham had faith in God, rather than Agamemnon's resignation to the gods, and continued to believe that God would return his son to him. Abraham performed a "teleological [i.e., considering the end or goal] suspension of the ethical," giving up what was most dear to him, and by virtue of the absurd, God gave it all back. It is interesting to note that Kierkegaard wrote this work right after he had given up to God what was most dear to him: Regine Olsen. Apparently believing that God would give her back to him, Kierkegaard was shocked when she became engaged to another man.

In the selection from *Concluding Unscientific Postscript,* reprinted here in the Howard and Edna Hong translation, Kierkegaard argues that whereas a logical system is possible, an existential system is not. Hegel's entire systematic enterprise is misguided because it assumes a finality that lived existence never has. When it comes to the important issues of life, such as knowledge of God, no system, no set of objective truths will give any real guidance. According to Kierkegaard, only subjective truth, "An objective uncertainty, held fast through appropriation with the most passionate inwardness," can be the truth for an existing person. Whereas one can never have objective certainty that God exists, one can make it true in one's own life by committing oneself completely and living as if it were true.

Written in Danish and presenting a pessimistic view of objective reason that was out of touch with the spirit of his time, it is not surprising that Kierkegaard's works were ignored for decades. The horror of World War I, together with the work done by Martin Heidegger in philosophy and Karl Barth in theology, brought Kierkegaard's pessimistic assessment of objectivism to prominence. Today Kierkegaard is acknowledged as the "father of existentialism" and is studied widely.

* * *

For representative collections of Kierkegaard's writings, see *A Kierkegaard Anthology,* edited by Robert Bretall (New York: Modern Library, 1936) and Walter A. Kaufmann, ed., *Existentialism from Dostoevsky to Sartre* (New York: Meridian Books, 1956). For biographies of Kierkegaard, see Walter Lowrie, *Kierkegaard* (Oxford: Oxford University Press, 1938) for comprehensive coverage, Walter Lowrie, *A Short Life of Kierkegaard* (Princeton, NJ: Princeton University Press, 1942) for a more succinct study, and Bruce H. Kirmmse, ed., *Encounters with Kierkegaard,* (Princeton, NJ: Princeton University Press, 1996) for descriptions of Kierkegaard by his contemporaries. There are a number of general overviews of Kierkegaard's thought, including H. Diem, *Kierkegaard: An Introduction,* translated by David Green (Richmond, VA: John Knox Press, 1966); Josiah Thompson, *Kierkegaard* (New York: Knopf, 1973); Alastair Hannay, *Kierkegaard* (London: Routledge & Kegan Paul, 1982); Diogenes Allen, *Three Outsiders: Pascal, Kierkegaard, Simone Weil* (Cambridge, MA: Cowley, 1983); and Patrick Gardiner, *Kierkegaard* (Oxford: Oxford University Press, 1988). For studies of specific aspects of Kierkegaard's thought, see Louis K. Dupre, *Kierkegaard as Theologian* (New York: Sheed and Ward, 1964); Niels Thulstrup, *Kierkegaard's Relation to Hegel,* translated by George L. Stengren (Princeton, NJ: Princeton University Press, 1980); John W. Elrod, *Kierkegaard and Christendom* (Princeton, NJ: Princeton University Press, 1981); C. Stephen Evans, *Kierkegaard's "Fragments" and "Postscript": The Religious Philosophy of Johannes Climacus* (Atlantic Highlands, NJ: Humanities Press, 1983); Merold Westphal, *Kierkegaard's Critique of Reason and Society* (Macon, GA: Mercer University Press, 1987); and C. Stephen Evans, *Passionate Reason: Making Sense of Kierkegaard's Philosophical Fragments* (Bloomington: Indiana University Press, 1992). For collections of essays, see H.A. Johnson and N. Thulstrup, eds., *A Kierkegaard Critique* (Chicago: Henry Regnery, 1967); Jerry H. Gill, ed., *Essays on Kierkegaard* (Minneapolis, MN: Burgess, 1969); Josiah Thompson, ed., *Kierkegaard: A Collection of Critical Essays* (Garden City, NY: Anchor Books, 1972); Harold Bloom, ed., *Søren Kierkegaard* (New York: Chelsea House, 1989); Célline Léon and Sylvia Walsh, eds., *Feminist Interpretations of Søren Kierkegaard* (College Park, PA: Pennsylvania State University Press, 1997); Alistair Hannay and Gordon Marino, eds., *The Cambridge Companion to Kierkegaard* (Cambridge: Cambridge University Press, 1997); and Jonathan Rée and Jane Chamberlain, eds., *Kierkegaard: A Critical Reader* (Oxford: Basil Blackwell, 1997).

FEAR AND TREMBLING (in part)

Is There a Teleological Suspension of the Ethical?

The ethical as such is the universal, and as the universal it applies to everyone, which from another angle means that it applies at all times. It rests immanent in itself, has nothing outside itself that is its ⟨*telos*⟩ [end, purpose] but is itself the ⟨*telos*⟩ for everything outside itself, and when the ethical has absorbed this into itself, it goes not further. The single individual, sensately and psychically qualified in immediacy, is the individual who has his ⟨*telos*⟩ in the universal, and it is his ethical task continually to express himself in this, to annul his singularity in order to become the universal. As soon as the single individual asserts himself in his singularity before the universal, he sins, and only by acknowledging this can he be reconciled again with the universal. Every time the single individual, after having entered the universal, feels an impulse to assert himself as the single individual, he is in a spiritual trial [*Anfægtelse*], from which he can work himself only by repentantly surrendering as the single individual in the universal. If this is the highest that can be said of man and his existence, then the ethical is of the same nature as a person's eternal salvation, which is his ⟨*telos*⟩ forevermore and at all times, since it would be a contradiction for this to be capable of being surrendered (that is, teleologically suspended), because as soon as this is suspended it is relinquished, whereas that which is suspended is not relinquished but is preserved in the higher, which is its ⟨*telos*⟩.

If this is the case, then Hegel is right in "The Good and Conscience," where he qualifies man only as the individual and considers this qualification as a "moral form of evil" (see especially *The Philosophy of Right*), which must be annulled [*ophævet*] in the teleology of the moral in such a way that the single individual who remains in that stage either sins or is immersed in spiritual trial. But Hegel is wrong in speaking about faith; he is wrong in not protesting loudly and clearly against Abraham's enjoying honor and glory as a father of faith when he ought to be sent back to a lower court and shown up as a murderer.

Faith is namely this paradox that the single individual is higher than the universal—yet, please note, in such a way that the movement repeats itself, so that after having been in the universal he as the single individual isolates himself as higher than the universal. If this is not faith, then Abraham is lost, then faith has never existed in the world precisely because it has always existed. For if the ethical—that is, social morality—is the highest and if there is in a person no residual incommensurability in some way such that this incommensurability is not evil (i.e., the single individual, who is to be expressed in the universal), then no categories are needed other than what Greek philosophy had or what can be deduced from them by consistent thought. Hegel should not have concealed this, for, after all, he had studied Greek philosophy.

People who are profoundly lacking in learning and are given to clichés are frequently heard to say that a light shines over the Christian world, whereas a darkness enshrouds paganism. This kind of talk has always struck me as strange, inasmuch as every more thorough thinker, every more earnest artist still regenerates himself in the eternal youth of the Greeks. The explanation for such a statement is that one does not know what one should say but only that one must say something. It is quite right to say that paganism did not have faith, but if something is supposed to have been said thereby, then one must have a clearer understanding of what faith is, for otherwise one falls into such clichés. It is easy to explain all existence, faith along with it, without having a conception of what faith is, and the one who counts on being admired for such an explanation is not such a bad calculator, for it is as Boileau says: *Un sot trouve toujours un plus sot, qui l'admire* [One fool always finds a bigger fool, who admires him].

Faith is precisely the paradox that the single individual as the single individual is higher than the universal, is justified before it, not as inferior to it but as superior—yet in such a way, please note, that it is the single individual who, after being subordinate as the single individual to the universal, now by means of the universal becomes the single individual who as the single individual is superior, that the single individual as the single individual stands in an absolute relation to the absolute. This position cannot be mediated, for all mediation takes place only by virtue of the universal; it is and remains for all eternity a paradox, impervious to thought. And yet faith is this paradox, or else (and I ask the reader to bear these consequences *in mente* [in mind] even though it would be too prolix for me to write them all down) or else faith has never existed simply because it has always existed, or else Abraham is lost.

It is certainly true that the single individual can easily confuse this paradox with spiritual trial [*Anfægtelse*], but it ought not to be concealed for that reason. It is certainly true that many persons may be so constituted that they are repulsed by it, but faith ought not therefore to be made into something else to enable one to have it, but one ought rather to admit to not having it, while those who have faith ought to be prepared to set forth some characteristics whereby the paradox can be distinguished from a spiritual trial.

Wanderer Above the Mist, 1817–1818, by Caspar David Friedrich (1774–1840). "Faith is precisely the paradox that the single individual as the single individual is higher than the universal. . . . This position cannot be mediated . . . it is and remains for all eternity a paradox, impervious to thought." Kierkegaard, *Fear and Trembling. (Marburg/Art Resource)*

The story of Abraham contains just such a teleological suspension of the ethical. There is no dearth of keen minds and careful scholars who have found analogies to it. What their wisdom amounts to is the beautiful proposition that basically everything is the same. If one looks more closely, I doubt very much that anyone in the whole wide world will find one single analogy, except for a later one, which proves nothing if it is certain that Abraham represents faith and that it is manifested normatively in him, whose life not only is the most paradoxical that can be thought but is also so paradoxical that it simply cannot be thought. He acts by virtue of the absurd, for it is precisely the absurd that he as the single individual is higher than the universal. This paradox cannot be mediated, for as soon as Abraham begins to do so, he has to confess that he was in a spiritual trial, and if that is the case, he will never sacrifice Isaac, or if he did sacrifice Isaac, then in repentance he must come back to the universal. He gets Isaac back again by virtue of the absurd. Therefore, Abraham is at no time a tragic hero but is something entirely different, either a murderer or a man of faith. Abraham does not have the middle term that saves the tragic hero. This is why I can understand a tragic hero but cannot understand Abraham, even though in a certain demented sense I admire him more than all others.

In ethical terms, Abraham's relation to Isaac is quite simply this: the father shall love the son more than himself. But within its own confines the ethical has various gradations. We shall see whether this story contains any higher expression for the ethical that can ethically explain his behavior, can ethically justify his suspending the ethical obligation to the son, but without moving beyond the teleology of the ethical.

When an enterprise of concern to a whole nation is impeded, when such a project is halted by divine displeasure, when the angry deity sends a dead calm that mocks every effort, when the soothsayer carries out his sad task and announces that the deity demands a young girl as sacrifice—then the father must heroically bring this sacrifice. He must nobly conceal his agony, even though he could wish he were "the lowly man who dares to weep" and not the king who must behave in a kingly manner. Although the lonely agony penetrates his breast and there are only three persons in the whole nation who know his agony, soon the whole nation will be initiated into his agony and also into his deed, that for the welfare of all he will sacrifice her, his daughter, this lovely young girl. O bosom! O fair cheeks, flaxen hair (v. 687). And the daughter's tears will agitate him, and the father will turn away his face, but the hero must raise the knife. And when the news of it reaches the father's house, the beautiful Greek maidens will blush with enthusiasm, and if the daughter was engaged, her betrothed will not be angry but will be proud to share in the father's deed, for the girl belonged more tenderly to him than to the father.

When the valiant judge who in the hour of need saved Israel binds God and himself in one breath by the same promise, he will heroically transform the young maiden's jubilation, the beloved daughter's joy to sorrow, and all Israel will sorrow with her over her virginal youth. But every freeborn man will understand, every resolute woman will admire Jephthah, and every virgin in Israel will wish to behave as his daughter did, because what good would it be for Jephthah to win the victory by means of a promise if he did not keep it—would not the victory be taken away from the people again?

When a son forgets his duty, when the state entrusts the sword of judgment to the father, when the laws demand punishment from the father's hand, then the father must heroically forget that the guilty one is his son, he must nobly hide his agony, but no one in the nation, not even the son, will fail to admire the father, and every time the Roman laws are interpreted, it will be remembered that many interpreted them more learnedly but no one more magnificently than Brutus.

But if Agamemnon, while a favorable wind was taking the fleet under full sail to its destination, had dispatched that messenger who fetched Iphigenia to be sacrificed; if Jephthah, without being bound by any promise that decided the fate of the nation, had said to his daughter: Grieve now for two months over your brief youth, and then I will sacrifice you; if Brutus had had a righteous son and yet had summoned the lictors to put him to death—who would have understood them? If, on being asked why they did this, these three men had answered: It is an ordeal in which we are being tried [forsøges]—would they have been better understood?

When in the crucial moment Agamemnon, Jephthah, and Brutus heroically have overcome the agony, heroically have lost the beloved, and have only to complete the task externally, there will never be a noble soul in the world without tears of compassion for their agony, of admiration for their deed. But if in the crucial moment these three men were to append to the heroic courage with which they bore the agony the little phrase: But it will not happen anyway—who then would understand them? If they went on to explain: This we believe by virtue of the absurd—who would understand them any better, for who would not readily understand that it was absurd, but who would understand that one could then believe it?

The difference between the tragic hero and Abraham is very obvious. The tragic hero is still within the ethical. He allows an expression of the ethical to have its ⟨*telos*⟩ in a higher expression of the ethical; he scales down the ethical relation between father and son or daughter and father to a feeling that has its dialectic in its relation to the idea of moral conduct. Here there can be no question of a teleological suspension of the ethical itself.

Abraham's situation is different. By his act he transgressed the ethical altogether and had a higher ⟨*telos*⟩ outside it, in relation to which he suspended it. For I certainly would like to know how Abraham's act can be related to the universal, whether any point of contact between what Abraham did and the universal can be found other than that Abraham transgressed it. It is not to save a nation, not to uphold the idea of the state that Abraham does it; it is not to appease the angry gods. If it were a matter of the deity's being angry, then he was, after all, angry only with Abraham, and Abraham's act is totally unrelated to the universal, is a purely private endeavor. Therefore, while the tragic hero is great because of his moral virtue, Abraham is great because of a purely personal virtue. There is no higher expression for the ethical in Abraham's life than that the father shall love the son. The ethical in the sense of the moral is entirely beside the point. Insofar as the universal was present, it was cryptically in Isaac, hidden, so to speak, in Isaac's loins, and must cry out with Isaac's mouth: Do not do this, you are destroying everything.

Why, then, does Abraham do it? For God's sake and—the two are wholly identical—for his own sake. He does it for God's sake because God demands this proof of his faith; he does it for his own sake so that he can prove it. The unity of the two is altogether correctly expressed in the word already used to describe this relationship. It is an ordeal, a temptation. A temptation—but what does that mean? As a rule, what tempts a person is something that will hold him back from doing his duty, but here the temptation is the ethical itself, which would hold him back from doing God's will. But what is duty? Duty is simply the expression for God's will.

Here the necessity of a new category for the understanding of Abraham becomes apparent. Paganism does not know such a relationship to the divine. The tragic hero does not enter into any private relationship to the divine, but the ethical is the divine, and thus the paradox therein can be mediated in the universal.

Abraham cannot be mediated; in other words, he cannot speak. As soon as I speak, I express the universal, and if I do not do so, no one can understand me. As soon as Abraham wants to express himself in the universal, he must declare that his situation is a spiritual trial [*Anfægtelse*], for he has no higher expression of the universal that ranks above the universal he violates.

Therefore, although Abraham arouses my admiration, he also appalls me. The person who denies himself and sacrifices himself because of duty gives up the finite in order to grasp the infinite and is adequately assured; the tragic hero gives up the certain for the even more certain, and the observer's eye views him with confidence. But the person who gives up the universal in order to grasp something even higher that is not the universal—what does he do? Is it possible that this can be anything other than a spiritual trial? And if it is possible, but the individual makes a mistake, what salvation is there for him? He suffers all the agony of the tragic hero, he shatters his joy in the world, he renounces everything, and perhaps at the same time he barricades himself from the sublime joy that was so precious to him that he would buy it at any price. The observer cannot understand him at all; neither can his eye rest upon him with confidence. Perhaps the believer's intention cannot be carried out at all, because it is inconceivable. Or if it could be done but the individual has misunderstood the deity—what salvation would there be for him? The tragic hero needs and demands tears, and where is the envious eye so arid that it could not weep with Agamemnon, but where is the soul so gone astray that it has the audacity to weep for Abraham? The tragic hero finishes his task at a specific moment in time, but as time passes he does what is no less significant: he visits the person encompassed by sorrow, who cannot breathe because of his anguished sighs, whose thoughts oppress him, heavy with tears. He appears to him, breaks the witchcraft of sorrow, loosens the bonds, evokes the tears, and the suffering one forgets his own sufferings in those of the tragic hero. One cannot weep over Abraham. One approaches him with a *horror religiosus,* as Israel approached Mount Sinai. What if he himself is distraught, what if he had made a mistake, this lonely man who climbs Mount Moriah, whose peak towers sky-high over the flatlands of Aulis, what if he is not a sleepwalker safely crossing the abyss while the one standing at the foot of the mountain looks up, shakes with anxiety, and then in his deference and horror does not even dare to call to him?—Thanks, once again thanks, to a man who, to a person overwhelmed by life's sorrows and left behind naked, reaches out the words, the leafage of language by which he can conceal his misery. Thanks to you, great Shakespeare, you who can say everything, everything, everything just as it is—and yet, why did you never articulate this torment? Did you perhaps reserve it for yourself, like the beloved's name that one cannot bear to have the world utter, for with his little secret that he cannot divulge the poet buys this power of the word to tell everybody else's dark secrets. A poet is not an apostle; he drives out devils only by the power of the devil.

But if the ethical is teleologically suspended in this manner, how does the single individual in whom it is suspended exist? He exists as the single individual in contrast to the universal. Does he sin, then, for from the point of view of the idea, this is the form of sin. Thus, even though the child does not sin, because it is not conscious of its existence as such, its existence, from the point of view of the idea, is nevertheless sin, and the ethical makes its claim upon it at all times. If it is denied that this form can be repeated in such a way that it is not sin, then judgment has fallen upon Abraham. How did Abraham exist? He had faith. This is the paradox by which he remains at the apex, the paradox that he cannot explain to anyone else, for the paradox is that he as the single individual places himself in an absolute relation to the absolute. Is he justified? Again, his justification is the paradoxical, for if he is, then he is justified not by virtue of being something universal but by virtue of being the single individual.

How does the single individual reassure himself that he is legitimate? It is a simple matter to level all existence to the idea of the state or the idea of a society. If this is done, it is also simple to mediate, for one never comes to the paradox that the single individual as the single individual is higher than the universal, something I can also express symbolically in a statement by Pythagoras to the effect that the odd number is more perfect than the even number. If occasionally there is any response at all these days with regard to the paradox, it is likely to be: One judges it by the result. Aware that he is a paradox who cannot be understood, a hero who has become a ⟨*skandalon*⟩ [offense] to his age will shout confidently to his contemporaries: The result will indeed prove that I was justified. This cry is rarely heard in our age, inasmuch as it does not produce heroes—this is its defect—and it likewise has the advantage that it produces few caricatures. When in our age we hear these words: It will be judged by the result— then we know at once with whom we have the honor of speaking. Those who talk this way are a numerous type whom I shall designate under the common name of assistant professors. With security in life, they live in their thoughts: they have a *permanent* position and a *secure* future in a well-organized state. They have hundreds, yes, even thousands of years between them and the earthquakes of existence; they are not afraid that such things can be repeated, for then what would the police and the newspapers say? Their life task is to judge the great men, judge them according to the result. Such behavior toward greatness betrays a strange mixture of arrogance and wretchedness— arrogance because they feel called to pass judgment, wretchedness because they feel that their lives are in no way allied with the lives of the great. Anyone with even a smattering *erectioris ingenii* [of nobility of nature] never becomes an utterly cold and clammy worm, and when he approaches greatness, he is never devoid of the thought that since the creation of the world it has been customary for the result to come last and that if one is truly going to learn something from greatness one must be particularly aware of the beginning. If the one who is to act wants to judge himself by the result, he will never begin. Although the result may give joy to the entire world, it cannot help the hero, for he would not know the result until the whole thing was over, and he would not become a hero by that but by making a beginning.

Moreover, in its dialectic the result (insofar as it is finitude's response to the infinite question) is altogether incongruous with the hero's existence. Or should Abraham's receiving Isaac by a *marvel* be able to prove that Abraham was justified in relating himself as the single individual to the universal? If Abraham actually had sacrificed Isaac, would he therefore have been less justified?

But we are curious about the result, just as we are curious about the way a book turns out. We do not want to know anything about the anxiety, the distress, the paradox. We carry on an esthetic flirtation with the result. It arrives just as unexpectedly but also just as effortlessly as a prize in a lottery, and when we have heard the result, we have built ourselves up. And yet no manacled robber of churches is so despicable a criminal as the one who plunders holiness in this way, and not even Judas, who sold his Lord for thirty pieces of silver, is more contemptible than someone who peddles greatness in this way.

It is against my very being to speak inhumanly about greatness, to make it a dim and nebulous far-distant shape or to let it be great but devoid of the emergence of the humanness without which it ceases to be great, for it is not what happens to me that makes me great but what I do, and certainly there is no one who believes that someone became great by winning the big lottery prize. A person might have been born in lowly circumstances, but I would still require him not to be so inhuman toward himself that he could imagine the king's castle only at a distance and ambiguously dream of its greatness, and destroy it at the same time he elevates it because he elevated it so basely. I require him to be man enough to tread confidently and with dignity there as well. He must not be so inhuman that he insolently violates everything by barging right off the street into the king's hall—he loses more thereby than the king. On the contrary, he should find a joy in observing every bidding of propriety with a happy and confident enthusiasm, which is precisely what makes him a free spirit. This is merely a metaphor, for that distinction is only a very imperfect expression of the distance of spirit. I require every person not to think so inhumanly of himself that he does not dare to enter those palaces where the memory of the chosen ones lives or even those where they themselves live. He is not to enter rudely and foist his affinity upon them. He is to be happy for every time he bows before them, but he is to be confident, free of spirit, and always more than a charwoman, for if he wants to be no more than that, he will never get in. And the very thing that is going to help him is the anxiety and distress in which the great were tried, for otherwise, if he has any backbone, they will only arouse his righteous envy. And anything that can be great only at a distance, that someone wants to make great with empty and hollow phrases—is destroyed by that very person.

Who was as great in the world as that favored woman, the mother of God, the Virgin Mary? And yet how do we speak of her? That she was the favored one among women does not make her great, and if it would not be so very odd for those who listen to be able to think just as inhumanly as those who speak, then every young girl might ask: Why am I not so favored? And if I had nothing else to say, I certainly would not dismiss such a question as stupid, because, viewed abstractly, vis-à-vis a favor, every person is just as entitled to it as the other. We leave out the distress, the anxiety, the paradox. My thoughts are as pure as anybody's, and he who can think this way surely has pure thoughts, and, if not, he can expect something horrible, for anyone who has once experienced these images cannot get rid of them again, and if he sins against them, they take a terrible revenge in a silent rage, which is more terrifying than the stridency of ten ravenous critics. To be sure, Mary bore the child wondrously, but she nevertheless did it "after the manner of women," and such a time is one of anxiety, distress, and paradox. The angel was indeed a ministering spirit, but he was not a meddlesome spirit who went to the other young maidens in Israel and said: Do not scorn Mary, the extraordinary is happening to her. The angel went only to Mary, and no one could understand her. Has any woman been as infringed upon as was Mary, and is it not true here also that the one whom God blesses he curses in the same breath? This is the spirit's view of Mary, and she is by no means—it is revolting to me to say it but even more so that people have inanely and unctuously made her out to be thus— she is by no means a lady idling in her finery and playing with a divine child. When, despite this, she said: Behold, I am the handmaid of the Lord—then she is great, and I believe it should not be difficult to explain why she became the mother of God. She needs worldly admiration as little as Abraham needs tears, for she was no heroine and he was no hero, but both of them became greater than these, not by being exempted in any way from the distress and the agony and the paradox, but became greater by means of these.

It is great when the poet in presenting his tragic hero for public admiration dares to say: Weep for him, for he deserves it. It is great to deserve the tears of those who deserve to shed tears. It is great that the poet dares to keep the crowd under restraint, dares to discipline men to examine themselves individually to see if they are worthy to weep for the hero, for the slop water of the snivellers is a debasement of the sacred.— But even greater than all this is the knight of faith's daring to say to the noble one who wants to weep for him: Do not weep for me, but weep for yourself.

We are touched, we look back to those beautiful times. Sweet sentimental longing leads us to the goal of our desire, to see Christ walking about in the promised land. We forget the anxiety, the distress, the paradox. Was it such a simple matter not to make a mistake? Was it not terrifying that this man walking around among the others was God? Was it not terrifying to sit down to eat with him? Was it such an easy matter to become an apostle? But the result, the eighteen centuries—that helps, that contributes to this mean deception whereby we deceive ourselves and others. I do not feel brave enough to wish to be contemporary with events like that, but I do not for that reason severely condemn those who made a mistake, nor do I depreciate those who saw what was right.

But I come back to Abraham. During the time before the result, either Abraham was a murderer every minute or we stand before a paradox that is higher than all mediations.

The story of Abraham contains, then, a teleological suspension of the ethical. As the single individual he became higher than the universal. This is the paradox, which cannot be mediated. How he entered into it is just as inexplicable as how he remains in it. If this is not Abraham's situation, then Abraham is not even a tragic hero but a murderer. It is thoughtless to want to go on calling him the father of faith, to speak of it to men who have an interest only in words. A person can become a tragic hero through his own strength—but not the knight of faith. When a person walks what is in one sense the hard road of the tragic hero, there are many who can give him advice, but he who walks the narrow road of faith has no one to advise him—no one understands him. Faith is a marvel, and yet no human being is excluded from it; for that which unites all human life is passion, and faith is a passion.

CONCLUDING UNSCIENTIFIC POSTSCRIPT (in part)

SECTION I, CHAPTER 2: POSSIBLE AND ACTUAL THESES BY LESSING

*   *   *

(A) A logical system can be given; (B) but a system of existence [Tilværelsens System] cannot be given.

(A) A logical system can be given.

α. If, however, a logical system is to be constructed, special care must be taken not to incorporate anything that is subject to the dialectic of existence, accordingly, anything that is [*er*] solely by existing [*være til*] or by having existed [*have været til*], not something that is [*er*] simply by being [*være*]. It follows quite simply that Hegel's matchless and matchlessly admired invention—the importation of movement into logic (not to mention that in every other passage one misses even his own attempt to make one believe that it is there)—simply confuses logic.* It is indeed curious to make

---

*The light-mindedness with which systematicians admit that Hegel has perhaps not been successful everywhere in importing movement into logic, much like the grocer who thinks that a few raisins do not matter when the purchase is large—his farcical docility is, of course, contempt for Hegel that not even his most vehement attacker has allowed himself. There have certainly been logical attempts prior to Hegel, but his method is everything. For him and for everyone who has intelligence enough to comprehend what it means to will something great, the absence of it at this or that point cannot be a trivial matter, as when a grocer and a customer bicker about whether there is a little underweight or overweight. Hegel himself has staked his whole reputation on the point of the method. But a method possesses the peculiar quality that, viewed abstractly, it is nothing at all; it is a method precisely in the process of being carried out; in being carried out it is a method, and where it is not carried out, it is not a method, and if there is no other method, there is no method at all. To turn Hegel into a rattlebrain must be reserved for his admirers; an attacker will always know how to honor him for having willed something great and having failed to achieve it.

Søren Kierkegaard, *Concluding Unscientific Postscript*, Section I, Chapter 2, "Possible and Actual Theses by Lessing"; Section II, Chapter 2, "Subjective Truth, Inwardness; Truth is Subjectivity," edited and translated by Howard V. Hong and Edna H. Hong (Princeton, NJ: Princeton University Press). Copyright © 1992 by Princeton University Press. Reprinted by permission of Princeton University Press.

movement the basis in a sphere in which movement is inconceivable or to have movement explain logic, whereas logic cannot explain movement.

On this point, however, I am very happy to be able to refer to a man who thinks soundly and fortunately is educated by the Greeks (rare qualities in our age!); a man who has known how to extricate himself and his thought from every trailing, groveling relation to Hegel, from whose fame everyone usually seeks to profit, if in no other way, then by going further, that is, by having absorbed Hegel; a man who has preferred to be content with Aristotle and with himself—I mean Trendlenburg (*Logische Untersuchungen*). One of his merits is that he comprehended movement as the inexplicable presupposition, as the common denominator in which being and thinking are united, and as their continued reciprocity. I cannot attempt here to show the relation of his conception to the Greeks, to Aristotelian thought, or to what, oddly enough, although in a popular sense only, bears a certain resemblance to his presentation: a small section in Plutarch's work on Isis and Osiris. It is by no means my view that Hegelian philosophy has not had a salutary influence on Trendlenburg, but it is fortunate that he has perceived that wanting to improve Hegel's structure, to go further etc., will not do (a mendacious approach by which many a botcher in our age arrogates Hegel's celebrity to himself and mendicantly fraternizes with him); on the other hand, it is fortunate that Trendlenburg, sober like a Greek thinker, without promising everything and without claiming to beatify all humankind, does indeed accomplish much and beatifies whoever would need his guidance in learning about the Greeks.

In a logical system, nothing may be incorporated that has a relation to existence, that is not indifferent to existence. The infinite advantage that the logical, by being the objective, possesses over all other thinking is in turn, subjectively viewed, restricted by its being a hypothesis, simply because it is indifferent to existence understood as actuality. This duplexity distinguishes the logical from the mathematical, which has no relation whatever toward or from existence [*Tilværelse*] but has only objectivity—not objectivity and the hypothetical as unity and contradiction in which it is negatively related to existence [*Existents*].

The logical system must not be a mystification, a ventriloquism, in which the content of existence [*Tilværelse*] emerges cunningly and surreptitiously, where logical thought is startled and finds what the Herr Professor or the licentiate has had up his sleeve. Judging between the two can be done more sharply by answering the question: In what sense is a category an abbreviation of existence, whether logical thinking is abstract after existence or abstract without any relation to existence. I would like to treat this question a little more extensively elsewhere, and even if it is not adequately answered, it is always something to have inquired about it in this way.

β. The dialectic of the beginning must be clarified. The almost amusing thing about it, that the beginning is and then in turn is not, because it is the beginning—this true dialectical remark has long enough been like a game that has been played in Hegelian society.

The system, so it is said, begins with the immediate; some, failing to be dialectical, are even oratorical enough to speak of the most immediate of all, although the comparative reflection contained here might indeed become dangerous for the beginning.*

---

*To show how would become too prolix here. Frequently it is not worth the trouble either, because, after a person has laboriously advanced an objection sharply, from a philosopher's rejoinder he discovers that his misunderstanding was not that he could not understand the idolized philosophy but rather that he had allowed himself to be persuaded to believe that the whole thing was supposed to be something—and not flabby thinking concealed by the most overbearing expressions.

The system begins with the immediate and therefore without presuppositions and therefore absolutely, that is, the beginning of the system is the absolute beginning. This is entirely correct and has indeed also been adequately admired. But why, then, before the system is begun, has that other equally important, definitely equally important, question not been clarified and its clear implications honored: *How does the system begin with the immediate, that is, does it begin with it immediately?* The answer to this must certainly be an unconditional no. If the system is assumed to be after existence (whereby a confusion with a system of existence is created), the system does indeed come afterward and consequently does not begin immediately with the immediate with which existence began, even though in another sense existence did not begin with it, because the immediate never is but is annulled when it is. The beginning of the system that begins with the immediate *is then itself achieved through reflection.*

Here is the difficulty, for if one does not let go of this one thought, deceptively or thoughtlessly or in breathless haste to have the system finished, this thought in all its simplicity is capable of deciding that there can be no system of existence and that a logical system must not boast of an absolute beginning, because such a beginning is just like pure being, a pure chimera.

In other words, if a beginning cannot be made immediately with the immediate (which would then be conceived as a fortuitous event or a miracle, that is, which would mean not to think), but this beginning must be achieved through reflection, then the question arises very simply (alas, if only I am not put in the doghouse on account of my simplicity, because everyone can understand my question—and consequently must feel ashamed of the questioner's popular knowledge): How do I bring to a halt the reflection set in motion in order to reach that beginning? Reflection has the notable quality of being infinite. But being infinite must in any case mean that it cannot stop of its own accord, because in stopping itself it indeed uses itself and can be stopped only in the same way as a sickness is cured if it is itself allowed to prescribe the remedy, that is, the sickness is promoted. Perhaps this infinity of reflection is the bad or spurious infinity. In that case, we are indeed almost finished, since the spurious infinity is reputedly something despicable that one must give up, the sooner the better. In that connection, may I not ask a question: How is it that Hegel and all Hegelians, who are generally supposed to be dialecticians, at this point become angry, yes, as angry as Germans? Or is "spurious" a dialectical qualification? From where does such a predicate enter logic? How do scorn and contempt and ways of frightening find a place as legitimate means of movement within logic, so that the absolute beginning is assumed by the individual because he is afraid of what his neighbors on all sides will think of him if he does not do it? Is not "spurious" an ethical category?*

What do I mean by speaking of the spurious infinity? I am charging the individual in question with not willing to stop the infinity of reflection. Am I requiring something of him, then? But on the other hand, in a genuinely speculative way, I assume that reflection stops of its own accord. Why, then, do I require something of him? And what do I require of him? I require a resolution. And in that I am right, for only in that way can reflection be stopped. But, on the other hand, it is never right for a philosopher to make sport of people and at one moment have reflection stop of its own accord in the absolute beginning and at the next moment taunt someone who has only one flaw,

---

*And if it is not that, it is in any case an esthetic category, as when Plutarch states that some have assumed one world because they feared that otherwise the result would be an unlimited and embarrassing infinity of worlds ⟨*euthus aoristou kai ksalepas apeirias hypolambanousas*⟩. (*De defectu oraculorum,* XXII).

that he is obtuse enough to believe the first, taunt him so as to help him in this fashion to the absolute beginning, which then occurs in two ways. But if a resolution is required, presuppositionlessness is abandoned. The beginning can occur only when reflection is stopped, and reflection can be stopped only by something else, and this something else is something altogether different from the logical, since it is a resolution. Only when the beginning, at which point reflection comes to a halt, is a breakthrough, so that the absolute beginning itself breaks forth through the endlessly perpetuated reflection—only then is the beginning presuppositionless. But if it is a break whereby reflection is broken off in order that the beginning can emerge, then this beginning is not absolute, since it has occurred by a ⟨*metabasis eis allo genos*⟩ [shifting from one genus to another].

When a beginning with the immediate is achieved by reflection, the immediate must mean something different from what it usually does. Hegelian logicians have correctly discerned this, and therefore they define the immediate, with which logic begins, as follows: the most abstract remainder after an exhaustive abstraction. There is no objection to this definition, but it is certainly objectionable that they do not respect what they themselves are saying, inasmuch as this definition indirectly states that there is no absolute beginning. "How is that?" I hear someone say. "When one has abstracted from everything, is there not then, etc.?" Indeed, *when* one has abstracted from everything. Let us be human beings. Like the act of reflection, this act of abstraction is infinite; so how do I bring it to a halt—and it is indeed first when . . . that . . . Let us even venture an imaginary construction in thought. Let that act of infinite abstraction be *in actu* [in actuality]; the beginning is not an act of abstraction but comes afterward. But then with what do I begin, now that there has been an abstraction from everything? Alas, at this point a Hegelian, deeply moved, perhaps would collapse on my chest and blissfully stammer: With nothing. And this is precisely what the system declares—that it begins with nothing. But I must pose my second question: How do I begin with this nothing? If, namely, the act of infinite abstraction is not the kind of trick of which two can very well be done at the same time, if, on the contrary, it is the most strenuous work that can be done—what then? Then all my strength will go into maintaining it. If I do not use all my strength, I do not abstract from everything. If, then, on this presupposition I make a beginning, I do not begin with nothing, simply because at the moment of beginning I did not abstract from everything. This means that if it is possible for a human being, thinking, to abstract from everything, it is impossible for him to do more, since this act, provided that it does not surpass human strength altogether, in any case completely exhausts it. To become tired of the act of abstraction and thus to manage to begin is only an explanation befitting grocers, who are not particular about a little irregularity.

The expression "to begin with nothing," even apart from its relation to the infinite act of abstraction, is itself deceptive. That is, to begin with nothing is neither more nor less than a new paraphrasing of the very dialectic of beginning. The beginning is and in turn is not, simply because it is the beginning, something that can also be expressed in this way: the beginning begins with nothing. It is merely a new expression, not a single step ahead. In the one instance, I only think a beginning *in abstracto;* in the other instance, I think the relation of the equally abstract beginning to a something with which a beginning is made. Now it is quite properly manifest that this something, indeed, the only something that corresponds to such a beginning, is nothing. But this is merely a tautological paraphrasing of the second thesis: the beginning is not. "The beginning is not" and "the beginning begins with nothing" are altogether identical theses, and I do not move from the spot.

What if, rather than speaking or dreaming of an absolute beginning, we speak of a leap? To want to be satisfied with a "mostly," an "as good as," a "one can almost say that," an "if you sleep on it until tomorrow, you may well say that" merely shows that one is related to Trop, who little by little went so far as to assume that having almost taken the bar examination was the same as having taken it. Everyone laughs at this, but when one chatters speculatively in the same manner in the realm of truth, in the shrine of science and scholarship, then it is good philosophy—genuine speculative philosophy. Lessing was no speculative philosopher; therefore he assumed the opposite, that an infinitely little distance makes the ditch infinitely broad, because the leap itself makes the ditch that broad.

It is very odd—the Hegelians, who in logic know that reflection is stopped by itself and that doubting everything flips over into its opposite by itself (a true sailor's yarn, that is, truly a sailor's yarn), know for daily use, however, when they are pleasant people, when they are like the rest of us (only more learned and gifted etc., something I shall always be willing to admit)—they know that reflection can be stopped only by a leap. Let us dwell on this point for a moment. If the individual does not stop reflection, he will be infinitized in reflection, that is, no decision is made.* By thus going astray in reflection, the individual really becomes objective, more and more he loses the decision of subjectivity and the return into himself. Yet it is assumed that reflection can stop itself objectively, whereas it is just the other way around; reflection cannot be stopped objectively, and when it is stopped subjectively, it does not stop of its own accord, but it is the subject who stops it.

For example, as soon as Rötscher (who in his book on Aristophanes does indeed understand the necessity of transition in the world-historical development, and who in the realm of logic must have understood the passage of reflection through itself to the absolute beginning) sets himself the task of interpreting Hamlet, he knows that reflection is stopped only by a resolution. He does not assume (shall I say "oddly enough"?), oddly enough, he does not assume that Hamlet finally arrived at the absolute beginning by continuing to reflect; but in logic he assumes (shall I say "oddly enough"?), oddly enough, there he most likely assumes that the passage of reflection through itself comes to a halt at the absolute beginning. This I do not understand, and it pains me not to understand it, because I have admiration for Rötscher's talent, for his classical education, for his esthetically sensitive and yet primitive conception of psychological phenomena.

What has been said here about a beginning in logic (that the same thing shows that there is no system of existence will be pursued in detail in b) is very plain and simple. I am almost embarrassed to say it or embarrassed to have to say it, embarrassed because of my situation—that a poor pamphlet writer, who would rather be worshiping on his knees before the system, should be constrained to say such a thing. What has been said could be stated in yet another way whereby it would perhaps make an impression on someone or other because the presentation would recall more specifically the scholarly disputes in the past. It would then become a question of the importance of the Hegelian phenomenology for the system, whether it is an introduction, whether it remains outside, and if it is an introduction, whether it is in turn incorporated in the system; further, whether Hegel may not even have the amazing merit of having written not only the system but two or even three systems, which always takes a matchless

---

*Perhaps the reader will recall that when the issue becomes objective, there is no question of an eternal happiness, because this lies precisely in subjectivity and in decision.

systematic head, and which nevertheless seems to be the case, since the system is completed more than once etc. Actually, all this has been said often enough, but frequently it has also been said in a confusing way. A large book has been written about it. First everything is said that Hegel has said, and thereafter consideration is given to this or that later addition, all of which merely diverts attention and shrouds in distracting prolixity what can be stated very briefly.

γ. In order to shed light on logic, it might be desirable to become oriented psychologically in the state of mind of someone who thinks the logical—what kind of dying to oneself is required for that purpose, and to what extent the imagination plays a part in it. The following is again another meager and very simple comment, but it may be quite true and not at all superfluous: a philosopher has gradually come to be such a marvelous creature that not even the most prodigal imagination has invented anything quite so fabulous. How, if at all, is the empirical *I* related to the pure *I–I*? Whoever wants to be a philosopher will certainly also want to be somewhat informed on this point and above all not want to become a ludicrous creature by being transmogrified— *eins, zwei, drei, kokolorum* [one, two, three, hocus pocus]—into speculative thought. If the person occupied with logical thought is also human enough not to forget that he is an existing individual, even if he has finished the system, the fantasticality and the charlatanry will gradually vanish. And even though it takes an eminently logical head to recast Hegel's logic, only sound common sense is needed for the person who at one time enthusiastically believed in the great thing Hegel claimed to have done and who demonstrated his enthusiasm by believing [*tro*] it, and his enthusiasm for Hegel by crediting [*tiltro*] him with it—and it takes only sound common sense to perceive that in many places Hegel behaved irresponsibly—not toward grocers, who believe only half of what a person says anyway, but toward enthusiastic youths who believed him. Even if such a young person was not exceptionally and splendidly endowed, yet when he has had the enthusiasm to believe the highest, as attributed to Hegel, when he has had the enthusiasm to despair over himself in a dubious moment in order not to abandon Hegel—when such a young person comes to himself again, he has a right to demand the nemesis of having laughter consume in Hegel what laughter may legitimately claim as its own. And such a young person has indeed vindicated Hegel in a way much different from that of many an adherent who in deceptive asides would now make Hegel everything, now a trifle.

(B) A system of existence cannot be given.

A system of existence [*Tilværelsens System*] cannot be given. Is there, then, not such a system? That is not at all the case. Neither is this implied in what has been said. Existence itself is a system—for God, but it cannot be a system for any existing [*bexis-terende*] spirit. System and conclusiveness correspond to each other, but existence is the very opposite. Abstractly viewed, system and existence cannot be thought conjointly, because in order to think existence, systematic thought must think it as annulled and consequently not as existing. Existence is the spacing that holds apart; the systematic is the conclusiveness that combines.

Actually there now develops a deception, an illusion, which *Fragments* has attempted to point out. I must now refer to this work, namely, to the question of whether the past is more necessary than the future. That is, when an existence is a thing of the past, it is indeed finished, it is indeed concluded, and to that extent it is turned over to the systematic view. Quite so—but for whom? Whoever is himself existing cannot gain this conclusiveness outside existence, a conclusiveness that corresponds to the eternity into which the past has entered. Even if a good-natured thinker is so absent-minded as to forget that he himself is existing, speculative thought and absentmindedness are still not quite the same thing. On the contrary, that he himself is existing implies the claim of existence upon him and that his existence, yes, if he is a great individual, that his existence at the present time may, as past, in turn have the validity of conclusiveness for a systematic thinker. But who, then, is this systematic thinker? Well, it is he who himself is outside existence and yet in existence, who in his eternity is forever concluded and yet includes existence within himself—it is God. So why the deception! Just because the world has lasted now for six thousand years, does existence therefore not have the very same claim upon the existing individual that it has always had, which is not that he in make-believe should be a contemplating spirit but that he in actuality should be an existing spirit. All understanding comes afterward. Whereas an individual existing now undeniably comes afterward in relation to the six thousand years that preceded, the curiously ironic consequence would emerge—if we assumed that he came to understand them systematically—that he would not come to understand himself as an existing being, because he himself would acquire no existence, because he himself would have nothing that should be understood afterward. It follows that such a thinker must be either the good Lord or a fantastical *quodlibet* [anything]. Certainly everyone will perceive the immorality in this, and certainly everyone will also perceive that what another author has observed regarding the Hegelian system is entirely in order: that through Hegel a system, the absolute system, was brought to completion—without having an ethics. By all means, let us smile at the ethical-religious fantasies of the Middle Ages in asceticism and the like, but above all let us not forget that the speculative, farcical exaggeration of becoming an *I–I*—and then *qua* human being often such a philistine that no enthusiast would have cared to lead such a life—is equally ludicrous.

So let us ask very simply, as a Greek youth would ask his master (and if the lofty wisdom can explain everything else but cannot answer a simple question, one surely sees that the world is out of joint), about the impossibility of a system of existence: Who is supposed to write or finish such a system? Surely a human being, unless we are to resume the peculiar talk about a human being's becoming speculative thought, a subject-object. Consequently, a human being—and surely a living, that is, an existing, human being. Or if the speculative thought that produces the system is the joint effort of these various thinkers, in what final conclusion does this fellowship combine? How does it come to light? Surely through a human being? And how, in turn, do the individual thinkers relate themselves to this effort; what are the middle terms between the particular and the world-historical; and in turn what sort of being is the one who is stringing it all on the systematic thread? Is he a human being or is he speculative thought? But if he is a human being, then he is indeed existing. Now, all in all, there are two ways for an existing individual: either he can do everything to forget that he is existing and thereby manage to become comic (the comic contradiction of wanting to be what one is not, for example, that a human being wants to be a bird is no more comic than the contradiction of not wanting to be what one is, as *in casu* [in this case] an existing individual, just as in the use of language it is comic when someone forgets his name, which signifies not so much forgetting his name as the singularity of his nature), because existence possesses the remarkable quality that an existing person exists whether he wants to or not; or he can direct all his attention to his existing. It is from this side that an objection must first be made to modern speculative thought, that it has not a false presupposition but a comic presupposition, occasioned by its having forgotten in a kind of world-historical absentmindedness what it means to be a human being, not what it means to be human in general, for even speculators might be swayed to consider that sort of thing, but what it means that we, you and I and he, are human beings, each one on his own.

The existing individual who directs all his attention to the actuality that he is existing will approvingly look upon those words of Lessing about a continued striving as a beautiful saying, not as something that gained its author immortal fame, because the saying is so very simple, but as something every attentive person must certify. The existing individual who forgets that he is existing will become more and more absentminded, and just as people occasionally set down the fruits of their *otium* [leisure] in books, so we may expect the expected existential system as the fruit of his absentmindedness—well, not all of us, but only those who are as absentminded as he is. Whereas the Hegelian system in absentmindedness goes ahead and becomes a system of existence, and what is more, is finished—without having an ethics (the very home of existence), that other simpler philosophy, presented by an existing individual for existing individuals, is especially intent upon advancing the ethical.

As soon as it is remembered that philosophizing is not speaking fantastically to fantastical beings but speaking to existing individuals, consequently that a decision about whether a continued striving is somewhat inferior to systematic conclusiveness is not to be made fantastically *in abstracto,* but that the question is what existing beings have to be satisfied with insofar as they are existing—then the continued striving will be unique in not involving illusion. Even if a person has achieved the highest, the repetition by which he must indeed fill out his existence, if he is not to go backward (or become a fantastical being), will again be a continued striving, because here in turn the conclusiveness is moved ahead and postponed. This is just like the Platonic conception of love; it is a want, and not only does that person feel a want who craves something he does not have but also that person who desires the continued possession of what he has. In the system and in the fifth act of the drama, one has a positive conclusiveness speculatively-fantastically and esthetically-fantastically, but such a conclusiveness is only for fantastical beings.

The continued striving is the expression of the existing subject's ethical lifeview. The continued striving must therefore not be understood metaphysically, but neither is there any individual who exists metaphysically. Thus through a misunderstanding a contrast could be drawn between systematic conclusiveness and the continued striving for truth. One might then be able, and perhaps has even tried, to bear in mind the Greek notion of continually wanting to be a learner. But that is only a misunderstanding in this sphere. On the contrary, ethically understood, the continued striving is the consciousness of being an existing individual, and the continued learning the expression of the perpetual actualization, which at no moment is finished as long as the subject is existing; the subject is aware of this and is therefore not deluded. But Greek philosophy had a continual relation to ethics. That was why continually wanting to be a learner was not regarded as a great discovery or the inspired undertaking of an exceptional individual, since it was neither more nor less than the understanding that one is existing and that to be conscious of this is no merit but to forget it is thoughtlessness.

So-called pantheistic systems have frequently been cited and attacked by saying that they cancel freedom and the distinction between good and evil. This is perhaps expressed just as definitely by saying that every such system fantastically volatilizes the concept *existence.* But this should be said not only of pantheistic systems, for it would have been better to show that every system must be pantheistic simply because of the conclusiveness. Existence must be annulled in the eternal before the system concludes itself. No existing remainder may be left behind, not even such a tiny little dingle-dangle as the existing Herr Professor who is writing the system. But the issue is not presented this way. No, the pantheistic systems are contested, partly with tumultuous aphorisms that again and again promise a new system, partly with a compilation that is supposed to be a system and has a separate paragraph in which it is declared that emphasis is placed on the concepts "existence" and "actuality." That such a paragraph mocks the entire system, that instead of being a paragraph in the system it is an absolute protest against the system, is of no consequence to busy systematic triflers. If the concept of existence is actually to be emphasized, this cannot be stated directly in a paragraph in a system, and all direct oaths and "the devil take me" only make the didacticizing upside-downness even more ludicrous. That existence is actually emphasized must be expressed in an essential form, and in relation to the illusiveness of existence this is an indirect form—that there is no system. Yet this must not in turn become a reassuring standardized formula, because the indirect expression will always be regenerated in the form. In committee deliberations, it is quite all right to include a dissenting vote, but a system that has a dissenting vote as a paragraph within it is a queer monstrosity. No wonder, then, that the system survives. It proudly ignores objections; and if it comes across a particular objection that appears to draw a little attention, the systematic entrepreneurs proceed to have a copyist make a copy of the objection, which is thereupon recorded in the system, and with the bookbinding the system is finished.

The systematic idea is subject-object, is the unity of thinking and being; existence, on the other hand, is precisely the separation. From this it by no means follows that existence is thoughtless, but existence has spaced and does space subject from object, thought from being. Objectively understood, thinking is pure thinking, which just as abstractly-objectively corresponds to its object, which in turn is therefore itself, and truth is the correspondence of thinking with itself. This objective thinking has no relation to the existing subjectivity, and while the difficult question always remains—namely, how the existing subject gains entrance into this objectivity in which subjectivity is pure abstract subjectivity (which again is an objective qualification and does not signify any existing human being)—it is certain that the existing subjectivity evaporates more and more. And finally, if it is possible that a human being can become such a thing and that all this is not something of which he at best can become cognizant through imagination, this existing subjectivity becomes a pure abstract co-knowledge [*Medviden*] in and knowledge of this pure relation between thinking and being, this pure identity, indeed this tautology, because here being does not mean that the thinking person is, but basically only that he is a thinker.

The existing subject, however, is existing, and so indeed is every human being. Yet let us not do the wrong of calling the objective tendency impious, pantheistic self-worship but rather view it as a venture in the comic, because the idea that from now on to the end of the world nothing should be said except what would suggest a further improvement in a nearly finished system is simply a systematic consequence for systematizers.

By beginning straightway with ethical categories against the objective tendency, one does wrong and fails to hit the mark, because one has nothing in common with the attacked. But by remaining within the metaphysical, one can employ the comic, which also is in the metaphysical sphere, in order to overtake such a transfigured professor. If a dancer could leap very high, we would admire him, but if he wanted to give the impression that he could fly—even though he could leap higher than any dancer had ever leapt before—let laughter overtake him. Leaping means to belong essentially to the earth and to respect the law of gravity so that the leap is merely the momentary, but flying means to be set free from telluric conditions, something that is reserved exclusively for winged creatures, perhaps also for inhabitants of the moon, perhaps—and perhaps that is also where the system will at long last find its true readers. To be a human being has been abolished, and every speculative thinker confuses himself with humankind, whereby he becomes something infinitely great and nothing at all. In absentmindedness, he confuses himself with humankind, just as the opposition press uses "we" and the skippers say "the devil take me." But having cursed for a long time, one finally returns to the direct statement, because all swearing cancels itself; and when one has learned that every urchin can say "we," one learns that it nevertheless means a little more to be one; and when one sees that every cellar dweller can play the game of being humankind, one finally perceives that to be simply and solely a human being means something more than playing party games this way. And one thing more—when a cellar dweller plays this game, everyone thinks it ludicrous; and yet it is just as ludicrous when the greatest human being does it. And in that regard one may laugh at him and, as is fitting, still have respect for his abilities, his learning, etc.

Section II, Chapter 2: Subjective Truth, Inwardness; Truth Is Subjectivity

Whether truth is defined more empirically as the agreement of thinking with being or more idealistically as the agreement of being with thinking, the point in each case is to pay scrupulous attention to what is understood by being and also to pay attention to whether the knowing human spirit might not be lured out into the indefinite and fantastically become something such as no *existing* human being has ever been or can be, a phantom with which the individual busies himself on occasion, yet without ever making it explicit to himself by means of dialectical middle terms how he gets out into this fantastical realm, what meaning it has for him to be there, whether the entire endeavor out there might not dissolve into a tautology within a rash, fantastical venture.

If, in the two definitions given, being is understood as empirical being, then truth itself is transformed into a *desideratum* [something wanted] and everything is placed in the process of becoming, because the empirical object is not finished, and the existing knowing spirit is itself in the process of becoming. Thus truth is an approximating whose beginning cannot be established absolutely, because there is no conclusion that has retroactive power. On the other hand, every beginning, when it is *made* (if it is not arbitrariness by not being conscious of this), does not occur by virtue of immanental thinking but is made by virtue of a resolution, essentially by virtue of faith. That the knowing spirit is an existing spirit, and that every human being is such a spirit existing for himself, I cannot repeat often enough, because the fantastical disregard of this has been the cause of much confusion. May no one misunderstand me. I am indeed a poor existing spirit like all other human beings, but if in a legitimate and honest way I could be assisted in becoming something extraordinary, the pure *I–I*, I would always be willing to give thanks for the gift and the good deed. If, however, it can occur only in the way mentioned earlier, by saying *eins, zwei, drei, kokolorum* or by tying a ribbon around the little finger and throwing it away in some remote place when the moon is full—then I would rather remain what I am, a poor existing individual human being.

The term "being" in those definitions must, then, be understood much more abstractly as the abstract rendition or the abstract prototype of what being *in concreto* is as empirical being. If it is understood in this way, nothing stands in the way of abstractly defining truth as something finished, because, viewed abstractly, the agreement between thinking and being is always finished, inasmuch as the beginning of the process of becoming lies precisely in the concretion that abstraction abstractly disregards.

But if being is understood in this way, the formula is a tautology; that is, thinking and being signify one and the same, and the agreement spoken of is only an abstract identity with itself. Therefore, none of the formulas says more than that truth is, if this is understood in such a way that the copula is accentuated—truth *is*—that is, truth is a redoubling. Truth is the first, but truth's other, that it *is*, is the same as the first; this, its being, is the abstract form of truth. In this way it is expressed that truth is not something simple but in an entirely abstract sense a redoubling, which is nevertheless canceled at the very same moment.

Abstraction may go on by paraphrasing this as much as it pleases—it will never come any further. As soon as the being of truth becomes empirically concrete, truth itself is in the process of becoming and is indeed in turn, by intimation, the agreement between thinking and being, and is indeed actually that way for God, but it is not that way for any existing spirit, because this spirit, itself existing, is in the process of becoming.

For the existing spirit *qua* existing spirit, the question about truth persists, because the abstract answer is only for that *abstractum* which an existing spirit becomes by abstracting from himself *qua* existing, which he can do only momentarily, although at such moments he still pays his debt to existence by existing nevertheless. Consequently, it is an existing spirit who asks about truth, presumably because he wants to exist in it, but in any case the questioner is conscious of being an existing individual human being. In this way I believe I am able to make myself understandable to every Greek and to every rational human being. If a German philosopher follows his inclination to put on an act and first transforms himself into a super-rational something, just as alchemists and sorcerers bedizen themselves fantastically, in order to answer the question about truth in an extremely satisfying way, this is of no more concern to me than his satisfying answer, which no doubt is extremely satisfying—if one is fantastically dressed up. But whether a German philosopher is or is not doing this can easily be ascertained by anyone who with enthusiasm concentrates his soul on willing to allow himself to be guided by a sage of that kind, and uncritically just uses his guidance compliantly by willing to form his existence according to it. When a person as a learner enthusiastically relates in this way to such a German professor, he accomplishes the most superb epigram upon him, because a speculator of that sort is anything but served by a learner's honest and enthusiastic zeal for expressing and accomplishing, for existentially appropriating his wisdom, since this wisdom is something that the Herr Professor himself has imagined and has written books about but has never attempted himself. It has not even occurred to him that it should be done. Like the customs clerk who, in the belief that his business was merely to write, wrote what he himself could not read, so there are speculative thinkers who merely write, and write that which, if it is to be read with the aid of action, if I may put it that way, proves to be nonsense, unless it is perhaps intended only for fantastical beings.

When for the existing spirit *qua* existing there is a question about truth, that abstract reduplication of truth recurs; but existence itself, existence itself in the questioner, who does indeed exist, holds the two factors apart, one from the other, and reflection shows two relations. To objective reflection, truth becomes something objective, an object, and the point is to disregard the subject. To subjective reflection, truth becomes appropriation, inwardness, subjectivity, and the point is to immerse oneself, existing, in subjectivity.

But what then? Are we to remain in this disjunction, or does mediation offer its kind assistance here, so that truth becomes subject-object? Why not? But can mediation then help the existing person so that he himself, as long as he is existing, becomes mediation, which is, after all, *sub specie aeterni,* whereas the poor existing one is existing? It certainly does not help to make a fool of a person, to entice him with the subject-object when he himself is prevented from entering into the state in which he can relate himself to it, prevented because he himself, by virtue of existing, is in the process of becoming. Of what help is it to explain how the eternal truth is to be understood eternally when the one to use the explanation is prevented from understanding it in this way because he is existing and is merely a fantast if he fancies himself to be *sub specie aeterni,* consequently when he must avail himself precisely of the explanation of how the eternal truth is to be understood in the category of time by someone who by existing is himself in time, something the honored professor himself admits, if not always, then every three months when he draws his salary.

With the subject-object of mediation, we have merely reverted to abstraction, inasmuch as the definition of truth as subject-object is exactly the same as: the truth is, that is, the truth is a redoubling. Consequently, the exalted wisdom has again been absentminded enough to forget that it was an existing spirit who asked about truth. Or is perhaps the existing spirit himself the subject-object? In that case, I am obliged to ask: Where is such an existing human being who is also a subject-object? Or shall we perhaps here again first transmute the existing spirit into a something in general and then explain everything except what was asked about: How an existing subject *in concreto* relates himself to the truth, or what then must be asked about: How the individual existing subject then relates himself to this something that seems to have not a little in common with a paper kite or with the lump of sugar that the Dutch used to hang from the ceiling and everyone would lick.

We return, then, to the two ways of reflection and have not forgotten that it is an existing spirit who is asking, simply an individual human being, and are not able to forget, either, that his existing is precisely what will prevent him from going both ways at once, and his concerned questions will prevent him from light-mindedly and fantastically becoming a subject-object. Now, then, which of the ways is the way of truth for the existing spirit? Only the fantastical *I-I* is simultaneously finished with both ways or advances methodically along both ways simultaneously, which for an existing human being is such an inhuman way of walking that I dare not recommend it.

Since the questioner specifically emphasizes that he is an existing person, the way to be commended is naturally the one that especially accentuates what it means to exist.

The way of objective reflection turns the subjective individual into something accidental and thereby turns existence into an indifferent, vanishing something. The way to the objective truth goes away from the subject, and while the subject and subjectivity become indifferent, the truth also becomes indifferent, and that is precisely its objective validity, because the interest, just like the decision, is subjectivity. The way of objective reflection now leads to abstract thinking, to mathematics, to historical knowledge of various kinds, and always leads away from the subjective individual, whose existence or nonexistence becomes, from an objective point of view, altogether properly, infinitely indifferent, altogether properly, because, as Hamlet says, existence and nonexistence have only subjective significance. At its maximum, this way will lead to a contradiction, and to the extent that the subject does not become totally indifferent to himself, this is merely an indication that his objective striving is not objective enough. At its maximum, it will lead to the contradiction that only objectivity has come about, whereas subjectivity has gone out, that is, the existing subjectivity that has made an attempt to become what in the abstract sense is called subjectivity, the abstract form of an abstract objectivity. And yet, viewed subjectively, the objectivity that has come about is at its maximum either a hypothesis or an approximation, because all eternal decision is rooted specifically in subjectivity.

But the objective way is of the opinion that it has a security that the subjective way does not have (of course, existence, what it means to exist, and objective security cannot be thought together). It is of the opinion that it avoids a danger that lies in wait for the subjective way, and at its maximum this danger is madness. In a solely subjective definition of truth, lunacy and truth are ultimately indistinguishable, because they may both have inwardness.* But one does not become lunatic by becoming objective. At this point I might perhaps add a little comment that does not seem superfluous in an objective age. Is the absence of inwardness also lunacy? The objective truth as such does not at all decide that the one stating it is sensible; on the contrary, it can even betray that the man is lunatic, although what he says is entirely true and especially objectively true.

I shall here allow myself to relate an incident that, without any modification whatever by me, comes directly from a madhouse. A patient in such an institution wants to run away and actually carries out his plan by jumping through a window. He now finds himself in the garden of the institution and wishes to take to the road of freedom. Then it occurs to him (shall I say that he was sagacious enough or lunatic enough to have this whimsical idea?): When you arrive in the city, you will be recognized and will very likely be taken back right away. What you need to do, then, is to convince everyone completely, by the objective truth of what you say, that all is well as far as your sanity is concerned. As he is walking along and pondering this, he sees a skittle ball lying on the ground. He picks it up and puts it in the tail of his coat. At every step he takes, this ball bumps him, if you please, on his r——, and every time it bumps him he says, "Boom! The earth is round." He arrives in the capital city and immediately visits one of his friends. He wants to convince him that he is not lunatic and therefore paces up and down the floor and continually says, "Boom! The earth is round!" But is the earth not round? Does the madhouse demand yet another sacrifice on account of this assumption, as in those days when everyone assumed it to be as flat as a pancake? Or is he lunatic, the man who hopes to prove that he is not lunatic by stating a truth universally accepted and universally regarded as objective? And yet, precisely by this it became clear to the physician that the patient was not yet cured, although the cure certainly could not revolve around getting him to assume that the earth is flat. But not everyone is a physician, and the demand of the times has considerable influence on the question of lunacy. Now and then, one would indeed almost be tempted to assume that the modern age, which has modernized Christianity, has also modernized Pilate's question, and that the need of the age to find something in which to repose declares itself in the question: What is lunacy? When an assistant professor, every time his coat-

---

*Even this is not true, however, because madness never has the inwardness of infinity. Its fixed idea is a kind of objective something, and the contradiction of madness lies in wanting to embrace it with passion. The decisive factor in madness is thus not the subjective, but the little finitude that becomes fixed, something the infinite can never become.

tail reminds him to say something, says *de omnibus dubitandum est* [everything must be doubted] and briskly writes away on a system in which there is sufficient internal evidence in every other sentence that the man has never doubted anything—he is not considered lunatic.

Don Quixote is the prototype of the subjective lunacy in which the passion of inwardness grasps a particular fixed finite idea. But when inwardness is absent, parroting lunacy sets in, which is just as comic, and it would be desirable for an imaginatively constructing psychologist to depict it by taking a handful of such philosophers and putting them together. When the insanity is a delirium of inwardness, the tragic and the comic are that the something that infinitely pertains to the unfortunate person is a fixed detail that pertains to no one else. But when the insanity is the absence of inwardness, the comic is that the something known by the blissful person is the truth, truth that pertains to the whole human race but does not in the least pertain to the highly honored parroter. This kind of insanity is more inhuman than the other. One shrinks from looking the first one in the eye, lest one discover the depth of his frantic state, but one does not dare to look at the other at all for fear of discovering that he does not have proper eyes but glass eyes and hair made from a floor mat, in short, that he is an artificial product. If one happens to meet a mentally deranged person of that sort, whose illness is simply that he has no mind, one listens to him in cold horror. One does not know whether one dares to believe that it is a human being with whom one is speaking, or perhaps a "walking stick," an artificial contrivance of Døbler that conceals in itself a barrel organ. To drink *Dus* with the executioner can indeed be unpleasant for a self-respecting man, but to get into a rational and speculative conversation with a walking stick—now that is almost enough to drive one crazy.

Subjective reflection turns inward toward subjectivity and in this inward deepening will be of the truth, and in such a way that, just as in the preceding, when objectivity was advanced, subjectivity vanished, here subjectivity as such becomes the final factor and objectivity the vanishing. Here it is not forgotten, even for a single moment, that the subject is existing, and that existing is a becoming, and that truth as the identity of thought and being is therefore a chimera of abstraction and truly only a longing of creation, not because truth is not an identity, but because the knower is an existing person, and thus truth cannot be an identity for him as long as he exists. If this is not held fast, then with the aid of speculative thought we promptly enter into the fantastical *I-I* that recent speculative thought certainly has used but without explaining how a particular individual relates himself to it, and, good Lord, of course no human being is more than a particular individual.

If the existing person could actually be outside himself, the truth would be something concluded for him. But where is this point? The *I–I* is a mathematical point that does not exist at all; accordingly anyone can readily take up this standpoint—no one stands in the way of anyone else. Only momentarily can a particular individual, existing, be in a unity of the infinite and the finite that transcends existing. This instant is the moment of passion. Modern speculative thought has mustered everything to enable the individual to transcend himself objectively, but this just cannot be done. Existence exercises its constraint, and if philosophers nowadays had not become pencil-pushers serving the trifling busyness of fantastical thinking, it would have discerned that suicide is the only somewhat practical interpretation of its attempt. But pencil pushing modern speculative thought takes a dim view of passion, and yet, for the existing person, passion is existence at its very highest—and we are, after all, existing persons. In passion, the existing subject is infinitized in the eternity of imagination and yet is also most definitely himself. The fantastical *I–I* is not infinitude and finitude in identity, since neither the one nor the other is actual; it is a fantastical union with a cloud, an unfruitful embrace, and the relation of the individual I to this mirage is never stated.

All essential knowing pertains to existence, or only the knowing whose relation to existence is essential is essential knowing. Essentially viewed, the knowing that does not inwardly in the reflection of inwardness pertain to existence is accidental knowing, and its degree and scope, essentially viewed, are a matter of indifference. That essential knowing is essentially related to existence does not, however, signify the above-mentioned abstract identity between thinking and being, nor does it signify that the knowledge is objectively related to something existent as its object, but it means that the knowledge is related to the knower, who is essentially an existing person, and that all essential knowing is therefore essentially related to existence and to existing. Therefore, only ethical and ethical-religious knowing is essential knowing. But all ethical and all ethical-religious knowing is essentially a relating to the existing of the knower.

Mediation is a mirage, just as the *I–I* is. Viewed abstractly, everything is and nothing becomes. Mediation cannot possibly find its place in abstraction, since it has movement as its presupposition. Objective knowledge can certainly have the existent as its object, but since the knowing subject is existing and himself in the process of becoming by existing, speculative thought must first explain how a particular existing subject relates himself to the knowledge of mediation, what he is at the moment, whether, for example, he is not at that very moment rather absentminded, and where he is, whether he is not on the moon. There is this continual talk about mediation and mediation. Is mediation, then, a human being, just as Per Degn assumes *Imprimatur* to be a human being? How does a human being go about becoming something of that sort? Is this dignity, this great *philosophicum,* attained by studying? Or does the magistrate give it away as he gives away sexton and grave-digger positions? Just try to become involved with these and other similar simple questions raised by a simple human being, who would so very much like to be mediation if he could become that in a legitimate and honorable manner, and not either by saying *eins, zwei, drei, kokolorum* or by forgetting that he himself is an existing human being, for whom existing is consequently something essential, and for whom existing ethically-religiously is a suitable *quantum satis* [sufficient amount]. To a speculative thinker it may seem *abgeschmackt* [in bad taste] to ask questions in this way, but it is especially important not to polemicize in the wrong place and hence not to begin fantastically-objectively a *pro* and *contra* as to whether or not there is mediation, but firmly to maintain what it means to be a human being.

In order to clarify the divergence of objective and subjective reflection, I shall now describe subjective reflection in its search back and inward into inwardness. At its highest, inwardness in an existing subject is passion; truth as a paradox corresponds to passion, and that truth becomes a paradox is grounded precisely in its relation to an existing subject. In this way the one corresponds to the other. In forgetting that one is an existing subject, one loses passion, and in return, truth does not become a paradox; but the knowing subject shifts from being human to being a fantastical something, and truth becomes a fantastical object for its knowing.

When the question about truth is asked objectively, truth is reflected upon objectively as an object to which the knower relates himself. What is reflected upon is not the relation but that what he relates himself to is the truth, the true. If only that to which he relates himself is the truth, the true, then the subject is in the truth. When the question about truth is asked subjectively, the individual's relation is reflected upon subjectively. If only the how of this relation is in truth, the individual is in truth, even if he in this way were to relate himself to untruth.*

Let us take the knowledge of God as an example. Objectively, what is reflected upon is that this is the true God; subjectively, that the individual relates himself to a something in *such a way* that his relation is in truth a God-relation. Now, on which side is the truth? Alas, must we not at this point resort to mediation and say: It is on neither side; it is in the mediation? Superbly stated, if only someone could say how an existing person goes about being in mediation, because to be in mediation is to be finished; to exist is to become. An existing person cannot be in two places at the same time, cannot be subject-object. When he is closest to being in two places at the same time, he is in passion; but passion is only momentary, and passion is the highest pitch of subjectivity.

The existing person who chooses the objective way now enters upon all approximating deliberation intended to bring forth God objectively, which is not achieved in all eternity, because God is a subject and hence only for subjectivity in inwardness. The existing person who chooses the subjective way instantly comprehends the whole dialectical difficulty because he must use some time, perhaps a long time, to find God objectively. He comprehends this dialectical difficulty in all its pain, because he must resort to God at that very moment, because every moment in which he does not have God is wasted.** At that very moment he has God, not by virtue of any objective deliberation but by virtue of the infinite passion of inwardness. The objective person is not bothered by dialectical difficulties such as what it means to put a whole research period into finding God, since it is indeed possible that the researcher would die tomorrow, and if he goes on living, he cannot very well regard God as something to be taken along at his convenience, since God is something one takes along a *tout prix* [at any price], which, in passion's understanding, is the true relationship of inwardness with God.

It is at this point, dialectically so very difficult, that the road swings off for the person who knows what it means to think dialectically and, existing, to think dialectically, which is quite different from sitting as a fantastical being at a desk and writing about something one has never done oneself, quite different from writing *de omnibus dubitandum* and then as an existing person being just as credulous as the most sensate human being. It is here that the road swings off, and the change is this: whereas objective knowledge goes along leisurely on the long road of approximation, itself not actuated by passion, to subjective knowledge every delay is a deadly peril and the decision so infinitely important that it is immediately urgent, as if the opportunity had already passed by unused.

Now, if the problem is to calculate where there is more truth (and, as stated, simultaneously to be on both sides equally is not granted to an existing person but is only a beatifying delusion for a deluded *I–I*), whether on the side of the person who

---

*The reader will note that what is being discussed here is essential truth, or the truth that is related essentially to existence, and that it is specifically in order to clarify it as inwardness or as subjectivity that the contrast is pointed out.

**In this way God is indeed a postulate, but not in the loose sense in which it is ordinarily taken. Instead, it becomes clear that this is the only way an existing person enters into a relationship with God: when the dialectical contradiction brings passion to despair and assists him in grasping God with "the category of despair" (faith), so that the postulate, far from being the arbitrary, is in fact *necessary* defense [*Nødværge*], self defense; in this way God is not a postulate, but the existing person's postulating of God is—a necessity [*Nødvendighed*].

only objectively seeks the true God and the approximating truth of the God-idea or on the side of the person who is infinitely concerned that he in truth relate himself to God with the infinite passion of need—then there can be no doubt about the answer for anyone who is not totally botched by scholarship and science. If someone who lives in the midst of Christianity enters, with knowledge of the true idea of God, the house of God, the house of the true God, and prays, but prays in untruth, and if someone lives in an idolatrous land but prays with all the passion of infinity, although his eyes are resting upon the image of an idol—where, then, is there more truth? The one prays in truth to God although he is worshiping an idol; the other prays in untruth to the true God and is therefore in truth worshiping an idol.

If someone objectively inquires into immortality, and someone else stakes the passion of the infinite on the uncertainty—where, then, is there more truth, and who has more certainty? The one has once and for all entered upon an approximation that never ends, because the certainty of immortality is rooted in subjectivity; the other is immortal and therefore struggles by contending with the uncertainty.

Let us consider Socrates. These days everyone is dabbling in a few proofs or demonstrations—one has many, another fewer. But Socrates! He poses the question objectively, problematically: if there is an immortality. So, compared with one of the modern thinkers with the three demonstrations, was he a doubter? Not at all. He stakes his whole life on this "if"; he dares to die, and with the passion of the infinite he has so ordered his whole life that it might be acceptable—if there is an immortality. Is there any better demonstration for the immortality of the soul? But those who have the three demonstrations do not order their lives accordingly. If there is an immortality, it must be nauseated by their way of living—is there any better counter-demonstration to the three demonstrations? The "fragment" of uncertainty helped Socrates, because he himself helped with the passion of infinity. The three demonstrations are of no benefit whatever to those others, because they are and remain slugs and, failing to demonstrate anything else, have demonstrated it by their three demonstrations.

In the same way a girl has perhaps possessed all the sweetness of being in love through a weak hope of being loved by the beloved, because she herself staked everything on this weak hope; on the other hand, many a wedded matron, who more than once has submitted to the strongest expression of erotic love, has certainly had demonstrations and yet, strangely enough, has not possessed *quod erat demonstrandum* [that which was to be demonstrated]. The Socratic ignorance was thus the expression, firmly maintained with all the passion of inwardness, of the relation of the eternal truth to an existing person, and therefore it must remain for him a paradox as long as he exists. Yet it is possible that in the Socratic ignorance there was more truth in Socrates than in the objective truth of the entire system that flirts with the demands of the times and adapts itself to assistant professors.

Objectively the emphasis is on what is said; subjectively the emphasis is on how it is said. This distinction applies even esthetically and is specifically expressed when we say that in the mouth of this or that person something that is truth can become untruth. Particular attention should be paid to this distinction in our day, for if one were to express in a single sentence the difference between ancient times and our time, one would no doubt have to say: In ancient times there were only a few individuals who knew the truth; now everyone knows it, but inwardness has an inverse relation to it. Viewed esthetically, the contradiction that emerges when truth becomes untruth in this and that person's mouth is best interpreted comically. Ethically-religiously, the emphasis is again on: *how*. But this is not to be understood as manner, modulation of voice, oral delivery, etc., but it is to be understood as the relation of the existing person, in his very existence, to what is said. Objectively, the question is only about categories of thought; subjectively, about inwardness. At its maximum, this "how" is the passion of the infinite, and the passion of the infinite is the very truth. But the passion of the infinite is precisely subjectivity, and thus subjectivity is truth. From the objective point of view, there is no infinite decision, and thus it is objectively correct that the distinction between good and evil is canceled, along with the principle of contradiction, and thereby also the infinite distinction between truth and falsehood. Only in subjectivity is there decision, whereas wanting to become objective is untruth. The passion of the infinite, not its content, is the deciding factor, for its content is precisely itself. In this way the subjective "how" and subjectivity are the truth.

But precisely because the subject is existing, the "how" that is subjectively emphasized is dialectical also with regard to time. In the moment of the decision of passion, where the road swings off from objective knowledge, it looks as if the infinite decision were thereby finished. But at the same moment, the existing person is in the temporal realm, and the subjective "how" is transformed into a striving that is motivated and repeatedly refreshed by the decisive passion of the infinite, but it is nevertheless a striving.

When subjectivity is truth, the definition of truth must also contain in itself an expression of the antithesis to objectivity, a memento of that fork in the road, and this expression will at the same time indicate the resilience of the inwardness. Here is such a definition of truth: *An objective uncertainty, held fast through appropriation with the most passionate inwardness, is the truth,* the highest truth there is for an existing person. At the point where the road swings off (and where that is cannot be stated objectively, since it is precisely subjectivity), objective knowledge is suspended. Objectively he then has only uncertainty, but this is precisely what intensifies the infinite passion of inwardness, and truth is precisely the daring venture of choosing the objective uncertainty with the passion of the infinite. I observe nature in order to find God, and I do indeed see omnipotence and wisdom, but I also see much that troubles and disturbs. The *summa summarum* [sum total] of this is an objective uncertainty, but the inwardness is so very great, precisely because it grasps this objective uncertainty with all the passion of the infinite. In a mathematical proposition, for example, the objectivity is given, but therefore its truth is also an indifferent truth.

But the definition of truth stated above is a paraphrasing of faith. Without risk, no faith. Faith is the contradiction between the infinite passion of inwardness and the objective uncertainty. If I am able to apprehend God objectively, I do not have faith; but because I cannot do this, I must have faith. If I want to keep myself in faith, I must continually see to it that I hold fast the objective uncertainty, see to it that in the objective uncertainty I am "out on 70,000 fathoms of water" and still have faith.

The thesis that subjectivity, inwardness, is truth contains the Socratic wisdom, the undying merit of which is to have paid attention to the essential meaning of existing, of the knower's being an existing person. That is why, in his ignorance, Socrates was in the truth in the highest sense within paganism. To comprehend this, that the misfortune of speculative thought is simply that it forgets again and again that the knower is an existing person, can already be rather difficult in our objective age. "But to go beyond Socrates when one has not even comprehended the Socratic—that, at least, is not Socratic." See "The Moral" in *Fragments.*

Just as in *Fragments,* let us from this point try a category of thought that actually does go beyond. Whether it is true or false is of no concern to me, since I am only imaginatively constructing, but this much is required, that it be clear that the Socratic is presupposed in it, so that I at least do not end up behind Socrates again.

When subjectivity, inwardness, is truth, then truth, objectively defined, is a paradox; and that truth is objectively a paradox shows precisely that subjectivity is truth, since the objectivity does indeed thrust away, and the objectivity's repulsion, or the expression for the objectivity's repulsion, is the resilience and dynamometer of inwardness. The paradox is the objective uncertainty that is the expression for the passion of inwardness that is truth. So much for the Socratic. The eternal, essential truth, that is, the truth that is related essentially to the existing person by pertaining essentially to what it means to exist (viewed Socratically, all other knowledge is accidental, its degree and scope indifferent), is a paradox. Nevertheless the eternal, essential truth is itself not at all a paradox, but it is a paradox by being related to an existing person. Socratic ignorance is an expression of the objective uncertainty; the inwardness of the existing person is truth. In anticipation of what will be discussed later, the following comment is made here: Socratic ignorance is an analogue to the category of the absurd, except that there is even less objective certainty in the repulsion exerted by the absurd, since there is only the certainty that it is absurd, and for that very reason there is infinitely greater resilience in the inwardness. The Socratic inwardness in existing is an analogue to faith, except that the inwardness of faith, corresponding not to the repulsion exerted by ignorance but to the repulsion exerted by the absurd, is infinitely deeper.

Viewed Socratically, the eternal essential truth is not at all paradoxical in itself, but only by being related to an existing person. This is expressed in another Socratic thesis: that all knowing is a recollecting. This thesis is an intimation of the beginning of speculative thought, but for that very reason Socrates did not pursue it; essentially it became Platonic. This is where the road swings off, and Socrates essentially emphasizes existing, whereas Plato, forgetting this, loses himself in speculative thought. Socrates' infinite merit is precisely that of being an *existing* thinker, not a speculative thinker who forgets what it means to exist. To Socrates, therefore, the thesis that all knowing is a recollecting has, at the moment of parting and as a continually annulled possibility of speculating, a double significance: (1) that the knower is essentially *integer* [uncorrupted] and that for him there is no other dubiousness with regard to knowledge of the eternal truth than this, that he exists, a dubiousness so essential and decisive to him that it signifies that existing, the inward deepening in and through existing, is truth; (2) that existence in temporality has no decisive significance, because there is continually the possibility of taking oneself back into eternity by recollecting, even though this possibility is continually annulled because the inward deepening in existing fills up time.*

---

*This may be the proper place to elucidate a dubiousness in the design of *Fragments,* a dubiousness that was due to my not wanting immediately to make the matter as dialectically difficult as it is, because in our day terminologies and the like are so muddled that it is almost impossible to safeguard oneself against confusion. In order, if possible, to elucidate properly the difference between the Socratic (which was supposed to be the philosophical, the pagan philosophical position) and the category of imaginatively constructed thought, which actually goes beyond the Socratic, I carried the Socratic back to the thesis that all knowing is a recollecting. It is commonly accepted as such, and only for the person who with a very special interest devotes himself to the Socratic, always returning to the sources, only for him will it be important to distinguish between Socrates and Plato on this point. The thesis certainly belongs to both of them, but Socrates continually parts with it because he wants to exist. By holding Socrates to the thesis that all knowing is recollecting, one turns him into a speculative philosopher instead of what he was, an existing thinker who understood existing as the essential. The thesis that all knowing is recollecting belongs to speculative thought, and recollecting is immanence, and from the point of view of speculation and the eternal there is no paradox. The difficulty, however, is that no human being is speculation, but the speculating person is an existing human being, subject to the claims of existence. To forget this is no merit, but to hold this fast is indeed a merit and that is precisely what Socrates did. To emphasize existence, which contains within it the

The great merit of the Socratic was precisely to emphasize that the knower is an existing person and that to exist is the essential. To go beyond Socrates by failing to understand this is nothing but a mediocre merit. This we must keep *in mente* [in mind] and then see whether the formula cannot be changed in such a way that one actually does go beyond the Socratic.

So, then, subjectivity, inwardness, is truth. Is there a *more inward* expression for it? Yes, if the discussion about "Subjectivity, inwardness, is truth" begins in this way: "Subjectivity is untruth." But let us not be in a hurry. Speculative thought also says that subjectivity is untruth but says it in the very opposite direction, namely, that objectivity is truth. Speculative thought defines subjectivity negatively in the direction of objectivity. The other definition, however, puts barriers in its own way at the very moment it wants to begin, which makes the inwardness so much more inward. Viewed Socratically, subjectivity is untruth if it refuses to comprehend that subjectivity is truth but wants, for example, to be objective. Here, on the other hand, in wanting to begin to become truth by becoming subjective, subjectivity is in the predicament of being untruth. Thus the work goes backward, that is, backward in inwardness. The way is so far from being in the direction of the objective that the beginning only lies even deeper in subjectivity.

But the subject cannot be untruth eternally or be presupposed to have been untruth eternally; he must have become that in time or he becomes that in time. The Socratic paradox consisted in this, that the eternal truth was related to an existing person. But now existence has accentuated the existing person a second time; a change so essential has taken place in him that he in no way can take himself back into eternity by Socratically recollecting. To do this is to speculate; to be able to do this but, by grasping the inward deepening in existence, to annul the possibility of doing it is the Socratic. But now the difficulty is that what accompanied Socrates as an annulled possibility has become an impossibility. If speculating was already of dubious merit in connection with the Socratic, it is now only confusion.

The paradox emerges when the eternal truth and existing are placed together, but each time existing is accentuated, the paradox becomes clearer and clearer. Viewed Socratically, the knower was an existing person, but now the existing person is accentuated in such a way that existence has made an essential change in him.

Let us now call the individual's untruth *sin*. Viewed eternally, he cannot be in sin or be presupposed to have been eternally in sin. Therefore, by coming into existence (for the beginning was that subjectivity is untruth), he becomes a sinner. He is not born

---

qualification of inwardness, is the Socratic, whereas the Platonic is to purse recollection and immanence. Basically Socrates is thereby beyond all speculation, because he does not have a fantastical beginning where the speculating person changes clothes and goes on and on and speculates, forgetting the most important thing, to exist. But precisely because Socrates is in this way beyond speculative thought, he acquires, when rightly depicted, a certain analogous likeness to what the imaginary construction set forth as that which truly goes beyond the Socratic: the truth as paradox is an analog to the paradox *sensu eminetiori* [in the more eminent sense]; the passion of inwardness in existing is then an analog to faith *sensu eminentiori*. That the difference is infinite nevertheless, that the designations in *Fragments* of that which truly goes beyond the Socratic are unchanged, I can easily show, but I was afraid to make complications by promptly using what seem to be the same designations, at least the same words, about the different things when the imaginary construction was to be presented as different from these. Now, I think there would be no objection to speaking of the paradox in connection with Socrates and faith, since it is quite correct to do so, provided that it is understood correctly. Besides, the ancient Greeks also use the word ⟨*pistis*⟩ [Faith], although by no means in the sense of the imaginary construction, and use it so as to make possible some very illuminating observations bearing upon its dissimilarity to faith *sensu eminentiori*, especially with reference to one of Aristotle's works where the term is employed.

as a sinner in the sense that he is presupposed to be a sinner before he is born, but he is born in sin and as a sinner. Indeed, we could call this *hereditary sin*. But if existence has in this way obtained power over him, he is prevented from taking himself back into eternity through recollection. If it is already paradoxical that the eternal truth is related to an existing person, now it is absolutely paradoxical that it is related to such an existing person. But the more difficult it is made for him, recollecting, to take himself out of existence, the more inward his existing can become in existence; and when it is made impossible for him, when he is lodged in existence in such a way that the back door of recollection is forever closed, then the inwardness becomes the deepest. But let us never forget that the Socratic merit was precisely to emphasize that the knower is existing, because the more difficult the matter becomes, the more one is tempted to rush along the easy road of speculative thought, away from terrors and decisions, to fame, honor, a life of ease, etc. If even Socrates comprehended the dubiousness of taking himself speculatively out of existence back into eternity, when there was no dubiousness for the existing person except that he existed and, of course, that existing was the essential—now it is impossible. He must go forward; to go backward is impossible.

Subjectivity is truth. The paradox came into existence through the relating of the eternal, essential truth to the existing person. Let us now go further; let us assume that the eternal, essential truth is itself the paradox. How does the paradox emerge? By placing the eternal, essential truth together with existing. Consequently, if we place it together in the truth itself, the truth becomes a paradox. The eternal truth has come into existence in time. That is the paradox. If the subject just mentioned was prevented by sin from taking himself back into eternity, now he is not to concern himself with this, because now the eternal, essential truth is not behind him but has come in front of him by existing itself or by having existed, so that if the individual, existing, does not lay hold of the truth in existence, he will never have it.

Existence can never be accentuated more sharply than it has been here. The fraud of speculative thought in wanting to recollect itself out of existence has been made impossible. This is the only point to be comprehended here, and every speculation that insists on being speculation shows *eo ipso* [precisely thereby] that it has not comprehended this. The individual can thrust all this away and resort to speculation, but to accept it and then want to cancel it through speculation is impossible, because it is specifically designed to prevent speculation.

When the eternal truth relates itself to an existing person, it becomes the paradox. Through the objective uncertainty and ignorance, the paradox thrusts away in the inwardness of the existing person. But since the paradox is not in itself the paradox, it does not thrust away intensely enough, for without risk, no faith; the more risk, the more faith; the more objective reliability, the less inwardness (since inwardness is subjectivity); the less objective reliability, the deeper is the possible inwardness. When the paradox itself is the paradox, it thrusts away by virtue of the absurd, and the corresponding passion of inwardness is faith.

But subjectivity, inwardness, is truth; if not, we have forgotten the Socratic merit. But when the retreat out of existence into eternity by way of recollection has been made impossible, then, with the truth facing one as the paradox, in the anxiety of sin and its pain, with the tremendous risk of objectivity, there is no stronger expression for inwardness than—to have faith. But without risk, no faith, not even the Socratic faith, to say nothing of the kind we are discussing here.

When Socrates believed that God is, he held fast the objective uncertainty with the entire passion of inwardness, and faith is precisely in this contradiction, in this risk. Now it is otherwise. Instead of the objective uncertainty, there is here the certainty that, viewed objectively, it is the absurd, and this absurdity, held fast in the passion of

inwardness, is faith. Compared with the earnestness of the absurd, the Socratic ignorance is like a witty jest, and compared with the strenuousness of faith, the Socratic existential inwardness resembles Greek nonchalance.

What, then, is the absurd? The absurd is that the eternal truth has come into existence in time, that God has come into existence, has been born, has grown up, etc., has
come into existence exactly as an individual human being, indistinguishable from any
other human being, inasmuch as all immediate recognizability is pre-Socratic paganism and from the Jewish point of view is idolatry. Every qualification of that which actually goes beyond the Socratic must essentially have a mark of standing in relation to
the god's having come into existence, because faith, *sensu strictissimo* [in the strictest
sense], as explicated in *Fragments*, refers to coming into existence. When Socrates believed that God is [*er til*], he no doubt perceived that where the road swings off there is
a road of objective approximation, for example, the observation of nature, world history, etc. His merit was precisely to shun this road, where the quantifying siren song
spellbinds and tricks the existing person. In relation to the absurd, the objective approximation resembles the comedy *Misforstaaelse paa Misforstaaelse* [Misunder-
standing upon Misunderstanding], which ordinarily is played by assistant professors
and speculative thinkers.

It is by way of the objective repulsion that the absurd is the dynamometer of faith
in inwardness. So, then, there is a man who wants to have faith; well, let the comedy
begin. He wants to have faith, but he wants to assure himself with the aid of objective
deliberation and approximation. What happens? With the aid of approximation, the absurd becomes something else; it becomes probable, it becomes more probable, it may
become to a high-degree and exceedingly probable. Now he is all set to believe it, and
he dares to say of himself that he does not believe as shoemakers and tailors and simple
folk do, but only after long deliberation. Now he is all set to believe it, but, lo and behold, now it has indeed become impossible to believe it. The almost probable, the probable, the to-a-high-degree and exceedingly probable—that he can almost know, or as
good as know, to a higher degree and exceedingly almost *know*—but *believe* it, that
cannot be done, for the absurd is precisely the object of faith and only that can be believed.

Or there is a man who says he has faith, but now he wants to make his faith clear
to himself; he wants to understand himself in his faith. Now the comedy begins again.
The object of faith becomes almost probable, it becomes as good as probable, it becomes probable, it becomes to a high degree and exceedingly probable. He has finished; he dares to say of himself that he does not believe as shoemakers and tailors or
other simple folk do but that he has also understood himself in his believing. What
wondrous understanding! On the contrary, he has learned to know something different
about faith than he believed and has learned to know that he no longer has faith, since
he almost knows, as good as knows, to a high degree and exceedingly almost knows.

Inasmuch as the absurd contains the element of coming into existence, the road
of approximation will also be that which confuses the absurd fact of coming into existence, which is the object of faith, with a simple historical fact, and then seeks historical certainty for that which is absurd precisely because it contains the contradiction
that something that can become historical only in direct opposition to all human understanding has become historical. This contradiction is the absurd, which can only be believed. If a historical certainty is obtained, one obtains merely the certainty that what is
certain is not what is the point in question. A witness can testify that he has believed it
and then testify that, far from being a historical certainty, it is in direct opposition to
his understanding, but such a witness repels in the same sense as the absurd repels, and
a witness who does not repel in this way is *eo ipso* a deceiver or a man who is talking

about something altogether different; and such a witness can be of no help except in obtaining certainty about something altogether different. One hundred thousand individual witnesses, who by the special nature of their testimony (that they have believed the absurd) remain individual witnesses, do not become something else en masse so that the absurd becomes less absurd. Why? Because one hundred thousand people individually have believed that it was absurd? Quite the contrary, those one hundred thousand witnesses repel exactly as the absurd does.

But I do not need to develop this further here. In *Fragments* (especially where the difference between the follower at first hand and the follower at second hand is annulled) and in Part One of this book, I have with sufficient care shown that all approximation is futile, since the point is rather to do away with introductory observations, reliabilities, demonstrations from effects, and the whole mob of pawnbrokers and guarantors, in order to get the absurd clear—so that one can believe if one will—I merely say that this must be extremely strenuous.

If speculative thought wants to become involved in this and, as always, say: From the point of view of the eternal, the divine, the theocentric, there is no paradox— I shall not be able to decide whether the speculative thinker is right, because I am only a poor existing human being who neither eternally nor divinely nor theocentrically is able to observe the eternal but must be content with existing. This much, however, is certain, that with speculative thought everything goes backward, back past the Socratic, which at least comprehended that for an existing person existing is the essential; and much less has speculative thought taken the time to comprehend what it means to be *situated* in existence the way the existing person is in the imaginary construction.

The difference between the Socratic position and the position that goes beyond the Socratic is clear enough and is essentially the same as in *Fragments,* for in the latter nothing has changed, and in the former the matter has only been made somewhat more difficult, but nevertheless not more difficult than it is. It has also become somewhat more difficult because, whereas in *Fragments* I set forth the thought-category of the paradox only in an imaginary construction, here I have also latently made an attempt to make clear the necessity of the paradox, and even though the attempt is somewhat weak, it is still something different from speculatively canceling the paradox.

Christianity has itself proclaimed itself to be the eternal, essential truth that has come into existence in time; it has proclaimed itself as *the paradox* and has required the inwardness of faith with regard to what is an offense to the Jews, foolishness to the Greeks—and an absurdity to the understanding. It cannot be expressed more strongly that subjectivity is truth and that objectivity only thrusts away, precisely by virtue of the absurd, and it seems strange that Christianity should have come into the world in order to be explained, alas, as if it were itself puzzled about itself and therefore came into the world to seek out the wise man, the speculative thinker, who can aid with the explanation. It cannot be expressed more inwardly that subjectivity is truth than when subjectivity is at first untruth, and yet subjectivity is truth.

*   *   *

The direct relationship with God is simply paganism, and only when the break has taken place, only then can there be a true God-relationship. But this break is indeed the first act of inwardness oriented to the definition that truth is inwardness. Nature is certainly the work of God, but only the work is directly present, not God. With regard to the individual human being, is this not acting like an illusive author, who nowhere sets forth his result in block letters or provides it beforehand in a preface? And why is God illusive?

Precisely because he is truth and in being illusive seeks to keep a person from untruth. The observer does not glide directly to the result but on his own must concern himself with finding it and thereby break the direct relation. But this break is the actual break-through of inwardness, an act of self-activity, the first designation of truth as inwardness.

Or is it not the case that God is so unnoticeable, so hidden yet present in his work, that a person might very well live on, marry, be respected and esteemed as husband, fa-ther, and captain of the popinjay shooting club, without discovering God in his work, without ever receiving any impression of the infinitude of the ethical, because he man-aged with an analogy to the speculative confusion of the ethical and the world-historical by managing with custom and tradition in the city where he lived? Just as a mother ad-monishes her child who is about to attend a party, "Now, mind your manners and watch the other polite children and behave as they do," so he, too, could live on and behave as he saw others behave. He would never do anything first and would never have any opin-ion unless he first knew that others had it, because "the others" would be his very first. On special occasions he would act like someone who does not know how to eat a course that is served at a banquet; he would reconnoiter until he saw how the others did it etc. Such a person could perhaps know ever so much, perhaps even know the system by rote; he could perhaps live in a Christian country, know how to bow his head every time God's name was mentioned, perhaps also see God in nature if he was in the company of others who saw God; in short, well, he could be a congenial party goer—and yet he would be deceived by the direct relation to truth, to the ethical, to God.

If one were to portray such a person in an imaginary construction, he would be a satire on what it is to be a human being. It is really the God-relationship that makes a human being a human being, but this is what he would lack. Yet no one would hesitate to consider him an actual human being (for the absence of inwardness is not seen di-rectly), although he would be more like a puppet character that very deceptively imi-tates all the human externalities—would even have children with his wife. At the end of his life, one would have to say that one thing had escaped him: he had not become aware of God. If God could have permitted a direct relationship, he would certainly have become aware. If God had taken the form, for example, of a rare, enormously large green bird, with a red beak, that perched in a tree on the embankment and perhaps even whistled in an unprecedented manner—then our party going man would surely have had his eyes opened; for the first time in his life he would have been able to be the first.

All paganism consists in this, that God is related directly to a human being, as the remarkably striking to the amazed. But the spiritual relationship with God in truth, that is, inwardness, is first conditioned by the actual breakthrough of inward deepening that corresponds to the divine cunning that God has nothing remarkable, nothing at all remarkable, about him—indeed, he is so far from being remarkable that he is invisible, and thus one does not suspect that he is there [*er til*], although his invisibility is in turn his omnipresence. But an omnipresent being is the very one who is seen everywhere, for example, as a police officer is—how illusive, then, that an omnipresent being is cognizable precisely by his being invisible,* simply and solely by this, because his

---

*In order to indicate how illusive the rhetorical can be, I shall show here how one could perhaps pro-duce an effect upon a listener rhetorically, even though what was said would be a dialectical retrogression. Suppose a pagan religious orator says that here on earth the god's temple is actually empty, but (and here the rhetorical begins) in heaven, where everything is more perfect, where water is air, and air is ether, there are also temples and shrines for the gods, but the difference is that the gods actually dwell in these temples—that the god actually dwells in the temple is dialectical retrogression, because his not dwelling in the temple is an expression for the spiritual relation to the invisible. But rhetorically it produces the effect.—Incidentally, I had in mind a specific passage by a Greek author, but I shall not quote him.

very visibility would annul his omnipresence. This relation between omnipresence and invisibility is like the relation between mystery and revelation, that the mystery expresses that the revelation is revelation in the stricter sense, that the mystery is the one and only mark by which it can be known, since otherwise a revelation becomes something like a police officer's omnipresence.

If God [*Gud*] wants to reveal himself in human form and provide a direct relation by taking, for example, the form of a man who is twelve feet tall, then that imaginatively constructed party goer and captain of the popinjay shooting club will surely become aware. But since God is unwilling to deceive, the spiritual relation in truth specifically requires that there be nothing at all remarkable about his form; then the party goer must say: There is nothing to see, not the slightest. If the god [*Guden*] has nothing whatever that is remarkable about him, the party goer is perhaps deceived in not becoming aware at all. But the god is without blame in this, and the actuality of this deception is continually also the possibility of the truth. But if the god has something remarkable about him, he deceives, inasmuch as a human being thus becomes aware of the untruth, and this awareness is also the impossibility of the truth.

In paganism, the direct relation is idolatry; in Christianity, everyone indeed knows that God cannot manifest himself in this way. But this knowledge is not inwardness at all, and in Christianity it can certainly happen with a rote knower that he becomes utterly "without God in the world," which was not the case in paganism, where there was still the untrue relation of idolatry. Idolatry is certainly a dismal substitute, but that the rubric "God" disappears completely is even more mistaken.

Accordingly, not even God relates himself directly to a derived spirit (and this is the wondrousness of creation: not to produce something that is nothing in relation to the Creator, but to produce something that is something and that in the true worship of God can use this something to become by itself nothing before God); even less can one human being relate himself in this way to another *in truth*. Nature, the totality of creation, is God's work, and yet God is not there, but within the individual human being there is a possibility (he is spirit according to his possibility) that in inwardness is awakened to a God-relationship, and then it is possible to see God everywhere. Compared with the spiritual relationship in inwardness, the sensate distinctions of the great, the amazing, the most crying-to-heaven superlatives of a southern nation are a retrogression to idolatry. Is it not as if an author wrote 166 folio volumes and the reader read and read, just as when someone observes and observes nature but does not discover that the meaning of this enormous work lies in the reader himself, because amazement at the many volumes and the five hundred lines to the page, which is similar to amazement at how immense nature is and how innumerable the animal species are, is not understanding.

With regard to the essential truth, a direct relation between spirit and spirit is unthinkable. If such a relation is assumed, it actually means that one party has ceased to be spirit, something that is not borne in mind by many a genius who both assists people *en masse* into the truth and is good-natured enough to think that applause, willingness to listen, signatures, etc. mean accepting the truth. Just as important as the truth, and of the two the even more important one, is the mode in which the truth is accepted, and it is of slight help if one gets millions to accept the truth if by the very mode of their acceptance they are transposed into untruth. And therefore all good-naturedness, all persuasion, all bargaining, all direct attraction with the aid of one's own person in consideration of one's suffering so much for the cause, of one's weeping over humankind, of one's being so enthusiastic, etc.—all such things are a misunderstanding, in relation to the truth a forgery by which, according to one's ability, one helps any number of people to acquire a semblance of truth.

THE PRESENT AGE (in part)

. . . The dialectic of antiquity was oriented to the eminent (the great individual—and then the crowd; one free man, and then the slaves); at present the dialectic of Christianity is oriented to representation (the majority perceive themselves in the representative and are liberated by the awareness that he is representing them in a kind of self-consciousness). The dialectic of the present age is oriented to equality, and its most logical implementation, albeit abortive, is leveling, the negative unity of the negative mutual reciprocity of individuals.

Anyone can see that leveling has its profound importance in the ascendancy of the category "generation" over the category "individuality." Whereas in antiquity the host of individuals existed, so to speak, in order to determine how much the excellent individual was worth, today the coinage standard has been changed so that about so and so many human beings *uniformly* make one individual; thus it is merely a matter of getting the proper number—and then one has significance. In antiquity the individual in the crowd had no significance whatsoever; the man of excellence stood for them all. The trend today is in the direction of mathematical equality, so that in all classes about so and so many uniformly make one individual. The eminent personage dared to consider everything permissible, the individuals in the crowd nothing at all. Nowadays we understand that so and so many people make one individual, and in all consistency we compute numbers (we call it joining together, but that is a euphemism) in connection with the most trivial things. For no other reason than to implement a whim, we add a few together and do it—that is, we dare to do it.

This is why eventually not even a very gifted person is able to liberate himself from reflection, for he soon realizes he is merely a fraction in something utterly trivial and misses the infinite liberation of the religious life. Even if a small group of people had the courage to meet death, we today would not say that each individual had the courage to do that, for what the individual fears more than death is reflection's judgment upon him, reflection's objection to his wanting to venture something as an individual. The individual does not belong to God, to himself, to the beloved, to his art, to his scholarship; no, just as a serf belongs to an estate, so the individual realizes that in every respect he belongs to an abstraction in which reflection subordinates him. If a group of people in our age could decide, each one individually, to give all his fortune to some good cause, it would not follow as a matter of course that the individual could decide to do it, and again not because he was irresolute about renouncing his fortune but because he feared the judgment of reflection much more than he feared poverty. If ten persons could agree to affirm the full and unqualified validity of erotic love or, with no crippling considerations, the limited justification of enthusiasm, it would not therefore follow that each of the ten would be able to do it, for they still would ambivalently love reflection's judgment even more than the rapture of love and the witnessing of enthusiasm with their spirit—therefore ten would have to agree on something in which it is a contradiction to be more than one. The idolized positive principle of sociality in our age is the consuming, demoralizing principle that in the thralldom of reflection

Søren Kierkegaard, "The Present Age," from *Two Ages,* edited and translated by Howard V. Hong and Edna H. Hong (Princeton, NJ: Princeton University Press, copyright 1978 by Howard V. Hong). Reprinted by permission.

transforms even virtues into *vitia splendida* [glittering vices]. And what is the basis of this other than a disregard for the separation of the religious individual before God in the responsibility of eternity. When dismay commences at this point, one seeks comfort in company, and thus reflection captures the individual for his whole life. And they who were not even aware of the beginning of this crisis automatically fall within the relation of reflection.

Leveling is not the action of one individual but a reflection-game in the hand of an abstract power. Just as one computes the diagonal in a parallelogram of forces, so also can the law of leveling be computed, for the individual who levels others is himself carried along, and so on. While the individual egotistically thinks he knows what he is doing, it must be said that they all know not what they do,* for just as inspired enthusiastic unanimity results in a something more that is not the individuals', a something more emerges here also. A demon that no individual can control is conjured up, and although the individual selfishly enjoys the abstraction during the brief moment of pleasure in the leveling, he is also underwriting his own downfall. The forward thrust of the enthusiast *may* end with his downfall, but the leveler's success is *e.o. ipso* his downfall. No period, no age, and therefore not the present one, either, can halt the scepticism of leveling, for the moment it wants to halt leveling, it will once again exemplify the law. It can be halted only if the individual, in individual separateness, gains the intrepidity of religiousness.

I once witnessed a fight in which three men shamefully mistreated a fourth. The crowd watched with indignation; their hostile muttering began to spur them to action: some of the crowd converged on one of the assailants and threw him down, etc. The avengers thereby exemplified the same law as the assailants. If I may be permitted to interject my own incidental person, I will finish the story. I approached one of the avengers and attempted to explain dialectically the inconsistency of their behavior, but apparently it was quite impossible for him to engage in anything like that, and he merely repeated: "He had it coming. Such a scoundrel deserves three against one." This borders on the comic, especially for the person who did not witness the beginning and then heard one man say of the other that he (the lone man) was three against one, and heard it the very moment when the opposite was the case—when there were three against him. In the first situation there was the comedy of contradiction in the same sense as "when the watchman said to a solitary person: Please break it up! Disperse!" The second situation had the comedy of self-contradiction. I gathered, however, that it was probably best for me to surrender all hope of ending this scepticism lest it be continued against me.

No particular individual (the eminent personage by reason of excellence and the dialectic of fate) will be able to halt the abstraction of leveling, for it is a negatively superior force, and the age of heroes is past. No assemblage will be able to halt the abstraction of leveling, for in the context of reflection the assemblage itself is in the service of leveling. Not even national individuality will be able to halt it, for the abstraction of leveling is related to a higher negativity: pure humanity. The abstraction of leveling, this spontaneous combustion of the human race, produced by the friction that occurs when the separateness of individual inwardness in the religious life is omitted, will stay with us, as they say of a tradewind that consumes everything. Yet by means of it every individual, each one separately, may in turn be religiously educated, in the highest sense may be helped to acquire the essentiality of the religious by means

*[See Luke 23:34.]

of the *examen rigorosum* [rigorous examination] of leveling. For the younger person, however firmly he adheres to what he admires as excellent, who realizes from the beginning that leveling is what the selfish individual and the selfish generation meant for evil, but what also can be the point of departure for the highest life, especially for the individual who in honesty before God wills it—for him it will be genuinely educative to live in an age of leveling. In the highest sense contemporaneity will develop him religiously as well as esthetically and intellectually, because the comic will come to be radically evident. For it is extremely comic to see the particular individual classed under the infinite abstraction "pure humanity" without any middle term, since all the communal concretions of individuality that temper the comic by relativity and strengthen the relative pathos are annihilated. But this again expresses the fact that rescue comes only through the essentiality of the religious in the particular individual. He will be encouraged to realize that the single individual who is high-minded enough to want it may find access to it through this very error. But the leveling must go on, it has to, just as offense must needs come into the world, but woe unto him by whom it comes.

It is frequently said that a reformation has to begin with each person's reformation of himself, but it has not happened that way, for the idea of reformation has given rise to a hero, who very likely bought his license to be a hero very dearly from God. By directly joining up with him, a few individuals get what was dearly bought at a better price, yes, at a good price, but then they do not get the highest, either. But, like the sharp Northeaster, the abstraction of leveling is a principle that forms no personal, intimate relation to any particular individual, but only the relation of abstraction, which is the same for all. No hero, then, suffers for others or helps others; leveling itself becomes the severe taskmaster who takes on the task of educating. And the person who learns the most from the education and reaches the top does not become the man of distinction, the outstanding hero—this is forestalled by leveling, which is utterly consistent, and he prevents it himself because he has grasped the meaning of leveling—no, he only becomes an essentially human being in the full sense of equality. This is the idea of religiousness. But the education is rigorous and the returns are apparently very small—apparently, for if the individual is unwilling to learn to be satisfied with himself in the essentiality of the religious life before God, to be satisfied with ruling over himself instead of over the world, to be satisfied as a pastor to be his own audience, as an author to be his own reader, etc., if he is unwilling to learn to be inspired by this as supreme because it expresses equality before God and equality with all men, then he will not escape from reflection, then with all his endowments he may for one delusive moment believe that it is he who is doing the leveling, until he himself succumbs to the leveling. It will do no good to appeal to and summon a Holger Danske* or a Martin Luther. Their age is past, and as a matter of fact it is indolence on the part of individuals to want such a one, it is a finite impatience that wants to have at cheap, second-hand prices the highest, which is dearly bought at first-hand. It will do no good to establish all sorts of organizations, for negatively something superior is introduced even though the myopic organization man cannot see it.

In its immediate and beautiful form, the principle of individuality prefigures the generation in the man of excellence, the leader, and has the subordinate individuals group around the representative. In its eternal truth, the principle of individuality uses

*[Danish folk-hero first eulogized in the medieval French poem *Ogier le Danois* or *Ogier de Danemarche*.]

the abstraction and equality of the generation as levelers and thereby religiously develops the cooperating individual into an essentially human being. For leveling is just as powerful with respect to the temporary as it is impotent with respect to the eternal. Reflection is a snare in which one is trapped, but in and through the Inspired leap of religiousness the situation changes and it is the snare that catapults one into the embrace of the eternal. Reflection is and remains the most persistent, unyielding creditor in existence. Up to now it has cunningly bought up every possible outlook on life, but the eternal life-view of the essentially religious it cannot buy; however, by means of glittering illusion it can tempt everybody away from all else, and by means of reminding people of the past it can discourage them from all else. But through the leap out into the depths one learns to help himself, learns to love all others as much as himself even though he is accused of arrogance and pride—for not accepting help—or of selfishness—for being unwilling to deceive others by helping them, that is, by helping them miss what is highest of all.

If anyone declares that what I set forth here is common knowledge and can be said by anyone, my answer is: So much the better, I am not looking for prominence. I have nothing against everyone's knowing it, unless the fact that everyone knows it and can say it should mean that it is taken away from me and turned over to the negative community. As long as I have permission to keep it, its value for me is not depreciated by everyone's knowing it.

For a long time the basic tendency of our modern age has been toward leveling by way of numerous upheavals; yet none of them was leveling because none was sufficiently abstract but had a concretion of actuality. An approximate leveling can take place through a clash of leaders resulting in the weakening of both, or through one leader's neutralizing the other, or through the union of the essentially weaker ones so they become stronger than the foremost leader. An approximate leveling can be accomplished by a particular social class or profession, for example, the clergy, the middle class, the farmers, by the people themselves, but all this is still only the movement of abstraction within the concretions of individuality.

For leveling really to take place, a phantom must first be raised, the spirit of leveling, a monstrous abstraction, an all-encompassing something that is nothing, a mirage—and this phantom is *the public*. Only in a passionless but reflective age can this phantom develop with the aid of the press, when the press itself becomes a phantom. There is no such thing as a public in spirited, passionate, tumultuous times, even when a people wants to actualize the idea of the barren desert, destroying and demoralizing everything. There are parties, and there is concretion. In such times the press will take on the character of a concretion in relation to the division. But just as sedentary professionals are particularly prone to fabricating fantastic illusions, so a sedentary reflective age devoid of passion will produce this phantom if the press is supposed to be the only thing which, though weak itself, maintains a kind of life in this somnolence. The public is the actual master of leveling, for when there is approximate leveling, something is doing the leveling, but the public is a monstrous nonentity.

The public is a concept that simply could not have appeared in antiquity, because the people were obliged to come forward *en masse in corpore* [as a whole] in the situation of action, were obliged to bear the responsibility for what was done by individuals in their midst, while in turn the individual was obliged to be present in person as the one specifically involved and had to submit to the summary court for approval or disapproval. Only when there is no strong communal life to give substance to the concretion will the press create this abstraction "the public," made up of unsubstantial individuals who are never united or never can be united in the simultaneity of any situation or organization and yet are claimed to be a whole. The public is a corps, outnumbering all the people together, but this corps can never be called up for inspection; indeed, it cannot even have so much as a single representative, because it is itself an abstraction. Nevertheless, if the age is reflective, devoid of passion, obliterating everything that is concrete, the public becomes the entity that is supposed to include everything. But once again this situation is the very expression of the fact that the single individual is assigned to himself.

Contemporaneity* with actual persons, each of whom is someone, in the actuality of the moment and the actual situation gives support to the single individual. But the existence of a public creates no situation and no community. After all, the single individual who reads is not a public, and then gradually many individuals read, perhaps all do, but there is no contemporaneity. The public may take a year and a day to assemble, and when it is assembled it still does not exist. The abstraction that individuals paralogistically form alienates individuals instead of helping them. The person who is with actual persons in the contemporaneity of the actual moment and the actual situation but has no opinion himself adopts the same opinion as the majority, or, if he is more argumentative, as the minority. But the majority and the minority are, it is well to note, actual human beings, and that is why solidarity with them is supportive.

The public, however, is an abstraction. In adopting the same opinion as these or those particular persons, one knows that they will be subject to the same danger as oneself, that they will go astray with one if the opinion is in error, etc. But to adopt the same opinion as the public is a deceptive consolation, for the public exists only *in abstracto*. Thus, although no majority has ever been so positively sure of being in the right and having the upper hand as the public is, this is slight consolation for the single individual, for the public is a phantom that does not allow any personal approach. If someone adopts the opinion of the public today and tomorrow is hissed and booed, he is hissed and booed by the public. A generation, a nation, a general assembly, a community, a man still have a responsibility to be something, can know shame for fickleness and disloyalty, but a public remains the public. A people, an assembly, a person can change in such a way that one may say: they are no longer the same; but the public can become the very opposite and is still the same—the public. But if the individual is not destroyed in the process, he will be educated by this very abstraction and this abstract discipline (in so far as he is not already educated in his own inwardness) to be satisfied in the highest religious sense with himself and his relationship to God, will be educated to make up his own mind instead of agreeing with the public, which annihilates all the relative concretions of individuality, to find rest within himself, at ease before God, instead of in counting and counting. And the ultimate difference between the modern era and antiquity will be that the aggregate is not the concretion that reinforces and educates the individual, yet without shaping him entirely, but is an abstraction that by means of its alienating, abstract equality helps him to become wholly educated—if he does not perish. The bleakness of antiquity was that the man of distinction was what *others could not be;* the inspiring aspect [of the modern era] will be that the person who has gained himself religiously is only what *all can be.*

The public is not a people, not a generation, not one's age, not a congregation, not an association, not some particular persons, for all these are what they are only by being concretions. Yes, not a single one of these who belong to a public is essentially

*[This central concept in Kierkegaard's writings is used here with reference to the engaged, nonspectator presence of the person.]

engaged in any way. For a few hours of the day he perhaps is part of the public, that is, during the hours when he is a nobody, because during the hours in which he is the specific person he is, he does not belong to the public. Composed of someones such as these, of individuals in the moments when they are nobodies, the public is a kind of colossal something, an abstract void and vacuum that is all and nothing. But on the same basis anyone can presume to have a public, and just as the Roman Catholic Church chimerically extended itself by appointing bishops in *partibus infidelium* [in non-Catholic countries], so too a public is something anyone can pick up, even a drunken sailor exhibiting a peep show, and in dialectical consistency the drunken sailor has absolutely the same right to a public as the most distinguished of men, the absolute right to place all these many, many zeros *in front of* his figure one. The public is all and nothing, the most dangerous of all powers and the most meaningless. One may speak to a whole nation in the name of the public, and yet the public is less than one ever so insignificant actual human being. The category "public" is reflection's mirage delusively making the individuals conceited, since everyone can arrogate to himself this mammoth, compared to which the concretions of actuality seem paltry. The public is the fairytale of an age of prudence, leading individuals to fancy* themselves greater than kings, but again the public is the cruel abstraction by which individuals will be religiously educated—or be destroyed.

Together with the passionlessness and reflectiveness of the age, the abstraction "the press" (for a newspaper, a periodical, is not a political concretion and is an individual only in an abstract sense) gives rise to the abstraction's phantom, "the public," which is the real leveler. Apart from its negative implications for the religious life, this too can have its significance. But in proportion to the scarcity of ideas, an age exhausted by a flash of enthusiasm will relax all the more readily in indolence, and even if we were to imagine that the press would become weaker and weaker for lack of events and ideas to stir the age, leveling becomes all the more a decadent urge, a sensate stimulation that excites momentarily and only makes the evil worse, the rescue more difficult, and the probability of destruction greater.

The demoralization of absolute monarchy and the decline of revolutionary periods have frequently been described, but the decline of an age devoid of passion is just as degenerate, even though less striking because of its ambiguity. Thus it may be of interest and significance to think about this. In this state of indolent laxity, more and more individuals will aspire to be nobodies in order to become the public, that abstract aggregate ridiculously formed by the participant's becoming a third party. That sluggish crowd which understands nothing itself and is unwilling to do anything, that gallery-public, now seeks to be entertained and indulges in the notion that everything anyone does is done so that it may have something to gossip about. Sluggishness crosses its legs and sits there like a snob, while everyone who is willing to work, the king and the public official and the teacher and the more intelligent journalist and the poet and the artist, all stretch and strain, so to speak, to drag along that sluggishness which snobbishly believes the others are horses.

If I were to imagine this public as a person (for even though some superior individuals temporarily are part of the public, they still have an intrinsic coordinating connection that stabilizes them, even if they do not reach the highest level of religiousness), I most likely would think of one of the Roman emperors, an imposing, well-fed

---

*Fortunately as an author I have never sought or had any public but have been happily content with "that single individual," and because of that restriction I have become almost proverbial.

figure suffering from boredom and therefore craving only the sensate titillation of laughter, for the divine gift of wit is not worldly enough. So this person, more sluggish than he is evil, but negatively domineering, saunters around looking for variety. Anyone who has read the ancient authors knows how many things an emperor could think up to beguile the time. In the same way the public keeps a dog for its amusement. This dog is the contemptible part of the literary world.* If a superior person shows up, perhaps even a man of distinction, the dog is goaded to attack him, and then the fun begins. The nasty dog tears at his coattails, indulges in all sorts of rough tricks, until the public is tired of it and says: That is enough now. So the public has done its leveling. The superior one, the stronger one, has been mistreated—and the dog, well, it remains a dog that even the public holds in contempt. In this way the leveling has been done by a third party; the public of nothingness has leveled through a third party that in and through its contemptibleness was already more than leveled and less than nothing. And the public is unrepentant, for after all it was not the public—in fact, it was the dog, just as one tells children: It was the cat that did it. And the public is unrepentant, because after all it was not really slander—it was just a bit of fun. Now if the person instrumental in the leveling had been remarkably intelligent, the indolent public would have been deceived, for then the instrument would have been just another disturbing factor, but if superiority is kept down by contemptibleness and contemptibleness kept down by itself, then this is the quittance of nothingness. And the public will be unrepentant, for it actually does not keep the dog, it merely subscribes; neither did it directly goad the dog to attack nor whistle it back. In the event of a lawsuit, the public would say: The dog is not mine; the dog has no owner. And if the dog is apprehended and sent to the school of veterinary medicine to be exterminated, the public could still say: It was really a good thing that the bad dog was exterminated; we all wanted it done—even the subscribers.

There may be someone who conscientiously studies such a situation, intent upon scrutinizing the superior one who is being mistreated, and he may think that it is a tragic calamity. I cannot agree with that at all, for the person who desires assistance in reaching what is highest does benefit by experiencing such a thing and should rather desire it, even if others may be disturbed on his behalf. No, the terrible thing is something else, the thought of the many human lives that are squandered or may easily be squandered. I will not even mention those who are lost or led astray to their downfall, who play the role of the dog for money, but of the many rootless ones, the superficial ones, the sensate, those who in snobbish indolence get no deeper impression of life than this foolish grinning, all the second-raters who are led into new temptation because in their limitation they even derive self-importance from having sympathy for the victims of the attack, without grasping that in such a situation the victims are always the strongest, without grasping that here it is dreadfully and yet ironically appropriate to say: Weep not for him, but weep for yourselves.

---

*[An allusion to *The Corsair*, a contemporary Danish publication given to anonymous lampoonery and gossip, widely read by numerous subscribers and others and feared by most people of position. Kierkegaard's pseudonymous works had been praised in *The Corsair*. To bring the anonymous P.L. Møller and M. Goldschmidt into the open, Kierkegaard under the name Frater Taciturnus of *Stages on Life's Way* ironically complained (*Fædrelandet*, Dec. 27, 1845) that he alone seemed to be praised in *The Corsair*. Thereupon for some months there was a series of cartoons and articles ridiculing Kierkegaard mercilessly and at times scurrilously. Publicly Kierkegaard lost the skirmish, but privately and also publicly in another sense Møller and Goldschmidt lost, and within a year both had left *The Corsair* and subsequently Denmark, Møller permanently. See Kierkegaard, *The Corsair Affair*.]

That is the basest kind of leveling, because it always corresponds to the denominator in relation to which all are made equal. Thus eternal life is also a kind of leveling, and yet it is not so, for the denominator is this: to be an essentially human person in the religious sense.

*   *   *

When the generation, which in fact has itself wanted to level, has wanted to be emancipated and to revolt, has wanted to demolish authority and thereby in the scepticism of association has itself occasioned the hopeless forest fire of abstraction, when through leveling by means of the scepticism of association the generation has eliminated individualities and all the organic concretions and has substituted humanity and numerical equality among men, when the generation momentarily has entertained itself with the broad vista of abstract infinity, which no elevation, none whatsoever, disturbs, and instead there is simply "nothing but air and sea"—that is the time when the work begins—then the individuals have to help themselves, each one individually.

It will no longer be as it once was, that individuals could look to the nearest eminence for orientation when things got somewhat hazy before their eyes. That time is now past. They either must be lost in the dizziness of abstract infinity or be saved infinitely in the essentiality of the religious life. Many may cry out in despair, but it will not help, for now it is too late. If formerly authority and power were misused in the world and brought down upon themselves the nemesis of revolution, then it was in fact powerlessness and weakness that aspired to stand on its own feet and therefore brought that nemesis down upon itself. And not one of the unrecognizable ones will dare give direct help, speak plainly, teach openly, assume decisive leadership of the crowd (instead of giving negative support and helping the individual to the same decisiveness he himself has). For that he would be dismissed because he would be dabbling in human sympathy's myopic ingenuity instead of obeying divine orders, the orders of the angry divinity yet so full of grace, for the development is still a forward movement, because all the individuals who are rescued gain the specific gravity of the religious life, gain its essentiality at first hand from God.

Then it will be said: "Look, everything is ready;* look, the cruelty of abstraction exposes the vanity of the finite in itself, look, the abyss of the infinite is opening up; look, the sharp scythe of leveling permits all, every single one, to leap over the blade—look, God is waiting! Leap, then, into the embrace of God.

*[See Luke 14:17.]

Karl Marx
1818–1883

It is hard to think of a more influential—or more controversial—nineteenth-century thinker than Karl Marx. Not content simply to develop a theory, Marx sought fundamental change in social, economic, and political structures. As he put it, "The philosophers have only *interpreted* the world in various ways; the point is, to *change it.*"

Marx was the third of nine children born to Heinrich and Henrietta Marx in the Rhineland town of Trier. His parents were of Jewish ancestry but had converted to Protestant Christianity to protect Heinrich's job as a government lawyer. In 1835, Karl went to the University of Bonn to study law. Hardly the model student, he spent much of his time drinking or writing love letters to his childhood sweetheart and then fiancée, Jenny von Westphalen. At his father's insistence, Marx transferred to the University of Berlin and began to focus on his studies. While there, he abandoned his legal training and began preparing for an academic career as a philosophy professor. He wrote a dissertation contrasting Democritus and Epicurus that was accepted by the University of Jena, and in 1841 Marx received his doctorate in philosophy.

But the leftist politics Marx had adopted while in Berlin made it impossible for him to obtain a university post, so in 1842 he took a position as editor of the *Rheinische Zeitung (Rhenish Gazette),* a liberal middle-class newspaper in Cologne. Marx was a successful editor—too successful for the government censors who suppressed the paper after an article by Marx on the poverty of the Mosel winemakers. Marx moved to Paris where he became coeditor of the new journal, the *Deutsch-Französische Jahrbücher (German-French Annals).* With his future seeming secure, Marx finally felt free to marry Jenny in 1843. But the

Jahrbücher closed almost immediately and once again he was unemployed. Fortunately, at about the same time, Marx received a sizable settlement from the shareholders of the *Rheinishe Zeitung,* and he and his new bride were able to live comfortably. Freed from his editing duties, Marx wrote extensively on economic and political matters. He also met the man who was to be his lifelong friend, collaborator, and financial backer: Friedrich Engels (1820–1895). Engels came from a family of wealthy textile industrialists and was, himself, the manager of his family's Manchester, England, branch. Together Marx and Engels produced *The Holy Family* (1845), Marx's first published book, which criticized a number of their fellow leftists.

While pursuing his writing projects, Marx was politically active among German communists living in Paris—activity that led to his expulsion from France in 1845. Living for a time in Brussels, Marx produced *The German Ideology* (1846) and *The Poverty of Philosophy* (1847) while continuing his political involvement. In 1847, he attended the congress of the newly formed Communist League in London. He and Engels were commissioned to produce an easy-to-read pamphlet outlining the league's doctrines. The result was the immensely influential *Manifesto of the Communist Party* (1848).

Following another attempt at editing an opposition newspaper in Cologne—and another expulsion by the government—Marx eventually settled in London. The next two decades were a time of poverty and hardship for the Marx family due as much to financial mismanagement as to lack of income. (Marx reflected often on the irony of his extensive work on capital when he had so little talent for managing it personally.) Marx received some income as a correspondent for the *New York Tribune;* but for the rest of his life, his primary source of income was Engels's gifts. In London, Marx became a fixture in the reading room of the British Museum, where he pored over government records, histories, and the writings of other economists, gathering data to document his thought. There he wrote *Critique of Political Economy* (1859) and began his *magnum opus, Das Kapital (Capital;* 1867). He also continued his political involvement, becoming the leader of the International Working Men's Association. He worked with the International until factional strife, particularly conflict with the anarchist Mikhail Aleksandrovich Bakunin (1814–1876), led Marx to dismantle the organization in 1872.

It wasn't until Marx's final years that he managed to gain some financial stability and to live the life of a bourgeois Victorian gentleman. But these years also brought tragedy and hardship of a different kind. Marx developed boils over his entire body and used creosote, opium, and arsenic, among other remedies, in a futile attempt to effect a cure. His beloved Jenny died in 1881 and his eldest daughter two years later. Shortly thereafter, Marx himself developed bronchitis and also died in 1883.

*   *   *

While a student in Berlin, Marx was influenced by Hegelian philosophy. Hegel had understood *history* as a progressive actualization of the Absolute, but he was somewhat ambiguous about the future. One group of followers, the Old Hegelians, argued in a reactionary way that this progressive actualization was now complete and that Christianity was the Absolute Religion, Hegelianism the Absolute Philosophy, and Prussia the Absolute State. Another group, the Young

Hegelians, led by Bruno Bauer (1809–1882), argued that the dialectical movement of history was continuing. To move to the next stage in this historical dialectic, they sought to expose the contradictions of the existing order.

Although Marx accepted Hegel's dialectical understanding of history, he became convinced that Hegel's philosophy (and that of the Young Hegelians) devalued humanity by its emphasis on the Absolute. Marx then drew on the materialism espoused in Ludwig Feuerbach's work, *The Essence of Christianity* (1841). Feuerbach had argued that Hegel's philosophy was nothing more than rationalized religion, asserting that humans were merely the "self-alienation," or loss of identity, of God. Instead, Feuerbach advocated an atheistic materialism that claimed that "God" was simply the self-alienation of humans. That is, all the divine characteristics were nothing more than idealized human characteristics objectified and projected onto an imagined deity.

In "The Critique of Hegel's Dialectic and General Philosophy," reprinted here from the Tom Bottomore translation of the *Economic and Philosophical Manuscripts of 1844,* Marx uses Feuerbach's work to present his criticism of Hegel. Marx expresses appreciation for Hegel's dialectical understanding of the "self-creation of man as a process" and points out that Hegel conceives of "objective man" as the result of "his own labor." But Hegel understood labor as being "abstract mental" labor, not the natural, embodied interaction with real objects that concerned Marx. On the other hand, although he appreciated Feuerbach's materialism, Marx held that his predecessor did not tie his criticism to historical development. "As far as Feuerbach is a materialist he does not deal with history, and as far as he considers history he is not a materialist," wrote Marx. Synthesizing the historical development of Hegel and the materialism of Feuerbach, Marx's theory has often been called "dialectical materialism" (though Marx himself did not use that term).

Marx also adapted Feuerbach's concept of alienation, applying it to political, social, and economic interactions. In the sections on "Alienated Labor" and "Private Property and Communism" from the *Economic and Philosophical Manuscripts of 1844,* given here, Marx explains how a capitalist system results in alienation for the worker. The worker's labor is alien to the worker because it belongs to the capitalist. In return for the worker's labor, the capitalist pays the worker a wage—a wage that competition keeps at a subsistence level. Yet the worker must continue to labor in order to survive. This means the worker is now self-alienated since the life activity, the essence of the worker, becomes "only a means for his existence." But alienation is not limited to individuals. Because they have different interests, workers, as an economic class, are alienated from those who own the means of production. This, in turn, gives rise to class struggle because the interests of one class are always in opposition to the interests of other economic classes. Only by having communal ownership of the means of production, that is, by abolishing private property, will such conflict be overcome. Only then will those who work control both the process and the product of their labor. The selection from *Manifesto of the Communist Party,* given here in the Samuel Moore translation, calls on the workers of the world to bring about such a revolutionary change in the modes of production.

Our selection from *The German Ideology,* translated by W. Lough, begins with an explanation of the difference between the Young and the Old Hegelians. Marx then gives a brief history of the modes of production and the types of ownership associated with each. He concludes by arguing that it is these modes of production, "the material activity and the material intercourse of men," that determine politics, law, religion, and philosophy.

Throughout his analysis of the human situation, Marx continually returned to these material forces of production, distribution, exchange, and consumption. In the Preface and Introduction to *A Contribution to the Critique of Political Economy,* reprinted here in the N.I. Stone translation, Marx explains how the real foundations of society are the productive forces and the relations of production. His brief overview of these forces serves as a helpful introduction to his method and program.

*   *   *

Isaiah Berlin's *Karl Marx: His Life and Environment* (1963; reprinted Oxford: Oxford University Press, 1996) is still considered by many to be the best general introduction to Marx's life and philosophy, whereas more recent studies include David McLellan, *Karl Marx: His Life and Thought* (New York: Harper & Row, 1973); David McLellan, *Karl Marx* (New York: Penguin Books, 1975); Peter Singer, *Marx* (Oxford: Oxford University Press, 1980); Allen W. Wood, *Karl Marx* (London: Routledge & Kegan Paul, 1981); and Jon Elster, *An Introduction to Karl Marx* (Cambridge: Cambridge University Press, 1986). The following are samples of the many more recent studies in particular areas of Marx's thought: Nicholas Lash, *A Matter of Hope: A Theologian's Reflections on the Thought of Karl Marx* (Notre Dame, IN: University of Notre Dame Press, 1982); Nancy Sue Love, *Marx, Nietzsche, and Modernity* (New York: Columbia University Press, 1986); Harold Mah, *The End of Philosophy, The Origin of "Ideology": Karl Marx and the Crisis of the Young Hegelians* (Berkeley: University of California Press, 1987); and Robert Meister, *Political Identity: Thinking Through Marx* (Cambridge, MA: Basil Blackwell, 1990). For an interesting criticism of Marx by one of his contemporaries, see M.A. Bakunin, *Bakunin on Anarchy: Selected Works by the Activist-Founder of World Anarchism,* edited and translated by Sam Dolgoff (New York: Knopf, 1972). For collections of critical essays, see Tom Bottomore, ed., *Modern Interpretations of Marx* (Oxford: Basil Blackwell, 1981); David McLellan, ed., *Marx: The First Hundred Years* (New York: St. Martin's Press, 1983); Terence Ball and James Farr, eds., *After Marx* (Cambridge: Cambridge University Press, 1984); and Terrell Carver, ed., *The Cambridge Companion to Marx* (Cambridge: Cambridge University Press, 1991).

ECONOMIC AND PHILOSOPHICAL
MANUSCRIPTS OF 1844 (in part)

ALIENATED LABOUR

[XXII] We have begun from the presuppositions of political economy. We have accepted its terminology and its laws. We presupposed private property; the separation of labour, capital and land, as also of wages, profit and rent; the division of labour; competition; the concept of exchange value, etc. From political economy itself, in its own words, we have shown that the worker sinks to the level of a commodity, and to a most miserable commodity; that the misery of the worker increases with the power and volume of his production; that the necessary result of competition is the accumulation of capital in a few hands, and thus a restoration of monopoly in a more terrible form; and finally that the distinction between capitalist and landlord, and between agricultural labourer and industrial worker, must disappear, and the whole of society divide into the two classes of property *owners* and *propertyless* workers.

Political economy begins with the fact of private property; it does not explain it. It conceives the *material* process of private property, as this occurs in reality, in general and abstract formulas which then serve it as laws. It does not *comprehend* these laws; that is, it does not show how they arise out of the nature of private property. Political economy provides no explanation of the basis for the distinction of labour from capital, of capital from land. When, for example, the relation of wages to profits is defined, this is explained in terms of the interests of capitalists; in other words, what should be explained is assumed. Similarly, competition is referred to at every point and is explained in terms of external conditions. Political economy tells us nothing about the extent to which these external and apparently accidental conditions are simply the expression of a necessary development. We have seen how exchange itself seems an accidental fact. The only motive forces which political economy recognizes are *avarice* and the *war between the avaricious, competition.*

Just because political economy fails to understand the interconnexions within this movement it was possible to oppose the doctrine of competition to that of monopoly, the doctrine of freedom of the crafts to that of the guilds, the doctrine of the division of landed property to that of the great estates; for competition, freedom of crafts, and the division of landed property were conceived only as accidental consequences brought about by will and force, rather than as necessary, inevitable and natural consequences of monopoly, the guild system and feudal property.

Thus we have now to grasp the real connexion between this whole system of alienation—private property, acquisitiveness, the separation of labour, capital and land, exchange and competition, value and the devaluation of man, monopoly and competition—and the system of *money.*

Let us not begin our explanation, as does the economist, from a legendary primordial condition. Such a primordial condition does not explain anything; it merely removes the question into a grey and nebulous distance. It asserts as a fact or event what

Economic and Philosophical Manuscripts (1844), from *Karl Marx: Early Writings,* edited and translated by T.B. Bottomore (New York: McGraw-Hill, 1964). Reprinted by permission of McGraw-Hill.

it should deduce, namely, the necessary relation between two things; for example, be-tween the division of labour and exchange. In the same way theology explains the ori-gin of evil by the fall of man; that is, it asserts as a historical fact what it should ex-plain.

We shall begin from a *contemporary* economic fact. The worker becomes poorer the more wealth he produces and the more his production increases in power and ex-tent. The worker becomes an ever cheaper commodity the more goods he creates. The *devaluation* of the human world increases in direct relation with the *increase in value* of the world of things. Labour does not only create goods; it also produces itself and the worker as a *commodity*, and indeed in the same proportion as it produces goods.

This fact simply implies that the object produced by labour, its product, now stands opposed to it as an *alien being*, as a *power independent* of the producer. The product of labour is labour which has been embodied in an object and turned into a physical thing; this product is an *objectification* of labour. The performance of work is at the same time its objectification. The performance of work appears in the sphere of political economy as a *vitiation* of the worker, objectification as a *loss* and as *servitude to the object,* and appropriation as *alienation.*

So much does the performance of work appear as vitiation that the worker is viti-ated to the point of starvation. So much does objectification appear as loss of the object that the worker is deprived of the most essential things not only of life but also of work. Labour itself becomes an object which he can acquire only by the greatest effort and with unpredictable interruptions. So much does the appropriation of the object ap-pear as alienation that the more objects the worker produces the fewer he can possess and the more he falls under the domination of his product, of capital.

All these consequences follow from the fact that the worker is related to the *product of his labour* as to an *alien* object. For it is clear on this presupposition that the more the worker expends himself in work the more powerful becomes the world of ob-jects which he creates in face of himself, the poorer he becomes in his inner life, and the less he belongs to himself. It is just the same as in religion. The more of himself man attributes to God the less he has left in himself. The worker puts his life into the object, and his life then belongs no longer to himself but to the object. The greater his activity, therefore, the less he possesses. What is embodied in the product of his labour is no longer his own. The greater this product is, therefore, the more he is diminished. The *alienation* of the worker in his product means not only that his labour becomes an object, assumes an *external* existence, but that it exists independently, *outside himself,* and alien to him, and that it stands opposed to him as an autonomous power. The life which he has given to the object sets itself against him as an alien and hostile force.

[XXIII] Let us now examine more closely the phenomenon of *objectification;* the worker's production and the *alienation* and *loss* of the object it produces, which is involved in it. The worker can create nothing without *nature,* without the *sensuous ex-ternal world.* The latter is the material in which his labour is realized, in which it is ac-tive, out of which and through which it produces things.

But just as nature affords the *means of existence* of labour, in the sense that labour cannot *live* without objects upon which it can be exercised, so also it provides the *means of existence* in a narrower sense; namely the means of physical existence for the *worker* himself. Thus, the more the worker *appropriates* the external world of sen-suous nature by his labour the more he deprives himself of *means of existence,* in two respects: first, that the sensuous external world becomes progressively less an object belonging to his labour or a means of existence of his labour, and secondly, that it be-comes progressively less a means of existence in the direct sense, a means for the physical subsistence of the worker.

In both respects, therefore, the worker becomes a slave of the object; first, in that he receives an *object of work,* i.e. receives *work,* and secondly, in that he receives *means of subsistence.* Thus the object enables him to exist, first as a worker and secondly, as a *physical subject.* The culmination of this enslavement is that he can only maintain himself as a *physical subject* so far as he is a *worker,* and that it is only as a *physical subject* that he is a worker.

   (The alienation of the worker in his object is expressed as follows in the laws of political economy: the more the worker produces the less he has to consume; the more value he creates the more worthless he becomes; the more refined his product the more crude and misshapen the worker; the more civilized the product the more barbarous the worker; the more powerful the work the more feeble the worker; the more the work manifests intelligence the more the worker declines in intelligence and becomes a slave of nature.)

   Political economy conceals the alienation in the nature of labour in so far as it does not examine the direct relationship between the worker (work) and production. Labour certainly produces marvels for the rich but it produces privation for the worker. It produces palaces, but hovels for the worker. It produces beauty, but deformity for the worker. It replaces labour by machinery, but it casts some of the workers back into a barbarous kind of work and turns the others into machines. It produces intelligence, but also stupidity and cretinism for the workers.

   The direct relationship of labour to its products is the relationship of the worker to the objects of his production. The relationship of property owners to the objects of

Child factory labor, 1908, North Carolina. Young children were often used in textile mills because of their agility and dexterity. According to Marx, factory workers such as this child are alienated or cut off from (1) the products they produce, (2) their own work activities, (3) themselves, and (4) each other. *(Lewis W. Hine/Courtesy George Eastman House, International Museum of Photography.)*

production and to production itself is merely a *consequence* of this first relationship and confirms it. We shall consider this second aspect later.

Thus, when we ask what is the important relationship of labour, we are concerned with the relationship of the *worker* to production.

So far we have considered the alienation of the worker only from one aspect; namely, *his relationship with the products of his labour.* However, alienation appears not merely in the result but also in the *process* of *production,* within *productive activity* itself. How could the worker stand in an alien relationship to the product of his activity if he did not alienate himself in the act of production itself? The product is indeed only the *résumé* of activity, of production. Consequently, if the product of labour is alienation, production itself must be active alienation—the alienation of activity and the activity of alienation. The alienation of the object of labour merely summarizes the alienation in the work activity itself.

What constitutes the alienation of labour? First, that the work is *external* to the worker, that it is not part of his nature; and that, consequently, he does not fulfil himself in his work but denies himself, has a feeling of misery rather than well-being, does not develop freely his mental and physical energies but is physically exhausted and mentally debased. The worker, therefore, feels himself at home only during his leisure time, whereas at work he feels homeless. His work is not voluntary but imposed, *forced labour.* It is not the satisfaction of a need, but only a *means* for satisfying other needs. Its alien character is clearly shown by the fact that as soon as there is no physical or other compulsion it is avoided like the plague. External labour, labour in which man alienates himself, is a labour of self-sacrifice, of mortification. Finally, the external character of work for the worker is shown by the fact that it is not his own work but work for someone else, that in work he does not belong to himself but to another person.

Just as in religion the spontaneous activity of human fantasy, of the human brain and heart, reacts independently as an alien activity of gods or devils upon the individual, so the activity of the worker is not his own spontaneous activity. It is another's activity and a loss of his own spontaneity.

We arrive at the result that man (the worker) feels himself to be freely active only in his animal functions—eating, drinking and procreating, or at most also in his dwelling and in personal adornment—while in his human functions he is reduced to an animal. The animal becomes human and the human becomes animal.

Eating, drinking and procreating are of course also genuine human functions. But abstractly considered, apart from the environment of human activities, and turned into final and sole ends, they are animal functions.

We have now considered the act of alienation of practical human activity, labour, from two aspects: (1) the relationship of the worker to the *product of labour* as an alien object which dominates him. This relationship is at the same time the relationship to the sensuous external world, to natural objects, as an alien and hostile world; (2) the relationship of labour to the *act of production* within *labour.* This is the relationship of the worker to his own activity as something alien and not belonging to him, activity as suffering (passivity), strength as powerlessness, creation as emasculation, the *personal* physical and mental energy of the worker, his personal life (for what is life but activity?), as an activity which is directed against himself, independent of him and not belonging to him. This is *self-alienation* as against the above mentioned alienation of the *thing.*

[XXIV] We have now to infer a third characteristic of *alienated labour* from the two we have considered.

Man is a species-being not only in the sense that he makes the community (his own as well as those of other things) his object both practically and theoretically, but also (and this is simply another expression for the same thing) in the sense that he treats himself as the present, living species, as a *universal* and consequently free being.

Species-life, for man as for animals, has its physical basis in the fact that man (like animals) lives from inorganic nature, and since man is more universal than an animal so the range of inorganic nature from which he lives is more universal. Plants, animals, minerals, air, light, etc. constitute, from the theoretical aspect, a part of human consciousness as objects of natural science and art; they are man's spiritual inorganic nature, his intellectual means of life, which he must first prepare for enjoyment and perpetuation. So also, from the practical aspect, they form a part of human life and activity. In practice man lives only from these natural products, whether in the form of food, heating, clothing, housing, etc. The universality of man appears in practice in the universality which makes the whole of nature into his inorganic body: (1) as a direct means of life; and equally (2) as the material object and instrument of his life activity. Nature is the inorganic body of man; that is to say nature, excluding the human body itself. To say that man *lives* from nature means that nature is his *body* with which he must remain in a continuous interchange in order not to die. The statement that the physical and mental life of man, and nature, are interdependent means simply that nature is interdependent with itself, for man is a part of nature.

Since alienated labour: (1) alienates nature from man; and (2) alienates man from himself, from his own active function, his life activity; so it alienates him from the species. It makes *species-life* into a means of individual life. In the first place it alienates species-life and individual life, and secondly, it turns the latter, as an abstraction, into the purpose of the former, also in its abstract and alienated form.

For labour, *life activity, productive life,* now appear to man only as *means* for the satisfaction of a need, the need to maintain his physical existence. Productive life is, however, species-life. It is life creating life. In the type of life activity resides the whole character of a species, its species character; and free, conscious activity is the species character of human beings. Life itself appears only as a *means of life*.

The animal is one with its life activity. It does not distinguish the activity from itself. It is *its activity*. But man makes his life activity itself an object of his will and consciousness. He has a conscious life activity. It is not a determination with which he is completely identified. Conscious life activity distinguishes man from the life activity of animals. Only for this reason is he a species-being. Or rather, he is only a self-conscious being, i.e. his own life is an object for him, because he is a species-being. Only for this reason is his activity free activity. Alienated labour reverses the relationship, in that man because he is a self conscious being makes his life activity, his *being,* only a means for his *existence*.

The practical construction of an *objective world,* the *manipulation* of inorganic nature, is the confirmation of man as a conscious species-being, i.e. a being who treats the species as his own being or himself as a species-being. Of course, animals also produce. They construct nests, dwellings, as in the case of bees, beavers, ants, etc. But they only produce what is strictly necessary for themselves or their young. They produce only in a single direction, while man produces universally. They produce only under the compulsion of direct physical needs, while man produces when he is free from physical need and only truly produces in freedom from such need. Animals produce only themselves, while man reproduces the whole of nature. The products of animal production belong directly to their physical bodies, while man is free in face of his product. Animals construct only in accordance with the standards and needs of the species to which they belong, while man knows how to produce in accordance with the standards of every species and knows how to apply the appropriate standard to the object. Thus man constructs also in accordance with the laws of beauty.

It is just in his work upon the objective world that man really proves himself as a *species-being*. This production is his active species-life. By means of it nature appears as his work and his reality. The object of labour is, therefore, the *objectification of man's species-life;* for he no longer reproduces himself merely intellectually, as in consciousness, but actively and in a real sense, and he sees his own reflection in a world which he has constructed. While, therefore, alienated labour takes away the object of production from man, it also takes away his *species-life,* his real objectivity as a species being, and changes his advantage over animals into a disadvantage in so far as his inorganic body, nature, is taken from him.

Just as alienated labour transforms free and self-directed activity into a means, so it transforms the species-life of man into a means of physical existence.

Consciousness, which man has from his species, is transformed through alienation so that species-life becomes only a means for him. (3) Thus alienated labour turns the *species life of man,* and also nature as his mental species-property, into an *alien* being and into a *means* for his *individual existence.* It alienates from man his own body, external nature, his mental life and his *human* life. (4) A direct consequence of the alienation of man from the product of his labour, from his life activity and from his species-life, is that *man* is *alienated* from other *men.* When man confronts himself he also confronts *other* men. What is true of man's relationship to his work, to the product of his work and to himself, is also true of his relationship to other men, to their labour and to the objects of their labour.

In general, the statement that man is alienated from his species-life means that each man is alienated from others, and that each of the others is likewise alienated from human life.

Human alienation, and above all the relation of man to himself, is first realized and expressed in the relationship between each man and other men. Thus in the relationship of alienated labour every man regards other men according to the standards and relationships in which he finds himself placed as a worker.

[XXV] We began with an economic fact, the alienation of the worker and his production. We have expressed this fact in conceptual terms as *alienated labour,* and in analysing the concept we have merely analysed an economic fact.

Let us now examine further how this concept of alienated labour must express and reveal itself in reality. If the product of labour is alien to me and confronts me as an alien power, to whom does it belong? If my own activity does not belong to me but is an alien, forced activity, to whom does it belong? To a being *other* than myself. And who is this being? The *gods?* It is apparent in the earliest stages of advanced production, e.g. temple building, etc. in Egypt, India, Mexico, and in the service rendered to gods, that the product belonged to the gods. But the gods alone were never the lords of labour. And no more was *nature.* What a contradiction it would be if the more man subjugates nature by his labour, and the more the marvels of the gods are rendered superfluous by the marvels of industry, the more he should abstain from his joy in producing and his enjoyment of the product for love of these powers.

The *alien* being to whom labour and the product of labour belong, to whose service labour is devoted, and to whose enjoyment the product of labour goes, can only be *man* himself. If the product of labour does not belong to the worker, but confronts him as an alien power, this can only be because it belongs to *a man other than the worker.*

If his activity is a torment to him it must be a source of enjoyment and pleasure to another. Not the gods, nor nature, but only man himself can be this alien power over men.

Consider the earlier statement that the relation of man to himself is first *realized, objectified,* through his relation to other men. If he is related to the product of his labour, his objectified labour, as to an *alien,* hostile, powerful and independent object, he is related in such a way that another alien, hostile, powerful and independent man is the lord of this object. If he is related to his own activity as to unfree activity, then he is related to it as activity in the service, and under the domination, coercion and yoke, of another man.

Every self-alienation of man, from himself and from nature, appears in the relation which he postulates between other men and himself and nature. Thus religious self-alienation is necessarily exemplified in the relation between laity and priest, or, since it is here a question of the spiritual world, between the laity and a mediator. In the real world of practice this self-alienation can only be expressed in the real, practical relation of man to his fellow men. The medium through which alienation occurs is itself a *practical* one. Through alienated labour, therefore, man not only produces his relation to the object and to the process of production as to alien and hostile men; he also produces the relation of other men to his production and his product, and the relation between himself and other men. Just as he creates his own production as a vitiation, a punishment, and his own product as a loss, as a product which does not belong to him, so he creates the domination of the non-producer over production and its product. As he alienates his own activity, so he bestows upon the stranger an activity which is not his own.

We have so far considered this relation only from the side of the worker, and later on we shall consider it also from the side of the non-worker.

Thus, through alienated labour the worker creates the relation of another man, who does not work and is outside the work process, to this labour. The relation of the worker to work also produces the relation of the capitalist (or whatever one likes to call the lord of labour) to work. *Private property* is, therefore, the product, the necessary result, of *alienated labour,* of the external relation of the worker to nature and to himself.

Private property is thus derived from the analysis of the concept of *alienated labour;* that is, alienated man, alienated labour, alienated life, and estranged man.

We have, of course, derived the concept of *alienated labour (alienated life)* from political economy, from an analysis of the *movement of private property.* But the analysis of this concept shows that although private property appears to be the basis and cause of alienated labour, it is rather a consequence of the latter, just as the gods are *fundamentally* not the cause but the product of confusions of human reason. At a later stage, however, there is a reciprocal influence.

Only in the final stage of the development of private property is its secret revealed, namely, that it is on one hand the *product* of alienated labour, and on the other hand the *means* by which labour is alienated, *the realization of this alienation.*

This elucidation throws light upon several unresolved controversies—

1. Political economy begins with labour as the real soul of production and then goes on to attribute nothing to labour and everything to private property. Proudhon, faced by this contradiction, has decided in favour of labour against private property. We perceive, however, that this apparent contradiction is the contradiction of *alienated labour* with itself and that political economy has merely formulated the laws of alienated labour.

We also observe, therefore, that *wages* and *private property* are identical, for wages, like the product or object of labour, labour itself remunerated, are only a necessary consequence of the alienation of labour. In the wage system labour appears not as an end in itself but as the servant of wages. We shall develop this point later on and here only bring out some of the [XXVI] consequences.

An enforced *increase in wages* (disregarding the other difficulties, and especially that such an anomaly could only be maintained by force) would be nothing more than a *better remuneration of slaves,* and would not restore, either to the worker or to the work, their human significance and worth.

Even the *equality of incomes* which Proudhon demands would only change the relation of the present-day worker to his work into a relation of all men to work. Society would then be conceived as an abstract capitalist.

2. From the relation of alienated labour to private property it also follows that the emancipation of society from private property, from servitude, takes the political form of the *emancipation of the workers;* not in the sense that only the latter's emancipation is involved, but because this emancipation includes the emancipation of humanity as a whole. For all human servitude is involved in the relation of the worker to production, and all the types of servitude are only modifications or consequences of this relation.

As we have discovered the concept of *private property* by an *analysis* of the concept of *alienated labour,* so with the aid of these two factors we can evolve all the *categories* of political economy, and in every category, e.g. trade, competition, capital, money, we shall discover only a particular and developed expression of these fundamental elements.

However, before considering this structure let us attempt to solve two problems.

1. To determine the general nature of *private property* as it has resulted from alienated labour, in its relation to *genuine human and social property.*

2. We have taken as a fact and analysed the *alienation of labour.* How does it happen, we may ask, that *man alienates his labour?* How is this alienation founded in the nature of human development? We have already done much to solve the problem in so far as we have *transformed* the question concerning the *origin of private property* into a question about the relation between *alienated labour* and the process of development of mankind. For in speaking of private property one believes oneself to be dealing with something external to mankind. But in speaking of labour one deals directly with mankind itself. This new formulation of the problem already contains its solution.

ad (1) *The general nature of private property and its relation to genuine human property.*

We have resolved alienated labour into two parts, which mutually determine each other, or rather, which constitute two different expressions of one and the same relation. *Appropriation* appears as *alienation* and *alienation* as *appropriation,* alienation as genuine acceptance in the community.

We have considered one aspect, *alienated* labour, in its bearing upon the *worker* himself, i.e. *the relation of alienated labour to itself.* And we have found as the necessary consequence of this relation the *property relation* of the *non-worker* to the *worker* and to labour. *Private property* as the material, summarized expression of alienated labour includes both relations; *the relation of the worker to labour, to the product of his labour and to the non-worker,* and the relation of the *non-worker to the worker and to the product of the latter's labour.*

We have already seen that in relation to the worker, who *appropriates* nature by his labour, appropriation appears as alienation, self-activity as activity for another and of another, living as the sacrifice of life, and production of the object as loss of the object to an alien power, an alien man. Let us now consider the relation of this *alien* man to the worker, to labour, and to the object of labour.

It should be noted first that everything which appears to the worker as an *activity of alienation,* appears to the non-worker as a *condition of alienation.* Secondly, the *real, practical* attitude (as a state of mind) of the worker in production and to the product appears to the non-worker who confronts him as a *theoretical* attitude.

[XXVII] Thirdly, the non-worker does everything against the worker which the latter does against himself, but he does not do against himself what he does against the worker.

Let us examine these three relationships more closely.*

PRIVATE PROPERTY AND COMMUNISM

. . . The antithesis between *propertylessness* and *property* is still an indeterminate antithesis, which is not conceived in its *active reference* to its intrinsic relations, not yet conceived as a contradiction, so long as it is not understood as an antithesis between *labour* and *capital.* Even without the advanced development of private property, e.g. in ancient Rome, in Turkey, etc. this antithesis may be expressed in a primitive form. In this form it does not yet *appear* as established by private property itself. But labour, the subjective essence of private property as the exclusion of property, and capital, objective labour as the exclusion of labour, constitute *private property* as the developed relation of the contradiction and thus a dynamic relation which drives towards its resolution.

ad ibidem. The supersession of self-estrangement follows the same course as self-estrangement. *Private property* is first considered only from its objective aspect, but with labour conceived as its essence. Its mode of existence is, therefore, *capital* which it is necessary to abolish "as such" (Proudhon). Or else the *specific form* of labour (labour which is brought to a common level, subdivided, and thus unfree) is regarded as the source of the *nocivity* of private property and of its existence alienated from man. Fourier, in accord with the Physiocrats, regards *agricultural labour* as being at least the exemplary kind of labour. Saint-Simon asserts on the contrary that *industrial labour* as such is the essence of labour, and consequently he desires the *exclusive* rule of the industrialists and an amelioration of the condition of the workers. Finally, *communism* is the positive expression of the abolition of private property, and in the first place of universal private property. In taking this relation in its *universal aspect* communism is, in its first form, only the generalization and fulfilment of the relation. As such it appears in a double form; the domination of material property looms so large that it aims to destroy everything which is incapable of being possessed by everyone as private property. It wishes to eliminate talent, etc. by *force.* Immediate physical possession seems to it the unique goal of life and existence. The role of *worker* is not abolished, but is extended to all men. The relation of private property remains the relation of the community to the world of things. Finally, this tendency to oppose general private property to private property is expressed in an animal form; *marriage* (which is incontestably a form of *exclusive private property*)

---

*[The manuscript breaks off unfinished at this point.]

is contrasted with the community of women, in which women become communal and common property. One may say that this idea of the *community of women* is the *open secret* of this entirely crude and unreflective communism. Just as women are to pass from marriage to universal prostitution, so the whole world of wealth (i.e. the objective being of man) is to pass from the relation of exclusive marriage with the private owner to the relation of universal prostitution with the community. This communism, which negates the *personality* of man in every sphere, is only the logical expression of private property, which is this negation. Universal *envy* setting itself up as a power is only a camouflaged form of cupidity which re-establishes itself and satisfies itself in a different way. The thoughts of every individual private property are *at least* directed against any *wealthier* private property, in the form of envy and the desire to reduce everything to a common level; so that this envy and levelling in fact constitute the essence of competition. Crude communism is only the culmination of such envy and levelling-down on the basis of a *preconceived* minimum. How little this abolition of private property represents a genuine appropriation is shown by the abstract negation of the whole world of culture and civilization, and the regression to the *unnatural* [IV] simplicity of the poor and wantless individual who has not only not surpassed private property but has not yet even attained to it.

The community is only a community of *work* and of *equality of wages* paid out by the communal capital, by the *community* as universal capitalist. The two sides of the relation are raised to a *supposed* universality; *labour* as a condition in which everyone is placed, and *capital* as the acknowledged universality and power of the community.

In the relationship with *woman,* as the prey and the handmaid of communal lust, is expressed the infinite degradation in which man exists for himself; for the secret of this relationship finds its *unequivocal,* incontestable, *open* and revealed expression in the relation of man to woman and in the way in which the *direct* and *natural* species-relationship is conceived. The immediate, natural and necessary relation of human being to human being is also the *relation* of *man* to *woman.* In this *natural* species-relationship man's relation to nature is directly his relation to man, and his relation to man is directly his relation to nature, to his own natural function. Thus, in this relation is *sensuously revealed,* reduced to an observable *fact,* the extent to which human nature has become nature for man and to which nature has become human nature for him. From this relationship man's whole level of development can be assessed. It follows from the character of this relationship how far *man* has become, and has understood himself as, a *species-being,* a *human being.* The relation of man to woman is the *most natural* relation of human being to human being. It indicates, therefore, how far man's *natural* behaviour has become *human,* and how far his *human* essence has become a *natural* essence for him, how far his *human nature* has become *nature* for him. It also shows how far man's needs have become *human* needs, and consequently how far the other person, as a person, has become one of his needs, and to what extent he is in his individual existence at the same time a social being. The first positive annulment of private property, crude communism, is, therefore, only a *phenomenal form* of the infamy of private property representing itself as positive community.

2. Communism (*a*) still political in nature, democratic or despotic; (*b*) with the abolition of the state, yet still incomplete and influenced by private property, that is, by the alienation of man. In both forms communism is already aware of being the reintegration of man, his return to himself, the supersession of man's self-alienation. But since it has not yet grasped the positive nature of private property, or the *human* nature of needs, it is still captured and contaminated by private property. It has well understood the concept, but not the essence.

3. *Communism* is the *positive* abolition of *private property,* of *human self-alienation,* and thus the real *appropriation* of *human* nature through and for man. It is, therefore, the return of man himself as a *social,* i.e. really human, being, a complete and conscious return which assimilates all the wealth of previous development. Communism as a fully developed naturalism is humanism and as a fully developed humanism is naturalism. It is the *definitive* resolution of the antagonism between man and nature, and between man and man. It is the true solution of the conflict between existence and essence, between objectification and self-affirmation, between freedom and necessity, between individual and species. It is the solution of the riddle of history and knows itself to be this solution.

[V] Thus the whole historical development, both the *real* genesis of communism (the birth of its empirical existence) and its thinking consciousness, is its comprehended and conscious process of becoming; whereas the other, still undeveloped, communism seeks in certain historical forms opposed to private property a *historical* justification founded upon what already exists, and to this end tears out of their context isolated elements of this development (Cabet and Villegardelle are pre-eminent among those who ride this hobby-horse) and asserts them as proofs of its historical pedigree. In doing so, it makes clear that by far the greater part of this development contradicts its own assertions, and that if it has ever existed its past existence refutes its pretension to *essential being.*

It is easy to understand the necessity which leads the whole revolutionary movement to find its empirical, as well as its theoretical, basis in the development of *private property,* and more precisely of the economic system.

This material, directly *perceptible* private property is the material and sensuous expression of *alienated human* life. Its movement—production and consumption—is the *sensuous* manifestation of the movement of all previous production, i.e. the realization or reality of man. Religion, the family, the state, law, morality, science, art, etc. are only *particular* forms of production and come under its general law. The positive supersession of *private property,* as the appropriation of *human* life, is, therefore, the positive supersession of all alienation, and the return of man from religion, the family, the state, etc. to his *human,* i.e. social life. Religious alienation as such occurs only in the sphere of *consciousness,* in the inner life of man, but economic alienation is that of *real life* and its supersession, therefore, affects both aspects. Of course, the development in different nations has a different beginning according to whether the actual and *established* life of the people is more in the realm of mind or more in the external world, is a real or ideal life. Communism begins where atheism begins (Owen), but atheism is at the outset still far from being *communism;* indeed it is still for the most part an abstraction.

Thus the philanthropy of atheism is at first only an abstract *philosophical* philanthropy, whereas that of communism is at once *real* and oriented towards *action.*

We have seen how, on the assumption that private property has been positively superseded, man produces man, himself and then other men; how the object which is the direct activity of his personality is at the same time his existence for other men and their existence for him. Similarly, the material of labour and man himself as a subject are the starting-point as well as the result of this movement (and because there must be this starting-point private property is a historical necessity). Therefore, the *social* character is the universal character of the whole movement; as society itself produces *man* as *man,* so it is *produced* by him. Activity and mind are social in their content as well as in their *origin;* they are *social* activity and social mind. The *human* significance of nature only exists for *social* man, because only in this case is nature a *bond* with other *men,* the basis of his existence for others and of their existence for him. Only then is nature the *basis* of his own *human* experience and a vital element of human reality. The *natural* existence of man has here become his *human* existence and nature itself has become human for him. Thus *society* is the accomplished union of man with nature, the veritable resurrection of nature, the realized naturalism of man and the realized humanism of nature.

[VI] Social activity and social mind by no means exist *only* in the form of activity or mind which is directly communal. Nevertheless, communal activity and mind, i.e. activity and mind which express and confirm themselves directly in a *real association* with other men, occur everywhere where this direct expression of sociability arises from the content of the activity or corresponds to the nature of mind.

Even when I carry out *scientific* work, etc., an activity which I can seldom conduct in direct association with other men, I perform a *social,* because *human,* act. It is not only the material of my activity—such as the language itself which the thinker uses—which is given to me as a social product. My *own existence* is a social activity. For this reason, what I myself produce I produce for society, and with the consciousness of acting as a social being.

My universal consciousness is only the *theoretical* form of that whose *living* form is the real community, the social entity, although at the present day this universal consciousness is an abstraction from real life and is opposed to it as an enemy. That is why the *activity* of my universal consciousness as such is my *theoretical* existence as a social being.

It is above all necessary to avoid postulating "society" once again as an abstraction confronting the individual. The individual *is* the *social being.* The manifestation of his life—even when it does not appear directly in the form of a communal manifestation, accomplished in association with other men—is, therefore, a manifestation and affirmation of *social life.* Individual human life and species-life are not different things, even though the mode of existence of individual life is necessarily either a more *specific* or a more *general* mode of species-life, or that of species-life a *specific* or more *general* mode of individual life.

In his *species-consciousness* man confirms his real *social life,* and reproduces his real existence in thought; while conversely, species-life confirms itself in species-consciousness and exists for itself in its universality as a thinking being. Though man is a unique individual—and it is just his particularity which makes him an individual, a really *individual* communal being—he is equally the *whole,* the ideal whole, the subjective existence of society as thought and experienced. He exists in reality as the representation and the real mind of social existence, and as the sum of human manifestations of life.

Thought and being are indeed *distinct* but they also form a unity. *Death* seems to be a harsh victory of the species over the individual and to contradict their unity; but the particular individual is only a *determinate species-being* and as such he is mortal.

4. Just as *private property* is only the sensuous expression of the fact that man is at the same time an *objective* fact for himself and becomes an alien and non-human object for himself; just as his manifestation of life is also his alienation of life and his self-realization a loss of reality, the emergence of an *alien* reality; so the positive supersession of private property, i.e. the *sensuous* appropriation of the human essence and of human life, of objective man and of human *creations,* by and for man, should not be taken only in the sense of *immediate,* exclusive *enjoyment,* or only in the sense of *possession* or *having.* Man appropriates his manifold being in an all-inclusive way, and thus as a whole man. All his *human* relations to the world—seeing, hearing,

smelling, tasting, touching, thinking, observing, feeling, desiring, acting, loving—in short, all the organs of his individuality, like the organs which are directly communal in form, [VII] are in their objective action (their *action in relation to the object*) the appropriation of this object, the appropriation of human reality. The way in which they react to the object is the confirmation of *human reality*.* It is human effectiveness and human *suffering,* for suffering humanly considered is an enjoyment of the self for man.

Private property has made us so stupid and partial that an object is only *ours* when we have it, when it exists for us as capital or when it is directly eaten, drunk, worn, inhabited, etc., in short, *utilized* in some way. But private property itself only conceives these various forms of possession as *means of life,* and the life for which they serve as means is the *life* of *private property*—labour and creation of capital.

Thus *all* the physical and intellectual senses have been replaced by the simple alienation of *all* these senses; the sense of *having.* The human being had to be reduced to this absolute poverty in order to be able to give birth to all his inner wealth. . . .

The supersession of private property is, therefore, the complete *emancipation* of all the human qualities and senses. It is such an emancipation because these qualities and senses have become *human,* from the subjective as well as the objective point of view. The eye has become a *human* eye when its *object* has become a *human,* social object, created by man and destined for him. The senses have, therefore, become directly theoreticians in practice. They relate themselves to the thing for the sake of the thing, but the thing itself is an *objective human* relation to itself and to man, and vice versa.** Need and enjoyment have thus lost their *egoistic* character and nature has lost its mere *utility* by the fact that its utilization has become *human* utilization.

Similarly, the senses and minds of other men have become my *own* appropriation. Thus besides these direct organs, *social* organs are constituted, in the form of society; for example, activity in direct association with others has become an organ for the manifestation of life and a mode of appropriation of *human* life.

It is evident that the human eye appreciates things in a different way from the crude, non-human eye, the human *ear* differently from the crude ear. As we have seen, it is only when the object becomes a *human* object, or objective *humanity,* that man does not become lost in it. This is only possible when man himself becomes a *social* object; when he himself becomes a social being and society becomes a being for him in this object.

On the one hand, it is only when objective reality everywhere becomes for man in society the reality of human faculties, human reality, and thus the reality of his own faculties, that all *objects* become for him the *objectification of himself.* The objects then confirm and realize his individuality, they are *his own* objects, i.e. man himself becomes the object. *The manner in which these objects* become his own depends upon the *nature of the object* and the nature of the corresponding faculty; for it is precisely the *determinate character* of this relation which constitutes the specific real mode of affirmation. The object is not the same for the *eye* as for the *ear,* for the ear as for the eye. The *distinctive character* of each faculty is precisely its *characteristic* essence and thus also the characteristic mode of its objectification, of its *objectively real,* living *being.* It is therefore not only in thought, [VIII] but through *all* the senses that man is affirmed in the objective world.

---

*It is, therefore, just as varied as the determinations of human nature and activities are diverse.

**In practice I can only relate myself in a human way to a thing when the thing is related in a human way to man.

Let us next consider the subjective aspect. Man's musical sense is only awakened by music. The most beautiful music has no meaning for the non-musical ear, is not an object for it, because my object can only be the confirmation of one of my own faculties. It can only be so for me in so far as my faculty exists for itself as a subjective capacity, because the meaning of an object for me extends only as far as the sense extends (only makes sense for an appropriate sense). For this reason, the *senses* of social man are *different* from those of non-social man. It is only through the objectively deployed wealth of the human being that the wealth of subjective *human* sensibility (a musical ear, an eye which is sensitive to the beauty of form, in short, senses which are capable of human satisfaction and which confirm themselves as human faculties) is cultivated or created. For it is not only the five senses, but also the so-called spiritual senses, the practical senses (desiring, loving, etc.), in brief, human sensibility and the human character of the senses, which can only come into being through the existence of *its* object, through humanized nature. The cultivation of the five senses is the work of all previous history. Sense which is subservient to crude needs has only a restricted meaning. For a starving man the human form of food does not exist, but only its abstract character as food. It could just as well exist in the most crude form, and it is impossible to say in what way this feeding-activity would differ from that of animals. The needy man, burdened with cares, has no appreciation of the most beautiful spectacle. The dealer in minerals sees only their commercial value, not their beauty or their particular characteristics; he has no mineralogical sense. Thus, the objectification of the human essence, both theoretically and practically, is necessary in order to *humanize* man's senses, and also to create the *human senses* corresponding to all the wealth of human and natural being.

Just as society at its beginnings finds, through the development of *private property* with its wealth and poverty (both intellectual and material), the materials necessary for this *cultural development,* so the fully constituted society produces man in all the plenitude of his being, the wealthy man endowed with all the senses, as an enduring reality. It is only in a social context that subjectivism and objectivism, spiritualism and materialism, activity and passivity, cease to be antinomies and thus cease to exist as such antinomies. The resolution of the *theoretical* contradictions is possible *only* through practical means, only through the *practical* energy of man. Their resolution is not by any means, therefore, only a problem of knowledge, but is a *real* problem of life which philosophy was unable to solve precisely because it saw there a purely theoretical problem.

It can be seen that the history of *industry* and industry as it *objectively* exists is an *open* book of the *human faculties,* and a human *psychology* which can be sensuously apprehended. This history has not so far been conceived in relation to human *nature,* but only from a superficial utilitarian point of view, since in the condition of alienation it was only possible to conceive real human faculties and *human* species-action in the form of general human existence, as religion, or as history in its abstract, general aspect as politics, art and literature, etc. *Everyday material industry* (which can be conceived as part of that general development; or equally, the general development can be conceived as a specific part of industry since all human activity up to the present has been labour, i.e. industry, self-alienated activity) shows us, in the form of *sensuous useful objects,* in an alienated form, the *essential human faculties* transformed into objects. No psychology for which this book, i.e. the most tangible and accessible part of history, remains closed, can become a *real* science with a genuine content. What is to be thought of a science which stays aloof from this enormous field of human labour, and which does not feel its own inadequacy even though this great wealth of human activity means nothing to it except perhaps what can be expressed in the single phrase—"need," "common need"?

The *natural sciences* have developed a tremendous activity and have assembled an ever-growing mass of data. But philosophy has remained alien to these sciences just as they have remained alien to philosophy. Their momentary *rapprochement* was only a *fantastic* illusion. There was a desire for union but the power to effect it was lacking. Historiography itself only takes natural science into account incidentally, regarding it as a factor making for enlightenment, for practical utility and for particular great discoveries. But natural science has penetrated all the more *practically* into human life through industry. It has transformed human life and prepared the emancipation of humanity, even though its immediate effect was to accentuate the dehumanization of man. *Industry* is the actual historical relationship of nature, and thus of natural science, to man. If industry is conceived as the *exoteric* manifestation of the essential human *faculties,* the *human* essence of nature and the *natural* essence of man can also be understood. Natural science will then abandon its abstract materialist, or rather idealist, orientation, and will become the basis of a *human* science, just as it has already become—though in an alienated form—the basis of actual human life. One basis for life and another for science is *a priori* a falsehood. Nature, as it develops in human history, in the act of genesis of human society, is the *actual* nature of man; thus nature, as it develops through industry, though in an *alienated* form, is truly *anthropological* nature.

Sense experience (*see* Feuerbach) must be the basis of all science. Science is only genuine science when it proceeds from sense experience, in the two forms of *sense perception* and *sensuous* need; i.e. only when it proceeds from nature. The whole of history is a preparation for "man" to become an object of *sense* perception, and for the development of human needs (the needs of man as such). History itself is a *real* part of *natural history,* of the development of nature into man. Natural science will one day incorporate the science of man, just as the science of man will incorporate natural science; there will be a *single* science.

Man is the direct object of natural science, because directly *perceptible nature* is for man directly human sense experience (an identical expression) in the form of the *other person* who is directly presented to him in a sensuous way. His own sense experience only exists as human sense experience for himself through the *other person.* But *nature* is the direct object of the *science of man.* The first object for man—man himself—is nature, sense experience; and the particular sensuous human faculties, which can only find objective realization in *natural* objects, can only attain self knowledge in the science of natural being. The element of thought itself, the element of the living manifestation of thought, language, is sensuous in character. The *social* reality of nature and *human* natural science, or the *natural science of man,* are identical expressions.

It will be seen from this how, in place of the *wealth* and *poverty* of political economy, we have the *wealthy* man and the plenitude of *human* need. The wealthy man is at the same time one who *needs* a complex of human manifestations of life, and whose own self-realization exists as an inner necessity, a *need.* Not only the wealth but also the *poverty* of man acquires, in a socialist perspective, a *human* and thus a social meaning. Poverty is the passive bond which leads man to experience a need for the greatest wealth, the *other* person. The sway of the objective entity within me, the sensuous eruption of my life-activity, is the passion which here becomes the *activity* of my being.

A being does not regard himself as independent unless he is his own master, and he is only his own master when he owes his existence to himself. A man who lives by the favour of another considers himself a dependent being. But I live completely by an-other person's favour when I owe to him not only the continuance of my life but also *its creation;* when he is its *source.* My life has necessarily such a cause outside itself if it is not my own creation. The idea of *creation* is thus one which it is difficult to elimi-nate from popular consciousness. This consciousness is *unable to conceive* that nature and man exist on their own account, because such an existence contradicts all the tan-gible facts of practical life.

The idea of the creation of the *earth* has received a severe blow from the science of geogeny, i.e. from the science which portrays the formation and development of the earth as a process of spontaneous generation. *Generatio aequivoca* (spontaneous gen-eration) is the only practical refutation of the theory of creation.

But it is easy indeed to say to the particular individual what Aristotle said: You are engendered by your father and mother, and consequently it is the coitus of two human beings, a human species-act, which has produced the human being. You see, therefore, that even in a physical sense man owes his existence to man. Consequently, it is not enough to keep in view only one of the two aspects, the *infinite* progression, and to ask further: who engendered my father and my grandfather? You must also keep in mind the *circular movement* which is perceptible in that progression, according to which man, in the act of generation reproduces himself; thus *man* always remains the subject. But you will reply: I grant you this circular movement, but you must in turn concede the progression, which leads ever further to the point where I ask; who created the first man and nature as a whole? I can only reply: your question is itself a product of abstraction. Ask yourself how you arrive at that question. Ask yourself whether your question does not arise from a point of view to which I cannot reply because it is a per-verted one. Ask yourself whether that progression exists as such for rational thought. If you ask a question about the creation of nature and man you abstract from nature and man. You suppose them *non-existent* and you want me to demonstrate that they *exist.* I reply: give up your abstraction and at the same time you abandon your question. Or else, if you want to maintain your abstraction, be consistent, and if you think of man and nature as non-existent, [XI] think of yourself too as non-existent, for you are also man and nature. Do not think, do not ask me any questions, for as soon as you think and ask questions your abstraction from the existence of nature and man becomes meaningless. Or are you such an egoist that you conceive everything as non-existent and yet want to exist yourself?

You may reply: I do not want to conceive the nothingness of nature, etc.; I only ask you about the act of its creation, just as I ask the anatomist about the formation of bones, etc.

Since, however, for socialist man, the *whole of what is called world history* is nothing but the creation of man by human labour, and the emergence of nature for man, he, therefore, has the evident and irrefutable proof of his *self-creation,* of his own *origins.* Once the essence of man and of nature, man as a natural being and nature as a human reality, has become evident in practical life, in sense experience, the quest for an *alien* being, a being above man and nature (a quest which is an avowal of the unre-ality of man and nature) becomes impossible in practice. *Atheism,* as a denial of this unreality, is no longer meaningful, for atheism is a *negation of God* and seeks to assert by this negation the *existence of man.* Socialism no longer requires such a roundabout method; it begins from the *theoretical* and *practical sense perception* of man and na-ture as essential beings. It is positive human *self-consciousness,* no longer a self-consciousness attained through the negation of religion; just as the *real life* of man is positive and no longer attained through the negation of private property, through *com-*

munism. Communism is the phase of negation of the negation and is, consequently, for the next stage of historical development, a real and necessary factor in the emancipation and rehabilitation of man. Communism is the necessary form and the dynamic principle of the immediate future, but communism is not itself the goal of human development—the form of human society.

CRITIQUE OF HEGEL'S DIALECTIC AND GENERAL PHILOSOPHY

This is perhaps an appropriate point at which to explain and substantiate what has been said, and to make some general comments upon Hegel's dialectic, especially as it is expounded in the *Phenomenology* and *Logic,* and upon its relation to the modern critical movement.

Modern German criticism was so much concerned with the past, and was so hampered by its involvement with its subject-matter, that it had a wholly uncritical attitude to the methods of criticism and completely ignored the partly formal, but in fact *essential* question—how do we now stand with regard to the Hegelian *dialectic?* This ignorance of the relationship of modern criticism to Hegel's general philosophy and his dialectic in particular was so great that critics such as Strauss and Bruno Bauer (the former in all his writings; the latter in his *Synoptiker,* where, in opposition to Strauss, he substitutes the "self-consciousness" of abstract man for the substance of "abstract nature," and even in *Das entdeckte Christentum)* were, at least implicitly, ensnared in Hegelian logic. Thus, for instance, in *Das entdeckte Christentum* it is argued: "As if self-consciousness in positing the world, that which is different, did not produce itself in producing its object; for it then annuls the difference between itself and what it has produced, since it exists only in this creation and movement, has its purpose only in this movement, etc." Or again: "They (the French materialists) could not see that the movement of the universe has only become real and unified in itself in so far as it is the movement of self-consciousness." These expressions not only do not differ from the Hegelian conception, but reproduce it textually.

[XII] How little these writers, in undertaking their criticism (Bauer in his *Synoptiker*), were aware of their relation to Hegel's dialectic, and how little such an awareness emerged from the criticism, is demonstrated by Bauer in his *Gute Sache der Freiheit* when, instead of replying to the indiscreet question put by Gruppe, "And now what is to be done with logic?," he transmits it to future critics.

Now that Feuerbach, in his "Thesen" in the *Anecdotis* and in greater detail in his *Philosophie der Zukunft,* has demolished the inner principle of the old dialectic and philosophy, the "Critical School," which was unable to do this itself but has seen it accomplished, has proclaimed itself the pure, decisive, absolute, and finally enlightened criticism, and in its spiritual pride has reduced the whole historical movement to the relation existing between itself and the rest of the world, which comes into the category of "the mass." It has reduced all dogmatic antitheses to the single dogmatic antithesis between its own cleverness and the stupidity of the world, between the critical Christ and mankind—"the rabble." At every moment of the day it has demonstrated its own excellence *vis-à-vis* the stupidity of the mass, and it has finally announced the critical *last judgment* by proclaiming that the day is at hand when the whole of fallen mankind will assemble before it and will be divided up into groups each of which will be handed its *testimonium paupertatis* (certificate of poverty). The Critical School has made public its superiority to all human feelings and to the world, above which it sits enthroned in sublime solitude, content to utter occasionally from its sarcastic lips the laughter of the Olympian gods. After all these entertaining antics of idealism (of Young Hegelianism) which is expiring in the form of criticism, the Critical School has not even now intimated that it was necessary to discuss critically its own source, the dialectic of Hegel; nor has it given any indication of its relation with the dialectic of Feuerbach. This is a procedure totally lacking in critical sense.

Feuerbach is the only person who has a *serious* and *critical* relation to Hegel's dialectic, who has made real discoveries in this field, and above all, who has vanquished the old philosophy. The magnitude of Feuerbach's achievement and the unassuming simplicity with which he presents his work to the world are in striking contrast with the behaviour of others.

Feuerbach's great achievement is—

1. to have shown that philosophy is nothing more than religion brought into thought and developed by thought, and that it is equally to be condemned as another form and mode of existence of human alienation;

2. to have founded *genuine materialism* and *positive science* by making the social relationship of "man to man" the basic principle of his theory;

3. to have opposed to the negation of the negation which claims to be the absolute positive, a self-subsistent principle positively founded on itself.

Feuerbach explains Hegel's dialectic, and at the same time justifies taking the positive phenomenon, that which is perceptible and indubitable, as the starting-point, in the following way.

Hegel begins from the alienation of substance (logically, from the infinite, the abstract universal) from the absolute and fixed abstraction; i.e. in ordinary language, from religion and theology. Secondly, he supersedes the infinite, and posits the real, the perceptible, the finite, and the particular. (Philosophy, supersession of religion and theology.) Thirdly, he then supersedes the positive and reestablishes the abstraction, the infinite. (Re-establishment of religion and theology.)

Thus Feuerbach conceives the negation of the negation as being *only* a contradiction within philosophy itself, which affirms theology (transcendence, etc.) after having superseded it, and thus affirms it in opposition to philosophy.

For the positing or self-affirmation and self-confirmation which is implied in the negation of the negation is regarded as a positing which is still uncertain, burdened with its contrary, doubtful of itself and thus incomplete, not demonstrated by its own existence, and implicit. [XIII] The positing which is perceptually indubitable and grounded upon itself is directly opposed to it.

In conceiving the negation of the negation, from the aspect of the positive relation inherent in it, as the only true positive, and from the aspect of the negative relation inherent in it, as the only true act and the self-confirming act of all being, Hegel has merely discovered an *abstract, logical* and *speculative* expression of the historical process, which is not yet the real history of man as a given subject, but only the history of the *act of creation,* of the *genesis of man.*

We shall explain both the abstract form of this process and the difference between the process as conceived by Hegel and by modern criticism, by Feuerbach in *Das Wesen des Christentums;* or rather, the critical form of this process which is still so uncritical in Hegel.

Let us examine Hegel's system. It is necessary to begin with the *Phenomenology,* because it is there that Hegel's philosophy was born and that its secret is to be found. [Marx's version of the table of contents from Hegel's *Phenomenology* which follows here has been deleted—F.B.]

*   *   *

Hegel's *Encyclopaedia* begins with logic, with *pure speculative thought,* and ends with *absolute knowledge,* the self-conscious and self-conceiving philosophical or absolute mind, i.e. the superhuman, abstract mind. The whole of the *Encyclopaedia* is nothing but the extended being of the philosophical mind, its self-objectification; and the philosophical mind is nothing but the alienated world-mind thinking within the bounds of its self-alienation, i.e. conceiving itself in an abstract manner. *Logic* is the *money* of the mind, the speculative *thought-value* of man and of nature, their essence indifferent to any real determinate character and thus unreal; *thought* which is *alienated* and abstract and ignores real nature and man. *The external character of this abstract thought . . . nature* as it exists for this abstract thought. Nature is external to it, loss of itself, and is only conceived as something external, as abstract thought, but alienated abstract thought. Finally, spirit, this thought which returns to its own origin and which, as anthropological, phenomenological, psychological, customary, artistic-religious spirit, is not valid for itself until it discovers itself and relates itself to itself as absolute knowledge in the absolute (i.e. abstract) spirit, and so receives its conscious and fitting existence. For its real mode of existence is *abstraction.*

Hegel commits a double error. The first appears most clearly in the *Phenomenology,* the birthplace of his philosophy. When Hegel conceives wealth, the power of the state, etc. as entities alienated from the human being, he conceives them only in their thought form. They are entities of thought and thus simply an alienation of *pure* (i.e. abstract) philosophical thought. The whole movement, therefore, ends in absolute knowledge. It is precisely abstract thought from which these objects are alienated, and which they confront with their presumptuous reality. The *philosopher,* himself an abstract form of alienated man, sets himself up as the *measure* of the alienated world. The whole *history of alienation,* and of the retraction of alienation, is, therefore, only the *history of the production* of abstract thought, i.e. of absolute, logical, speculative thought. *Estrangement,* which thus forms the real interest of this alienation and of the supersession of this alienation, is the opposition of *in itself* and *for itself,* of *consciousness* and *self-consciousness,* of *object* and *subject,* i.e. the opposition in thought itself between abstract thought and sensible reality or real sensuous existence. All other contradictions and movements are merely the *appearance,* the *cloak,* the *exoteric* form of these two opposites which are alone important and which constitute the *significance* of the other, profane contradictions. It is not the fact that the human being *objectifies* himself *inhumanly,* in opposition to himself, but that he *objectifies* himself by *distinction* from and in *opposition* to abstract thought, which constitutes alienation as it exists and as it has to be transcended.

[XVIII] The appropriation of man's objectified and alienated faculties is thus, in the first place, only an *appropriation* which occurs in *consciousness,* in *pure thought,* i.e. *in abstraction.* It is the appropriation of these objects as thoughts and as movements of thought. For this reason, despite its thoroughly negative and critical appearance, and despite the genuine criticism which it contains and which often anticipates later developments, there is already implicit in the *Phenomenology,* as a germ, as a potentiality and a secret, the uncritical positivism and uncritical idealism of Hegel's later works—the philosophical dissolution and restoration of the existing empirical world. *Secondly,* the vindication of the objective world for man (for example, the recognition that sense perception is not *abstract* sense perception but *human* sense perception, that religion, wealth, etc. are only the alienated reality of *human* objectification, of *human* faculties put to work, and are, therefore, a way to genuine *human* reality), this appropriation, or the insight into this process, appears in Hegel as the recognition of *sensuousness, religion,* state power, etc. as *mental* phenomena, for *mind* alone is the true essence of man, and the true form of mind is thinking mind, the logical, speculative mind. The *human character* of nature, of historically produced nature, of man's products, is shown by their being *products* of abstract mind, and thus phases of *mind, entities of thought.* The *Phenomenology is* a concealed, unclear and mystifying criticism, but in so far as it grasps the *alienation* of man (even though man appears only as mind) all the elements of criticism are contained in it, and are often *presented* and *worked out* in a manner which goes far beyond Hegel's own point of view. The sections devoted to the "unhappy consciousness," the "honest consciousness," the struggle between the "noble" and the "base" consciousness, etc., etc. contain the *critical* elements (though still in an alienated form) of whole areas such as religion, the state, civil life, etc. Just as the *entity,* the *object,* appears as an entity of thought, so also the *subject* is always *consciousness* or *self-consciousness;* or rather, the object appears only as abstract consciousness and man as *self-consciousness.* Thus the distinctive forms of alienation which are manifested are only different forms of consciousness and self-consciousness. Since abstract consciousness (the form in which the object is conceived) is in *itself* merely a distinctive moment of self-consciousness, the outcome of the movement is the identity of self-consciousness and consciousness—absolute knowledge—the movement of abstract thought not directed outwards but proceeding within itself; i.e. the dialectic of pure thought is the result.

[XXIII] The outstanding achievement of Hegel's *Phenomenology*—the dialectic of negativity as the moving and creating principle—is, first, that Hegel grasps the self-creation of man as a process, objectification as loss of the object, as alienation and transcendence of this alienation, and that he, therefore, grasps the nature of *labour,* and conceives objective man (true, because real man) as the result of his *own* labour. The *real,* active orientation of man to himself as a species-being, or the affirmation of himself as a real species-being (i.e. as a human being) is only possible so far as he really brings forth all his *species-powers* (which is only possible through the co-operative endeavours of mankind and as an outcome of history) and treats these powers as objects, which can only be done at first in the form of alienation.

We shall next show in detail Hegel's one-sidedness and limitations, as revealed in the final chapter of the *Phenomenology,* on absolute knowledge; a chapter which contains the concentrated spirit of the *Phenomenology,* its relation to the dialectic, and also Hegel's *consciousness* of both and of their interrelations.

For the present, let us make these preliminary observations: Hegel's standpoint is that of modern political economy. He conceives *labour* as the *essence,* the self-confirming essence of man; he observes only the positive side of labour, not its negative side. Labour is *man's coming to be for himself* within *alienation,* or as an alienated man. Labour as Hegel understands and recognizes it is *abstract mental labour.* Thus, that which above all constitutes the *essence* of philosophy, the *alienation of man knowing himself,* or *alienated* science *thinking* itself, Hegel grasps as its essence. Consequently, he is able to bring together the separate elements of earlier philosophy and to present his own as the philosophy. What other philosophers did, that is, to conceive separate elements of nature and of human life as phases of self-consciousness and indeed of abstract self-consciousness, Hegel *knows* by doing philosophy; therefore, his science is absolute.

Let us now turn to our subject.

Absolute knowledge. The final chapter of the "Phenomenology."

The main point is that the *object of consciousness* is nothing else but *self-consciousness,* that the object is only *objectified* self-consciousness, self-consciousness as an object. (Positing man = self-consciousness.)

It is necessary, therefore, to surmount the *object of consciousness. Objectivity* as such is regarded as an alienated human relationship which does not correspond with the *essence of man,* self-consciousness. The reappropriation of the objective essence of man, which was produced as something alien and determined by alienation, signifies the supersession not only of *alienation* but also of *objectivity;* that is, man is regarded as a *non-objective, spiritual* being.

The process of *overcoming the object of consciousness* is described by Hegel as follows: The *object* does not reveal itself only as *returning* into the Self (according to Hegel that is a *one-sided* conception of the movement, considering only one aspect). Man is equated with self. The Self, however, is only man conceived *abstractly* and produced by abstraction. Man is self-referring. His eye, his ear, etc. are *self-referring;* every one of his faculties has this quality of *self-*reference. But it is entirely false to say on that account, "*Self-consciousness* has eyes, ears, faculties." Self-consciousness is rather a quality of human nature, of the human eye, etc.; human nature is not a quality of [XXIV] *self-consciousness.*

The Self, abstracted and determined for itself, is man as an *abstract egoist,* purely abstract *egoism* raised to the level of thought. (We shall return to this point later.)

For Hegel, *human life, man,* is equivalent to *self-consciousness.* All alienation of human life is, therefore, *nothing* but *alienation of self-consciousness.* The alienation of self-consciousness is not regarded as the *expression,* reflected in knowledge and thought, of the *real* alienation of human life. Instead, *actual* alienation, that which appears real, is in its *innermost* hidden nature (which philosophy first discloses) only the *phenomenal being* of the alienation of real human life, of *self-consciousness.* The science which comprehends this is therefore called *Phenomenology.* All reappropriation of alienated objective life appears, therefore, as an incorporation in self-consciousness. The person who takes possession of his being is only the self-consciousness which takes possession of objective being; the return of the object into the Self is, therefore, the reappropriation of the object.

Expressed in a *more comprehensive* way the *supersession of the object of consciousness* means: (1) that the object as such presents itself to consciousness as something disappearing; (2) that it is the alienation of self-consciousness which establishes "thinghood"; (3) that this alienation has *positive* as well as *negative* significance; (4) that it has this significance not only *for us* or in itself, but also *for self-consciousness itself;* (5) that for *self-consciousness* the negative of the object, its self-supersession, has *positive* significance, or self-consciousness *knows* thereby the nullity of the object in that self-consciousness alienates itself, for in this alienation it establishes *itself* as object or, for the sake of the indivisible unity of *being-for-itself,* establishes the object as itself; (6) that, on the other hand, this other "moment" is equally present, that self-consciousness has superseded and reabsorbed this alienation and objectivity, and is thus *at home* in its other being as such; (7) that this is the movement of consciousness, and consciousness is, therefore, the totality of its "moments"; (8) that similarly, consciousness must have related itself to the object in all its determinations, and have conceived it in terms of each of them. This totality of determinations makes the object *intrinsically* a *spiritual being,* and it becomes truly so for consciousness by the apprehension of every one of these determinations as the Self, or by what was called earlier the *spiritual* attitude towards them.

ad (1) That the object as such presents itself to consciousness as something disappearing is the above-mentioned *return of the object into the Self.*

ad (2) *The alienation of self-consciousness* establishes *"thinghood."* Because man equals self-consciousness, his alienated objective being or *"thinghood"* is equivalent to *alienated self-consciousness,* and "thinghood" is established by this alienation. ("Thinghood" is that which is *an object for him,* and an object for him is really only that which is an essential object, consequently his *objective* essence. And since it is not the real *man,* nor *nature*—man being *human nature*—who becomes as such a subject, but only an abstraction of man, self-consciousness, "thinghood" can only be *alienated self-consciousness.*) It is quite understandable that a living, natural being endowed with objective (i.e. material) faculties should have *real natural objects* of its being, and equally that its self-alienation should be the establishment of a *real,* objective world, but in the form of *externality,* as a world which does not belong to, and dominates, its being. There is nothing incomprehensible or mysterious about this. The converse, rather, would be mysterious. But it is equally clear that a self-consciousness, i.e. its alienation, can only establish *"thinghood,"* i.e. only an abstract thing, a thing created by abstraction and not a real thing. It is [XXVI] clear, moreover, that "thinghood" is totally lacking in *independence,* in *being,* vis-à-vis self-consciousness; it is a mere *construct* established by self-consciousness. And what is established is not self-confirming; it is the confirmation of the act of establishing, which for an instant, but only for an instant, fixes its energy as a product and *apparently* confers upon it the role of an independent, real being.

When real, corporeal *man,* with his feet firmly planted on the solid ground, inhaling and exhaling all the powers of nature, *posits* his real objective faculties, as a result of his alienation, as alien objects, the *positing* is not the subject of this act but the subjectivity of *objective* faculties whose action must also, therefore, be *objective.* An objective being acts objectively, and it would not act objectively if objectivity were not part of its essential being. It creates and establishes *only objects, because* it is established by objects, and because it is fundamentally *natural.* In the act of establishing it does not descend from its "pure activity" to the *creation of objects;* its *objective* product simply confirms its *objective* activity, its activity as an objective, natural being.

We see here how consistent naturalism or humanism is distinguished from both idealism and materialism, and at the same time constitutes their unifying truth. We see also that only naturalism is able to comprehend the process of world history.

Man is directly a *natural being.* As a natural being, and as a living natural being he is, on the one hand, endowed with *natural powers* and *faculties,* which exist in him as tendencies and abilities, as *drives.* On the other hand, as a natural, embodied, sentient, objective being he is a *suffering,* conditioned and limited being, like animals and plants. The *objects* of his drives exist outside himself as *objects* independent of him, yet they are *objects* of his *needs,* essential *objects* which are indispensable to the exercise and confirmation of his faculties. The fact that man is an *embodied,* living, real, sentient, objective being with natural powers, means that he has *real, sensuous objects* as the objects of his being, or that he can only express his being in real, sensuous objects. *To be* objective, natural, sentient and at the same time to have object, nature and sense outside oneself, or to be oneself object, nature and sense for a third person, is the same thing. *Hunger* is a natural *need;* it requires, therefore, a *nature* outside itself, an *object* outside itself, in order to be satisfied and stilled. Hunger is the objective need of a body for an *object* which exists outside itself and which is essential for its integration and the expression of its nature. The sun is an *object,* a necessary and life-assuring object, for the plant, just as the plant is an object for the sun, an *expression* of the sun's life-giving power and *objective* essential powers.

A being which does not have its nature outside itself is not a *natural* being and does not share in the being of nature. A being which has no object outside itself is not an objective being. A being which is not itself an object for a third being has no being for its *object,* i.e. it is not objectively related and its being is not objective.

[XXVII] A non-objective being is a *non-being.* Suppose a being which neither is an object itself nor has an object. In the first place, such a being would be the *only* being; no other being would exist outside itself and it would be solitary and alone. For as soon as there exist objects outside myself, as soon as I am not *alone,* I am *another, another reality* from the object outside me. For this third object I am thus an *other reality* than itself, i.e. *its object.* To suppose a being which is not the object of another being would be to suppose that *no* objective being exists. As soon as I have an object, this object has me for its object. But a *non-objective* being is an unreal, non-sensuous, merely conceived being; i.e. a merely imagined being, an abstraction. To be *sensuous,* i.e. real, is to be an object of sense or *sensuous* object, and thus to have sensuous objects outside oneself, objects of one's sensations. To be sentient is to *suffer* (to experience).

Man as an objective sentient being is a *suffering* being, and since he feels his suffering, a *passionate* being. Passion is man's faculties striving to attain their object.

But man is not merely a natural being; he is a *human* natural being. He is a being for himself, and, therefore, a *species-being;* and as such he has to express and authenticate himself in being as well as in thought. Consequently, *human* objects are not natural objects as they present themselves directly, nor is *human sense,* as it is immediately and objectively *given, human* sensibility and human objectivity. Neither objective nature nor subjective nature is directly presented in a form adequate to the *human* being. And as everything natural must have its *origin* so *man* has his process of genesis, *history,* which is for him, however, a conscious process and thus one which is consciously self-transcending. (We shall return to this point later.)

Thirdly, since this establishment of "thinghood" is itself only an appearance, an act which contradicts the nature of pure activity, it has to be annulled again and "thinghood" has to be denied.

ad 3, 4, 5, 6. (3) This alienation of consciousness has not only a negative but also a positive significance, and (4) it has this positive significance not only for us or in itself, but for consciousness itself. (5) For *consciousness* the negation of the object, or its annulling of itself by that means, has positive significance; it *knows* the nullity of the object by the fact that it alienates *itself,* for in this alienation it *knows* itself as the object or, for the sake of the indivisible unit of *being-for self,* knows the object as itself. (6) On the other hand, this other "moment" is equally present, but consciousness has superseded and reabsorbed this alienation and objectivity and is thus *at home in its other being as such.*

We have already seen that the appropriation of alienated objective being, or the supersession of objectivity in the form of *alienation* (which has to develop from indifferent otherness to real antagonistic alienation), signifies for Hegel also, or primarily, the supersession of *objectivity,* since it is not the determinate character of the object but its *objective* character which is the scandal of alienation for self-consciousness. The object is therefore negative, self-annulling, a *nullity.* This nullity of the object has a positive significance because it knows this nullity, objective being, as its *self-alienation,* and knows that this nullity exists only through its self-alienation. . . .

The way in which consciousness is, and in which something is for it, is *knowing.* Knowing is its only act. Thus something comes to exist for consciousness so far as it *knows* this *something.* Knowing is its only objective relation. It knows, then, the nullity of the object (i.e. knows the non-existence of the distinction between itself and the object, the non-existence of the object for it) because it knows the object as its *self-alienation.* That is to say, it knows itself (knows knowing as an object), because the object is only the semblance of an object, a deception, which is intrinsically nothing but knowing itself which has confronted itself with itself, has established in face of itself a *nullity,* a "something" which has no objective existence outside the knowing itself. Knowing knows that in relating itself to an object it is only *outside* itself, alienates itself, and that *it* only *appears* to itself as an object; or in other words, that that which appears to it as an object is only itself.

On the other hand, Hegel says, this other "moment" is present at the same time; namely, that consciousness has equally superseded and reabsorbed this alienation and objectivity, and consequently is at *home in its other being as such.*

In this discussion all the illusions of speculation are assembled.

First, consciousness—self-consciousness—is *at home in its other being as such.* It is, therefore—if we abstract from Hegel's abstraction and substitute the self-consciousness of man for self-consciousness—*at home in its other being as such.* This implies, first, that consciousness (knowing as knowing, thinking as thinking) claims to be directly the *other* of itself, the sensuous world, reality, life; it is thought over-reaching itself in thought (Feuerbach). This aspect is contained in it, in so far as consciousness as mere consciousness is offended not by the alienated objectivity but by *objectivity* as such.

Secondly, it implies that self-conscious man, in so far as he has recognized and superseded the spiritual world (or the universal spiritual mode of existence of his world) then confirms it again in this alienated form and presents it as his true existence; he re-establishes it and claims to *be at home in his other being.* Thus, for example, after superseding religion, when he has recognized religion as a product of self-alienation, he then finds a confirmation of himself in *religion as religion. This is* the root of Hegel's false positivism, or of his merely *apparent* criticism; what Feuerbach calls the positing, negation and re-establishment of religion or theology, but which has to be conceived in a more general way. Thus reason is at home in unreason as such. Man, who has recognized that he leads an alienated life in law, politics, etc. leads his true human life in this alienated life as such. Self-affirmation, in contradiction with itself, with the knowledge and the nature of the object, is thus the true *knowledge* and *life.*

There can no longer be any question about Hegel's compromise with religion, the state, etc., for this falsehood is the falsehood of his whole argument.

[XXIX] If I *know* religion as *alienated* human self-consciousness what I know in it as religion is not my self-consciousness but my alienated self-consciousness confirmed in it. Thus my own self, and the self-consciousness which is its essence, is not confirmed in *religion* but in the *abolition* and *supersession* of religion.

In Hegel, therefore, the negation of the negation is not the confirmation of true being by the negation of illusory being. It is the confirmation of illusory being, or of self-alienating being in its denial; or the denial of this illusory being as an objective being existing outside man and independently of him, and its transformation into a subject.

The act of *supersession* plays a strange part in which denial and preservation, denial and affirmation, are linked together. Thus, for example, in Hegel's *Philosophy of Right, private right* superseded equals *morality,* morality superseded equals the *family,* the family superseded equals *civil society,* civil society superseded equals the *state,* and the state superseded equals *world history.* But in *actuality* private right, morality, the family, civil society, the state, etc. remain; only they have become "moments," modes of existence of man, which have no validity in isolation but which mutually dissolve and engender one another. *They are "moments" of the movement.*

In their actual existence this mobile nature is concealed. It is first revealed in thought, in philosophy; consequently, my true religious existence is my existence in the *philosophy of religion,* my true political existence is my existence in the *philosophy of right,* my true natural existence is my existence in the *philosophy of nature,* my true artistic existence is my existence in the *philosophy of art,* and my true human existence is my existence in *philosophy.* In the same way, the true existence of religion, the state, nature and art, is the *philosophy* of religion, of the state, of nature, and of art. But if the philosophy of religion is the only true existence of religion I am only truly religious as a *philosopher of religion,* and I deny actual religious sentiment and the actual *religious* man. At the same time, however, I *confirm* them, partly in my own existence or in the alien existence with which I confront them (for this *is* only their philosophical expression), and partly in their own original form, since they are for me the merely *apparent* other being, allegories, the lineaments of their own true existence (i.e. of my *philosophical* existence) concealed by sensuous draperies.

In the same way, *quality* superseded equals *quantity,* quantity superseded equals measure, measure superseded equals *being,* being superseded equals *phenomenal being,* phenomenal being superseded equals *actuality,* actuality superseded equals the *concept,* the concept superseded equals *objectivity,* objectivity superseded equals the *absolute* idea, the absolute idea superseded equals *nature,* nature superseded equals *subjective* spirit, subjective spirit superseded equals *ethical* objective spirit, *ethical* spirit superseded equals *art,* art superseded equals *religion,* and religion superseded equals *absolute knowledge.*

On the other hand, this supersession is supersession of an entity of thought; thus, private property as *thought* is superseded in the *thought* of morality. And since thought imagines itself to be, without mediation, the other aspect of itself, namely *sensuous reality,* and takes its own action for *real, sensuous action,* this supersession in thought, which leaves its object in existence in the real world, believes itself to have really overcome it. On the other hand, since the object has now become for it a "moment" of thought, it is regarded in its real existence as a confirmation of thought, of self-consciousness, of abstraction.

[XXX] From the one aspect the existent which Hegel *supersedes* in philosophy is not therefore the *actual* religion, state or nature, but religion itself as an object of knowledge, i.e. *dogmatics;* and similarly with *jurisprudence, political science* and *natural science.* From this aspect, therefore, he stands in opposition both to the actual being and to the direct, non-philosophical science (or the non-philosophical *concepts*) of this being. Thus he contradicts the conventional conceptions.

From the other aspect, the religious man, etc. can find in Hegel his ultimate confirmation.

We have now to consider the *positive* moments of Hegel's dialectic, within the condition of alienation.

(a) Supersession as an objective movement which reabsorbs alienation into itself. This is the insight, expressed within alienation, into the *appropriation* of the objective being through the supersession of its alienation. It is the alienated insight into the *real objectification* of man, into the real appropriation of his objective being by the destruction of the *alienated* character of the objective world, by the annulment of its alienated mode of existence. In the same way, atheism as the annulment of God is the emergence of theoretical humanism, and communism as the annulment of private property is the vindication of real human life as man's property. The latter is also the emergence of practical humanism, for atheism is humanism mediated to itself by the annulment of religion, while communism is humanism mediated to itself by the annulment of private property. It is only by the supersession of this mediation (which is, however, a necessary pre-condition) that the self-originating *positive* humanism can appear.

But atheism and communism are not flight or abstraction from, nor loss of, the objective world which men have created by the objectification of their faculties. They are not an impoverished return to unnatural, primitive simplicity. They are rather the first real emergence, the genuine actualization, of man's nature as something real.

Thus Hegel, in so far as he sees the positive significance of the self-referring negation (though in an alienated mode) conceives man's self-estrangement, alienation of being, loss of objectivity and reality, as self-discovery, change of nature, objectification and realization. In short, Hegel conceives labour as man's *act of self-creation* (though in abstract terms); he grasps man's relation to himself as an alien being and the emergence of *species-consciousness* and *species-life* as the demonstration of his alien being.

(b) But in Hegel, apart from, or rather as a consequence of, the inversion we have already described, this act of genesis appears, in the first place, as one which is merely *formal,* because it is abstract, and because human nature itself is treated as merely *abstract, thinking nature,* as self-consciousness.

Secondly, because the conception is *formal* and *abstract* the annulment of alienation becomes a confirmation of alienation. For Hegel, this movement of *self-creation* and *self-objectification* in the form of *self-estrangement* is the *absolute* and hence final *expression of human life,* which has its end in itself, is at peace with itself and at one with its own nature.

This movement, in its abstract [XXXI] form as dialectic, is regarded therefore as *truly human life,* and since it is nevertheless an abstraction, an alienation of human life, it is regarded as a divine process and thus as the *divine process* of mankind; it is a process which man's abstract, pure, absolute being, as distinguished from himself, traverses.

Thirdly, this process must have a bearer, a subject; but the subject first emerges as a result. This result, the subject knowing itself as absolute self-consciousness, is therefore *God, absolute spirit, the self-knowing and self-manifesting idea.* Real man and real nature become mere predicates, symbols of this concealed unreal man and unreal nature. Subject and predicate have, therefore, an inverted relation to each other; *a mystical subject-object,* or a *subjectivity reaching beyond the object,* the *absolute subject* as a process of self-alienation and of return from alienation into itself, and at the same time of reabsorption of this alienation, the *subject* as this process; pure, *unceasing* revolving within itself.

First, the formal and abstract conception of man's act of self-creation or self-objectification.

Since Hegel equates man with self-consciousness, the alienated object, the alienated real being of man, is simply *consciousness,* merely the thought of alienation, its abstract and hence vacuous and unreal expression, the *negation*. The annulment of alienation is also, therefore, merely an abstract and vacuous annulment of this empty abstraction, the *negation of the negation*. The replete, living, sensuous, concrete activity of self-objectification is, therefore, reduced to a mere abstraction, *absolute negativity,* an abstraction which is then crystallized as such and is conceived as an independent activity, as activity itself. Since this so-called negativity is merely the *abstract, vacuous* form of that real living act, its content can only be a formal content produced by abstraction from all content. They are, therefore, general, abstract *forms of abstraction* which refer to any content and are thus neutral towards, and valid for, any content; forms of thought, logical forms which are detached from *real* spirit and *real* nature. (We shall expound later the *logical* content of absolute negativity.)

Hegel's positive achievement in his speculative logic is to show that the *determinate concepts,* the universal *fixed thought-forms,* in their independence from nature and spirit, are a necessary result of the general alienation of human nature and also of human thought; and to depict them as a whole as moments in the process of abstraction. For example, being superseded is essence, essence superseded is concept, the concept superseded is . . . the absolute idea. But what is the absolute idea? It must supersede itself if it does not want to traverse the whole process of abstraction again from the beginning and to rest content with being a totality of abstractions or a self-comprehending abstraction. But the self-comprehending abstraction knows itself to be nothing; it must abandon itself, the abstraction, and so arrives at an entity which is its exact opposite, *nature.* The whole *Logic* is therefore, a demonstration that abstract thought is nothing for itself, that the absolute idea is nothing for itself, that only *nature* is something.

[XXXII] The absolute idea, the *abstract* idea which *"regarded* from the aspect of its unity with itself, is *intuition"* (Hegel's *Encyclopaedia,* 3rd ed., p. 222), and which "in its own absolute truth *resolves* to let the moment of its particularity or of initial determination and other-being, the *immediate idea,* as its reflection, *emerge freely from itself as nature"* (ibid.); this whole idea which behaves in such a strange and fanciful way and which has given the Hegelians such terrible headaches is throughout nothing but *abstraction,* i.e. the abstract thinker. It is abstraction which, made wise by experience and enlightened about its own truth, resolves under various (false and still abstract) conditions to *abandon* itself, and to establish its other being, the particular, the determinate, in place of its self-absorption, non-being, universality and indeterminateness; and which resolves to let nature, which it concealed within itself only as an abstraction, as an entity of thought, *emerge freely from itself.* That is, it decides to forsake abstraction and to observe nature free from abstraction. The abstract idea, which without mediation becomes *intuition,* is nothing but abstract thought which abandons itself and decides for *intuition.* This whole transition from logic to the philosophy of nature is simply the transition from *abstracting* to *intuiting,* a transition which is extremely difficult for the abstract thinker to accomplish and which he therefore describes in such strange terms. The *mystical feeling* which drives the philosopher from abstract thinking to intuition is *ennui,* the longing for a content.

(Man alienated from himself is also the thinker alienated from his *being,* i.e. from his natural and human life. His thoughts are consequently spirits existing outside nature and man. In his *Logic* Hegel has imprisoned all these spirits together, and has conceived each of them first as negation, i.e. as *alienation of human* thought, and secondly as negation of the negation, i.e. as the supersession of this alienation and as the real expression of human thought. But since this negation of the negation is itself still confined within the alienation, it is in part a restoration of these fixed spiritual forms in their alienation, in part an immobilization in the final act, the act of self-reference, as the true being of these spiritual forms.* Further, in so far as this abstraction conceives itself, and experiences an increasing weariness of itself, there appears in Hegel an abandonment of abstract thought which moves solely in the sphere of thought, devoid of eyes, ears, teeth, everything, and a resolve to recognize *nature* as being and to go over to intuition.)

[XXXIII] But *nature* too, taken abstractly, for itself, and rigidly separated from man, is *nothing* for man. It goes without saying that the abstract thinker who has committed himself to intuition, intuits nature abstractly. As nature lay enclosed in the thinker in a form which was obscure and mysterious even to himself, as absolute idea, as an entity of thought, so in truth, when he let it emerge from himself it was still only *abstract nature,* nature as an *entity of thought,* but now with the significance that it is the other-being of thought, is real, intuited nature, distinguished from abstract thought. Or, to speak in human language, the abstract thinker discovers from intuiting nature that the entities which he thought to create out of nothing, out of pure abstraction, to create in the divine dialectic as the pure products of thought endlessly shuttling back and forth in itself and never regarding external reality, are simply *abstractions* from *natural characteristics.* The whole of nature, therefore, reiterates to him the logical abstractions, but in a sensuous, external form. He *analyses* nature and these abstractions again. His intuition of nature is, therefore, simply the act of confirmation of his abstraction from the intuition of nature; his conscious re-enactment of the process of generating his abstraction. Thus, for example, Time equals Negativity which refers to itself (loc. cit., p. 238). In the natural form, superseded Movement as Matter corresponds to superseded Becoming as Being. In the *natural* form Light is *Reflection-in-itself.* Body as *Moon* and *Comet* is the natural form of the antithesis which, according to the *Logic,* is on the one hand the *positive grounded upon itself,* and on the other hand, the *negative grounded upon itself.* The Earth is the *natural* form of the logical *ground,* as the negative unity of the antithesis, etc.

Nature as nature, i.e. so far as it is sensuously distinguished from that secret sense concealed within it, nature separated and distinguished from these abstractions is *nothing* (a *nullity demonstrating its nullity*), is *devoid of sense,* or has only the sense of an external thing which has been superseded.

"In the finite-*teleological* view is to be found the correct premise that nature does not contain within itself the absolute purpose" (loc. cit., p. 225). Its purpose is the confirmation of abstraction. "Nature has shown itself to be the idea in the *form* of *other-being.* Since the idea is in this form the negative of itself, or *external to itself,* nature is not just relatively external *vis-à-vis* this idea, but *externality* constitutes the form in which it exists as nature" (loc. cit., p. 227).

Externality should not be understood here as the *self-externalizing world of sense,* open to the light and to man's senses. It has to be taken here in the sense of alienation, as error, a defect, that which ought not to be. For that which is true is still the idea. Nature is merely the form of its other-being. And since abstract thought is *being,* that which is ex-

---

*That is, Hegel substitutes the act of abstraction revolving within itself, for these fixed abstractions. In so doing, he has first of all the merit of having indicated the source of all these inappropriate concepts which originally belonged to different philosophies, and of having brought them together and established the comprehensive range of abstractions, instead of some particular abstraction, as the object of criticism. We shall see later why Hegel separates though from the *subject.* It is already clear, however, that if man is not human the expression of his nature cannot be human, and consequently thought itself could not be conceived as an expression of man's nature, as the expression of a human and natural subject, with eyes, ears, etc. living in society, in the world, and in nature.

ternal to it is by its nature a merely *external thing*. The abstract thinker recognizes at the same time that *sensuousness, externality* in contrast to thought which shuttles back and forth *within itself,* is the essence of nature. But at the same time he expresses this antithesis in such a way that this *externality* of nature, and its *contrast* with thought, appears as a deficiency, and that nature distinguished from abstraction appears as a deficient being. [XXXIV] A being which is deficient, not simply for me or in my eyes, but in itself, has something outside itself which it lacks. That is to say, its being is something other than itself. For the abstract thinker, nature must therefore supersede itself, because it is already posited by him as a potentially *superseded* being.

"*For us,* spirit has *nature as its premise,* being the truth of nature and thereby its *absolute primus.* In this truth nature has *vanished,* and spirit has surrendered itself as the idea which has attained being-for-itself, whose *object,* as well as the *subject,* is the *concept.* This identity is *absolute negativity,* for whereas in nature the concept has its perfect external objectivity, here its alienation has been superseded and the concept has become identical with itself. It is this identity only so far as it is a return from nature" (loc. cit., p. 392).

"*Revelation,* as the *abstract* idea, is unmediated transition to, the *coming-to-be* of, nature; as the revelation of the spirit, which is free, it is the establishment of nature as *its own* world, an establishment which, as reflection, is simultaneously the *presupposition* of the world as independently existing nature. Revelation in conception is the creation of nature as spirit's own being, in which it acquires the *affirmation* and *truth* of its freedom." "*The absolute is spirit;* this is the highest definition of the absolute."

MANIFESTO OF THE COMMUNIST PARTY (in part)

A spectre is haunting Europe—the spectre of Communism. All the powers of old Europe have entered into a holy alliance to exorcise this spectre: Pope and Czar, Metternich and Guizot, French Radicals and German police spies.

Where is the party in opposition that has not been decried as communistic by its opponents in power? Where the opposition that has not hurled back the branding reproach of Communism against the more advanced opposition parties, as well as against its reactionary adversaries?

Two things result from this fact:

I. Communism is already acknowledged by all European powers to be itself a power.

II. It is high time that Communists should openly, in the face of the whole world, publish their views, their aims, their tendencies, and meet this nursery tale of the spectre of Communism with a manifesto of the party itself.

To this end, Communists of various nationalities have assembled in London and sketched the following manifesto, to be published in the English, French, German, Italian, Flemish, and Danish languages.

CHAPTER I: BOURGEOIS AND PROLETARIANS*

The History of all hitherto existing society** is the history of class struggles.

Freeman and slave, patrician and plebeian, lord and serf, guild-master*** and journeyman, in a word, oppressor and oppressed stood in constant opposition to one another, carried on an uninterrupted, now hidden, now open fight, a fight that each time ended either in a revolutionary reconstitution of society at large, or in the common ruin of the contending classes.

In the earlier epochs of history we find almost everywhere a complicated arrangement of society into various orders, a manifold gradation of social rank. In ancient Rome we have patricians, knights, plebeians, slaves; in the Middle Ages, feudal lords, vassals, guild-masters, journeymen, apprentices, serfs; in almost all of these classes, again, subordinate gradations.

The modern bourgeois society that has sprouted from the ruins of feudal society has not done away with class antagonisms. It has but established new classes, new conditions of oppression, new forms of struggle in place of the old ones.

Our epoch, the epoch of the bourgeoisie, possesses, however, this distinctive feature: it has simplified the class antagonisms. Society as a whole is more and more splitting up into two great hostile camps, into two great classes directly facing each other—bourgeoisie and proletariat.

From the serfs of the Middle Ages sprang the chartered burghers of the earliest towns. From these burgesses the first elements of the bourgeoisie were developed.

The discovery of America, the rounding of the Cape, opened up fresh ground for the rising bourgeoisie. The East Indian and Chinese markets, the colonization of America, trade with the colonies, the increase in the means of exchange and in commodities generally, gave to commerce, to navigation, to industry, an impulse never before known, and thereby, to the revolutionary element in the tottering feudal society, a rapid development.

The feudal system of industry, in which industrial production was monopolized by closed guilds, now no longer sufficed for the growing wants of the new markets. The manufacturing system took its place. The guild-masters were pushed aside by the manufacturing middle class; division of labor between the different corporate guilds vanished in the face of division of labor in each single workshop.

Meantime the markets kept ever growing, the demand ever rising. Even manufacture no longer sufficed. Thereupon, steam and machinery revolutionized industrial

---

*By *bourgeoisie* is meant the class of modern capitalists, owners of the means of social production, and employers of wage labor; by *proletariat,* the class of modern wage laborers who, having no means of production of their own, are reduced to selling their labor power in order to live.

**That is, all *written* history. In 1837, the pre-history of society, the social organization existing previous to recorded history, was all but unknown. Since then Haxthausen discovered common ownership of land in Russia; Maurer proved it to be the social foundation from which all Teutonic races started in history, and, by and by, village communities were found to be, or to have been, the primitive form of society everywhere from India to Ireland. The inner organization of this primitive communistic society was laid bare, in its typical form, by Morgan's crowning discovery of the true nature of the *gens* and its relation to the *tribe.* With the dissolution of these primeval communities society begins to be differentiated into separate and finally antagonistic classes. I have attempted to retrace this process of dissolution in *The Origin of the Family, Private Property and the State.*

***[Guild-master, that is, a full member of a guild, a master within, not a head of a guild.]

production. The place of manufacture was taken by the giant, modern industry, the place of the industrial middle class, by industrial millionaires—the leaders of whole industrial armies, the modern bourgeois.

Modern industry has established the world market, for which the discovery of America paved the way. This market has given an immense development to commerce, to navigation, to communication by land. This development has, in its turn, reacted on the extension of industry; and in proportion as industry, commerce, navigation, railways extended, in the same proportion the bourgeoisie developed, increased its capital, and pushed into the background every class handed down from the Middle Ages.

We see, therefore, how the modern bourgeoisie is itself the product of a long course of development, of a series of revolutions in the modes of production and of exchange.

Each step in the development of the bourgeoisie was accompanied by a corresponding political advance of that class. An oppressed class under the sway of the feudal nobility, it became an armed and self-governing association in the medieval commune:* here independent urban republic (as in Italy and Germany); there, taxable "third estate" of the monarchy (as in France); afterwards, in the period of manufacture proper, serving either the semi-feudal or the absolute monarchy as a counterpoise against the nobility, and, in fact, cornerstone of the great monarchies in general. The bourgeoisie has at last, since the establishment of modern industry and of the world market, conquered for itself, in the modern representative state, exclusive political sway. The executive of the modern state is but a committee for managing the common affairs of the whole bourgeoisie.

The bourgeoisie has played a most revolutionary role in history.

The bourgeoisie, wherever it has got the upper hand, has put an end to all feudal, patriarchal, idyllic relations. It has pitilessly torn asunder the motley feudal ties that bound man to his "natural superiors," and has left no other bond between man and man than naked self-interest, than callous "cash payment." It has drowned the most heavenly ecstasies of religious fervor, of chivalrous enthusiasm, of philistine sentimentalism, in the icy water of egotistical calculation. It has resolved personal worth into exchange value, and in place of the numberless indefeasible chartered freedoms has set up that single, unconscionable freedom—Free Trade. In one word, for exploitation, veiled by religious and political illusions, it has substituted naked, shameless, direct, brutal exploitation.

The bourgeoisie has stripped of its halo every occupation hitherto honored and looked up to with reverent awe. It has converted the physician, the lawyer, the priest, the poet, the man of science, into its paid wage laborers.

The bourgeoisie has torn away from the family its sentimental veil, and has reduced the family relation to a mere money relation.

The bourgeoisie has disclosed how it came to pass that the brutal display of vigor in the Middle Ages which reactionaries so much admire found its fitting complement in the most slothful indolence. It has been the first to show what man's activity can bring about. It has accomplished wonders far surpassing Egyptian pyramids, Roman

---

*"Commune" was the name taken in France by the nascent towns even before they had conquered from their feudal lords and masters local self-government and political rights as the "Third Estate." Generally speaking, for the economic development of the bourgeoisie, England is here taken as the typical country; for its political development, France.

aqueducts, and Gothic cathedrals; it has conducted expeditions that put in the shade all former migrations of nations and crusades.

The bourgeoisie cannot exist without constantly revolutionizing the instruments of production, and thereby the relations of production, and with them the whole relations of society. Conservation of the old modes of production in unaltered form was, on the contrary, the first condition of existence for all earlier industrial classes. Constant revolutionizing of production, uninterrupted disturbance of all social conditions, everlasting uncertainty and agitation distinguish the bourgeois epoch from all earlier ones. All fixed, fast-frozen relations with their train of ancient and venerable prejudices and opinions are swept away; all new-formed ones become antiquated before they can ossify. All that is solid melts in air, all that is holy is profaned, and man is at last compelled to face with sober senses his real conditions of life and his relations with his kind.

The need of a constantly expanding market for its products chases the bourgeoisie over the whole surface of the globe. It must nestle everywhere, settle everywhere, establish connections everywhere.

The bourgeoisie has through its exploitation of the world market given a cosmopolitan character to production and consumption in every country. To the great chagrin of reactionaries it has drawn from under the feet of industry the national ground on which it stood. All old-established national industries have been destroyed or are daily being destroyed. They are dislodged by new industries whose introduction becomes a life and death question for all civilized nations; by industries that no longer work up indigenous raw material, but raw material drawn from the remotest zones; industries whose products are consumed, not only at home, but in every quarter of the globe. In place of the old wants, satisfied by the production of the country, we find new wants, requiring for their satisfaction the products of distant lands and climes. In place of the old local and national seclusion and self-sufficiency we have intercourse in every direction, universal inter-dependence of nations. And as in material, so also in intellectual production. The intellectual creations of individual nations become common property. National one-sidedness and narrow-mindedness become more and more impossible, and from the numerous national and local literatures there arises a world literature.

The bourgeoisie, by the rapid improvement of all instruments of production, by the immensely facilitated means of communication, draws all nations, even the most barbarian, into civilization. The cheap prices of its commodities are the heavy artillery with which it batters down all Chinese walls, with which it forces the barbarians' intensely obstinate hatred of foreigners to capitulate. It compels all nations, on pain of extinction, to adopt the bourgeois mode of production; it compels them to introduce what it calls civilization into their midst, i.e., to become bourgeois themselves. In a word, it creates a world after its own image.

The bourgeoisie has subjected the country to the rule of the towns. It has created enormous cities, has greatly increased the urban population as compared with the rural, and has thus rescued a considerable part of the population from the idiocy of rural life. Just as it has made the country dependent on the towns, so it has made barbarian and semi-barbarian countries dependent on the civilized ones, nations of peasants on nations of bourgeois, the East on the West.

More and more the bourgeoisie keeps doing away with the scattered state of the population, of the means of production, and of property. It has agglomerated population, centralized means of production, and has concentrated property in a few hands. The necessary consequence of this was political centralization. Independent, or but loosely connected provinces, with separate interests, laws, governments and systems of taxation, became lumped together into one nation, with one government, one code of laws, one national class interest, one frontier and one customs tariff.

The bourgeoisie during its rule of scarce one hundred years has created more massive and more colossal productive forces than have all preceding generations together. Subjection of nature's forces to man, machinery, application of chemistry to industry and agriculture, steam-navigation, railways, electric telegraphs, clearing of whole continents for cultivation, canalization of rivers, whole populations conjured out of the ground—what earlier century had even a presentiment that such productive forces slumbered in the lap of social labor?

We see, then, that the means of production and of exchange which served as the foundation for the growth of the bourgeoisie were generated in feudal society. At a certain stage in the development of these means of production and of exchange, the conditions under which feudal society produced and exchanged, the feudal organization of agriculture and manufacturing industry, in a word, the feudal relations of property became no longer compatible with the already developed productive forces; they became so many fetters. They had to be burst asunder; they were burst asunder.

Into their place stepped free competition, accompanied by a social and political constitution adapted to it, and by the economic and political sway of the bourgeois class.

A similar movement is going on before our own eyes. Modern bourgeois society with its relations of production, of exchange and of property, a society that has conjured up such gigantic means of production and of exchange, is like the sorcerer who is no longer able to control the powers of the nether world whom he has called up by his spells. For many a decade past the history of industry and commerce is but the history of the revolt of modern productive forces against modern conditions of production, against the property relations that are the conditions for the existence of the bourgeoisie and of its rule. It is enough to mention the commercial crises that by their periodical return put the existence of the entire bourgeois society on trial, each time more threateningly. In these crises a great part not only of the existing products, but also of the previously created productive forces, are periodically destroyed. In these crises there breaks out an epidemic that, in all earlier epochs, would have seemed an absurdity—the epidemic of over-production. Society suddenly finds itself put back into a state of momentary barbarism; it appears as if a famine, a universal war of devastation had cut off the supply of every means of subsistence; industry and commerce seem to be destroyed. And why? Because there is too much civilization, too much means of subsistence, too much industry, too much commerce. The productive forces at the disposal of society no longer tend to further the development of the conditions of bourgeois property; on the contrary, they have become too powerful for these conditions, by which they are fettered, and no sooner do they overcome these fetters than they bring disorder into the whole of bourgeois society, endanger the existence of bourgeois property. The conditions of bourgeois society are too narrow to comprise the wealth created by them. And how does the bourgeoisie get over these crises? On the one hand by enforced destruction of a mass of productive forces; on the other, by the conquest of new markets and by the more thorough exploitation of the old ones. That is to say, by paving the way for more extensive and more destructive crises, and by diminishing the means whereby crises are prevented.

The weapons with which the bourgeoisie felled feudalism to the ground are now turned against the bourgeoisie itself.

But not only has the bourgeoisie forged the weapons that bring death to itself; it has also called into existence the men who are to wield those weapons—the modern working class, the proletarians.

In proportion as the bourgeoisie, i.e., capital, is developed, in the same proportion is the proletariat, the modern working class, developed—a class of laborers, who live only so long as they find work, and who find work only so long as their labor increases capital. These laborers, who must sell themselves piecemeal, are a commodity like every other article of commerce, and are consequently exposed to all the vicissitudes of competition, to all the fluctuations of the market.

Owing to the extensive use of machinery and to division of labor, the work of the proletarians has lost all individual character, and, consequently all charm for the workman. He becomes an appendage of the machine, and it is only the most simple, most monotonous, and most easily acquired knack that is required of him. Hence, the cost of production of a workman is restricted almost entirely to the means of subsistence that he requires for his maintenance and for the propagation of his race. But the price of a commodity, and therefore also of labor, is equal to its cost of production. In proportion, therefore, as the repulsiveness of the work increases, the wage decreases. Nay more, in proportion the burden of toil also increases, whether by prolongation of the working hours, by increase of the work exacted in a given time, or by increased speed of the machinery, etc.

Modern industry has converted the little workshop of the patriarchal master into the great factory of the industrial capitalist. Masses of laborers, crowded into the factory, are organized like soldiers. As privates of the industrial army they are placed under the command of a perfect hierarchy of officers and sergeants. Not only are they slaves of the bourgeois class and of the bourgeois state; they are daily and hourly enslaved by the machine, by the overseer, and, above all, by the individual bourgeois manufacturer himself. The more openly this despotism proclaims gain to be its end and aim, the more petty, the more hateful, and the more embittering it is.

The less the skill and exertion of strength implied in manual labor—in other words, the more modern industry develops—the more is the labor of men superseded by that of women. Differences of age and sex have no longer any distinctive social validity for the working class. All are instruments of labor, more or less expensive to use, according to their age and sex.

No sooner has the laborer received his wages in cash, for the moment escaping exploitation by the manufacturer, than he is set upon by the other portions of the bourgeoisie—the landlord, the shopkeeper, the pawnbroker, etc.

The lower strata of the middle class—the small tradespeople, shopkeepers, and retired tradesmen generally, the handicraftsmen and peasants—all these sink gradually into the proletariat, partly because their diminutive capital does not suffice for the scale on which modern industry is carried on and is swamped in the competition with the large capitalists, partly because their specialized skill is rendered worthless by new methods of production. Thus the proletariat is recruited from all classes of the population.

The proletariat goes through various stages of development. With its birth begins its struggle with the bourgeoisie. At first the contest is carried on by individual laborers, then by the workpeople of a factory, then by the operatives of one trade, in one locality, against the individual bourgeois who directly exploits them. They direct their attacks not against the bourgeois conditions of production, but against the instruments of production themselves; they destroy imported wares that compete with their labor, they smash machinery to pieces, they set factories ablaze, they seek to restore by force the vanished status of the workman of the Middle Ages.

At this stage the laborers still form an incoherent mass scattered over the whole country, and broken up by their mutual competition. If anywhere they unite to form more compact bodies, this is not yet the consequence of their own active union, but of the union of the bourgeoisie, which class, in order to attain its own political ends, is compelled to set the whole proletariat in motion, and is, moreover, still able to do so for a time. At this stage, therefore, the proletarians do not fight their enemies, but the enemies of their enemies, the remnants of absolute monarchy, the landowners, the non-industrial bourgeois, the petty bourgeoisie. Thus the whole historical movement is concentrated in the hands of the bourgeoisie; every victory so obtained is a victory for the bourgeoisie.

But with the development of industry the proletariat not only increases in number; it becomes concentrated in greater masses, its strength grows, and it feels that strength more. The various interests and conditions of life within the ranks of the proletariat are more and more equalized, in proportion as machinery obliterates all distinctions of labor and nearly everywhere reduces wages to the same low level. The growing competition among the bourgeois and the resulting commercial crises make the wages of the workers ever more fluctuating. The unceasing improvement of machinery, ever more rapidly developing, makes their livelihood more and more precarious; the collisions between individual workmen and individual bourgeois take more and more the character of collisions between two classes. Thereupon the workers begin to form combinations (trade unions) against the bourgeoisie; they club together in order to keep up the rate of wages; they found permanent associations in order to make provision beforehand for these occasional revolts. Here and there the contest breaks out into riots.

Now and then the workers are victorious, but only for a time. The real fruit of their battles lies not in the immediate result but in the ever expanding union of the workers. This union is furthered by the improved means of communication which are created by modern industry, and which place the workers of different localities in contact with one another. It was just this contact that was needed to centralize the numerous local struggles, all of the same character, into one national struggle between classes. But every class struggle is a political struggle. And that union, which the burghers of the Middle Ages, with their miserable highways, required centuries to attain, the modern proletarians, thanks to railways achieve in a few years.

This organization of the proletarians into a class, and consequently into a political party, is continually being upset again by the competition between the workers themselves. But it ever rises up again, stronger, firmer, mightier. It compels legislative recognition of particular interests of the workers by taking advantage of the divisions among the bourgeoisie itself. Thus the Ten Hour bill in England was carried.

Altogether, collisions between the classes of the old society further the course of development of the proletariat in many ways. The bourgeoisie finds itself involved in a constant battle—at first with the aristocracy; later on, with those portions of the bourgeoisie itself whose interests have become antagonistic to the progress of industry; at all times with the bourgeoisie of foreign countries. In all these battles it sees itself compelled to appeal to the proletariat, to ask for its help, and thus to drag it into the political arena. The bourgeoisie itself, therefore, supplies the proletariat with its own elements of political and general education; in other words, it furnishes the proletariat with weapons for fighting the bourgeoisie.

Further, as we have already seen, entire sections of the ruling classes are, by the advance of industry, precipitated into the proletariat, or are at least threatened in their conditions of existence. These also supply the proletariat with fresh elements of enlightenment and progress.

Finally, in times when the class struggle nears the decisive hour, the process of dissolution going on within the ruling class, in fact within the whole range of old society, assumes such a violent, glaring character that a small section of the ruling class cuts itself adrift and joins the revolutionary class, the class that holds the future in its hands. Just as, therefore, at an earlier period a section of the nobility went over to the bourgeoisie, so now a portion of the bourgeoisie goes over to the proletariat, and in particular, a portion of the bourgeois ideologists who have raised themselves to the level of comprehending theoretically the historical movement as a whole.

Of all the classes that stand face to face with the bourgeoisie today, the proletariat alone is a really revolutionary class. The other classes decay and finally disappear in the face of modern industry; the proletariat is its special and essential product.

The lower middle class, the small manufacturer, the shopkeeper, the artisan, the peasant—all these fight against the bourgeoisie, to save from extinction their existence as fractions of the middle class. They are, therefore, not revolutionary but conservative. Nay more, they are reactionary, for they try to roll back the wheel of history. If by chance they are revolutionary they are so only in view of their impending transfer into the proletariat; they thus defend not their present but their future interests; they desert their own standpoint to adopt that of the proletariat.

The "dangerous class," the social scum (*Lumpenproletariat*), that passively rotting mass thrown off by the lowest layers of old society, may here and there be swept into the movement by a proletarian revolution; its conditions of life, however, prepare it far more for the part of a bribed tool of reactionary intrigue.

The social conditions of the old society no longer exist for the proletariat. The proletarian is without property; his relation to his wife and children has no longer anything in common with bourgeois family relations; modern industrial labor, modern subjection to capital, the same in England as in France, in America as in Germany, has stripped him of every trace of national character. Law, morality, religion are to him so many bourgeois prejudices, behind which lurk in ambush just as many bourgeois interests.

All the preceding classes that got the upper hand sought to fortify their already acquired status by subjecting society at large to their conditions of appropriation. The proletarians cannot become masters of the productive forces of society except by abolishing their own previous mode of appropriation, and thereby also every other previous mode of appropriation. They have nothing of their own to secure and to fortify; their mission is to destroy all previous securities for, and insurances of, individual property.

All previous historical movements were movements of minorities, or in the interest of minorities. The proletarian movement is the self-conscious, independent movement of the immense majority, in the interest of the immense majority. The proletariat, the lowest stratum of our present society, cannot stir, cannot raise itself up, without the whole superincumbent strata of official society being sprung into the air.

Though not in substance, yet in form, the struggle of the proletariat with the bourgeoisie is at first a national struggle. The proletariat of each country must, of course, first of all settle matters with its own bourgeoisie.

In depicting the most general phases of the development of the proletariat we traced the more or less veiled civil war raging within existing society, up to the point where that war breaks out into open revolution, and where the violent overthrow of the bourgeoisie lays the foundation for the sway of the proletariat.

Hitherto, every form of society has been based, as we have already seen, on the antagonism of oppressing and oppressed classes. But in order to oppress a class certain conditions must be assured to it under which it can, at least, continue its slavish existence. The serf, in the period of serfdom, raised himself to membership in the commune, just as the petty bourgeois, under the yoke of feudal absolutism, managed to develop into a bourgeois. The modern laborer, on the contrary, instead of rising with the progress of industry, sinks deeper and deeper below the conditions of existence of his own class. He becomes a pauper, and pauperism develops more rapidly than population and wealth. And here it becomes evident that the bourgeoisie is unfit any longer to be the ruling class in society and to impose its conditions of existence upon society as an overriding law. It is unfit to rule because it is incompetent to assure an existence to its slave within his slavery, because it cannot help letting him sink into such a state that it has to feed him, instead of being fed by him. Society can no longer live under this bourgeoisie, in other words, its existence is no longer compatible with society.

The essential condition for the existence and sway of the bourgeois class is the formation and augmentation of capital; the condition for capital is wage labor. Wage labor rests exclusively on competition between the laborers. The advance of industry, whose involuntary promoter is the bourgeoisie, replaces the isolation of the laborers, due to competition, by their revolutionary combination, due to association. The development of modern industry, therefore, cuts from under its feet the very foundation on which the bourgeoisie produces and appropriates products. What the bourgeoisie, therefore, produces above all are its own grave-diggers. Its fall and the victory of the proletariat are equally inevitable.

*   *   *

[The specific measures called for by the Communist Party] will, of course, be different in different countries.

Nevertheless, in the most advanced countries the following will be pretty generally applicable:

1. Abolition of property in land and application of all rents of land to public purposes.
2. A heavy progressive or graduated income tax.
3. Abolition of all right of inheritance.
4. Confiscation of the property of all emigrants and rebels.
5. Centralization of credit in the hands of the state by means of a national bank with state capital and an exclusive monopoly.
6. Centralization of the means of communication and transport in the hands of the state.
7. Extension of factories and instruments of production owned by the state; the bringing into cultivation of waste lands, and the improvement of the soil generally in accordance with a common plan.
8. Equal obligation of all to work. Establishment of industrial armies, especially for agriculture.
9. Combination of agriculture with manufacturing industries; gradual abolition of the distinction between town and country by a more equable distribution of the population over the country.
10. Free education for all children in public schools. Abolition of child factory labor in its present form. Combination of education with industrial production, etc.

*   *   *

CHAPTER IV: POSITION OF THE COMMUNISTS IN RELATION TO THE VARIOUS EXISTING OPPOSITION PARTIES

Section II has made clear the relations of the Communists to the existing working class parties, such as the Chartists in England and the Agrarian Reformers in America.

The Communists fight for the attainment of the immediate aims, for the enforcement of the momentary interests of the working class; but in the movement of the present they also represent and take care of the future of that movement. In France the Communists ally themselves with the Social-Democrats* against the conservative and radical bourgeoisie, reserving, however, the right to take up a critical position in regard to phrases and illusions traditionally handed down from the great Revolution.

In Switzerland they support the Radicals without losing sight of the fact that this party consists of antagonistic elements, partly of Democratic Socialists, in the French sense, partly of radical bourgeois.

Capital and Labour," cartoon from *Punch* magazine, 1843. The cartoon shows the suffering of the workers and their families that makes possible the bourgeois capitalists' high life. It was in response to conditions such as this that Marx and Engels wrote in *The Communist Manifesto* (1848), "The proletarians have nothing to lose but their chains. They have a world to win. Workingmen of all countries, unite!" *(Library of Congress)*

*The party then represented in Parliament by Ledru-Rollin, in literature by Louis Blanc, in the daily press by the *Réforme.* The name of Social-Democracy signifies, with these its inventors, a section of the Democratic or Republican Party more or less tinged with Socialism.

In Poland they support the party that insists on an agrarian revolution as the prime condition for national emancipation, that party which fomented the insurrection of Cracow in 1846.

In Germany they fight with the bourgeoisie whenever it acts in a revolutionary way, against the absolute monarchy, the feudal squirearchy, and the petty bourgeoisie.

But they never cease for a single instant to instil into the working class the clearest possible recognition of the hostile antagonism between bourgeoisie and proletariat, in order that the German workers may straightway use, as so many weapons against the bourgeoisie, the social and political conditions that the bourgeoisie must necessarily introduce along with its supremacy, and in order that, after the fall of the reactionary classes in Germany, the fight against the bourgeoisie itself may immediately begin.

The Communists turn their attention chiefly to Germany because that country is on the eve of a bourgeois revolution that is bound to be carried out under more advanced conditions of European civilization and with a much more developed proletariat than what existed in England in the 17th and in France in the 18th century, and because the bourgeois revolution in Germany will be but the prelude to an immediately following proletarian revolution.

In short, the Communists everywhere support every revolutionary movement against the existing social and political order of things.

In all these movements they bring to the front as the leading question in each case the property question, no matter what its degree of development at the time.

Finally, they labor everywhere for the union and agreement of the democratic parties of all countries.

The Communists disdain to conceal their views and aims. They openly declare that their ends can be attained only by the forcible overthrow of all existing social conditions. Let the ruling classes tremble at a Communist revolution. The proletarians have nothing to lose but their chains. They have a world to win.

Workingmen of all countries, unite!

THE GERMAN IDEOLOGY (in part)

IDEOLOGY IN GENERAL,
GERMAN IDEOLOGY IN PARTICULAR

German criticism has, right up to its latest efforts, never quitted the realm of philosophy. Far from examining its general philosophic premises, the whole body of its inquiries has actually sprung from the soil of a definite philosophical system, that of Hegel. Not only in their answers but in their very questions there was a mystification. This dependence on Hegel is the reason why not one of these modern critics has even

Karl Marx and Frederick Engels, *The German Ideology,* translated by W. Lough, edited by S. Ryazanskaya (Moscow, USSR: Progress Publishers, 1964), Vol. I, Chapter I "Feuerbach," Section A "Ideology in General, German Ideology in Particular."

attempted a comprehensive criticism of the Hegelian system, however much each professes to have advanced beyond Hegel. Their polemics against Hegel and against one another are confined to this—each extracts one side of the Hegelian system and turns this against the whole system as well as against the sides extracted by the others. To begin with they extracted pure unfalsified Hegelian categories such as "substance" and "self-consciousness," later they desecrated these categories with more secular names such as "species," "the Unique," "Man," etc.

The entire body of German philosophical criticism from Strauss to Stirner is confined to criticism of *religious* conceptions. The critics started from real religion and actual theology. What religious consciousness and a religious conception really meant was determined variously as they went along. Their advance consisted in subsuming the allegedly dominant metaphysical, political, juridical, moral and other conceptions under the class of religious or theological conceptions; and similarly in pronouncing political, juridical, moral consciousness as religious or theological, and the political, juridical, moral man—*"man"* in the last resort—as religious. The dominance of religion was taken for granted. Gradually every dominant relationship was pronounced a religious relationship and transformed into a cult, a cult of law, a cult of the State, etc. On all sides it was only a question of dogmas and belief in dogmas. The world was sanctified to an ever-increasing extent till at last our venerable Saint Max was able to canonise it *en bloc* and thus dispose of it once for all.

The Old Hegelians had *comprehended* everything as soon as it was reduced to an Hegelian logical category. The Young Hegelians *criticised* everything by attributing to it religious conceptions or by pronouncing it a theological matter. The Young Hegelians are in agreement with the Old Hegelians in their belief in the rule of religion, of concepts, of a universal principle in the existing world. Only, the one party attacks this dominion as usurpation, while the other extols it as legitimate.

Since the Young Hegelians consider conceptions, thoughts, ideas, in fact all the products of consciousness, to which they attribute an independent existence, as the real chains of men (just as the Old Hegelians declared them the true bonds of human society) it is evident that the Young Hegelians have to fight only against these illusions of the consciousness. Since, according to their fantasy, the relationships of men, all their doings, their chains and their limitations are products of their consciousness, the Young Hegelians logically put to men the moral postulate of exchanging their present consciousness for human, critical or egoistic consciousness, and thus of removing their limitations. This demand to change consciousness amounts to a demand to interpret reality in another way, i.e., to recognise it by means of another interpretation. The Young-Hegelian ideologists, in spite of their allegedly "world-shattering" statements, are the staunchest conservatives. The most recent of them have found the correct expression for their activity when they declare they are only fighting against *"phrases."* They forget, however, that to these phrases they themselves are only opposing other phrases, and that they are in no way combating the real existing world when they are merely combating the phrases of this world. The only results which this philosophic criticism could achieve were a few (and at that thoroughly one-sided) elucidations of Christianity from the point of view of religious history; all the rest of their assertions are only further embellishments of their claim to have furnished, in these unimportant elucidations, discoveries of universal importance.

It has not occurred to any one of these philosophers to inquire into the connection of German philosophy with German reality, the relation of their criticism to their own material surroundings.

The premises from which we begin are not arbitrary ones, not dogmas, but real premises from which abstraction can only be made in the imagination. They are the real individuals, their activity and the material conditions under which they live, both those which they find already existing and those produced by their activity. These premises can thus be verified in a purely empirical way.

The first premise of all human history is, of course, the existence of living human individuals. Thus the first fact to be established is the physical organisation of these individuals and their consequent relation to the rest of nature. Of course, we cannot here go either into the actual physical nature of man, or into the natural conditions in which man finds himself—geological, orohydrographical, climatic and so on. The writing of history must always set out from these natural bases and their modification in the course of history through the action of men.

Men can be distinguished from animals by consciousness, by religion or anything else you like. They themselves begin to distinguish themselves from animals as soon as they begin to *produce* their means of subsistence, a step which is conditioned by their physical organisation. By producing their means of subsistence men are indirectly producing their actual material life.

The way in which men produce their means of subsistence depends first of all on the nature of the actual means of subsistence they find in existence and have to reproduce. This mode of production must not be considered simply as being the reproduction of the physical existence of the individuals. Rather it is a definite form of activity of these individuals, a definite form of expressing their life, a definite *mode of life* on their part. As individuals express their life, so they are. What they are, therefore, coincides with their production, both with *what* they produce and with *how* they produce. The nature of individuals thus depends on the material conditions determining their production.

This production only makes its appearance with the *increase of population.* In its turn this presupposes the *intercourse* of individuals with one another. The form of this intercourse is again determined by production.

The relations of different nations among themselves depend upon the extent to which each has developed its productive forces, the division of labour and internal intercourse. This statement is generally recognised. But not only the relation of one nation to others, but also the whole internal structure of the nation itself depends on the stage of development reached by its production and its internal and external intercourse. How far the productive forces of a nation are developed is shown most manifestly by the degree to which the division of labour has been carried. Each new productive force, insofar as it is not merely a quantitative extension of productive forces already known (for instance the bringing into cultivation of fresh land), causes a further development of the division of labour.

The division of labour inside a nation leads at first to the separation of industrial and commercial from agricultural labour, and hence to the separation of *town* and *country* and to the conflict of their interests. Its further development leads to the separation of commercial from industrial labour. At the same time through the division of labour inside these various branches there develop various divisions among the individuals co-operating in definite kinds of labour. The relative position of these individual groups is determined by the methods employed in agriculture, industry and commerce (patriarchalism, slavery, estates, classes). These same conditions are to be seen (given a more developed intercourse) in the relations of different nations to one another.

The various stages of development in the division of labour are just so many different forms of ownership, i.e., the existing stage in the division of labour determines also the relations of individuals to one another with reference to the material, instrument, and product of labour.

The first form of ownership is tribal ownership. It corresponds to the undeveloped stage of production, at which a people lives by hunting and fishing, by the rearing of beasts or, in the highest stage, agriculture. In the latter case it presupposes a great mass of uncultivated stretches of land. The division of labour is at this stage still very elementary and is confined to a further extension of the natural division of labour existing in the family. The social structure is, therefore, limited to an extension of the family; patriarchal family chieftains, below them the members of the tribe, finally slaves. The slavery latent in the family only develops gradually with the increase of population, the growth of wants, and with the extension of external relations, both of war and of barter.

The second form is the ancient communal and State ownership which proceeds especially from the union of several tribes into a *city* by agreement or by conquest, and which is still accompanied by slavery. Beside communal ownership we already find movable, and later also immovable, private property developing, but as an abnormal form subordinate to communal ownership. The citizens hold power over their labouring slaves only in their community, and on this account alone, therefore, they are bound to the form of communal ownership. It is the communal private property which compels the active citizens to remain in this spontaneously derived form of association over against their slaves. For this reason the whole structure of society based on this communal ownership, and with it the power of the people, decays in the same measure as, in particular, immovable private property evolves. The division of labour is already more developed. We already find the antagonism of town and country; later the antagonism between those states which represent town interests and those which represent country interests, and inside the towns themselves the antagonism between industry and maritime commerce. The class relation between citizens and slaves is now completely developed.

This whole interpretation of history appears to be contradicted by the fact of conquest. Up till now violence, war, pillage, murder and robbery, etc., have been accepted as the driving force of history. Here we must limit ourselves to the chief points and take, therefore, only the most striking example—the destruction of an old civilisation by a barbarous people and the resulting formation of an entirely new organisation of society. (Rome and the barbarians; feudalism and Gaul; the Byzantine Empire and the Turks.) With the conquering barbarian people war itself is still, as indicated above, a regular form of intercourse, which is the more eagerly exploited as the increase in population together with the traditional and, for it, the only possible, crude mode of production gives rise to the need for new means of production. In Italy, on the other hand, the concentration of landed property (caused not only by buying-up and indebtedness but also by inheritance, since loose living being rife and marriage rare, the old families gradually died out and their possessions fell into the hands of a few) and its conversion into grazing-land (caused not only by the usual economic forces still operative today but by the importation of plundered and tribute-corn and the resultant lack of demand for Italian corn) brought about the almost total disappearance of the free population. The very slaves died out again and again, and had constantly to be replaced by new ones. Slavery remained the basis of the whole productive system. The plebeians, midway between freemen and slaves, never succeeded in becoming more than a proletarian rabble. Rome indeed never became more than a city; its connection with the provinces was almost exclusively political and could, therefore, easily be broken again by political events.

With the development of private property, we find here for the first time the same conditions which we shall find again, only on a more extensive scale, with modern private property. On the one hand, the concentration of private property, which began very early in Rome (as the Licinian agrarian law proves) and proceeded very rapidly from the time of the civil wars and especially under the Emperors; on the other hand, coupled with this, the transformation of the plebeian small peasantry into a proletariat, which, however, owing to its intermediate position between propertied citizens and slaves, never achieved an independent development.

The third form of ownership is feudal or estate property. If antiquity started out from the *town* and its little territory, the Middle Ages started out from the *country*. This different starting-point was determined by the sparseness of the population at that time, which was scattered over a large area and which received no large increase from the conquerors. In contrast to Greece and Rome, feudal development at the outset, therefore, extends over a much wider territory, prepared by the Roman conquests and the spread of agriculture at first associated with it. The last centuries of the declining Roman Empire and its conquest by the barbarians destroyed a number of productive forces; agriculture had declined, industry had decayed for want of a market, trade had died out or been violently suspended, the rural and urban population had decreased. From these conditions and the mode of organisation of the conquest determined by them, feudal property developed under the influence of the Germanic military constitution. Like tribal and communal ownership, it is based again on a community, but the directly producing class standing over against it is not, as in the case of the ancient community, the slaves, but the enserfed small peasantry. As soon as feudalism is fully developed, there also arises antagonism to the towns. The hierarchical structure of landownership, and the armed bodies of retainers associated with it, gave the nobility power over the serfs. This feudal organisation was, just as much as the ancient communal ownership, an association against a subjected producing class; but the form of association and the relation to the direct producers were different because of the different conditions of production.

This feudal system of landownership had its counterpart in the *towns* in the shape of corporative property, the feudal organisation of trades. Here property consisted chiefly in the labour of each individual person. The necessity for association against the organised robber-nobility, the need for communal covered markets in an age when the industrialist was at the same time a merchant, the growing competition of the escaped serfs swarming into the rising towns, the feudal structure of the whole country: these combined to bring about the *guilds*. The gradually accumulated small capital of individual craftsmen and their stable numbers, as against the growing population, evolved the relation of journeyman and apprentice, which brought into being in the towns a hierarchy similar to that in the country.

Thus the chief form of property during the feudal epoch consisted on the one hand of landed property with serf labour chained to it, and on the other of the labour of the individual with small capital commanding the labour of journeymen. The organisation of both was determined by the restricted conditions of production—the small-scale and primitive cultivation of the land, and the craft type of industry. There was little division of labour in the heyday of feudalism. Each country bore in itself the antithesis of town and country; the division into estates was certainly strongly marked; but apart from the differentiation of princes, nobility, clergy and peasants in the country, and masters, journeymen, apprentices and soon also the rabble of casual labourers in the towns, no division of importance took place. In agriculture it was rendered difficult by the strip-system, beside which the cottage industry of the peasants themselves emerged. In industry there was no division of labour at all in the individual trades themselves, and very little between them. The separation of industry and commerce was found already in existence in older towns; in the newer it only developed later, when the towns entered into mutual relations.

The grouping of larger territories into feudal kingdoms was a necessity for the landed nobility as for the towns. The organisation of the ruling class, the nobility, had, therefore, everywhere a monarch at its head.

The fact is, therefore, that definite individuals who are productively active in a definite way enter into these definite social and political relations. Empirical observation must in each separate instance bring out empirically, and without any mystification and speculation, the connection of the social and political structure with production. The social structure and the State are continually evolving out of the life-process of definite individuals, but of individuals, not as they may appear in their own or other people's imagination, but as they *really* are; i.e., as they operate, produce materially, and hence as they work under definite material limits, presuppositions and conditions independent of their will.

The production of ideas, of conceptions, of consciousness, is at first directly interwoven with the material activity and the material intercourse of men, the language of real life. Conceiving, thinking, the mental intercourse of men, appear at this stage as the direct efflux of their material behaviour. The same applies to mental production as expressed in the language of politics, laws, morality, religion, metaphysics, etc., of a people. Men are the producers of their conceptions, ideas, etc.—real, active men, as they are conditioned by a definite development of their productive forces and of the intercourse corresponding to these, up to its furthest forms. Consciousness can never be anything else than conscious existence, and the existence of men is their actual life-process. If in all ideology men and their circumstances appear upside-down as in a *camera obscura*, this phenomenon arises just as much from their historical life-process as the inversion of objects on the retina does from their physical life-process.

In direct contrast to German philosophy which descends from heaven to earth, here we ascend from earth to heaven. That is to say, we do not set out from what men say, imagine, conceive, nor from men as narrated, thought of, imagined, conceived, in order to arrive at men in the flesh. We set out from real, active men, and on the basis of their real life-process we demonstrate the development of the ideological reflexes and echoes of this life-process. The phantoms formed in the human brain are also, necessarily, sublimates of their material life-process, which is empirically verifiable and bound to material premises. Morality, religion, metaphysics, all the rest of ideology and their corresponding forms of consciousness, thus no longer retain the semblance of independence. They have no history, no development; but men, developing their material production and their material intercourse, alter, along with this their real existence, their thinking and the products of their thinking. Life is not determined by consciousness, but consciousness by life. In the first method of approach the starting-point is consciousness taken as the living individual; in the second method, which conforms to real life, it is the real living individuals themselves, and consciousness is considered solely as *their* consciousness.

This method of approach is not devoid of premises. It starts out from the real premises and does not abandon them for a moment. Its premises are men, not in any fantastic isolation and rigidity, but in their actual, empirically perceptible process of development under definite conditions. As soon as this active life-process is described, history ceases to be a collection of dead facts as it is with the empiricists (themselves still abstract), or an imagined activity of imagined subjects, as with the idealists.

Where speculation ends—in real life—there real, positive science begins: the representation of the practical activity, of the practical process of development of men. Empty talk about consciousness ceases, and real knowledge has to take its place. When reality is depicted, philosophy as an independent branch of knowledge loses its medium of existence. At the best its place can only be taken by a summing-up of the most general results, abstractions which arise from the observation of the historical development of men. Viewed apart from real history, these abstractions have in themselves no value whatsoever. They can only serve to facilitate the arrangement of historical material, to indicate the sequence of its separate strata. But they by no means afford a recipe or schema, as does philosophy, for neatly trimming the epochs of history. On the contrary, our difficulties begin only when we set about the observation and the arrangement—the real depiction—of our historical material, whether of a past epoch or of the present. The removal of these difficulties is governed by premises which it is quite impossible to state here, but which only the study of the actual life process and the activity of the individuals of each epoch will make evident. We shall select here some of these abstractions, which we use in contradistinction to the ideologists, and shall illustrate them by historical examples.

A CONTRIBUTION TO THE CRITIQUE OF POLITICAL ECONOMY (in part)

Author's Preface

*   *   *

In the social production which men carry on they enter into definite relations that are indispensable and independent of their will; these relations of production correspond to a definite stage of development of their material powers of production. The sum total of these relations of production constitutes the economic structure of society—the real foundation, on which rise legal and political superstructures and to which correspond definite forms of social consciousness. The mode of production in material life determines the general character of the social, political and spiritual processes of life. It is not the consciousness of men that determines their existence, but, on the contrary, their social existence determines their consciousness. At a certain stage of their development, the material forces of production in society come in conflict with the existing relations of production, or—what is but a legal expression for the same thing—with the property relations within which they had been at work before. From forms of development of the forces of production these relations turn into their fetters. Then comes the period of social revolution. With the change of the economic foundation the entire immense superstructure is more or less rapidly transformed. In considering such transformations the distinction should always be made between the material transformation of the economic conditions of production which can be determined with the precision of natural science, and the legal, political, religious, aesthetic or philosophic—in short ideological forms in which men become conscious of this conflict and fight it out. Just as our opinion of an individual is not based on what he thinks of himself, so can we not judge of such a period of transformation by its own consciousness; on the contrary, this consciousness must rather be explained from the contradictions of material life, from the existing conflict between the social forces of production and the relations of production. No social order ever disappears before all the productive forces, for which there is room in it, have been developed; and new higher relations of production never appear before the material conditions of their existence have matured in the womb of the old society. Therefore, mankind always takes up only such problems as it can solve; since, looking at the matter more closely, we will always find that the problem itself arises only when the material conditions necessary for its solution already exist or are at least in the process of formation. In broad outlines we can designate the Asiatic, the ancient, the feudal, and the modern bourgeois methods of production as so many epochs in the progress of the economic formation of society. The bourgeois relations of production are the last antagonistic form of the social process of production—antagonistic not in the sense of individual antagonism, but of one arising from conditions surrounding the life of individuals in society; at the same time the productive forces developing in the womb of bourgeois society create the material conditions for the solution of that antagonism. This social formation constitutes, therefore, the closing chapter of the prehistoric stage of human society.

*   *   *

Introduction

1. PRODUCTION IN GENERAL

The subject of our discussion is first of all *material* production by individuals as determined by society, naturally constitutes the starting point. The individual and isolated hunter or fisher who forms the starting point with Smith and Ricardo, belongs to the insipid illusions of the eighteenth century. They are Robinsonades which do not by any means represent, as students of the history of civilization imagine, a reaction against over-refinement and a return to a misunderstood natural life. They are no more based on such a naturalism than is Rosseau's "contract social," which makes naturally independent individuals come in contact and have mutual intercourse by contract. They are the fiction and only the aesthetic fiction of the small and great Robinsonades. They are, moreover, the anticipation of "bourgeois society," which had been in course of development since the sixteenth century and made gigantic strides towards maturity in the eighteenth. In this society of free competition the individual appears free from the bonds of nature, etc., which in former epochs of history made him a part of a definite, limited human conglomeration. To the prophets of the eighteenth century, on whose shoulders Smith and Ricardo are still standing, this eighteenth century individual, constituting the joint product of the dissolution of the feudal form of society and of the new forces of production which had developed since the sixteenth century, appears as an ideal whose existence belongs to the past; not as a result of history, but as its starting point.

Since that individual appeared to be in conformity with nature and [corresponded] to their conception of human nature, [he was regarded] not as a product of history, but of nature. This illusion has been characteristic of every new epoch in the past. Steuart, who, as an aristocrat, stood more firmly on historical ground, contrary to the spirit of the eighteenth century, escaped this simplicity of view. The further back we go into history, the more the individual and, therefore, the producing individual seems to depend on and constitute a part of a larger whole: at first it is, quite naturally, the family and the clan, which is but an enlarged family; later on, it is the community growing up in its different forms out of the clash and the amalgamation of clans. It is but in the eighteenth century, in "bourgeois society," that the different forms of social union confront the individual as a mere means to his private ends, as an outward necessity. But the period in which this view of the isolated individual becomes prevalent, is the very one in which the interrelations of society (general from this point of view) have reached the highest state of development. Man is in the most literal sense of the word a *zoon politikon,* not only a social animal, but an animal which can develop into an individual only in society. Production by isolated individuals outside of society— something which might happen as an exception to a civilized man who by accident got into the wilderness and already dynamically possessed within himself the forces of society—is as great an absurdity as the idea of the development of language without individuals living together and talking to one another. We need not dwell on this any longer. It would not be necessary to touch upon this point at all, were not the vagary which had its justification and sense with the people of the eighteenth century transplanted in all earnest into the field of political economy by Baatiat, Carey, Proudhon and others. Proudhon and others naturally find it very pleasant, when they do not know the historical origin of a certain economic phenomenon, to give it a quasi historico-philosophical explanation by going into mythology. Adam or Prometheus hit upon the scheme cut and dried, whereupon it was adopted, etc. Nothing is more tediously dry than the dreaming *locus communis.*

Whenever we speak, therefore, of production, we always have in mind production at a certain stage of social development, or production by social individuals. Hence, it might seem that in order to speak of production at all, we must either trace the historical process of development through its various phases, or declare at the outset that we are dealing with a certain historical period, as, e.g., with modern capitalistic production which, as a matter of fact, constitutes the subject proper of this work. But all stages of production have certain landmarks in common, common purposes. *Production in general* is an abstraction, but it is a rational abstraction, in so far as it singles out and fixes the common features, thereby saving us repetition. Yet these general or common features discovered by comparison constitute something very complex, whose constituent elements have different destinations. Some of these elements belong to all epochs, others are common to a few. Some of them are common to the most modern as well as to the most ancient epochs. No production is conceivable without them; but while even the most completely developed languages have laws and conditions in common with the least developed ones, what is characteristic of their development are the points of departure from the general and common. The conditions which generally govern production must be differentiated in order that the essential points of difference be not lost sight of in view of the general uniformity which is due to the fact that the subject, mankind, and the object, nature, remain the same. The failure to remember this one fact is the source of all the wisdom of modern economists who are trying to prove the eternal nature and harmony of existing social conditions. Thus they say, e.g., that no production is possible without some instrument of production, let that instrument be only the hand; that none is possible without past accumulated labor, even if that labor consist of mere skill which has been accumulated and concentrated in the hand of the savage by repeated exercise. Capital is, among other things, also an instrument of production, also past impersonal labor. Hence capital is a universal, eternal natural phenomenon; which is true if we disregard the specific properties which turn an "instrument of production" and "stored up labor" into capital. The entire history of production appears to a man like Carey, e.g., as a malicious perversion on the part of governments.

If there is no production in general, there is also no general production. Production is always some special branch of production or an aggregate, as, e.g., agriculture, stock raising, manufactures, etc. But political economy is not technology. The connection between the general destinations of production at a given stage of social development and the particular forms of production, is to be developed elsewhere (later on).

Finally, production is not only of a special kind. It is always a certain body politic, a social personality that is engaged on a larger or smaller aggregate of branches of production. The connection between the real process and its scientific presentation also falls outside of the scope of this treatise. [We must thus distinguish between] production in general, special branches of production and production as a whole.

It is the fashion with economists to open their works with a general introduction, which is entitled "production" (see, e.g., John Stuart Mill) and deals with the general "requisites of production."

This general introductory part treats or is supposed to treat:

1. Of the conditions without which production is impossible, i.e., of the most essential conditions of production. As a matter of fact, however, it dwindles down, as we shall see, to a few very simple definitions, which flatten out into shallow tautologies;

2. Of conditions which further production more or less, as, e.g., Adam Smith's [discussion of] a progressive and stagnant state of society.

In order to give scientific value to what serves with him as a mere summary, it would be necessary to study the *degree of productivity* by periods in the development of individual nations; such a study falls outside of the scope of the present subject, and in so far as it does belong here is to be brought out in connection with the discussion of competition, accumulation, etc. The commonly accepted view of the matter gives a general answer to the effect that an industrial nation is at the height of its production at the moment when it reaches its historical climax in all respects. Or, that certain races, climates, natural conditions, such as distance from the sea, fertility of the soil, etc., are more favorable to production than others. That again comes down to the tautology that the facility of creating wealth depends on the extent to which its elements are present both subjectively and objectively. As a matter of fact a nation is at its industrial height so long as its main object is not gain, but the process of gaining. In that respect the Yankees stand above the English.

But all that is not what the economists are really after in the general introductory part. Their object is rather to represent production in contradistinction to distribution— see Mill, e.g.—as subject to eternal laws independent of history, and then to substitute bourgeois relations, in an underhand way, as immutable natural laws of society *in abstracto*. This is the more or less conscious aim of the entire proceeding. On the contrary, when it comes to distribution, mankind is supposed to have indulged in all sorts of arbitrary action. Quite apart from the fact that they violently break the ties which bind production and distribution together, so much must be clear from the outset: that, no matter how greatly the systems of distribution may vary at different stages of society, it should be possible here, as in the case of production, to discover the common features and to confound and eliminate all historical differences in formulating *general human* laws. E.g., the slave, the serf, the wage-worker—all receive a quantity of food, which enables them to exist as slave, serf, and wage-worker. The conqueror, the official, the landlord, the monk, or the levite, who respectively live on tribute, taxes, rent, alms, and the tithe,—all receive [a part] of the social product which is determined by laws different from those which determine the part received by the slave, etc. The two main points which all economists place under this head, are: first, property; second, the protection of the latter by the administration of justice, police, etc. The objections to these two points can be stated very briefly.

1. All production is appropriation of nature by the individual within and through a definite form of society. In that sense it is a tautology to say that property (appropriation) is a condition of production. But it becomes ridiculous, when from that one jumps at once to a definite form of property, e.g., private property (which implies, besides, as a prerequisite the existence of an opposite form, viz., absence of property). History points rather to common property (e.g., among the Hindus, Slavs, ancient Celts, etc.) as the primitive form, which still plays an important part at a much later period as communal property. The question as to whether wealth grows more rapidly under this or that form of property, is not even raised here as yet. But that there can be no such a thing as production, nor, consequently, society, where property does not exist in any form, is a tautology. Appropriation which does not appropriate is a *contradictio* in *subjecto*.

2. Protection of property, etc. Reduced to their real meaning, these commonplaces express more than what their preachers know, namely, that every form of production creates its own legal relations, forms of government, etc. The crudity and the shortcomings of the conception lie in the tendency to see but an accidental reflective connection in what constitutes an organic union. The bourgeois economists have a vague notion that it is better to carry on production under the modern police, than it was, e.g., under club-law. They forget that club law is also law, and that the right of the stronger continues to exist in other forms even under their "government of law."

When the social conditions corresponding to a certain stage of production are in a state of formation or disappearance, disturbances of production naturally arise, although differing in extent and effect.

To sum up: all the stages of production have certain destinations in common, which we generalize in thought; but the so-called general conditions of all production are nothing but abstract conceptions which do not go to make up any real stage in the history of production.

2. THE GENERAL RELATION OF PRODUCTION TO DISTRIBUTION, EXCHANGE, AND CONSUMPTION

Before going into a further analysis of production, it is necessary to look at the various divisions which economists put side by side with it. The most shallow conception is as follows: By production, the members of society appropriate (produce and shape) the products of nature to human wants; distribution determines the proportion in which the individual participates in this production; exchange brings him the particular products into which he wishes to turn the quantity secured by him through distribution; finally, through consumption the products become objects of use and enjoyment, of individual appropriation. Production yields goods adopted to our needs; distribution distributes them according to social laws; exchange distributes further what has already been distributed, according to individual wants; finally, in consumption the product drops out of the social movement, becoming the direct object of the individual want which it serves and satisfies in use. Production thus appears as the starting point; consumption as the final end; and distribution and exchange as the middle; the latter has a double aspect, distribution being defined as a process carried on by society, while exchange, as one proceeding from the individual. In production the person is embodied in things, in [consumption] things are embodied in persons; in distribution, society assumes the part of go-between of production and consumption in the form of generally prevailing rules; in exchange this is accomplished by the accidental make-up of the individual.

Distribution determines what proportion (quantity) of the products the individual is to receive; exchange determines the products in which the individual desires to receive his share allotted to him by distribution.

Production, distribution, exchange, and consumption thus form a perfect connection, production standing for the general, distribution and exchange for the special, and consumption for the individual, in which all are joined together. To be sure this is a connection, but it does not go very deep. Production is determined [according to the economists] by universal natural laws, while distribution depends on social chance: distribution can, therefore, have a more or less stimulating effect on production: exchange lies between the two as a formal social movement, and the final act of consumption which is considered not only as a final purpose, but also as a final aim, falls, properly, outside of the scope of economics, except in so far as it reacts on the starting point and causes the entire process to begin all over again.

The opponents of the economists—whether economists themselves or not—who reproach them with tearing apart, like barbarians, what is an organic whole, either stand on common ground with them or are *below* them. Nothing is more common than the charge that the economists have been considering production as an end in itself, too much to the exclusion of everything else. The same has been said with regard to distribution. This accusation is itself based on the economic conception that distribution exists side by side with production as a self-contained, independent sphere. Or [they are accused] that the various factors are not treated by them in their connection as a whole. As though it were the text books that impress this separation upon life and not life upon the text books; and the subject at issue were a dialectic balancing of conceptions and not an analysis of real conditions.

a. Production is at the same time also consumption. Twofold consumption, subjective and objective. The individual who develops his faculties in production, is also expending them, consuming them in the act of production, just as procreation is in its way a consumption of vital powers. In the second place, production is consumption of means of production which are used and used up and partly (as, e.g., in burning) reduced to their natural elements. The same is true of the consumption of raw materials which do not remain in their natural form and state, being greatly absorbed in the process. The act of production is, therefore, in all its aspects an act of consumption as well. But this is admitted by economists. Production as directly identical with consumption, consumption as directly coincident with production, they call productive consumption. This identity of production and consumption finds its expression in

Spinoza's proposition, *Determinatio est negatio*. But this definition of productive consumption is resorted to just for the purpose of distinguishing between consumption as identical with production and consumption proper, which is defined as its destructive counterpart. Let us then consider consumption proper.

Consumption is directly also production, just as in nature the consumption of the elements and of chemical matter constitutes production of plants. It is clear, that in nutrition, e.g., which is but one form of consumption, man produces his own body; but it is equally true of every kind of consumption, which goes to produce the human being in one way or another. [It is] consumptive production. But, say the economists, this production which is identical with consumption, is a second production resulting from the destruction of the product of the first. In the first, the producer transforms himself into things; in the second, things are transformed into human beings. Consequently, this consumptive production—although constituting a direct unity of production and consumption—differs essentially from production proper. The direct unity in which production coincides with consumption and consumption with production, does not interfere with their direct duality.

Production is thus at the same time consumption, and consumption is at the same time production. Each is directly its own counterpart. But at the same time an intermediary movement goes on between the two. Production furthers consumption by creating material for the latter which otherwise would lack its object. But consumption in its turn furthers production, by providing for the products the individual for whom they are products. The product receives its last finishing touches in consumption. A railroad on which no one rides, which is, consequently not used up, not consumed, is but a potential railroad, and not a real one. Without production, no consumption; but, on the other hand, without consumption, no production; since production would then be without a purpose. Consumption produces production in two ways.

In the first place, in that the product first becomes a real product in consumption; e.g., a garment becomes a real garment only through the act of being worn; a dwelling which is not inhabited, is really no dwelling; consequently, a product as distinguished from a mere natural object, proves to be such, first *becomes* a product in consumption. Consumption gives the product the finishing touch by annihilating it, since a product is the [result] of production not only as the material embodiment of activity, but also as a mere object for the active subject.

In the second place, consumption produces production by creating the necessity for new production, i.e., by providing the ideal, inward, impelling cause which constitutes the prerequisite of production. Consumption furnishes the impulse for production as well as its object, which plays in production the part of its guiding aim. It is clear that while production furnishes the material object of consumption, consumption provides the ideal object of production, as its image, its want, its impulse and its purpose. It furnishes the object of production in its subjective form. No wants, no production. But consumption reproduces the want.

In its turn, production—

First, furnishes consumption with its material, its object. Consumption without an object is no consumption, hence production works in this direction by producing consumption.

Second. But it is not only the object that production provides for consumption. It gives consumption its definite outline, its character, its finish. Just as consumption gives the product its finishing touch as a product, production puts the finishing touch on consumption. For the object is not simply an object in general, but a definite object, which is consumed in a certain definite manner prescribed in its turn by production.

Hunger is hunger; but the hunger that is satisfied with cooked meat eaten with fork and knife is a different kind of hunger from the one that devours raw meat with the aid of hands, nails, and teeth. Not only the object of consumption, but also the manner of consumption is produced by production; that is to say, consumption is created by production not only objectively, but also subjectively. Production thus creates the consumers.

Third. Production not only supplies the want with material, but supplies the material with a want. When consumption emerges from its first stage of natural crudeness and directness—and its continuation in that state would in itself be the result of a production still remaining in a state of natural crudeness—it is itself furthered by its object as a moving spring. The want of it which consumption experiences is created by its appreciation of the product. The object of art, as well as any other product, creates an artistic and beauty-enjoying public. Production thus produces not only an object for the individual, but also an individual for the object.

Production thus produces consumption: first, by furnishing the latter with material; second, by determining the manner of consumption; third, by creating in consumers a want for its products as objects of consumption. It thus produces the object, the manner, and the moving spring of consumption. In the same manner, consumption [creates] the *disposition* of the producer by setting him up as an aim and by stimulating wants. The identity of consumption and production thus appears to be a three fold one.

First, direct identity: production is consumption; consumption is production. Consumptive production. Productive consumption. Economists call both productive consumption, but make one distinction by calling the former reproduction, and the latter productive consumption. All inquiries into the former deal with productive and unproductive labor; those into the latter treat of productive and unproductive consumption.

Second. Each appears as the means of the other and as being brought about by the other, which is expressed as their mutual interdependence; a relation, by virtue of which they appear as mutually connected and indispensable, yet remaining outside of each other.

Production creates the material as the outward object of consumption; consumption creates the want as the inward object, the purpose of production. Without production, no consumption; without consumption, no production; this maxim figures in political economy in many forms.

Third. Production is not only directly consumption and consumption directly production; nor is production merely a means of consumption and consumption the purpose of production. In other words, not only does each furnish the other with its object; production, the material object of consumption; consumption, the ideal object of production. On the contrary, either one is not only directly the other, not only a means of furthering the other, but while it is taking place, creates the other as such for itself. Consumption completes the act of production by giving the finishing touch to the product as such, by destroying the latter, by breaking up its independent material form; by bringing to a state of readiness, through the necessity of repetition, the disposition to produce developed in the first act of production; that is to say, it is not only the concluding act through which the product becomes a product, but also [the one] through which the producer becomes a producer. On the other hand, production produces consumption, by determining the manner of consumption, and further, by creating the incentive for consumption, the very ability to consume, in the form of want. This latter identity mentioned under point 3, is much discussed in political economy in connection with the treatment of the relations of demand and supply, of objects and wants, of natural wants and those created by society.

Hence, it is the simplest matter with a Hegelian to treat production and consumption as identical. And this has been done not only by socialist writers of fiction but even by economists, e.g., Say; the latter maintained that if we consider a nation as a whole, or mankind *in abstracto*—her production is at the same time her consumption. Storch pointed out Say's error by calling attention to the fact that a nation does not entirely consume her product, but also creates means of production, fixed capital, etc. To consider society as a single individual is moreover a false mode of speculative reasoning. With an individual, production and consumption appear as different aspects of one act. The important point to be emphasized here is that if production and consumption be considered as activities of one individual or of separate individuals, they appear at any rate as aspects of one process in which production forms the actual starting point and is, therefore, the predominating factor. Consumption, as a natural necessity, as a want, constitutes an internal factor of productive activity, but the latter is the starting point of realization and, therefore, its predominating factor, the act into which the entire process resolves itself in the end. The individual produces a certain article and turns again into himself by consuming it; but he returns as a productive and a self-reproducing individual. Consumption thus appears as a factor of production.

In society, however, the relation of the producer to his product, as soon as it is completed, is an outward one, and the return of the product to the individual depends on his relations to other individuals. He does not take immediate possession of it. Nor does the direct appropriation of the product constitute his purpose, when he produces in society. Between the producer and the product distribution steps in, which determines by social laws his share in the world of products; that is to say, distribution steps in between production and consumption.

Does distribution form an independent sphere standing side by side with and outside of production?

b. Production and Distribution. In perusing the common treatises on economics one can not help being struck with the fact that everything is treated there twice; e.g., under distribution, there figure rent, wages, interest, and profit; while under production we find land, labor, and capital as agents of production. As regards capital, it is at once clear that it is counted twice: first, as an agent of production; second, as a source of income; as determining factors and definite forms of distribution, interest and profit figure as such also in production, since they are forms, in which capital increases and grows, and are consequently factors of its own production. Interest and profit, as forms of distribution, imply the existence of capital as an agent of production. They are forms of distribution which have for their prerequisite capital as an agent of production. They are also forms of reproduction of capital.

In the same manner, wages is wage-labor when considered under another head; the definite character which labor has in one case as an agent of production, appears in the other as a form of distribution. If labor were not fixed as wage-labor, its manner of participation in distribution would not appear as wages, as is the case, e.g., under slavery. Finally, rent—to take at once the most developed form of distribution—by means of which landed property receives its share of the products, implies the existence of large landed property (properly speaking, agriculture on a large scale) as an agent of production, and not simply land, no more than wages represents simply labor. The relations and methods of distribution appear, therefore, merely as the reverse sides of the agents of production. An individual who participates in production as a wage laborer, receives his share of the products, i.e., of the results of production, in the form of wages. The subdivisions and organization of distribution are determined by the subdivisions and organization of production. Distribution is itself a product of production, not only in so far as the material goods are concerned, since only the results of production can be distributed; but also as regards its form, since the definite manner of participation in production determines the particular form of distribution, the form under which participation in distribution takes place. It is quite an illusion to place land under production, rent under distribution, etc.

Economists, like Ricardo, who are accused above all of having paid exclusive attention to production, define distribution, therefore, as the exclusive subject of political economy, because they instinctively regard the forms of distribution as the clearest forms in which the agents of production find expression in a given society.

To the single individual distribution naturally appears as a law established by society determining his position in the sphere of production, within which he produces, and thus antedating production. At the outset the individual has no capital, no landed property. From his birth he is assigned to wage-labor by the social process of distribution. But this very condition of being assigned to wage-labor is the result of the existence of capital and landed property as independent agents of production.

From the point of view of society as a whole, distribution seems to antedate and to determine production in another way as well, as a pre-economic fact, so to say. A conquering people divides the land among the conquerors establishing thereby a certain division and form of landed property and determining the character of production; or, it turns the conquered people into slaves and thus makes slave labor the basis of production. Or, a nation, by revolution, breaks up large estates into small parcels of land and by this new distribution imparts to production a new character. Or, legislation perpetuates land ownership in large families or distributes labor as an hereditary privilege and thus fixes it in castes.

In all of these cases, and they are all historic, it is not distribution that seems to be organized and determined by production, but on the contrary, production by distribution.

In the most shallow conception of distribution, the latter appears as a distribution of products and to that extent as further removed from and quasi-independent of production. But before distribution means distribution of products, it is first, a distribution of the means of production, and second, what is practically another wording of the same fact, it is a distribution of the members of society among the various kinds of production (the subjection of individuals to certain conditions of production). The distribution of products is manifestly a result of this distribution, which is bound up with the process of production and determines the very organization of the latter. To treat of production apart from the distribution which is comprised in it, is plainly an idle abstraction. Conversely, we know the character of the distribution of products the moment we are given the nature of that other distribution which forms originally a factor of production. Ricardo, who was concerned with the analysis of production as it is organized in modern society and who was the economist of production *par excellence,* for that very reason declares not production but distribution as the subject proper of modern economics. We have here another evidence of the insipidity of the economists who treat production as an eternal truth, and banish history to the domain of distribution.

What relation to production this distribution, which has a determining influence on production itself, assumes, is plainly a question which falls within the province of production. Should it be maintained that at least to the extent that production depends on a certain distribution of the instruments of production, distribution in that sense precedes production and constitutes its prerequisite; it may be replied that production has in fact its prerequisite conditions, which form factors of it. These may appear at first to have a natural origin. By the very process of production they are changed from natural to historical, and if they appear during one period as a natural prerequisite of production, they formed at other periods its historical result. Within the sphere of production itself they are undergoing a constant change. E.g., the application of machinery produces a change in the distribution of the instruments of production as well as in that of products, and modern land ownership on a large scale is as much the result of modern trade and modern industry, as that of the application of the latter to agriculture.

All of these questions resolve themselves in the last instance to this: How do general historical conditions affect production and what part does it play at all in the course of history? It is evident that this question can be taken up only in connection with the discussion and analysis of production.

Yet in the trivial form in which these questions are raised above, they can be answered just as briefly. In the case of all conquests three ways lie open. The conquering people may impose its own methods of production upon the conquered (e.g., the English in Ireland in the nineteenth century, partly also in India); or, it may allow everything to remain as it was contenting itself with tribute (e.g., the Turks and the Romans); or, the two systems by mutually modifying each other may result in something new, a synthesis (which partly resulted from the Germanic conquests). In all of these conquests the method of production, be it of the conquerors, the conquered, or the one resulting from a combination of both, determines the nature of the new distribution which comes into play. Although the latter appears now as the prerequisite condition of the new period of production, it is in itself but a product of production, not of production belonging to history in general, but of production relating to a definite historical period. The Mongols with their devastations in Russia, e.g., acted in accordance with their system of production, for which sufficient pastures on large uninhabited stretches of country are the main prerequisite. The Germanic barbarians, with whom agriculture carried on with the aid of serfs was the traditional system of production and who were accustomed to lonely life in the country, could introduce the same conditions in the Roman provinces so much easier since the concentration of landed property which had taken place there, did away completely with the older systems of agriculture. There is a prevalent tradition that in certain periods robbery constituted the only source of living. But in order to be able to plunder, there must be something to plunder, i.e., there must be production. And even the method of plunder is determined by the method of production. A stockjobbing nation, e.g., can not be robbed in the same manner as a nation of shepherds.

In the case of the slave the instrument of production is robbed directly. But then the production of the country in whose interest he is robbed, must be so organized as to admit of slave labor, or (as in South America, etc.) a system of production must be introduced adapted to slavery.

Laws may perpetuate an instrument of production, e.g., land, in certain families. These laws assume an economic importance if large landed property is in harmony with the system of production prevailing in society, as is the case, e.g., in England. In France agriculture had been carried on on a small scale in spite of the large estates, and the latter were, therefore, broken up by the Revolution. But how about the legislative attempt to perpetuate the minute subdivision of the land? In spite of these laws land ownership is concentrating again. The effect of legislation on the maintenance of a system of distribution and its resultant influence on production are to be determined elsewhere.

c. Exchange and Circulation. Circulation is but a certain aspect of exchange, or it may be defined as exchange considered as a whole. Since *exchange* is an intermediary factor between production and its dependent distribution, on the one hand, and consumption, on the other; and since the latter appears but as a constituent of production, exchange is manifestly also a constituent part of production.

In the first place, it is clear that the exchange of activities and abilities which takes place in the sphere of production falls directly within the latter and constitutes one of its essential elements. In the second place, the same is true of the exchange of products, in so far as it is a means of completing a certain product, designed for immediate consumption. To that extent exchange constitutes an act included in production. Thirdly, the so-called exchange between dealers and dealers' is by virtue of its organization determined by production, and is itself a species of productive activity. Exchange appears to be independent of and indifferent to production only in the last stage when products are exchanged directly for consumption. But in the first place, there is no exchange without a division of labor, whether natural or as a result of historical development; secondly, private exchange implies the existence of private production; thirdly, the intensity of exchange, as well as its extent and character are determined by the degree of development and organization of production, as, e.g., exchange between city and country, exchange in the country, in the city, etc. Exchange thus appears in all its aspects to be directly included in or determined by production.

The result we arrive at is not that production, distribution, exchange, and consumption are identical, but that they are all members of one entity, different sides of one unit. Production predominates not only over production itself in the opposite sense of that term, but over the other elements as well. With it the process constantly starts over again. That exchange and consumption can not be the predominating elements is self evident. The same is true of distribution in the narrow sense of distribution of products; as for distribution in the sense of distribution of the agents of production, it is itself but a factor of production. A definite [form of] production thus determines the [forms of] consumption, distribution, exchange, and *also the mutual relations between these various elements.* Of course, production *in its one-sided form* is in its turn influenced by other elements; e.g., with the expansion of the market, i.e., of the sphere of exchange, production grows in volume and is subdivided to a greater extent.

With a change in distribution, production undergoes a change; as, e.g., in the case of concentration of capital, of a change in the distribution of population in city and country, etc. Finally, the demands of consumption also influence production. A mutual interaction takes place between the various elements. Such is the case with every organic body.

3. THE METHOD OF POLITICAL ECONOMY

When we consider a given country from a politico-economic standpoint, we begin with its population, then analyze the latter according to its subdivision into classes, location in city, country, or by the sea, occupation in different branches of production; then we study its exports and imports, annual production and consumption, prices of commodities, etc. It seems to be the correct procedure to commence with the real and concrete aspect of conditions as they are; in the case of political economy, to commence with population which is the basis and the author of the entire productive activity of society. Yet, on closer consideration it proves to be wrong. Population is an abstraction, if we leave out, e.g., the classes of which it consists. These classes, again, are but an empty word, unless we know what are the elements on which they are based, such as wage-labor, capital. etc. These imply, in their turn, exchange, division of labor, prices, etc. Capital, e.g., does not mean anything without wage-labor, value, money, price, etc. If we start out, therefore, with population, we do so with a chaotic conception of the whole, and by closer analysis we will gradually arrive at simpler ideas; thus we shall proceed from the imaginary concrete to less and less complex abstractions, until we get at the simplest conception. This once attained, we might start on our return journey until we would finally come back to population, but this time not as a chaotic notion of an integral whole, but as a rich aggregate of many conceptions and relations. The former method is the one which political economy had adopted in the past at its inception. The economists of the seventeenth century, e.g., always started out with the living aggregate: population, nation, state, several states, etc., but in the end they invariably arrived, by means of analysis, at certain leading, abstract general principles, such as division of labor, money, value, etc. As soon as these separate elements had been more or less established by abstract reasoning there arose the systems of political economy which start from simple conceptions, such as labor, division of labor, demand, exchange value, and conclude with state, international exchange and world market. The latter is manifestly the scientifically correct method. The concrete is concrete, because it is a combination of many objects with different destinations, i.e., a unity of diverse elements. In our thought, it therefore appears as a process of synthesis, as a result, and not as a starting point, although it is the real starting point and, therefore, also the starting point of observation and conception. By the former method the complete conception passes into an abstract definition; by the latter, the abstract definitions lead to the reproduction of the concrete subject in the course of reasoning. Hegel fell into the error, therefore, of considering the real as the result of self-coordinating, self-absorbed, and spontaneously operating thought, while the method of advancing from the abstract to the concrete is but a way of thinking by which the concrete is grasped and is reproduced in our mind as a concrete. It is by no means, however, the process which itself generates the concrete. The simplest economic category, say, exchange value, implies the existence of population, population that is engaged in production under certain conditions; it also implies the existence of certain types of family, clan, or state, etc. It can have no other existence except as an abstract one-sided relation of an already given concrete and living aggregate.

As a category, however, exchange value leads an antediluvian existence. And since our philosophic consciousness is so arranged that only the image of the man that it conceives appears to it as the real man and the world as it conceives it, as the real world; it mistakes the movement of categories for the real act of production (which unfortunately receives only its impetus from outside) whose result is the world; that is true—here we have, however, again a tautology—in so far as the concrete aggregate is a thought aggregate, in so far as the concrete subject of our thought is in fact a product of thought, of comprehension; not, however, in the sense of a product of a self-emanating conception which works outside of and stands above observation and imagination, but of a mental consummation of observation and imagination. The whole, as it appears in our heads as a thought-aggregate, is the product of a thinking mind which grasps the world in the only way open to it, a way which differs from the one employed by the artistic, religious, or practical mind. The concrete subject continues to lead an independent existence after it has been grasped, as it did before, outside of the head, so long as the head contemplates it only speculatively, theoretically. So that in the employment of the theoretical method [in political economy], the subject, society, must constantly be kept in mind as the premise from which we start.

But have these simple categories no independent historical or natural existence antedating the more concrete ones? *Ça depend.* For instance, in his *Philosophy of Law* Hegel rightly starts out with possession, as the simplest legal relation of individuals. But there is no such thing as possession before the family or the relations of lord and serf, which are a great deal more concrete relations, have come into existence. On the other hand, one would be right in saying that there are families and clans which only *possess,* but do not *own* things. The simpler category thus appears as a relation of simple family and clan communities with respect to property. In earlier society the category appears as a simple relation of a developed organism, but the concrete substratum from which springs the relation of possession, is always implied. One can imagine an isolated savage in possession of things. But in that case possession is no legal relation. It is not true that the family came as the result of the historical evolution of possession. On the contrary, the latter always implies the existence of this "more concrete category of law." Yet so much may be said, that the simple categories are the expression of relations in which the less developed concrete entity may have been realized without entering into the manifold relations and bearings which are mentally expressed in the concrete category; but when the concrete entity attains fuller development it will retain the same category as a subordinate relation.

Money may exist and actually had existed in history before capital, or banks, or wage-labor came into existence. With that in mind, it may be said that the more simple category can serve as an expression of the predominant relations of an undeveloped whole or of the subordinate relations of a more developed whole, [relations] which had historically existed before the whole developed in the direction expressed in the more concrete category. In so far, the laws of abstract reasoning which ascends from the most simple to the complex, correspond to the actual process of history.

On the other hand, it may be said that there are highly developed but historically unripe forms of society in which the highest economic forms are to be found, such as co-operation, advanced division of labor, etc., and yet there is no money in existence, e.g., Peru.

In Slavic communities also, money, as well as exchange to which it owes its existence, does not appear at all or very little within the separate communities, but it appears on their boundaries in their inter-communal traffic; in general, it is erroneous to consider exchange as a constituent element originating within the community. It appears at first more in the mutual relations between different communities, than in those between the members of the same community. Furthermore, although money begins to play its part everywhere at an early stage, it plays in antiquity the part of a predominant element only in one-sidedly developed nations, viz., trading nations, and even in most cultured antiquity, in Greece and Rome, it attains its full development, which constitutes the prerequisite of modern bourgeois society, only in the period of their decay. Thus, this quite simple category attained its culmination in the past only at the most advanced stages of society. Even then it did not pervade all economic relations; in Rome, e.g., at the time of its highest development taxes and payments in kind remained the basis. As a matter of fact, the money system was fully developed there only so far as the army was concerned; it never came to dominate the entire system of labor.

Thus, although the simple category may have existed historically before the more concrete one, it can attain its complete internal and external development only in complex forms of society, while the more concrete category has reached its full development in a less advanced form of society.

Labor is quite a simple category. The idea of labor in that sense, as labor in general, is also very old. Yet, "labor" thus simply defined by political economy is as much a modern category, as the conditions which have given rise to this simple abstraction. The monetary system, e.g., defines wealth quite objectively, as a thing in money. Compared with this point of view, it was a great step forward, when the industrial or commercial system came to see the source of wealth not in the object but in the activity of persons, viz., in commercial and industrial labor. But even the latter was thus considered only in the limited sense of a money producing activity. The physiocratic system [marks still further progress] in that it considers a certain form of labor, viz., agriculture, as the source of wealth, and wealth itself not in the disguise of money, but as a product in general, as the general result of labor. But corresponding to the limitations of the activity, this product is still only a natural product. Agriculture is productive, land is the source of production *par excellence.* It was a tremendous advance on the part of Adam Smith to throw aside all limitations which mark wealth-producing activity and [to define it] as labor in general, neither industrial, nor commercial, nor agricultural, or one as much as the other. Along with the universal character of wealth-creating activity we have now the universal character of the object defined as wealth, viz., product in general, or labor in general, but as past incorporated labor. How difficult and great was the transition, is evident from the way Adam Smith himself falls back from time to time into the physiocratic system. Now, it might seem as though this amounted simply to finding an abstract expression for the simplest relation into which men have been mutually entering as producers from times of yore, no matter under what form of society. In one sense this is true. In another it is not.

The indifference as to the particular kind of labor implies the existence of a highly developed aggregate of different species of concrete labor, none of which is any longer the predominant one. So do the most general abstractions commonly arise only where there is the highest concrete development, where one feature appears to be jointly possessed by many, and to be common to all. Then it can not be thought of any longer in one particular form. On the other hand, this abstraction of labor is but the result of a concrete aggregate of different kinds of labor. The indifference to the particular kind of labor corresponds to a form of society in which individuals pass with ease from one kind of work to another, which makes it immaterial to them what particular kind of work may fall to their share. Labor has become here, not only categorically but really, a means of creating wealth in general and is no longer grown together with the individual into one particular destination. This state of affairs has found its highest development in the most modern of bourgeois societies, the United States. It is only here that the abstraction of the category "labor," "labor in general," labor *sans phrase,* the starting point of modern political economy, becomes realized in practice. Thus, the simplest abstraction which modern political economy sets up as its starting point, and which expresses a relation dating back to antiquity and prevalent under all forms of society, appears in this abstraction truly realized only as a category of the most modern society. It might be said that what appears in the United States as an historical product—viz., the indifference as to the particular kind of labor—appears among the Russians, e.g., as a natural disposition. But it makes all the difference in the world whether barbarians have a natural predisposition which makes them applicable alike to everything, or whether civilized people apply themselves to everything. And, besides, this indifference of the Russians as to the kind of work they do, corresponds to their traditional practice of remaining in the rut of a quite definite occupation until they are thrown out of it by external influences.

This example of labor strikingly shows how even the most abstract categories, in spite of their applicability to all epochs—just because of their abstract character—are by the very definiteness of the abstraction a product of historical conditions as well, and are fully applicable only to and under those conditions.

The bourgeois society is the most highly developed and most highly differentiated historical organization of production. The categories which serve as the expression of its conditions and the comprehension of its own organization enable it at the
same time to gain an insight into the organization and the conditions of production
which had prevailed under all the past forms of society, on the ruins and constituent elements of which it has arisen, and of which it still drags along some unsurmounted
remnants, while what had formerly been mere intimation has now developed to complete significance. The anatomy of the human being is the key to the anatomy of the
ape. But the intimations of a higher animal in lower ones can be understood only if the
animal of the higher order is already known. The bourgeois economy furnishes a key
to ancient economy, etc. This is, however, by no means true of the method of those
economists who blot out all historical differences and see the bourgeois form in all
forms of society. One can understand the nature of tribute, tithes, etc., after one has
learned the nature of rent. But they must not be considered identical.

Since, furthermore, bourgeois society is but a form resulting from the development of antagonistic elements, some relations belonging to earlier forms of society are
frequently to be found in it but in a crippled state or as a travesty of their former self,
as, e.g., communal property. While it may be said, therefore, that the categories of
bourgeois economy contain what is true of all other forms of society, the statement is
to be taken *cum grano salis*. They may contain these in a developed, or crippled, or
caricatured form, but always essentially different. The so-called historical development
amounts in the last analysis to this, that the last form considers its predecessors as
stages leading up to itself and perceives them always one-sidedly, since it is very seldom and only under certain conditions that it is capable of self-criticism; of course, we
do not speak here of such historical periods which appear to their own contemporaries
as periods of decay. The Christian religion became capable to assist us to an objective
view of past mythologies as soon as it was ready for self-criticism to a certain extent,
dynamei so-to-say. In the same way bourgeois political economy first came to understand the feudal, the ancient, and the oriental societies as soon as the self-criticism of
the bourgeois society had commenced. So far as bourgeois political economy has not
gone into the mythology of purely identifying the bourgeois system with the past, its
criticism of the feudal system against which it still had to wage war resembled Christian criticism of the heathen religions or Protestant criticism of Catholicism.

In the study of economic categories, as in the case of every historical and social
science, it must be borne in mind that as in reality so in our mind the subject, in this
case modern bourgeois society, is given and that the categories are therefore but forms
of expression, manifestations of existence, and frequently but one-sided aspects of this
subject, this definite society; and that, therefore, the origin of [political economy] as a
science does not by any means date from the time to which it is referred *as such*. This
is to be firmly held in mind because it has an immediate and important bearing on the
matter of the subdivisions of the science.

For instance, nothing seems more natural than to start with rent, with landed
property, since it is bound up with land, the source of all production and all existence,
and with the first form of production in all more or less settled communities, viz., agriculture. But nothing would be more erroneous. Under all forms of society there is a
certain industry which predominates over all the rest and whose condition therefore determines the rank and influence of all the rest.

It is the universal light with which all the other colors are tinged and are modified through its peculiarity. It is a special ether which determines the specific gravity of
everything that appears in it.

Let us take for example pastoral nations (mere hunting and fishing tribes are not as yet at the point from which real development commences). They engage in a certain form of agriculture, sporadically. The nature of land-ownership is determined thereby. It is held in common and retains this form more or less according to the extent to which these nations hold on to traditions; such, e.g., is land-ownership among the Slavs. Among nations whose agriculture is carried on by a settled population— the settled state constituting a great advance—where agriculture is the predominant industry, such as in ancient and feudal societies, even the manufacturing industry and its organization, as well as the forms of property which pertain to it, have more or less the characteristic features of the prevailing system of land ownership; [society] is then either entirely dependent upon agriculture, as in the case of ancient Rome, or, as in the Middle Ages, it imitates in its city relations the forms of organization prevailing in the country. Even capital, with the exception of pure money capital, has, in the form of the traditional working tool, the characteristics of land ownership in the Middle Ages.

The reverse is true of bourgeois society. Agriculture comes to be more and more merely a branch of industry and is completely dominated by capital. The same is true of rent. In all the forms of society in which land ownership is the prevalent form, the influence of the natural element is the predominant one. In those where capital predominates the prevailing element is the one historically created by society. Rent can not be understood without capital, nor can capital], without rent. Capital is the all dominating economic power of bourgeois society. It must form the starting point as well as the end and be developed before land-ownership is. After each has been considered separately, their mutual relation must be analyzed.

It would thus be impractical and wrong to arrange the economic categories in the order in which they were the determining factors in the course of history. Their order of sequence is rather determined by the relation which they bear to one another in modern bourgeois society, and which is the exact opposite of what seems to be their natural order or the order of their historical development. What we are interested in is not the place which economic relations occupy in the historical succession of different forms of society. Still less are we interested in the order of their succession "in idea" *(Proudhon),* which is but a hazy conception of the course of history. We are interested in their organic connection within modern bourgeois society.

The sharp line of demarkation (abstract precision) which so clearly distinguished the trading nations of antiquity, such as the Phoenicians and the Carthagenians, was due to that very predominance of agriculture. Capital as trading or money capital appears in that abstraction, where capital does not constitute as yet the predominating element of society. The Lombardians and the Jews occupied the same position among the agricultural nations of the middle ages.

As a further illustration of the fact that the same category plays different parts at different stages of society, we may mention the following: one of the latest forms of bourgeois society, viz., stock companies, appear also at its beginning in the form of the great chartered monopolistic trading companies.

The conception of national wealth which is imperceptibly formed in the minds of the economists of the seventeenth century, and which partly continues to be entertained by those of the eighteenth century, is that wealth is produced solely for the state, but that the power of the latter is proportional to that wealth. It was as yet an unconsciously hypocritical way in which wealth announced itself and its own production as the aim of modern states considering the latter merely as a means to the production of wealth.

The order of treatment must manifestly be as follows: first, the general abstract definitions which are more or less applicable to all forms of society, but in the sense indicated above. Second, the categories which go to make up the inner organization of bourgeois society and constitute the foundations of the principal classes; capital, wage-labor, landed property; their mutual relations; city and country; the three great social classes, the exchange between them; circulation, credit (private). Third, the organization of bourgeois society in the form of a state, considered in relation to itself; the "unproductive" classes; taxes; public debts; public credit; population; colonies; emigration. Fourth, the international organization of production; international division of labor; international exchange; import and export; rate of exchange. Fifth, the world market and crises.

4. PRODUCTION, MEANS OF PRODUCTION, AND CONDITIONS OF PRODUCTION. THE RELATIONS OF PRODUCTION AND DISTRIBUTION. THE CONNECTION BETWEEN FORM OF STATE AND PROPERTY ON THE ONE HAND AND RELATIONS OF PRODUCTION AND DISTRIBUTION ON THE OTHER. LEGAL RELATIONS. FAMILY RELATIONS.

Notes on the points to be mentioned here and not to be omitted:*

1. *War* attains complete development before peace; how certain economic phenomena, such as wage-labor, machinery, etc., are developed at an earlier date through war and in armies than within bourgeois society. The connection between productive force and the means of communication is made especially plain in the case of the army.

2. The relation between the idealistic and realistic methods of writing history; namely, the so-called history of civilization which is all a history of religion and states.

In this connection something may be said of the different methods hitherto employed in writing history. The so-called objective [method]. The subjective. (The moral and others). The philosophic.

3. *Secondary and tertiary*. Conditions of production which have been taken over or transplanted; in general, those that are not original. Here [is to be treated] the effect of international relations.

4. Objections to the materialistic character of this view. Its relation to naturalistic materialism.

5. The dialectics of the conceptions productive force (means of production) and relation of production, dialectics whose limits are to be determined and which does not do away with the concrete difference.

6. The unequal relation between the development of material production and art, for instance. In general, the conception of progress is not to be taken in the sense of the usual abstraction. In the case of art, etc., it is not so important and difficult to under-

---

*[The "notes" Marx includes here are extremely fragmentary giving only a listing of issues he plans to discuss later.]

stand this disproportion as in that of practical social relations, e.g., the relation between education in the United States and Europe. The really difficult point, however, that is to be discussed here is that of the unequal development of relations of production as legal relations. As, e.g., the connection between Roman civil law (this is less true of criminal and public law) and modern production.

7. This conception of development appears to imply necessity. On the other hand, justification of accident. Varia. (Freedom and other points). (The effect of means of communication). World history does not always appear in history as the result of world history.

8. The starting point [is to be found] in certain facts of nature embodied subjectively and objectively in clans, races, etc.

It is well known that certain periods of highest development of art stand in no direct connection with the general development of society, nor with the material basis and the skeleton structure of its organization. Witness the example of the Greeks as compared with the modern nations or even Shakespeare. As regards certain forms of art, as e.g., the epos, it is admitted that they can never be produced in the world-epoch making form as soon as art as such comes into existence; in other words, that in the domain of art certain important forms of it are possible only at a low stage of its development. If that be true of the mutual relations of different forms of art within the domain of art itself, it is far less surprising that the same is true of the relation of art as a whole to the general development of society. The difficulty lies only in the general formulation of these contradictions. No sooner are they specified than they are explained. Let us take for instance the relation of Greek art and of that of Shakespeare's time to our own. It is a well known fact that Greek mythology was not only the arsenal of Greek art, but also the very ground from which it had sprung. Is the view of nature and of social relations which shaped Greek imagination and Greek [art] possible in the age of automatic machinery, and railways, and locomotives, and electric telegraphs? Where does Vulcan come in as against Roberts & Co.; Jupiter, as against the lightning rod; and Hermes, as against the Credit Mobilier? All mythology masters and dominates and shapes the forces of nature in and through the imagination; hence it disappears as soon as man gains mastery over the forces of nature. What becomes of the Goddess Fame side by side with Printing House Square?* Greek art presupposes the existence of Greek mythology, i.e., that nature and even the form of society are wrought up in popular fancy in an unconsciously artistic fashion. That is its material. Not, however, any mythology taken at random, nor any accidental unconsciously artistic laboration of nature (including under the latter all objects, hence [also] society). Egyptian mythology could never be the soil or womb which would give birth to Greek art. But in any event [there had to be] a mythology. In no event [could Greek art originate] in a society which excludes any mythological explanation of nature, any mythological attitude towards it and which requires from the artist an imagination free from mythology.

Looking at it from another side: is Achilles possible side by side with powder and lead? Or is the Iliad at all compatible with the printing press and steam press? Does not singing and reciting and the muses necessarily go out of existence with the appearance of the printer's bar, and do not, therefore, disappear the prerequisites of epic poetry?

But the difficulty is not in grasping the idea that Greek art and epos are bound up with certain forms of social development. It rather lies in understanding why they still

*[The *Times* building in London.]

constitute with us a source of aesthetic enjoyment and in certain respects prevail as the standard and model beyond attainment. A man can not become a child again unless he becomes childish. But does he not enjoy the artless ways of the child and must he not strive to reproduce its truth on a higher plane? Is not the character of every epoch revived perfectly true to nature in child nature? Why should the social childhood of mankind, where it had obtained its most beautiful development, not exert an eternal charm as an age that will never return? There are ill-bred children and precocious children. Many of the ancient nations belong to the latter class. The Greeks were normal children. The charm their art has for us does not conflict with the primitive character of the social order from which it had sprung. It is rather the product of the latter, and is rather due to the fact that the unripe social conditions under which the art arose and under which alone it could appear can never return.

CHARLES SANDERS PEIRCE
1839–1914

Charles Sanders Peirce (pronounced "Purse") was born in Cambridge, Massachusetts, to Benjamin and Sarah Hunt Mills Peirce. His father was a noted mathematician and professor of astronomy and mathematics at Harvard. Like John Stuart Mill and Søren Kierkegaard, Charles Peirce received his most significant schooling from his father. From an early age, his father taught him mathematics and science, encouraging Peirce in his youthful laboratory experiments. Though Peirce did graduate from both Cambridge High School and Harvard, he did not distinguish himself academically at either institution and had trouble adapting socially. During his college years, he spent much of his time with his father, discussing the elder Peirce's mathematical studies. Following graduation from Harvard in 1859, Peirce studied chemistry at the Lawrence Scientific School. There he met and then married his first wife, Harriet Melusina Fay. In addition to this change in his social life, Peirce's academic performance improved, and in 1863 he graduated from Lawrence *summa cum laude*.

While Peirce was still in school, his father arranged a job for him with the United States Coast and Geodetic Survey. Peirce worked for this agency over the next thirty years but nevertheless found time for a number of other pursuits. He worked as an astronomer at Harvard, continued to perform scientific experiments, read and wrote extensively in philosophy, and lectured on logic at Johns Hopkins University. Peirce also helped form the Metaphysical Club, an informal gathering of friends to discuss philosophical matters. The club included such well-known thinkers as William James and Oliver Wendell Holmes. Though esteemed by his fellow philosophers, Peirce's difficult personality and reputation for "loose living" kept him from a professorship. Peirce's "inability to exercise the proper moral self-control" (James's description) eventually led to a divorce from Harriet Fay in 1883. The following year Peirce married a French woman named Juliette Froisy.

In 1891, Peirce received a small legacy, retired from his job with the U.S. Coast and Geodetic Survey, and moved to Milford, Pennsylvania, where he lived a reclusive life while writing on philosophical themes. His works received virtually no recognition during his lifetime, and on his death his second wife sold all his papers to Harvard for five hundred dollars.

* * *

Peirce has been called a "philosopher's philosopher." His writings are often difficult for beginning students, partly because of the technical way in which he expresses his ideas. In addition, he developed four more-or-less complete systems, abandoning each in favor of the next. Despite his esoteric and variegated writing, in 1877 and 1878 Peirce published a pair of essays for a general audience in *Popular Science Monthly*. These became his most important works.

These essays, "The Fixation of Belief" and "How to Make Our Ideas Clear," are given here (complete). Together they develop Peirce's famous theory of pragmatism. Peirce begins with a brief history of knowledge, concluding that all inquiry begins with doubt. In order to lead to belief, this doubt must be "real and living," the actual state in which we find ourselves.

Peirce's second essay continues this theme by contrasting the invented doubt of thinkers such as Descartes to genuine inquiry. Peirce defines real doubt as an irritating condition that "most frequently . . . arise[s] from some indecision, however momentary, in our action." This kind of doubt stimulates the mind, leading us to seek relief—to find the "calm and satisfactory" state of belief. "Belief" has three properties: (1) "It is something that we are aware of"; (2) "it appeases the irritation of doubt"; and (3) "it involves the establishment in our nature of a rule of action, or, say for short, a *habit*." Belief, then, not only cuts off doubt, it involves and leads to action, so that "different beliefs are distinguished by the different modes of action to which they give rise."

To understand what a belief *means,* then, we must look at what actions or habits it produces:

> Consider what effects, that might conceivably have practical bearings, we conceive the object of our conception to have. Then, our conception of these effects is the whole of our conception of the object.

Although one writer has called this famous quotation from our reading "the least clear recommendation of how to make our ideas clear in the history of philosophy," it nevertheless gives the essence of Peirce's pragmatism. To conceive of an object clearly is to anticipate certain practical effects that can be empirically verified. Any idea that cannot be empirically verified and that is without "practical anticipations" is meaningless; "only practical distinctions have a meaning." Furthermore, if two apparently disparate ideas have the same practical effects, they are in fact only one idea.

Peirce then explained four methods of moving from doubt to belief: (1) tenacity, accepting one alternative to the doubt and rejecting all possible criticism of it; (2) authority, submitting to the state's or the church's tenaciously held beliefs;

(3) the *a priori* method, relying on the inclination to believe; and (4) science. Peirce argued for the scientific method, because it was concerned with examining the practical effects that make up one's conception of an object. Furthermore, unlike the other three methods, scientific inquiry is "animated by a cheerful hope that the processes of investigation, if only pushed far enough, will give one certain solution to each question to which they [the inquirers] apply it." Peirce assumed that in any diligently pursued scientific study, "a force outside of themselves" will lead all scientists involved in the investigation to the same conclusion.

Peirce has been called the father of pragmatism, and his work clearly influenced William James and John Dewey. Apart from the pragmatists, echoes of Peirce's writing can be heard in the verification criterion of meaning of the logical positivists and in the mandate of the later Wittgenstein that "the meaning is the use." Since the publication of his collected essays in the middle of the century, there has been renewed interest in Peirce's thought.

*   *   *

For general works on pragmatism (which include sections on Peirce and which place his thought in a wider context), see Edward C. Moore, *American Pragmatism: Peirce, James and Dewey* (New York: Columbia University Press, 1961); H.S. Thayer, "Pragmatism," in D.J. O'Connor, ed., *A Critical History of Western Philosophy* (New York: The Free Press, 1964); Amelie O. Rorty, ed., *Pragmatic Philosophy* (New York: Anchor Doubleday, 1966); Frederick Copleston, *A History of Philosophy, Vol. VIII* (Garden City, NY: Anchor Doubleday, 1967); A.J. Ayer, *The Origins of Pragmatism: Studies in the Philosophy of Charles Sanders Peirce and William James* (San Francisco: Freeman, Cooper, 1968); H.S. Thayer, *Meaning and Action: A Critical History of Pragmatism* (Indianapolis, IN: Bobbs-Merrill, 1968); Charles Moore, *The Pragmatic Movement in America* (New York: George Braziller, 1970); Israel Scheffler, *Four Pragmatists: A Critical Introduction to Peirce, James, Mead, and Dewey* (New York: Humanities Press, 1974); John E. Smith, *Purpose and Thought: The Meaning of Pragmatism* (New Haven, CT: Yale University Press, 1978); and Richard Rorty, *The Consequences of Pragmatism* (Minneapolis: University of Minnesota Press, 1982).

All of Peirce's works have been collected in the eight-volume set, *Collected Papers of Charles Sanders Peirce*, edited by Charles Hartshorne and Paul Weiss (Cambridge, MA: Harvard University Press, 1931–1935, 1958)—Volumes I, V, and VI contain the most important philosophical material. For a biography of Peirce, see Joseph Brent, *Charles Sanders Peirce: A Life* (Bloomington: Indiana University Press, 1993). The most comprehensive study of Peirce is James Feibleman, *An Introduction to Peirce's Philosophy* (New York: Harper & Brothers, 1946), whereas Murray G. Murphey, *The Development of Peirce's Philosophy* (Cambridge, MA: Harvard University Press, 1961) is a standard. Manley Thompson, *The Pragmatic Philosophy of C.S. Peirce* (Chicago: University of Chicago Press, 1953); W.B. Gallie, *Peirce and Pragmatism* (New York: Dover, 1966); Robert F. Almeder, *The Philosophy of Charles S. Peirce: A Critical Introduction* (Totowa, NJ: Rowman and Littlefield, 1980); and Christopher Hookway, *Peirce* (New York: Routledge, 1985) also provide helpful introductions. For collections of essays, see Philip P. Wiener and Frederic H. Young, eds., *Studies in the Philosophy of Charles Sanders Peirce* (Cambridge, MA: Harvard

University Press, 1952); Edward C. Moore and Richard S. Robin, eds., *Studies in the Philosophy of Charles Sanders Peirce*, Second Series (Amherst: University of Massachusetts Press, 1964); Richard J. Bernstein, ed., *Perspectives on Peirce* (New Haven, CT: Yale University Press, 1965); Kenneth Laine Ketner, ed., *Peirce and Contemporary Thought* (New York: Fordham University Press, 1995); and Jacqueline Brunning and Paul Forster, eds., *The Rule of Reason: The Philosophy of Charles Sanders Peirce* (Toronto: University of Toronto Press, 1997).

THE FIXATION OF BELIEF

Few persons care to study logic, because everybody conceives himself to be proficient enough in the art of reasoning already. But I observe that this satisfaction is limited to one's own ratiocination, and does not extend to that of other men.

We come to the full possession of our power of drawing inferences, the last of all our faculties; for it is not so much a natural gift as a long and difficult art. The history of its practice would make a grand subject for a book. The medieval schoolman, following the Romans, made logic the earliest of a boy's studies after grammar, as being very easy. So it was as they understood it. Its fundamental principle, according to them, was, that all knowledge rests either on authority or reason; but that whatever is deduced by reason depends ultimately on a premiss derived from authority. Accordingly, as soon as a boy was perfect in the syllogistic procedure, his intellectual kit of tools was held to be complete.

To Roger Bacon, that remarkable mind who in the middle of the thirteenth century was almost a scientific man, the schoolmen's conception of reasoning appeared only an obstacle to truth. He saw that experience alone teaches anything—a proposition which to us seems easy to understand, because a distinct conception of experience has been handed down to us from former generations; which to him likewise seemed perfectly clear, because its difficulties had not yet unfolded themselves. Of all kinds of experience, the best, he thought, was interior illumination, which teaches many things about Nature which the external senses could never discover, such as the transubstantiation of bread.

Four centuries later, the more celebrated Bacon, in the first book of his *Novum Organum,* gave his clear account of experience as something which must be open to verification and reexamination. But, superior as Lord Bacon's conception is to earlier notions, a modern reader who is not in awe of his grandiloquence is chiefly struck by the inadequacy of his view of scientific procedure. That we have only to make some crude experiments, to draw up briefs of the results in certain blank forms, to go through these by rule, checking off everything disproved and setting down the alternatives, and that thus in a few years physical science would be finished up—what an idea! "He wrote on science like a Lord Chancellor," indeed, as Harvey, a genuine man of science said.

The early scientists, Copernicus, Tycho Brahe, Kepler, Galileo, Harvey, and Gilbert, had methods more like those of their modern brethren. Kepler undertook to draw a curve through the places of Mars, and to state the times occupied by the planet

Guaranty Building, Buffalo, New York, 1895, designed by Louis Sullivan (1856–1924). Sullivan's building epitomizes the pragmatic approach to architecture summarized in his famous dictum, "form follows function." Both the exterior and interior designs complement the purpose for which this building was constructed. (*The Buffalo and Erie County Historical Society*)

in describing the different parts of the curve; but perhaps his greatest service to science was in impressing on men's minds that this was the thing to be done if they wished to improve astronomy; that they were not to content themselves with inquiring whether one system of epicycles was better than another but that they were to sit down to the figures and find out what the curve, in truth, was. He accomplished this by his incomparable energy and courage, blundering along in the most inconceivable way (to us), from one irrational hypothesis to another, until, after trying twenty-two of these, he fell, by the mere exhaustion of his invention, upon the orbit which a mind well furnished with the weapons of modern logic would have tried almost at the outset.

In the same way, every work of science great enough to be well remembered for a few generations affords some exemplification of the defective state of the art of reasoning of the time when it was written; and each chief step in science has been a lesson in logic. It was so when Lavoisier and his contemporaries took up the study of Chemistry. The old chemist's maxim had been, "Lege, lege, lege, labora, ora, et relege." Lavoisier's method was not to read and pray, but to dream that some long and complicated chemical process would have a certain effect, to put it into practice with dull patience, after its inevitable failure, to dream that with some modification it would have another result, and to end by publishing the last dream as a fact: his way was to carry his mind into his laboratory, and literally to make of his alembics and cucurbits instruments of thought, giving a new conception of reasoning as something which was to be done with one's eyes open, in manipulating real things instead of words and fancies.

The Darwinian controversy is, in large part, a question of logic. Mr. Darwin proposed to apply the statistical method to biology. The same thing has been done in a widely different branch of science, the theory of gases. Though unable to say what the movements of any particular molecule of gas would be on a certain hypothesis regarding the constitution of this class of bodies, Clausius and Maxwell were yet able, eight years before the publication of Darwin's immortal work, by the application of the doctrine of probabilities, to predict that in the long run such and such a proportion of the molecules would, under given circumstances, acquire such and such velocities; that there would take place, every second, such and such a number of collisions, etc.; and from these propositions were able to deduce certain properties of gases, especially in regard to their heat-relations. In like manner, Darwin, while unable to say what the operation of variation and natural selection in any individual case will be, demonstrates that in the long run they will, or would, adapt animals to their circumstances. Whether or not existing animal forms are due to such action, or what position the theory ought to take, forms the subject of a discussion in which questions of fact and questions of logic are curiously interlaced.

The object of reasoning is to find out, from the consideration of what we already know, something else which we do not know. Consequently, reasoning is good if it be such as to give a true conclusion from true premises, and not otherwise. Thus, the question of validity is purely one of fact and not of thinking. A being the facts stated in the premises and B being that concluded, the question is, whether these facts are really so related that if A were B would generally be. If so, the inference is valid; if not, not. It is not in the least the question whether, when the premises are accepted by the mind, we feel an impulse to accept the conclusion also. It is true that we do generally reason correctly by nature. But that is an accident; the true conclusion would remain true if we had no impulse to accept it; and the false one would remain false, though we could not resist the tendency to believe in it.

We are, doubtless, in the main logical animals, but we are not perfectly so. Most of us, for example, are naturally more sanguine and hopeful than logic would justify.

We seem to be so constituted that in the absence of any facts to go upon we are happy and self-satisfied; so that the effect of experience is continually to contract our hopes and aspirations. Yet a lifetime of the application of this corrective does not usually eradicate our sanguine disposition. Where hope is unchecked by any experience, it is likely that our optimism is extravagant. Logicality in regard to practical matters (if this be understood, not in the old sense, but as consisting in a wise union of security with fruitfulness of reasoning) is the most useful quality an animal can possess, and might, therefore, result from the action of natural selection; but outside of these it is probably of more advantage to the animal to have his mind filled with pleasing and encouraging visions, independently of their truth; and thus, upon unpractical subjects, natural selection might occasion a fallacious tendency of thought.

That which determines us, from given premises, to draw one inference rather than another, is some habit of mind, whether it be constitutional or acquired. The habit is good or otherwise, according as it produces true conclusions from true premises or not; and an inference is regarded as valid or not, without reference to the truth or falsity of its conclusion specially, but according as the habit which determines it is such as to produce true conclusions in general or not. The particular habit of mind which governs this or that inference may be formulated in a proposition whose truth depends on the validity of the inferences which the habit determines; and such a formula is called a *guiding principle* of inference. Suppose, for example, that we observe that a rotating disk of copper quickly comes to rest when placed between the poles of a magnet, and we infer that this will happen with every disk of copper. The guiding principle is, that what is true of one piece of copper is true of another. Such a guiding principle with regard to copper would be much safer than with regard to many other substances—brass, for example.

A book might be written to signalize all the most important of these guiding principles of reasoning. It would probably be we must confess, of no service to a person whose thought is directed wholly to practical subjects, and whose activity moves along thoroughly-beaten paths. The problems that present themselves to such a mind are matters of routine which he has learned once for all to handle in learning his business. But let a man venture into an unfamiliar field, or where his results are not continually checked by experience, and all history shows that the most masculine intellect will ofttimes lose his orientation and waste his efforts in directions which bring him no nearer to his goal, or even carry him entirely astray. He is like a ship in the open sea, with no one on board who understands the rules of navigation. And in such a case some general study of the guiding principles of reasoning would be sure to be found useful.

The subject could hardly be treated, however, without being first limited; since almost any fact may serve as a guiding principle. But it so happens that there exists a division among facts, such that in one class are all those which are absolutely essential as guiding principles, while in the others are all which have any other interest as objects of research. This division is between those which are necessarily taken for granted in asking why a certain conclusion is thought to follow from certain premises, and those which are not implied in such a question. A moment's thought will show that a variety of facts are already assumed when the logical question is first asked. It is implied, for instance, that there are such states of mind as doubt and belief—that a passage from one to the other is possible, the object of thought remaining the same, and that this transition is subject to some rules by which all minds are alike bound. As these are facts which we must already know before we can have any clear conception of reasoning at all, it cannot be supposed to be any longer of much interest to inquire into their truth or falsity. On the other hand, it is easy to believe that those rules of reasoning which are deduced from the very idea of the process are the ones which are the most essential; and, indeed, that so long as it conforms to these it will, at least, not lead to false conclusions from true premises. In point of fact, the importance of what may be deduced from the assumptions involved in the logical question turns out to be greater than might be supposed, and this for reasons which it is difficult to exhibit at the outset. The only one which I shall here mention is, that conceptions which are really products of logical reflection, without being readily seen to be so, mingle with our ordinary thoughts, and are frequently the causes of great confusion. This is the case, for example, with the conception of quality. A quality, as such, is never an object of observation. We can see that a thing is blue or green, but the quality of being blue and the quality of being green are not things which we see; they are products of logical reflections. The truth is, that common-sense, or thought as it first emerges above the level of the narrowly practical, is deeply imbued with that bad logical quality to which the epithet *metaphysical* is commonly applied; and nothing can clear it up but a severe course of logic.

We generally know when we wish to ask a question and when we wish to pronounce a judgment, for there is a dissimilarity between the sensation of doubting and that of believing.

But this is not all which distinguishes doubt from belief. There is a practical difference. Our beliefs guide our desires and shape our actions. The Assassins, or followers of the Old Man of the Mountain, used to rush into death at his least command, because they believed that obedience to him would insure everlasting felicity. Had they doubted this, they would not have acted as they did. So it is with every belief, according to its degree. The feeling of believing is a more or less sure indication of there being established in our nature some habit which will determine our actions. Doubt never has such an effect.

Nor must we overlook a third point of difference. Doubt is an uneasy and dissatisfied state from which we struggle to free ourselves and pass into the state of belief; while the latter is a calm and satisfactory state which we do not wish to avoid, or to change to a belief in anything else. On the contrary, we cling tenaciously, not merely to believing, but to believing just what we do believe.

Thus, both doubt and belief have positive effects upon us, though very different ones. Belief does not make us act at once, but puts us into such a condition that we shall behave in some certain way, when the occasion arises. Doubt has not the least such active effect, but stimulates us to inquiry until it is destroyed. This reminds us of the irritation of a nerve and the reflex action produced thereby; while for the analogue of belief, in the nervous system, we must look to what are called nervous associations—for example, to that habit of the nerves in consequence of which the smell of a peach will make the mouth water.

The irritation of doubt causes a struggle to attain a state of belief. I shall term this struggle *Inquiry*, though it must be admitted that this is sometimes not a very apt designation.

The irritation of doubt is the only immediate motive for the struggle to attain belief. It is certainly best for us that our beliefs should be such as may truly guide our actions so as to satisfy our desires; and this reflection will make us reject every belief which does not seem to have been so formed as to insure this result. But it will only do so by creating a doubt in the place of that belief. With the doubt, therefore, the struggle begins, and with the cessation of doubt it ends. Hence, the sole object of inquiry is the settlement of opinion. We may fancy that this is not enough for us, and that we seek, not merely an opinion, but a true opinion. But put this fancy to the test, and it proves groundless; for as soon as a firm belief is reached we are entirely satisfied, whether the belief be true or false. And it is clear that nothing out of the sphere of our knowledge can be our object, for nothing which does not affect the mind can be the motive for mental effort. The most that can be maintained is, that we seek for a belief that we shall *think* to be true. But we think each one of our beliefs to be true, and, indeed, it is mere tautology to say so.

That the settlement of opinion is the sole end of inquiry is a very important proposition. It sweeps away, at once, various vague and erroneous conceptions of proof. A few of these may be noticed here.

1. Some philosophers have imagined that to start an inquiry it was only necessary to utter a question whether orally or by setting it down upon paper, and have even recommended us to begin our studies with questioning everything! But the mere putting of a proposition into the interrogative form does not stimulate the mind to any struggle after belief. There must be a real and living doubt, and without this all discussion is idle.

2. It is a very common idea that a demonstration must rest on some ultimate and absolutely indubitable propositions. These, according to one school, are first principles of a general nature; according to another, are first sensations. But, in point of fact, an inquiry, to have that completely satisfactory result called demonstration, has only to start with propositions perfectly free from all actual doubt. If the premises are not in fact doubted at all, they cannot be more satisfactory than they are.

3. Some people seem to love to argue a point after all the world is fully convinced of it. But no further advance can be made. When doubt ceases, mental action on the subject comes to an end; and, if it did go on, it would be without a purpose.

If the settlement of opinion is the sole object of inquiry, and if belief is of the nature of a habit, why should we not attain the desired end, by taking as answer to a question any we may fancy, and constantly reiterating it to ourselves, dwelling on all which may conduce to that belief, and learning to turn with contempt and hatred from anything that might disturb it? This simple and direct method is really pursued by many men. I remember once being entreated not to read a certain newspaper lest it might change my opinion upon free-trade. "Lest I might be entrapped by its fallacies and misstatements," was the form of expression. "You are not," my friend said, "a special student of political economy. You might, therefore, easily be deceived by fallacious arguments upon the subject. You might, then, if you read this paper, be led to believe in protection. But you admit that free-trade is the true doctrine; and you do not wish to believe what is not true." I have often known this system to be deliberately adopted. Still oftener, the instinctive dislike of an undecided state of mind, exaggerated into a vague dread of doubt, makes men cling spasmodically to the views they already take. The man feels that, if he only holds to his belief without wavering, it will be entirely satisfactory. Nor can it be denied that a steady and immovable faith yields great peace of mind. It may, indeed, give rise to inconveniences, as if a man should resolutely continue to believe that fire would not burn him, or that he would be eternally damned if he received his *ingesta* otherwise than through a stomach pump. But then the man who adopts this method will not allow that its inconveniences are greater than its advantages. He will say, "I hold steadfastly to the truth, and the truth is always wholesome." And in many cases it may very well be that the pleasure he derives from his calm faith overbalances any inconveniences resulting from its deceptive character. Thus, if it be true that death is annihilation, then the man who believes that he will certainly go straight to heaven when he dies, provided he has fulfilled certain simple observances in this life, has a cheap pleasure which will not be followed by the least disappointment. A similar consideration seems to have weight with many persons in religious topics, for we frequently hear it said, "Oh, I could not believe so-and-so, because I should be wretched if I did." When an ostrich buries its head in the sand as danger approaches, it very likely takes the happiest course. It hides the danger, and then calmly says there is no danger; and, if it feels perfectly sure there is none, why should it raise its head to see? A man may go through life, systematically keeping out of view all that might cause a change in his opinions, and if he only succeeds—basing his method, as he does, on two fundamental psychological laws—I do not see what can be said against his doing so. It would be an egotistical impertinence to object that his procedure is irrational, for that only amounts to saying that his method of settling belief is not ours. He does not propose to himself to be rational, and, indeed, will often talk with scorn of man's weak and illusive reason. So let him think as he pleases.

But this method of fixing belief, which may be called the method of tenacity, will be unable to hold its ground in practice. The social impulse is against it. The man who adopts it will find that other men think differently from him, and it will be apt to occur to him, in some saner moment, that their opinions are quite as good as his own, and this will shake his confidence in his belief. This conception, that another man's thought or sentiment may be equivalent to one's own, is a distinctly new step, and a highly important one. It arises from an impulse too strong in man to be suppressed without danger of destroying the human species. Unless we make ourselves hermits we shall necessarily influence each other's opinions; so that the problem becomes how to fix belief, not in the individual merely, but in the community.

Let the will of the state act, then? instead of that of the individual. Let an institution be created which shall have for its object to keep correct doctrines before the attention of the people, to reiterate them perpetually, and to teach them to the young; having at the same time power to prevent contrary doctrines from being taught, advocated, or expressed. Let all possible causes of a change of mind be removed from men's apprehensions. Let them be kept ignorant, lest they should learn of some reason to think otherwise than they do. Let their passions be enlisted, so that they may regard private and unusual opinions with hatred and horror. Then, let all men who reject the established belief be terrified into silence. Let the people turn out and tar-and-feather such men, or let inquisitions be made into the manner of thinking of suspected persons, and when they are found guilty of forbidden beliefs, let them be subjected to some signal punishment. When complete agreement could not otherwise be reached, a general massacre of all who have not thought in a certain way has proved a very effective means of settling opinion in a country. If the power to do this be wanting, let a list of opinions be drawn up, to which no man of the least independence of thought can assent, and let the faithful be required to accept all these propositions, in order to segregate them as radically as possible from the influence of the rest of the world.

This method has, from the earliest times, been one of the chief means of upholding correct theological and political doctrines, and of preserving their universal or catholic character. In Rome, especially, it has been practised from the days of Numa Pompilius to those of Pius Nonus. This is the most perfect example in history; but wherever there is a priesthood—and no religion has been without one—this method has been more or less made use of. Wherever there is an aristocracy, or a guild, or any association of a class of men whose interests depend, or are supposed to depend, on certain propositions, there will be inevitably found some traces of this natural product of social feeling. Cruelties always accompany this system; and when it is consistently carried out, they become atrocities of the most horrible kind in the eyes of any rational

man. Nor should this occasion surprise, for the officer of a society does not feel justified in surrendering the interests of that society for the sake of mercy, as he might his
own private interests. It is natural, therefore, that sympathy and fellowship should thus
produce a most ruthless power.

In judging this method of fixing belief, which may be called the method of authority, we must, in the first place, allow its immeasurable mental and moral superiority to the method of tenacity. Its success is proportionately greater; and, in fact, it has
over and over again worked the most majestic results. The mere structures of stone
which it has caused to be put together—in Siam, for example, in Egypt, and in Europe—have many of them a sublimity hardly more than rivaled by the greatest works
of Nature. And, except the geological epochs, there are no periods of time so vast as
those which are measured by some of these organized faiths. If we scrutinize the matter closely, we shall find that there has not been one of their creeds which has remained
always the same; yet the change is so slow as to be imperceptible during one person's
life, so that individual belief remains sensibly fixed. For the mass of mankind, then,
there is perhaps no better method than this. If it is their highest impulse to be intellectual slaves, then slaves they ought to remain.

But no institution can undertake to regulate opinions upon every subject. Only
the most important ones can be attended to, and on the rest men's minds must be left to
the action of natural causes. This imperfection will be no source of weakness so long
as men are in such a state of culture that one opinion does not influence another—that
is, so long as they cannot put two and two together. But in the most priest ridden states
some individuals will be found who are raised above that condition. These men possess a wider sort of social feeling; they see that men in other countries and in other
ages have held to very different doctrines from those which they themselves have been
brought up to believe; and they cannot help seeing that it is the mere accident of their
having been taught as they have, and of their having been surrounded with the manners
and associations they have, that has caused them to believe as they do and not far differently. Nor can their candour resist the reflection that there is no reason to rate their
own views at a higher value than those of other nations and other centuries; thus giving
rise to doubts in their minds.

They will further perceive that such doubts as these must exist in their minds
with reference to every belief which seems to be determined by the caprice either of
themselves or of those who originated the popular opinions. The willful adherence to a
belief, and the arbitrary forcing of it upon others, must, therefore, both be given up. A
different new method of settling opinions must be adopted, that shall not only produce
an impulse to believe, but shall also decide what proposition it is which is to be believed. Let the action of natural preferences be unimpeded, then, and under their influence let men, conversing together and regarding matters in different lights, gradually
develop beliefs in harmony with natural causes. This method resembles that by which
conceptions of art have been brought to maturity. The most perfect example of it is to
be found in the history of metaphysical philosophy. Systems of this sort have not usually rested upon any observed facts, at least not in any great degree. They have been
chiefly adopted because their fundamental propositions seemed "agreeable to reason."
This is an apt expression; it does not mean that which agrees with experience, but that
which we find ourselves inclined to believe. Plato, for example, finds it agreeable to
reason that the distances of the celestial spheres from one another should be proportional to the different lengths of strings which produce harmonious chords. Many
philosophers have been led to their main conclusions by considerations like this; but
this is the lowest and least developed form which the method takes, for it is clear that

another man might find Kepler's theory, that the celestial spheres are proportional to the inscribed and circumscribed spheres of the different regular solids, more agreeable to his reason. But the shock of opinions will soon lead men to rest on preferences of a far more universal nature. Take, for example, the doctrine that man only acts selfishly—that is, from the consideration that acting in one way will afford him more pleasure than acting in another. This rests on no fact in the world, but it has had a wide acceptance as being the only reasonable theory.

This method is far more intellectual and respectable from the point of view of reason than either of the others which we have noticed. Indeed, as long as no better method can be applied, it ought to be followed, since it is then the expression of instinct which must be the ultimate cause of belief in all cases. But its failure has been the most manifest. It makes of inquiry something similar to the development of taste; but taste, unfortunately, is always more or less a matter of fashion, and accordingly metaphysicians have never come to any fixed agreement, but the pendulum has swung backward and forward between a more material and a more spiritual philosophy, from the earliest times to the latest. And so from this, which has been called the *a priori* method, we are driven, in Lord Bacon's phrase, to a true induction. We have examined this *a priori* method as something which promised to deliver our opinions from their accidental and capricious element. But development, while it is a process which eliminates the effect of some casual circumstances, only magnifies that of others. This method, therefore, does not differ in a very essential way from that of authority. The government may not have lifted its finger to influence my convictions; I may have been left outwardly quite free to choose, we will say, between monogamy and polygamy, and, appealing to my conscience only, I may have concluded that the latter practice is in itself licentious. But when I come to see that the chief obstacle to the spread of Christianity among a people of as high culture as the Hindoos has been a conviction of the immorality of our way of treating women, I cannot help seeing that, though governments do not interfere, sentiments in their development will be very greatly determined by accidental causes. Now, there are some people, among whom I must suppose that my reader is to be found, who, when they see that any belief of theirs is determined by any circumstance extraneous to the facts, will from that moment not merely admit in words that that belief is doubtful, but will experience a real doubt of it, so that it ceases in some degree at least to be a belief.

To satisfy our doubts, therefore, it is necessary that a method should be found by which our beliefs may be determined by nothing human, but by some external permanency—by something upon which our thinking has no effect. Some mystics imagine that they have such a method in a private inspiration from on high. But that is only a form of the method of tenacity, in which the conception of truth as something public is not yet developed. Our external permanency would not be external, in our sense, if it was restricted in its influence to one individual. It must be something which affects, or might affect, every man. And, though these affections are necessarily as various as are individual conditions, yet the method must be such that the ultimate conclusion of every man shall be the same. Such is the method of science. Its fundamental hypothesis, restated in more familiar language, is this: There are Real things, whose characters are entirely independent of our opinions about them; those Reals affect our senses according to regular laws, and, though our sensations are as different as our relations to the objects, yet, by taking advantage of the laws of perception, we can ascertain by reasoning how things really and truly are; and any man, if he have sufficient experience and he reason enough about it, will be led to the one True conclusion. The new conception here involved is that of Reality. It may be asked how I know that there are any

Reals. If this hypothesis is the sole support of my method of inquiry, my method of inquiry must not be used to support my hypothesis. The reply is this: 1. If investigation cannot be regarded as proving that there are Real things, it at least does not lead to a contrary conclusion; but the method and the conception on which it is based remain ever in harmony. No doubts of the method, therefore, necessarily arise from its practice, as is the case with all the others. 2. The feeling which gives rise to any method of fixing belief is a dissatisfaction at two repugnant propositions. But here already is a vague concession that there is some *one* thing which a proposition should represent. Nobody, therefore, can really doubt that there are Reals, for, if he did, doubt would not be a source of dissatisfaction. The hypothesis, therefore, is one which every mind admits. So that the social impulse does not cause men to doubt it. 3. Everybody uses the scientific method about a great many things, and only ceases to use it when he does not know how to apply it. 4. Experience of the method has not led us to doubt it, but, on the contrary, scientific investigation has had the most wonderful triumphs in the way of settling opinion. These afford the explanation of my not doubting the method or the hypothesis which it supposes; and not having any doubt, nor believing that anybody else whom I could influence has, it would be the merest babble for me to say more about it. If there be anybody with a living doubt upon the subject, let him consider it.

To describe the method of scientific investigation is the object of this series of papers. At present I have only room to notice some points of contrast between it and other methods of fixing belief.

This is the only one of the four methods which presents any distinction of a right and a wrong way. If I adopt the method of tenacity, and shut myself out from all influences, whatever I think necessary to doing this, is necessary according to that method. So with the method of authority: the state may try to put down heresy by means which, from a scientific point of view, seem very ill-calculated to accomplish its purposes; but the only test *on that method* is what the state thinks; so that it cannot pursue the method wrongly. So with the *a priori* method. The very essence of it is to think as one is inclined to think. All metaphysicians will be sure to do that, however they may be inclined to judge each other to be perversely wrong. The Hegelian system recognizes every natural tendency of thought as logical, although it be certain to be abolished by counter-tendencies. Hegel thinks there is a regular system in the succession of these tendencies, in consequence of which, after drifting one way and the other for a long time, opinion will at last go right. And it is true that metaphysicians do get the right ideas at last; Hegel's system of Nature represents tolerably the science of his day; and one may be sure that whatever scientific investigation shall have put out of doubt will presently receive *a priori* demonstration on the part of the metaphysicians. But with the scientific method the case is different. I may start with known and observed facts to proceed to the unknown; and yet the rules which I follow in doing so may not be such as investigation would approve. The test of whether I am truly following the method is not an immediate appeal to my feelings and purposes, but, on the contrary, itself involves the application of the method. Hence it is that bad reasoning as well as good reasoning is possible; and this fact is the foundation of the practical side of logic.

It is not to be supposed that the first three methods of settling opinion present no advantage whatever over the scientific method. On the contrary, each has some peculiar convenience of its own. The *a priori* method is distinguished for its comfortable conclusions. It is the nature of the process to adopt whatever belief we are inclined to, and there are certain flatteries to the vanity of man which we all believe by nature, until we are awakened from our pleasing dream by rough facts. The method of authority will always govern the mass of mankind; and those who wield the various forms of organized force in the state will never be convinced that dangerous reasoning ought not to be suppressed in some way. If liberty of speech is to be untrammeled from the grosser forms of constraint, then uniformity of opinion will be secured by a moral terrorism to which the respectability of society will give its thorough approval. Following the method of authority is the path of peace. Certain non-conformities are permitted; certain others (considered unsafe) are forbidden. These are different in different countries and in different ages; but, wherever you are, let it be known that you seriously hold a tabooed belief, and you may be perfectly sure of being treated with a cruelty less brutal but more refined than hunting you like a wolf. Thus, the greatest intellectual benefactors of mankind have never dared, and dare not now, to utter the whole of their thought; and thus a shade of *prima facie* doubt is cast upon every proposition which is considered essential to the security of society. Singularly enough, the persecution does not all come from without; but a man torments himself and is oftentimes most distressed at finding himself believing propositions which he has been brought up to regard with aversion. The peaceful and sympathetic man will, therefore, find it hard to resist the temptation to submit his opinions to authority. But most of all I admire the method of tenacity for its strength, simplicity, and directness. Men who pursue it are distinguished for their decision of character, which becomes very easy with such a mental rule. They do not waste time in trying to make up their minds what they want, but, fastening like lightning upon whatever alternative comes first, they hold to it to the end, whatever happens, without an instant's irresolution. This is one of the splendid qualities which generally accompany brilliant, unlasting success. It is impossible not to envy the man who can dismiss reason, although we know how it must turn out at last.

Such are the advantages which the other methods of settling opinion have over scientific investigation. A man should consider well of them; and then he should consider that, after all, he wishes his opinions to coincide with the fact, and that there is no reason why the results of those three first methods should do so. To bring about this effect is the prerogative of the method of science. Upon such considerations he has to make his choice—a choice which is far more than the adoption of any intellectual opinion, which is one of the ruling decisions of his life, to which, when once made, he is bound to adhere. The force of habit will sometimes cause a man to hold on to old beliefs, after he is in a condition to see that they have no sound basis. But reflection upon the state of the case will overcome these habits, and he ought to allow reflection its full weight. People sometimes shrink from doing this, having an idea that beliefs are wholesome which they cannot help feeling rest on nothing. But let such persons suppose an analogous though different case from their own. Let them ask themselves what they would say to a reformed Mussulman who should hesitate to give up his old notions in regard to the relations of the sexes; or to a reformed Catholic who should still shrink from reading the Bible. Would they not say that these persons ought to consider the matter fully, and clearly understand the new doctrine, and then ought to embrace it, in its entirety? But, above all, let it be considered that what is more wholesome than any particular belief is integrity of belief, and that to avoid looking into the support of any belief from a fear that it may turn out rotten is quite as immoral as it is disadvantageous. The person who confesses that there is such a thing as truth, which is distinguished from falsehood simply by this, that if acted on it should, on full consideration, carry us to the point we aim at and not astray, and then, though convinced of this, dares not know the truth and seeks to avoid it, is in a sorry state of mind indeed.

Yes, the other methods do have their merits: a clear logical conscience does cost something—just as any virtue, just as all that we cherish, costs us dear. But we should not desire it to be otherwise. The genius of a man's logical method should be loved and reverenced as his bride, whom he has chosen from all the world. He need not contemn the others; on the contrary, he may honor them deeply, and in doing so he only honors her the more. But she is the one that he has chosen, and he knows that he was right in making that choice. And having made it, he will work and fight for her, and will not complain that there are blows to take, hoping that there may be as many and as hard to give, and will strive to be the worthy knight and champion of her from the blaze of whose splendors he draws his inspiration and his courage.

HOW TO MAKE OUR IDEAS CLEAR

Whoever has looked into a modern treatise on logic of the common sort, will doubtless remember the two distinctions between *clear* and *obscure* conceptions, and between *distinct* and *confused* conceptions. They have lain in the books now for nigh two centuries, unimproved and unmodified, and are generally reckoned by logicians as among the gems of their doctrine.

A clear idea is defined as one which is so apprehended that it will be recognized wherever it is met with, and so that no other will be mistaken for it. If it fails of this clearness, it is said to be obscure.

This is rather a neat bit of philosophical terminology; yet, since it is clearness that they were defining, I wish the logicians had made their definition a little more plain. Never to fail to recognize an idea, and under no circumstances to mistake another for it, let it come in how recondite a form it may, would indeed imply such prodigious force and clearness of intellect as is seldom met with in this world. On the other hand, merely to have such an acquaintance with the idea as to have become familiar with it, and to have lost all hesitancy in recognizing it in ordinary cases, hardly seems to deserve the name of clearness of apprehension, since after all it only amounts to a subjective feeling of mastery which may be entirely mistaken. I take it, however, that when the logicians speak of "clearness," they mean nothing more than such a familiarity with an idea, since they regard the quality as but a small merit, which needs to be supplemented by another, which they call *distinctness*.

A distinct idea is defined as one which contains nothing which is not clear. This is technical language; by the contents of an idea logicians understand whatever is contained in its definition. So that an idea is *distinctly* apprehended, according to them, when we can give a precise definition of it, in abstract terms. Here the professional logicians leave the subject; and I would not have troubled the reader with what they have to say, if it were not such a striking example of how they have been slumbering through ages of intellectual activity, listlessly disregarding the enginery of modern thought, and never dreaming of applying its lessons to the improvement of logic. It is easy to show that the doctrine that familiar use and abstract distinctness make the perfection of apprehension has its only true place in philosophies which have long been extinct; and it is now time to formulate the method of attaining to a more perfect clearness of thought, such as we see and admire in the thinkers of our own time.

When Descartes set about the reconstruction of philosophy, his first step was to (theoretically) permit scepticism and to discard the practice of the schoolmen of looking to authority as the ultimate source of truth. That done, he sought a more natural fountain of true principles, and thought he found it in the human mind; thus passing, in the directest way, from the method of authority to that of apriority, as described in my first paper. Self-consciousness was to furnish us with our fundamental truths, and to decide what was agreeable to reason. But since, evidently, not all ideas are true, he was led to note, as the first condition of infallibility, that they must be clear. The distinction between an idea seeming clear and really being so, never occurred to him. Trusting to introspection, as he did, even for a knowledge of external things, why should he question its testimony in respect to the contents of our own minds? But then, I suppose, seeing men, who seemed to be quite clear and positive, holding opposite opinions upon fundamental principles, he was further led to say that clearness of ideas is not sufficient, but that they need also to be distinct, i.e., to have nothing unclear about them. What he probably meant by this (for he did not explain himself with precision) was, that they must sustain the test of dialectical examination; that they must not only seem clear at the outset, but that discussion must never be able to bring to light points of obscurity connected with them.

Such was the distinction of Descartes, and one sees that it was precisely on the level of his philosophy. It was somewhat developed by Leibniz. This great and singular genius was as remarkable for what he failed to see as for what he saw. That a piece of mechanism could not do work perpetually without being fed with power in some form, was a thing perfectly apparent to him; yet he did not understand that the machinery of the mind can only transform knowledge, but never originate it, unless it be fed with facts of observation. He thus missed the most essential point of the Cartesian philosophy, which is, that to accept propositions which seem perfectly evident to us is a thing which, whether it be logical or illogical, we cannot help doing. Instead of regarding the matter in this way, he sought to reduce the first principles of science to two classes, those which cannot be denied without self-contradiction, and those which result from the principle of sufficient reason (of which more anon), and was apparently unaware of the great difference between his position and that of Descartes. So he reverted to the old trivialities of logic; and, above all, abstract definitions played a great part in his philosophy. It was quite natural, therefore, that on observing that the method of Descartes laboured under the difficulty that we may seem to ourselves to have clear apprehensions of ideas which in truth are very hazy, no better remedy occurred to him than to require an abstract definition of every important term. Accordingly, in adopting the distinction of *clear* and *distinct* notions, he described the latter quality as the clear apprehension of everything contained in the definition; and the books have ever since copied his words. There is no danger that his chimerical scheme will ever again be over-valued. Nothing new can ever be learned by analyzing definitions. Nevertheless, our existing beliefs can be set in order by this process, and order is an essential element of intellectual economy, as of every other. It may be acknowledged, therefore, that the books are right in making familiarity with a notion the first step toward clearness of apprehension, and the defining of it the second. But in omitting all mention of any higher perspicuity of thought, they simply mirror a philosophy which was exploded a hundred years ago. That much-admired "ornament of logic"—the doctrine of clearness and distinctness—may be pretty enough, but it is high time to relegate to our cabinet of curiosities the antique *bijou,* and to wear about us something better adapted to modern uses.

The very first lesson that we have a right to demand that logic shall teach us is, how to make our ideas clear; and a most important one it is, depreciated only by minds who stand in need of it. To know what we think, to be masters of our own meaning, will make a solid foundation for great and weighty thought. It is most easily learned by those whose ideas are meagre and restricted; and far happier they than such as wallow helplessly in a rich mud of conceptions. A nation, it is true, may, in the course of generations overcome the disadvantage of an excessive wealth of language and its natural concomitant, a vast, unfathomable deep of ideas. We may see it in history, slowly perfecting its literary forms, sloughing at length its metaphysics, and, by virtue of the untirable patience which is often a compensation, attaining great excellence in every branch of mental acquirement. The page of history is not yet unrolled that is to tell us whether such a people will or will not in the long run prevail over one whose ideas (like the words of their language) are few, but which possesses a wonderful mastery over those which it has. For an individual, however, there can be no question that a few clear ideas are worth more than many confused ones. A young man would hardly be persuaded to sacrifice the greater part of his thoughts to save the rest; and the muddled head is the least apt to see the necessity of such a sacrifice. Him we can usually only commiserate, as a person with a congenital defect. Time will help him, but intellectual maturity with regard to clearness is apt to come rather late. This seems an unfortunate arrangement of Nature, inasmuch as clearness is of less use to a man settled in life, whose errors have in great measure had their effect, than it would be to one whose path lay before him. It is terrible to see how a single unclear idea, a single formula without meaning, lurking in a young man's head, will sometimes act like an obstruction of inert matter in an artery, hindering the nutrition of the brain and condemning its victim to pine away in the fullness of his intellectual vigour and in the midst of intellectual plenty. Many a man has cherished for years as his hobby some vague shadow of an idea, too meaningless to be positively false; he has, nevertheless, passionately loved it, has made it his companion by day and by night, and has given to it his strength and his life, leaving all other occupations for its sake, and in short has lived with it and for it, until it has become, as it were, flesh of his flesh and bone of his bone; and then he has waked up some bright morning to find it gone, clean vanished away like the beautiful Melusina of the fable, and the essence of his life gone with it. I have myself known such a man; and who can tell how many histories of circle-squarers, metaphysicians, astrologers, and what not, may not be told in the old German [French!] story?

The principles set forth in the first part of this essay lead, at once, to a method of reaching a clearness of thought of higher grade than the "distinctness" of the logicians. It was there noticed that the action of thought is excited by the irritation of doubt, and ceases when belief is attained; so that the production of belief is the sole function of thought. All these words, however, are too strong for my purpose. It is as if I had described the phenomena as they appear under a mental microscope. Doubt and Belief, as the words are commonly employed, relate to religious or other grave discussions. But here I use them to designate the starting of any question, no matter how small or how great, and the resolution of it. If, for instance, in a horse-car, I pull out my purse and find a five-cent nickel and five coppers, I decide, while my hand is going to the purse, in which way I will pay my fare. To call such a question Doubt, and my decision Belief, is certainly to use words very disproportionate to the occasion. To speak of such a doubt as causing an irritation which needs to be appeased, suggests a temper which is uncomfortable to the verge of insanity. Yet, looking at the matter minutely, it must be admitted that, if there is the least hesitation as to whether I shall pay the five coppers or the nickel (as there will be sure to be, unless I act from some previously contracted habit in the matter), though irritation is too strong a word, yet I am excited to such small mental activity as may be necessary to deciding how I shall act. Most frequently doubts arise from some indecision, however momentary, in our action. Sometimes it is not so. I have, for example, to wait in a railway-station, and to pass the time I read the advertisements on the walls. I compare the advantages of different trains and different routes which I never expect to take, merely fancying myself to be in a state of hesitancy, because I am bored with having nothing to trouble me. Feigned hesitancy, whether feigned for mere amusement or with a lofty purpose, plays a great part in the production of scientific inquiry. However the doubt may originate, it stimulates the mind to an activity which may be slight or energetic, calm or turbulent. Images pass rapidly through consciousness, one incessantly melting into another, until at last, when all is over—it may be in a fraction of a second, in an hour, or after long years—we find ourselves decided as to how we should act under such circumstances as those which occasioned our hesitation. In other words, we have attained belief.

In this process we observe two sorts of elements of consciousness, the distinction between which may best be made clear by means of an illustration. In a piece of music there are the separate notes, and there is the air. A single tone may be prolonged for an hour or a day, and it exists as perfectly in each second of that time as in the whole taken together; so that, as long as it is sounding, it might be present to a sense from which everything in the past was as completely absent as the future itself. But it is different with the air, the performance of which occupies a certain time, during the portions of which only portions of it are played. It consists in an orderliness in the succession of sounds which strike the ear at different times; and to perceive it there must be some continuity of consciousness which makes the events of a lapse of time present to us. We certainly only perceive the air by hearing the separate notes; yet we cannot be said to directly hear it, for we hear only what is present at the instant, and an orderliness of succession cannot exist in an instant. These two sorts of objects, what we are *immediately* conscious of and what we are *mediately* conscious of, are found in all consciousness. Some elements (the sensations) are completely present at every instant so long as they last, while others (like thought) are actions having beginning, middle, and end, and consist in a congruence in the succession of sensations which flow through the mind. They cannot be immediately present to us, but must cover some portion of the past or future. Thought is a thread of melody running through the succession of our sensations.

We may add that just as a piece of music may be written in parts, each part having its own air, so various systems of relationship of succession subsist together between the same sensations. These different systems are distinguished by having different motives, ideas, or functions. Thought is only one such system, for its sole motive, idea, and function is to produce belief, and whatever does not concern that purpose belongs to some other system of relations. The action of thinking may incidentally have other results; it may serve to amuse us, for example, and among *dilettanti* it is not rare to find those who have so perverted thought to the purposes of pleasure that it seems to vex them to think that the questions upon which they delight to exercise it may ever get finally settled; and a positive discovery which takes a favourite subject out of the arena of literary debate is met with ill-concealed dislike. This disposition is the very debauchery of thought. But the soul and meaning of thought, abstracted from the other elements which accompany it, though it may be voluntarily thwarted, can never be made to direct itself toward anything but the production of belief. Thought in action has for its only possible motive the attainment of thought at rest; and whatever does not refer to belief is no part of the thought itself.

And what, then, is belief? It is the demi-cadence which closes a musical phrase in the symphony of our intellectual life. We have seen that it has just three properties: First, it is something that we are aware of; second, it appeases the irritation of doubt;

and, third, it involves the establishment in our nature of a rule of action, or, say for short, a *habit*. As it appeases the irritation of doubt, which is the motive for thinking, thought relaxes, and comes to rest for a moment when belief is reached. But, since belief is a rule for action, the application of which involves further doubt and further thought, at the same time that it is a stopping-place, it is also a new starting-place for thought. That is why I have permitted myself to call it thought at rest, although thought is essentially an action. The *final* upshot of thinking is the exercise of volition, and of this thought no longer forms a part; but belief is only a stadium of mental action, an effect upon our nature due to thought, which will influence future thinking.

The essence of belief is the establishment of a habit; and different beliefs are distinguished by the different modes of action to which they give rise. If beliefs do not differ in this respect, if they appease the same doubt by producing the same rule of action, then no mere differences in the manner of consciousness of them can make them different beliefs, any more than playing a tune in different keys is playing different tunes. Imaginary distinctions are often drawn between beliefs which differ only in their mode of expression;—the wrangling which ensues is real enough, however. To believe that any objects are arranged among themselves as in Fig. 1, and to believe that they are arranged [as] in Fig. 2, are one and the same belief; yet it is conceivable that a man should assert one proposition and deny the other.

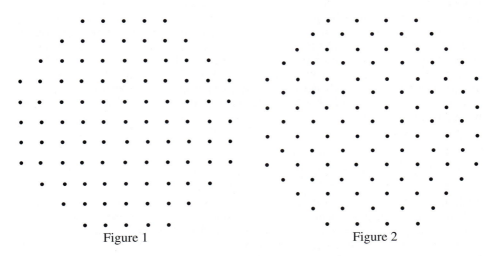

Figure 1   Figure 2

Such false distinctions do as much harm as the confusion of beliefs really different, and are among the pitfalls of which we ought constantly to beware, especially when we are upon metaphysical ground. One singular deception of this sort, which often occurs, is to mistake the sensation produced by our own unclearness of thought for a character of the object we are thinking. Instead of perceiving that the obscurity is purely subjective, we fancy that we contemplate a quality of the object which is essentially mysterious; and if our conception be afterward presented to us in a clear form we do not recognize it as the same, owing to the absence of the feeling of unintelligibility. So long as this deception lasts, it obviously puts an impassable barrier in the way of perspicuous thinking; so that it equally interests the opponents of rational thought to perpetuate it, and its adherents to guard against it.

Another such deception is to mistake a mere difference in the grammatical construction of two words for a distinction between the ideas they express. In this pedantic age, when the general mob of writers attend so much more to words than to things, this error is common enough. When I just said that thought is an *action,* and that it consists in a *relation,* although a person performs an action but not a relation, which can only be the result of an action, yet there was no inconsistency in what I said, but only a grammatical vagueness.

From all these sophisms we shall be perfectly safe so long as we reflect that the whole function of thought is to produce habits of action; and that whatever there is connected with a thought, but irrelevant to its purpose, is an accretion to it, but no part of it. If there be a unity among our sensations which has no reference to how we shall act on a given occasion, as when we listen to a piece of music, why we do not call that thinking. To develop its meaning, we have, therefore, simply to determine what habits it produces, for what a thing means is simply what habits it involves. Now, the identity of a habit depends on how it might lead us to act, not merely under such circumstances as are likely to arise, but under such as might possibly occur, no matter how improbable they may be. What the habit is depends on *when* and *how* it causes us to act. As for the *when,* every stimulus to action is derived from perception; as for the *how,* every purpose of action is to produce some sensible result. Thus, we come down to what is tangible and conceivably practical, as the root of every real distinction of thought, no matter how subtle it may be; and there is no distinction of meaning so fine as to consist in anything but a possible difference of practice.

To see what this principle leads to, consider in the light of it such a doctrine as that of transubstantiation. The Protestant churches generally hold that the elements of the sacrament are flesh and blood only in a tropical sense; they nourish our souls as meat and the juice of it would our bodies. But the Catholics maintain that they are literally just meat and blood; although they possess all the sensible qualities of wafer-cakes and diluted wine. But we can have no conception of wine except what may enter into a belief, either—

1. That this, that, or the other, is wine; or,
2. That wine possesses certain properties.

Such beliefs are nothing but self-notifications that we should, upon occasion, act in regard to such things as we believe to be wine according to the qualities which we believe wine to possess. The occasion of such action would be some sensible perception, the motive of it to produce some sensible result. Thus our action has exclusive reference to what affects the senses, our habit has the same bearing as our action, our belief the same as our habit, our conception the same as our belief; and we can consequently mean nothing by wine but what has certain effects, direct or indirect, upon our senses; and to talk of something as having all the sensible characters of wine, yet being in reality blood, is senseless jargon. Now, it is not my object to pursue the theological question; and having used it as a logical example I drop it, without caring to anticipate the theologian's reply. I only desire to point out how impossible it is that we should have an idea in our minds which relates to anything but conceived sensible effects of things. Our idea of anything *is* our idea of its sensible effects; and if we fancy that we have any other we deceive ourselves, and mistake a mere sensation accompanying the thought for a part of the thought itself. It is absurd to say that thought has any meaning unrelated to its only function. It is foolish for Catholics and Protestants to fancy themselves in disagreement about the elements of the sacrament, if they agree in regard to all their sensible effects, here and hereafter.

It appears, then, that the rule for attaining the third grade of clearness of apprehension is as follows: Consider what effects, that might conceivably have practical bearings, we conceive the object of our conception to have. Then, our conception of these effects is the whole of our conception of the object.

Let us illustrate this rule by some examples; and, to begin with the simplest one possible, let us ask what we mean by calling a thing *hard*. Evidently that it will not be scratched by many other substances. The whole conception of this quality, as of every other, lies in its conceived effects. There is absolutely no difference between a hard thing and a soft thing so long as they are not brought to the test. Suppose, then, that a diamond could be crystallized in the midst of a cushion of soft cotton, and should remain there until it was finally burned up. Would it be false to say that that diamond was soft? This seems a foolish question, and would be so, in fact, except in the realm of logic. There such questions are often of the greatest utility as serving to bring logical principles into sharper relief than real discussions ever could. In studying logic we must not put them aside with hasty answers, but must consider them with attentive care, in order to make out the principles involved. We may, in the present case, modify our question, and ask what prevents us from saying that all hard bodies remain perfectly soft until they are touched, when their hardness increases with the pressure until they are scratched. Reflection will show that the reply is this: there would be no *falsity* in such modes of speech. They would involve a modification of our present usage of speech with regard to the words hard and soft, but not of their meanings. For they represent no fact to be different from what it is; only they involve arrangements of facts which would be exceedingly maladroit. This leads us to remark that the question of what would occur under circumstances which do not actually arise is not a question of fact, but only of the most perspicuous arrangement of them. For example, the question of free-will and fate in its simplest form, stripped of verbiage, is something like this: I have done something of which I am ashamed; could I, by an effort of the will, have resisted the temptation, and done otherwise? The philosophical reply is, that this is not a question of fact, but only of the arrangement of facts. Arranging them so as to exhibit what is particularly pertinent to my question—namely, that I ought to blame myself for having done wrong—it is perfectly true to say that, if I had willed to do otherwise than I did, I should have done otherwise. On the other hand, arranging the facts so as to exhibit another important consideration, it is equally true that, when a temptation has once been allowed to work, it will, if it has a certain force, produce its effect, let me struggle how I may. There is no objection to a contradiction in what would result from a false supposition. The *reductio ad absurdum* consists in showing that contradictory results would follow from a hypothesis which is consequently judged to be false. Many questions are involved in the free-will discussion, and I am far from desiring to say that both sides are equally right. On the contrary, I am of opinion that one side denies important facts, and that the other does not. But what I do say is, that the above single question was the origin of the whole doubt; that, had it not been for this question, the controversy would never have arisen; and that this question is perfectly solved in the manner which I have indicated.

Let us next seek a clear idea of Weight. This is another very easy case. To say that a body is heavy means simply that, in the absence of opposing force, it will fall. This (neglecting certain specifications of how it will fall, etc., which exist in the mind of the physicist who uses the word) is evidently the whole conception of weight. It is a fair question whether some particular facts may not account for gravity; but what we mean by the force itself is completely involved in its effects.

This leads us to undertake an account of the idea of Force in general. This is the great conception which, developed in the early part of the seventeenth century from the rude idea of a cause, and constantly improved upon since, has shown us how to explain all the changes of motion which bodies experience, and how to think about all physical phenomena; which has given birth to modern science, and changed the face of the globe; and which, aside from its more special uses, has played a principal part in directing the course of modern thought, and in furthering modern social development. It is, therefore, worth some pains to comprehend it. According to our rule, we must begin by asking what is the immediate use of thinking about force; and the answer is, that we thus account for changes of motion. If bodies were left to themselves, without the intervention of forces, every motion would continue unchanged both in velocity and in direction. Furthermore, change of motion never takes place abruptly; if its direction is changed, it is always through a curve without angles; if its velocity alters, it is by degrees. The gradual changes which are constantly taking place are conceived by geometers to be compounded together according to the rules of the parallelogram of forces. If the reader does not already know what this is, he will find it, I hope, to his advantage to endeavour to follow the following explanation; but if mathematics are insupportable to him, pray let him skip three paragraphs rather than that we should part company here.

A *path* is a line whose beginning and end are distinguished. Two paths are considered to be equivalent, which, beginning at the same point, lead to the same point. Thus the two paths, A B C D E and A F G H E (Fig. 3), are equivalent. Paths which do *not* begin at the same point are considered to be equivalent, provided that, on moving either of them without turning it, but keeping it always parallel to its original position, when its beginning coincides with that of the other path, the ends also coincide. Paths are considered as geometrically added together, when one begins where the other ends; thus the path A E is conceived to be a sum of A B, B C, C D, and D E. In the parallelogram of Fig. 4 the diagonal A C is the sum of A B and B C; or, since A D is geometrically equivalent to B C, A C is the geometrical sum of A B and A D.

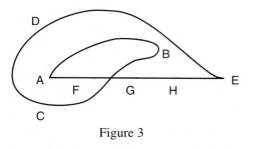

Figure 3

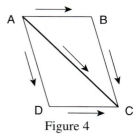

Figure 4

All this is purely conventional. It simply amounts to this: that we choose to call paths having the relations I have described equal or added. But, though it is a convention, it is a convention with a good reason. The rule for geometrical addition may be applied not only to paths, but to any other things which can be represented by paths. Now, as a path is determined by the varying direction and distance of the point which moves over it from the starting-point, it follows that anything which from its beginning to its end is determined by a varying direction and a varying magnitude is capable of being represented by a line. Accordingly, *velocities* may be represented by lines, for they have only directions and rates. The same thing is true of *accelerations*, or changes of velocities. This is evident enough in the case of velocities; and it becomes evident for accelerations if we consider that precisely what velocities are to positions—namely, states of change of them—that accelerations are to velocities.

The so-called "parallelogram of forces" is simply a rule for compounding accelerations. The rule is, to represent the accelerations by paths, and then to geometrically add the paths. The geometers, however, not only use the "parallelogram of forces" to compound different accelerations, but also to resolve one acceleration into a sum of several. Let A B (Fig. 5) be the path which represents a certain acceleration—say, such a change in the motion of a body that at the end of one second the body will, under the influence of that change, be in a position different from what it would have had if its motion had continued unchanged such that a path equivalent to A B would lead from the latter position to the former.

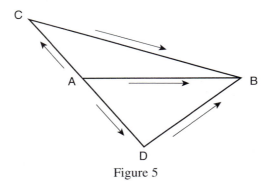

Figure 5

This acceleration may be considered as the sum of the accelerations represented by A C and C B. It may also be considered as the sum of the very different accelerations represented by A D and D B, where A D is almost the opposite of A C. And it is clear that there is an immense variety of ways in which A B might be resolved into the sum of two accelerations.

After this tedious explanation, which I hope, in view of the extraordinary interest of the conception of force, may not have exhausted the reader's patience, we are prepared at last to state the grand fact which this conception embodies. This fact is that if the actual changes of motion which the different particles of bodies experience are each resolved in its appropriate way, each component acceleration is precisely such as is prescribed by a certain law of Nature, according to which bodies, in the relative positions which the bodies in question actually have at the moment, always receive certain accelerations, which, being compounded by geometrical addition, give the acceleration which the body actually experiences.

This is the only fact which the idea of force represents, and whoever will take the trouble clearly to apprehend what this fact is, perfectly comprehends what force is. Whether we ought to say that a force is an acceleration, or that it *causes* an acceleration, is a mere question of propriety of language, which has no more to do with our real meaning than the difference between the French idiom "*Il fait froid*" and its English equivalent "*It is cold.*" Yet it is surprising to see how this simple affair has muddled men's minds. In how many profound treatises is not force spoken of as a "mysterious entity," which seems to be only a way of confessing that the author despairs of ever getting a clear notion of what the word means! In a recent admired work on *Analytic Mechanics* it is stated that we understand precisely the effect of force, but what force itself is we do not understand! This is simply a self-contradiction. The idea which the word force excites in our minds has no other function than to affect our actions, and these actions can have no reference to force otherwise than through its effects. Consequently, if we know what the effects of force are, we are acquainted with every fact which is implied in saying that a force exists, and there is nothing more to know. The truth is, there is some vague notion afloat that a question may mean something which the mind cannot conceive; and when some hair-splitting philosophers have been confronted with the absurdity of such a view, they have invented an empty distinction between positive and negative conceptions, in the attempt to give their non-idea a form not obviously nonsensical. The nullity of it is sufficiently plain from the considerations given a few pages back; and, apart from those considerations, the quibbling character of the distinction must have struck every mind accustomed to real thinking.

Let us now approach the subject of logic, and consider a conception which particularly concerns it, that of *reality*. Taking clearness in the sense of familiarity, no idea could be clearer than this. Every child uses it with perfect confidence, never dreaming that he does not understand it. As for clearness in its second grade, however, it would probably puzzle most men, even among those of a reflective turn of mind, to give an abstract definition of the real. Yet such a definition may perhaps be reached by considering the points of difference between reality and its opposite, fiction. A figment is a product of somebody's imagination; it has such characters as his thought impresses upon it. That those characters are independent of how you or I think is an external reality. There are, however, phenomena within our own minds, dependent upon our thought, which are at the same time real in the sense that we really think them. But though their characters depend on how we think, they do not depend on what we think those characters to be. Thus, a dream has a real existence as a mental phenomenon, if somebody has really dreamt it; that he dreamt so and so, does not depend on what anybody thinks was dreamt, but is completely independent of all opinion on the subject. On the other hand, considering, not the fact of dreaming, but the thing dreamt, it retains its peculiarities by virtue of no other fact than that it was dreamt to possess them. Thus we may define the real as that whose characters are independent of what anybody may think them to be.

But, however satisfactory such a definition may be found, it would be a great mistake to suppose that it makes the idea of reality perfectly clear. Here, then, let us apply our rules. According to them, reality, like every other quality, consists in the peculiar sensible effects which things partaking of it produce. The only effect which real things have is to cause belief, for all the sensations which they excite emerge into consciousness in the form of beliefs. The question therefore is, how is true belief (or belief in the real) distinguished from false belief (or belief in fiction). Now, as we have seen in the former paper,* the ideas of truth and falsehood, in their full development, appertain exclusively to the experiential method of settling opinion. A person who arbitrarily chooses the propositions which he will adopt can use the word truth only to emphasize the expression of his determination to hold on to his choice. Of course, the method

*["The Fixation of Belief" (1877), see above p. 374ff.]

of tenacity never prevailed exclusively; reason is too natural to men for that. But in the literature of the dark ages we find some fine examples of it. When Scotus Erigena is commenting upon a poetical passage in which Helleborus is spoken of as having caused the death of Socrates, he does not hesitate to inform the inquiring reader that Helleborus and Socrates were two eminent Greek philosophers, and that the latter, having been overcome in argument by the former, took the matter to heart and died of it! What sort of an idea of truth could a man have who could adopt and teach, without the qualification of a perhaps, an opinion taken so entirely at random? The real spirit of Socrates, who I hope would have been delighted to have been "overcome in argument," because he would have learned something by it, is in curious contrast with the naive idea of the glossist, for whom (as for "the born missionary" of today) discussion would seem to have been simply a struggle. When philosophy began to awake from its long slumber, and before theology completely dominated it, the practice seems to have been for each professor to seize upon any philosophical position he found unoccupied and which seemed a strong one, to intrench himself in it, and to sally forth from time to time to give battle to the others. Thus, even the scanty records we possess of those disputes enable us to make out a dozen or more opinions held by different teachers at one time concerning the question of nominalism and realism. Read the opening part of the *Historia Calamitatum* of Abelard, who was certainly as philosophical as any of his contemporaries, and see the spirit of combat which it breathes. For him, the truth is simply his particular stronghold. When the method of authority prevailed, the truth meant little more than the Catholic faith. All the efforts of the scholastic doctors are directed toward harmonizing their faith in Aristotle and their faith in the Church, and one may search their ponderous folios through without finding an argument which goes any further. It is noticeable that where different faiths flourish side by side, renegades are looked upon with contempt even by the party whose belief they adopt; so completely has the idea of loyalty replaced that of truth seeking. Since the time of Descartes, the defect in the conception of truth has been less apparent. Still, it will sometimes strike a scientific man that the philosophers have been less intent on finding out what the facts are, than on inquiring what belief is most in harmony with their system. It is hard to convince a follower of the *a priori* method by adducing facts; but show him that an opinion he is defending is inconsistent with what he has laid down elsewhere, and he will be very apt to retract it. These minds do not seem to believe that disputation is ever to cease; they seem to think that the opinion which is natural for one man is not so for another, and that belief will, consequently, never be settled. In contenting themselves with fixing their own opinions by a method which would lead another man to a different result, they betray their feeble hold of the conception of what truth is.

On the other hand, all the followers of science are animated by a cheerful hope that the processes of investigation, if only pushed far enough, will give one certain solution to each question to which they apply it. One man may investigate the velocity of light by studying the transits of Venus and the aberration of the stars; another by the oppositions of Mars and the eclipses of Jupiter's satellites; a third by the method of Fizeau; a fourth by that of Foucault; a fifth by the motions of the curves of Lissajoux; a sixth, a seventh, an eighth, and a ninth, may follow the different methods of comparing the measures of statical and dynamical electricity. They may at first obtain different results, but, as each perfects his method and his processes, the results are found to move steadily together toward a destined centre. So with all scientific research. Different minds may set out with the most antagonistic views, but the progress of investigation carries them by a force outside of themselves to one and the same conclusion. This activity of thought by which we are carried, not where we wish, but to a fore-ordained goal, is like the operation of destiny. No modification of the point of view taken, no selection of other facts for study, no natural bent of mind even, can enable a man to escape the predestinate opinion. This great hope is embodied in the conception of truth and reality. The opinion which is fated to be ultimately agreed to by all who investigate, is what we mean by the truth, and the object represented in this opinion is the real. That is the way I would explain reality.

But it may be said that this view is directly opposed to the abstract definition which we have given of reality, inasmuch as it makes the characters of the real depend on what is ultimately thought about them. But the answer to this is that, on the one hand, reality is independent, not necessarily of thought in general, but only of what you or I or any finite number of men may think about it; and that, on the other hand, though the object of the final opinion depends on what that opinion is, yet what that opinion is does not depend on what you or I or any man thinks. Our perversity and that of others may indefinitely postpone the settlement of opinion; it might even conceivably cause an arbitrary proposition to be universally accepted as long as the human race should last. Yet even that would not change the nature of the belief, which alone could be the result of investigation carried sufficiently far; and if, after the extinction of our race, another should arise with faculties and disposition for investigation, that true opinion must be the one which they would ultimately come to. "Truth crushed to earth shall rise again," and the opinion which would finally result from investigation does not depend on how anybody may actually think. But the reality of that which is real does depend on the real fact that investigation is destined to lead, at last, if continued long enough, to a belief in it.

But I may be asked what I have to say to all the minute facts of history, forgotten never to be recovered, to the lost books of the ancients, to the buried secrets.

> Full many a gem of purest ray serene
>   The dark, unfathomed caves of ocean bear;
> Full many a flower is born to blush unseen,
>   And waste its sweetness on the desert air.

Do these things not really exist because they are hopelessly beyond the reach of our knowledge? And then, after the universe is dead (according to the prediction of some scientists), and all life has ceased forever, will not the shock of atoms continue though there will be no mind to know it? To this I reply that, though in no possible state of knowledge can any number be great enough to express the relation between the amount of what rests unknown to the amount of the known, yet it is unphilosophical to suppose that, with regard to any given question (which has any clear meaning), investigation would not bring forth a solution of it, if it were carried far enough. Who would have said, a few years ago, that we could ever know of what substances stars are made whose light may have been longer in reaching us than the human race has existed? Who can be sure of what we shall not know in a few hundred years? Who can guess what would be the result of continuing the pursuit of science for ten thousand years, with the activity of the last hundred? And if it were to go on for a million, or a billion, or any number of years you please, how is it possible to say that there is any question which might not ultimately be solved?

But it may be objected, "Why make so much of these remote considerations, especially when it is your principle that only practical distinctions have a meaning?" Well, I must confess that it makes very little difference whether we say that a stone on the bottom of the ocean, in complete darkness, is brilliant or not—that is to say, that it *probably* makes no difference, remembering always that that stone *may* be fished up tomorrow. But that there are gems at the bottom of the sea, flowers in the untravelled desert, etc., are propositions which, like that about a diamond being hard when it is not pressed, concern much more the arrangement of our language than they do the meaning of our ideas.

It seems to me, however, that we have, by the application of our rule, reached so clear an apprehension of what we mean by reality, and of the fact which the idea rests on, that we should not, perhaps, be making a pretension so presumptuous as it would be singular, if we were to offer a metaphysical theory of existence for universal acceptance among those who employ the scientific method of fixing belief. However, as metaphysics is a subject much more curious than useful, the knowledge of which, like that of a sunken reef, serves chiefly to enable us to keep clear of it, I will not trouble the reader with any more Ontology at this moment. I have already been led much further into that path than I should have desired; and I have given the reader such a dose of mathematics, psychology, and all that is most abstruse, that I fear he may already have left me, and that what I am now writing is for the compositor and proofreader exclusively. I trusted to the importance of the subject. There is no royal road to logic, and really valuable ideas can only be had at the price of close attention. But I know that in the matter of ideas the public prefer the cheap and nasty; and in my next paper I am going to return to the easily intelligible, and not wander from it again. The reader who has been at the pains of wading through this paper, shall be rewarded in the next one by seeing how beautifully what has been developed in this tedious way can be applied to the ascertainment of the rules of scientific reasoning.

We have, hitherto, not crossed the threshold of scientific logic. It is certainly important to know how to make our ideas clear, but they may be ever so clear without being true. How to make them so, we have next to study. How to give birth to those vital and procreative ideas which multiply into a thousand forms and diffuse themselves everywhere, advancing civilization and making the dignity of man, is an art not yet reduced to rules, but of the secret of which the history of science affords some hints.

WILLIAM JAMES
1842–1910

William James was born into one of the leading families of New York City. His grandfather, a strict Calvinist and also named William, was an Irish immigrant who had amassed a fortune in real estate. His father, Henry, rejected the grandfather's religion and became an unorthodox mystic. His mother, Mary, was also a child of wealth, and his brother, Henry Jr., became a famous novelist. The life of the James family was one of creative anarchy. Their dinner table was animated with lively debate in which the children were expected to hold their own with such guests as Ralph Waldo Emerson, Washington Irving, and Oliver Wendell Holmes. To encourage intellectual freedom, and to avoid the rigidity of his own joyless upbringing, Henry Sr. put his children into as many different schools as possible. The family moved often, restlessly wandering back and forth across the Atlantic, alighting temporarily in London, Paris, New York, Geneva, Newport, Bonn, and Albany.

William James reflected his family's wanderlust in his academic pursuits. He studied art for a time before joining an expedition to the Amazon basin as an apprentice naturalist. He then traveled to Germany to study physiology, before returning to the United States to complete a degree in medicine at Harvard Medical School in 1869. In 1872, James was appointed to teach physiology and anatomy at Harvard. His intellectual roving and his unwillingness to be bound by the usual academic disciplines continued when he moved in 1875 to psychology and later to philosophy. He subsequently marveled at his audacity:

> I originally studied medicine in order to be a physiologist, but I drifted into psychology and philosophy from a sort of fatality. I never had any philosophic instruction and the first lecture on psychology I ever heard was the first one I ever gave.

In 1878, James married Alice Howe Gibbens, and they had five children. Although James had experienced ill health as a young man (including smallpox contracted in Brazil), his strength seemed to improve following marriage.

In 1890, William James published his first major work, *The Principles of Psychology*. A two-volume work, *Principles* was one of the first attempts to treat psychology as a legitimate, experimental science, and it quickly became the standard work in the field. James did intense philosophical research over the next seventeen years and published his results: *The Will to Believe and Other Essays* (1897), *Varieties of Religious Experience* (1902), and *Pragmatism* (1907). During this period, he continued to teach at Harvard and to lecture throughout the United States and Europe. Resigning from Harvard in 1907, James gave a series of lectures published as *A Pluralistic Universe* (1909) and *The Meaning of Truth* (1909). James died in 1910, and his last complete work, *Essays in Radical Empiricism,* was published posthumously.

At the time of his death, James was considered the embodiment of American philosophy. All accounts indicate that in addition to his large intellect and breadth of learning, James was a generous, open-minded, and sociable person. One historian of philosophy went so far as to describe him as "one of the sweetest men who ever lived."

*   *   *

If Peirce is a philosopher's philosopher, then James is the common person's philosopher. What his thought may lack in technical precision, it makes up for in both expressiveness and concern for common problems. Yet James's engaging style and lack of jargon left him open to charges of imprecision and carelessness.

James's popular style is apparent in an address he gave to the Yale Philosophical Club, published in 1891. In "The Moral Philosopher and the Moral Life," reprinted here (complete), James argues that the most universal ethical principle is "that *the essence of good is simply to satisfy demand* . . . demand . . . for anything under the sun." Demands are never intrinsically "good" or "bad." In fact, "good" and "bad" have no "absolute natures." Such terms are only "objects of feeling and desire which have no foothold or anchorage in Being, apart from the existence of actually living minds." Although James acknowledges that there might be a *divine* mind that established a stable and systematic moral universe based on divine desires, our knowledge of such a universe will always be fragmentary and incomplete. James concludes that "The ethical philosopher, therefore, whenever he ventures to say which course of action is the best, is on no essentially different level from the common man."

In his most famous work, the series of lectures published as *Pragmatism,* James begins by distinguishing between two human temperaments: the tough-minded and the tender-minded. The tough-minded are those who are empirically oriented—those who "go by facts." By contrast, the tender-minded are rationalists who "go by principles." According to James, the history of philosophy is largely the story of the clash between these two attitudes: "The tough think of the tender as sentimentalists and softheads. The tender feel the tough to be unrefined, callous, or brutal." The tough-minded approach to philosophy has the virtue of being connected to "facts," but it tends to exclude religion. The tender-minded approach allows for religion but is unconnected to the realities of everyday life. The result is that for the ordinary person, "Empiricist writers give him materialism, rationalists give him something religious, but to that religion 'actual things are blank.'"

James believes that pragmatism is a method that reconciles these opposing temperaments. Borrowing from Peirce, James develops pragmatism as "a method of settling metaphysical disputes that otherwise might be interminable." As a theory of meaning, pragmatism asks what practical effects a belief has, whether that belief is tough- or tender-minded. To discover what a belief *means* is to find what difference such a belief makes "in concrete fact and in conduct consequent upon that fact, imposed on somebody, somehow, somewhere, and somewhen." The proper goal of philosophy is to discover "what definite difference it will make to you and me, at definite instants of our life, if this world-formula or that world-formula be the true one."

But James went further than Peirce and claims that pragmatism provides a theory of *truth* as well as of meaning. Peirce had continued to hold a traditional correspondence theory of truth: An assertion was true if it corresponded with a fact. Instead, James says that an idea *becomes* true if it allows the individual to gain "satisfactory relations with other parts of our experience." These relations are not fixed—they are dynamic, just as our experience is dynamic. As James puts it,

> *True ideas are those that we can assimilate, validate, corroborate, and verify. False ideas are those that we cannot.* That is the practical difference it makes to us to have true ideas, that therefore is the meaning of truth. . . .

Though it was written earlier, James's famous essay on religion, "The Will to Believe," anticipated elements of his mature pragmatism. Defining a genuine option as one that is living, forced, and momentous, James argues that there is no reason not to make such a choice for religious belief. Those who would argue that one should withhold religious beliefs until there is sensible proof are "telling us . . . that to yield to our fear of it being error is wiser and better than to yield to our hope that it may be true." Instead, says James, we have the "right to believe"—even if the data are inconclusive.

Critics have pointed out that James's "will to believe" could lead to virtually any conclusion one considers living, forced, and momentous. Furthermore, his theory of pragmatism could be used to make any belief true—provided it produced beneficial results. As H.S. Thayer pointed out, "Standards of veracity thus go slack on the very occasions in which, ordinarily, they need the tightest rein, where passion and personal interests are most in play."* This fact, along with a number of other objections, led Peirce to change the name of *his* philosophy to "pragmaticism," to distinguish it from James's thought. For his part, James claimed that he was only presenting a way of discovering truth, not redefining it. It was left to others such as John Dewey to reformulate the pragmatic theory of truth more precisely.

*   *   *

---

*H.S. Thayer, "Pragmatism," in D.J. O'Connor, ed., *A Critical History of Western Philosophy* (New York: The Free Press, 1964), p. 451.

For general works on pragmatism, see the introduction to Peirce (page 371). For biographies of James, see Gay Wilson Allen, *William James: A Biography* (New York: Viking Press, 1967); Jacques Barzun, *A Stroll with William James* (New York: Harper & Row, 1983); and Daniel W. Bjork, *William James: The Center of His Vision* (New York: Columbia University Press, 1988). The standard study of James's thought is Ralph Barton Perry, *The Thought and Character of William James*, 2 volumes (Boston: Little, Brown, 1935). Other general introductions to his thought include Bernard P. Brennan, *William James* (New York: Twayne, 1968); Ellen Kappy Suckiel, *The Pragmatic Philosophy of William James* (Notre Dame, IN: University of Notre Dame Press, 1982); Graham Bird, *William James* (London: Routledge & Kegan Paul, 1986); and Gerald E. Myers, *William James: His Life and Thought* (New Haven, CT: Yale University Press, 1986). Collections of essays include Doris Olin, ed., *William James Pragmatism in Focus* (London: Routledge, 1992); and Ruth Anna Putnam, ed., *The Cambridge Companion to William James* (Cambridge: Cambridge University Press, 1997). For studies devoted to James's religious theories, see Stephen T. Davis, *Faith, Skepticism, and Evidence: An Essay in Religious Epistemology* (Lewisburg, PA: Bucknell University Press, 1978); Robert J. Vanden Burgt, *The Religious Philosophy of William James* (Chicago: Nelson-Hall, 1981); Robert J. O'Connell, *William James on the Courage to Believe* (New York: Fordham University Press, 1984); Eugene Fontinell, *Self, God, and Immortality: A Jamesian Investigation* (Philadelphia: Temple University Press, 1986); and Ellen Kappy Suckiel, *Heaven's Champion: William James's Philosophy of Religion* (Notre Dame, IN: University of Notre Dame Press, 1997). For studies of James's psychology, see Bruce Wilshire, *William James and Phenomenology: A Study of "The Principles of Psychology"* (Bloomington: Indiana University Press, 1968); John Wild, *The Radical Empiricism of William James* (Garden City, NY: Doubleday, 1969); and James M. Edie, *William James and Phenomenology* (Bloomington: Indiana University Press, 1987).

THE MORAL PHILOSOPHER
AND THE MORAL LIFE

The main purpose of this paper is to show that there is no such thing possible as an ethical philosophy dogmatically made up in advance. We all help to determine the content of ethical philosophy so far as we contribute to the race's moral life. In other words, there can be no final truth in ethics any more than in physics, until the last man has had his experience and said his say. In the one case as in the other, however, the hypotheses which we now make while waiting, and the acts to which they prompt us, are among the indispensable conditions which determine what that "say" shall be.

First of all, what is the position of him who seeks an ethical philosophy? To begin with, he must be distinguished from all those who are satisfied to be ethical sceptics. He will not be a sceptic; therefore so far from ethical scepticism being one possible fruit of ethical philosophizing, it can only be regarded as that residual alternative to all philosophy which from the outset menaces every would-be philosopher who may give up the quest discouraged, and renounce his original aim. That aim is to find an account of the moral relations that obtain among things, which will weave them into the unity of a stable system, and make of the world what one may call a genuine universe from the ethical point of view. So far as the world resists reduction to the form of unity, so far as ethical propositions seem unstable, so far does the philosopher fail of his ideal. The subject-matter of his study is the ideals he finds existing in the world; the purpose which guides him is this ideal of his own, of getting them into a certain form. This ideal is thus a factor in ethical philosophy whose legitimate presence must never be overlooked; it is a positive contribution which the philosopher himself necessarily makes to the problem. But it is his only positive contribution. At the outset of his inquiry he ought to have no other ideals. Were he interested peculiarly in the triumph of any one kind of good, he would *pro tanto* cease to be a judicial investigator, and become an advocate for some limited element of the case.

There are three questions in ethics which must be kept apart. Let them be called respectively the *psychological* question, the metaphysical question, and the casuistic question. The psychological question asks after the historical origin of our moral ideas and judgments; the metaphysical question asks what the very meaning of the words "good," "ill," and "obligation" are; the casuistic question asks what is the measure of the various goods and ills which men recognize, so that the philosopher may settle the true order of human obligations.

1. The psychological question is for most disputants the only question. When your ordinary doctor of divinity has proved to his own satisfaction that an altogether unique faculty called "conscience" must be postulated to tell us what is right and what is wrong; or when your popular-science enthusiast has proclaimed that "apriorism" is an exploded superstition, and that our moral judgments have gradually resulted from the teaching of the environment, each of these persons thinks that ethics is settled and nothing more is to be said. The familiar pair of names, *Intuitionist* and *Evolutionist,* so commonly used now to connote all possible differences in ethical opinion, really refer to the psychological question alone. The discussion of this question hinges so much upon particular details that it is impossible to enter upon it at all within the limits of this paper. I will therefore only express dogmatically my own belief, which is this— that the Benthams, the Mills, and the Bains have done a lasting service in taking so many of our human ideals and showing how they must have arisen from the association with acts of simple bodily pleasures and reliefs from pain. Association with many remote pleasures will unquestionably make a thing significant of goodness in our minds; and the more vaguely the goodness is conceived of, the more mysterious will its source appear to be. But it is surely impossible to explain all our sentiments and preferences in this simple way. The more minutely psychology studies human nature, the more clearly it finds there traces of secondary affections, relating the impressions of the environment with one another and with our impulses in quite different ways from those mere associations of coexistence and succession which are practically all that pure empiricism can admit. Take the love of drunkenness; take bashfulness, the terror of high places, the tendency to seasickness, to faint at the sight of blood, the susceptibility to musical sounds; take the emotion of the comical, the passion for poetry, for mathematics, or for metaphysics—no one of these things can be wholly explained by either association or utility. They *go with* other things that can be so explained, no doubt; and some of them are prophetic of future utilities, since there is nothing in us for which some use may not be found. But their origin is in incidental complications to

our cerebral structure, a structure whose original features arose with no reference to the perception of such discords and harmonies as these.

Well, a vast number of our moral perceptions also are certainly of this secondary and brain-born kind. They deal with directly felt fitnesses between things, and often fly in the teeth of all the prepossessions of habit and presumptions of utility. The moment you get beyond the coarser and more commonplace moral maxims, the Decalogues and *Poor Richard's Almanacs,* you fall into schemes and positions which to the eye of common-sense are fantastic and over-strained. The sense for abstract justice which some persons have is as excentric a variation, from the natural-history point of view, as is the passion for music or for the higher philosophical consistencies which consumes the soul of others. The feeling of the inward dignity of certain spiritual attitudes, as peace, serenity, simplicity, veracity; and of the essential vulgarity of others, as queru-lousness, anxiety, egoistic fussiness, etc.—are quite inexplicable except by an innate preference of the more ideal attitude for its own pure sake. The nobler thing *tastes* bet-ter, and that is all that we can say. "Experience" of consequences may truly teach us what things are *wicked,* but what have consequences to do with what is *mean* and *vul-gar?* If a man has shot his wife's paramour, by reason of what subtile repugnancy in things is it that we are so disgusted when we hear that the wife and the husband have made it up and are living comfortably together again? Or if the hypothesis were of-fered us of a world in which Messrs. Fourier's and Bellamy's and Morris's utopias should all be outdone, and millions kept permanently happy on the one simple condi-tion that a certain lost soul on the far-off edge of things should lead a life of lonely tor-ture, what except a specifical and independent sort of emotion can it be which would make us immediately feel, even though an impulse arose within us to clutch at the hap-piness so offered, how hideous a thing would be its enjoyment when deliberately ac-cepted as the fruit of such a bargain? To what, once more, but subtile brain-born feel-ings of discord can be due all these recent protests against the entire race-tradition of retributive justice?—I refer to Tolstoy with his ideas of non-resistance, to Mr. Bellamy with his substitution of oblivion for repentance (in his novel of Dr. Heidenhain's Process), to M. Guyau with his radical condemnation of the punitive ideal. All these subtilities of the moral sensibility go as much beyond what can be ciphered out from the "laws of association" as the delicacies of sentiment possible between a pair of young lovers go beyond such precepts of the "etiquette to be observed during engage-ment" as are printed in manuals of social form.

No! Purely inward forces are certainly at work here. All the higher, more pene-trating ideals are revolutionary. They present themselves far less in the guise of effects of past experience than in that of probable causes of future experience, factors to which the environment and the lessons it has so far taught us must learn to bend.

This is all I can say of the psychological question now. In the last chapter of a re-cent work* I have sought to prove in a general way the existence, in our thought, of re-lations which do not merely repeat the couplings of experience. Our ideals have cer-tainly many sources. They are not all explicable as signifying corporeal pleasures to be gained, and pains to be escaped. And for having so constantly perceived this psycho-logical fact, we must applaud the intuitionist school. Whether or not such applause must be extended to that school's other characteristics will appear as we take up the following questions.

The Principles of Psychology (New York, H. Holt, 1890).

The next one in order is the metaphysical question, of what we mean by the words "obligation," "good," and "ill."

2. First of all, it appears that such words can have no application or relevancy in a world in which no sentient life exists. Imagine an absolutely material world, containing only physical and chemical facts, and existing from eternity without a God, without even an interested spectator: would there be any sense in saying of that world that one of its states is better than another? Or if there were two such worlds possible, would there be any rhyme or reason in calling one good and the other bad—good or bad positively, I mean, and apart from the fact that one might relate itself better than the other to the philosopher's private interests? But we must leave these private interests out of the account, for the philosopher is a mental fact, and we are asking whether goods and evils and obligations exist in physical facts *per se*. Surely there is no *status* for good and evil to exist in, in a purely insentient world. How can one physical fact, considered simply as a physical fact, be "better" than another? Betterness is not a physical relation. In its mere material capacity, a thing can no more be good or bad than it can be pleasant or painful. Good for what? Good for the production of another physical fact, do you say? But what in a purely physical universe demands the production of that other fact? Physical facts simply *are* or *are not;* and neither when present or absent, can they be supposed to make demands. If they do, they can only do so by having desires; and then they have ceased to be purely physical facts, and have become facts of conscious sensibility. Goodness, badness, and obligation must be *realized* somewhere in order really to exist; and the first step in ethical philosophy is to see that no merely inorganic "nature of things" can realize them. Neither moral relations nor the moral law can swing *in vacuo*. Their only habitat can be a mind which feels them; and no world composed of merely physical facts can possibly be a world to which ethical propositions apply.

The moment one sentient being, however, is made a part of the universe, there is a chance for goods and evils really to exist. Moral relations now have their *status*, in that being's consciousness. So far as he feels anything to be good, he *makes* it good. It is good, for him; and being good for him, is absolutely good, for he is the sole creator of values in that universe, and outside of his opinion things have no moral character at all.

In such a universe as that it would of course be absurd to raise the question of whether the solitary thinker's judgments of good and ill are true or not. Truth supposes a standard outside of the thinker to which he must conform; but here the thinker is a sort of divinity, subject to no higher judge. Let us call the supposed universe which he inhabits a *moral solitude*. In such a moral solitude it is clear that there can be no outward obligation, and that the only trouble the god-like thinker is liable to have will be over the consistency of his own several ideals with one another. Some of these will no doubt be more pungent and appealing than the rest, their goodness will have a profounder, more penetrating taste; they will return to haunt him with more obstinate regrets if violated. So the thinker will have to order his life with them as its chief determinants, or else remain inwardly discordant and unhappy. Into whatever equilibrium he may settle, though, and however he may straighten out his system, it will be a right system; for beyond the facts of his own subjectivity there is nothing moral in the world.

If now we introduce a second thinker with his likes and dislikes into the universe, the ethical situation becomes much more complex, and several possibilities are immediately seen to obtain.

One of these is that the thinkers may ignore each other's attitude about good and evil altogether, and each continue to indulge his own preferences, indifferent to what the other may feel or do. In such a case we have a world with twice as much of the ethical quality in it as our moral solitude, only it is without ethical unity. The same object is good or bad there, according as you measure it by the view which this one or that one of the thinkers takes. Nor can you find any possible ground in such a world for saying that one thinker's opinion is more correct than the other's, or that either has the truer moral sense. Such a world, in short, is not a moral universe but a moral dualism. Not only is there no single point of view within it from which the values of things can be unequivocally judged, but there is not even a demand for such a point of view, since the two thinkers are supposed to be indifferent to each other's thoughts and acts. Multiply the thinkers into a pluralism, and we find realized for us in the ethical sphere something like that world which the antique sceptics conceived of—in which individual minds are the measures of all things, and in which no one "objective" truth, but only a multitude of "subjective" opinions, can be found.

But this is the kind of world with which the philosopher, so long as he holds to the hope of a philosophy, will not put up. Among the various ideals represented, there must be, he thinks, some which have the more truth or authority; and to these the others ought to yield, so that system and subordination may reign. Here in the word "ought" the notion of *obligation* comes emphatically into view, and the next thing in order must be to make its meaning clear.

Since the outcome of the discussion so far has been to show us that nothing can be good or right except so far as some consciousness feels it to be good or thinks it to be right, we perceive on the very threshold that the real superiority and authority which are postulated by the philosopher to reside in some of the opinions, and the really inferior character which he supposes must belong to others, cannot be explained by any abstract moral "nature of things" existing antecedently to the concrete thinkers themselves with their ideals. Like the positive attributes good and bad, the comparative ones better and worse must be *realized* in order to be real. If one ideal judgment be objectively better than another, that betterness must be made flesh by being lodged concretely in some one's actual perception. It cannot float in the atmosphere, for it is not a sort of meteorological phenomenon, like the aurora borealis or the zodiacal light. Its *esse* is *percipi*, like the *esse* of the ideals themselves between which it obtains. The philosopher, therefore, who seeks to know which ideal ought to have supreme weight and which one ought to be subordinated, must trace the *ought* itself to the *de facto* constitution of some existing consciousness, behind which, as one of the data of the universe, he as a purely ethical philosopher is unable to go. This consciousness must make the one ideal right by feeling it to be right, the other wrong by feeling it to be wrong. But now what particular consciousness in the universe can enjoy this prerogative of obliging others to conform to a rule which it lays down?

If one of the thinkers were obviously divine, while all the rest were human, there would probably be no practical dispute about the matter. The divine thought would be the model, to which the others should conform. But still the theoretic question would remain, What is the ground of the obligation, even here?

In our first essays at answering this question, there is an inevitable tendency to slip into an assumption which ordinary men follow when they are disputing with one another about questions of good and bad. They imagine an abstract moral order in which the objective truth resides; and each tries to prove that this preexisting order is more accurately reflected in his own ideas than in those of his adversary. It is because one disputant is backed by this overarching abstract order that we think the other should submit. Even so, when it is a question no longer of two finite thinkers, but of God and ourselves—we follow our usual habit, and imagine a sort of *de jure* relation, which antedates and overarches the mere facts, and would make it right that we should conform our thoughts to God's thoughts, even though he made no claim to that effect, and though we preferred *de facto* to go on thinking for ourselves.

But the moment we take a steady look at the question, *we see not only that without a claim actually made by some concrete person there can be no obligation, but that there is some obligation wherever there is a claim.* Claim and obligation are, in fact, coextensive terms; they cover each other exactly. Our ordinary attitude of regarding ourselves as subject to an overarching system of moral relations, true "in themselves," is therefore either an out-and-out superstition, or else it must be treated as a merely provisional abstraction from that real Thinker in whose actual demand upon us to think as he does our obligation must be ultimately based. In a theistic-ethical philosophy that thinker in question is, of course, the Deity to whom the existence of the universe is due.

I know well how hard it is for those who are accustomed to what I have called the superstitious view, to realize that every *de facto* claim creates in so far forth an obligation. We inveterately think that something which we call the "validity" of the claim is what gives to it its obligatory character, and that this validity is something outside of the claim's mere existence as a matter of fact. It rains down upon the claim, we think, from some sublime dimension of being, which the moral law inhabits, much as upon the steel of the compass-needle the influence of the Pole rains down from out of the starry heavens. But again, how can such an inorganic abstract character of imperativeness, additional to the imperativeness which is in the concrete claim itself, *exist?* Take any demand, however slight, which any creature, however weak, may make. Ought it not, for its own sole sake, to be satisfied? If not, prove why not. The only possible kind of proof you could adduce would be the exhibition of another creature who should make a demand that ran the other way. The only possible reason there can be why any phenomenon ought to exist is that such a phenomenon actually is desired. Any desire is imperative to the extent of its amount; it *makes* itself valid by the fact that it exists at all. Some desires, truly enough, are small desires; they are put forward by insignificant persons, and we customarily make light of the obligations which they bring. But the fact that such personal demands as these impose small obligations does not keep the largest obligations from being personal demands.

If we must talk impersonally, to be sure we can say that "the universe" requires, exacts, or makes obligatory such or such an action, whenever it expresses itself through the desires of such or such a creature. But it is better not to talk about the universe in this personified way, unless we believe in a universal or divine consciousness which actually exists. If there be such a consciousness, then its demands carry the most of obligation simply because they are the greatest in amount. But it is even then not *abstractly* right that we should respect them. It is only *concretely* right—or right after the fact, and by virtue of the fact, that they are actually made. Suppose we do not respect them, as seems largely to be the case in this queer world. That ought not to be, we say; that is wrong. But in what way is this fact of wrongness made more acceptable or intelligible when we imagine it to consist rather in the laceration of an *a priori* ideal order than in the disappointment of a living personal God? Do we, perhaps, think that we cover God and protect him and make his impotence over us less ultimate, when we back him up with this *a priori* blanket from which he may draw some warmth of further appeal? But the only force of appeal to *us*, which either a living God or an abstract ideal order can wield, is found in the "everlasting ruby vaults" of our own human hearts, as they happen to beat responsive and not irresponsive to the claim. So far as they do feel it when made by a living consciousness, it is life answering to life. A claim thus livingly acknowledged is acknowledged with a solidity and fulness which no thought of an "ideal" backing can render more complete; while if, on the other hand, the heart's response is withheld, the stubborn phenomenon is there of an impotence in the claims which the universe embodies, which no talk about an eternal nature of things can gloze over or dispel. An ineffective *a priori* order is as impotent a thing as an ineffective God; and in the eye of philosophy, it is as hard a thing to explain.

We may now consider that what we distinguished as the metaphysical question in ethical philosophy is sufficiently answered, and that we have learned what the words "good," "bad," and "obligation" severally mean. They mean no absolute natures, independent of personal support. They are objects of feeling and desire, which have no foothold or anchorage in Being, apart from the existence of actually living minds.

Wherever such minds exist, with judgments of good and ill, and demands upon one another, there is an ethical world in its essential features. Were all other things, gods and men and starry heavens, blotted out from this universe, and were there left but one rock with two loving souls upon it, that rock would have as thoroughly moral a constitution as any possible world which the eternities and immensities could harbor. It would be a tragic constitution, because the rock's inhabitants would die. But while they lived, there would be real good things and real bad things in the universe; there would be obligations, claims, and expectations; obediences, refusals, and disappointments; compunctions and longings for harmony to come again, and inward peace of conscience when it was restored; there would, in short, be a moral life, whose active energy would have no limit but the intensity of interest in each other with which the hero and heroine might be endowed.

We, on this terrestrial globe, so far as the visible facts go, are just like the inhabitants of such a rock. Whether a God exist, or whether no God exist, in yon blue heaven above us bent, we form at any rate an ethical republic here below. And the first reflection which this leads to is that ethics have as genuine and real a foothold in a universe where the highest consciousness is human, as in a universe where there is a God as well. "The religion of humanity" affords a basis for ethics as well as theism does. Whether the purely human system can gratify the philosopher's demand as well as the other is a different question, which we ourselves must answer ere we close.

3. The last fundamental question in *Ethics* was, it will be remembered, the casuistic question. Here we are, in a world where the existence of a divine thinker has been and perhaps always will be doubted by some of the lookers-on, and where, in spite of the presence of a large number of ideals in which human beings agree, there are a mass of others about which no general consensus obtains. It is hardly necessary to present a literary picture of this, for the facts are too well known. The wars of the flesh and the spirit in each man, the concupiscences of different individuals pursuing the same unshareable material or social prizes, the ideals which contrast so according to races, circumstances, temperaments, philosophical beliefs, etc.—all form a maze of apparently inextricable confusion with no obvious Ariadne's thread to lead one out. Yet the philosopher, just because he is a philosopher, adds his own peculiar ideal to the confusion (with which if he were willing to be a sceptic he would be passably content), and insists that over all these individual opinions there is a *system of truth* which he can discover if he only takes sufficient pains.

We stand ourselves at present in the place of that philosopher, and must not fail to realize all the features that the situation comports. In the first place we will not be sceptics; we hold to it that there is a truth to be ascertained. But in the second place we have just gained the insight that that truth cannot be a self-proclaiming set of laws, or an abstract "moral reason," but can only exist in act, or in the shape of an opinion held by some thinker really to be found. There is, however, no visible thinker invested with authority. Shall we then simply proclaim our own ideals as the lawgiving ones? No; for if we are true philosophers we must throw our own spontaneous ideals, even the dearest, impartially in with that total mass of ideals which are fairly to be judged. But how then can we as philosophers ever find a test; how avoid complete moral scepticism on the one hand, and on the other escape bringing a wayward personal standard of our own along with us, on which we simply pin our faith?

The dilemma is a hard one, nor does it grow a bit more easy as we revolve it in our minds. The entire undertaking of the philosopher obliges him to seek an impartial test. That test, however, must be incarnated in the demand of some actually existent person; and how can he pick out the person save by an act in which his own sympathies and prepossessions are implied?

One method indeed presents itself, and has as a matter of history been taken by the more serious ethical schools. If the heap of things demanded proved on inspection less chaotic than at first they seemed, if they furnished their own relative test and measure, then the casuistic problem would be solved. If it were found that all goods qua goods contained a common essence, then the amount of this essence involved in any one good would show its rank in the scale of goodness, and order could be quickly made; for this essence would be *the* good upon which all thinkers were agreed, the relatively objective and universal good that the philosopher seeks. Even his own private ideals would be measured by their share of it, and find their rightful place among the rest.

Various essences of good have thus been found and proposed as bases of the ethical system. Thus, to be a mean between two extremes; to be recognized by a special intuitive faculty; to make the agent happy for the moment; to make others as well as him happy in the long run; to add to his perfection or dignity; to harm no one; to follow from reason or flow from universal law; to be in accordance with the will of God; to promote the survival of the human species on this planet—are so many tests, each of which has been maintained by somebody to constitute the essence of all good things or actions so far as they are good.

No one of the measures that have been actually proposed has, however, given general satisfaction. Some are obviously not universally present in all cases—e.g., the character of harming no one, or that of following a universal law; for the best course is often cruel; and many acts are reckoned good on the sole condition that they be exceptions, and serve not as examples of a universal law. Other characters, such as following the will of God, are unascertainable and vague. Others again, like survival, are quite indeterminate in their consequences, and leave us in the lurch where we most need their help: a philosopher of the Sioux Nation, for example, will be certain to use the survival-criterion in a very different way from ourselves. The best, on the whole, of these marks and measures of goodness seems to be the capacity to bring happiness. But in order not to break down fatally, this test must be taken to cover innumerable acts and impulses that never aim at happiness; so that, after all, in seeking for a universal principle we inevitably are carried onward to the *most* universal principle—that *the essence of good is simply to satisfy demand.* The demand may be for anything under the sun. There is really no more ground for supposing that all our demands can be accounted for by one universal underlying kind of motive than there is ground for supposing that all physical phenomena are cases of a single law. The elementary forces in ethics are probably as plural as those of physics are. The various ideals have no common character apart from the fact that they are ideals. No single abstract principle can be so used as to yield to the philosopher anything like a scientifically accurate and genuinely useful casuistic scale.

A look at another peculiarity of the ethical universe, as we find it, will still further show us the philosopher's perplexities. As a purely theoretic problem, namely, the casuistic question would hardly ever come up at all. If the ethical philosopher were only asking after the best *imaginable* system of goods he would indeed have an easy task; for all demands as such are *prima facie* respectable, and the best simply imaginary world would be one in which *every* demand was gratified as soon as made. Such a world would, however, have to have a physical constitution entirely different from that of the one which we inhabit. It would need not only a space, but a time, of *n*-dimensions, to include all the acts and experiences incompatible with one another here below, which would then go on in conjunction—such as spending our money, yet growing rich; taking our holiday, yet getting ahead with our work; shooting and fishing, yet doing no hurt to the beasts; gaining no end of experience, yet keeping our youthful freshness of heart; and the like. There can be no question that such a system of things, however brought about, would be the absolutely ideal system; and that if a philosopher could create universes *a priori*, and provide all the mechanical conditions, that is the sort of universe which we should unhesitatingly create.

But this world of ours is made on an entirely different pattern, and the casuistic question here is most tragically practical. The actually possible in this world is vastly narrower than all that is demanded; and there is always a *pinch* between the ideal and the actual which can only be got through by leaving part of the ideal behind. There is hardly a good which we can imagine except as competing for the possession of the same bit of space and time with some other imagined good. Every end of desire that presents itself appears exclusive of some other end of desire. Shall a man drink and smoke, *or* keep his nerves in condition?—he cannot do both. Shall he follow his fancy for Amelia, *or* for Henrietta?—both cannot be the choice of his heart. Shall he have the dear old Republican party, *or* a spirit of unsophistication in public affairs?—he cannot have both, etc. So that the ethical philosopher's demand for the right scale of subordination in ideals is the fruit of an altogether practical need. Some part of the ideal must be butchered, and he needs to know which part. It is a tragic situation, and no mere speculative conundrum, with which he has to deal.

Now we are blinded to the real difficulty of the philosopher's task by the fact that we are born into a society whose ideals are largely ordered already. If we follow the ideal which is conventionally highest, the others which we butcher either die and do not return to haunt us; or if they come back and accuse us of murder, every one applauds us for turning to them a deaf ear. In other words, our environment encourages us not to be philosophers but partisans. The philosopher, however, cannot, so long as he clings to his own ideal of objectivity, rule out any ideal from being heard. He is confident, and rightly confident, that the simple taking counsel of his own intuitive preferences would be certain to end in a mutilation of the fulness of the truth. The poet Heine is said to have written "Bunsen" in the place of "*Gott*" in his copy of that author's work entitled *God in History*, so as to make it read "Bunsen in der Geschichte." Now, with no disrespect to the good and learned Baron, is it not safe to say that any single philosopher, however wide his sympathies, must be just such a *Bunsen in der Geschichte* of the moral world, so soon as he attempts to put his own ideas of order into that howling mob of desires, each struggling to get breathing-room for the ideal to which it clings? The very best of men must not only be insensible, but be ludicrously and peculiarly insensible, to many goods. As a militant, fighting free-handed that the goods to which he is sensible may not be submerged and lost from out of life, the philosopher, like every other human being, is in a natural position. But think of Zeno and of Epicurus, think of Calvin and of Paley, think of Kant and Schopenhauer, of Herbert Spencer and John Henry Newman, no longer as one-sided champions of special ideals, but as schoolmasters deciding what all must think—and what more grotesque topic could a satirist wish for on which to exercise his pen? The fabled attempt of Mrs. Partington to arrest the rising tide of the North Atlantic with her broom was a reasonable spectacle compared with their effort to substitute the content of their clean-shaven systems for that exuberant mass of goods with which all human nature is in travail, and groaning to bring to the light of day. Think, furthermore, of such individual moralists, no longer as mere schoolmasters, but as pontiffs armed with the temporal power, and having authority in every concrete case of conflict to order which good shall be butchered and which shall be suffered to survive—and the notion really turns one pale. All one's slumbering revolutionary instincts waken at the thought of any single moralist wielding such powers of life and death. Better chaos forever than an order based on any closet-philosopher's rule, even though he were the most enlightened possible member of his tribe. No! if the philosopher is to keep his judicial position, he must never become one of the parties to the fray.

What can he do, then, it will now be asked, except to fall back on scepticism and give up the notion of being a philosopher at all?

But do we not already see a perfectly definite path of escape which is open to him just because he is a philosopher, and not the champion of one particular ideal? Since everything which is demanded is by that fact a good, must not the guiding principle for ethical philosophy (since all demands conjointly cannot be satisfied in this poor world) be simply to satisfy at all times *as many demands as we can?* That act must be the best act, accordingly, which makes for the *best whole,* in the sense of awakening the least sum of dissatisfactions. In the casuistic scale, therefore, those ideals must be written highest which *prevail at the least cost,* or by whose realization the least possible number of other ideals are destroyed. Since victory and defeat there must be, the victory to be philosophically prayed for is that of the more inclusive side—of the side which even in the hour of triumph will to some degree do justice to the ideals in which the vanquished party's interests lay. The course of history is nothing but the story of men's struggles from generation to generation to find the more and more inclusive order. *Invent some manner* of realizing your own ideals which will also satisfy the alien demands—that and that only is the path of peace! Following this path, society has shaken itself into one sort of relative equilibrium after another by a series of social discoveries quite analogous to those of science. Polyandry and polygamy and slavery, private warfare and liberty to kill, judicial torture and arbitrary royal power have slowly succumbed to actually aroused complaints; and though some one's ideals are unquestionably the worse off for each improvement, yet a vastly greater total number of them find shelter in our civilized society than in the older savage ways. So far then, and up to date, the casuistic scale is made for the philosopher already far better than he can ever make it for himself. An experiment of the most searching kind has proved that the laws and usages of the land are what yield the maximum of satisfaction to the thinkers taken all together. The presumption in cases of conflict must always be in favor of the conventionally recognized good. The philosopher must be a conservative, and in the construction of his casuistic scale must put the things most in accordance with the customs of the community on top.

And yet if he be a true philosopher he must see that there is nothing final in any actually given equilibrium of human ideals, but that, as our present laws and customs have fought and conquered other past ones, so they will in their turn be overthrown by any newly discovered order which will hush up the complaints that they still give rise to, without producing others louder still. "Rules are made for man, not man for rules"—that one sentence is enough to immortalize Green's *Prolegomena to Ethics.* And although a man always risks much when he breaks away from established rules and strives to realize a larger ideal whole than they permit, yet the philosopher must allow that it is at all times open to any one to make the experiment, provided he fear not to stake his life and character upon the throw. The pinch is always here. Pent in under every system of moral rules are innumerable persons whom it weighs upon, and goods which it represses; and these are always rumbling and grumbling in the background, and ready for any issue by which they may get free. See the abuses which the institution of private property covers, so that even today it is shamelessly asserted among us that one of the prime functions of the national government is to help the adroiter citizens to grow rich. See the unnamed and unnamable sorrows which the tyranny, on the whole so beneficent, of the marriage-institution brings to so many, both of the married and the unwed. See the wholesale loss of opportunity under our *regime* of so-called equality and industrialism, with the drummer and the counter-jumper in the saddle, for so many faculties and graces which could flourish in the feudal world. See our kindliness for the humble and the outcast, how it wars with that stern weeding-out which until now has been the condition of every perfection in the breed. See everywhere the struggle and the squeeze; and everlastingly the problem how to make them less. The anarchists, nihilists, and free-lovers; the free-silverites, socialists, and single-tax men; the free-traders and civil-service reformers; the prohibitionists and anti-vivisectionists; the radical Darwinians with their idea of the suppression of the weak— these and all the conservative sentiments of society arrayed against them, are simply deciding through actual experiment by what sort of conduct the maximum amount of good can be gained and kept in this world. These experiments are to be judged, not *a priori,* but by actual finding, after the fact of their making, how much more outcry or how much appeasement comes about. What closet-solutions can possibly anticipate the result of trials made on such a scale? Or what can any superficial theorist's judgment be worth, in a world where every one of hundreds of ideals has its special champion already provided in the shape of some genius expressly born to feel it, and to fight to death in its behalf? The pure philosopher can only follow the windings of the spectacle, confident that the line of least resistance will always be towards the richer and the more inclusive arrangement, and that by one tack after another some approach to the kingdom of heaven is incessantly made.

4. All this amounts to saying that, so far as the casuistic question goes, ethical science is just like physical science, and instead of being deducible all at once from abstract principles, must simply bide its time, and be ready to revise its conclusions from day to day. The presumption of course, in both sciences, always is that the vulgarly accepted opinions are true, and the right casuistic order that which public opinion believes in; and surely it would be folly quite as great, in most of us, to strike out independently and to aim at originality in ethics as in physics. Every now and then, however, some one is born with the right to be original, and his revolutionary thought or action may bear prosperous fruit. He may replace old "laws of nature" by better ones; he may, by breaking old moral rules in a certain place, bring in a total condition of things more ideal than would have followed had the rules been kept.

On the whole, then, we must conclude that no philosophy of ethics is possible in the old-fashioned absolute sense of the term. Everywhere the ethical philosopher must wait on facts. The thinkers who create the ideals come he knows not whence, their sensibilities are evolved he knows not how; and the question as to which of two conflicting ideals will give the best universe then and there, can be answered by him only through the aid of the experience of other men. I said some time ago, in treating of the "first" question, that the intuitional moralists deserve credit for keeping most clearly to the psychological facts. They do much to spoil this merit on the whole, however, by mixing with it that dogmatic temper which, by absolute distinctions and unconditional "thou shalt nots," changes a growing, elastic, and continuous life into a superstitious system of relics and dead bones. In point of fact, there are no absolute evils, and there are no non-moral goods; and the *highest* ethical life—however few may be called to bear its burdens—consists at all times in the breaking of rules which have grown too narrow for the actual case. There is but one unconditional commandment, which is that we should seek incessantly, with fear and trembling, so to vote and to act as to bring about the very largest total universe of good which we can see. Abstract rules indeed can help; but they help the less in proportion as our intuitions are more piercing, and our vocation is the stronger for the moral life. For every real dilemma is in literal strictness a unique situation; and the exact combination of ideals realized and ideals disappointed which each decision creates is always a universe without a precedent, and for which no adequate previous rule exists. The philosopher, then, *qua* philosopher, is no better able to determine the best universe in the concrete emergency than other men. He sees, indeed, somewhat better than most men what the question always is—not a question of this good or that good simply taken, but of the two total universes with which these goods respectively belong. He knows that he must vote always for the richer universe, for the good which seems most organizable, most fit to enter into complex combinations, most apt to be a member of a more inclusive whole. But which particular universe this is he cannot know for certain in advance; he only knows that if he makes a bad mistake the cries of the wounded will soon inform him of the fact. In all this the philosopher is just like the rest of us non-philosophers, so far as we are just and sympathetic instinctively, and so far as we are open to the voice of complaint. His function is in fact indistinguishable from that of the best kind of statesman at the present day. His books upon ethics, therefore, so far as they truly touch the moral life, must more and more ally themselves with a literature which is confessedly tentative and suggestive rather than dogmatic—I mean with novels and dramas of the deeper sort, with sermons, with books on statecraft and philanthropy and social and economical reform. Treated in this way ethical treatises may be voluminous and luminous as well; but they never can be final, except in their abstractest and vaguest features; and they must more and more abandon the old-fashioned, clear-cut, and would-be "scientific" form.

5. The chief of all the reasons why concrete ethics cannot be final is that they have to wait on metaphysical and theological beliefs. I said some time back that real ethical relations existed in a purely human world. They would exist even in what we called a moral solitude if the thinker had various ideals which took hold of him in turn. His self of one day would make demands on his self of another; and some of the demands might be urgent and tyrannical, while others were gentle and easily put aside. We call the tyrannical demands *imperatives*. If we ignore these we do not hear the last of it. The good which we have wounded returns to plague us with interminable crops of consequential damages, compunctions, and regrets. Obligation can thus exist inside a single thinker's consciousness; and perfect peace can abide with him only so far as he lives according to some sort of a casuistic scale which keeps his more imperative

goods on top. It is the nature of these goods to be cruel to their rivals. Nothing shall avail when weighed in the balance against them. They call out all the mercilessness in our disposition, and do not easily forgive us if we are so soft-hearted as to shrink from sacrifice in their behalf.

The deepest difference, practically, in the moral life of man is the difference between the easy-going and the strenuous mood. When in the easy-going mood the shrinking from present ill is our ruling consideration. The strenuous mood, on the contrary, makes us quite indifferent to present ill, if only the greater ideal be attained. The capacity for the strenuous mood probably lies slumbering in every man, but it has more difficulty in some than in others in waking up. It needs the wilder passions to arouse it, the big fears, loves, and indignations; or else the deeply penetrating appeal of some one of the higher fidelities, like justice, truth, or freedom. Strong relief is a necessity of its vision; and a world where all the mountains are brought down and all the valleys are exalted is no congenial place for its habitation. This is why in a solitary thinker this mood might slumber on forever without waking. His various ideals, known to him to be mere preferences of his own, are too nearly of the same denominational value: he can play fast or loose with them at will. This too is why, in a merely human world without a God, the appeal to our moral energy falls short of its maximal stimulating power. Life, to be sure, is even in such a world a genuinely ethical symphony; but it is played in the compass of a couple of poor octaves, and the infinite scale of values fails to open up. Many of us, indeed—like Sir James Stephen in those eloquent *Essays by a Barrister*—would openly laugh at the very idea of the strenuous mood being awakened in us by those claims of remote posterity which constitute the last appeal of the religion of humanity. We do not love these men of the future keenly enough; and we love them perhaps the less the more we hear of their evolutionized perfection, their high average longevity and education, their freedom from war and crime, their relative immunity from pain and zymotic disease, and all their other negative superiorities. This is all too finite, we say; we see too well the vacuum beyond. It lacks the note of infinitude and mystery, and may all be dealt with in the don't-care mood. No need of agonizing ourselves or making others agonize for these good creatures just at present.

When, however, we believe that a God is there, and that he is one of the claimants, the infinite perspective opens out. The scale of the symphony is incalculably prolonged. The more imperative ideals now begin to speak with an altogether new objectivity and significance, and to utter the penetrating, shattering, tragically challenging note of appeal. They ring out like the call of Victor Hugo's alpine eagle, *"qui parle au precipice et que le gouffre entend,"* ["who speaks from the precipice and the abyss hears"] and the strenuous mood awakens at the sound. It saith among the trumpets, ha, ha! it smelleth the battle afar off, the thunder of the captains and the shouting. Its blood is up; and cruelty to the lesser claims, so far from being a deterrent element, does but add to the stern joy with which it leaps to answer to the greater. All through history, in the periodical conflicts of puritanism with the don't-care temper, we see the antagonism of the strenuous and genial moods, and the contrast between the ethics of infinite and mysterious obligation from on high, and those of prudence and the satisfaction of merely finite need.

The capacity of the strenuous mood lies so deep down among our natural human possibilities that even if there were no metaphysical or traditional grounds for believing in a God, men would postulate one simply as a pretext for living hard, and getting out of the game of existence its keenest possibilities of zest. Our attitude towards concrete evils is entirely different in a world where we believe there are none but finite demanders, from what it is in one where we joyously face tragedy for an infinite demander's sake. Every sort of energy and endurance, of courage and capacity for handling life's evils, is set free in those who have religious faith. For this reason the strenuous type of character will on the battlefield of human history always outwear the easy-going type, and religion will drive irreligion to the wall.

It would seem, too—and this is my final conclusion—that the stable and systematic moral universe for which the ethical philosopher asks is fully possible only in a world where there is a divine thinker with all-enveloping demands. If such a thinker existed, his way of subordinating the demands to one another would be the finally valid casuistic scale; his claims would be the most appealing; his ideal universe would be the most inclusive realizable whole. If he now exist, then actualized in his thought already must be that ethical philosophy which we seek as the pattern which our own must evermore approach. In the interests of our own ideal of systematically unified moral truth, therefore, we, as would-be philosophers, must postulate a divine thinker, and pray for the victory of the religious cause. Meanwhile, exactly what the thought of the infinite thinker may be is hidden from us even were we sure of his existence; so that our postulation of him after all serves only to let loose in us the strenuous mood. But this is what it does in all men, even those who have no interest in philosophy. The ethical philosopher, therefore, whenever he ventures to say which course of action is the best, is on no essentially different level from the common man. "See, I have set before thee this day life and good and death and evil; therefore, choose life that thou and thy seed may live"—when this challenge comes to us, it is simply our total character and personal genius that are on trial; and if we invoke any so-called philosophy, our choice and use of that also are but revelations of our personal aptitude or incapacity for moral life. From this unsparing practical ordeal no professor's lectures and no array of books can save us. The solving word, for the learned and the unlearned man alike, lies in the last resort in the dumb willingnesses and unwillingnesses of their interior characters, and nowhere else. It is not in heaven, neither is it beyond the sea; but the word is very nigh unto thee, in thy mouth and in thy heart, that thou mayest do it.

THE WILL TO BELIEVE

In the recently published *Life* by Leslie Stephen of his brother, Fitz-James, there is an account of a school to which the latter went when he was a boy. The teacher, a certain Mr. Guest, used to converse with his pupils in this wise: "Gurney, what is the difference between justification and sanctification?—Stephen, prove the omnipotence of God!" etc. In the midst of our Harvard freethinking and indifference we are prone to imagine that here at your good old orthodox College conversation continues to be somewhat upon this order; and to show you that we at Harvard have not lost all interest in these vital subjects, I have brought with me tonight something like a sermon on justification by faith to read to you,—I mean an essay in justification of faith, a defence of our right to adopt a believing attitude in religious matters, in spite of the fact that our merely logical intellect may not have been coerced. "The Will to Believe," accordingly, is the title of my paper.

I have long defended to my own students the lawfulness of voluntarily adopted faith; but as soon as they have got well imbued with the logical spirit, they have as a rule refused to admit my contention to be lawful philosophically, even though in point of fact they were personally all the time chock-full of some faith or other themselves. I am all the while, however, so profoundly convinced that my own position is correct, that your invitation has seemed to me a good occasion to make my statements more clear. Perhaps your minds will be more open than those with which I have hitherto had to deal. I will be as little technical as I can, though I must begin by setting up some technical distinctions that will help us in the end.

I. Let us give the name of *hypothesis* to anything that may be proposed to our belief; and just as the electricians speak of live and dead wires, let us speak of any hypothesis as either *live* or *dead*. A live hypothesis is one which appeals as a real possibility to him to whom it is proposed. If I ask you to believe in the Mahdi, the notion makes no electric connection with your nature,—it refuses to scintillate with any credibility at all. As an hypothesis it is completely dead. To an Arab, however (even if he be not one of the Mahdi's followers), the hypothesis is among the mind's possibilities: it is alive. This shows that deadness and liveness in an hypothesis are not intrinsic properties, but relations to the individual thinker. They are measured by his willingness to act. The maximum of liveness in an hypothesis means willingness to act irrevocably. Practically, that means belief; but there is some believing tendency wherever there is willingness to act at all.

Next, let us call the decision between two hypotheses an option. Options may be of several kinds. They may be—1, *living* or *dead*; 2, *forced* or *avoidable;* 3, *momentous* or *trivial;* and for our purposes we may call an option a *genuine* option when it is of the forced, living, and momentous kind.

1. A living option is one in which both hypotheses are live ones. If I say to you: "Be a theosophist or be a Mohammedan," it is probably a dead option, because for you neither hypothesis is likely to be alive. But if I say: "Be an agnostic or be a Christian," it is otherwise: trained as you are, each hypothesis makes some appeal, however small, to your belief.

2. Next, if I say to you: "Choose between going out with your umbrella or without it," I do not offer you a genuine option, for it is not forced. You can easily avoid it by not going out at all. Similarly, if I say, "Either love me or hate me," "Either call my theory true or call it false," your option is avoidable. You may remain indifferent to me, neither loving nor hating, and you may decline to offer any judgment as to my theory. But if I say, "Either accept this truth or go without it," I put on you a forced option, for there is no standing place outside of the alternative. Every dilemma based on a complete logical disjunction, with no possibility of not choosing, is an option of this forced kind.

3. Finally, if I were Dr. Nansen and proposed to you to join my North Pole expedition, your option would be momentous; for this would probably be your only similar opportunity, and your choice now would either exclude you from the North Pole sort of immortality altogether or put at least the chance of it into your hands. He who refuses to embrace a unique opportunity loses the prize as surely as if he tried and failed. *Per contra,* the option is trivial when the opportunity is not unique, when the stake is insignificant, or when the decision is reversible if it later prove unwise. Such trivial options abound in the scientific life. A chemist finds an hypothesis live enough to spend a year in its verification: he believes in it to that extent. But if his experiments prove inconclusive either way, he is quit for his loss of time, no vital harm being done.

It will facilitate our discussion if we keep all these distinctions well in mind.

II. The next matter to consider is the actual psychology of human opinion. When we look at certain facts, it seems as if our passional and volitional nature lay at the root of all our convictions. When we look at others, it seems as if they could do nothing when the intellect had once said its say. Let us take the latter facts up first.

Does it not seem preposterous on the very face of it to talk of our opinions being modifiable at will? Can our will either help or hinder our intellect in its perceptions of truth? Can we, by just willing it, believe that Abraham Lincoln's existence is a myth, and that the portraits of him in *McClure's Magazine* are all of some one else? Can we, by any effort of our will, or by any strength of wish that it were true, believe ourselves well and about when we are roaring with rheumatism in bed, or feel certain that the sum of the two one-dollar bills in our pocket must be a hundred dollars? We can say any of these things, but we are absolutely impotent to believe them; and of just such things is the whole fabric of the truths that we do believe in made up,—matters of fact, immediate or remote, as Hume said, and relations between ideas, which are either there or not there for us if we see them so, and which if not there cannot be put there by any action of our own.

In Pascal's *Thoughts* there is a celebrated passage known in literature as Pascal's wager. In it he tries to force us into Christianity by reasoning as if our concern with truth resembled our concern with the stakes in a game of chance. Translated freely his words are these: You must either believe or not believe that God is—which will you do? Your human reason cannot say. A game is going on between you and the nature of things which at the day of judgment will bring out either heads or tails. Weigh what your gains and your losses would be if you should stake all you have on heads, or God's existence: if you win in such case, you gain eternal beatitude; if you lose, you lose nothing at all. If there were an infinity of chances, and only one for God in this wager, still you ought to stake your all on God; for though you surely risk a finite loss by this procedure, any finite loss is reasonable, even a certain one is reasonable, if there is but the possibility of infinite gain. Go, then, and take holy water, and have masses said; belief will come and stupefy your scruples,—*Cela vous fera croire et vous abêtira* [That will make you believe and make you stupid]. Why should you not? At bottom, what have you to lose?

You probably feel that when religious faith expresses itself thus, in the language of the gaming-table, it is put to its last trumps. Surely Pascal's own personal belief in masses and holy water had far other springs; and this celebrated page of his is but an argument for others, a last desperate snatch at a weapon against the hardness of the unbelieving heart. We feel that a faith in masses and holy water adopted wilfully after such a mechanical calculation would lack the inner soul of faith's reality; and if we were ourselves in the place of the Deity, we should probably take particular pleasure in cutting off believers of this pattern from their infinite reward. It is evident that unless there be some pre-existing tendency to believe in masses and holy water, the option offered to the will by Pascal is not a living option. Certainly no Turk ever took to masses and holy water on its account; and even to us Protestants these means of salvation seem such foregone impossibilities that Pascal's logic, invoked for them specifically, leaves us unmoved. As well might the Mahdi write to us, saying, "I am the Expected One whom God has created in his effulgence. You shall be infinitely happy if you confess me; otherwise you shall be cut off from the light of the sun. Weigh, then, your infinite gain if I am genuine against your finite sacrifice if I am not!" His logic would be that of Pascal; but he would vainly use it on us, for the hypothesis he offers us is dead. No tendency to act on it exists in us to any degree.

The talk of believing by our volition seems, then, from one point of view, simply silly. From another point of view it is worse than silly, it is vile. When one turns to the magnificent edifice of the physical sciences, and sees how it was reared; what thousands of disinterested moral lives of men lie buried in its mere foundations; what patience and postponement, what choking down of preference, what submission to the icy laws of outer fact are wrought into its very stones and mortar; how absolutely impersonal it stands in its vast augustness,—then how besotted and contemptible seems every little sentimentalist who comes blowing his voluntary smoke-wreaths, and pretending to decide things from out of his private dream! Can we wonder if those bred in the rugged and manly school of science should feel like spewing such subjectivism out of their mouths? The whole system of loyalties which grow up in the schools of science go dead against its toleration; so that it is only natural that those who have caught the scientific fever should pass over to the opposite extreme, and write sometimes as if the incorruptibly truthful intellect ought positively to prefer bitterness and unacceptableness to the heart in its cup.

> It fortifies my soul to know
> That, though I perish, Truth is so—

sings Clough, while Huxley exclaims: "My only consolation lies in the reflection that, however bad our posterity may become, so far as they hold by the plain rule of not pretending to believe what they have no reason to believe, because it may be to their advantage so to pretend [the word 'pretend' is surely here redundant], they will not have reached the lowest depth of immorality." And that delicious *enfant terrible* Clifford writes: "Belief is desecrated when given to unproved and unquestioned statements for the solace and private pleasure of the believer. . . . Whoso would deserve well of his fellows in this matter will guard the purity of his belief with a very fanaticism of jealous care, lest at any time it should rest on an unworthy object, and catch a stain which can never be wiped away. . . . If [a] belief has been accepted on insufficient evidence [even though the belief be true, as Clifford on the same page explains] the pleasure is a stolen one. . . . It is sinful because it is stolen in defiance of our duty to mankind. That duty is to guard ourselves from such beliefs as from a pestilence which may shortly master our own body and then spread to the rest of the town. . . . It is wrong always, everywhere, and for every one, to believe anything upon insufficient evidence."

III. All this strikes one as healthy, even when expressed, as by Clifford, with somewhat too much of robustious pathos in the voice. Free-will and simple wishing do seem, in the matter of our credences, to be only fifth wheels to the coach. Yet if any one should thereupon assume that intellectual insight is what remains after wish and will and sentimental preference have taken wing, or that pure reason is what then settles our opinions, he would fly quite as directly in the teeth of the facts.

It is only our already dead hypotheses that our willing nature is unable to bring to life again. But what has made them dead for us is for the most part a previous action of our willing nature of an antagonistic kind. When I say "willing nature," I do not mean only such deliberate volitions as may have set up habits of belief that we cannot now escape from,—I mean all such factors of belief as fear and hope, prejudice and passion, imitation and partisanship, the circumpressure of our caste and set. As a matter of fact we find ourselves believing, we hardly know how or why. Mr. Balfour gives the name of "authority" to all those influences, born of the intellectual climate, that make hypotheses possible or impossible for us, alive or dead. Here in this room, we all of us believe in molecules and the conservation of energy, in democracy and necessary progress, in Protestant Christianity and the duty of fighting for "the doctrine of the immortal Monroe," all for no reasons worthy of the name. We see into these matters with no more inner clearness, and probably with much less, than any disbeliever in them might possess. His unconventionality would probably have some grounds to show for its conclusions; but for us, not insight, but the *prestige* of the opinions, is what makes the spark shoot from them and light up our sleeping magazines of faith. Our reason is quite satisfied, in nine hundred and ninety-nine cases out of every thousand of us, if it can find a few arguments that will do to recite in case our credulity is criticised by some one else. Our faith is faith in some one else's faith, and in the greatest matters this is most the case. Our belief in truth itself, for instance, that there is a truth, and that our minds and it are made for each other,—what is it but a passionate affirmation of desire, in which our social system backs us up? We want to have a truth; we want to believe that our experiments and studies and discussions must put us in a continually better and better position towards it; and on this line we agree to fight out our thinking lives. But if a pyrrhonistic sceptic asks us *how we know* all this, can our logic find a reply? No! certainly it cannot. It is just one volition against another,—we are willing to go in for life upon a trust or assumption which he, for his part, does not care to make.

As a rule we disbelieve all facts and theories for which we have no use. Clifford's cosmic emotions find no use for Christian feelings. Huxley belabors the bishops because there is no use for sacerdotalism in his scheme of life. Newman, on the contrary, goes over to Romanism, and finds all sorts of reasons good for staying there, because a priestly system is for him an organic need and delight. Why do so few "scientists" even look at the evidence for telepathy, so called? Because they think, as a leading biologist, now dead, once said to me, that even if such a thing were true, scientists ought to band together to keep it suppressed and concealed. It would undo the uniformity of Nature and all sorts of other things without which scientists cannot carry on their pursuits. But if this very man had been shown something which as a scientist he might do with telepathy, he might not only have examined the evidence, but even have found it good enough. This very law which the logicians would impose upon us—if I may give the name of logicians to those who would rule out our willing nature here—is based on nothing but their own natural wish to exclude all elements for which they, in their professional quality of logicians, can find no use.

Evidently, then, our non-intellectual nature does influence our convictions. There are passional tendencies and volitions which run before and others which come after belief, and it is only the latter that are too late for the fair; and they are not too late when the previous passional work has been already in their own direction. Pascal's argument, instead of being powerless, then seems a regular clincher, and is the last stroke needed to make our faith in masses and holy water complete. The state of things is evidently far from simple; and pure insight and logic, whatever they might do ideally, are not the only things that really do produce our creeds.

IV. Our next duty, having recognized this mixed-up state of affairs, is to ask whether it be simply reprehensible and pathological, or whether, on the contrary, we must treat it as a normal element in making up our minds. The thesis I defend is, briefly stated, this: *Our passional nature not only lawfully may, but must, decide an option between propositions, whenever it is a genuine option that cannot by its nature be decided on intellectual grounds; for to say, under such circumstances, "Do not decide, but leave the question open," is itself a passional decision,—just like deciding yes or no,—and is attended with the same risk of losing the truth.* The thesis thus abstractly expressed will, I trust, soon become quite clear. But I must first indulge in a bit more of preliminary work.

V. It will be observed that for the purposes of this discussion we are on "dogmatic" ground,—ground, I mean, which leaves systematic philosophical scepticism altogether out of account. The postulate that there is truth, and that it is the destiny of our minds to attain it, we are deliberately resolving to make, though the sceptic will not make it. We part company with him, therefore, absolutely, at this point. But the faith that truth exists, and that our minds can find it, may be held in two ways. We may talk of the *empiricist* way and of the *absolutist* way of believing in truth. The absolutists in this matter say that we not only can attain to knowing truth, but we can *know when* we have attained to knowing it; while the empiricists think that although we may attain it, we cannot infallibly know when. To *know* is one thing, and to know for certain *that* we know is another. One may hold to the first being possible without the second; hence the empiricists and the absolutists, although neither of them is a sceptic in the usual philosophic sense of the term, show very different degrees of dogmatism in their lives.

If we look at the history of opinions, we see that the empiricist tendency has largely prevailed in science, while in philosophy the absolutist tendency has had everything its own way. The characteristic sort of happiness, indeed, which philosophies yield has mainly consisted in the conviction felt by each successive school or system that by it bottom-certitude had been attained. "Other philosophies are collections of opinions, mostly false; my philosophy gives standing-ground forever,"—who does not recognize in this the key-note of every system worthy of the name? A system, to be a system at all, must come as a *closed* system, reversible in this or that detail, perchance, but in its essential features never!

Scholastic orthodoxy, to which one must always go when one wishes to find perfectly clear statement, has beautifully elaborated this absolutist conviction in a doctrine which it calls that of "objective evidence." If, for example, I am unable to doubt that I now exist before you, that two is less than three, or that if all men are mortal then I am mortal too, it is because these things illumine my intellect irresistibly. The final ground of this objective evidence possessed by certain propositions is the *adæquatio intellectûs nostri cum rê* [adequacy of our mind to the matter]. The certitude it brings involves an *aptitudinem ad extorquendum certum assensum* [aptitude for eliciting a definite assent] on the part of the truth envisaged, and on the side of the subject a *quietem in cognitione* [resting in knowledge], when once the object is mentally received, that leaves no possibility of doubt behind; and in the whole transaction nothing operates but the *entitas ipsa* [very entity] of the object and the *entitas ipsa* of the mind. We slouchy modern thinkers dislike to talk in Latin,—indeed, we dislike to talk in set terms at all; but at bottom our own state of mind is very much like this whenever we uncritically abandon ourselves: You believe in objective evidence, and I do. Of some things we feel that we are certain: we know, and we know that we do know. There is something that gives a click inside of us, a bell that strikes twelve, when the hands of our mental clock have swept the dial and meet over the meridian hour. The greatest empiricists among us are only empiricists on reflection: when left to their instincts, they dogmatize like infallible popes. When the Cliffords tell us how sinful it is to be Christians on such "insufficient evidence," insufficiency is really the last thing they have in mind. For them the evidence is absolutely sufficient, only it makes the other way. They believe so completely in an anti-Christian order of the universe that there is no living option: Christianity is a dead hypothesis from the start.

VI. But now, since we are all such absolutists by instinct, what in our quality of students of philosophy ought we to do about the fact? Shall we espouse and indorse it? Or shall we treat it as a weakness of our nature from which we must free ourselves, if we can?

I sincerely believe that the latter course is the only one we can follow as reflective men. Objective evidence and certitude are doubtless very fine ideals to play with, but where on this moonlit and dream-visited planet are they found? I am, therefore, myself a complete empiricist so far as my theory of human knowledge goes. I live, to be sure, by the practical faith that we must go on experiencing and thinking over our experience, for only thus can our opinions grow more true; but to hold any one of them—I absolutely do not care which—as if it never could be reinterpretable or corrigible, I believe to be a tremendously mistaken attitude, and I think that the whole history of philosophy will bear me out. There is but one indefectibly certain truth, and that is the truth that pyrrhonistic scepticism itself leaves standing,—the truth that the present phenomenon of consciousness exists. That, however, is the bare starting-point of knowledge, the mere admission of a stuff to be philosophized about. The various philosophies are but so many attempts at expressing what this stuff really is. And if we repair to our libraries what disagreement do we discover! Where is a certainly true answer found? Apart from abstract propositions of comparison (such as two and two are the same as four), propositions which tell us nothing by themselves about concrete reality, we find no proposition ever regarded by any one as evidently certain that has not either been called a falsehood, or at least had its truth sincerely questioned by some one else. The transcending of the axioms of geometry, not in play but in earnest, by certain of our contemporaries (as Zöllner and Charles H. Hinton), and the rejection of the whole Aristotelian logic by the Hegelians, are striking instances in point.

No concrete test of what is really true has ever been agreed upon. Some make the criterion external to the moment of perception, putting it either in revelation, the *consensus gentium* [agreement of the people], the instincts of the heart, or the systematized experience of the race. Others make the perceptive moment its own test,—Descartes, for instance, with his clear and distinct ideas guaranteed by the veracity of God; Reid with his "common-sense"; and Kant with his forms of synthetic judgment *a priori*. The inconceivability of the opposite; the capacity to be verified by sense; the possession of complete organic unity or self-relation, realized when a thing is its own other,—are standards which, in turn, have been used. The much lauded objective evidence is never triumphantly there; it is a mere aspiration or *Grenzbegriff*, marking the infinitely remote ideal of our thinking life. To claim that certain truths now possess it, is simply to say that when you think them true and they *are* true, then their evidence is objective, otherwise it is not. But practically one's conviction that the evidence one goes by is of the real objective brand, is only one more subjective opinion added to the lot. For what a contradictory array of opinions have objective evidence and absolute certitude been claimed! The world is rational through and through,—its existence is an ultimate brute fact; there is a personal God,—a personal God is inconceivable; there is an extramental physical world immediately known,—the mind can only know its own ideas; a moral imperative exists,—obligation is only the resultant of desires; a permanent spiritual principle is in every one,—there are only shifting states of mind; there is an endless chain of causes,—there is an absolute first cause; an eternal necessity,—a freedom; a purpose,—no purpose; a primal One,—a primal Many; a universal continuity,—an essential discontinuity in things; an infinity,—no infinity. There is this,—there is that; there is indeed nothing which some one has not thought absolutely true, while his neighbor deemed it absolutely false; and not an absolutist among them seems ever to have considered that the trouble may all the time be essential, and that the intellect, even with truth directly in its grasp, may have no infallible signal for knowing whether it be truth or no. When, indeed, one remembers that the most striking practical application to life of the doctrine of objective certitude has been the conscientious labors of the Holy Office of the Inquisition, one feels less tempted than ever to lend the doctrine a respectful ear.

But please observe, now, that when as empiricists we give up the doctrine of objective certitude, we do not thereby give up the quest or hope of truth itself. We still pin our faith on its existence, and still believe that we gain an ever better position towards it by systematically continuing to roll up experiences and think. Our great difference from the scholastic lies in the way we face. The strength of his system lies in the principles, the origin, the *terminus a quo* [starting point] of his thought; for us the strength is in the outcome, the upshot, the *terminus ad quem* [conclusion]. Not where it comes from but what it leads to is to decide. It matters not to an empiricist from what quarter an hypothesis may come to him: he may have acquired it by fair means or by foul; passion may have whispered or accident suggested it; but if the total drift of thinking continues to confirm it, that is what he means by its being true.

VII. One more point, small but important, and our preliminaries are done. There are two ways of looking at our duty in the matter of opinion,—ways entirely different, and yet ways about whose difference the theory of knowledge seems hitherto to have shown very little concern. *We must know the truth, and we must avoid error,*—these are our first and great commandments as would-be knowers; but they are not two ways of stating an identical commandment, they are two separable laws. Although it may indeed happen that when we believe the truth *A,* we escape as an incidental consequence from believing the falsehood *B,* it hardly ever happens that by merely disbelieving *B* we necessarily believe *A.* We may in escaping *B* fall into believing other falsehoods, *C* or *D,* just as bad as *B,* or we may escape *B* by not believing anything at all, not even *A.*

Believe truth! Shun error!—these, we see, are two materially different laws; and by choosing between them we may end by coloring differently our whole intellectual life. We may regard the chase for truth as paramount, and the avoidance of error as secondary; or we may, on the other hand, treat the avoidance of error as more imperative, and let truth take its chance. Clifford, in the instructive passage which I have quoted, exhorts us to the latter course. Believe nothing, he tells us, keep your mind in suspense forever, rather than by closing it on insufficient evidence incur the awful risk of believing lies. You, on the other hand, may think that the risk of being in error is a very small matter when compared with the blessings of real knowledge, and be ready to be duped many times in your investigation rather than postpone indefinitely the chance of guessing true. I myself find it impossible to go with Clifford. We must remember that these feelings of our duty about either truth or error are in any case only expressions of our passional life. Biologically considered, our minds are as ready to grind out falsehood as veracity, and he who says, "Better go without belief forever than believe a lie!" merely shows his own preponderant private horror of becoming a dupe. He may be critical of many of his desires and fears, but this fear he slavishly obeys. He cannot imagine any one questioning its binding force. For my own part, I have also a horror of being duped; but I can believe that worse things than being duped may happen to a man in this world: so Clifford's exhortation has to my ears a thoroughly fantastic sound. It is like a general informing his soldiers that it is better to keep out of battle forever than to risk a single wound. Not so are victories either over enemies or over nature gained. Our errors are surely not such awfully solemn things. In a world where we are so certain to incur them in spite of all our caution, a certain lightness of heart seems healthier than this excessive nervousness on their behalf. At any rate, it seems the fittest thing for the empiricist philosopher.

VIII.   And now, after all this introduction, let us go straight at our question. I have said, and now repeat it, that not only as a matter of fact do we find our passional nature influencing us in our opinions, but that there are some options between opinions in which this influence must be regarded both as an inevitable and as a lawful determinant of our choice.

I fear here that some of you my hearers will begin to scent danger, and lend an inhospitable ear. Two first steps of passion you have indeed had to admit as necessary,—we must think so as to avoid dupery, and we must think so as to gain truth; but the surest path to those ideal consummations, you will probably consider, is from now onwards to take no further passional step.

Well, of course, I agree as far as the facts will allow. Wherever the option between losing truth and gaining it is not momentous, we can throw the chance of *gaining truth* away, and at any rate save ourselves from any chance of *believing falsehood,* by not making up our minds at all till objective evidence has come. In scientific questions, this is almost always the case; and even in human affairs in general, the need of acting is seldom so urgent that a false belief to act on is better than no belief at all. Law courts, indeed, have to decide on the best evidence attainable for the moment, because a judge's duty is to make law as well as to ascertain it, and (as a learned judge once said to me) few cases are worth spending much time over: the great thing is to have them decided on any acceptable principle, and got out of the way. But in our dealings with objective nature we obviously are recorders, not makers, of the truth; and decisions for the mere sake of deciding promptly and getting on to the next business would be wholly out of place. Throughout the breadth of physical nature facts are what they are quite independently of us, and seldom is there any such hurry about them that the risks of being duped by believing a premature theory need be faced. The questions here are always trivial options, the hypotheses are hardly living (at any rate not living for us spectators), the choice between believing truth or falsehood is seldom forced. The attitude of sceptical balance is therefore the absolutely wise one if we would escape mistakes. What difference, indeed, does it make to most of us whether we have or have not a theory of the Rontgen rays, whether we believe or not in mind-stuff, or have a conviction about the causality of conscious states? It makes no difference. Such options are not forced on us. On every account it is better not to make them, but still keep weighing reasons *pro et contra* with an indifferent hand.

I speak, of course, here of the purely judging mind. For purposes of discovery such indifference is to be less highly recommended, and science would be far less advanced than she is if the passionate desires of individuals to get their own faiths confirmed had been kept out of the game. See for example the sagacity which Spencer and Weismann now display. On the other hand, if you want an absolute duffer in an investigation, you must, after all, take the man who has no interest whatever in its results: he is the warranted incapable, the positive fool. The most useful investigator, because the most sensitive observer, is always he whose eager interest in one side of the question is balanced by an equally keen nervousness lest he become deceived.* Science has orga-

*Compare Wilfrid Ward's Essay, "The Wish to Believe," in his *Witness to the Unseen* (New York: Macmillan, 1893).

nized this nervousness into a regular *technique,* her so-called method of verification; and she has fallen so deeply in love with the method that one may even say she has ceased to care for truth by itself at all. It is only truth as technically verified that interests her. The truth of truths might come in merely affirmative form, and she would decline to touch it. Such truth as that, she might repeat with Clifford, would be stolen in defiance of her duty to mankind. Human passions, however, are stronger than technical rules. "*Le coeur a ses raisons,*" as Pascal says, "*que la raison ne connait pas*" ["The heart has reasons which reason does not know"]; and however indifferent to all but the bare rules of the game the umpire, the abstract intellect, may be, the concrete players who furnish him the materials to judge of are usually, each one of them, in love with some pet "live hypothesis" of his own. Let us agree, however, that wherever there is no forced option, the dispassionately judicial intellect with no pet hypothesis, saving us, as it does, from dupery at any rate, ought to be our ideal.

The question next arises: Are there not somewhere forced options in our speculative questions, and can we (as men who may be interested at least as much in positively gaining truth as in merely escaping dupery) always wait with impunity till the coercive evidence shall have arrived? It seems *a priori* improbable that the truth should be so nicely adjusted to our needs and powers as that. In the great boarding-house of nature, the cakes and the butter and the syrup seldom come out so even and leave the plates so clean. Indeed, we should view them with scientific suspicion if they did.

IX. *Moral questions* immediately present themselves as questions whose solution cannot wait for sensible proof. A moral question is a question not of what sensibly exists, but of what is good, or would be good if it did exist. Science can tell us what exists; but to compare the worths, both of what exists and of what does not exist, we must consult not science, but what Pascal calls our heart. Science herself consults her heart when she lays it down that the infinite ascertainment of fact and correction of false belief are the supreme goods for man. Challenge the statement, and science can only repeat it oracularly, or else prove it by showing that such ascertainment and correction bring man all sorts of other goods which man's heart in turn declares. The question of having moral beliefs at all or not having them is decided by our will. Are our moral preferences true or false, or are they only odd biological phenomena, making things good or bad for us, but in themselves indifferent? How can your pure intellect decide? If your heart does not want a world of moral reality, your head will assuredly never make you believe in one. Mephistophelian scepticism, indeed, will satisfy the head's play-instincts much better than any rigorous idealism can. Some men (even at the student age) are so naturally cool-hearted that the moralistic hypothesis never has for them any pungent life, and in their supercilious presence the hot young moralist always feels strangely ill at ease. The appearance of knowingness is on their side, of *naïveté* and gullibility on his. Yet, in the inarticulate heart of him, he clings to it that he is not a dupe, and that there is a realm in which (as Emerson says) all their wit and intellectual superiority is no better than the cunning of a fox. Moral scepticism can no more be refuted or proved by logic than intellectual scepticism can. When we stick to it that there is truth (be it of either kind), we do so with our whole nature, and resolve to stand or fall by the results. The sceptic with his whole nature adopts the doubting attitude; but which of us is the wiser, Omniscience only knows.

Turn now from these wide questions of good to a certain class of questions of fact, questions concerning personal relations, states of mind between one man and another. *Do you like me or not?*—for example. Whether you do or not depends, in countless instances, on whether I meet you half-way, am willing to assume that you must like me, and show you trust, and expectation. The previous faith on my part in your liking's existence is in such cases what makes your liking come. But if I stand aloof, and refuse to budge an inch until I have objective evidence, until you shall have done something apt, as the absolutists say, *ad extorquendum assensum meum* [to extort my consent], ten to one your liking never comes. How many women's hearts are vanquished by the mere sanguine insistence of some man that they *must* love him! He will not consent to the hypothesis that they cannot. The desire for a certain kind of truth here brings about that special truth's existence; and so it is in innumerable cases of other sorts. Who gains promotions, boons, appointments, but the man in whose life they are seen to play the part of live hypotheses, who discounts them, sacrifices other things for their sake before they have come, and takes risks for them in advance? His faith acts on the powers above him as a claim, and creates its own verification.

A social organism of any sort whatever, large or small, is what it is because each member proceeds to his own duty with a trust that the other members will simultaneously do theirs. Wherever a desired result is achieved by the co-operation of many independent persons, its existence as a fact is a pure consequence of the precursive faith in one another of those immediately concerned. A government, an army, a commercial system, a ship, a college, an athletic team, all exist on this condition, without which not only is nothing achieved, but nothing is even attempted. A whole train of passengers (individually brave enough) will be looted by a few highwaymen, simply because the latter can count on one another, while each passenger fears that if he makes a movement of resistance, he will be shot before any one else backs him up. If we believed that the whole car-full would rise at once with us, we should each severally rise, and train-robbing would never even be attempted. There are, then, cases where a fact cannot come at all unless a preliminary faith exists in its coming. *And where faith in a fact can help create the fact*, that would be an insane logic which should say that faith running ahead of scientific evidence is the "lowest kind of immorality" into which a thinking being can fall. Yet such is the logic by which our scientific absolutists pretend to regulate our lives!

X. In truths dependent on our personal action, then, faith based on desire is certainly a lawful and possibly an indispensable thing.

But now, it will be said, these are all childish human cases, and have nothing to do with great cosmical matters, like the question of religious faith. Let us then pass on to that. Religions differ so much in their accidents that in discussing the religious question we must make it very generic and broad. What then do we now mean by the religious hypothesis? Science says things are; morality says some things are better than other things; and religion says essentially two things.

First, she says that the best things are the more eternal things, the overlapping things, the things in the universe that throw the last stone, so to speak, and say the final word. "Perfection is eternal,"—this phrase of Charles Secrétan seems a good way of putting this first affirmation of religion, an affirmation which obviously cannot yet be verified scientifically at all.

The second affirmation of religion is that we are better off even now if we believe her first affirmation to be true.

Now, let us consider what the logical elements of this situation are *in case the religious hypothesis in both its branches be really true*. (Of course, we must admit that possibility at the outset. If we are to discuss the question at all, it must involve a living option. If for any of you religion be a hypothesis that cannot, by any living possibility be true, then you need go no farther. I speak to the "saving remnant" alone.) So proceeding, we see, first, that religion offers itself as a *momentous* option. We are supposed to gain, even now, by our belief, and to lose by our non-belief, a certain vital good. Secondly, religion is a *forced* option, so far as that good goes. We cannot escape the issue by remaining sceptical and waiting for more light, because, although we do avoid error in that way *if religion be untrue,* we lose the good, *if it be true,* just as certainly as if we positively chose to disbelieve. It is as if a man should hesitate indefinitely to ask a certain woman to marry him because he was not perfectly sure that she would prove an angel after he brought her home. Would he not cut himself off from that particular angel-possibility as decisively as if he went and married some one else? Scepticism, then, is not avoidance of option; it is option of a certain particular kind of risk. *Better risk loss of truth than chance of error,*—that is your faith-vetoer's exact position. He is actively playing his stake as much as the believer is; he is backing the field against the religious hypothesis, just as the believer is backing the religious hypothesis against the field. To preach scepticism to us as a duty until "sufficient evidence" for religion be found, is tantamount therefore to telling us, when in presence of the religious hypothesis, that to yield to our fear of its being error is wiser and better than to yield to our hope that it may be true. It is not intellect against all passions, then; it is only intellect with one passion laying down its law. And by what, forsooth, is the supreme wisdom of this passion warranted? Dupery for dupery, what proof is there that dupery through hope is so much worse than dupery through fear? I, for one, can see no proof; and I simply refuse obedience to the scientist's command to imitate his kind of option, in a case where my own stake is important enough to give me the right to choose my own form of risk. If religion be true and the evidence for it be still insufficient, I do not wish, by putting your extinguisher upon my nature (which feels to me as if it had after all some business in this matter), to forfeit my sole chance in life of getting upon the winning side,—that chance depending, of course, on my willingness to run the risk of acting as if my passional need of taking the world religiously might be prophetic and right.

All this is on the supposition that it really may be prophetic and right, and that, even to us who are discussing the matter, religion is a live hypothesis which may be true. Now, to most of us religion comes in a still further way that makes a veto on our active faith even more illogical. The more perfect and more eternal aspect of the universe is represented in our religions as having personal form. The universe is no longer a mere *It* to us, but a *Thou,* if we are religious; and any relation that may be possible from person to person might be possible here. For instance, although in one sense we are passive portions of the universe, in another we show a curious autonomy, as if we were small active centres on our own account. We feel, too, as if the appeal of religion to us were made to our own active good-will, as if evidence might be forever withheld from us unless we met the hypothesis half-way. To take a trivial illustration: just as a man who in a company of gentlemen made no advances, asked a warrant for every concession, and believed no one's word without proof, would cut himself off by such churlishness from all the social rewards that a more trusting spirit would earn,—so here, one who should shut himself up in snarling logicality and try to make the gods extort his recognition willy-nilly, or not get it at all, might cut himself off forever from his only opportunity of making the gods' acquaintance. This feeling, forced on us we know not whence, that by obstinately believing that there are gods (although not to do so would be so easy both for our logic and our life) we are doing the universe the deepest service we can, seems part of the living essence of the religious hypothesis. If the hypothesis were true in all its parts, including this one, then pure intellectualism, with its veto on our making willing advances, would be an absurdity; and some participation of our sympathetic nature would be logically required. I, therefore, for one, cannot see my way to accepting the agnostic rules for truth-seeking, or wilfully agree to keep my willing nature out of the game. I cannot do so for this plain reason, that *a rule of thinking which would absolutely prevent me from acknowledging certain kinds of truth if those kinds of truth were really there, would be an irrational rule*. That for me is the long and short of the formal logic of the situation, no matter what the kinds of truth might materially be.

I confess I do not see how this logic can be escaped. But sad experience makes me fear that some of you may still shrink from radically saying with me, *in abstracto,* that we have the right to believe at our own risk any hypothesis that is live enough to tempt our will. I suspect, however, that if this is so, it is because you have got away from the abstract logical point of view altogether, and are thinking (perhaps without realizing it) of some particular religious hypothesis which for you is dead. The freedom to "believe what we will" you apply to the case of some patent superstition; and the faith you think of is the faith defined by the schoolboy when he said, "Faith is when you believe something that you know ain't true." I can only repeat that this is misapprehension. *In concreto,* the freedom to believe can only cover living options which the intellect of the individual cannot by itself resolve; and living options never seem absurdities to him who has them to consider. When I look at the religious question as it really puts itself to concrete men, and when I think of all the possibilities which both practically and theoretically it involves, then this command that we shall put a stopper on our heart, instincts, and courage, and *wait*—acting of course meanwhile more or less as if religion were not true*—till doomsday, or till such time as our intellect and senses working together may have raked in evidence enough,—this command, I say, seems to me the queerest idol ever manufactured in the philosophic cave. Were we scholastic absolutists, there might be more excuse. If we had an infallible intellect with its objective certitudes, we might feel ourselves disloyal to such a perfect organ of knowledge in not trusting to it exclusively, in not waiting for its releasing word. But if we are empiricists, if we believe that no bell in us tolls to let us know for certain when truth is in our grasp, then it seems a piece of idle fantasticality to preach so solemnly our duty of waiting for the bell. Indeed we *may* wait if we will,—I hope you do not think that I am denying that,—but if we do so, we do so at our peril as much as if we believed. In either case we *act*, taking our life in our hands. No one of us ought to issue vetoes to the other, nor should we bandy words of abuse. We ought, on the contrary, delicately and profoundly to respect one another's mental freedom: then only shall we bring about the intellectual republic; then only shall we have that spirit of inner tolerance without which all our outer tolerance is soulless, and which is empiricism's glory; then only shall we live and let live, in speculative as well as in practical things.

I began by a reference to Fitz James Stephen; let me end by a quotation from him. "What do you think of yourself? What do you think of the world? . . . These are questions with which all must deal as it seems good to them. They are riddles of the Sphinx, and in

---

*Since belief is measured by action, he who forbids us to believe religion to be true, necessarily also forbids us to act as we should if we did believe it to be true. The whole defence of religious faith hinges upon action. If the action required or inspired by the religious hypothesis is in no way different from that dictated by the naturalistic hypothesis, then religious faith is a pure superfluity, better pruned away, and controversy about its legitimacy is a piece of idle trifling, unworthy of serious minds. I myself believe, of course, that the religious hypothesis gives to the world an expression which specifically determines our reactions, and makes them in a large part unlike what they might be on a purely naturalistic scheme of belief.

some way or other we must deal with them. . . . In all important transactions of life we have to take a leap in the dark. . . . If we decide to leave the riddles unanswered, that is a choice; if we waver in our answer, that, too, is a choice: but whatever choice we make, we make it at our peril. If a man chooses to turn his back altogether on God and the future, no one can prevent him; no one can show beyond reasonable doubt that *he* is mistaken. If a man thinks otherwise and acts as he thinks, I do not see that any one can prove that he is mistaken. Each must act as he thinks best; and if he is wrong, so much the worse for him. We stand on a mountain pass in the midst of whirling snow and blinding mist, through which we get glimpses now and then of paths which may be deceptive. If we stand still we shall be frozen to death. If we take the wrong road we shall be dashed to pieces. We do not certainly know whether there is any right one. What must we do? 'Be strong and of a good courage.' Act for the best, hope for the best, and take what comes. . . . If death ends all, we cannot meet death better."*

PRAGMATISM (in part)

Lecture I: The Present Dilemma in Philosophy

*   *   *

Philosophy is at once the most sublime and the most trivial of human pursuits. It works in the minutest crannies and it opens out the widest vistas. It "bakes no bread," as has been said, but it can inspire our souls with courage; and repugnant as its manners, its doubting and challenging, its quibbling and dialectics, often are to common people, no one of us can get along without the far-flashing beams of light it sends over the world's perspectives. These illuminations at least, and the contrast-effects of darkness and mystery that accompany them, give to what it says an interest that is much more than professional.

The history of philosophy is to a great extent that of a certain clash of human temperaments. Undignified as such a treatment may seem to some of my colleagues, I shall have to take account of this clash and explain a good many of the divergencies of philosophers by it. Of whatever temperament a professional philosopher is, he tries, when philosophizing, to sink the fact of his temperament. Temperament is no conventionally recognized reason, so he urges impersonal reasons only for his conclusions. Yet his temperament really gives him a stronger bias than any of his more strictly objective premises. It loads the evidence for him one way or the other, making for a more sentimental or a more hard-hearted view of the universe, just as this fact or that principle would. He *trusts* his temperament. Wanting a universe that suits it, he believes in any representation of the universe that does suit it. He feels men of opposite temper to be out of key with the world's character, and in his heart considers them incompetent

*Liberty, Equality, Fraternity, p. 353, 2nd edition (London, 1874).

and "not in it," in the philosophic business, even though they may far excel him in dialectical ability.

Yet in the forum he can make no claim, on the bare ground of his temperament, to superior discernment or authority. There arises thus a certain insincerity in our philosophic discussions: the potentest of all our premises is never mentioned. I am sure it would contribute to clearness if in these lectures we should break this rule and mention it, and I accordingly feel free to do so.

Of course I am talking here of very positively marked men, men of radical idiosyncracy, who have set their stamp and likeness on philosophy and figure in its history. Plato, Locke, Hegel, Spencer, are such temperamental thinkers. Most of us have, of course, no very definite intellectual temperament, we are a mixture of opposite ingredients, each one present very moderately. We hardly know our own preferences in abstract matters; some of us are easily talked out of them, and end by following the fashion or taking up with the beliefs of the most impressive philosopher in our neighborhood, whoever he may be. But the one thing that has *counted* so far in philosophy is that a man should *see* things, see them straight in his own peculiar way, and be dissatisfied with any opposite way of seeing them. There is no reason to suppose that this strong temperamental vision is from now onward to count no longer in the history of man's beliefs.

Now the particular difference of temperament that I have in mind in making these remarks is one that has counted in literature, art, government, and manners as well as in philosophy. In manners we find formalists and free-and-easy persons. In government, authoritarians and anarchists. In literature, purists or academicals, and realists. In art, classics and romantics. You recognize these contrasts as familiar; well, in philosophy we have a very similar contrast expressed in the pair of terms "rationalist" and "empiricist," "empiricist" meaning your lover of facts in all their crude variety, "rationalist" meaning your devotee to abstract and eternal principles. No one can live an hour without both facts and principles, so it is a difference rather of emphasis; yet it breeds antipathies of the most pungent character between those who lay the emphasis differently; and we shall find it extraordinarily convenient to express a certain contrast in men's ways of taking their universe, by talking of the "empiricist" and of the "rationalist" temper. These terms make the contrast simple and massive.

More simple and massive then are usually the men of whom the terms are predicated. For every sort of permutation and combination is possible in human nature; and if I now proceed to define more fully what I have in mind when I speak of rationalists and empiricists, by adding to each of those titles some secondary qualifying characteristics, I beg you to regard my conduct as to a certain extent arbitrary. I select types of combination that nature offers very frequently, but by no means uniformly, and I select them solely for their convenience in helping me to my ulterior purpose of characterizing pragmatism. Historically we find the terms "intellectualism" and "sensationalism" used as synonyms of "rationalism" and "empiricism." Well, nature seems to combine most frequently with intellectualism an idealistic and optimistic tendency. Empiricists on the other hand are not uncommonly materialistic, and their optimism is apt to be decidedly conditional and tremulous. Rationalism is always monistic. It starts from wholes and universals, and makes much of the unity of things. Empiricism starts from the parts, and makes of the whole a collection—is not averse therefore to calling itself pluralistic. Rationalism usually considers itself more religious than empiricism, but there is much to say about this claim, so I merely mention it. It is a true claim when the individual rationalist is what is called a man of feeling, and when the individual empiricist prides himself on being hard-headed. In that case the rationalist will usually also be in favor of what is called free-will, and the empiricist will be a fatalist—I use the terms most popularly current. The rationalist finally will be of dogmatic temper in his affirmations, while the empiricist may be more sceptical and open to discussion.

I will write these traits down in two columns. I think you will practically recognize the two types of mental make-up that I mean if I head the columns by the titles "tender-minded" and "tough-minded" respectively.

The Tender-Minded	**The Tough-Minded**
Rationalistic (going by "principles"),	Empiricist (going by "facts"),
Intellectualistic,	Sensationalistic,
Idealistic,	Materialistic,
Optimistic,	Pessimistic,
Religious,	Irreligious,
Free-willist,	Fatalistic,
Monistic,	Pluralistic,
Dogmatical.	Skeptical.

Pray postpone for a moment the question whether the two contrasted mixtures which I have written down are each inwardly coherent and self-consistent or not. . . . It suffices for our immediate purpose that tender-minded and tough-minded people, characterized as I have written them down, do both exist. Each of you probably knows some well-marked example of each type, and you know what each example thinks of the example on the other side of the line. They have a low opinion of each other. Their antagonism, whenever as individuals their temperaments have been intense, has formed in all ages a part of the philosophic atmosphere of the time. It forms a part of the philosophic atmosphere to-day. The tough think of the tender as sentimentalists and softheads. The tender feel the tough to be unrefined, callous, or brutal. Their mutual reaction is very much like that that takes place when Bostonian tourists mingle with a population like that of Cripple Creek. Each type believes the other to be inferior to itself; but disdain in the one case is mingled with amusement, in the other it has a dash of fear.

Now, as I have already insisted, few of us are tender-foot Bostonians pure and simple, and few are typical Rocky Mountain toughs, in philosophy. Most of us have a hankering for the good things on both sides of the line. Facts are good, of course—give us lots of facts. Principles are good—give us plenty of principles. The world is indubitably one if you look at it in one way, but as indubitably is it many, if you look at it in another. It is both one and many—let us adopt a sort of pluralistic monism. Everything of course is necessarily determined, and yet of course our wills are free: a sort of free-will determinism is the true philosophy. The evil of the parts is undeniable, but the whole can't be evil: so practical pessimism may be combined with metaphysical optimism. And so forth—your ordinary philosophic layman never being a radical, never straightening out his system, but living vaguely in one plausible compartment of it or another to suit the temptations of successive hours.

But some of us are more than mere laymen in philosophy. We are worthy of the name of amateur athletes, and are vexed by too much inconsistency and vacillation in our creed. We cannot preserve a good intellectual conscience so long as we keep mixing incompatibles from opposite sides of the line.

*   *   *

LECTURE II: WHAT PRAGMATISM MEANS

Some years ago, being with a camping party in the mountains, I returned from a solitary ramble to find every one engaged in a ferocious metaphysical dispute. The *corpus* of the dispute was a squirrel—a live squirrel supposed to be clinging to one side of a tree-trunk; while over against the tree's opposite side a human being was imagined to stand. This human witness tries to get sight of the squirrel by moving rapidly round the tree, but no matter how fast he goes, the squirrel moves as fast in the opposite direction, and always keeps the tree between himself and the man, so that never a glimpse of him is caught. The resultant metaphysical problem now is this: *Does the man go round the squirrel or not?* He goes round the tree, sure enough, and the squirrel is on the tree; but does he go round the squirrel? In the unlimited leisure of the wilderness, discussion had been worn threadbare. Everyone had taken sides, and was obstinate; and the numbers on both sides were even. Each side, when I appeared therefore appealed to me to make it a majority. Mindful of the scholastic adage that whenever you meet a contradiction you must make a distinction, I immediately sought and found one, as follows: "Which party is right," I said, "depends on what you *practically mean* by 'going round' the squirrel. If you mean passing from the north of him to the east, then to the south, then to the west, and then to the north of him again, obviously the man does go round him, for he occupies these successive positions. But if on the contrary you mean being first in front of him, then on the right of him, then behind him, then on his left, and finally in front again, it is quite as obvious that the man fails to go round him, for by the compensating movements the squirrel makes, he keeps his belly turned towards the man all the time, and his back turned away. Make the distinction, and there is no occasion for any farther dispute. You are both right and both wrong according as you conceive the verb 'to go round' in one practical fashion or the other."

Although one or two of the hotter disputants called my speech a shuffling evasion, saying they wanted no quibbling or scholastic hair-splitting, but meant just plain honest English "round," the majority seemed to think that the distinction had assuaged the dispute.

I tell this trivial anecdote because it is a peculiarly simple example of what I wish now to speak of as *the pragmatic method*. The pragmatic method is primarily a method of settling metaphysical disputes that otherwise might be interminable. Is the world one or many?—fated or free?—material or spiritual?—here are notions either of which may or may not hold good of the world; and disputes over such notions are unending. The pragmatic method in such cases is to try to interpret each notion by tracing its respective practical consequences. What difference would it practically make to any one if this notion rather than that notion were true? If no practical difference whatever can be traced, then the alternatives mean practically the same thing, and all dispute is idle. Whenever a dispute is serious, we ought to be able to show some practical difference that must follow from one side or the other's being right.

A glance at the history of the idea will show you still better what pragmatism means. The term is derived from the same Greek word ⟨*pragma*⟩, meaning action, from which our words "practice" and "practical" come. It was first introduced into philosophy by Mr. Charles Peirce in 1878. In an article entitled "How to Make Our Ideas Clear," in the *Popular Science Monthly* for January of that year. Mr. Peirce, after pointing out that our beliefs are really rules for action, said that, to develop a thought's meaning, we need only determine what conduct it is fitted to produce: that conduct is for us its sole significance. And the tangible fact at the root of all our thought-distinctions, however subtle, is that there is no one of them so fine as to consist in anything but a possible difference of practice. To attain perfect clearness in our thoughts of an object, then, we need only consider what conceivable effects of a practical kind the object may involve—what sensations we are to expect from it, and what reactions we must prepare. Our conception of these effects, whether immediate or remote, is then for us the whole of our conception of the object, so far as that conception has positive significance at all.

This is the principle of Peirce, the principle of pragmatism. It lay entirely unnoticed by any one for twenty years, until I, in an address before Professor Howison's philosophical union at the University of California, brought it forward again and made a special application of it to religion. By that date (1898) the times seemed ripe for its reception. The word "pragmatism" spread, and at present it fairly spots the pages of the philosophic journals. On all hands we find the "pragmatic movement" spoken of, sometimes with respect, sometimes with contumely, seldom with clear understanding. It is evident that the term applies itself conveniently to a number of tendencies that hitherto have lacked a collective name, and that it has "come to stay."

To take in the importance of Peirce's principle, one must get accustomed to applying it to concrete cases. I found a few years ago that Ostwald, the illustrious Leipzig chemist, had been making perfectly distinct use of the principle of pragmatism in his lectures on the philosophy of science, though he had not called it by that name.

"All realities influence our practice," he wrote me, "and that influence is their meaning for us. I am accustomed to put questions to my classes in this way: In what respects would the world be different if this alternative or that were true? If I can find nothing that would become different, then the alternative has no sense."

That is, the rival views mean practically the same thing, and meaning, other than practical, there is for us none. Ostwald in a published lecture gives this example of what he means. Chemists have long wrangled over the inner constitution of certain bodies called "tautomerous." Their properties seemed equally consistent with the notion that an instable hydrogen atom oscillates inside of them, or that they are instable mixtures of two bodies. Controversy raged, but never was decided. "It would never have begun," says Ostwald, "if the combatants had asked themselves what particular experimental fact could have been made different by one or the other view being correct. For it would then have appeared that no difference of fact could possibly ensue; and the quarrel was as unreal as if, theorizing in primitive times about the raising of dough by yeast, one party should have invoked a 'brownie,' while another insisted on an 'elf' as the true cause of the phenomenon."*

It is astonishing to see how many philosophical disputes collapse into insignificance the moment you subject them to this simple test of tracing a concrete consequence. There can *be* no difference anywhere that doesn't *make* a difference elsewhere—no difference in abstract truth that doesn't express itself in a difference in concrete fact and in conduct consequent upon that fact, imposed on somebody, somehow, somewhere, and somewhen. The whole function of philosophy ought to be to find

---

*"Theorie und Praxis," *Zeitsch. des Oesterreichischen Ingenieur u. Architecten-Vereines,* 1905, Nr. 4 u. 6. I find a still more radical pragmatism than Ostwald's in an address by Professor W.S. Franklin: "I think that the sickliest notion of physics, even if a student gets it, is that it is 'the science of masses, molecules, and the ether.' And I think that the healthiest notion, even if a student does not wholly get it, is that physics is the science of the ways of taking hold of bodies and pushing them!" (*Science,* January 2, 1903.)

out what definite difference it will make to you and me, at definite instants of our life, if this world-formula or that world-formula be the true one.

There is absolutely nothing new in the pragmatic method. Socrates was an adept at it. Aristotle used it methodically. Locke, Berkeley, and Hume made momentous contributions to truth by its means. Shadworth Hodgson keeps insisting that realities are only what they are "known as." But these forerunners of pragmatism used it in fragments: they were preluders only. Not until in our time has it generalized itself, become conscious of a universal mission, pretended to a conquering destiny. I believe in that destiny, and I hope I may end by inspiring you with my belief.

Pragmatism represents a perfectly familiar attitude in philosophy, the empiricist attitude, but it represents it, as it seems to me, both in a more radical and in a less objectionable form than it has ever yet assumed. A pragmatist turns his back resolutely and once for all upon a lot of inveterate habits dear to professional philosophers. He turns away from abstraction and insufficiency, from verbal solutions, from bad *a priori* reasons, from fixed principles, closed systems, and pretended absolutes and origins. He turns towards concreteness and adequacy, towards facts, towards action and towards power. That means the empiricist temper regnant and the rationalist temper sincerely given up. It means the open air and possibilities of nature, as against dogma, artificiality, and the pretence of finality in truth.

At the same time it does not stand for any special results. It is a method only. But the general triumph of that method would mean an enormous change in what I called in my last lecture the "temperament" of philosophy. Teachers of the ultra-rationalistic type would be frozen out, much as the courtier type is frozen out in republics, as the ultramontane type of priest is frozen out in protestant lands. Science and metaphysics would come much nearer together, would in fact work absolutely hand in hand.

Metaphysics has usually followed a very primitive kind of quest. You know how men have always hankered after unlawful magic, and you know what a great part in magic words have always played. If you have his name, or the formula of incantation that binds him, you can control the spirit, genie, afrite, or whatever the power may be. Solomon knew the names of all the spirits, and having their names, he held them subject to his will. So the universe has always appeared to the natural mind as a kind of enigma, of which the key must be sought in the shape of some illuminating or power-bringing word or name. That word names the universe's *principle*, and to possess it is after a fashion to possess the universe itself. "God," "Matter," "Reason," "the Absolute," "Energy," are so many solving names. You can rest when you have them. You are at the end of your metaphysical quest.

But if you follow the pragmatic method, you cannot look on any such word as closing your quest. You must bring out of each word its practical cash-value, set it at work within the stream of your experience. It appears less as a solution, then, than as a program for more work, and more particularly as an indication of the ways in which existing realities may be *changed*.

Theories thus become instruments, not answers to enigmas, in which we can rest. We don't lie back upon them, we move forward, and, on occasion, make nature over again by their aid. Pragmatism unstiffens all our theories, limbers them up and sets each one at work. Being nothing essentially new, it harmonizes with many ancient philosophic tendencies. It agrees with nominalism for instance, in always appealing to particulars; with utilitarianism in emphasizing practical aspects; with positivism in its disdain for verbal solutions, useless questions and metaphysical abstractions.

All these, you see, are *anti-intellectualist* tendencies. Against rationalism as a pretension and a method pragmatism is fully armed and militant. But, at the outset, at least, it stands for no particular results. It has no dogmas, and no doctrines save its method. As the young Italian pragmatist Papini has well said, it lies in the midst of our theories, like a corridor in a hotel. Innumerable chambers open out of it. In one you may find a man writing an atheistic volume; in the next some one on his knees praying for faith and strength; in a third a chemist investigating a body's properties. In a fourth a system of idealistic metaphysics is being excogitated; in a fifth the impossibility of metaphysics is being shown. But they all own the corridor, and all must pass through it if they want a practicable way of getting into or out of their respective rooms.

No particular results then, so far, but only an attitude of orientation, is what the pragmatic method means. *The attitude of looking away from first things, principles, "categories," supposed necessities; and of looking towards last things, fruits, consequences, facts.*

So much for the pragmatic method! You may say that I have been praising it rather than explaining it to you, but I shall presently explain it abundantly enough by showing how it works on some familiar problems. Meanwhile the word pragmatism has come to be used in a still wider sense, as meaning also a certain *theory of truth*. I mean to give a whole lecture to the statement of that theory, after first paving the way, so I can be very brief now. But brevity is hard to follow, so I ask for your redoubled attention for a quarter of an hour. If much remains obscure, I hope to make it clearer in the later lectures.

One of the most successfully cultivated branches of philosophy in our time is what is called inductive logic, the study of the conditions under which our sciences have evolved. Writers on this subject have begun to show a singular unanimity as to what the laws of nature and elements of fact mean, when formulated by mathematicians, physicists and chemists. When the first mathematical, logical, and natural uniformities, the first laws, were discovered, men were so carried away by the clearness, beauty and simplification that resulted, that they believed themselves to have deciphered authentically the eternal thoughts of the Almighty. His mind also thundered and reverberated in syllogisms. He also thought in conic sections, squares and roots and ratios, and geometrized like Euclid. He made Kepler's laws for the planets to follow; he made velocity increase proportionally to the time in falling bodies; he made the law of the sines for light to obey when refracted; he established the classes, orders, families and genera of plants and animals, and fixed the distances between them. He thought the archetypes of all things, and devised their variations; and when we rediscover any one of these his wondrous institutions, we seize his mind in its very literal intention.

But as the sciences have developed farther, the notion has gained ground that most, perhaps all, of our laws are only approximations. The laws themselves, moreover, have grown so numerous that there is no counting them; and so many rival formulations are proposed in all the branches of science that investigators have become accustomed to the notion that no theory is absolutely a transcript of reality, but that any one of them may from some point of view be useful. Their great use is to summarize old facts and to lead to new ones. They are only a man-made language, a conceptual shorthand, as some one calls them, in which we write our reports of nature; and languages, as is well known, tolerate much choice of expression and many dialects.

Thus human arbitrariness has driven divine necessity from scientific logic. If I mention the names of Sigwart, Mach, Ostwald, Pearson, Milhaud, Poincare, Duhem, Ruyssen, those of you who are students will easily identify the tendency I speak of, and will think of additional names.

Riding now on the front of this wave of scientific logic Messrs. Schiller and Dewey appear with their pragmatistic account of what truth everywhere signifies.

Everywhere, these teachers say, "truth" in our ideas and beliefs means the same thing that it means in science. It means, they say, nothing but this, *that ideas (which themselves are but parts of our experience) become true just in so far as they help us to get into satisfactory relation with other parts of our experience,* to summarize them and get about among them by conceptual short-cuts instead of following the interminable succession of particular phenomena. Any idea upon which we can ride, so to speak; any idea that will carry us prosperously from any one part of our experience to any other part, linking things satisfactorily, working securely, simplifying, saving labor; is true for just so much, true in so far forth, true *instrumentally*. This is the "instrumental" view of truth taught so successfully at Chicago, the view that truth in our ideas means their power to "work," promulgated so brilliantly at Oxford.

Messrs. Dewey, Schiller and their allies, in reaching this general conception of all truth, have only followed the example of geologists, biologists and philologists. In the establishment of these other sciences, the successful stroke was always to take some simple process actually observable in operation—as denudation by weather, say, or variation from parental type, or change of dialect by incorporation of new words and pronunciations—and then to generalize it, making it apply to all times, and produce great results by summating its effects through the ages.

The observable process which Schiller and Dewey particularly singled out for generalization is the familiar one by which any individual settles into new opinions. The process here is always the same. The individual has a stock of old opinions already, but he meets a new experience that puts them to a strain. Somebody contradicts them; or in a reflective moment he discovers that they contradict each other; or he hears of facts with which they are incompatible; or desires arise in him which they cease to satisfy. The result is an inward trouble to which his mind till then had been a stranger, and from which he seeks to escape by modifying his previous mass of opinions. He saves as much of it as he can, for in this matter of belief we are all extreme conservatives. So he tries to change first this opinion, and then that (for they resist change very variously), until at last some new idea comes up which he can graft upon the ancient stock with a minimum of disturbance of the latter, some idea that mediates between the stock and the new experience and runs them into one another most felicitously and expediently.

This new idea is then adopted as the true one. It preserves the older stock of truths with a minimum of modification, stretching them just enough to make them admit the novelty, but conceiving that in ways as familiar as the case leaves possible. An *outrée* [exaggerated] explanation, violating all our preconceptions, would never pass for a true account of a novelty. We should scratch round industriously till we found something less excentric. The most violent revolutions in an individual's beliefs leave most of his old order standing. Time and space, cause and effect, nature and history, and one's own biography remain untouched. New truth is always a go-between, a smoother-over of transitions. It marries old opinion to new fact so as ever to show a minimum of jolt, a maximum of continuity. We hold a theory true just in proportion to its success in solving this "problem of maxima and minima." But success in solving this problem is eminently a matter of approximation. We say this theory solves it on the whole more satisfactorily than that theory; but that means more satisfactorily to ourselves, and individuals will emphasize their points of satisfaction differently. To a certain degree, therefore, everything here is plastic.

The point I now urge you to observe particularly is the part played by the older truths. Failure to take account of it is the source of much of the unjust criticism levelled against pragmatism. Their influence is absolutely controlling. Loyalty to them is the first principle—in most cases it is the only principle; for by far the most usual way of handling phenomena so novel that they would make for a serious rearrangement of our preconception is to ignore them altogether, or to abuse those who bear witness for them.

You doubtless wish examples of this process of truth's growth, and the only trouble is their superabundance. The simplest case of new truth is of course the mere numerical addition of new kinds of facts, or of new single facts of old kinds, to our experience—an addition that involves no alteration in the old beliefs. Day follows day, and its contents are simply added. The new contents themselves are not true, they simply *come* and *are*. Truth is *what we say about them*, and when we say that they have come, truth is satisfied by the plain additive formula.

But often the day's contents oblige a rearrangement. If I should now utter piercing shrieks and act like a maniac on this platform, it would make many of you revise your ideas as to the probable worth of my philosophy. "Radium" came the other day as part of the day's content, and seemed for a moment to contradict our ideas of the whole order of nature, that order having come to be identified with what is called the conservation of energy. The mere sight of radium paying heat away indefinitely out of its own pocket seemed to violate that conservation. What to think? If the radiations from it were nothing but an escape of unsuspected "potential" energy, pre-existent inside of the atoms, the principle of conservation would be saved. The discovery of "helium" as the radiation's outcome, opened a way to this belief. So Ramsay's view is generally held to be true, because, although it extends our old ideas of energy, it causes a minimum of alteration in their nature.

I need not multiply instances. A new opinion counts as "true" just in proportion as it gratifies the individual's desire to assimilate the novel in his experience to his beliefs in stock. It must both lean on old truth and grasp new fact; and its success (as I said a moment ago) in doing this, is a matter for the individual's appreciation. When old truth grows, then, by new truth's addition, it is for subjective reasons. We are in the process and obey the reasons. That new idea is truest which performs most felicitously its function of satisfying our double urgency. It makes itself true, gets itself classed as true, by the way it works; grafting itself then upon the ancient body of truth, which thus grows much as a tree grows by the activity of a new layer of cambium.

Now Dewey and Schiller proceed to generalize this observation and to apply it to the most ancient parts of truth. They also once were plastic. They also were called true for human reasons. They also mediated between still earlier truths and what in those days were novel observations. Purely objective truth, truth in whose establishment the function of giving human satisfaction in marrying previous parts of experience with newer parts played no role whatever, is nowhere to be found. The reasons why we call things true is the reason why they *are* true, for "to be true" *means* only to perform this marriage-function.

The trail of the human serpent is thus over everything. Truth independent; truth that we *find* merely; truth no longer malleable to human need; truth incorrigible, in a word; such truth exists indeed superabundantly—or is supposed to exist by rationalistically minded thinkers; but then it means only the dead heart of the living tree, and its being there means only that truth also has its paleontology, and its "prescription," and may grow stiff with years of veteran service and petrified in men's regard by sheer antiquity. But how plastic even the oldest truths nevertheless really are has been vividly shown in our day by the transformation of logical and mathematical ideas, a transformation which seems even to be invading physics. The ancient formulas are reinterpreted as special expressions of much wider principles, principles that our ancestors never got a glimpse of in their present shape and formulation.

Mr. Schiller still gives to all this view of truth the name of "Humanism," but, for this doctrine too, the name of pragmatism seems fairly to be in the ascendant, so I will treat it under the name of pragmatism in these lectures.

Such then would be the scope of pragmatism—first, a method; and second, a genetic theory of what is meant by truth. And these two things must be our future topics.

What I have said of the theory of truth will, I am sure, have appeared obscure and unsatisfactory to most of you by reason of its brevity. I shall make amends for that hereafter. In a lecture on "common sense" I shall try to show what I mean by truths grown petrified by antiquity. In another lecture I shall expatiate on the idea that our thoughts become true in proportion as they successfully exert their go between function. In a third I shall show how hard it is to discriminate subjective from objective factors in Truth's development. You may not follow me wholly in these lectures; and if you do, you may not wholly agree with me. But you will, I know, regard me at least as serious, and treat my effort with respectful consideration.

You will probably be surprised to learn, then, that Messrs. Schiller's and Dewey's theories have suffered a hailstorm of contempt and ridicule. All rationalism has risen against them. In influential quarters Mr. Schiller, in particular, has been treated like an impudent schoolboy who deserves a spanking. I should not mention this, but for the fact that it throws so much sidelight upon that rationalistic temper to which I have opposed the temper of pragmatism. Pragmatism is uncomfortable away from facts. Rationalism is comfortable only in the presence of abstractions. This pragmatist talk about truths in the plural, about their utility and satisfactoriness, about the success with which they "work," etc., suggests to the typical intellectualist mind a sort of coarse lame second-rate makeshift article of truth. Such truths are not real truth. Such tests are merely subjective. As against this, objective truth must be something non-utilitarian, haughty, refined, remote, august, exalted. It must be an absolute correspondence of our thoughts with an equally absolute reality. It must be what we *ought* to think unconditionally. The conditioned ways in which we *do* think are so much irrelevance and matter for psychology. Down with psychology, up with logic, in all this question!

See the exquisite contrast of the types of mind! The pragmatist clings to facts and concreteness, observes truth at its work in particular cases, and generalizes. Truth, for him, becomes a class-name for all sorts of definite working-values in experience. For the rationalist it remains a pure abstraction, to the bare name of which we must defer. When the pragmatist undertakes to show in detail just why we must defer, the rationalist is unable to recognize the concretes from which his own abstraction is taken. He accuses us of *denying* truth; whereas we have only sought to trace exactly why people follow it and always ought to follow it. Your typical ultra-abstractionist fairly shudders at concreteness: other things equal, he positively prefers the pale and spectral. If the two universes were offered, he would always choose the skinny outline rather than the rich thicket of reality. It is so much purer, clearer, nobler.

I hope that as these lectures go on, the concreteness and closeness to facts of the pragmatism which they advocate may be what approves itself to you as its most satisfactory peculiarity. It only follows here the example of the sister-sciences, interpreting the unobserved by the observed. It brings old and new harmoniously together. It converts the absolutely empty notion of a static relation of "correspondence" (what that may mean we must ask later) between our minds and reality, into that of a rich and active commerce (that any one may follow in detail and understand) between particular thoughts of ours, and the great universe of other experiences in which they play their parts and have their uses.

But enough of this at present? The justification of what I say must be postponed. I wish now to add a word in further explanation of the claim I made at our last meeting, that pragmatism may be a happy harmonizer of empiricist ways of thinking with the more religious demands of human beings.

Men who are strongly of the fact-loving temperament, you may remember me to have said, are liable to be kept at a distance by the small sympathy with facts which that philosophy from the present-day fashion of idealism offers them. It is far too intellectualistic. Old fashioned theism was bad enough, with its notion of God as an exalted monarch, made up of a lot of unintelligible or preposterous "attributes"; but, so long as it held strongly by the argument from design, it kept some touch with concrete realities. Since, however, Darwinism has once for all displaced design from the minds of the "scientific," theism has lost that foothold; and some kind of an immanent or pantheistic deity working in things rather than above them is, if any, the kind recommended to our contemporary imagination. Aspirants to a philosophic religion turn, as a rule, more hopefully nowadays towards idealistic pantheism than towards the older dualistic theism, in spite of the fact that the latter still counts able defenders.

But, as I said in my first lecture, the brand of pantheism offered is hard for them to assimilate if they are lovers of facts, or empirically minded. It is the absolutistic brand, spurning the dust and reared upon pure logic. It keeps no connexion whatever with concreteness. Affirming the Absolute Mind, which is its substitute for God, to be the rational presupposition of all particulars of fact, whatever they may be, it remains supremely indifferent to what the particular facts in our world actually are. Be they what they may, the Absolute will father them. Like the sick lion in Esop's fable, all footprints lead into his den, but *nulla vestigia retrorsum* [no footprints were left]. You cannot redescend into the world of particulars by the Absolute's aid, or deduce any necessary consequences of detail important for your life from your idea of his nature. He gives you indeed the assurance that all is well with *Him*, and for his eternal way of thinking; but thereupon he leaves you to be finitely saved by your own temporal devices.

Far be it from me to deny the majesty of this conception, or its capacity to yield religious comfort to a most respectable class of minds. But from the human point of view, no one can pretend that it doesn't suffer from the faults of remoteness and abstractness. It is eminently a product of what I have ventured to call the rationalistic temper. It disdains empiricism's needs. It substitutes a pallid outline for the real world's richness. It is dapper, it is noble in the bad sense, in the sense in which to be noble is to be inapt for humble service. In this real world of sweat and dirt, it seems to me that when a view of things is "noble," that ought to count as a presumption against its truth, and as a philosophic disqualification. The prince of darkness may be a gentleman, as we are told he is, but whatever the God of earth and heaven is, he can surely be no gentleman. His menial services are needed in the dust of our human trials, even more than his dignity is needed in the empyrean.

Now pragmatism, devoted though she be to facts, has no such materialistic bias as ordinary empiricism labors under. Moreover, she has no objection whatever to the realizing of abstractions, so long as you get about among particulars with their aid and they actually carry you somewhere. Interested in no conclusions but those which our minds and our experiences work out together, she has no *a priori* prejudices against theology. *If theological ideas prove to have a value for concrete life, they will be true, for pragmatism, in the sense of being good for so much. For how much more they are true, will depend entirely on their relations to the other truths that also have to be acknowledged.*

What I said just now about the Absolute, of transcendental idealism, is a case in point. First, I called it majestic and said it yielded religious comfort to a class of minds, and then I accused it of remoteness and sterility. But so far as it affords such comfort, it surely is not sterile; it has that amount of value; it performs a concrete function. As a good pragmatist, I myself ought to call the Absolute true "in so far forth," then; and I unhesitatingly now do so.

But what does *true in so far forth* mean in this case? To answer, we need only apply the pragmatic method. What do believers in the Absolute mean by saying that their belief affords them comfort? They mean that since, in the Absolute finite evil is "overruled" already, we may, therefore, whenever we wish, treat the temporal as if it were potentially the eternal, be sure that we can trust its outcome, and, without sin, dismiss our fear and drop the worry of our finite responsibility. In short, they mean that we have a right ever and anon to take a moral holiday, to let the world wag in its own way, feeling that its issues are in better hands than ours and are none of our business.

The universe is a system of which the individual members may relax their anxieties occasionally, in which the don't-care mood is also right for men, and moral holidays in order,—that, if I mistake not, is part, at least, of what the Absolute is "known-as," that is the great difference in our particular experiences which his being true makes, for us, that is his cash-value when he is pragmatically interpreted. Farther than that the ordinary lay-reader in philosophy who thinks favorably of absolute idealism does not venture to sharpen his conceptions. He can use the Absolute for so much, and so much is very precious. He is pained at hearing you speak incredulously of the Absolute, therefore, and disregards your criticisms because they deal with aspects of the conception that he fails to follow.

If the Absolute means this, and means no more than this, who can possibly deny the truth of it? To deny it would be to insist that men should never relax, and that holidays are never in order.

I am well aware how odd it must seem to some of you to hear me say that an idea is "true" so long as to believe it is profitable to our lives. That it is *good,* for as much as it profits, you will gladly admit. If what we do by its aid is good, you will allow the idea itself to be good in so far forth, for we are the better for possessing it. But is it not a strange misuse of the word "truth," you will say, to call ideas also "true" for this reason?

To answer this difficulty fully is impossible at this stage of my account. You touch here upon the very central point of Messrs. Schiller's, Dewey's and my own doctrine of truth, which I can not discuss with detail until my sixth lecture. Let me now say only this, that truth is *one species of good,* and not, as is usually supposed, a category distinct from good, and co-ordinate with it. *The true is the name of whatever proves itself to be good in the way of belief, and good, too, for definite, assignable reasons.* Surely you must admit this, that if there were no good for life in true ideas, or if the knowledge of them were positively disadvantageous and false ideas the only useful ones, then the current notion that truth is divine and precious, and its pursuit a duty, could never have grown up or become a dogma. In a world like that, our duty would be to shun truth, rather. But in this world, just as certain foods are not only agreeable to our taste, but good for our teeth, our stomach, and our tissues; so certain ideas are not only agreeable to think about, or agreeable as supporting other ideas that we are fond of, but they are also helpful in life's practical struggles. If there be any life that it is really better we should lead, and if there be any idea which, if believed in, would help us to lead that life, then it would be really *better for us* to believe in that idea, *unless, indeed, belief in it incidentally clashed with other greater vital benefits.*

"What would be better for us to believe!" This sounds very like a definition of truth. It comes very near to saying "what we *ought* to believe": and in *that* definition none of you would find any oddity. Ought we ever not to believe what it is *better for us* to believe? And can we then keep the notion of what is better for us, and what is true for us, permanently apart?

Pragmatism says no, and I fully agree with her. Probably you also agree, so far as the abstract statement goes, but with a suspicion that if we practically did believe everything that made for good in our own personal lives, we should be found indulging all kinds of fancies about this world's affairs, and all kinds of sentimental superstitions about a world hereafter. Your suspicion here is undoubtedly well founded, and it is evident that something happens when you pass from the abstract to the concrete that complicates the situation.

I said just now that what is better for us to believe is true *unless the belief incidentally clashes with some other vital benefit*. Now in real life what vital benefits is any particular belief of ours most liable to clash with? What indeed except the vital benefits yielded by *other beliefs* when these prove incompatible with the first ones? In other words, the greatest enemy of any one of our truths may be the rest of our truths. Truths have once for all this desperate instinct of self-preservation and of desire to extinguish whatever contradicts them. My belief in the Absolute, based on the good it does me, must run the gauntlet of all my other beliefs. Grant that it may be true in giving me a moral holiday. Nevertheless, as I conceive it,—and let me speak now confidentially, as it were, and merely in my own private person,—it clashes with other truths of mine whose benefits I hate to give up on its account. It happens to be associated with a kind of logic of which I am the enemy, I find that it entangles me in metaphysical paradoxes that are inacceptable, etc., etc. But as I have enough trouble in life already without adding the trouble of carrying these intellectual inconsistencies, I personally just give up the Absolute. I just *take* my moral holidays; or else as a professional philosopher, I try to justify them by some other principle.

If I could restrict my notion of the Absolute to its bare holiday-giving value, it wouldn't clash with my other truths. But we can not easily thus restrict our hypotheses. They carry supernumerary features, and these it is that clash so. My disbelief in the Absolute means then disbelief in those other supernumerary features, for I fully believe in the legitimacy of taking moral holidays.

You see by this what I meant when I called pragmatism a mediator and reconciler and said, borrowing the word from Papini, that she "unstiffens" our theories. She has in fact no prejudices whatever, no obstructive dogmas, no rigid canons of what shall count as proof. She is completely genial. She will entertain any hypothesis, she will consider any evidence. It follows that in the religious field she is at a great advantage both over positivistic empiricism, with its anti-theological bias, and over religious rationalism, with its exclusive interest in the remote, the noble, the simple, and the abstract in the way of conception.

In short, she widens the field of search for God. Rationalism sticks to logic and the empyrean. Empiricism sticks to the external senses. Pragmatism is willing to take anything, to follow either logic or the senses and to count the humblest and most personal experiences. She will count mystical experiences if they have practical consequences. She will take a God who lives in the very dirt of private fact—if that should seem a likely place to find him.

Her only test of probable truth is what works best in the way of leading us, what fits every part of life best and combines with the collectivity of experience's demands, nothing being omitted. If theological ideas should do this, if the notion of God, in particular, should prove to do it, how could pragmatism possibly deny God's existence? She could see no meaning in treating as "not true" a notion that was pragmatically so successful. What other kind of truth could there be, for her, than all this agreement with concrete reality?

In my last lecture I shall return again to the relations of pragmatism with religion. But you see already how democratic she is. Her manners are as various and flexible, her resources as rich and endless, and her conclusions as friendly as those of mother nature.

*   *   *

LECTURE IV: THE ONE AND THE MANY

We saw in the last lecture that the pragmatic method, in its dealings with certain concepts, instead of ending with admiring contemplation, plunges forward into the river of experience with them and prolongs the perspective by their means. Design, free-will, the absolute mind, spirit instead of matter, have for their sole meaning a better promise as to this world's outcome. Be they false or be they true, the meaning of them is this meliorism. I have sometimes thought of the phenomenon called "total reflexion" in Optics as a good symbol of the relation between abstract ideas and concrete realities, as pragmatism conceives it. Hold a tumbler of water a little above your eyes and look up through the water at its surface—or better still look similarly through the flat wall of an aquarium. You will then see an extraordinarily brilliant reflected image say of a candle-flame, or any other clear object, situated on the opposite side of the vessel. No ray, under these circumstances gets beyond the water's surface: every ray is totally reflected back into the depths again. Now let the water represent the world of sensible facts, and let the air above it represent the world of abstract ideas. Both worlds are real, of course, and interact; but they interact only at their boundary, and the *locus* of everything that lives, and happens to us, so far as full experience goes, is the water. We are like fishes swimming in the sea of sense, bounded above by the superior element, but unable to breathe it pure or penetrate it. We get our oxygen from it, however, we touch it incessantly, now in this part, now in that, and every time we touch it, we turn back into the water with our course re-determined and re-energized. The abstract ideas of which the air consists are indispensable for life, but irrespirable by themselves, as it were, and only active in their re-directing function. All similes are halting, but this one rather takes my fancy. It shows how something, not sufficient for life in itself, may nevertheless be an effective determinant of life elsewhere.

In this present hour I wish to illustrate the pragmatic method by one more application. I wish to turn its light upon the ancient problem of "the one and the many." I suspect that in but few of you has this problem occasioned sleepless nights, and I should not be astonished if some of you told me it had never vexed you at all. I myself have come, by long brooding over it, to consider it the most central of all philosophic problems, central because so pregnant. I mean by this that if you know whether a man is a decided monist or a decided pluralist, you perhaps know more about the rest of his opinions than if you give him any other name ending in *ist*. To believe in the one or in the many, that is the classification with the maximum number of consequences. So bear with me for an hour while I try to inspire you with my own interest in this problem.

Philosophy has often been defined as the quest or the vision of the world's unity. Few persons ever challenge this definition, which is true as far as it goes, for philosophy has indeed manifested above all things its interest in unity. But how about the variety in things? Is that such an irrelevant matter? If instead of using the term philosophy, we talk in general of our intellect and its needs, we quickly see that unity is only one of them. Acquaintance with the details of fact is always reckoned, along with their reduction to system, as an indispensable mark of mental greatness. Your "scholarly" mind, of encyclopedic, philological type, your man essentially of *learning*, has never lacked for praise along with your philosopher. What our intellect really aims at is neither variety nor unity taken singly, but *totality*.* In this, acquaintance with reality's diversities is as important as understanding their connexion. Curiosity goes *pari passu* with the systematizing passion.

In spite of this obvious fact the unity of things has always been considered more *illustrious,* as it were, than their variety. When a young man first conceives the notion that the whole world forms one great fact, with all its parts moving abreast, as it were, and interlocked, he feels as if he were enjoying a great insight, and looks superciliously on all who still fall short of this sublime conception. Taken thus abstractly as it first comes to one, the monistic insight is so vague as hardly to seem worth defending intellectually. Yet probably every one in this audience in some way cherishes it. A certain abstract monism, a certain emotional response to the character of oneness, as if it were a feature of the world not co-ordinate with its manyness, but vastly more excellent and eminent, is so prevalent in educated circles that we might almost call it a part of philosophic common sense. Of *course* the world is One, we say. How else could it be a world at all? Empiricists as a rule, are as stout monists of this abstract kind as rationalists are.

The difference is that the empiricists are less dazzled. Unity doesn't blind them to everything else, doesn't quench their curiosity for special facts, whereas there is a kind of rationalist who is sure to interpret abstract unity mystically and to forget everything else, to treat it as a principle; to admire and worship it; and thereupon to come to a full stop intellectually.

"The world is One!"—the formula may become a sort of number-worship. "Three" and "seven" have, it is true, been reckoned sacred numbers; but, abstractly taken, why is "one" more excellent than "forty-three," or than "two million and ten"? In this first vague conviction of the world's unity, there is so little to take hold of that we hardly know what we mean by it.

The only way to get forward with our notion is to treat it pragmatically. Granting the oneness to exist, what facts will be different in consequence? What will the unity be known as? The world is One—yes, but *how* one. What is the practical value of the oneness for us.

Asking such questions, we pass from the vague to the definite, from the abstract to the concrete. Many distinct ways in which a oneness predicated of the universe might make a difference, come to view. I will note successively the more obvious of these ways.

1. First, the world is at least *one subject of discourse*. If its manyness were so irremediable as to permit *no* union whatever of its parts, not even our minds could "mean" the whole of it at once: they would be like eyes trying to look in opposite di-

---

*Compare A. Bellanger: *Les concepts de Cause, et l'activité intentionelle de l'Esprit.* (Paris: Alcan, 1905), p. 79ff.

rections. But in point of fact we mean to cover the whole of it by our abstract term "world" or "universe," which expressly intends that no part shall be left out. Such unity of discourse carries obviously no farther monistic specifications. A "chaos," once so named, has as much unity of discourse as a cosmos. It is an odd fact that many monists consider a great victory scored for their side when pluralists say "the universe is many." " 'The Universe'!" they chuckle—"his speech bewrayeth him. He stands confessed of monism out of his own mouth." Well, let things be one in so far forth! You can then fling such a word as universe at the whole collection of them, but what matters it? It still remains to be ascertained whether they are one in any further or more valuable sense.

2. Are they, for example, *continuous?* Can you pass from one to another, keeping always in your one universe without any danger of falling out? In other words, do the parts of our universe *hang together*, instead of being like detached grains of sand?

Even grains of sand hang together through the space in which they are embedded, and if you can in any way move through such space, you can pass continuously from number one of them to number two. Space and time are thus vehicles of continuity by which the world's parts hang together. The practical difference to us, resultant from these forms of union, is immense. Our whole motor life is based upon them.

3. There are innumerable other paths of practical continuity among things. Lines of *influence* can be traced by which they hang together. Following any such line you pass from one thing to another till you may have covered a good part of the universe's extent. Gravity and heat-conduction are such all-uniting influences, so far as the physical world goes. Electric, luminous and chemical influences follow similar lines of influence. But opaque and inert bodies interrupt the continuity here, so that you have to step round them, or change your mode of progress if you wish to get farther on that day. Practically, you have then lost your universe's unity, *so far as it was constituted by those first lines of influence.*

There are innumerable kinds of connexion that special things have with other special things; and the *ensemble* of any one of these connexions forms one sort of system by which things are conjoined. Thus men are conjoined in a vast network of *acquaintanceship*. Brown knows Jones, Jones knows Robinson, etc.; and *by choosing your farther intermediaries rightly* you may carry a message from Jones to the Empress of China, or the Chief of the African Pigmies, or to any one else in the inhabited world. But you are stopped short, as by a nonconductor, when you choose one man wrong in this experiment. What may be called love systems are grafted on the acquaintance-system. A loves (or hates) B; B loves (or hates) C, etc. But these systems are smaller than the great acquaintance-system that they presuppose.

Human efforts are daily unifying the world more and more in definite systematic ways. We found colonial, postal, consular, commercial systems, all the parts of which obey definite influences that propagate themselves within the system but not to facts outside of it. The result is innumerable little hangings-together of the world's parts within the larger hangings together, little worlds, not only of discourse but of operation, within the wider universe. Each system exemplifies one type or grade of union, its parts being strung on that peculiar kind of relation, and the same part may figure in many different systems, as a man may hold various offices and belong to several clubs. From this "systematic" point of view, therefore, the pragmatic value of the world's unity is that all these definite networks actually and practically exist. Some are more enveloping and extensive, some less so; they are superposed upon each other; and between them all they let no individual elementary part of the universe escape. Enormous as is the amount of disconnexion among things (for these systematic influences and conjunctions follow rigidly exclusive paths), everything that exists is influenced in some way by something else, if you can only pick the way out rightly. Loosely speaking, and in general, it may be said that all things cohere and adhere to each other somehow, and that the universe exists practically in reticulated or concatenated forms which make of it a continuous or "integrated" affair. Any kind of influence whatever helps to make the world one, so far as you can follow it from next to next. You may then say that "the world *is* One,"—meaning in these respects, namely, and just so far as they obtain. But just as definitely is it not One, so far as they do not obtain; and there is no species of connexion which will not fail, if, instead of choosing conductors for it you choose non-conductors. You are then arrested at your very first step and have to write the world down as a pure *many* from that particular point of view. If our intellect had been as much interested in disjunctive as it is in conjunctive relations, philosophy would have equally successfully celebrated the world's *disunion*.

The great point is to notice that the oneness and the manyness are absolutely co-ordinate here. Neither is primordial or more essential or excellent than the other. Just as with space, whose separating of things seems exactly on a par with its uniting of them, but sometimes one function and sometimes the other is what comes home to us most, so, in our general dealings with the world of influences, we now need conductors and now need non-conductors, and wisdom lies in knowing which is which at the appropriate moment.

4. All these systems of influence or non-influence may be listed under the general problem of the world's *causal unity*. If the minor causal influences among things should converge towards one common causal origin of them in the past, one great first cause for all that is, one might then speak of the absolute causal unity of the world. God's *fiat* on creation's day has figured in traditional philosophy as such an absolute cause and origin. Transcendental Idealism, translating "creation" into "thinking" (or "willing to think") calls the divine act "eternal" rather than "first"; but the union of the many here is absolute, just the same—the many would not *be*, save for the One. Against this notion of the unity of origin of all things there has always stood the pluralistic notion of an eternal self-existing many in the shape of atoms or even of spiritual units of some sort. The alternative has doubtless a pragmatic meaning, but perhaps, as far as these lectures go, we had better leave the question of unity of origin unsettled.

5. The most important sort of union that obtains among things, pragmatically speaking, is their *generic unity*. Things exist in kinds, there are many specimens in each kind, and what the "kind" implies for one specimen, it implies also for every other specimen of that kind. We can easily conceive that every fact in the world might be singular, that is, unlike any other fact and sole of its kind. In such a world of singulars our logic would be useless, for logic works by predicating of the single instance what is true of all its kind. With no two things alike in the world, we should be unable to reason from our past experiences to our future ones. The existence of so much generic unity in things is thus perhaps the most momentous pragmatic specification of what it may mean to say "the world is One." *Absolute* generic unity would obtain if there were one *summum genus* under which all things without exception could be eventually subsumed. "Beings," "thinkables," "experiences," would be candidates for this position. Whether the alternatives expressed by such words have any pragmatic significance or not, is another question which I prefer to leave unsettled just now.

6. Another specification of what the phrase "the world is one" may mean is *unity of purpose*. An enormous number of things in the world subserve a common purpose. All the man-made systems, administrative, industrial, military, or what not, exist each for its controlling purpose. Every living being pursues its own peculiar purposes. They

co-operate, according to the degree of their development, in collective or tribal purposes, larger ends thus enveloping lesser ones, until an absolutely single, final and climacteric purpose subserved by all things without exception might conceivably be reached. It is needless to say that the appearances conflict with such a view. Any resultant, as I said in my third lecture, *may* have been purposed in advance, but none of the results we actually know in this world have in point of fact been purposed in advance in all their details. Men and nations start with a vague notion of being rich, or great, or good. Each step they make brings unforeseen chances into sight, and shuts out older vistas, and the specifications of the general purpose have to be daily changed. What is reached in the end may be better or worse than what was proposed, but it is always more complex and different.

Our different purposes also are at war with each other. Where one can't crush the other out, they compromise; and the result is again different from what any one distinctly proposed beforehand. Vaguely and generally, much of what was purposed may be gained; but everything makes strongly for the view that our world is incompletely unified teleologically and is still trying to get its unification better organized.

Whoever claims *absolute* teleological unity, saying that there is one purpose that every detail of the universe subserves, dogmatizes at his own risk. Theologians who dogmatize thus find it more and more impossible, as our acquaintance with the warring interests of the world's parts grows more concrete, to imagine what the one climacteric purpose may possibly be like. We see indeed that certain evils minister to ulterior goods, that the bitter makes the cocktail better, and that a bit of danger or hardship puts us agreeably to our trumps. We can vaguely generalize this into the doctrine that all the evil in the universe is but instrumental to its greater perfection. But the scale of the evil actually in sight defies all human tolerance; and transcendental idealism, in the pages of a Bradley or a Royce, brings us no farther than the book of Job did—God's ways are not our ways, so let us put our hands upon our mouth. A God who can relish such superfluities of horror is no God for human beings to appeal to. His animal spirits are too high. In other words the "Absolute" with his one purpose, is not the manlike God of common people.

7. *Aesthetic union* among things also obtains, and is very analogous to teleological union. Things tell a story. Their parts hang together so as to work out a climax. They play into each other's hands expressively. Retrospectively, we can see that altho no definite purpose presided over a chain of events, yet the events fell into a dramatic form, with a start, a middle, and a finish. In point of fact all stories end; and here again the point of view of many is the more natural one to take. The world is full of partial stories that run parallel to one another, beginning and ending at odd times. They mutually interlace and interfere at points, but we can not unify them completely in our minds. In following your life-history, I must temporarily turn my attention from my own. Even a biographer of twins would have to press them alternately upon his reader's attention.

It follows that whoever says that the whole world tells one story utters another of those monistic dogmas that a man believes at his risk. It is easy to see the world's history pluralistically, as a rope of which each fibre tells a separate tale; but to conceive of each cross section of the rope as an absolutely single fact, and to sum the whole longitudinal series into one being living an undivided life, is harder. We have indeed the analogy of embryology to help us. The microscopist makes a hundred flat cross-sections of a given embryo, and mentally unites them into one solid whole. But the great world's ingredients, so far as they are beings, seem, like the rope's fibres, to be discontinuous, cross-wise, and to cohere only in the longitudinal direction. Followed in that direction they are many. Even the embryologist, when he follows the *development* of his object, has to treat the history of each single organ in turn. *Absolute* aesthetic union is thus another barely abstract ideal. The world appears as something more epic than dramatic.

So far, then, we see how the world is unified by its many systems, kinds, purposes, and dramas. That there is more union in all these ways than openly appears is certainly true. That there *may* be one sovereign purpose, system, kind, and story, is a legitimate hypothesis. All I say here is that it is rash to affirm this dogmatically without better evidence than we possess at present.

8. The *great* monistic *denkmittel* for a hundred years past has been the notion of *the one Knower*. The many exist only as objects for his thought—exist in his dream, as it were; and *as he knows them,* they have one purpose, form one system, tell one tale for him. This notion of an *all enveloping noetic unity* in things is the sublimest achievement of intellectualist philosophy. Those who believe in the Absolute, as the all-knower is termed, usually say that they do so for coercive reasons, which clear thinkers can not evade. The Absolute has far-reaching practical consequences, to some of which I drew attention in my second lecture. Many kinds of difference important to us would surely follow from its being true. I can not here enter into all the logical proofs of such a Being's existence, farther than to say that none of them seem to me sound. I must therefore treat the notion of an All-Knower simply as an hypothesis, exactly on a par logically with the pluralist notion that there is no point of view, no focus of information extant, from which the entire content of the universe is visible at once. "God's conscience," says Professor Royce,* "forms in its wholeness one luminously transparent conscious moment"—this is the type of noetic unity on which rationalism insists. Empiricism on the other hand is satisfied with the type of noetic unity that is humanly familiar. Everything gets known by *some* knower along with something else; but the knowers may in the end be irreducibly many, and the greatest knower of them all may yet not know the whole of everything, or even know what he does know at one single stroke:—he may be liable to forget. Whichever type obtained, the world would still be a universe noetically. Its parts would be conjoined by knowledge, but in the one case the knowledge would be absolutely unified, in the other it would be strung along and overlapped.

The notion of one instantaneous or eternal Knower—either adjective here means the same thing—is, as I said, the great intellectualist achievement of our time. It has practically driven out that conception of "Substance" which earlier philosophers set such store by, and by which so much unifying work used to be done—universal substance which alone has being in and from itself, and of which all the particulars of experience are but forms to which it gives support. Substance has succumbed to the pragmatic criticisms of the English school. It appears now only as another name for the fact that phenomena as they come are actually grouped and given in coherent forms, the very forms in which we finite knowers experience or think them together. These forms of conjunction are as much parts of the tissue of experience as are the terms which they connect; and it is a great pragmatic achievement for recent idealism to have made the world hang together in these directly representable ways instead of drawing its unity from the "inherence" of its parts—whatever that may mean—in an unimaginable principle behind the scenes.

The Conception of God (New York, 1897), p. 292.

"The world is One," therefore, just so far as we experience it to be concatenated, One by as many definite conjunctions as appear. But then also *not* One by just as many definite *dis*-junctions as we find. The oneness and the manyness of it thus obtain in respects which can be separately named. It is neither a universe pure and simple nor a multiverse pure and simple. And its various manners of being One suggest, for their accurate ascertainment, so many distinct programs of scientific work. Thus the pragmatic question "What is the oneness known as? What practical difference will it make?" saves us from all feverish excitement over it as a principle of sublimity and carries us forward into the stream of experience with a cool head. The stream may indeed reveal far more connexion and union than we now suspect, but we are not entitled on pragmatic principles to claim absolute oneness in any respect in advance.

It is so difficult to see definitely what absolute oneness can mean, that probably the majority of you are satisfied with the sober attitude which we have reached. Nevertheless there are possibly some radically monistic souls among you who are not content to leave the one and the many on a par. Union of various grades, union of diverse types, union that stops at non-conductors, union that merely goes from next to next, and means in many cases outer nextness only, and not a more internal bond, union of concatenation, in short; all that sort of thing seems to you a halfway stage of thought. The oneness of things, superior to their manyness, you think must also be more deeply true, must be the more real aspect of the world. The pragmatic view, you are sure, gives us a universe imperfectly rational. The real universe must form an unconditional unit of being, something consolidated, with its parts co-implicated through and through. Only then could we consider our estate completely rational.

There is no doubt whatever that this ultra monistic way of thinking means a great deal to many minds. "One Life, One Truth, One Love, One Principle, One Good, One God"—I quote from a Christian Science leaflet which the day's mail brings into my hands—beyond doubt such a confession of faith has pragmatically an emotional value, and beyond doubt the word "One" contributes to the value quite as much as the other words. But if we try to realize *intellectually* what we can possibly *mean* by such a glut of oneness we are thrown right back upon our pragmatistic determinations again. It means either the mere name One, the universe of discourse; or it means the sum total of all the ascertainable particular conjunctions and concatenations; or, finally, it means some one vehicle of conjunction treated as all-inclusive, like one origin, one purpose, or one knower. In point of fact it always means one knower to those who take it intellectually to-day. The one knower involves, they think, the other forms of conjunction. His world must have all its parts co-implicated in the one logical aesthetical-teleological unit-picture which is his eternal dream.

The character of the absolute knower's picture is however so impossible for us to represent clearly, that we may fairly suppose that the authority which absolute monism undoubtedly possesses, and probably always will possess over some persons, draws its strength far less from intellectual than from mystical grounds. To interpret absolute monism worthily, be a mystic. Mystical states of mind in every degree are shown by history, usually tho not always, to make for the monistic view. This is no proper occasion to enter upon the general subject of mysticism, but I will quote one mystical pronouncement to show just what I mean. The paragon of all monistic systems is the Vedanta philosophy of Hindostan, and the paragon of Vedantist missionaries was the late Swami Vivekananda who visited our land some years ago. The method of Vedantism is the mystical method. You do not reason, but after going through a certain discipline *you see,* and having seen, you can report the truth. Vivekananda thus reports the truth in one of his lectures here:

Where is there any more misery for him who sees this Oneness in the universe, this One-ness of life, Oneness of everything? . . . This separation between man and man, man and woman, man and child, nation from nation, earth from moon, moon from sun, this separa-tion between atom and atom is the cause really of all the misery, and the Vedanta says this separation does not exist, it is not real. It is merely apparent, on the surface. In the heart of things there is unity still. If you go inside you find that unity between man and man, women and children, races and races, high and low, rich and poor, the gods and men: all are One, and animals too, if you go deep enough, and he who has attained to that has no more delusion. . . . Where is there any more delusion for him? What can delude him? He knows the reality of everything, the secret of everything. Where is there any more misery for him? What does he desire? He has traced the reality of everything unto the Lord, that centre, that Unity of everything, and that is Eternal Bliss, Eternal Knowledge, Eternal Ex-istence. Neither death nor disease nor sorrow nor misery nor discontent is There . . . In the Centre, the reality, there is no one to be mourned for, no one to be sorry for. He has pene-trated everything, the Pure One, the Formless, the Bodiless, the Stainless, He the Knower, He the great Poet, the Self-Existent, He who is giving to every one what he deserves.

Observe how radical the character of the monism here is. Separation is not sim-ply overcome by the One, it is denied to exist. There is no many. We are not parts of the One; It has no parts; and since in a sense we undeniably are, it must be that each of us is the One, indivisibly and totally. *An Absolute One, and I that One,*—surely we have here a religion which, emotionally considered, has a high pragmatic value; it im-parts a perfect sumptuosity of security. As our Swami says in another place:

When man has seen himself as One with the infinite Being of the universe, when all sepa-rateness has ceased, when all men, all women, all angels, all gods, all animals, all plants, the whole universe has been melted into that oneness, then all fear disappears. Whom to fear? Can I hurt myself? Can I kill myself? Can I injure myself? Do you fear yourself? Then will all sorrow disappear. What can cause me sorrow? I am the One Existence of the universe. Then all jealousies will disappear; of whom to be jealous? Of myself? Then all bad feelings disappear. Against whom shall I have this bad feeling? Against myself? There is none in the universe but me . . . kill out this differentiation, kill out this supersti-tion that there are many. "He who, in this world of many, sees that One; he who, in this mass of insentiency, sees that One Sentient Being; he who in this world of shadow, catches that Reality, unto him belongs eternal peace, unto none else, unto none else."

We all have some ear for this monistic music: it elevates and reassures. We all have at least the germ of mysticism in us. And when our idealists recite their argu-ments for the Absolute, saying that the slightest union admitted anywhere carries logi-cally absolute Oneness with it, and that the slightest separation admitted anywhere log-ically carries disunion remediless and complete, I cannot help suspecting that the palpable weak places in the intellectual reasonings they use are protected from their own criticism by a mystical feeling that, logic or no logic, absolute Oneness must somehow at any cost be true. Oneness overcomes *moral* separateness at any rate. In the passion of love we have the mystic germ of what might mean a total union of all sen-tient life. This mystical germ wakes up in us on hearing the monistic utterances, ac-knowledges their authority, and assigns to intellectual considerations a secondary place.

I will dwell no longer on these religious and moral aspects of the question in this lecture. When I come to my final lecture there will be something more to say.

Leave then out of consideration for the moment the authority which mystical in-sights may be conjectured eventually to possess; treat the problem of the One and the

Many in a purely intellectual way; and we see clearly enough where pragmatism stands. With her criterion of the practical differences that theories make, we see that she must equally abjure absolute monism and absolute pluralism. The world is One just so far as its parts hang together by any definite connexion. It is many just so far as any definite connexion fails to obtain. And finally it is growing more and more unified by those systems of connexion at least which human energy keeps framing as time goes on.

It is possible to imagine alternative universes to the one we know, in which the most various grades and types of union should be embodied. Thus the lowest grade of universe would be a world of mere *withness*, of which the parts were only strung together by the conjunction "and." Such a universe is even now the collection of our several inner lives. The spaces and times of your imagination, the objects and events of your day-dreams are not only more or less incoherent *inter se,* but are wholly out of definite relation with the similar contents of any one else's mind. Our various reveries now as we sit here compenetrate each other idly without influencing or interfering. They coexist, but in no order and in no receptacle, being the nearest approach to an absolute "many" that we can conceive. We can not even imagine any reason why they *should* be known all together, and we can imagine even less, if they were known together, how they could be known as one systematic whole.

But add our sensations and bodily actions, and the union mounts to a much higher grade. Our *audita et visa* [hearing and seeing] and our acts fall into those receptacles of time and space in which each event finds its date and place. They form "things" and are of "kinds" too, and can be classed. Yet we can imagine a world of things and of kinds in which the causal interactions with which we are so familiar should not exist. Everything there might be inert towards everything else, and refuse to propagate its influence. Or gross mechanical influences might pass, but no chemical action. Such worlds would be far less unified than ours. Again there might be complete physico-chemical interaction, but no minds; or minds, but altogether private ones, with no social life; or social life limited to acquaintance, but no love; or love, but no customs or institutions that should systematize it. No one of these grades of universe would be absolutely irrational or disintegrated, inferior tho it might appear when looked at from the higher grades. For instance, if our minds should ever become "telepathically" connected, so that we knew immediately, or could under certain conditions know immediately, each what the other was thinking, the world we now live in would appear to the thinkers in that world to have been of an inferior grade.

With the whole of past eternity open for our conjectures to range in, it may be lawful to wonder whether the various kinds of union now realized in the universe that we inhabit may not possibly have been successively evolved after the fashion in which we now see human systems evolving in consequence of human needs. If such an hypothesis were legitimate, total oneness would appear at the end of things rather than at their origin. In other words the notion of the "Absolute" would have to be replaced by that of the "Ultimate." The two notions would have the same content—the maximally unified content of fact, namely—but their time-relations would be positively reversed.*

After discussing the unity of the universe in this pragmatic way, you ought to see why I said in my second lecture, borrowing the word from my friend G. Papini, that pragmatism tends to *unstiffen* all our theories. The world's oneness has generally been

---

*Compare on the Ultimate, Mr. Schiller's essay "Activity and Substance," in his book entitled *Humanism,* p. 204.

affirmed abstractly only, and as if any one who questioned it must be an idiot. The temper of monists has been so vehement, as almost at times to be convulsive; and this way of holding a doctrine does not easily go with reasonable discussion and the drawing of distinctions. The theory of the Absolute, in particular, has had to be an article of faith, affirmed dogmatically and exclusively. The One and All, first in the order of being and of knowing, logically necessary itself, and uniting all lesser things in the bonds of mutual necessity, how could it allow of any mitigation of its inner rigidity? The slightest suspicion of pluralism, the minutest wiggle of independence of any one of its parts from the control of the totality would ruin it. Absolute unity brooks no degrees,—as well might you claim absolute purity for a glass of water because it contains but a single little cholera-germ. The independence, however infinitesimal, of a part, however small, would be to the Absolute as fatal as a cholera-germ.

Pluralism on the other hand has no need of this dogmatic rigoristic temper. Provided you grant *some* separation among things, some tremor of independence, some free play of parts on one another, some real novelty or chance, however minute, she is amply satisfied, and will allow you any amount, however great, of real union. How much of union there may be is a question that she thinks can only be decided empirically. The amount may be enormous, colossal; but absolute monism is shattered if, along with all the union, there has to be granted the slightest modicum, the most incipient nascency, or the most residual trace, of a separation that is not "overcome."

Pragmatism, pending the final empirical ascertainment of just what the balance of union and disunion among things may be, must obviously range herself upon the pluralistic side. Some day, she admits, even total union, with one knower, one origin, and a universe consolidated in every conceivable way, may turn out to be the most acceptable of all hypotheses. Meanwhile the opposite hypothesis, of a world imperfectly unified still, and perhaps always to remain so, must be sincerely entertained. This latter hypothesis is pluralism's doctrine. Since absolute monism forbids its being even considered seriously, branding it as irrational from the start, it is clear that pragmatism must turn its back on absolute monism, and follow pluralism's more empirical path.

This leaves us with the common-sense world, in which we find things partly joined and partly disjoined. "Things," then, and their "conjunctions"—what do such words mean, pragmatically handled? In my next lecture, I will apply the pragmatic method to the stage of philosophizing known as Common Sense.

FRIEDRICH NIETZSCHE
1844–1900

Friedrich Wilhelm Nietzsche was born in Röcken, Prussia, in 1844. He was named in honor of the Prussian king, Friedrich Wilhelm IV, whose birthday, October 15, he shared. Nietzsche's father, Ludwig Nietzsche, was a Lutheran minister and his mother, Franziska Oehler Nietzsche, was the daughter of a Lutheran minister. When Nietzsche was only five years old, his father died from what was called "softening of the brain," after a year of mental instability. The rest of Nietzsche's childhood was spent in a household of women, including his widowed mother, his sister, his anxiety-prone paternal grandmother, and two maiden aunts.

Following grade school, Nietzsche attended a famous boarding school at Pforta, where he did outstanding work. However, while there, Nietzsche suffered migraine headaches, which continued to afflict him until he experienced a mental breakdown in 1889. The medicine he took to relieve the headaches upset his stomach and left him nauseous. For much of his adult life, he alternated between the extremes of headaches and nausea with only short periods of health in between.

In 1864, he enrolled at the University of Bonn to study theology and classical philology (linguistics), but he left within a year. By this time, he had given up whatever religious faith he had and was no longer interested in theology. He then moved to the University of Leipzig to continue his studies in philology. His professor at Leipzig, Friedrich Ritschl, was so impressed with Nietzsche's work that he published some of his papers and later recommended him for a chair of classical philology at the University of Basel. In 1869, at the unusual age of only twenty-four, Nietzsche was given the chair as an associate professor. He had produced neither a doctoral dissertation nor the additional book normally required of an associate professor, but Leipzig immediately awarded him a doctorate without examination or thesis, and within a year he was promoted to full professor at Basel.

In 1872, Nietzsche published his first book, *The Birth of Tragedy*, which included a laudatory section on Richard Wagner's music. Over the next four years, Nietzsche wrote four meditations (published collectively in English as *Thoughts Out of Season*), the last of which was another tribute to Wagner. During this period, Nietzsche and Wagner were close friends; and Nietzsche often visited Wagner's villa on Lake Lucerne. But by 1878, they had broken relations over Wagner's nationalism and anti-Semitism.

Nietzsche's health began to deteriorate, and he was forced to resign from the university in 1879. Over the next ten years, Nietzsche traveled and devoted all his remaining energy to writing, publishing such books as *The Gay Science* (1882), *Thus Spoke Zarathustra* (1883–1885), *Beyond Good and Evil* (1886), *On the Genealogy of Morality* (1887), and his final denunciation of his former friend, *The Case of Wagner* (1888).

By the end of 1888, Nietzsche showed signs of oncoming madness, and in January 1889 he collapsed in the street in Turin, Italy, while hugging the neck of a horse. For the next eleven years until his death in 1900, he lived in the care of his mother and sister. Works that he had written in 1888, including *The Will to Power, Twilight of the Idols, The Anti-Christ,* and his outrageous autobiography *Ecco Homo* (which includes chapter headings such as "Why I Am So Clever"), were published after distorted editing by his sister. Only in the twentieth century have unedited versions of these works become available.

The cause of Nietzsche's insanity has been vigorously debated. Critics have held that his ideas caused it and claim to have found evidence of insanity in many of his writings. His sister romanticized that he went mad because Germany spurned him. More likely explanations are that he contracted syphilis during a rare sexual escapade while a young man or that he simply inherited a brain disease from his father.

* * *

Nietzsche's style of writing in epigrams, aphorisms, stories, poetry, and essays virtually defies an editor to systematically summarize his thought. Even though Nietzsche never sought to build a system, there are recurring, interwoven themes represented by the selections given here.

In *The Birth of Tragedy,* translated by Francis Golffing, Nietzsche presents a distinction between Apollonian and Dionysian tendencies in art. The Apollonian tendency (named for the Greek god of the sun, Apollo) represents the harmony and restraint exemplified by Greek sculpture and architecture. The Dionysian tendency (named for the Greek god of wine and revelry, Dionysos) represents wild abandonment as exemplified by the drunken sexual frenzies of the Dionysian cult festivals or the music of Beethoven's Ninth Symphony. Greek tragedy arises as a synthesis of Apollonian form and Dionysian urges. But Greek tragedy is in turn superseded by Greek rationalism as exemplified by Socrates: the theoretical man who optimistically sees knowledge as the panacea to the problems of life. What is needed now, Nietzsche argues, is a new synthesis of these Dionysian and Apollonian tendencies by an "artistic" Socrates. Such a

Socratic figure would be a creative genius who would honestly face the harshness of life without losing a clear rational analytic perspective.

In order to produce new values, such a creative genius must be free from all constraints, including moral constraints that would limit creativity by imposing "universal" standards. In the first essay of *On the Genealogy of Morality,* given here in the Carol Diethe translation, Nietzsche shows how such a limiting morality developed as he distinguishes between "master morality" and "slave morality." Master morality is basically affirmative and defines itself on its own terms. In this morality, "good" means that which is noble, powerful, and beautiful, and which belongs to the highest rank; and "bad" signifies that which is base, low-minded, and unworthy of greatness. On the other hand, slave morality is basically negative and claims to find values "out there," ordained by God or some other transcendent law-giver. It is born out of resentment and identifies the "good" with such base sentiments as humility and pity. Instead of "bad," this morality uses the vindictive term "evil" to castigate all who would stand against it. Nietzsche claims that beginning with the Jews, and completed by the Christians, this slave morality had infected all of Europe with its life-denying poison. What is now needed is a "transvaluation of all values," which would move us "beyond good and evil."

In affirming the master morality, the creative genius must begin by proclaiming the death of God. With the death of God, slave morality—and all values dependent on some external law-giver—collapses and the individual is free to create self-defined values. By the "death of God," Nietzsche does not mean that there once was a diety who got old and passed away, nor that people no longer should live holy lives. Rather, Nietzsche claims that all *absolutes* have collapsed and there is no transcendent basis in any area—whether religion, philosophy, science, or politics—for making meaning out of life. The brief selection here from *Thus Spoke Zarathustra,* translated by Walter Kaufmann, is one of several passages in which Nietzsche announces the death of God.

In our selection from *Twilight of the Idols,* also translated by Kaufmann, Nietzsche examines how philosophers have tried to find something transcendent, something permanent. Beginning with the Pre-Socratic thinker Parmenides, philosophers have been unwilling to accept the actual transitory world of "becoming." Instead they have denigrated this world, labeling it "apparent," and have in its place invented an immutable world of "being." But, as Nietzsche explains, "Any distinction between a 'true' and an 'apparent' world—whether in the Christian manner or in the manner of Kant . . . is only a suggestion of decadence, a symptom of the *decline of life.*"

The genius who can embrace "becoming," who acknowledges the death of all external values, could become an *Ōbermensch* ("overman" or "superman"). Such an overman would be a this-world antithesis to God and would affirm life without any resentment. The overman would be to humans as humans are to apes. But, most important, the overman would be one who acknowledges and celebrates the *will to power.* Nietzsche explains the nature of this force in our short selection from *The Will to Power,* translated by Kaufmann and R. J. Hollingdale.

According to Nietzsche, all human behavior can be understood in terms of the will to power and every relationship between persons is a power relationship. In master morality, the hero asserts the will to power by taking direct action. In slave morality, as explicated in our final selection from Kaufmann's translation of *The Anti-Christ,* the will to power is perverted into resentment in order to gain the imaginary powers of revenge and pity.

But the will to power can also be expressed *within* the person. That is, more than gaining power over others, the will to power can lead to power over the self. The overman will be the one who uses power in this way to "overcome his animal nature, organize the chaos of his passions, sublimate his impulses, and give style to his character,"* becoming completely free and self-created.

Ironically, despite his distaste for anti-Semitism and his emphasis on the *self-overcoming* aspects of the will to power, Nietzsche was hailed as a hero by the Nazis. They used his emphases on the master morality and the will to power as a justification for their atrocities. Nietzsche's sister, Elisabeth, married a German anti-Semite and in her old age eagerly received Adolph Hitler at the Nietzsche Archives. However, despite its unfortunate association with the Nazis, Nietzsche's thought has continued to be influential, as his insights have been developed by existentialists, phenomenologists, psychoanalysts, poststructuralists, and deconstructionists, as well as poets and novelists.

*   *   *

A representative sampling of Neitzsche's thought can be found in *The Portable Nietzsche,* edited by Walter A. Kaufmann (New York: Viking Press, 1968). The best general introduction to Nietzsche's thought remains Walter A. Kaufmann, *Nietzsche: Philosopher, Psychologist, Antichrist* (Princeton, NJ: Princeton University Press, 1968). Recent overviews include Richard Schacht, *Nietzsche* (London: Routledge, 1983); Alexander Nehamas, *Nietzsche: Life as Literature* (Cambridge, MA: Harvard University Press, 1985); Graham Parke, *Composing the Soul* (Chicago: University of Chicago Press, 1994); John Richardson, *Nietzsche's System* (Oxford: Oxford University Press, 1995); and Michael Tanner, *Nietzsche* (Oxford: Oxford University Press, 1995). Ivo Frenzel, *Friedrich Nietzsche: An Illustrated Biography,* translated by Joachim Neugroschel (New York: Pegasus, 1967); and Sander L. Gilman, ed., *Conversations with Nietzsche: A Life in the Words of His Contemporaries,* translated by David J. Parent (New York: Oxford University Press, 1987), provide general biographies, whereas H.F. Peters, *Zarathustra's Sister: The Case of Elisabeth and Friedrich Nietzsche* (New York: Crown, 1977), presents a fascinating history of the expropriation of Nietzsche's thought in the service of German anti-Semitism. Walter A. Kaufmann, *Nietzsche, Heidegger, and Buber* (New York: McGraw-Hill, 1980); Allan Megill, *Prophets of Extremity: Nietzsche, Heidegger, Foucault, Derrida* (Berkeley: University of California Press, 1985); and Paul S. Miklowitz, *Metaphysics to Metafictions: Hegel, Nietzsche, and the End of Philosophy* (Albany, NY: SUNY Press, 1999) show the connections between Nietzsche and other important thinkers. For collections of critical essays, see Robert C. Solomon, ed., *Nietzsche: A Collection of Critical Essays* (Garden City, NY: Anchor Doubleday, 1973); Harold Bloom, ed., *Friedrich Nietzsche* (New York: Chelsea House, 1987); Richard Schacht, ed., *Nietzsche, Genealogy, Morality: Essays on*

---

*Walter Kaufmann, *Nietzsche: Philosopher, Psychologist, Antichrist* (Princeton, NJ: Princeton University Press, 1950), p. 316.

Nietzsche's On the Genealogy of Morals (Berkeley: University of California Press, 1994); Peter Sedgwick, ed., *Nietzsche: A Critical Reader* (Oxford: Basil Blackwell, 1995); Bernd Magnus and Kathleen Higgins, *The Cambridge Companion to Nietzsche* (Cambridge: Cambridge University Press, 1996); Kelly Oliver and Marilyn Pearsall, eds., *Feminist Interpretations of Nietzsche* (College Park, PA: Pennsylvania State University Press, 1998); and Daniel W. Conway, Nietzsche: Critical Assessments, four volumes (London: Routledge, 1998). Finally, Robert C. Solomon and Kathleen M. Higgins, eds., *Reading Nietzsche* (New York: Oxford University Press, 1988) provide helpful introductory essays on several of Nietzsche's works, while Daniel W. Conway, *Nietzsche's Dangerous Game: Philosophy in the Twilight of the Idols* (Cambridge: Cambridge University Press, 1997) focuses on Nietzsche's later work.

THE BIRTH OF TRAGEDY (in part)

I. Much will have been gained for esthetics once we have succeeded in apprehending directly—rather than merely *ascertaining*—that art owes its continuous evolution to the Apollonian-Dionysiac duality, even as the propagation of the species depends on the duality of the sexes, their constant conflicts and periodic acts of reconciliation. I have borrowed my adjectives from the Greeks, who developed their mystical doctrines of art through plausible *embodiments,* not through purely conceptual means. It is by those two art-sponsoring deities, Apollo and Dionysos, that we are made to recognize the tremendous split, as regards both origins and objectives, between the plastic, Apollonian arts and the non-visual art of music inspired by Dionysos. The two creative tendencies developed alongside one another, usually in fierce opposition, each by its taunts forcing the other to more energetic production, both perpetuating in a discordant concord that agon which the term art but feebly denominates: until at last, by the thaumaturgy of an Hellenic act of will, the pair accepted the yoke of marriage and, in this condition, begot Attic tragedy, which exhibits the salient features of both parents.

To reach a closer understanding of both these tendencies, let us begin by viewing them as the separate art realms of *dream* and *intoxication,* two physiological phenomena standing toward one another in much the same relationship as the Apollonian and Dionysiac. It was in a dream, according to Lucretius, that the marvelous gods and goddesses first presented themselves to the minds of men. That great sculptor, Phidias, beheld in a dream the entrancing bodies of more-than-human beings, and likewise, if anyone had asked the Greek poets about the mystery of poetic creation, they too would have referred him to dreams and instructed him much as Hans Sachs instructs us in *Die Meistersinger:*

My friend, it is the poet's work
Dreams to interpret and to mark.
Believe me that man's true conceit
In a dream becomes complete:
All poetry we ever read
Is but true dreams interpreted.

The fair illusion of the dream sphere, in the production of which every man proves himself an accomplished artist, is a precondition not only of all plastic art, but even, as we shall see presently, of a wide range of poetry. Here we enjoy an immediate apprehension of form, all shapes speak to us directly, nothing seems indifferent or redundant. Despite the high intensity with which these dream realities exist for us, we still have a residual sensation that they are illusions; at least such has been my experience—and the frequency, not to say normality, of the experience is borne out in many passages of the poets. Men of philosophical disposition are known for their constant premonition that our everyday reality, too, is an illusion, hiding another, totally different kind of reality. It was Schopenhauer who considered the ability to view at certain times all men and things as mere phantoms or dream images to be the true mark of philosophic talent. The person who is responsive to the stimuli of art behaves toward the reality of dream much the way the philosopher behaves toward the reality of existence: he observes exactly and enjoys his observations, for it is by these images that he interprets life, by these processes that he rehearses it. Nor is it by pleasant images only that such plausible connections are made: the whole divine comedy of life, including its somber aspects, its sudden balkings, impish accidents, anxious expectations, moves past him, not quite like a shadow play—for it is he himself, after all, who lives and suffers through these scenes—yet never without giving a fleeting sense of illusion; and I imagine that many persons have reassured themselves amidst the perils of dream by calling out, "It is a dream! I want it to go on." I have even heard of people spinning out the causality of one and the same dream over three or more successive nights. All these facts clearly bear witness that our innermost being, the common substratum of humanity, experiences dreams with deep delight and a sense of real necessity. This deep and happy sense of the necessity of dream experiences was expressed by the Greeks in the image of Apollo. Apollo is at once the god of all plastic powers and the soothsaying god. He who is etymologically the "lucent" one, the god of light, reigns also over the fair illusion of our inner world of fantasy. The perfection of these conditions in contrast to our imperfectly understood waking reality, as well as our profound awareness of nature's healing powers during the interval of sleep and dream, furnishes a symbolic analogue to the soothsaying faculty and quite generally to the arts, which make life possible and worth living. But the image of Apollo must incorporate that thin line which the dream image may not cross, under penalty of becoming pathological, of imposing itself on us as crass reality: a discreet limitation, a freedom from all extravagant urges, the sapient tranquillity of the plastic god. His eye must be sunlike, in keeping with his origin. Even at those moments when he is angry and ill-tempered there lies upon him the consecration of fair illusion. In an eccentric way one might say of Apollo what Schopenhauer says, in the first part of *The World as Will and Idea,* of man caught in the veil of Maya: "Even as on an immense, raging sea, assailed by huge wave crests, a man sits in a little rowboat trusting his frail craft, so, amidst the furious torments of this world, the individual sits tranquilly, supported by the *principium individuationis* and relying on it." One might say that the unshakable confidence in that principle has received its most magnificent expression in Apollo, and that Apollo himself may be regarded as the marvelous divine image of the *principium individuationis,* whose looks and gestures radiate the full delight, wisdom, and beauty of "illusion."

In the same context Schopenhauer has described for us the tremendous awe which seizes man when he suddenly begins to doubt the cognitive modes of experience, in other words, when in a given instance the law of causation seems to suspend itself. If we add to this awe the glorious transport which arises in man, even from the very depths of nature, at the shattering of the *principium individuationis,* then we are in a position to apprehend the essence of Dionysiac rapture, whose closest analogy is furnished by physical intoxication. Dionysiac stirrings arise either through the influence of those narcotic potions of which all primitive races speak in their hymns, or through the powerful approach of spring, which penetrates with joy the whole frame of nature. So stirred, the individual forgets himself completely. It is the Same Dionysiac power which in medieval Germany drove ever increasing crowds of people singing and dancing from place to place; we recognize in these St. John's and St. Vitus' dancers the bacchic choruses of the Greeks, who had their precursors in Asia Minor and as far back as Babylon and the orgiastic Sacaea. There are people who, either from lack of experience or out of sheer stupidity, turn away from such phenomena, and, strong in the sense of their own sanity, label them either mockingly or pityingly "endemic diseases." These benighted souls have no idea how cadaverous and ghostly their "sanity" appears as the intense throng of Dionysiac revelers sweeps past them.

Not only does the bond between man and man come to be forged once more by the magic of the Dionysiac rite, but nature itself, long alienated or subjugated, rises again to celebrate the reconciliation with her prodigal son, man. The earth offers its gifts voluntarily, and the savage beasts of mountain and desert approach in peace. The chariot of Dionysos is bedecked with flowers and garlands; panthers and tigers stride beneath his yoke. If one were to convert Beethoven's "Paean to Joy" into a painting, and refuse to curb the imagination when that multitude prostrates itself reverently in the dust, one might form some apprehension of Dionysiac ritual. Now the slave emerges as a freeman; all the rigid, hostile walls which either necessity or despotism has erected between men are shattered. Now that the gospel of universal harmony is sounded, each individual becomes not only reconciled to his fellow but actually at one with him—as though the veil of Maya had been torn apart and there remained only shreds floating before the vision of mystical Oneness. Man now expresses himself through song and dance as the member of a higher community; he has forgotten how to walk, how to speak, and is on the brink of taking wing as he dances. Each of his gestures betokens enchantment; through him sounds a supernatural power, the same power which makes the animals speak and the earth render up milk and honey. He feels himself to be godlike and strides with the same elation and ecstasy as the gods he has seen in his dreams. No longer the *artist,* he has himself become a *work of art: the productive power of the whole universe is now manifest in his transport, to the glorious satisfaction of the primordial One. The finest clay, the most precious marble— man—is here kneaded and hewn, and the chisel blows of the Dionysiac world artist* are accompanied by the cry of the Eleusinian mystagogues: "Do you fall on your knees, multitudes, do you divine your creator?"

II. So far we have examined the Apollonian and Dionysiac states as the product of formative forces arising directly from nature without the mediation of the human artist. At this stage artistic urges are satisfied directly, on the one hand through the imagery of dreams, whose perfection is quite independent of the intellectual rank, the artistic development of the individual; on the other hand, through an ecstatic reality which once

Starry Night, 1889, by Vincent van Gogh (1853-1890). Oil on Canvas, 29' x 36 1/4" (73.7 x 92.1 cm). (©*The Museum of Modern Art, New York, Acquired through the Lillie P. Bliss Bequest.*) of It is hard not to think of the paintings of Nietzsche's contemporary Vincent van Gogh when reading Nietzsche's words: "If one were to convert Beethoven's Paean to Joy' into a painting, and refuse to curb the imagination when that multitude prostrates itself reverently in the dust, one might form some appre-hension of Dionysiac ritual," Photograph (c) 2000.

again takes no account of the individual and may even destroy him, or else redeem him through a mystical experience of the collective. In relation to these immediate creative conditions of nature every artist must appear as "imitator," either as the Apollonian dream artist or the Dionysiac ecstatic artist, or, finally (as in Greek tragedy, for exam-ple) as dream and ecstatic artist in one. We might picture to ourselves how the last of these, in a state of Dionysiac intoxication and mystical self-abrogation, wandering apart from the reveling throng, sinks upon the ground, and how there is then revealed to him his own condition—complete oneness with the essence of the universe—in a dream similitude.

Having set down these general premises and distinctions, we now turn to the Greeks in order to realize to what degree the formative forces of nature were devel-oped in them. Such an inquiry will enable us to assess properly the relation of the Greek artist to his prototypes or, to use Aristotle's expression, his "imitation of na-ture." Of the dreams the Greeks dreamed it is not possible to speak with any certainty, despite the extant dream literature and the large number of dream anecdotes. But con-sidering the incredible accuracy of their eyes, their keen and unabashed delight in colors, one can hardly be wrong in assuming that their dreams too showed a strict consequence of lines and contours, hues and groupings, a progression of scenes similar to their best bas-reliefs. The perfection of these dream scenes might almost tempt us to consider the dreaming Greek as a Homer and Homer as a dreaming Greek; which would be as though the modern man were to compare himself in his dreaming to Shakespeare.

Yet there is another point about which we do not have to conjecture at all: I mean the profound gap separating the Dionysiac Greeks from the Dionysiac barbarians. Throughout the range of ancient civilization (leaving the newer civilizations out of account for the moment) we find evidence of Dionysiac celebrations which stand to the Greek type in much the same relation as the bearded satyr, whose name and attributes are derived from the he-goat, stands to the god Dionysos. The central concern of such celebrations was, almost universally, a complete sexual promiscuity overriding every form of established tribal law; all the savage urges of the mind were unleashed on those occasions until they reached that paroxysm of lust and cruelty which has always struck me as the "witches' cauldron" *par excellence.* It would appear that the Greeks were for a while quite immune from these feverish excesses which must have reached them by every known land or sea route. What kept Greece safe was the proud, imposing image of Apollo, who in holding up the head of the Gorgon to those brutal and grotesque Dionysiac forces subdued them. Doric art has immortalized Apollo's majestic rejection of all license. But resistance became difficult, even impossible, as soon as similar urges began to break forth from the deep substratum of Hellenism itself. Soon the function of the Delphic god developed into something quite different and much more limited: all he could hope to accomplish now was to wrest the destructive weapon, by a timely gesture of pacification, from his opponent's hand. That act of pacification represents the most important event in the history of Greek ritual; every department of life now shows symptoms of a revolutionary change. The two great antagonists have been reconciled. Each feels obliged henceforth to keep to his bounds, each will honor the other by the bestowal of periodic gifts, while the cleavage remains fundamentally the same. And yet, if we examine what happened to the Dionysiac powers under the pressure of that treaty we notice a great difference: in the place of the Babylonian Sacaea, with their throwback of men to the condition of apes and tigers, we now see entirely new rites celebrated: rites of universal redemption, of glorious transfiguration. Only now has it become possible to speak of nature's celebrating an aesthetic triumph; only now has the abrogation of the *principium individuationis* become an aesthetic event. That terrible witches' brew concocted of lust and cruelty has lost all power under the new conditions. Yet the peculiar blending of emotions in the heart of the Dionysiac reveler—his ambiguity if you will—seems still to hark back (as the medicinal drug harks back to the deadly poison) to the days when the infliction of pain was experienced as joy while a sense of supreme triumph elicited cries of anguish from the heart. For now in every exuberant joy there is heard an undertone of terror, or else a wistful lament over an irrecoverable loss. It is as though in these Greek festivals a sentimental trait of nature were coming to the fore, as though nature were bemoaning the fact of her fragmentation, her decomposition into separate individuals. The chants and gestures of these revelers, so ambiguous in their motivation, represented an absolute *novum* in the world of the Homeric Greeks; their Dionysiac music, in especial, spread abroad terror and a deep shudder. It is true: music had long been familiar to the Greeks as an Apollonian art, as a regular beat like that of waves lapping the shore, a plastic rhythm expressly developed for the portrayal of Apollonian conditions. Apollo's music was a Doric architecture of sound—of barely hinted sounds such as are proper to the cithara. Those very elements which characterize Dionysiac music and, after it, music quite generally: the heart-shaking power of tone, the uniform stream of melody, the incomparable resources of harmony—all those elements had been carefully kept at a distance as being inconsonant with the Apollonian norm. In the Dionysiac dithyramb man is incited to strain his symbolic faculties to the utmost; something quite unheard of is now clamoring to be heard: the desire to tear asunder the veil of Maya, to sink back into the original oneness of nature; the desire to express the very essence of nature symbolically. Thus an entirely new set of symbols springs into being. First all the symbols pertaining to physical features: mouth, face, the spoken word, the dance movement which coordinates the limbs and bends them to its rhythm. Then suddenly all the rest of the symbolic forces—music and rhythm as such, dynamics, harmony—assert themselves with great energy. In order to comprehend this total emancipation of all the symbolic powers one must have reached the same measure of inner freedom those powers themselves were making manifest; which is to say that the votary of Dionysos could not be understood except by his own kind. It is not difficult to imagine the awed surprise with which the Apollonian Greek must have looked on him. And that surprise would be further increased as the latter realized, with a shudder, that all this was not so alien to him after all, that his Apollonian consciousness was but a thin veil hiding from him the whole Dionysiac realm.

III. In order to comprehend this we must take down the elaborate edifice of Apollonian culture stone by stone until we discover its foundations. At first the eye is struck by the marvelous shapes of the Olympian gods who stand upon its pediments, and whose exploits, in shining bas-relief, adorn its friezes. The fact that among them we find Apollo as one god among many, making no claim to a privileged position, should not mislead us. The same drive that found its most complete representation in Apollo generated the whole Olympian world, and in this sense we may consider Apollo the father of that world. But what was the radical need out of which that illustrious society of Olympian beings sprang?

Whoever approaches the Olympians with a different religion in his heart, seeking moral elevation, sanctity, spirituality, loving-kindness, will presently be forced to turn away from them in ill-humored disappointment. Nothing in these deities reminds us of asceticism, high intellect, or duty: we are confronted by luxuriant, triumphant *existence,* which deifies the good and the bad indifferently. And the beholder may find himself dismayed in the presence of such overflowing life and ask himself what potion these heady people must have drunk in order to behold, in whatever direction they looked, Helen laughing back at them, the beguiling image of their own existence. But we shall call out to this beholder, who has already turned his back: Don't go! Listen first to what the Greeks themselves have to say of this life, which spreads itself before you with such puzzling serenity. An old legend has it that King Midas hunted a long time in the woods for the wise Silenus, companion of Dionysos, without being able to catch him. When he had finally caught him the king asked him what he considered man's greatest good. The daemon remained sullen and uncommunicative until finally, forced by the king, he broke into a shrill laugh and spoke: "Ephemeral wretch, begotten by accident and toil, why do you force me to tell you what it would be your greatest boon not to hear? What would be best for you is quite beyond your reach: not to have been born, not to be, to be *nothing.* But the second best is to die soon."

What is the relation of the Olympian gods to this popular wisdom? It is that of the entranced vision of the martyr to his torment.

Now the Olympian magic mountain opens itself before us, showing us its very roots. The Greeks were keenly aware of the terrors and horrors of existence; in order to be able to live at all they had to place before them the shining fantasy of the Olympians. Their tremendous distrust of the titanic forces of nature: *Moira,* mercilessly enthroned beyond the knowable world; the vulture which fed upon the great philanthropist Prometheus; the terrible lot drawn by wise Oedipus; the curse on the house of Atreus which brought Orestes to the murder of his mother: that whole Panic philosophy, in short, with its mythic examples, by which the gloomy Etruscans perished, the Greeks conquered—or at least hid from view—again and again by means of this artificial Olympus. In order to live at all the Greeks had to construct these deities. The Apollonian need for beauty had to develop the Olympian hierarchy of joy by slow degrees from the original titanic hierarchy of terror, as roses are seen to break from a thorny thicket. How else could life have been borne by a race so hypersensitive, so emotionally intense, so equipped for suffering? The same drive which called art into being as a completion and consummation of existence, and as a guarantee of further existence, gave rise also to that Olympian realm which acted as a transfiguring mirror to the Hellenic will. The gods justified human life by living it themselves—the only satisfactory theodicy ever invented. To exist in the clear sunlight of such deities was now felt to be the highest good, and the only real grief suffered by Homeric man was inspired by the thought of leaving that sunlight, especially when the departure seemed imminent. Now it became possible to stand the wisdom of Silenus on its head and proclaim that it was the worst evil for man to die soon, and second worst for him to die at all. Such laments as arise now arise over short-lived Achilles, over the generations ephemeral as leaves, the decline of the heroic age. It is not unbecoming to even the greatest hero to yearn for an afterlife, though it be as a day laborer. So impetuously, during the Apollonian phase, does man's will desire to remain on earth, so identified does he become with existence, that even his lament turns to a song of praise.

It should have become apparent by now that the harmony with nature which we late-comers regard with such nostalgia, and for which Schiller has coined the cant term naive, is by no means a simple and inevitable condition to be found at the gateway to every culture, a kind of paradise. Such a belief could have been endorsed only by a period for which Rousseau's Emile was an artist and Homer just such an artist nurtured in the bosom of nature. Whenever we encounter "naïveté" in art, we are face to face with the ripest fruit of Apollonian culture—which must always triumph first over titans, kill monsters, and overcome the somber contemplation of actuality, the intense susceptibility to suffering, by means of illusions strenuously and zestfully entertained. But how rare are the instances of true naïveté, of that complete identification with the beauty of appearance! It is this achievement which makes Homer so magnificent—Homer, who, as a single individual, stood to Apollonian popular culture in the same relation as the individual dream artist to the oneiric capacity of a race and of nature generally. The naïveté of Homer must be viewed as a complete victory of Apollonian illusion. Nature often uses illusions of this sort in order to accomplish its secret purposes. The true goal is covered over by a phantasm. We stretch out our hands to the latter, while nature, aided by our deception, attains the former. In the case of the Greeks it was the will wishing to behold itself in the work of art, in the transcendence of genius; but in order so to behold itself its creatures had first to view themselves as glorious, to transpose themselves to a higher sphere, without having that sphere of pure contemplation either challenge them or upbraid them with insufficiency. It was in that sphere of beauty that the Greeks saw the Olympians as their mirror images; it was by means of that aesthetic mirror that the Greek will opposed suffering and the somber wisdom of suffering which always accompanies artisic talent. As a monument to its victory stands Homer, the naive artist.

* * *

XV. . . . The influence of Socrates (like a shadow cast by the evening sun, ever lengthening into the future) has prompted generation after generation to reconsider the foundations of its art—art taken in its deepest and broadest sense—and as that influence is eternal it also guarantees the eternity of artistic endeavor. But before people were able to realize that all art is intimately dependent on the Greeks from Homer to Socrates, they had necessarily toward the Greeks the same attitude that the Athenians had toward Socrates. Practically every era of Western civilization has at one time or another tried to liberate itself from the Greeks, in deep dissatisfaction because whatever they themselves achieved, seemingly quite original and sincerely admired, lost color and life when held against the Greek model and shrank to a botched copy, a caricature. Time and again a hearty anger has been felt against that presumptuous little nation which had the nerve to brand, for all time, whatever was not created on its own soil as "barbaric." Who are these people, whose historical splendor was ephemeral, their institutions ridiculously narrow, their mores dubious and sometimes objectionable, who yet pretend to the special place among the nations which genius claims among the crowd? None of the later detractors was fortunate enough to find the cup of hemlock with which such a being could be disposed of once and for all: all the poisons of envy, slander, and rage have proved insufficient to destroy that complacent magnificence. And so people have continued to be both ashamed and fearful of the Greeks—though now and again someone has come along who has acknowledged the full truth: that the Greeks are the chariot drivers of every subsequent culture, but that, almost always, chariot and horses are of too poor a quality for the drivers, who then make sport of driving the chariot into the abyss—which they themselves clear with the bold leap of Achilles.

In order to see Socrates as one of these charioteers, it is necessary only to view him as the prototype of an entirely new mode of existence. He is the great exemplar of that theoretical man whose significance and aims we must now attempt to understand. Like the artist, *theoretical* man takes infinite pleasure in all that exists and is thus saved from the practical ethics of pessimism, with its lynx eyes that shine only in the dark. But while the artist, having unveiled the truth garment by garment, remains with his gaze fixed on what is still hidden, theoretical man takes delight in the cast garments and finds his highest satisfaction in the unveiling process itself, which proves to him his own power. Science could not have developed as it has done if its sole concern had been that one naked goddess. For then the adepts of science would have felt like people trying to dig a hole through the earth, each of whom soon realizes that though he toil in lifelong labor he will excavate only an infinitesimal fraction of the great distance and that even this fraction will be covered over before his eyes by another's efforts, so that a third man would do well to find a new spot for his tunneling. Moreover, once it has been proved beyond question that the Antipodes can never be reached by such a direct method, what person in his right mind would want to go on digging—unless it were for the accidental benefit of striking some precious metal or hitting upon a law of nature? For this reason Lessing, most honest of theoretical men, dared to say that the search for truth was more important to him than truth itself and thereby revealed the innermost secret of inquiry, to the surprise and annoyance of his fellows. Yet, sure enough, alongside sporadic perceptions such as this one of Lessing's, which represented an act of honesty as well as high-spirited defiance, we find a type of deep-seated illusion, first manifested in Socrates: the illusion that thought, guided by the thread of causation, might plumb the farthest abysses of being and even *correct* it. This grand metaphysical illusion has become integral to the scientific endeavor and again and again leads science to those far limits of its inquiry where it becomes art—*which, in this mechanism, is what is really intended.*

If we examine Socrates in the light of this idea, he strikes us as the first who was able not only to live under the guidance of that instinctive scientific certainty but to die by it, which is much more difficult. For this reason the image of the dying Socrates— mortal man freed by knowledge and argument from the fear of death—is the emblem which, hanging above the portal of every science, reminds the adept that his mission is to make existence appear intelligible and thereby justified. If arguments prove insufficient, the element of myth may be used to strengthen them—that myth which I have described as the necessary consequence, and ultimate intention, of all science.

Once we have fully realized how, after Socrates, the mystagogue of science, one school of philosophers after another came upon the scene and departed; how generation after generation of inquirers, spurred by an insatiable thirst for knowledge, explored every aspect of the universe; and how by that ecumenical concern a common net of knowledge was spread over the whole globe, affording glimpses into the workings of an entire solar system—once we have realized all this, and the monumental pyramid of present-day knowledge, we cannot help viewing Socrates as the vortex and turning point of Western civilization. For if we imagine that immense store of energy used, not for the purposes of knowledge, but for the practical, egotistical ends of individuals and nations, we may readily see the consequence: universal wars of extermination and constant migrations of peoples would have weakened man's instinctive zest for life to such an extent that, suicide having become a matter of course, duty might have commanded the son to kill his parents, the friend his friend, as among the Fiji islanders. We know that such wholesale slaughter prevails wherever art in some form or other—especially as religion or science—has not served as antidote to barbarism.

As against this practical pessimism, Socrates represents the archetype of the theoretical optimist, who, strong in the belief that nature can be fathomed, considers knowledge to be the true panacea and error to be radical evil. To Socratic man the one noble and truly human occupation was that of laying bare the workings of nature, of separating true knowledge from illusion and error. So it happened that ever since Socrates the mechanism of concepts, judgments, and syllogisms has come to be regarded as the highest exercise of man's powers, nature's most admirable gift. Socrates and his successors, down to our own day, have considered all moral and sentimental accomplishments—noble deeds, compassion, self-sacrifice, heroism, even that spiritual calm, so difficult of attainment, which the Apollonian Greek called *sophrosyne*— to be ultimately derived from the dialectic of knowledge, and therefore teachable. Whoever has tasted the delight of a Socratic perception, experienced how it moves to encompass the whole world of phenomena in ever widening circles, knows no sharper incentive to life than his desire to complete the conquest, to weave the net absolutely tight. To such a person the Platonic Socrates appears as the teacher of an entirely new form of "Greek serenity" and affirmation. This positive attitude toward existence must release itself in actions for the most part pedagogic, exercised upon noble youths, to the end of producing genius. But science, spurred on by its energetic notions, approaches irresistibly those outer limits where the optimism implicit in logic must collapse. For the periphery of science has an infinite number of points. Every noble and gifted man has, before reaching the mid-point of his career, come up against some point of the periphery that defied his understanding, quite apart from the fact that we have no way of knowing how the area of the circle is ever to be fully charted. When the inquirer, having pushed to the circumference, realizes how logic in that place curls about itself and bites its own tail, he is struck with a new kind of perception: a tragic perception, which requires, to make it tolerable, the remedy of art.

If we look about us today, with eyes refreshed and fortified by the spectacle of the Greeks, we shall see how the insatiable zest for knowledge, prefigured in Socrates, has been transformed into tragic resignation and the need for art; while, to be sure, on a lower level that same zest appears as hostile to all art and especially to the truly tragic, Dionysiac art, as I have tried to show paradigmatically in the subversion of Aeschylean art by Socratism.

At this point we find ourselves, not without trepidation, knocking at the gates of present and future. Will this dialectic inversion lead to ever new configurations of genius, above all to that of Socrates as the practitioner of music? Will the all-encompassing net of art (whether under the name of religion or science) be woven ever more tightly and delicately? Or will it be torn to shreds by the restless and barbaric activities of our present day? Deeply concerned, yet not unhopeful, we stand aside for a little while as spectators privileged to witness these tremendous struggles and transitions. Alas, it is the spell inherent in such battles that he who watches them must also fight them.

*   *   *

XXV. Music and tragic myth are equally expressive of the Dionysiac talent of a nation and cannot be divorced from one another. Both have their origin in a realm of art which lies beyond the Apollonian; both shed their transfiguring light on a region in whose rapt harmony dissonance and the horror of existence fade away in enchantment. Confident of their supreme powers, they both toy with the sting of displeasure, and by their toying they both justify the existence of even the "worst possible world." Thus the Dionysiac element, as against the Apollonian, proves itself to be the eternal and original power of art, since it calls into being the entire world of phenomena. Yet in the midst of that world a new transfiguring light is needed to catch and hold in life the stream of individual forms. If we could imagine an incarnation of dissonance—and what is man if not that?—that dissonance, in order to endure life, would need a marvelous illusion to cover it with a veil of beauty. This is the proper artistic intention of Apollo, in whose name are gathered together all those countless illusions of fair semblance which at any moment make life worth living and whet our appetite for the next moment.

But only so much of the Dionysiac substratum of the universe may enter an individual consciousness as can be dealt with by that Apollonian transfiguration; so that these two prime agencies must develop in strict proportion, conformable to the laws of eternal justice. Whenever the Dionysiac forces become too obstreperous, as is the case today, we are safe in assuming that Apollo is close at hand, though wrapped in a cloud, and that the rich effects of his beauty will be witnessed by a later generation.

The reader may intuit these effects if he has ever, though only in a dream, been carried back to the ancient Hellenic way of life. Walking beneath high Ionic peristyles, looking toward a horizon defined by pure and noble lines, seeing on either hand the glorified reflections of his shape in gleaming marble and all about him men moving solemnly or delicately, with harmonious sounds and rhythmic gestures: would he not then, overwhelmed by this steady stream of beauty, be forced to raise his hands to Apollo and call out: "Blessed Greeks! how great must be your Dionysos, if the Delic god thinks such enchantments necessary to cure you of your dithyrambic madness!" To one so moved, an ancient Athenian with the august countenance of Aeschylus might reply: "But you should add, extraordinary stranger, what suffering must this race have endured in order to achieve such beauty! Now come with me to the tragedy and let us sacrifice in the temple of both gods."

ON THE GENEALOGY OF MORALITY (in part)

"GOOD AND EVIL," "GOOD AND BAD"

1.—These English psychologists, who have to be thanked for having made the only attempts so far to write a history of the emergence of morality,—provide us with a small riddle in the form of themselves; in fact, I admit that as living riddles they have a significant advantage over their books—*they are actually interesting!* These English psychologists—just what do they want? You always find them at the same task, whether they want to or not, pushing the *partie honteuse* of our inner world to the foreground, and looking for what is really effective, guiding and decisive for our development where man's intellectual pride would least wish to find it (for example, in the *vis inertiae* of habit, or in forgetfulness, or in a blind and random coupling of ideas, or in something purely passive, automatic, reflexive, molecular and thoroughly stupid)— what is it that actually drives these psychologists in precisely *this* direction all the time? Is it a secret, malicious, mean instinct to belittle man, which is perhaps unacknowledged? Or perhaps a pessimistic suspicion, the mistrust of disillusioned, surly idealists who have turned poisonous and green? Or a certain subterranean animosity and *rancune* towards Christianity (and Plato), which has perhaps not even passed the threshold of the consciousness? Or even a lewd taste for the strange, for the painful paradox, for the dubious and nonsensical in life? Or finally—a bit of everything, a bit of meanness, a bit of gloominess, a bit of anti-Christianity, a bit of a thrill and need for pepper? . . . But people tell me that they are just old, cold, boring frogs crawling round men and hopping into them as if they were in their element, namely a *swamp.* I am resistant to hearing this and, indeed, I do not believe it; and if it is permissible to wish where it is impossible to know, I sincerely hope that the reverse is true,—that these analysts holding a microscope to the soul are actually brave, generous and proud animals, who know how to control their own pleasure and pain and have been taught to sacrifice desirability to truth, every truth, even a plain, bitter, ugly, foul, unchristian, immoral truth . . . Because there are such truths.

On the Genealogy of Morality, first essay: "Good and Evil," "Good and Bad" (complete), translated by Carol Diethe from Friedrich Nietzsche, *On the Genealogy of Morality,* edited by Keith Ansell-Pearson (Cambridge: Cambridge University Press, 1994). Reprinted by permission of Cambridge University Press.

2. So you have to respect the good spirits which preside in these historians of morality! But it is unfortunately a fact that *historical spirit* itself is lacking in them, they have been left in the lurch by all the good spirits of history itself! As is now established philosophical practice, they all think in a way that is *essentially* unhistorical; this can't be doubted. The idiocy of their moral genealogy is revealed at the outset when it is a question of conveying the descent of the concept and judgment of "good." "Originally"—they decree—"unegoistic acts were praised and called good by their recipients, in other words, by the people to whom they were *useful;* later, everyone *forgot* the origin of the praise and because such acts had always been *routinely* praised as good, people began also to experience them as good—as if they were something good *as such."* We can see at once: this first deduction contains all the typical traits of idiosyncratic English psychologists, we have "usefulness," "forgetting," "routine" and finally "error," all as the basis of a respect for values of which the higher man has hitherto been proud, as though it were a sort of general privilege of mankind. This pride *must be* humbled, this valuation devalued: has that been achieved? . . . Now for me, it is obvious that the real breeding-ground for the concept "good" has been sought and located in the wrong place by this theory: the judgment "good" does *not* emanate from those to whom goodness is shown! Instead it has been "the good" themselves, meaning the noble, the mighty, the high-placed and the high-minded, who saw and judged themselves and their actions as good, I mean first-rate, in contrast to everything lowly, low-minded, common and plebeian. It was from this *pathos of distance* that they first claimed the right to create values and give these values names: usefulness was none of their concern! The standpoint of usefulness is as alien and inappropriate as it can be to such a heated eruption of the highest rank-ordering and rank-defining value judgments: this is the point where feeling reaches the opposite of the low temperatures needed for any calculation of prudence or reckoning of usefulness,—and not just for once, for one exceptional moment, but permanently. The pathos of nobility and distance, as I said, the continuing and predominant feeling of complete and fundamental superiority of a higher ruling kind in relation to a lower kind, to those "below"—that is the origin of the antithesis "good" and "bad." (The seigneurial privilege of giving names even allows us to conceive of the origin of language itself as a manifestation of the power of the rulers: they say "this is so and so," they set their seal on everything and every occurrence with a sound and thereby take possession of it, as it were.) It is because of this origin that the word "good" is *not* absolutely necessarily attached to "unegoistic" actions: as the superstition of these moral genealogists would have it. On the contrary, it is only with a *decline* of aristocratic value-judgments that this whole antithesis between "egoistic" and "unegoistic" forces itself more and more on man's conscience,— it is, to use my language, the *herd instinct* which, with that, finally gets its word in (and makes *words*). And even then it takes long enough for this instinct to become sufficiently dominant for the valuation of moral values to become enmeshed and embedded in the antithesis (as is the case in contemporary Europe, for example: the prejudice which takes "moral," "unegoistic" and *"desinteresse"* as equivalent terms already rules with the power of a "fixed idea" and mental illness).

3. But secondly: quite apart from the fact that that hypothesis about the descent of the value judgment "good'' is historically untenable, it also suffers from an inner psychological contradiction. The usefulness of unegoistic behaviour is supposed to be the origin of the esteem in which it is held, and this origin is supposed to have been forgotten:—but how was such forgetting *possible?* Did the usefulness of such behaviour suddenly cease at some point? The opposite is the case: it is that this usefulness has

been a permanent part of our everyday experience, something, then, which has been constantly stressed anew; consequently, instead of fading from consciousness, instead of becoming forgettable, it must have impressed itself on consciousness with ever greater clarity. How much more sensible is the opposite theory (that doesn't make it any more true—), which is held, for example, by Herbert Spencer: he judges the concept "good" as essentially the same as "useful," "practical," so that in their judgments "good" and "bad," people sum up and sanction their *unforgotten, unforgettable* experiences of what is useful-practical, harmful impractical. According to this theory, good is what has always shown itself to be useful: so it can claim validity as "valuable in the highest degree," as "valuable as such." This route towards an explanation is wrong, as I said, but at least the explanation in itself is rational and psychologically tenable.

4.—I was given a pointer in the *right* direction by the question as to what the terms for "good," as used in different languages, mean from the etymological point of view: then I found that they all led me back to the *same conceptual transformation,*—that everywhere, "noble," "aristocratic" in social terms is the basic concept from which, necessarily, "good" in the sense of "spiritually noble," "aristocratic," of "spiritually high-minded," "spiritually privileged" developed: a development which always runs parallel with that other one which ultimately transfers "common," "plebeian," "low" into the concept "bad." The best example for the latter is the German word *"schlecht"* (bad) itself which is identical with *"schlicht"* (plain, simple)—compare *"schlechtweg"* (plainly), *"schlechterdings"* (simply)—which originally referred to the simple, the common man with no derogatory implication, but simply in contrast to the nobility. Round about the time of the Thirty Years War, late enough, then, this meaning shifted into its current usage. To me, this seems an *essential* insight into moral genealogy; that it has been discovered so late is due to the obstructing influence which the democratic bias within the modern world exercises over all questions of descent. And this is the case in the apparently most objective of fields, natural science and physiology, which I shall just allude to here. The havoc this prejudice can wreak, once it is unbridled to the point of hatred, particularly for morality and history, can be seen in the famous case of Buckle; the *plebeianism* of the modern spirit, which began in England, broke out there once again on its native soil as violently as a volcano of mud and with that salted, over-loud, vulgar loquacity with which all volcanoes have spoken up till now.—

5.—With regard to *our* problem, which can justifiably be called a *quiet* problem and which fastidiously addresses itself to only a few ears, it is of no little interest to discover that, in these words and roots which denote "good," we can often detect the main nuance which made the noble feel they were men of higher rank. True, in most cases they might give themselves names which simply show superiority of power (such as "the mighty," "the masters," "the commanders") or the most visible sign of this superiority, such as "the rich," "the propertied" (that is the meaning of *arya;* and the equivalent in Iranian and Slavic). But the names also show a *typical character trait:* and this is what concerns us here. For example, they call themselves "the truthful": led by the Greek aristocracy, whose mouthpiece is the Megarian poet Theognis. The word used specifically for this purpose, ⟨*esthlos*⟩*, means, according to its root, one who *is,* who

---

*[This word seems originally to have meant "genuine, real"; it later becomes one of the most commonly used words for "noble."]

has reality, who really exists and is true; then, with a subjective transformation, it becomes the slogan and catch-phrase of the aristocracy and is completely assimilated with the sense of "aristocratic," in contrast to the *deceitful* common man, as taken and shown by Theognis,—until, finally, with the decline of the aristocracy, the word remains as a term for spiritual *noblesse,* and, as it were, ripens and sweetens. Cowardice is underlined in the word ⟨*kakos*⟩ [weak, ugly, cowardly, worthless] and in ⟨*deilos*⟩ [cowardly (and thus despicable)] (the plebeian in contrast to the ⟨*agathos*⟩: perhaps this gives a clue as to where we should look for the etymological derivation of the ambiguous term ⟨*agathos*⟩ [capable, useful, good]. In the Latin word *malus* [bad, evil] (to which I juxtapose ⟨*melas*⟩ [dark, black]) the common man could be characterized as the dark-skinned and especially the dark-haired man ("hic niger est—")*, as the pre-Aryan occupant of Italian soil who could most easily be distinguished from the blond race which had become dominant, namely the Aryan conquering race, by its colour; at any rate, I have found exactly the same with Gaelic peoples,—fin (for example in Fingal), the word designating the aristocracy and finally the good, noble, pure, was originally a blond person in contrast to the dark-skinned, dark-haired native inhabitants. By the way, the Celts were a completely blond race; it is wrong to connect those traces of an essentially dark-haired population, which can be seen on carefully prepared ethnological maps in Germany, with any Celtic descent and mixing of blood in such a connection, as Virchow does: it is more a case of the *pre-Aryan* population of Germany emerging at these points. (The same holds good for virtually the whole of Europe: to all intents and purposes the subject race has ended up by regaining the upper hand in skin colour, shortness of forehead and perhaps even in intellectual and social instincts: who can give any guarantee that modern democracy, the even more modern anarchism, and indeed that predilection for the "commune," the most primitive form of social structure which is common to all Europe's socialists, are not in essence a huge *counter-attack*—and that the conquering *master race,* that of the Aryans, is not physiologically being defeated as well? . . .) I think I can interpret the Latin *bonus* [good] as "the 'warrior' ": providing I am correct in tracing *bonus* back to an older *duonus* (compare *bel-lum* ** = *duellum* = *duen-lum,* which seems to me to contain that *duonus*). Therefore *bonus* as a man of war, of division (duo), as warrior: one can see what made up a man's "goodness" in ancient Rome. Take our German *"gut"*: does it not mean "the god-like man," the man "of godlike race"? And is it not identical with the popular (originally noble), name of the Goths. The grounds for this supposition will not be gone into here.

6.—If the highest caste is at the same time the *clerical* caste and therefore chooses a title for its overall description which calls its priestly function to mind, this does not yet constitute an exception to the rule that the concept of political superiority always resolves itself into the concept of psychological superiority (although this may be the occasion giving rise to exceptions). This is an example of the first juxtaposition of "pure" and "impure" as signs of different estates; and later "good" and "bad" develop in a direction which no longer refers to social standing. In addition, people should be wary of taking these terms "pure" and "impure" too seriously, too far or even symbolically: all ancient man's concepts were originally understood—to a degree we can

*["That man is a dangerous character," literally "He is black." (Horace, *Satires* I, 85.)]
**[Both "bellum" and "duellum" mean "war" in Latin.]

scarcely imagine—as crude, coarse, detached, narrow, direct and in particular *unsymbolic*. From the outset the "pure man" was just a man who washed, avoided certain foods which cause skin complaints, did not sleep with the filthy women from the lower orders and had a horror of blood,—nothing more, not much more! And yet the very nature of an essentially priestly aristocracy shows how contradictory valuations could become dangerously internalized and sharpened, precisely in such an aristocracy at an early stage; and in fact clefts were finally driven between man and man which even an Achilles of free-thinking would shudder to cross. From the very beginning there has been something *unhealthy* about these priestly aristocracies and in the customs dominant there, which are turned away from action and which are partly brooding and partly emotionally explosive, resulting in the almost inevitable bowel complaints and neurasthenia which have plagued the clergy down the ages; but as for the remedy they themselves found for their sickness,—surely one must say that its after-effects have shown it to be a hundred times more dangerous than the disease it was meant to cure? People are still ill from the after-effects of these priestly quack-cures! For example, think of certain diets (avoidance of meat), of fasting, sexual abstinence, the flight "into the desert" (Wier-Mitchell's bed-rest, admittedly without the subsequent overfeeding and weight-gain which constitute the most effective antidote to all hysteria brought on by the ascetic ideal): think, too, of the whole metaphysics of the clergy, which is antagonistic towards the senses, making men lazy and refined, think, too, of their Fakir-like and Brahmin-like self-hypnotizing—Brahminism as crystal ball and fixed idea—and the final, all-too-comprehensible general disenchantment with its radical cure, *nothingness* (or God:—the yearning for a *unio mystica* with God is the Buddhist yearning for nothingness, Nirvâna—and no more!) Priests make *everything* more dangerous, not just medicaments and healing arts but pride, revenge, acumen, debauchery, love, lust for power, virtue, sickness;—in any case, with some justification one could add that man first became an *interesting animal* on the foundation of this *essentially dangerous* form of human existence, the priest, and that the human soul became *deep* in the higher sense and turned *evil* for the first time—and of course, these are the two basic forms of man's superiority, hitherto, over other animals! . . .

7.—You will have already guessed how easy it was for the priestly method of valuation to split off from the chivalric-aristocratic method and then to develop further into the opposite of the latter; this receives a special impetus when the priestly caste and warrior caste confront one another in jealousy and cannot agree on the prize of war. The chivalric-aristocratic value-judgments are based on a powerful physicality, a blossoming, rich, even effervescent good health which includes the things needed to maintain it, war, adventure, hunting, dancing, jousting and everything else that contains strong, free, happy action. The priestly-aristocratic method of valuation—as we have seen—has different criteria: woe betide it when it comes to war! As we know, priests make the most *evil enemies*—but why? Because they are the most powerless. Out of this powerlessness, their hate swells into something huge and uncanny to a most intellectual and poisonous level. The greatest haters in world history, and the most intelligent [*die geist-reichsten Hasser*], *have always been priests:—nobody else's intelligence* [*Geist*] stands a chance against the intelligence [*Geist*] of priestly revenge.*)

---

*[The German term *Geist* and its derivatives are generally rendered by "spirit" and its derivatives, but can also, as in this sentence, be translated as "intelligence" and, as elsewhere, "mind," "intellectual," etc.— translator's note.]

The history of mankind would be far too stupid a thing if it had not had the intellect [*Geist*] of the powerless injected into it:—let us take the best example straight away. Nothing which has been done on earth against "the noble," "the mighty," "the masters" and "the rulers," is worth mentioning compared with what *the Jews* have done against them: the Jews, that priestly people, which in the last resort was able to gain satisfaction from its enemies and conquerors only through a radical revaluation of their values, that is, through an act of the most deliberate revenge. Only this was fitting for a priestly people with the most entrenched priestly vengefulness. It was the Jews who, rejecting the aristocratic value equation (good = noble = powerful = beautiful = happy = blessed) ventured, with awe-inspiring consistency, to bring about a reversal and held it in the teeth of their unfathomable hatred (the hatred of the powerless), saying, "Only those who suffer are good, only the poor, the powerless, the lowly are good; the suffering, the deprived, the sick, the ugly, are the only pious people, the only ones saved, salvation is for them alone, whereas you rich, the noble and powerful, you are eternally wicked, cruel, lustful, insatiate, godless, you will also be eternally wretched, cursed and damned!" . . . We know who became heir to this Jewish revaluation . . . With regard to the huge and incalculably disastrous initiative taken by the Jews with this most fundamental of all declarations of war, I recall the words I wrote on another occasion [*Beyond Good and Evil*]—namely, that *the slaves' revolt in morality* begins with the Jews: a revolt which has two thousand years of history behind it and which has only been lost sight of because—it was victorious . . .

8.—But you don't understand that? You don't have eyes for something which needed two millennia to achieve victory? . . . There is nothing surprising about that: all *long* things are difficult to see, to see round. But *that* is what happened: from the trunk of the tree of revenge and hatred, Jewish hatred—the deepest and most sublime, indeed a hatred which created ideals and changed values, the like of which has never been seen on earth—there grew something just as incomparable, a *new love,* the deepest and most sublime kind of love: and what other trunk could it have grown out of? . . . But don't make the mistake of thinking that it had grown forth, as a denial of the thirst for revenge, as the opposite of Jewish hatred! No, the reverse is true! This love grew out of the hatred, as its crown, as the triumphant crown expanding ever wider in the purest brightness and radiance of the sun, the crown which, as it were, in the realm of light and height, was pursuing the aims of that hatred, victory, spoils, seduction with the same urgency with which the roots of that hatred were burrowing ever more thoroughly and greedily into everything that was deep and evil. This Jesus of Nazareth, as the embodiment of the gospel of love, this "redeemer" bringing salvation and victory to the poor, the sick, to sinners—was he not seduction in its most sinister and irresistible form, seduction and the circuitous route to just those very *Jewish* values and innovative ideals? Did Israel not reach the pinnacle of her sublime vengefulness via this very "redeemer," this apparent opponent of and disperser of Israel? Is it not part of a secret black art of a truly *great* politics of revenge, a far-sighted, subterranean revenge, slow to grip and calculating, that Israel had to denounce her actual instrument of revenge before all the world as a mortal enemy and nail him to the cross so that "all the world," namely all Israel's enemies, could safely nibble at this bait? And could anyone, on the other hand, using all the ingenuity of his intellect, think up a more *dangerous* bait? Something to equal the enticing, intoxicating, benumbing, corrupting power of that symbol of the "holy cross," to equal that horrible paradox of a "God on the Cross," to equal that mystery of an unthinkable final act of extreme cruelty and self crucifixion of God for the *salvation of mankind?* . . . At least it is certain that *sub hoc* *signo** Israel, with its revenge and revaluation of all former values, has triumphed repeatedly over all other ideals, all *nobler* ideals.—

9.—"But why do you talk about *nobler* ideals! Let's bow to the facts: the people have won—or 'the slaves,' the 'plebeians,' 'the herd,' or whatever you want to call them— if the Jews made this come about, good for them! No people ever had a more world-historic mission. 'The Masters' are deposed; the morality of the common people has triumphed. You might take this victory for blood-poisoning (it did mix the races up)— I do not deny it; but undoubtedly this intoxication has *succeeded.* The 'salvation' of the human race (I mean, from 'the Masters') is well on course; everything is being made appreciably Jewish, Christian or plebeian (never mind the words!). The passage of this poison through the whole body of mankind seems unstoppable, even though its tempo and pace, from now on, might tend to be slower, softer, quieter, calmer—there is no hurry . . . With this in view, does the church still have a vital role, indeed, does it have a right to exist? Or could one do without it? *Quaeritur* [That is the question]. It seems that the Church rather slows down and blocks the passage of poison instead of accelerating it? Well, that might be what makes it useful . . . Certainly it is by now crude and boorish, something which is repugnant to a more tender intellect, to a truly modern taste. Should not the church at least try to be more refined? . . . Nowadays it alienates, more than it seduces . . . Who amongst us would be a freethinker if it were not for the Church? We loathe the Church, *not* its poison . . . Apart from the Church, we too love the poison . . ."—This is the epilogue by a "free-thinker" to my speech, an honest animal as he clearly shows himself to be, and moreover a democrat; he had listened to me up to that point, and could not stand listening to my silence. As a matter of fact, there is much for me to keep silent about at this point.—

10. The beginning of the slaves' revolt in morality occurs when *ressentiment* itself turns creative and gives birth to values: the *ressentiment* of those beings who, being denied the proper response of action, compensate for it only with imaginary revenge. Whereas all noble morality grows out of a triumphant saying "yes" to itself, slave morality says "no" on principle to everything that is "outside," "other," "non-self": and *this* "no" is its creative deed. This reversal of the evaluating glance—this *inevitable* orientation to the outside instead of back onto itself—is a feature of *ressentiment:* in order to come about, slave morality first has to have an opposing, external world, it needs, physiologically speaking, external stimuli in order to act at all,—its action is basically a reaction. The opposite is the case with the noble method of valuation: this acts and grows spontaneously, seeking out its opposite only so that it can say "yes" to itself even more thankfully and exultantly,—its negative concept "low," "common," "bad" is only a pale contrast created after the event compared to its positive basic concept, saturated with life and passion, "We the noble, the good, the beautiful and the happy!" When the noble method of valuation makes a mistake and sins against reality, this happens in relation to the sphere with which it is *not* sufficiently familiar, a true knowledge of which it has indeed rigidly resisted: in some circumstances, it misjudges the sphere it despises, that of the common man, the rabble; on the other hand, we should bear in mind that the distortion which results from the feeling of contempt, disdain and

*[The Emperor Constantine once had a vision of a cross with the attached legend: "By this, conquer." This phrase was eventually transformed into the Latin: "*In hoc signo vinces*" ("In this sign you will conquer"). "*Sub hoc signo*" ("Under this sign") is presumably to be understood as a variant of "*In hoc signo.*"]

superciliousness, always assuming that the image of the despised person is *distorted,* remains far behind the distortion with which the entrenched hatred and revenge of the powerless man attacks his opponent—in effigy of course. Indeed, contempt has too much negligence, nonchalance, complacency and impatience, even too much personal cheerfulness mixed into it, for it to be in a position to transform its object into a real caricature and monster. Nor should one fail to hear the almost kindly nuances which the Greek nobility, for example, places in all words which it uses to distinguish itself from the rabble; a sort of sympathy, consideration and indulgence incessantly permeates and sugars them, with the result that nearly all words referring to the common man remain as expressions for "unhappy," "pitiable" (compare ⟨*deilos*⟩ [timid, fearful], ⟨*deilaios*⟩ [timidity], ⟨*poneros*⟩ [bad, wicked, slothful], ⟨*moxtharos*⟩ [wearisome labor, toil], the last two actually designating the common man as slave worker and beast of burden)—and on the other hand, "bad," "low" and "unhappy" have never ceased to reverberate in the Greek ear in a tone in which "unhappy" predominates: this is a legacy of the old, nobler, aristocratic method of valuation, which does not deny itself even in contempt (philologists will remember the sense in which ⟨*oizuros*⟩ [to have pain], ⟨*anolbos*⟩ [not prosperous, unfortunate], ⟨*tlemon*⟩ [one who endures or suffers], ⟨*dustuxein*⟩ [one who has bad luck], ⟨*tsumphora*⟩ [accident, misfortune] are used). The "well-born" felt they were "the happy"; they did not need first of all to construct their happiness artificially by looking at their enemies, or in some cases by talking themselves into it, *lying themselves into it* (as all men of *ressentiment* are wont to do); and also, as complete men bursting with strength and therefore *necessarily* active, they knew they must not separate happiness from action,—being active is by necessity counted as part of happiness (this is the etymological derivation of ⟨*eu prattein*⟩ [do well])—all very much the opposite of "happiness" at the level of the powerless, the oppressed, and those rankled with poisonous and hostile feelings, for whom it manifests itself as essentially a narcotic, an anaesthetic, rest, peace, "sabbath," relaxation of the mind and stretching of the limbs, in short as something *passive.* While the noble man is confident and frank with himself (⟨*gennaios*⟩, "of noble birth," underlines the nuance "upright" and probably "naive" as well), the man of *ressentiment* is neither upright nor naive, nor honest and straight with himself. His soul *squints;* his mind loves dark corners, secret paths and back-doors, everything secretive appeals to him as being *his* world, *his* security, *his* comfort; he knows all about keeping quiet, not forgetting, waiting, temporarily humbling and abasing himself. A race of such men of *ressentiment* will inevitably end up *cleverer* than any noble race, and will respect cleverness to a quite different degree as well: namely, as a condition of existence of the first rank, whilst the cleverness of noble men can easily have a subtle aftertaste of luxury and refinement about it:—precisely because in this area, it is nowhere near as important as the complete certainty of function of the governing *unconscious* instincts, nor indeed as important as a certain lack of cleverness, such as a daring charge at danger or at the enemy, or those frenzied sudden fits of anger, love, reverence, gratitude and revenge by which noble souls down the ages have recognized one another. When *ressentiment* does occur in the noble man himself, it is consumed and exhausted in an immediate reaction, and therefore it does not *poison,* on the other hand, it does not occur at all in countless cases where it is unavoidable for all who are weak and powerless. To be unable to take his enemies, his misfortunes and even his *misdeeds* seriously for long—that is the sign of strong, rounded natures with a superabundance of a power which is flexible, formative, healing and can make one forget (a good example from the modern world is Mirabeau, who had no recall for the insults and slights directed at him and who could not forgive, simply because he—forgot.) A man like this shakes from him, with one shrug, many worms which would have burrowed into another man; here and here alone is it possible, assuming that this is possible at all on earth truly to "*love* your neighbour" [Matt. 5:43]. How much respect a noble man has for his enemies!—and a respect of that sort is a bridge to love . . . For he insists on having his enemy to himself, as a mark of distinction, indeed he will tolerate as enemies none other than such as have nothing to be despised and a *great deal* to be honoured! Against this, imagine "the enemy" as conceived of by the man of *ressentiment*—and here we have his deed, his creation: he has conceived of the "evil enemy," *"the evil one"* as a basic idea to which he now thinks up a copy and counterpart, the "good one"—himself! . . .

11. Exactly the opposite is true of the noble man who conceives of the basic idea "good" by himself, in advance and spontaneously, and only then creates a notion of "bad"! This "bad" of noble origin and that "evil" from the cauldron of unassuaged hatred—the first is an afterthought, an aside, a complementary colour, whilst the other is the original, the beginning, the actual *deed* in the conception of slave morality—how different are the two words "bad" and "evil," although both seem to be the opposite for the same concept, "good"! But it is not the same concept "good"; on the contrary, one should ask who is actually evil in the sense of the morality of *ressentiment.* The stern reply is: *precisely* the "good" person of the other morality, the noble, powerful, dominating man, but re-touched, re-interpreted and reviewed through the poisonous eye of *ressentiment.* Here there is one point which we would be the last to deny: anyone who came to know these "good men" as enemies came to know nothing but *"evil enemies,"* the same people who are so strongly held in check by custom, respect, habit, gratitude and even more through spying on one another and through peer-group jealousy, who, on the other hand, behave towards one another by showing such resourcefulness in consideration, self-control, delicacy, loyalty, pride and friendship,—they are not much better than uncaged beasts of prey in the world outside where the strange, the foreign, begin. There they enjoy freedom from every social constraint, in the wilderness they compensate for the tension which is caused by being closed in and fenced in by the peace of the community for so long, they *return* to the innocent conscience of the wild beast, as exultant monsters, who perhaps go away having committed a hideous succession of murder, arson, rape and torture, in a mood of bravado and spiritual equilibrium as though they had simply played a student's prank, convinced that poets will now have something to sing about and celebrate for quite some time. At the centre of all these noble races we cannot fail to see the blond beast of prey, the magnificent *blond beast* avidly prowling round for spoil and victory; this hidden centre needs release from time to time, the beast must out again, must return to the wild:—Roman, Arabian, Germanic, Japanese nobility, Homeric heroes, Scandinavian Vikings—in this requirement they are all alike. It was the noble races which left the concept of "barbarian" in their traces wherever they went; even their highest culture betrays the fact that they were conscious of this and indeed proud of it (for example, when Pericles, in that famous funeral oration, tells his Athenians, "Our daring has forced a path to every land and sea, erecting timeless memorials to itself everywhere for good *and ill"* [Thucydides II.39ff.]). This "daring" of the noble races, mad, absurd and sudden in the way it manifests itself, the unpredictability and even the improbability of their undertakings—Pericles singles out the ⟨*hrathumia*⟩ of the Athenians for praise—their unconcern and scorn for safety, body, life, comfort, their shocking cheerfulness, and depth of delight in all destruction, in all the debauches of victory and cruelty—all this, for those who suffered under it, was summed up in the image of the "barbarian," the "evil

enemy," perhaps the "Goth" or the "Vandal." The deep and icy mistrust which the German arouses as soon as he comes to power, which we see again even today—is still the aftermath of that inextinguishable horror with which Europe viewed the raging of the blond Germanic beast for centuries (although between the old Germanic peoples and us Germans there is scarcely an idea in common, let alone a blood relationship). I once remarked on Hesiod's dilemma when he thought up the series of cultural eras and tried to express them in gold, silver and iron: he could find no other solution to the contradiction presented to him by the magnificent but at the same time so shockingly violent world of Homer than to make two eras out of one, which he now placed one behind the other—first the era of heroes and demigods from Troy and Thebes, as that world which remained in the memory of the noble races which had their ancestors in it; then the iron era, as that same world appeared to the descendants of the downtrodden, robbed, ill-treated, and those carried off and sold: as an era of iron, hard, as I said, cold, cruel, lacking feeling and conscience, crushing everything and coating it with blood. Assuming that what is at any rate believed as "truth" were indeed true, that it is the *meaning of all culture* to breed a tame and civilized animal, a *household pet,* out of the beast of prey "man," then one would undoubtedly have to view all instinctive reaction and instinctive ressentiment, by means of which the noble races and their ideals were finally wrecked and overpowered, as the actual *instruments of culture;* which, however, is not to say that the *bearers* of these instincts were themselves representatives of the culture. Instead, the opposite would be not only probable—no! it is *visible* today! These bearers of oppressive, vindictive instincts, the descendants of all European and non-European slavery, in particular of all pre-Aryan population—represent the *decline* of mankind! These "instruments of culture" are a disgrace to man, more a grounds for suspicion of, or an argument against, "culture" in general! We may be quite justified in retaining our fear of the blond beast at the centre of every noble race and remain on our guard: but who would not, a hundred times over, prefer to fear if he can admire at the same time, rather than not fear, but thereby permanently retain the disgusting spectacle of the failed, the stunted, the wasted away and the poisoned? And is that not our fate? What constitutes *our* aversion to "man" today?—for we *suffer* from man, no doubt about that.—*Not* fear; rather, the fact that we have nothing to fear from man; that "man" is first and foremost a teeming mass of worms; that the "tame man," who is incurably mediocre and unedifying, has already learnt to view himself as the aim and pinnacle, the meaning of history, the "higher man";—yes, the fact that he has a certain right to feel like that in so far as he feels distanced from the superabundance of failed, sickly, tired and exhausted people of whom today's Europe is beginning to reek, and in so far as he is at least relatively successful, at least still capable of living, at least saying "yes" to life . . .

12.—At this juncture I cannot suppress a sigh and one last hope. What do I find absolutely intolerable? Something which I just cannot cope alone with and which suffocates me and makes me feel faint? Bad air! Bad air! That something failed comes near me, that I have to smell the bowels of a failed soul! . . . Apart from that, what cannot be borne in the way of need, deprivation, bad weather, disease, toil, solitude? Basically we can cope with everything else, born as we are to an underground and battling existence; again and again we keep coming up to the light, again and again we experience our golden hour of victory,—and then there we stand, the way we were born, unbreakable, tense, ready for new, more difficult and distant things, like a bow which is merely stretched tauter by affliction.—But from time to time grant me—assuming that there are divine benefactresses beyond good and evil—a glimpse, grant me just one glimpse of something perfect, completely finished, happy, powerful, triumphant, which still leaves something to fear! A glimpse of a man who justifies man *himself,* a stroke of luck, an instance of a man who makes up for and redeems man, and enables us to retain our *faith in mankind!* . . . For the matter stands like so: the stunting and levelling of European man conceals *our* greatest danger, because the sight of this makes us tired . . . Today we see nothing that wants to expand, we suspect that things will just continue to decline, getting thinner, better-natured, cleverer, more comfortable, more mediocre, more indifferent, more Chinese, more Christian—no doubt about it, man is getting "better" all the time . . . Right here is where the destiny of Europe lies—in losing our fear of man we have also lost our love for him, our respect for him, our hope in him and even our will to be man. The sight of man now makes us tired—what is nihilism today if it is not *that?*. . . We are tired of *man* . . .

13. —But let us return: the problem of the *other* origin of "good," of good as thought up by the man of *ressentiment,* demands its solution. There is nothing strange about the fact that lambs bear a grudge towards large birds of prey: but that is no reason to blame the large birds of prey for carrying off the little lambs. And if the lambs say to each other, "These birds of prey are evil; and whoever is least like a bird of prey and most like its opposite, a lamb,—is good, isn't he?," then there is no reason to raise objections to this setting-up of an ideal beyond the fact that the birds of prey will view it somewhat derisively, and will perhaps say, "We don't bear any grudge at all towards these good lambs, in fact we love them, nothing is tastier than a tender lamb."—It is just as absurd to ask strength *not* to express itself as strength, not to be a desire to overthrow, crush, become master, to be a thirst for enemies, resistance and triumphs, as it is to ask weakness to express itself as strength. A quantum of force is just such a quantum of drive, will, action, in fact it is nothing but this driving, willing and acting, and only the seduction of language (and the fundamental errors of reason petrified within it), which construes and misconstrues all actions as conditional upon an agency, a "subject," can make it appear otherwise. And just as the common people separates lightning from its flash and takes the latter to be a *deed,* something performed by a subject, which is called lightning, popular morality separates strength from the manifestations of strength, as though there were an indifferent substratum behind the strong person which had the *freedom* to manifest strength or not. But there is no such substratum; there is no "being" behind the deed, its effect and what becomes of it; "the doer" is invented as an afterthought,—the doing is everything. Basically, the common people double a deed; when they see lightning, they make a doing-a-deed out of it: they posit the same event, first as cause and then as its effect. The scientists do no better when they say "force moves, force causes" and such like,—all our science, in spite of its coolness and freedom from emotion, still stands exposed to the seduction of language and has not ridded itself of the changelings foisted upon it, the "subjects" (the atom is, for example, just such a changeling, likewise the Kantian "thing-in-itself"): no wonder, then, if the entrenched, secretly smouldering emotions of revenge and hatred put this belief to their own use and, in fact, do not defend any belief more passionately than that *the strong are free* to be weak, and the birds of prey are free to be lambs:—in this way, they gain the right to make the birds of prey *responsible* for being birds of prey . . . When the oppressed, the downtrodden, the violated say to each other with the vindictive cunning of powerlessness: "Let us be different from evil people, let us be good! And a good person is anyone who does not rape, does not harm anyone, who does not attack, does not retaliate, who leaves the taking of revenge to God, who keeps hidden as we do, avoids all evil and asks little from life in general, like us who are patient,

humble and upright"—this means, if heard coolly and impartially, nothing more than "We weak people are just weak; it is good to do nothing *for which we are not strong enough*"—but this grim state of affairs, this cleverness of the lowest rank which even insects possess (which play dead, in order not to "do too much" when in great danger), has, thanks to the counterfeiting and self-deception of powerlessness, clothed itself in the finery of self-denying, quiet, patient virtue, as though the weakness of the weak were itself—I mean its *essence,* its effect, its whole unique, unavoidable, irredeemable reality—a voluntary achievement, something wanted, chosen, a *deed,* an *accomplishment.* This type of man *needs* to believe in an unbiased "subject" with freedom of choice, because he has an instinct of self-preservation and self-affirmation in which every lie is sanctified. The reason the subject (or, as we more colloquially say, *the soul*) has been, until now, the best doctrine on earth, is perhaps because it facilitated that sublime self-deception whereby the majority of the dying, the weak and the oppressed of every kind could construe weakness itself as freedom, and their particular mode of existence as an *accomplishment.*

14.—Would anyone like to have a little look down into the secret of how *ideals are fabricated* on this earth? Who has enough pluck? . . . Come on! Here we have a clear glimpse into this dark workshop. Just wait one moment, Mr. Nosy Daredevil: your eyes will have to become used to this false, shimmering light . . . There! That's enough! Now you can speak! What's happening down there? Tell me what you see, you with your most dangerous curiosity—now *I* am the one who's listening.

—"I cannot see anything but I can hear all the better. There is a guarded, malicious little rumour-mongering and whispering from every nook and cranny. I think people are telling lies; a sugary mildness clings to every sound. Lies are turning weakness into an *accomplishment,* no doubt about it—it's just as you said."

—Go on!

—"and impotence which doesn't retaliate is being turned into 'goodness'; timid baseness is being turned into 'humility'; submission to people one hates is being turned into 'obedience' (actually towards someone who, they say, orders this submission—they call him God). The inoffensiveness of the weakling, the very cowardice with which he is richly endowed, his standing-by-the-door, his inevitable position of having to wait, are all given good names such as 'patience,' which is also called *the* virtue; not-being-able-to-take revenge is called not-wanting-to-take-revenge, it might even be forgiveness ('for they know not what they do [Luke 23:34]—but we know what they are doing!'). They are also talking about 'loving your enemy' and sweating while they do it."

—Go on!

—"They are miserable, without a doubt, all these rumour-mongers and clandestine forgers, even if they do crouch close together for warmth—but they tell me that their misery means they are God's chosen and select, after all, people beat the dogs they love best; perhaps this misery is just a preparation, a test, a training, it might be even more than that—something which will one day be balanced up and paid back with enormous interest in gold, no! in happiness. They call that 'bliss.'"

—Go on!

—"They are now informing me that not only are they better than the powerful, the masters of the world whose spittle they have to lick (*not* from fear, not at all from fear! but because God orders them to honour those in authority [Rom. 13:1])—not only are they better, but they have a 'better time,' or at least will have a better time one day. But enough! enough! I can't bear it any longer. Bad air! Bad air! This workshop where *ideals are fabricated*—it seems to me just to stink of lies."

—No! Wait a moment! You haven't said anything yet about the masterpieces of those black magicians who can turn anything black into whiteness, milk and innocence:—haven't you noticed their perfect *raffinement,* their boldest, subtlest, most ingenious and mendacious stunt? Pay attention! These cellar rats full of revenge and hatred—what do they turn revenge and hatred into? Have you ever heard these words? Would you suspect, if you just went by what they said, that the men around you were nothing but men of *ressentiment?* . . .

—"I understand, I'll open my ears once more (oh! oh! oh! and *hold* my nose). Now, at last, I can hear what they have been saying so often: 'We good people—*we are the just*'—what they are demanding is not called retribution, but 'the triumph of *justice*'; what they hate is not their enemy, oh no! they hate '*injustice,*' 'godlessness'; what they believe and hope for is not the prospect of revenge, the delirium of sweet revenge (—Homer early on dubbed it " 'sweeter than honey' "), but the victory of God, the *just* God, over the Godless; all that remains for them to love on earth are not their brothers in hate but their 'brothers in love,' as they say, all good and just people on earth."

—And what do they call that which serves as a consolation for all the sufferings of the world—their phantasmagoria of anticipated future bliss?

—"What? Do I hear correctly? They call it 'the last judgment,' the coming of *their* kingdom, the 'kingdom of God'—but *in the meantime* they live 'in faith,' 'in love,' 'in hope.' "

Enough! Enough!

15. Faith in what? Love of what? Hope for what?—These weaklings—in fact *they,* too, want to be the powerful one day, this is beyond doubt, one day *their* "kingdom" will come too—"the kingdom of God" *simpliciter* is their name for it, as I said: they are so humble about everything! Just to experience *that,* you need to live long, well beyond death,—yes, you need eternal life in order to be able to gain eternal recompense in "the kingdom of God" for that life on earth "in faith," "in love," "in hope." Recompense for what? Recompense through what . . . It seems to me that Dante made a gross error when, with awe-inspiring naivete he placed the inscription over the gateway to his hell: "Eternal love created me as well":—at any rate, this inscription would have a better claim to stand over the gateway to Christian Paradise and its "eternal bliss": "Eternal *hate* created me as well" assuming that a true statement can be placed above the gateway to a lie! For what is the bliss of this Paradise? . . . We might have guessed already; but it is better to be expressly shown it by no less an authority in such matters than Thomas Aquinas, the great teacher and saint. "The blessed in the heavenly kingdom," he says as meekly as a lamb, "will see the torment of the damned *so that they may even more thoroughly enjoy their blessedness.*"* Or, if you want it even more forcefully, for example from the mouth of a triumphant Church Father [Tertullian] who advised his Christians against the cruel voluptuousness of the public spectacles—but why? "Faith offers us much more"—he says, *De Spectaculis.* Chs. 29ff—"something *much stronger,* thanks to salvation, quite other joys are at our command; instead of athletes we have our martyrs; we want blood, well then, we have the blood of Christ . . . But think what awaits us on the day of his second coming, of his triumph!"—and then the enraptured visionary goes on: "But there are yet other spectacles: that final and everlasting day of judgement, that day that was not expected and was even laughed at by the nations, when the whole old world and all it gave birth to are consumed in one fire. What an ample breadth of sights there will be then! *At which one shall I gaze in wonder? At which shall I laugh? At which rejoice? At which exult,* when I see so many great *kings* who were proclaimed to have been taken up into

*[These passages are given in Latin by Nietzsche.]

heaven, groaning in the deepest darkness together with those who claimed to have witnessed their apotheosis and with Jove himself. And when I see those [provincial] governors, persecutors of the Lord's name, melting in flames more savage than those with which they insolently raged against Christians! When I see those wise philosophers who persuaded their disciples that nothing was of any concern to god and who affirmed to them either that we have no souls or that our souls will not return to their original bodies! Now they are ashamed before those disciples, as they are burned together with them. Also the poets trembling before the tribunal not of Minos or of Radamanthus, but of the unexpected Christ! Then the tragic actors will be easier to hear because they will be in better voice [i.e. screaming even louder] in their own tragedy. Then the actors of pantomime will be easy to recognize, being much more nimble than usual because of the fire. Then the charioteer will be on view, all red in a wheel of flame and the athletes, thrown not in the gymnasia but into the fire. Unless even then I don't want to see them alive, preferring to cast an *insatiable* gaze on those who raged against the Lord. "This is he," I will say, "that son of a carpenter or prostitute [Nietzsche adds:] (Tertullian refers to the Jews from now on, as is shown by what follows and in particular by this well-known description of the mother of Jesus from the Talmud) that destroyer of the Sabbath, that Samaritan, that man who had a devil. He it is whom you bought from Judas, who was beaten with a reed and with fists, who was defiled with spit and had gall and vinegar to drink. He it is whom his disciples secretly took away so that it might be said that he had risen again, or whom the gardener removed so that his lettuces would not be harmed by the crowd of visitors." What praetor or consul or quaestor or priest will grant you from his largesse the chance of seeing and *exulting in such things?* And yet to some extent we have such things already *through faith,* made present in the imagining spirit. Furthermore what sorts of things are those which the eye has not seen nor the ear heard, and which have not come into the human heart? (I Cor. 2:9) I believe that they are more pleasing than the circus or both of the enclosures [first and fourth rank of seats, or, according to others, the comic and the tragic stages] or than any race-track."*

(*Per fidem* [By my faith]: that is what is written.)

16. Let us draw to a close. The two *opposing* values "good and bad," "good and evil" have fought a terrible battle for thousands of years on earth; and although the latter has been dominant for a long time, there is still no lack of places where the battle remains undecided. You could even say that, in the meantime, it has reached ever greater heights but at the same time has become ever deeper and more intellectual: so that there is, today, perhaps no more distinguishing feature of the *"higher nature,"* the intellectual nature, than to be divided in this sense and really and truly a battle ground for these opposites. The symbol of this fight, written in a script which has hitherto remained legible throughout human history, is "Rome against Judea, Judea against Rome":—up to now there has been no greater event than *this* battle, *this* question, *this* contradiction of mortal enemies. Rome saw the Jew as something contrary to nature, as though he were its polar opposite, a monster; in Rome, the Jew was looked upon as *convicted* of hatred against the whole of mankind: rightly, if one is right in linking the well being and future of the human race with the unconditional rule of aristocratic values, Roman values. What, on the other hand, did the Jews feel about Rome? We can guess from a thousand indicators; but it is enough to call once more to mind the Apocalypse of John, the wildest of all outbursts ever written which revenge has on its conscience. (By the way, we must not underestimate the profound consistency of Christian

---

*[These passages are given in Latin by Nietzsche.]

instinct in inscribing this book of hate to the disciple of love, the very same to whom it attributed that passionately ecstatic gospel—: there is some truth in this, however much literary counterfeiting might have been necessary to the purpose.) So the Romans were the strong and noble, stronger and nobler than anybody hitherto who had lived or been dreamt of on earth; their every relic and inscription brings delight, provided one can guess *what* it is that is doing the writing there. By contrast, the Jews were a priestly nation of *ressentiment par excellence,* possessing an unparalleled genius for popular morality: compare peoples with similar talents, such as the Chinese or the Germans, with the Jews, and you will realize who are first rate and who are fifth. Which of them has *prevailed* for the time being, Rome or Judea? But there is no trace of doubt: just consider whom you bow down to in Rome itself; today, as though to the embodiment of the highest values and not just in Rome, but over nearly half the earth, everywhere where man has become tame or wants to become tame, to *three Jews,* as we know, and *one Jewess* (to Jesus of Nazareth, Peter the Fisherman, Paul the Carpet-Weaver and the mother of Jesus mentioned first, whose name was Mary). This is very remarkable: without a doubt Rome has been defeated. However, in the Renaissance there was a brilliant, uncanny reawakening of the classical ideal, of the noble method of valuing everything: Rome itself woke up, as though from suspended animation, under the pressure of the new, Judaic Rome built over it, which looked like an ecumenical synagogue and was called "Church": but Judea triumphed again at once, thanks to that basically proletarian (German and English) *ressentiment*-movement which people called the Reformation, including its inevitable consequence, the restoration of the church,—as well as the restoration of the ancient, tomb-like silence of classical Rome. In an even more decisive and profound sense than then, Judea once again triumphed over the classical ideal with the French Revolution: the last political nobility in Europe, that of the *French* seventeenth and eighteenth centuries, collapsed under the *ressentiment*-instincts of the rabble,—the world had never heard greater rejoicing and more uproarious enthusiasm! True, the most dreadful and unexpected thing happened in the middle: the ancient ideal itself appeared *bodily* and with unheard-of splendour before the eye and conscience of mankind, and once again, stronger, simpler and more penetrating than ever, in answer to the old, mendacious *ressentiment* slogan of *priority for the majority,* of man's will to baseness, abasement, levelling, decline and decay, there rang out the terrible and enchanting counter-slogan: *priority for the few!* Like a last signpost to the *other* path, Napoleon appeared as a man more unique and late-born for his times than ever a man had been before, and in him, the problem of the *noble ideal itself* was made flesh—just think *what* a problem that is: Napoleon, this synthesis of monster [*Unmensch*] and *Öbermensch* . . .

17. —Was it over after that? Was that greatest among all conflicts of ideals placed *ad acta* for ever? Or just postponed, postponed indefinitely? . . . Won't there have to be an even more terrible flaring up of the old flame, one prepared much longer in advance? And more: shouldn't one desire *that* with all one's strength? or will it, even? or even promote it? . . . Whoever, like my readers, now starts to ponder these points and reflect further, will have difficulty coming to a speedy conclusion,—reason enough, then, for me to come to a conclusion myself, assuming that it has been sufficiently clear for some time what I want, what I actually want with that dangerous slogan which is written on the spine of my last book, *Beyond Good and Evil* . . . at least this does *not* mean "Beyond Good and Bad."—

NOTE: I take the opportunity presented to me by this essay, of publicly and formally expressing a wish which I have only expressed in occasional conversations with scholars up till now: that is that some Faculty of Philosophy should do the great service of promoting the study of *the history of morality* by means of a series of academic prize essays:—perhaps this book might serve to give a powerful impetus in such a direction. With regard to such a possibility, I raise the following question for consideration: it merits the attention of philologists and historians as well as those who are actually philosophers by profession:

> "What signposts does linguistics, especially the study of etymology, give to the history of the evolution of moral concepts?"

—On the other hand, it is just as essential to win the support of physiologists and doctors for these problems (on the *value* of all previous valuations): we can leave it to the professional philosophers to act as advocates and mediators in this, once they have completely succeeded in transforming the originally so reserved and suspicious relationship between philosophy, physiology and medicine into the most cordial and fruitful exchange. Indeed, every table of values, every "thou shalt" known to history or the study of ethnology, needs first and foremost a *physiological* elucidation and interpretation, rather than a psychological one; and all of them await critical study from medical science. The question: what is this or that table of values and "morals" *worth*? needs to be asked from different angles; in particular, the question "value for *what*?" cannot be examined too finely. Something, for example, which obviously had value with regard to the longest possible life-span of a race (or to the improvement of its abilities to adapt to a particular climate, or to maintaining the greatest number) would not have anything like the same value if it was a question of developing a stronger type. The good of the majority and the good of the minority are conflicting moral stand-points: we leave it to the naivety of English biologists to view the first as higher in value as *such . . . All* sciences must, from now on, prepare the way for the future work of the philosopher: this work being understood to mean that the philosopher has to solve the *problem of values* and that he has to decide on the *hierarchy of values.*

THUS SPOKE ZARATHUSTRA (in part)

ZARATHUSTRA'S PROLOGUE

[1] When Zarathustra was thirty years old he left his home and the lake of his home and went into the mountains. Here he enjoyed his spirit and his solitude, and for ten years did not tire of it. But at last a change came over his heart, and one morning he rose with the dawn, stepped before the sun, and spoke to it thus:

"You great star, what would your happiness be had you not those for whom you shine?

"For ten years you have climbed to my cave: you would have tired of your light and of the journey had it not been for me and my eagle and my serpent.

"But we waited for you every morning, took your overflow from you, and blessed you for it.

"Behold, I am weary of my wisdom, like a bee that has gathered too much honey; I need hands outstretched to receive it.

"I would give away and distribute, until the wise among men find joy once again in their folly, and the poor in their riches.

"For that I must descend to the depths, as you do in the evening when you go behind the sea and still bring light to the underworld, you over rich star.

"Like you, I must go *under*—go down, as is said by man, to whom I want to descend.

"So bless me then, you quiet eye that can look even upon an all-too-great happiness without envy!

"Bless the cup that wants to overflow, that the water may flow from it golden and carry everywhere the reflection of your delight.

"Behold, this cup wants to become empty again, and Zarathustra wants to become man again."

Thus Zarathustra began to go under.

[2] Zarathustra descended alone from the mountains, encountering no one. But when he came into the forest, all at once there stood before him an old man who had left his holy cottage to look for roots in the woods. And thus spoke the old man to Zarathustra:

"No stranger to me is this wanderer: many years ago he passed this way. Zarathustra he was called, but he has changed. At that time you carried your ashes to the mountains; would you now carry your fire into the valleys? Do you not fear to be punished as an arsonist?

"Yes, I recognize Zarathustra. His eyes are pure, and around his mouth there hides no disgust. Does he not walk like a dancer?

"Zarathustra has changed, Zarathustra has become a child, Zarathustra is an awakened one; what do you now want among the sleepers? You lived in your solitude as in the sea, and the sea carried you. Alas, would you now climb ashore? Alas, would you again drag your own body?"

Zarathustra answered: "I love man."

"Why," asked the saint, "did I go into the forest and the desert? Was it not because I loved man all-too-much? Now I love God; man I love not. Man is for me too imperfect a thing. Love of man would kill me."

Zarathustra answered: "Did I speak of love? I bring men a gift."

"Give them nothing!" said the saint. "Rather, take part of their load and help them to bear it—that will be best for them, if only it does you good! And if you want to give them something, give no more than alms, and let them beg for that!"

"No," answered Zarathustra. "I give no alms. For that I am not poor enough."

The saint laughed at Zarathustra and spoke thus: "Then see to it that they accept your treasures. They are suspicious of hermits and do not believe that we come with gifts. Our steps sound too lonely through the streets. And what if at night, in their beds, they hear a man walk by long before the sun has risen—they probably ask themselves, Where is the thief going?

"Do not go to man. Stay in the forest! Go rather even to the animals! Why do you not want to be as I am—a bear among bears, a bird among birds?"

"And what is the saint doing in the forest?" asked Zarathustra.

The saint answered: "I make songs and sing them; and when I make songs, I laugh, cry, and hum: thus I praise God. With singing, crying, laughing, and humming, I praise the god who is my god. But what do you bring us as a gift?"

When Zarathustra had heard these words he bade the saint farewell and said: "What could I have to give you? But let me go quickly lest I take something from you!" And thus they separated, the old one and the man, laughing as two boys laugh.

But when Zarathustra was alone he spoke thus to his heart: "Could it be possible? This old saint in the forest has not yet heard anything of this, that God is *dead!*"

[3] When Zarathustra came into the next town, which lies on the edge of the forest, he found many people gathered together in the market place; for it had been promised that there would be a tightrope walker. And Zarathustra spoke thus to the people:

"I teach you the overman. Man is something that shall be overcome. What have you done to overcome him?

"All beings so far have created something beyond themselves; and do you want to be the ebb of this great flood and even go back to the beasts rather than overcome man? What is the ape to man? A laughingstock or a painful embarrassment. And man shall be just that for the overman: a laughingstock or a painful embarrassment. You have made your way from worm to man, and much in you is still worm. Once you were apes, and even now, too, man is more ape than any ape.

"Whoever is the wisest among you is also a mere conflict and cross between plant and ghost. But do I bid you become ghosts or plants?

"Behold, I teach you the overman. The overman is the meaning of the earth. Let your will say: the overman *shall be* the meaning of the earth! I beseech you, my brothers, *remain faithful to the earth,* and do not believe those who speak to you of otherworldly hopes! Poison-mixers are they, whether they know it or not. Despisers of life are they, decaying and poisoned themselves, of whom the earth is weary: so let them go.

"Once the sin against God was the greatest sin; but God died, and these sinners died with him. To sin against the earth is now the most dreadful thing, and to esteem the entrails of the unknowable higher than the meaning of the earth.

"Once the soul looked contemptuously upon the body, and then this contempt was the highest: she wanted the body meager, ghastly, and starved. Thus she hoped to escape it and the earth. Oh, this soul herself was still meager, ghastly, and starved: and cruelty was the lust of this soul. But you, too, my brothers, tell me: what does your body proclaim of your soul? Is not your soul poverty and filth and wretched contentment?

"Verily, a polluted stream is man. One must be a sea to be able to receive a polluted stream without becoming unclean. Behold, I teach you the overman: he is this sea; in him your great contempt can go under.

"What is the greatest experience you can have? It is the hour of the great contempt. The hour in which your happiness, too, arouses your disgust, and even your reason and your virtue.

"The hour when you say, 'What matters my happiness? It is poverty and filth and wretched contentment. But my happiness ought to justify existence itself.'

"The hour when you say, 'What matters my reason? Does it crave knowledge as the lion his food? It is poverty and filth and wretched contentment.'

"The hour when you say, 'What matters my virtue? As yet it has not made me rage. How weary I am of my good and my evil! All that is poverty and filth and wretched contentment.'

"The hour when you say, 'What matters my justice? I do not see that I am flames and fuel. But the just are flames and fuel.'

"The hour when you say, 'What matters my pity? Is not pity the cross on which he is nailed who loves man? But my pity is no crucifixion.'

"Have you yet spoken thus? Have you yet cried thus? Oh, that I might have heard you cry thus!

"Not your sin but your thrift cries to heaven; your meanness even in your sin cries to heaven.

"Where is the lightning to lick you with its tongue? Where is the frenzy with which you should be inoculated?

"Behold, I teach you the overman: he is this lightning, he is this frenzy."

When Zarathustra had spoken thus, one of the people cried: "Now we have heard enough about the tightrope walker; now let us see him tool." And all the people laughed at Zarathustra. But the tightrope walker, believing that the word concerned him, began his performance.

TWILIGHT OF THE IDOLS (in part)

MAXIMS AND ARROWS

1. Idleness is the beginning of all psychology. What? Should psychology be a vice?*

2. Even the most courageous among us only rarely has the courage for that which he really knows.

3. To live alone one must be a beast or a god, says Aristotle. Leaving out the third case: one must be both—a philosopher.

4. "All truth is simple." Is that not doubly a lie?

5. I want, once and for all, *not* to know many things. Wisdom sets limits to knowledge too.

6. In our own wild nature we find the best recreation from our un-nature, from our spirituality.

*There is a German proverb: "Idleness is the beginning of all vices."

7. What? Is man merely a mistake of God's? Or God merely a mistake of man's?

8. *Out of life's school of war:* What does not destroy me, makes me stronger.

9. Help yourself, then everyone will help you. Principle of neighbor-love.

10. Not to perpetrate cowardice against one's own acts! Not to leave them in the lurch afterward! The bite of conscience is indecent.

11. Can an ass be tragic? To perish under a burden one can neither bear nor throw off? The case of the philosopher.

12. If we have our own *why* of life, we shall get along with almost any *how*. Man does *not* strive for pleasure; only the Englishman does.

13. Man has created woman—out of what? Out of a rib of his god—of his "ideal."

14. What? You search? You would multiply yourself by ten, by a hundred? You seek followers? Seek zeros!

15. Posthumous men—*I*, for example—are understood worse than timely ones, but *heard* better. More precisely: we are never understood—*hence* our authority.

16. *Among women:* "Truth? Oh, you don't know truth. Is it not an attempt to assassinate all our *pudeurs?*"

17. That is an artist as I love artists, modest in his needs—. he really wants only two things, his bread and his art—*panem et Circen.**

18. Whoever does not know how to lay his will into things, at least lays some *meaning* into them: that means, he has the faith that they already obey a will. (Principle of "faith.")

19. What? You elected virtue and the swelled bosom and yet you leer enviously at the advantages of those without qualms? But virtue involves *renouncing* "advantages." (Inscription for an anti-Semite's door.)

20. The perfect woman perpetrates literature as she perpetrates a small sin: as an experiment, in passing, looking around to see if anybody notices it—and to make sure that somebody does.

21. To venture into all sorts of situations in which one may not have any sham virtues, where, like the tightrope walker on his rope, one either stands or falls—or gets away.

22. "Evil men have no songs." How is it, then, that the Russians have songs?

---

panem et circenses, "bread and circuses"—here changed by Nietzsche into "bread and Circe," art being compared to the Homeric sorceress.

23. "German spirit": for the past eighteen years a contradiction in terms.

24. By searching out origins, one becomes a crab, The historian looks backward; eventually he also *believes* backward.

25. Contentment protects even against colds. Has a woman who knew herself to be well dressed ever caught cold? I am assuming that she was barely dressed.

26. I mistrust all systematizers and I avoid them. The *will* to a system is a lack of integrity.

27. Women are considered profound. My? Because one never fathoms their depths. Women aren't even shallow.

28. If a woman has manly virtues, one feels like running away; and if she has no manly virtues, she herself runs away.

29. "How much conscience has had to chew on in the past! And what excellent teeth it had! And today—what is lacking?" A dentist's question.

30. One rarely rushes into a single error. Rushing into the first one, one always does too much. So one usually perpetrates another one—and now one does too little.

31. When stepped on, a worm doubles up. That is clever. In that way he lessens the probability of being stepped on again. In the language of morality: *humility*.

32. There is a hatred of lies and simulation, stemming from an easily provoked sense of honor. There is another such hatred, from cowardice, since lies are for*bidden* by a divine commandment. Too cowardly to lie.

33. How little is required for pleasure! The sound of a bagpipe. Without music, life would be an error. The German imagines even God singing songs.

34. *On ne peut penser et écrire qu'assis** (G. Flaubert). There I have caught you, nihilist! The sedentary life is the very sin against the Holy Spirit. Only thoughts reached by walking have value.

35. There are cases in which we are like horses, we psychologists, and become restless: we see our own shadow wavering up and down before us. A psychologist must turn his eyes from himself to eye anything at all.

36. Whether we immoralists are *harming* virtue? just as little as anarchists harm princes. Only since the latter are shot at do they again sit securely on their thrones. Moral: *morality must be shot at.*

37. You run *ahead?* Are you doing it as a shepherd? Or as an exception? A third case would be the fugitive. *First* question of conscience.

---

*"One can think and write, except sitting."

38. Are you genuine? Or merely an actor? A representative? Or that which is represented? In the end, perhaps you are merely a copy of an actor. *Second* question of conscience.

39. *The disappointed one speaks.* I searched for great human beings; I always found only the *apes* of their ideals.

40. Are you one who looks on? Or one who lends a hand? Or one who looks away and walks off? *Third* question of conscience.

41. Do you want to walk along? Or walk ahead? Or walk by yourself? One must know *what* one wants and *that* one wants. *Fourth* question of conscience.

42. Those were steps for me, and I have climbed up over them: to that end I had to pass over them. Yet they thought that I wanted to retire on them.

43. What does it matter if *I* remain right. I am much too right. And he who laughs best today will also laugh last.

44. The formula of my happiness: a Yes, a No, a straight line, a *goal.*

THE PROBLEM OF SOCRATES

[1] Concerning life, the wisest men of all ages have judged alike: *it is no good.* Always and everywhere one has heard the same sound from their mouths—a sound full of doubt, full of melancholy, full of weariness of life, full of resistance to life. Even Socrates said, as He died; "To live—that means to be sick a long time: I owe Asclepius the Savior a rooster." Even Socrates was tired of it. What does that evidence? What does it evince? Formerly one would have said (—oh, it has been said, and loud enough, and especially by our pessimists): "At least something of all this must be true! The consensus of the sages evidences the truth." Shall we still talk like that today? *May* we? "At least something must be *sick* here," *we* retort. These wisest men of all ages— they should first be scrutinized closely. Were they all perhaps shaky on their legs? late? tottery? decadents? Could it be that wisdom appears on earth as a raven, inspired by a little whiff of carrion?

[2] This irreverent thought that the great sages are *types of decline* first occurred to me precisely in a case where it is most strongly opposed by both scholarly and unscholarly prejudice: I recognized Socrates and Plato to be symptoms of degeneration, tools of the Greek dissolution, pseudo-Greek, anti-Greek *(Birth of Tragedy,* 1872). The consensus of the sages—I comprehended this ever more clearly—proves least of all that they were right in what they agreed on: it shows rather that they themselves, these wisest men, agreed in some *physiological* respect, and hence adopted the same negative attitude to life—*had to* adopt it. Judgments, judgments of value, concerning life, for it or against it, can, in the end, never be true: they have value only as symptoms, they are worthy of consideration only as symptoms; in themselves such judgments are stupidities. One must by all means stretch out one's fingers and make the attempt to

grasp this amazing finesse, *that the value of life cannot be estimated.* Not by the living, for they are an interested party, even a bone of contention, and not judges; not by the dead, for a different reason. For a philosopher to see a problem in the value of life is thus an objection to him, a question mark concerning his wisdom, an un-wisdom. Indeed? All these great wise men—they were not only decadents but not wise at all? But I return to the problem of Socrates.

[3] In origin, Socrates belonged to the lowest class: Socrates was plebs. We know, we can still see for ourselves, how ugly he was. But ugliness, in itself an objection, is among the Greeks almost a refutation. Was Socrates a Greek at all? Ugliness is often enough the expression of a development that has been crossed, *thwarted* by crossing. Or it appears as declining development. The anthropologists among the criminologists tell us that the typical criminal is ugly: *monstrum in fronte, monstrum in animo.* But the criminal is a decadent. Was Socrates a typical criminal? At least that would not be contradicted by the famous judgment of the physiognomist which sounded so offensive to the friends of Socrates. A foreigner who knew about faces once passed through Athens and told Socrates to his face that he *was a monstrum—* that he harbored in himself all the bad vices and appetites. And Socrates merely answered: "You know me, sir!"

[4] Socrates' decadence is suggested not only by the admitted wantonness and anarchy of his instincts, but also by the hypertrophy of the logical faculty and that *sarcasm of the rachitic* which distinguishes him. Nor should we forget those auditory hallucinations which, as "the *daimonion* of Socrates," have been interpreted religiously. Everything in him is exaggerated, *buffo,* a caricature, everything is at the same time concealed, ulterior, subterranean. I seek to comprehend what idiosyncrasy begot that Socratic equation of reason, virtue, and happiness: that most bizarre of all equations, which. moreover, is opposed to all the instincts of the earlier Greeks.

[5] With Socrates, Greek taste changes in favor of dialectics. What really happened there? Above all, a *noble* taste is thus vanquished; with dialectics the plebs come to the top. Before Socrates, dialectic manners were repudiated in good society: they were considered bad manners, they were compromising. The young were warned against them. Furthermore, all such presentations of one's reasons were distrusted. Honest things, like honest men, do not carry their reasons in their hands like that. It is indecent to show all five fingers. What must first be proved is worth little. Wherever authority still forms part of good bearing, where one does not give reasons but commands, the dialectician is a kind of buffoon: one laughs at him, one does not take him seriously. Socrates was the buffoon who *got himself taken seriously:* what really happened there?

[6] One chooses dialectic only when one has no other means. One knows that one arouses mistrust with it, that it is not very persuasive. Nothing is easier to erase than a dialectical effect: the experience of every meeting at which there are speeches proves this. It can only be *self-defense* for those who no longer have other weapons. One must have to *enforce* one's right: until one reaches that point, one makes no use of it. The Jews were dialecticians for that reason; Reynard the Fox was one—and Socrates too?

[7] Is the irony of Socrates an expression of revolt? Of plebeian *ressentiment?* Does he, as one oppressed, enjoy his own ferocity in the knife-thrusts of his syllogisms? Does he *avenge* himself on the noble people whom he fascinates? As a dialectician, one holds a merciless tool in one's hand; one can become a tyrant by means of it; one compromises those one conquers. The dialectician leaves it to his opponent to prove that he is no idiot: be makes one furious and helpless at the same time. The di-

alectician renders the intellect of his opponent powerless. Indeed? Is dialectic only, a form of *revenge* in Socrates?

[8] I have given to understand how it was that Socrates could repel: it is therefore all the more necessary to explain his fascination. That he discovered a new kind of *agon* ["contest"], that he became its first fencing master for the noble circles of Athens, is one point. He fascinated by appealing to the agonistic impulse of the Greeks-he introduced a variation into the wrestling match between young men and youths. Socrates was also a great *erotic*.

[9] But Socrates guessed even more. He saw *through* his noble Athenians; he comprehended that his own case, his idiosyncrasy, was no longer exceptional. The same kind of degeneration was quietly developing everywhere: old Athens was coming to an end. And Socrates understood that all the world *needed* him—his means, his cure, his personal artifice of self-preservation. Everywhere the instincts were in anarchy; everywhere one was within five paces of excess: *monstrum in animo* was the general danger. "The impulses want to play the tyrant; one must invent a *counter-tyrant* who is stronger." When the physiognomist had revealed to Socrates who he was—a cave of bad appetites—the great master of irony let slip another word which is the key to Ms character. "This is true," he said, "but I mastered them all." *How* did Socrates become master over *himself?* His case was, at bottom, merely the extreme case only the most striking instance of what was then beginning to be a universal distress: no one was any longer master over himself, the instincts turned *against* each other. He fascinated, being this extreme case; his awe-inspiring ugliness proclaimed him as such to all who could see; he fascinated, of course, even more as an answer, a solution, an apparent *cure* of this case.

[10] When one finds it necessary to turn *reason* into a tyrant, as Socrates did, the danger cannot be slight that something else will play the tyrant. Rationality was then hit upon as the savior; neither Socrates nor his "patients" had any choice about being rational: it was *de rigeur,* it was their last resort. The fanaticism with which all Greek reflection throws itself upon rationality betrays a desperate situation; there was danger, there was but one choice: either to perish or—to be *absurdly rational.* The moralism of the Greek philosophers from Plato on is pathologically conditioned; so is their esteem of dialectics. Reason-virtue-happiness, that means merely that one must imitate Socrates and counter the dark appetites with a permanent daylight—the daylight of reason. One must be clever, clear, bright at any price: any concession to the instincts, to the unconscious, leads *downward.*

[11] I have given to understand how it was that Socrates fascinated he seemed to be a physician, a savior. Is it necessary to go on to demonstrate the error in his faith in "rationality at any price"? It is a self-deception on the part of philosophers and moralists if they believe that they are extricating themselves from decadence when they merely wage war against it. Extrication lies beyond their strength: what they choose as a means, as salvation, is itself but another expression of decadence; they change its expression, but they do not get rid of decadence itself. Socrates was a misunderstanding; *the whole improvement—morality, including the Christian, was a misunderstanding.* The most blinding daylight; rationality at any price; life, bright, cold, cautious, conscious, without instinct, in opposition to the instincts—all this too was a mere disease, another disease, and by no means a return to "virtue," to "health," to happiness. To *have* to fight the instincts—that is the formula of decadence: as long as life *is ascending,* happiness equals instinct.

[12] Did he himself still comprehend this, this most brilliant of all self-outwitters? Was this what he said to himself in the end, in the *wisdom* of his courage to die?

Socrates *wanted* to die: not Athens, but he himself chose the hemlock; he forced Athens to sentence him. "Socrates is no physician," he said softly to himself; "here death alone is the physician. Socrates himself has merely been sick a long time."

"REASON" IN PHILOSOPHY

[1] You ask me which of the philosophers' traits are really idiosyncrasies? For example, their lack of historical sense, their hatred of the very idea of becoming, their Egypticism. They think that they show their *respect* for a subject when they de-historicize it, *sub specie aeterni*—when they turn it into a mummy. All that philosophers have handled for thousands of years have been concept-mummies; nothing real escaped their grasp alive. When these honorable idolators of concepts worship something, they kill it and stuff it; they threaten the life of everything they worship. Death, change, old age, as well as procreation and growth, are to their minds objections—even refutations. Whatever has being does not become; whatever becomes does not have being. Now they all believe, desperately even, in what has being. But since they never grasp it, they seek for reasons why it is kept from them. "There must be mere appearance, there must be some deception which prevents us from perceiving that which has being: where is the deceiver?"

"We have found him," they cry ecstatically; "it is the senses! These senses, which are so immoral in other ways too, deceive us concerning the *true* world. Moral: let us free ourselves from the deception of the senses, from becoming, from history, from lies; history is nothing but faith in the senses, faith in lies. Moral: let us say No to all who have faith in the senses, to all the rest of mankind; they are all 'mob.' Let us be philosophers! Let us be mummies! Let us represent monotono-theism by adopting the expression of a gravedigger! And above all, away with the body, this wretched *idée fixe* of the senses, disfigured by all the fallacies of logic, refuted, even impossible, although it is impudent enough to behave as if it were real!"

[2] With the highest respect, I except the name of *Heraclitus*. When the rest of the philosophic folk rejected the testimony of the senses because they showed multiplicity and change, he rejected their testimony because they showed things as if they had permanence and unity. Heraclitus too did the senses an injustice. They lie neither in the way the Eleatics believed, nor as he believed—they do not lie at all. What we *make* of their testimony, that alone introduces lies; for example, the lie of unity, the lie of thinghood, of substance, of permanence. "Reason" is the cause of our falsification of the testimony of the senses. Insofar as the senses show becoming, passing away, and change, they do not lie. But Heraclitus will remain eternally right with his assertion that being is an empty fiction. The "apparent" world is the only one: the "true" world is merely added by a lie.

[3] And what magnificent instruments of observation we possess in our senses! This nose, for example, of which no philosopher has yet spoken with reverence and gratitude, is actually the most delicate instrument so far at our disposal: it is able to detect minimal differences of motion which even a spectroscope cannot detect. Today we possess science precisely to the extent to which we have decided to *accept* the testimony of the senses—to the extent to which we sharpen them further, arm them, and have learned to think them through. The rest is miscarriage and not-yet-science-in

other words, metaphysics, theology, psychology, epistemology—or formal science, a doctrine of signs, such as logic and that applied logic which is called mathematics. In them reality is not encountered at all, not even as a problem—no more than the question of the value of such a sign-convention as logic.

[4] The other idiosyncrasy of the philosophers is no less dangerous; it consists in confusing the last and the first. They place that which comes at the end—unfortunately! for it ought not to come at all!—namely, the "highest concepts," which means the most general, the emptiest concepts, the last smoke of evaporating reality, in the beginning, *as* the beginning. This again is nothing but their way of showing reverence: the higher *may* not grow out of the lower, may not have grown at all. Moral: whatever is of the first rank must be *causa sui* [self-caused]. Origin out of something else is considered an objection, a questioning of value. All the highest values are of the first rank; all the highest concepts, that which has being, the unconditional, the good, the true, the perfect—all these cannot have become and must therefore be *causa sui*. All these, moreover, cannot be unlike each other or in contradiction to each other. Thus they arrive at their stupendous concept, "God." That which is last, thinnest, and emptiest is put first, as *the* cause, as *ens realissimum* [the most real being]. Why did mankind have to take seriously the brain afflictions of sick web-spinners? They have paid dearly for it!

[5] At long last, let us contrast the very different manner in which we conceive the problem of error and appearance. (I say "we" for politeness' sake.) Formerly, alteration, change, any becoming at all, were taken as proof of mere appearance, as an indication that there must be something which led us astray. Today, conversely, precisely insofar as the prejudice of reason forces us to posit unity, identity, permanence, substance, cause, thinghood, being, we see ourselves somehow caught in error, compelled into error. So certain are we, on the basis of rigorous examination, that this is where the error lies.

It is no different in this case than with the movement of the sun: there our eye is the constant advocate of error, here it is our language. In its origin language belongs in the age of the most rudimentary form of psychology. We enter a realm of crude fetishism when we summon before consciousness the basic presuppositions of the metaphysics of language, in plain talk, the presuppositions of reason. Everywhere it sees a doer and doing; it believes in will as *the* cause; it believes in the ego, in the ego as being, in the ego as substance, and it projects this faith in the ego-substance upon all things—only thereby does it first *create* the concept of "thing." Everywhere "being" is projected by thought, pushed underneath, as the cause; the concept of being follows, and is a derivative of, the concept of ego. In the beginning there is that great calamity of an error that the will is something which is effective, that will is a capacity. Today we know that it is only a word.

Very much later, in a world which was in a thousand ways more enlightened, philosophers, to their great surprise, became aware of the sureness, the subjective certainty, in our handling of the categories of reason: they concluded that these categories could not be derived from anything empirical—for everything empirical plainly contradicted them. Whence, then, were they derived?

And in India, as in Greece, the same mistake was made: "We must once have been at home in a higher world (instead of a very much lower one, which would have been the truth); we must have been divine, for we have reason!" Indeed, nothing has yet possessed a more naive power of persuasion than the error concerning being, as it has been formulated by the Eleatics, for example. After all, every word we say and every sentence speak in its favor. Even the opponents of the Eleatics still succumbed to the seduction of their concept of being: Democritus, among others, when he invented his atom. "Reason" in language—oh, what an old deceptive female she is! I am afraid we are not rid of God because we still have faith in grammar.

[6] It will be appreciated if I condense so essential and so new an insight into four theses. In that way I facilitate comprehension; in that way I provoke contradiction.

First proposition. The reasons for which "this" world has been characterized as "apparent" are the very reasons which indicate its reality; any other kind of reality is absolutely indemonstrable.

Second proposition. The criteria which have been bestowed on the "true being" of things are the criteria of not-being, of *naught;* the "true world" has been constructed out of contradiction to the actual world: indeed an apparent world, insofar as it is merely a moral-optical illusion.

Third proposition. To invent fables about a world "other" than this one has no meaning at all, unless an instinct of slander, detraction, and suspicion against life has gained the upper hand in us: in that case, we avenge ourselves against life with a phantasmagoria of "another," a "better" life.

Fourth proposition. Any distinction between a "true" and an "apparent" world— whether in the Christian manner or in the manner of Kant (in the end, an underhanded Christian)—is only a suggestion of decadence, a symptom of the *decline of life.* That the artist esteems appearance higher than reality is no objection to this proposition. For "appearance" in this case means reality *once more,* only by way of selection, reinforcement, and correction. The tragic artist is no pessimist: he is precisely the one who says Yes to everything questionable, even to the terrible—he is *Dionysian.*

HOW THE "TRUE WORLD" FINALLY BECAME A FABLE

THE HISTORY OF AN ERROR

1. The true world—attainable for the sage, the pious, the virtuous man; he lives in it, *he is it.*

(The oldest form of the idea, relatively sensible, simple, and persuasive. A circumlocution for the sentence, "I, Plato, *am* the truth.")

2. The true world—unattainable for now, but promised for the sage, the pious, the virtuous man ("for the sinner who repents")

(Progress of the idea: it becomes more subtle, insidious, incomprehensible—*it becomes female,* it becomes Christian.)

3. The true world—unattainable, indemonstrable, unpromisable; but the very thought of it—a consolation, an obligation, an imperative.

(At bottom, the old sun, but seen through mist and skepticism. The idea has become elusive, pale, Nordic, Königsbergian [i.e., Kantian].)

4. The true world—unattainable? At any rate, unattained. And being unattained, also *unknown.* Consequently, not *consoling,* redeeming, or obligating: how could something unknown obligate us?

(Gray morning. The first yawn of reason. The cockcrow of positivism.)

5. The "true" world—an idea which is no longer good for anything, not even obligating—an idea which has become useless and superfluous—*consequently,* a refuted idea: let us abolish it!

(Bright day; breakfast; return of *bon sens* and cheerfulness; Plato's embarrassed blush; pandemonium of all free spirits.)

6. The true world—we have abolished. What world has remained? The apparent one perhaps? But no! *With the true world we have also abolished the apparent one.*

(Noon; moment of the briefest shadow; end of the longest error; high point of humanity; INCIPIT ZARATHUSTRA.)

Morality as Anti-Nature

[1] All passions have a phase when they are merely disastrous, when they drag down their victim with the weight of stupidity—and a later, very much later phase when they wed the spirit, when they "spiritualize" themselves. Formerly, in view of the element of stupidity in passion, war was declared on passion itself, its destruction was plotted; all the old moral monsters are agreed on this: *il faut tuer les passions* [one must kill the passions]. The most famous formula for this is to be found in the New Testament, in that Sermon on the Mount, where, incidentally, things are by no means looked at from a height. There it is said, for example, with particular reference to sexuality: "If thy eye offend thee, pluck it out." Fortunately, no Christian acts in accordance with this precept. *Destroying* the passions and cravings, merely as a preventive measure against their stupidity and the unpleasant consequences of this stupidity—today this itself strikes us as merely another acute form of stupidity. We no longer admire dentists who "pluck out" teeth so that they will not hurt any more.

To be fair, it should be admitted, however, that on the ground out of which Christianity grew, the concept of the *"spiritualization* of passion" could never have been formed. After all the first church, as is well known, fought against the "intelligent" in favor of the "poor in spirit." How could one expect from it an intelligent war against passion? The church fights passion with excision in every sense: its practice, its "cure," is *castratism.* It never asks: "How can one spiritualize, beautify, deify a craving?" It has at all times laid the stress of discipline on extirpation (of sensuality, of pride, of the lust to rule, of avarice, of vengefulness). But an attack on the roots of passion means an attack on the roots of life: the practice of the church *is hostile to life.*

[2] The same means in the fight against a craving—castration, extirpation—is instinctively chosen by those who are too weak-willed, too degenerate, to be able to impose moderation on themselves; by those who are so constituted that they require *La Trappe,* [The Trappist Order] to use a figure of speech, or (without any figure of speech) some kind of definitive declaration of hostility, a *cleft* between themselves and the passion. Radical means are indispensable only for the degenerate; the weakness of the will—or, to speak more definitely, the inability not to respond to a stimulus—is itself merely another form of degeneration. The radical hostility, the deadly hostility against sensuality, is always a symptom to reflect on: it entitles us to suppositions concerning the total state of one who is excessive in this manner.

This hostility, this hatred, by the way, reaches its climax only when such types lack even the firmness for this radical cure, for this renunciation of their "devil." One should survey the whole history of the priests and philosophers, including the artists: the most poisonous things against the senses have been said not by the impotent, nor by ascetics, but by the impossible ascetics, by those who really were in dire need of being ascetics.

[3] The spiritualization of sensuality is called *love:* it represents a great triumph over Christianity. Another triumph is our spiritualization of *hostility.* It consists in a profound appreciation of the value of having enemies: in short, it means acting and thinking in the opposite way from that which has been the rule. The church always wanted the destruction of its enemies; we, we immoralists and Antichristians, find our advantage in this, that the church exists. In the political realm too, hostility has now become more spiritual—much more sensible, much more thoughtful, much more *considerate.* Almost every party understands how it is in the interest of its own self-preservation that the opposition should not lose all strength; the same is true of power politics. A new creation in particular—the new *Reich,* for example—needs enemies more than friends: in opposition alone does it *feel* itself necessary, in opposition alone does it *become* necessary.

Our attitude to the "internal enemy" is no different: here too we have spiritualized hostility; here too we have come to appreciate its value. The price of fruitfulness is to be rich in internal opposition; one remains young only as long as the soul does not stretch itself and desire peace. Nothing has become more alien to us than that desideratum of former times, "peace of soul," the *Christian* desideratum; there is nothing we envy less than the moralistic cow and the fat happiness of the good conscience. One has renounced the *great* life when one renounces war.

In many cases, to be sure, "peace of soul" is merely a misunderstanding—something else, which lacks only a more honest name. Without further ado or prejudice, a few examples. "Peace of soul" can be, for one, the gentle radiation of a rich animality into the moral (or religious) sphere. Or the beginning of weariness, the first shadow of evening, of any kind of evening. Or a sign that the air is humid, that south winds are approaching. Or unrecognized gratitude for a good digestion (sometimes called "love of man"). Or the attainment of calm by a convalescent who feels a new relish in all things and waits. Or the state which follows a thorough satisfaction of our dominant passion, the well-being of a rare repletion. Or the senile weakness of our will, our cravings, our vices. Or laziness, persuaded by vanity to give itself moral airs. Or the emergence of certainty, even a dreadful certainty, after long tension and torture by uncertainty. Or the expression of maturity and mastery in the midst of doing, creating, working, and willing—calm breathing, *attained* "freedom of the will." *Twilight of the Idols*—who knows? perhaps also only a kind of "peace of soul."

[4] I reduce a principle to a formula. Every naturalism in morality—that is, every healthy morality—is dominated by an instinct of life; some commandment of life is fulfilled by a determinate canon of "shalt" and "shalt not"; some inhibition and hostile element on the path of life is thus removed. *Anti-natural* morality—that is, almost every morality which has so far been taught, revered, and preached—turns, conversely, *against* the instincts of life: it is *condemnation* of these instincts, now secret, now outspoken and impudent. When it says, "God looks at the heart," it says No to both the lowest and the highest desires of life, and posits God as the *enemy* of *life.* The saint in whom God delights is the ideal eunuch. Life has come to an end where the "kingdom of God" begins.

[5] Once one has comprehended the outrage of such a revolt against life as has become almost sacrosanct in Christian morality, one has, fortunately, also comprehended something else: the futility, apparentness, absurdity, and *mendaciousness* of such a revolt. A condemnation of life by the living remains in the end a mere symptom of a certain kind of life: the question whether it is justified or unjustified is not even

raised thereby. One would require a position *outside* of life, and yet have to know it as well as one, as many, as all who have lived it, in order to be permitted even to touch the problem of the *value* of life: reasons enough to comprehend that this problem is for us an unapproachable problem. When we speak of values, we speak with the inspiration, with the way of looking at things, which is part of life: life itself forces us to posit values; life itself values through us when we posit values. From this it follows that even that anti-natural morality which conceives of God as the counter-concept and condemnation of life is only a value judgment of life—but of what life? of what kind of life? I have already given the answer: of declining, weakened, weary, condemned life. Morality, as it has so far been understood—as it has in the end been formulated once more by Schopenhauer, as "negation of the will to life"—is; the very *instinct of decadence,* which makes an imperative of itself. It says: *"Perish!"* It is a condemnation pronounced by the condemned.

[6] Let us finally consider how naive it is altogether to say: "Man *ought* to be such and such!" Reality shows us an enchanting wealth of types, the abundance of a lavish play and change of forms—and some wretched loafer of a moralist comments: "No! Man ought to be different." He even knows what man should be like, this wretched bigot and prig: he paints himself on the wall and comments, *"Ecce homo!"* But even when the moralist addresses himself only to the single human being and says to him, "You ought to be such and such!" he does not cease to make himself ridiculous. The single human being is a piece of *fatum* from the front and from the rear, one law more, one necessity more for all that is yet to come and to be. To say to him, "Change yourself!" is to demand that everything be changed, even retroactively. And indeed there have been consistent moralists who wanted man to be different, that is, virtuous—they wanted him remade in their own image as a prig: to that end, they *negated* the world! No small madness! No modest kind of immodesty!

Morality, insofar as it *condemns* for its own sake, and not out of regard for the concerns, considerations, and contrivances of life, is a specific error with which one ought to have no pity—an *idiosyncrasy of degenerates* which has caused immeasurable harm.

We others, we immoralists, have, conversely, made room in our hearts for every kind of understanding, comprehending, and *approving.* We do not easily negate; we make it a point of honor to be *affirmers.* More and more, our eyes have opened to that economy which needs and knows how to utilize all that the holy witlessness of the priest, of the *diseased* reason in the priest, rejects—that economy in the law of life which finds an advantage even in the disgusting species of the prigs, the priests, the virtuous. *What* advantage? But we ourselves, we immoralists, are the answer.

THE FOUR GREAT ERRORS

[1] *The error of confusing cause and effect.* There is no more dangerous error than that of mistaking the effect for the cause-. I call it the real corruption of reason. Yet this error belongs among the most ancient and recent habits of mankind. It is even hallowed among us and goes by the name of "religion" or "morality." Every single sentence which religion and morality formulate contains it; priests and legislators of moral codes are the originators of this corruption of reason.

I give an example. Everybody knows the book of the famous Cornaro in which he recommends his slender diet as a recipe for a long and happy life—a virtuous one too. Few books have been read so much; even now thousands of copies are sold in England every year. I do not doubt that scarcely any book (except the Bible, as is meet) has done as much harm, has *shortened* as many lives, as this well-intentioned *curiosum.* The reason: the mistaking of the effect for the cause. The worthy Italian thought his diet was the *cause* of his long life, whereas the precondition for a long life, the extraordinary slowness of his metabolism, the consumption of so little, was the cause of his slender diet. He was not free to eat little *or* much; his frugality was not a matter of "free will": he became sick when he ate more. But whoever is no carp not only does well to eat properly, but needs to. A scholar in our time, with his rapid consumption of nervous energy, would simply destroy himself with Cornaro's diet. *Crede experto* ["Believe him who has tried!"]

[2] The most general formula on which every religion and morality is founded is: "Do this and that, refrain from this and that—then you will be happy! Otherwise. . . ." Every morality, every religion, is this imperative; I call it the great original sin of reason, the *immortal unreason.* In my mouth, this formula is changed into its opposite— first example of my "revaluation of all values": a well-turned-out human being, a "happy one," *must* perform certain actions and shrinks instinctively from other actions; he carries the order, which he represents physiologically, into his relations with other human beings and things. In a formula: his virtue is the *effect* of his happiness. A long life, many descendants—this is not the wages of virtue; rather virtue itself is that slowing down of the metabolism which leads, among other things, also to a long life, many descendants—in short, to *Cornarism.*

The church and morality say: "A generation, a people, are destroyed by license and luxury." My *recovered* reason says: when a people approaches destruction, when it degenerates physiologically, then license and luxury *follow* from this (namely, the craving for ever stronger and more frequent stimulation, as every exhausted nature knows it). This young man turns pale early and wilts; his friends say; that is due to this or that disease. I say: that he became diseased, that he did not resist the disease, was already the effect of art impoverished life or hereditary exhaustion. The newspaper reader says: this party destroys itself by making such a mistake. My *higher* politics says: a party which makes such mistakes has reached its end; it has lost its sureness of instinct. Every mistake in every sense is the effect of the degeneration of instinct, of the disintegration of the will: one could almost define what is bad in this way. All that is good is instinct—and hence easy, necessary, free. Laboriousness is an objection; the god is typically different from the hero. (In my language light feet are the first attribute of divinity.)

[3] *The error of a false causality.* People have believed at all times that they knew what a cause is; but whence did we take our knowledge—or more precisely, our faith that we had such knowledge? From the realm of the famous "inner facts," of which not a single one has so far proved to be factual. We believed ourselves to be causal in the act of willing: we thought that here at least we caught causality in the act. Nor did one doubt that all the antecedents of an act, its causes, were to be sought in consciousness and would be found there once sought—as "motives": else one would not have been free and responsible for it. Finally, who would have denied that a thought is caused? that the ego causes the thought?

Of these three "inward facts" which seem to guarantee causality, the first and most persuasive is that of the will as cause. The conception of a consciousness ("spirit") as a cause, and later also that of the ego as cause (the "subject"), are only afterbirths: first the causality of the will was firmly accepted as given, as *empirical.*

Meanwhile we have thought better of it. Today we no longer believe a word of all this. The "inner world" is full of phantoms and will-o'-the-wisps: the will is one of them. The will no longer moves anything, hence does not explain anything either—it merely accompanies vents; it can also be absent. The so-called *motive:* another error. Merely a surface phenomenon of consciousness, something alongside the deed that is more likely to cover up the antecedents of the deeds than to represent them. And as for the *ego!* That has become a fable, a fiction, a play on words: it has altogether ceased to think, feel, or will!

What follows from this? There are no mental causes at all. The whole of the allegedly empirical evidence for that has gone to the devil. That is what follows! And what a fine abuse we had perpetrated with this "empirical, evidence"; we *created* the world on this basis as a world of causes, a world of will, a world of spirits. The most ancient and enduring psychology was at work here and did not do anything else: all that happened was considered a doing, all doing the effect of a will; the world became to it a multiplicity of doers; a doer (a "subject") was slipped under all that happened. It was out of himself that man projected his three "inner facts"—that in which he believed most firmly, the will, the spirit, the ego. He even took the concept of being from, the concept of the ego; he posited "things" as "being," in his image, in accordance with his concept of the ego as a cause. Small wonder that later he always found in things only that *which he had put into them.* The thing itself, to say it once more, the concept of thing is a mere reflex of the faith in the ego as cause. And even your atom, my dear mechanists and physicists—how much error, how much rudimentary psychology is still residual in your atom! Not to mention the "thing-in-itself," the *horrendum pudendum* of the metaphysicians! The error of the spirit as cause mistaken for reality! And made the very measure of reality! And called God!

[4] *The error of Imaginary causes.* To begin with dreams: *ex post facto*, a cause is slipped under a particular sensation (for example, one following a far-off cannon shot)—often a whole little novel in which the dreamer turns up as the protagonist. The sensation endures meanwhile in a kind of resonance: it waits, as it were, until the causal instinct permits it to step into the foreground now no longer as a chance occurrence, but as "meaning." The cannon shot appears in a *causal* mode, in an apparent reversal of time. What is really later, the motivation, is experienced first—often with a hundred details which pass like lightning—and the shot *follows.* What has happened? The representations which were *produced* by a certain state have been misunderstood as its causes.

In fact, we do the same thing when awake. Most of our general feeling—every kind of inhibition, pressure, tension, and explosion in the play and counterplay of our organs, and particularly the state of the *nervus sympathicus*—excite our causal instinct: we want to have a reason for feeling this way or that—for feeling bad or for feeling good. We are never satisfied merely to state the fact that we feel this way or that; we admit this fact only—become conscious of it only—when we have furnished some kind of motivation. Memory, which swings into action in such cases, unknown to us, brings up earlier states of the same kind, together with the causal interpretations associated with them—not their real causes. The faith, to be sure, that such representations, such accompanying conscious processes, are the causes, is also brought forth by memory. Thus originates a habitual acceptance of a particular causal interpretation, which, as a matter of fact, inhibits any investigation into the real cause—even precludes it.

[5] *The psychological explanation of this.* To derive something unknown from something familiar relieves, comforts, and satisfies, besides giving a feeling of power. With the unknown, one is confronted with danger, discomfort, and care; the first instinct is to abolish these painful states. First principle: any explanation is better than none. Since at bottom it is merely a matter of wishing to be rid of oppressive representations, one is not too particular about the means of getting rid of them: the first representation that explains the unknown as familiar feels so good that one "considers it true." The proof of pleasure ("of strength") as a criterion of truth.

The causal instinct is thus conditional upon, and excited by, the feeling of fear. The "why?" shall, if at all possible, not give the cause for its own sake so much as for a *particular kind of cause*—a cause that is comforting, liberating, and relieving. That it is something already familiar, experienced, and inscribed in the memory, which is posited as a cause, that is the first consequence of this need. That which is new and strange and has not been experienced before, is excluded as a cause. Thus one searches not only for some kind of explanation to serve as a cause, but for a particularly selected and preferred kind of explanation—that which has most quickly and most frequently abolished the feeling of the strange, new, and hitherto unexperienced: the *most habitual* explanations. Consequence: one kind of positing of causes predominates more and more, is concentrated into a system, and finally emerges as *dominant*, that is, as simply precluding other causes and explanations. The banker immediately thinks of "business," the Christian of "sin," and the girl of her love.

[6] *The whole realm of morality and religion belongs under this concept of imaginary causes.* The "explanation" of *disagreeable* general feelings. They are produced by beings that are hostile to us (evil spirits: the most famous case—the misunderstanding of the hysterical as witches). They are produced by acts which cannot be approved (the feeling of "sin," of "sinfulness," is slipped under a physiological discomfort; one always finds reasons for being dissatisfied with oneself). They are produced as punishments, as payment for something we should not have done, for what we should not have *been* (impudently generalized by Schopenhauer into a principle in which morality appears as what it really is—as the very poisoner and slanderer of life: "Every great pain, whether physical or spiritual, declares what we deserve; for it could not come to us if we did not deserve it. (*World as Will and Representation* II, 666). They are produced as effects of ill-considered actions that turn out badly. (Here the affects, the senses, are posited as causes, as "guilty"; and physiological calamities are interpreted with the help of other calamities as "deserved.")

The "explanation" of *agreeable* general feelings. They are produced by trust in God. They are produced by the consciousness of good deeds (the so-called "good conscience"—a physiological state which at times looks so much like good digestion that it is hard to tell them apart). They are produced by the successful termination of some enterprise (a naïve fallacy: the successful termination of some enterprise does not by any means give a hypochondriac or a Pascal agreeable general feelings). They are produced by faith, charity, and hope—the Christian virtues.

In truth, all these supposed explanations are resultant states and, as it were, translations of pleasurable or unpleasurable feelings into a false dialect: one is in a state of hope *because* the basic physiological feeling is once again strong and rich; one trusts in God *because* the feeling of fullness and strength gives a sense of rest. Morality and religion belong altogether to the *psychology of error:* in every single case, cause and effect are confused; or truth is confused with the effects of *believing* something to be true; or a state of consciousness is confused with its causes.

[7] *The error of free will.* Today we no longer have any pity for the concept of "free will": we know only too well what it really is—the foulest of all theologians' artifices, aimed at making mankind "responsible" in their sense, that is, *dependent upon them.* Here I simply supply the psychology of all "making responsible."

Wherever responsibilities are sought, it is usually the instinct of wanting to judge and punish which is at work. Becoming has been deprived of its innocence when any being-such-and-such is traced back to will, to purposes, to acts of responsibility: the doctrine of the will has been invented essentially for the purpose of punishment, that is, because one wanted to impute guilt. The entire old psychology, the psychology of will, was conditioned by the fact that its originators, the priests at the head of ancient communities, wanted to create for themselves the right to punish—or wanted to create this right for God. Men were considered "free" so that they might be judged and punished—so that they might become *guilty:* consequently, every act had to be considered as willed, and the origin of every act had to be considered as lying within the consciousness (and thus the most fundamental counterfeit in *psychologicis* was made the principle of psychology itself).

Today, as we have entered into the reverse movement and we immoralists are trying with all our strength to take the concept of guilt and the concept of punishment out of the world again, and to cleanse psychology, history, nature, and social institutions and sanctions of them, there is in our eyes no more radical opposition than that of the theologians, who continue with the concept of a "moral world-order" to infect the innocence of becoming by means of "punishment" and "guilt." Christianity is a metaphysics of the hangman.

[8] What alone can be *our* doctrine? That no one *gives* man his qualities—neither God, nor society, nor his parents and ancestors, nor he himself. (The nonsense of the last idea was taught as "intelligible freedom" by Kant—perhaps by Plato already.) No one is responsible for man's being there at all, for his being such-and-such, or for his being in these circumstances or in this environment. The fatality of his essence is not to be disentangled from the fatality of all that has been and will be. Man is not the effect of some special purpose, of a will, and end; nor is he the object of an attempt to attain an "ideal of humanity" or an "ideal of happiness" or an "ideal of morality." It is absurd to wish to devolve one's essence on some end or other. We have invented the concept of "end": in reality there is no end.

One is necessary, one is a piece of fatefulness, one belongs to the whole, one is in the whole; there is nothing which could judge, measure, compare, or sentence our being, for that would mean judging, measuring, comparing, or sentencing the whole. But there nothing besides the whole. That nobody is held responsible any longer, that the mode of being may not be traced back to a *causa prima,* that the world does not form a unity either as a sensorium or as "spirit"— alone is the great liberation; with this alone is the innocence of becoming restored. The concept of "God" was until now the greatest objection to existence. We deny God, we deny the responsibility in God: only thereby do we redeem the world.

THE WILL TO POWER (in part)

And do you know what "the world" is to me? Shall I show it to you in my mirror? This world: a monster of energy, without beginning, without end; a firm, iron magnitude of force that does not grow bigger or smaller, that does not expend itself but only transforms itself, as a whole, of unalterable size, a household without expenses or losses, but likewise without increase or income; enclosed by "nothingness" as by a boundary; not something blurry or wasted, not something endlessly extended, but set in a definite space as a definite force, and not a space that might be "empty" here or there, but rather as force throughout, as a play of forces and waves of forces, at the same time one and many, increasing here and at the same time decreasing there; a sea of forces flowing and rushing together, eternally changing, eternally flooding back, with tremendous years of recurrence, with an ebb and a flood of its forms; out of the simplest forms striving toward the most complex, out of the stillest, most rigid, coldest forms toward the hottest, most turbulent, most self-contradictory, and then again returning home to the simple out of this abundance, out of the play of contradictions back to the joy of concord, still affirming itself in this uniformity of its courses and its years, blessing itself as that which must return eternally, as a becoming that knows no satiety, no disgust, no weariness: this, my *Dionysian* world of the eternally self-creating, the eternally self-destroying, this mystery world of the twofold voluptuous delight, my "beyond good and evil," without goal, unless the joy of the circle is itself a goal; without will, unless a ring feels good-will toward itself—do you want a *name* for this world? A *solution* for all its riddles? A light for you, too, you best-concealed, strongest, most intrepid, most midnightly men?—This *world is the will to power—and nothing besides!* And you yourselves are also this will to power—and nothing besides!

THE ANTI-CHRIST (in part)

FIRST BOOK: ATTEMPT AT A CRITIQUE OF CHRISTIANITY

*   *   *

2. What is good? Everything that heightens the feeling of power in man, the will to power, power itself.

What is bad? Everything that is born of weakness.

Friedrich Nietzsche, *The Will to Power*, edited by Walter Kaufmann, translated by Walter Kaufmann and R.J. Hollingdale (New York: Random House, 1967), §1067, pp. 449–50. Copyright © 1967 by Random House, Inc.

The Anti-Christ, from *The Portable Nietzsche,* translated and edited by Walter Kaufmann. Copyright 1954 by the Viking Press, renewed © 1982 by Viking Penguin Inc. Used by permission of Viking Penguin, a division of Penguin Books USA Inc.

What is happiness? The feeling that power is *growing,* that resistance is overcome.

Not contentedness but more power; not peace but war; not virtue but fitness (Renaissance virtue, *virtù,* virtue that is moraline*-free).

The weak and the failures shall perish: first principle of our love of man. And they shall even be given every possible assistance.

What is more harmful than any vice? Active pity for all the failures and all the weak: Christianity.

3. The problem I thus pose is not what shall succeed mankind in the sequence of living beings (man is an *end*), but what type of man shall be *bred,* shall be *willed,* for being higher in value, worthier of life, more certain of a future.

Even in the past this higher type has appeared often—but as a fortunate accident, as an exception, never as something *willed.* In fact, this has been the type most dreaded—almost *the* dreadful—and from dread the opposite type was willed, bred, and *attained:* the domestic animal, the herd animal, the sick human animal—the Christian.

4. Mankind does *not* represent a development toward something better or stronger or higher in the sense accepted today. "Progress" is merely a modern idea, that is, a false idea. The European of today is vastly inferior in value to the European of the Renaissance: further development is altogether *not* according to any necessity in the direction of elevation, enhancement, or strength.

In another sense, success in individual cases is constantly encountered in the most widely different places and cultures: here we really do find a *higher type,* which is, in relation to mankind as a whole, a kind of overman. Such fortunate accidents of great success have always been possible and will perhaps always be possible. And even whole families, tribes, or peoples may occasionally represent such a *bull's-eye.*

5. Christianity should not be beautified and embellished: it has waged deadly war against this higher type of man; it has placed all the basic instincts of this type under the ban; and out of these instincts it has distilled evil and the Evil One: the strong man as the typically reprehensible man, the "reprobate." Christianity has sided with all that is weak and base, with all failures; it has made an ideal of whatever *contradicts* the instinct of the strong life to preserve itself; it has corrupted the reason even of those strongest in spirit by teaching men to consider the supreme values of the spirit as something sinful, as something that leads into error—as temptations. The most pitiful example: the corruption of Pascal, who believed in the corruption of his reason through original sin when it had in fact been corrupted only by his Christianity.

6. It is a painful, horrible spectacle that has dawned on me: I have drawn back the curtain from the *corruption* of man. In my mouth, this word is at least free from one suspicion: that it might involve a moral accusation of man. It is meant—let me emphasize this once more—*moraline-free.* So much so that I experience this corruption most strongly precisely where men have so far aspired most deliberately to "virtue" and "godliness." I understand corruption, as you will guess, in the sense of decadence: it is my contention that all the values in which mankind now sums up its supreme desiderata are *decadence-values.*

I call an animal, a species, or an individual corrupt when it loses its instincts, when it chooses, when it prefers, what is disadvantageous for it. A history of "lofty sentiments," of the "ideals of mankind"—and it is possible that I shall have to write it—would almost explain too *why* man is so corrupt. Life itself is to my mind the instinct for growth, for durability, for an accumulation of forces, for *power:* where the will to power is lacking there is decline. It is my contention that all the supreme values

---

*The coinage of a man who neither smoked nor drank coffee.

of mankind *lack* this will—that the values which are symptomatic of decline, *nihilistic* values, are lording it under the holiest name.

7. Christianity is called the religion of *pity.* Pity stands opposed to the tonic emotions which heighten our vitality: it has a depressing effect. We are deprived of strength when we feel pity. That loss of strength which suffering as such inflicts on life is still further increased and multiplied by pity. Pity makes suffering contagious. Under certain circumstances, it may engender a total loss of life and vitality out of all proportion to the magnitude of the cause (as in the case of the death of the Nazarene). That is the first consideration, but there is a more important one.

Suppose we measure pity by the value of the reactions it usually produces; then its perilous nature appears in an even brighter light. Quite in general, pity crosses the law of development, which is the law of *selection.* It preserves what is ripe for destruction; it defends those who have been disinherited and condemned by life; and by the abundance of the failures of all kinds which it keeps alive, it gives life itself a gloomy and questionable aspect.

Some have dared to call pity a virtue (in every *noble* ethic it is considered a weakness); and as if this were not enough, it has been made *the* virtue, the basis and source of all virtues. To be sure—one should always keep this in mind—this was done by a philosophy that was nihilistic and had inscribed the *negation of life* upon its shield. Schopenhauer was consistent enough: pity negates life and renders it *more deserving of negation.*

Pity is the *practice* of nihilism. To repeat: this depressive and contagious instinct crosses those instincts which aim at the preservation of life and at the enhancement of its value. It multiplies misery and conserves all that is miserable, and is thus a prime instrument of the advancement of decadence: pity persuades men to *nothingness!* Of course, one does not say "nothingness" but "beyond" or "God," or "*true* life," or Nirvana, salvation, blessedness.

This innocent rhetoric from the realm of the religious-moral idiosyncrasy appears much less innocent as soon as we realize which tendency it is that here shrouds itself in sublime words: *hostility against life.* Schopenhauer was hostile to life; therefore pity became a virtue for him.

Aristotle, as is well known, considered pity a pathological and dangerous condition, which one would be well advised to attack now and then with a purge: he understood tragedy as a purge. From the standpoint of the instinct of life, a remedy certainly seems necessary for such a pathological and dangerous accumulation of pity as it is represented by the case of Schopenhauer (and unfortunately by our entire literary and artistic decadence from St. Petersburg to Paris, from Tolstoy to Wagner)—to puncture it and make it *burst.*

In our whole unhealthy modernity there is nothing more unhealthy than Christian pity. To be physicians *here,* to be inexorable here, to wield the scalpel *here*—that is *our* part, that is *our* love of man, that is how we are philosophers, we *Hyperboreans.*

*   *   *

62. With this I am at the end and I pronounce my judgment. I *condemn* Christianity. I raise against the Christian church the most terrible of all accusations that any accuser ever uttered. It is to me the highest of all conceivable corruptions. It has had the will to the last corruption that is even possible. The Christian church has left nothing untouched by its corruption; it has turned every value into an un-value, every truth into a lie, every integrity into a vileness of the soul. Let anyone dare to speak to me of

its "humanitarian" blessings! To *abolish* any distress ran counter to its deepest advantages: it lived on distress, it *created* distress to eternalize *itself.*

The worm of sin, for example: with this distress the church first enriched mankind. The "equality of souls before God," this falsehood, this *pretext* for the rancor of all the base-minded, this explosive of a concept which eventually became revolution, modern idea, and the principle of decline of the whole order of society—is *Christian* dynamite. "Humanitarian" blessings of Christianity! To breed out of *humanitas* a self-contradiction, an art of self-violation, a will to lie at any price, a repugnance, a contempt for all good and honest instincts! Those are some of the blessings of Christianity!

Parasitism as the *only* practice of the church; with its ideal of anemia, of "holiness," draining all blood, all love, all hope for life; the beyond as the will to negate every reality; the cross as the mark of recognition for the most subterranean conspiracy that ever existed—against health, beauty, whatever has turned out well, courage, spirit, *graciousness* of the soul, *against life itself.*

This eternal indictment of Christianity I will write on all walls, wherever there are walls—I have letters to make even the blind see.

I call Christianity the one great curse, the one great innermost corruption, the one great instinct of revenge, for which no means is poisonous, stealthy, subterranean, *small* enough—I call it the one immortal blemish of mankind.

And time is reckoned from the *dies nefastus* with which this calamity began— after the *first* day of Christianity! *Why not rather after its last day? After today?* Revaluation of all values!